WILEY GAAP

Financial Statement Disclosures Manual

Subscriber Update Service

BECOME A SUBSCRIBER!
Did you purchase this product from a bookstore?

If you did, it's important for you to become a subscriber. John Wiley & Sons, Inc. may publish, on a periodic basis, supplements and new editions to reflect the latest changes in the subject matter that you **need to know** in order to stay competitive in this ever-changing industry. By contacting the Wiley office nearest you, you'll receive any current update at no additional charge. In addition, you'll receive future updates and revised or related volumes on a 30-day examination review.

If you purchased this product directly from John Wiley & Sons, Inc., we have already recorded your subscription for this update service.

To become a subscriber, please call **1-877-762-2974** or send your name, company name (if applicable), address, and the title of the product to

mailing address:	**Supplement Department**
	John Wiley & Sons, Inc.
	One Wiley Drive
	Somerset, NJ 08875
e-mail:	**subscriber@wiley.com**
fax:	**1-732-302-2300**
online:	**www.wiley.com**

For customers outside the United States, please contact the Wiley office nearest you:

Professional & Reference Division
John Wiley & Sons Canada, Ltd.
22 Worcester Road
Etobicoke, Ontario M9W 1L1
CANADA
Phone: 416-236-4433
Phone: 1-800-567-4797
Fax: 416-236-4447
Email: canada@jwiley.com

John Wiley & Sons Australia, Ltd.
33 Park Road
P.O. Box 1226
Milton, Queensland 4064
AUSTRALIA
Phone: 61-7-3859-9755
Fax: 61-7-3859-9715
Email: brisbane@johnwiley.com.au

John Wiley & Sons, Ltd.
The Atrium
Southern Gate, Chichester
West Sussex, PO19 8SQ
ENGLAND
Phone: 44-1243 779777
Fax: 44-1243 775878
Email: customer@wiley.co.uk

John Wiley & Sons (Asia) Pte. Ltd.
2 Clementi Loop #02-01
SINGAPORE 129809
Phone: 65-64632400
Fax: 65-64634604/5/6
Customer Service: 65-64604280
Email: enquiry@wiley.com.sg

WILEY GAAP

Financial Statement Disclosures Manual

Joanne M. Flood

WILEY

Library of Congress Cataloging-in-Publication Data is Available:

ISBN 9781118572085 (Hardback)
ISBN 9781119365723 (ePub)
ISBN 9781119365747 (ePDF)

Cover Design and Image: Wiley

SKY10025571_031221

CONTENTS

PREFACE

Wiley GAAP: Financial Statements Disclosure Manual provides summaries of authoritative literature, practice alerts, and hundreds of examples of presentations and disclosures. It is organized to align fully with the structure of the FASB Codification. Chapters begin with a summary of the authoritative literature, including scope, scope exceptions, and technical alerts of relevant FASB Updates, and an alert with common areas of disclosure concerns. The remainder of each chapter contains detailed illustrations of presentations and disclosures. This organization facilitates the primary objective of the book—to assist financial statement preparers and practitioners in resolving the myriad practical problems faced in presenting financial statements.

As a bonus, a comprehensive presentation and disclosure checklist, available online to all *Wiley GAAP: Financial Statement Disclosure Manual* purchasers, offers practical guidance on preparing financial statements for commercial entities in accordance with GAAP. For easy reference and research, the checklist also follows the order of the Codification. To download the checklist, go to www.wiley.com/go/FSDM2021 (password: Flood).

The author's wish is that this book will serve preparers, practitioners, faculty, and students as a reliable reference tool to facilitate their understanding of, and ability to, present financial statements in accordance with the authoritative literature.

On the Horizon. Significant accounting changes are on the horizon. In the next year, the FASB is expected to make strides on the following major projects and others:

- Conceptual framework projects on elements, measurement, and presentation
- Identifiable intangible assets
- Disclosure framework revisions on income taxes, inventory, interim reporting, government acquisitions
- Disaggregation of performance information
- Not-for-profit reporting of gifts-in-kind
- Segment reporting
- Numerous narrow scope projects

This volume is current through ASU 2020-06. Readers are encouraged to check the FASB website for status updates to FASB projects.

Joanne M. Flood
September 2020

ABOUT THE AUTHOR

Joanne M. Flood, CPA, is an author and independent consultant on accounting and auditing technical topics and e-learning. She has experience as an auditor in both an international firm and a local firm and worked as a senior manager in the AICPA's Professional Development group. She received her MBA summa cum laude in accounting from Adelphi University and her bachelor's degree in English from Molloy College.

While in public accounting, Joanne worked on major clients in retail, manufacturing, and finance and on small business clients in construction, manufacturing, and professional services. At the AICPA, she developed and wrote e-learning, text, and instructor-led training courses on U.S. and international standards. She also produced training materials in a wide variety of media, including print, video, and audio, and pioneered the AICPA's e-learning product line. Joanne resides on Long Island, New York, with her daughter, Elizabeth. She is the author of the following Wiley publications:

Financial Disclosure Checklist

Wiley GAAP 2021: Interpretation and Application of Generally Accepted Accounting Principles

Wiley Practitioner's Guide to GAAS 2021: Covering all SASs, SSAEs, SSARSs, and Interpretations

Wiley GAAP: Financial Statement Disclosures Manual (Wiley Regulatory Reporting)

Wiley Revenue Recognition

1 ASC 105 GENERALLY ACCEPTED ACCOUNTING PRINCIPLES

AUTHORITATIVE LITERATURE

Accounting Standards Codification (ASC) Topic 105 establishes the FASB Accounting Standards Codification™ (the Codification) as the source of authoritative GAAP. ASC 105 contains no disclosure or presentation requirements.

What Is GAAP?

The Codification (ASC) is the:

> . . . *source of authoritative generally accepted accounting principles (GAAP) recognized by the FASB to be applied by nongovernmental entities. Rules and interpretive releases of the Securities and Exchange Commission (SEC) under authority of federal securities laws are also sources of authoritative GAAP for SEC registrants. In addition to the SEC's rules and interpretive releases, the SEC staff issues Staff Accounting Bulletins that represent practices followed by the staff in administering SEC disclosure requirements, and it utilizes SEC Staff Announcements and Observer comments made at Emerging Issues Task Force meetings to publicly announce its views on certain accounting issues for SEC registrants. ASC 105-10-05-1*

In the absence of authoritative guidance, the Codification offers the following approach:

> *If the guidance for a transaction or event is not specified within a source of authoritative GAAP for that entity, an entity shall first consider accounting principles for similar transactions or events within a source of authoritative GAAP for that entity and then consider nonauthoritative guidance from other sources. An entity shall not follow the accounting treatment specified in accounting guidance for similar transactions or events in cases in which those accounting principles either prohibit the application of the accounting treatment to the particular transaction or event or indicate that the accounting treatment should not be applied by analogy. ASC 105-10-05-2*

The Codification lists some possible nonauthoritative sources:

- Practices that are widely recognized and prevalent either generally or in the industry
- FASB Concepts Statements
- American Institute of Certified Public Accountants (AICPA) Issues Papers
- International Financial Reporting Standards of the International Accounting Standards Board
- Pronouncements of professional associations or regulatory agencies
- Technical Information Service Inquiries and Replies included in AICPA Technical Practice Aids
- Accounting textbooks, handbooks, and articles
  (ASC 105-10-05-3)

GAAP is concerned with:

- The measurement of economic activity,
- The time when such measurements are to be made and recorded,
- The disclosures surrounding this activity, and
- The preparation and presentation of summarized economic information in the form of financial statements.

Accounting Principles and Concepts

There are two broad categories of accounting principles—recognition and disclosure.

Recognition Principles Recognition principles determine the timing and measurement of items that enter the accounting cycle and impact the financial statements. These are reflected in quantitative standards that require economic information to be reflected numerically.

Disclosure Principles Disclosure principles deal with factors that are not always quantifiable. Disclosures involve qualitative information that is an essential ingredient of a full set of financial statements. Their absence would make the financial statements misleading by omitting information relevant to the decision-making needs of the reader. Disclosure principles also complement recognition principles by dictating that disclosures:

- Expand on some quantitative data,
- Explain assumptions underlying the numerical information, and
- Provide additional information on accounting policies, contingencies, uncertainties, etc.

These are essential to fully understand the performance and financial condition of the reporting enterprise.

The Concept of Materiality

Chapter 3 of CON 8 discusses how materiality differs from relevance and that materiality assessments can be properly made only by those with an understanding of the entity's facts and circumstances. Following are the relevant passages:

> *QC11. Relevance and materiality are defined by what influences or makes a difference to an investor or other decision maker; however, these two concepts can be distinguished from each other. Relevance is a general notion about what type of information is useful to investors. Materiality is entity specific. The omission or misstatement of an item in a financial report is material if, in light of surrounding circumstances, the magnitude of the item is such that it is probable that the judgment of a reasonable person relying upon the report would have been changed or influenced by the inclusion or correction of the item.*

QC11A. A decision not to disclose certain information or recognize an economic phenomenon may be made, for example, because the amounts involved are too small to make a difference to an investor or other decision maker (they are immaterial). However, magnitude by itself, without regard to the nature of the item and the circumstances in which the judgment has to be made, generally is not a sufficient basis for a materiality judgment.

QC11B. No general standards of materiality could be formulated to take into account all the considerations that enter into judgments made by an experienced reasonable provider of financial information. This is because materiality judgments can properly be made only by those that understand the reporting entity's pertinent facts and circumstances. Whenever an authoritative body imposes materiality rules or standards, it is substituting generalized collective judgments for specific individual judgments, and there is no reason to suppose that the collective judgments always are superior.

Descriptions of Materiality

Materiality has great significance in understanding, researching, and implementing GAAP and affects the entire scope of financial reporting. Disputes over financial statement presentations often turn on the materiality of items that were, or were not, recognized, measured, and presented in certain ways.

Materiality is described by the FASB in Statement of Financial Concepts 8 (CON 8), *Qualitative Characteristics of Accounting Information*:

Information is material if omitting it or misstating it could influence decisions that users make on the basis of the financial information of a specific reporting entity. In other words, materiality is an entity-specific aspect of relevance based on the nature or magnitude or both of the items to which the information relates in the contest of an individual entity's financial report.

The Supreme Court has held that a fact is material if there is:

a substantial likelihood that the disclosure of the omitted fact would have been viewed by the reasonable investor as having significantly altered the "total mix" of information made available.

Due to its inherent subjectivity, the FASB definition does not provide specific or quantitative guidance in distinguishing material information from immaterial information. The individual accountant must exercise professional judgment in evaluating information and concluding on its materiality. Materiality as a criterion has both quantitative and qualitative aspects, and items should not be deemed *immaterial* unless all potentially applicable quantitative and qualitative aspects are given full consideration and found not relevant.

SAB Topics 1.M (SAB 99) and 1.N (SAB 108) contain guidance from the SEC staff on assessing materiality during the preparation of financial statements. That guidance references the Supreme Court opinion and the definition in CON 2, which has been superseded by CON 8. The SEC in Staff Accounting Bulletin (SAB) Topics 1.M (SAB 99) and 1.N (SAB 108) provides useful discussions of this issue. SAB Topic 1.M indicates that:

a matter is material if there is a substantial likelihood that a reasonable person would consider it important.

Although not strictly applicable to nonpublic preparers of financial statements, the SEC guidance is worthy of consideration by all accountants and auditors. Among other things, Topic 1.M notes that deliberate application of nonacceptable accounting methods cannot be justified merely because the impact on the financial statements is deemed to be immaterial. Topic 1.N also usefully reminds preparers and others that materiality has both quantitative and qualitative dimensions, and both must be given full consideration. Topic 1.N has added to the literature of materiality with its discussion of considerations applicable to prior period restatements.

Quantitative Factors Quantitatively, materiality has been defined in relatively few pronouncements, which speaks to the great difficulty of setting precise measures for materiality. For example, in ASC 280-10-50, which addresses segment disclosures, a material segment or customer is defined in ASC 280-10-50-12 as representing 10% or more of the reporting entity's revenues (although, even given this rule, qualitative considerations may cause smaller segments to be deemed reportable). The Securities and Exchange Commission has, in several of its pronouncements, defined materiality as 1% of total assets for receivables from officers and stockholders, 5% of total assets for separate balance sheet disclosure of items, and 10% of total revenue for disclosure of oil and gas producing activities.

Qualitative Factors In addition to quantitative assessments, preparers should consider qualitative factors, such as company-specific trends and performance metrics. Information from analysts' reports and investor calls may provide an indication of what is important to reasonable investors and should be considered.

Although materiality judgments have traditionally been primarily based on quantitative assessments, the nature of a transaction or event can affect a determination of whether that transaction or event is material. Examples of items that involve an otherwise immaterial amount but that would be material include:

- A transaction that, if recorded, changes a profit to a loss or changes compliance with ratios in a debt covenant to noncompliance,
- A transaction that might be judged immaterial if it occurred as part of routine operations may be material if its occurrence helps meet certain objectives. For example, a transaction that allows management to achieve a target or obtain a bonus that otherwise would not become due would be considered material, regardless of the actual amount involved.
- Offers to buy or sell assets for more or less than book value, and
- Litigation proceedings against the company pursuant to price-fixing or antitrust allegations, and active negotiations regarding their settlement.

Degree of Precision Another factor in judging materiality is the degree of precision that may be attained when making an estimate. For example, accounts payable can usually be estimated more accurately than a possible loss from the incurrence of an asset retirement obligation. An error amount that would be material in estimating accounts payable might be acceptable in estimating the retirement obligation.

DISCLOSURE AND PRESENTATION REQUIREMENTS

This topic has no disclosure and presentation Subtopics.

2 ASC 205 PRESENTATION OF FINANCIAL STATEMENTS

AUTHORITATIVE LITERATURE

Subtopics

ASC 205, *Presentation of Financial Statements*, is divided into four subtopics:

- ASC 205-10, *Overall*
- ASC 205-20, *Discontinued Operations*
- ASC 205-30, *Liquidation Basis of Accounting*
- ASC 205-40, *Going Concern*

Scope and Scope Exceptions

ASC 205-10 The guidance in ASC 205-10 applies to:

- All subtopics in ASC 205-10 unless explicitly excluded
- Business entities and not-for-profit entities
  (ASC 205-10-15-1)

ASC 205-20 The guidance in 205-20 applies to either:
- A component of an entity or a group of components that is disposed of or is classified as held for sale, *or*
- A business or nonprofit entity that, on acquisition, is classified as held for sale.
  (ASC 205-20-15-2)

The guidance does *not* apply to oil and gas properties that use the full-cost method of accounting prescribed by the SEC. (ASC 205-20-15-3)

ASC 205-30 ASC 205-30 does not apply to companies registered under the Investment Company Act of 1945. (ASC 205-30-15-1)

ASC 205-40 ASC 205-40 applies to all entities. (ASC 205-40-15-1)

PRACTICE ALERT

While SEC comments pertain to public entities, their comments can provide valuable practice pointers for nonpublic entity financial statement preparers. In the areas covered in this Topic, the SEC has commented in recent years that preparers should consider carefully:

- Why current earnings before taxes and depreciation are not comparable to the corresponding prior period measures due to the reclassifications of devices from inventory to property, plant, and equipment and the lack of inclusion of periodic depreciation expenses related to equipment leasing revenue.
- Whether the operations they have disposed of meet the criteria to be accounted for as discontinued operations.
- Whether the discontinued operations meet the criteria for classification as a component or group of components of an entity, or an entity that represents a strategic shift that will have a major effect on the entity's operations and financial results and meets the other criteria in ASC 205-20-45-1B.
- Whether the assets classified as held for use meet the criteria in ASC 360.
- Why the entity's expected sale of a component is not reflected as held for sale and discontinued operations.

- Whether assets held for sale or disposal were tested for impairment in prior periods or in the current period.
- The factors used to present, or not present, assets held for sale separately on the statement of financial position,.
- The timeline of events leading to an asset sale.
- Why gain or loss on a sale of the disposition is not disclosed.
- Known trends, events, or uncertainties that are reasonably likely to impact future liquidity and/or going concern.

Preparers would be prudent to document their conclusions on any of the above items.

DISCLOSURES AND PRESENTATION REQUIREMENTS

ASC 205-10, *Overall*

Comparative Statements To increase the usefulness of financial statements, many entities include financial statements for one or more prior years in their annual reports. Some also include five- or ten-year summaries of condensed financial information. While not required, ASC 205-10-45-1 emphasizes that the presentation of comparative financial statements in annual reports enhances the usefulness of such reports and brings out more clearly the nature and trends of current changes affecting the enterprise. Comparative presentations demonstrate the fact that the statements for a series of periods are far more significant than those for a single period and that the accounts for one period are but an installment of what is essentially a continuous history.

Full Set of Financial Statements A full set of financial statements consists of:

1. Financial position at the end of the period.
2. Earnings (net income), which may be shown in a separate statement or within one continuous statement of comprehensive income.
3. Comprehensive income for the period in one statement or two consecutive statements.
4. Cash flows during the period.
5. Investments by and distributions to the owners during the period.
   (ASC 205-10-45-1A)

Order of Data The order of data is not prescribed. However, for tabular information, it is good practice to present information by year with the most current year appearing consistently in either the first or last column.

Changes Affecting Comparability Comparative information should be consistent. Any exceptions to comparability must be disclosed as a reclassification, and accounting change, or correction of an error, as described in ASC 250. (ASC 205-10-45-3) To the extent they remain significant, notes to financial statements should be repeated in comparative statements or at least referred to. (ASC 205-10-45-4 and 50-2)

Presentation Here are the presentation items required for GAAP:

- Include name of entity for which statements are being presented (if d/b/a is different name from legal name, indicate both).
- Titles of statements should be appropriate (certain titles denote and should be reserved for GAAP financial statements; other titles denote other comprehensive basis of accounting [OCBOA] financial statements).
- Dates and periods covered should be clearly stated.

- If comparative statements are presented, repeat or at least refer to notes from prior years to the extent they continue to be significant. (FASB ASC 205-10-45-4 and 50-2)
- Differences between "economic" entity and legal entity being presented should be noted (e.g., consolidated or not, subsidiaries included and excluded, combined statements, etc.). Disclose summarized financial information for previously unconsolidated subsidiaries.

Disclosure There is only one required disclosure for this subsection listed in the Codification:

For reclassifications or other reasons, if changes have occurred in the manner or basis of presenting corresponding items in two or more periods, disclose the explanation of the change. (FASB ASC 205-10-50-1)

ASC 205-20, *Discontinued Operations*

Determining When a Disposal Should Be Presented as a Discontinued Operation The unit of account for a discontinued operation is:

- A component of an entity,
- A group of components of an entity, or
- A business or nonprofit entity.
  (ASC 205-20-45-1A)

The guidance describes a discontinued operation as a disposal of a component, group of components, or an entity that:

- Represents a strategic shift that has (or will have) a major effect on an entity's operations and financial results.
  and
- Is:
  - disposed of by sale,
  - meets the criteria to be classified as held for sale, or
  - disposed of by other than sale (for example by abandonment, exchange, or distribution to owner).
    (ASC 205-20-45-1B)

The guidance goes on to state that a strategic shift could include:

- A major geographical area of operations,
- A major line of business,
- A major equity method investment, or
- Other major parts of an entity.
  (ASC 205-20-45-1C)

A component is classified as held for sale when all of the following criteria are met:

- Management has the authority to approve and commits to a plan to sell.
- The component is available for immediate sale.
- Management has initiated a program to complete the plan to sell.
- A buyer is being actively sought.
- The sale is probable.

- The transfer will qualify for recognition as a completed sale within one year.
- The sale price being marketed is reasonable.
- It is unlikely that the plan to sell will not be withdrawn or undergo significant changes unless the limited exceptions under ASC 205-20-45-1G are met.
  (ASC 205-20-44-1E and ASC 360-010-45-9)

Presentation—Income Statement A discontinued operation is reported as such in the period in which the discontinued operation has been disposed of by sale or other means or is classified as held for sale. (ASC 205-20-45-3)

In the period in which a component of an entity is reported as a discontinued operation:	
Item	*Presentation*
Results of operations of that component	Report as a separate component of income, net of tax, before the cumulative effect of accounting changes. (ASC 205-20-45-1B and 45-3A)
Any gain or loss recognized on disposal or loss recognized on classification as held for sale	Report separately on the face of the income statement or disclose in the notes. (ASC 205-20-45-3B and 205-20-50-1b)
The income statements of any prior periods being presented	Restate to also reflect the results of operations of the component as discontinued operations. (ASC 205-20-45-3)

Gain or loss is calculated based on guidance in other Topics. For example, if the discontinued operation is within the scope of ASC 360, *Property, Plant, and Equipment*, guidance can be found in that Topic. (ASC 205-20-45-3C)

The following types of debt should be allocated to discontinued operations:

- Interest on debt assumed by the buyer.
- Interest on debt required to be repaid as a result.
  (ASC 205-20-45-6)

In subsequent periods, adjustments to amounts previously reported may be needed because, for example, of resolution of contingencies related to disposal or operations of the discontinued business or settlement of employee benefit obligations. If adjustments are needed, they should be presented separately in the discontinued operations section where income is reported. (ASC 205-20-45-4 and 45-5 and 50-3A)

Presentation—Balance Sheet The assets and liabilities of a disposal group must be presented separately, and not offset, on the face of the balance sheet or by reference in the notes. When the discontinued operation is initially classified as held for sale and from prior periods presented, the major classes of assets and liabilities should be disclosed on the face of the statement of financial position or in the notes. (FASB ASC 205-10-45-10 and 45-11) and the entity does not have to reclassify previously reported amounts.

Disclosures for Assets Sold or Held for Sale For all types of discontinued operations, disclosures include:

- For periods in which a discontinued operation has been disposed of or is classified as held-for-sale:
  - The facts and circumstances leading to the disposal or expected disposal;
  - The expected manner and timing of the disposal;

- If not separately presented on the face of the income statement as part of discontinued operations, gain or loss recognized on the disposal or loss recognized on classification as held for sale in accordance with the relevant guidance in other subtopics; and
- The segment in which the discontinued operation is reported under Topic 280. (FASB ASC 205-20-50-1)

Change to a Plan of Sale If an entity changes its plan of sale, in the period in which that decision is made, it must disclose in the notes:

- The facts and circumstances leading to the decision.
- The effect of the change on the results of operations for all periods presented. (FASB ASC 205-20-50-3)
- The nature and amount of adjustments to amounts previously reported in discontinued operations directly related to discontinued operations. (FASB ASC 205-20-50-3A)

Continuing Involvement After disposal an entity may have significant continuing involvement because of a supply agreement, guarantee, equity method involvement, etc. For as long as the discontinued operation is presented separately, the entity must present information about the entity's significant continuing involvement with a discontinued operation after the disposal date. (FASB ASC 205-20-50-4A)

For each discontinued operation in which the entity retains significant continuing involvement after the disposal date, the entity must disclose:

- Description of the nature of the activities that give rise to the continuing involvement.
- Period of time the involvement is expected to continue.
- The amount of any cash flows.
- Revenues or expenses in continuing operations after the disposal transaction that were eliminated in consolidated financial statements as intra-entity transactions
- Where an entity retains an equity method investment after disposal:
  - The pretax income of the investee.
  - The ownership interest in the discontinued operation before and after disposal.
  - The ownership interest in the investee after the disposal transaction.
  - Share of the income or loss of the investee in the period after the disposal and where on the income statement that is reported. (FASB ASC 205-20-50-4B)

Disclosures Required for a Discontinued Operation Comprising a Component or Group of Components of an Entity For discontinued operations, to the extent not presented on the face of the financial statements as part of discontinued operations, the entity must disclose:

- Pretax profit or loss.
- Major classes of line items making up the pretax profit or loss.
- For the periods in which the results of discontinued operations are presented in the income statement either:
  - the total operating and investing cash flows of the discontinued operation, or
  - the depreciation, amortization, capital expenditures, and significant operating and investing noncash items.
- The pretax profit or loss attributable to the parent if the discontinued operation includes a noncontrolling interest.

- Carrying amounts of major classes of assets and liabilities included in discontinued operations for the period in which it is classified as held for sale and all prior periods presented.
(FASB ASC 205-20-50-5B)

If the above disclosures are provided in a note, the following amounts, if not considered major, may be aggregated in one line:

- For the initial period in which a disposal group is classified as held for sale and all prior periods,
  - reconciliation of the amounts disclosed in the last bullet of ASC 205-20-50-5B above and
  - total assets and liabilities classified as held for sale that are presented separately on the face of the statement of financial position.
- For the periods in which the results of operations of the discontinued operations are recorded in the income statement, the amounts disclosed above and the after-tax profit or loss from discontinued operations.
(FASB ASC 205-20-50-5C and 5D)

Disclosures Required for a Discontinued Operation Comprising an Equity Method Investment

- The entity must disclose summarized information about the assets, liabilities, and results of operations of the investee if that information was disclosed in periods before the disposal. (FASB ASC 205-20-50-7)

ASC 205-30, *Liquidation Basis of Accounting*

Determining When to Apply the Liquidation Basis of Accounting Guidance requires financial statements to be prepared using the liquidation basis of accounting when liquidation is imminent. (ASC 205-30-25-1) For example, if a calendar year entity determines on March 1 that liquidation is imminent, it must calculate net asset balances as of March 1 and present a statement of net assets as of its March 31 quarterly financial statements.

Liquidation is considered imminent when:

- A plan for liquidation is approved by the person or persons with the authority to make such a plan effective, and the likelihood is remote that the execution of the plan will be blocked by other parties or the entity will return from liquidation, or
- A plan for liquidation is being imposed by other forces, such as involuntary bankruptcy, and the likelihood is remote that the entity will return from liquidation.
(ASC 205-30-25-2)

Measuring Assets and Liabilities The financial statements prepared under the liquidation basis of accounting are intended to "report the amount of cash or other consideration that an investor might reasonably be expected to receive after liquidation." (ASU 2013-07, BC13) Assets should be measured at the amount the entity expects to collect upon sale. This may or may not be fair value because fair value assumes an orderly sale. (ASC 205-30-30-1) Therefore, an asset sale during a liquidation may or may not approximate fair value. The following should also be considered:

- Previously unrecognized assets, such as internally generated trademarks and patents, should be recognized. These items may be presented in the aggregate, but must separately record any expected disposal or selling costs. Expected selling costs should be included in the accrual of estimated disposal costs. (ASC 205-30-25-4)

- Liabilities should be recognized in accordance with relevant guidance in other Topics. However, some estimates, like timing of payments, may change and should be recorded. In addition, an entity should not assume that it will legally be released from its obligations. (ASC 205-30-30-2)
- Estimated costs to dispose of assets or other items to be sold in liquidation should be accrued, but discount provisions should not be applied (ASC 205-30-25-6 and 205-30-30-3). Those costs should be presented in the aggregate, but separate from the related assets or items. If and when it has a reasonable basis for estimation, the entity should accrue costs and income expected to be incurred or earned through the end of the liquidation. (ASC 205-30-25-6 and 7)
- Income expected to be collected during liquidation should be accrued, but the entity should exercise care in making that estimate.
- The entity must estimate the costs that it will incur during liquidation if it has a basis for the estimation.

Presentation An entity using the liquidation basis of accounting must apply it prospectively from the day the liquidation becomes imminent and change the form of its financial statements to:

- A statement of net assets in liquidation, as of the end of the reporting period, that presents the entity's net assets available for distribution to investors, and
- A statement of changes in net assets in liquidation that present only changes in net assets occurring during the period since liquidation became imminent.
  (ASC 205-30-45-1 and 45-2 and ASC 205-30-20)

While the standards do not require a statement of net assets as of the date the liquidation becomes imminent, that information is necessary to prepare a statement of changes in net assets for the first period in which liquidation becomes imminent. (ASU 2013-07, BC 17)

Disclosure The entity must disclose information required by other Topics relevant to understanding the statement of net assets in liquidation and statement of changes in net assets in liquidation, informing readers about:

- The amount of cash or other consideration that the entity expects to collect and
- The amount that the entity is obligated or expects to be obligated to pay during the course of liquidation.
  (FASB ASC 205-30-50-1)

The entity must also disclose all of the following for financial statements using the liquidation basis of accounting:

- That the financial statements are prepared using the liquidation basis of accounting.
- The facts and circumstances surrounding the adoption of the liquidation basis of accounting and the entity's determination that liquidation is imminent.
- The entity's plan for liquidation, including a description of:
  - The manner by which it plans to dispose of its assets.
  - Other items it expects to sell that it had not previously recognized as assets (for example, trademarks).

- ○ The manner by which it plans to settle its liabilities.
    - ○ The expected date by which the entity expects to complete its liquidation.
- Methods and significant assumptions used to measure assets and liabilities.
- Any subsequent changes to those methods and assumptions.
- The type and amount of costs and income accrued in the statement of net assets in liquidation.
- The period over which those costs are expected to be paid or income earned.
(FASB ASC 205-30-50-2)

The entity should also consider information that would help the reader to better understand the proceedings and where to obtain additional information, including:

- Which subsidiaries are included in the filing
- The bankruptcy jurisdiction
- Key hearings
- Agreements reached with creditors
- The status of any debtor-in-possession and exit financings

It should be noted that disclosures, such as debt covenant violations, required by other Topics may be affected by the filing.

ASC 205-40, *Going Concern*

The Codification essentially, with some exceptions, mirrors going-concern requirements for auditors currently found in PCAOB and AICPA standards. Management must perform, at least annually, an evaluation of the entity's ability to continue as a going concern within one year after the financial statements are issued or, when applicable, available to be issued.

Overall Guidance Management must perform two steps:

1. Evaluate, in the aggregate, conditions and events that are known or reasonably knowable at the evaluation date, and
2. Assess whether it is probable that the entity will be able to meet its obligations that are due within one year after the date that the financial statements are issued or available to be issued.
(ASC 205-30-50-3 and 50-4)

The going concern probability threshold is the same used for accounting for contingencies—more likely than not.

Consideration of Management's Plans When making going concern assessments, management may consider mitigating plans to determine whether substantial doubt is alleviated. These plans can be considered only if both of the following conditions are met:

- It is probable that the plan will be effectively implemented with the year.
- It is probable that the plan when implemented will mitigate the conditions or events that raise substantial doubt about going concern.
(ASC 205- 30-50-6 and 50-7)

In order for these plans to be considered, generally, management or those with authority must approve the plans before the issuance date of the financial statements.

Disclosure Requirements

Management Conclusion	*Disclosures*
Conditions do not give rise to substantial doubt.	No specific disclosures are required.
Substantial doubt exists but is alleviated by management's plans.	In a separate note or part of another note, for example, on debt, information that enables users to assess: • Principal conditions or events that raised substantial doubt, • Management's evaluation of the significance of those conditions or events in relation to the entity's ability to meet its obligations, and • Management's plans that alleviated those concerns. (ASC 205-40-50-12)

After considering all the facts and management's plans, management concludes that substantial doubt remains.	A separate note with:
	• A statement that there is substantial doubt about the entity's ability to continue as a going concern within one year after the date that the financial statements are issued or available to be issued.
	• Disclosures that allow users to understand:
	  ○ Principal conditions or events that raised substantial doubt,
	  ○ Management's evaluation of the significance of those conditions or events in relation to the entity's ability to meet its obligations, and
	  ○ Management's plans to mitigate the conditions or events. (ASC 205-40-50-13)

In subsequent years	Present the above disclosures in subsequent financial statements as long as substantial doubt exists. If any changes in conditions or events occur, they should be explained. It is expected that as more is known, the disclosure will become more extensive. If the substantial doubt is resolved in a subsequent period, the entity must disclose how it was resolved. (ASC 205-40-50-14)

PRESENTATION AND DISCLOSURE EXAMPLES

Example 2.1: Reclassification

During the first quarter of fiscal 20X3, the Company evaluated the impact of the organizational restructuring program (see Note X) on the determination of its operating segments and reporting units. The Company concluded that its operating and reportable segments continue to be Candles, Home Furnishings, and Body Care. However, based on the organizational changes that result from the organizational restructuring and the impact on the information used by the Chief Operating Decision Maker (CODM), the Company reclassified the revenues and costs associated with one brand from the Body Care to the Candles operating segment. The revenues and costs associated with the reclassification of one brand from Body Care to Candles Care have been reflected for the fiscal years ending 20X3 and 20X2. Further, the Company has reclassified amounts presented for depreciation and amortization to reflect the fully allocated amounts included in Operating income (loss) of the segments.

Example 2.2: Income Statement Presentation for Discontinued Operations—Face of the Income Statement

	20X3	*20X2*
Income from continuing operations before income taxes	$ 598	$ 583
Income taxes	239	233
Income from continuing operations	359	350
Discontinued operations (Note X)		
Loss from operations of discontinued component	1,165	1,045
Loss on disposal of discontinued component	167	
Income tax benefit	(532)	(418)
Loss on discontinued operations	800	627
Net income	$ (441)	$ (277)

This example shows the loss on disposal on the face of the income statement. Alternatively, the amount can be shown in the notes to the financial statements, as long as the disclosure identifies the caption in the income statement in which the loss is included.

Example 2.3: Computing the Gain or Loss on Disposal in the Year in Which the Discontinued Operation Is Classified as Held for Sale

Today's Telecommunications has decided to close its pager division, which is a component of the reporting entity. This represents a strategic shift to focus on other divisions of the business. Today's Telecommunications has committed to a plan to sell the assets and liabilities of the division and has properly reclassified the division as held-for-sale at that date. The following conditions apply:

- The division has incurred $1,750 in losses from operations from the beginning of the year to the date it was reclassified as held-for-sale.
- The fair value of the assets and liabilities of the division are $10,775.
- Brokers' commissions and other costs to sell are estimated to be $1,650.
- The carrying value of the assets and liabilities of the division is $12,525 before the adjustments (depreciation, amortization, adjustment of valuation accounts, and similar periodic adjustments) are made.
- The adjustments reduce the carrying value of the assets and liabilities by $125.
- Losses from operations of the division from the date it is classified as held-for-sale to the end of the fiscal year are $580. (This loss does not include the GAAP adjustments noted above.)
- Anticipated future losses from operations of the division from the end of this fiscal year to the expected sales date are $1,999.
- The tax rate is 40%.

The income statement presentation of discontinued operations would be:

Discontinued operations (Note X)	
Loss from operations of discontinued division, net of tax of $982	$1,473
Loss on disposal of discontinued division, net of tax of $1,310	1,965
Loss on discontinued operations	$3,438

The loss from operations of the discontinued pager division is the sum of the $1,750 loss incurred prior to the date the assets and liabilities were classified as held-for-sale, plus the $125 adjustments that were recorded, plus the $580 loss incurred from the date the division was classified as held-for-sale to the end of the fiscal year. The sum ($2,455) less the tax effects of $982 ($2,455 × 40%) is the loss from operations of $1,473.

The loss on disposal is the difference between the carrying value of the division and its fair value less costs to sell. The carrying value of the division is $12,400 ($12,525 less the adjustments of $125). The fair value of the division less costs to sell is $9,125 ($10,775 fair value less costs to sell of $1,650). The difference of $3,275 less the tax effects of $1,310 ($3,275 × 40%) is the loss on disposal of $1,965. The anticipated future losses from operations of the division will be reported in discontinued operations in the future period in which they occur. They are not included in the loss on disposal in the current fiscal year.

Example 2.4: Discontinued Operations—Adjustment of Loss Repeated in a Prior Period as a Discontinued Operation

Continuing the previous example, the sale of Today's Telecommunications' pager division, which is a component of the entity, closed in the year subsequent to the fiscal year in which the assets and liabilities were classified as held-for-sale.

- The actual sales price less costs to sell was $9,725.
- The net carrying value of the assets and liabilities on the date of sale was $12,225.
- The loss from operations from the end of the fiscal year to the date of sale was $2,045.
- The tax rate is 40%.

The income statement presentation of discontinued operations would be:

Discontinued operations (Note X)	
Loss from operations of discontinued division, net of tax of $818	1,227
Gain on disposal of discontinued division, net of tax of $310	465
Loss on discontinued operations	762

The loss from operations of the discontinued pager division is the $2,045 less the tax effects of $818 ($2,045 × 40%). The loss on disposal is the difference between the carrying value of the division and its sales price less the loss recognized in the prior period. The carrying value of the division was $12,225; the sales price less costs to sell was $9,725, for an actual loss of $2,500. The loss recognized in the prior period was $3,275, so an adjustment of $775 ($2,500 less $3,275) is necessary. The tax effects on the adjustment are $310 ($775 × 40%), so the net adjustment is a gain of $465 ($775 – $310).

Example 2.5: Discontinued Operations Reporting—in Periods after the Sale, Including Adjustment for Contingency

The Hewitt Candy Company sells its entire candy cane production line, recognizing a gain of $155,000 on the transaction prior to applicable taxes of $54,000. During the year in which the sale was completed, Hewitt lost $23,000 on its operation of the candy cane line, while it also lost $72,000 during the preceding year. Applicable tax reductions during these years were $8,000 and $25,000, respectively. It reports these results in the following portion of its income statement:

	20X0	20X1
Discontinued operations:		
Loss from operations of discontinued candy cane division (net of applicable taxes of $25,000 and $8,000)	$(47,000)	$(15,000)
Gain on disposal of candy cane division (net of applicable taxes of $54,000)	—	101,000

A clause in the sale agreement stipulates that Hewitt must reimburse the buyer for any maintenance problems found in the equipment. In the following year, the two parties negotiate a payment by Hewitt of $39,000 to address claims made under this clause. The applicable tax reduction associated with this payment is $14,000. It reports these results in the following portion of its income statement:

	20X0	20X1	20X2
Discontinued operations:			
Loss from operations of discontinued candy cane division (net of applicable taxes of $25,000 and $8,000)	$(47,000)	$(15,000)	--
Gain on disposal of candy cane division (net of applicable taxes of $54,000)	--	101,000	--
Adjustment to gain on disposal of candy cane division (net of applicable taxes of $14,000)	--	--	$(25,000)

Example 2.6: Discontinued Operations—Note Disclosure in Years Subsequent to the Year in Which the Discontinued Operation Was Classified as Held for Sale

In the fourth quarter of fiscal 20X0, the Company decided to discontinue operations of the Up Fashion division. This represents a strategic shift in operations that has a major impact on the Company's operations and financial results and has been accounted for as discontinued operations This strategy will allow the Company to focus its efforts on improving Little Miss Division sales and profitability, expanding internationally, and continuing to develop its miss tween business. The Company closed 17 Up Fashion stores in the first fiscal quarter of 20X1 and during the second fiscal quarter of 20X1, closed the remaining 18 Up Fashion stores. The results of the Up Fashion stores closed to date, net of income tax benefit, which consists of 35 and 49 stores for the fiscal years ended July 2, 20X1 and July 3, 20X0, respectively, have been presented as a discontinued operation in the accompanying consolidated statements of operations and comprehensive income (loss) for all periods presented and are as follows:

	Fiscal Year Ended
	July 2, 20X1
Net sales	$10,205
Cost of sales, including production and occupancy	17,378
Gross margin	(7,173)
Selling, general and administrative expenses	5,351
Loss from discontinued operations, before income tax benefit	(12,524)
Tax benefit	(5,939)
Loss from discontinued operations, net of tax benefit	$(6,585)

Example 2.7: Discontinued Operations—Note Disclosure in Years Subsequent to the Year in Which the Discontinued Operation Was Classified as Held for Sale

In the second quarter of 20X2, following termination of the Home Décor agreement, the Company disclosed its intention to explore strategic alternatives regarding its European Home Decor business of the International Division.

On September 23, 20X2, the Company announced that it had received an irrevocable offer from Davis Investors, a subsidiary of The Lawson Group (the "Purchaser") to acquire the Company's European business operations (the "Home Décor Business"). The transaction was structured as an equity sale with the Purchaser acquiring the Home Décor Business with its operating assets and liabilities.

In addition to approving the sale of the Home Décor Business in the third quarter of 20X2, the Company's Board of Directors approved a plan to sell substantially all of the remaining operations of the International Division. On December 31, 20X2, the Company closed the sale of the Home Décor Business contemplated by the Sale and Purchase Agreement (the SPA) dated November 22, 20X2 as amended to complete the sale). Approximately $70 million has been accrued at December 31, 20X2 under a working capital adjustment provision. The draft working capital adjustment submitted by the Company to the Purchaser is subject to a dispute resolution provision as provided for in the SPA. The Company is actively marketing for sale the businesses in South Korea, mainland China, Australia, and New Zealand and expects to complete the dispositions within the one year period associated with held for sale assets. Collectively, the European Home Décor Business sale and other planned dispositions represent a strategic shift that has a major impact on the Company's operations and financial results and has been accounted for as discontinued operations. The retained sourcing and trading operations of the former International Division are presented as Other in Note X, Segment Information.

The Company has presented the operating results of the European Home Décor Business as well as the entities to be sold within discontinued operations, net of tax in the consolidated statements of operations for all periods presented. The related assets and liabilities of the disposal groups are presented as current and non-current assets and liabilities of discontinued operations in the consolidated balance sheets as of December 31, 20X1 and December 26, 20X2. Cash flows from the Company's discontinued operations are presented in the consolidated statements of cash flows for all periods. Certain portions of the former International Division assets and operations are being retained or did not meet the held for sale criteria at December 31, 20X2 and, therefore, remain in continuing operations.

The loss on classification as discontinued operations relating to the remaining entities was measured at the lower of carrying value or estimated fair value less costs to sell and is included in the valuation allowance in the balance sheet as shown below. Completion of the sale of the remaining international operations may be for amounts different from the current estimates and will be evaluated each reporting period until the dispositions are complete.

In accordance with the Company's annual goodwill impairment test $15 million of goodwill in the Australia/New Zealand reporting unit was considered impaired in the third quarter of 20X2 based on a decrease in the long-term projected cash flows and related estimated terminal value of that business.

Restructuring charges incurred by the International Division that previously had been presented as part of Corporate costs have been included in the measurement and presentation of discontinued operations in all periods presented.

The SPA contains customary warranties of the Company and the Purchaser, with the Company's warranties limited to an aggregate of EURO 10 million. The Company will provide various transition and product sourcing services to the Purchaser for a period of 6 to 24 months under a separate agreement after the closing. Also, as part of the disposition, the Company retained responsibility for the frozen defined benefits pension plan in the United Kingdom.

As part of the European Home Décor Business sale transaction, the Purchaser shall indemnify and hold the Company harmless in connection with any guarantees in place as of September 23, 20X2 and given by Company in respect of the liabilities or obligations of the European Home Décor Business. Further, if the Purchaser wishes to terminate any such guarantee or cease to comply with any underlying obligation that is subject to such a guarantee, the Purchaser shall obtain an unconditional and irrevocable release of the guarantee. However, the Company is contingently liable in the event of a breach by the Purchaser of any such obligation. The Company does not believe it is probable it would be required to perform under any of these guarantees or such underlying obligations.

The major components of discontinued operations, net of tax presented in the consolidated statements of operations for the years ended December 31, 20X2 and December 26, 20X1 include the following.

(In millions)	*20X2*	*20X1*
Sales	$2,564	$2,758
Cost of goods sold and occupancy costs	2,019	2,119
Operating expenses	573	617
Asset impairments	90	—
Restructuring charges	11	90
Interest income	1	2
Interest expense	**(5)**	(2)
Other income (expense), net	**(2)**	—
Loss on sale or held for sale classification	**(223)**	—
Income tax expense (benefit)	**(208)**	16
Discontinued operations, net of tax	**$(150)**	$(84)

Disposition of the European Home Décor Business on December 31, 20X2 resulted in a pretax loss on sale of $108 million and is included in the table above. The tax benefit associated with discontinued operations differs from the statutory rate due to the mix of earnings and loss in the various jurisdictions, the impact of various permanent items and other factors.

Assets and liabilities of discontinued operations presented in the consolidated balance sheets at December 31, 20X2, and December 26, 20X1 are included in the following table. Because the sale of the European Home Décor Business was completed before year-end 20X2, the assets and liabilities of that business are not included as of December 31, 20X2.

(In millions)		20X2		20X1
Assets				
Cash and cash equivalents		$ 44		$ 209
Receivables, net		88		420
Inventories		82		292
Prepaid expenses and other current assets		4		35
Property and equipment, net		31		—
Other assets		6		—
Valuation allowance		(113)		—
Current assets of discontinued operations		$ 142		$ 956
Property and equipment, net		$ —		$ 119
Goodwill		—		15
Other assets		—		48
Noncurrent assets of discontinued operations		$ —		$ 182
Liabilities				
Trade accounts payable		$ 60		$ 331
Accrued expenses and other current liabilities		27		282
Income taxes payable		2		4
Short-term borrowings and current maturities of long-term debt		9		5
Deferred income taxes and other long-term liabilities		6		—
Current liabilities of discontinued operations		$ 104		$ 622
Deferred income taxes and other long-term liabilities		$ —		$ 40
Long-term debt, net of current maturities		—		6
Noncurrent liabilities of discontinued operations		$ —		$ 46

Cash flows from discontinued operations included depreciation and amortization of $19 million, $30 million, and $36 million for the years ended December 31, 20X2 and December 26, 20X1 respectively, as well as capital expenditures of $9 million, $19 million, and $27 million for the years ended December 31, 20X2 and December 26, 20X1, respectively.

Example 2.8: Note—Discontinued Operation—Not a Strategic Shift

In fiscal year 20X7, we expanded into container shipping services as a new business sector to provide related transportation logistics services to customers in the United States and in Canada. We have signed cooperation agreements with ShipCo Canada to provide freight logistics services and container shipping services to them in the United States. To ensure effective and high-quality services provided to our customers in the United States, we established a joint venture, LRB Shipping Center Corp., in the second quarter of fiscal 20X7 with a U.S. local freight forwarder, Meta Global Logistics Inc. The joint venture ended in December 20X7 and we continue to operate shipping business through our other subsidiaries. Since LRB Center's operating revenue was less than 1% of the Company's consolidated revenue and the termination did not constitute a strategic shift that would have a major effect on the Company's operations and financial results, the results of operations for LRB Center was not reported as discontinued operations in the financial statements.

Example 2.9: Basis of Presentation—Liquidation Basis of Accounting

As a result of poor performance and lack of new capital contributions, XYZ Company has determined that liquidation was imminent as of June 1, 20X1 and adopted the liquidation basis of accounting at that date. XYZ calculated the net asset balances as of June 1 and presented a statement of changes in net assets as of June 30. The company adjusted the beginning balance of net assets as of June 1, 20X1 when preparing its quarterly report. Assets have been measured and are presented at the amounts of cash proceeds that the Company expects to get from liquidation. The Company has presented its internally developed trade name and other intellectual property assets which were not previously recognized under generally accepted accounting principles (GAAP), but are recognized under the liquidation basis of accounting. The company has also accrued for costs it expects to incur during the liquidation process.

Example 2.10: Statement of Net Assets in Liquidation

XYZ Company
Statement of Net Assets in Liquidation
As of June 30, 20X1

Assets

Cash and cash equivalents at carrying value	$ 3,300
Trade receivables, Net	1,536
Property, plant, and equipment, Net	6,518
Liquidation basis of accounting, Items previously not recognized	818
Total Assets	**$12,172**
Liabilities	
Accounts payable	$216
Taxes payable	66
Notes payable	450
Due to related parties	348

Estimated costs to liquidate	<u>32</u>
Total liabilities	**<u>1,112</u>**
Net assets	**$11,060**

Practice Pointer: Notice that in the example above, the entity initially measures its assets to reflect the amount it expects to receive in cash or other consideration. The assets include items previously unrecognized, like trademarks and patents that the company expects to sell. These are valued in the Statement of Net Assets at the amounts of proceeds the entity expects to realize. Assets are reported gross. The costs to dispose of the assets are presented separately in estimated costs to liquidate. The statement is unclassified and presents the total net assets in liquidation.

Example 2.11: Statement of Changes in Net Assets in Liquidation

XYZ Company
Statement of Changes in Net Assets in Liquidation
for the Period June 1, 20X1 through June 30, 20X1

Net assets as of June 1, under liquidation basis	*$18,574*
Adjustment for accrued liquidation costs	(8,795)
Net assets adjusted as of June 1, 20X1 under liquidation of accounting	**9,779**
Net operations	5,187
Liquidation basis of accounting remeasurement loss on accrued costs to dispose of assets and liabilities	(668)
Subsequent period remeasurement adjustment on assets	2,927
Liquidation basis of accounting remeasurement loss on items previously not recognized	(527)
Net assets as of June 30, 20X1 under liquidation basis	**$16,030**

Example 2.12: Note—Liquidation Is Imminent

Liquidation of Company As a result of poor performance and lack of new capital contributions, the Company's Board of Directors concluded in a meeting held September 18, 20X0 that the implementation of a Formal Plan of Complete Dissolution and Liquidation is in the best interest of the Company and its shareholders. Subsequently, the Plan was submitted to ABC's shareholders as of October 28, 20X0 for approval at the Company's annual meeting held on December 4, 20X0. The Plan of Complete Dissolution and Liquidation was approved by the shareholders at the annual meeting.

Plan of Liquidation As a result of the adoption of the Plan of Complete Dissolution and Liquidation, ABC's activities are now limited to: selling, collecting, or otherwise realizing the value of its remaining assets; making tax and other regulatory filings; winding down the Company's remaining business activities; paying (or adequately providing for the payment) of valid creditor claims and obligations; and making liquidation distributions to ABC's shareholders.

Currently, ABC's assets consist primarily of cash, recoverable income taxes, and notes receivable. The Company believes that its current cash position and cash generated from the collection of its remaining assets will be sufficient to meet its current obligations, to fund ABC's wind-down operations, and allow the Company to pay liquidation distributions (see Note X). The Company expects to complete its liquidation over the ensuing 6 to 12 months.

Financial Statement Presentation In preparing these financial statements, the Company has evaluated events and transactions for potential recognition through March 2, 20X1, the date the financial statements were issued.

The consolidated financial statements include the accounts of ABC, Inc. and Forest Commerce Center, Inc., the Company's real estate subsidiary whose assets were sold at March 31, 20X0. Upon consolidation, all intercompany accounts and transactions are eliminated.

The Company considers cash and other highly liquid investments, with less than 90-day maturities, as cash and cash equivalents. Cash and cash equivalents are stated at cost, which approximates liquidation value. The majority of cash and cash equivalents were federally insured.

Adoption of the Liquidation Basis of Accounting As a result of the Company's shareholders' approval of the Plan of Complete Dissolution, the Company adopted the liquidation basis of accounting effective December 5, 20X1. This basis of accounting is considered appropriate when liquidation of a company is imminent. Under this basis of accounting, assets are valued at the expected cash proceeds from liquidation, and liabilities are stated in accordance with GAAP that otherwise applies. The entity is also required to accrue and separately present costs that it expects to incur and the income it expects to earn during the expected duration of the liquidation. The conversion from the going concern to liquidation basis of accounting required management to make significant estimates and judgments to record assets and liabilities. These estimates are subject to change based upon the timing of potential sales and further deterioration of the market.

The Company will continue to incur operating costs and receive income on its investments and cash and cash equivalents throughout the liquidation period. On a regular basis management evaluates assumptions, judgments, and estimates that can have a significant impact on reported assets in liquidation based on the most recent information available to us, and when necessary makes changes accordingly. Actual costs and income may differ from estimates, which might reduce assets available in liquidation to be ultimately distributed to shareholders.

Accrued Liquidation Costs The Company is required to make significant estimates and exercise judgment in determining accrued liquidation costs. The Company reviewed all operating expenses and contractual commitments such as payroll and related expenses, lease termination costs, professional fees, and other outside services to determine the estimated costs to be incurred during the liquidation period. Accordingly, estimated expenses anticipated to occur from December 5, 20X0 through final liquidation were accrued in the consolidated statement of net assets as of December 31, 20X0 and March 31, 20X1 prepared on a liquidation basis.

The accrued costs expected to be incurred in liquidation and recorded payments, since March 31, 20X0 made related to the accrued liquidation costs are as follows:

Accrued Liquidation Costs	As Booked March 31, 20X0	Adjustments to Reserve	Payments	Balance at December 31, 20X0
Payroll related costs	$ 777	$0	$ (363)	$ 192
Contractual commitments	52	0	(52)	0
Professional services	144	0	(1)	143
Insurance, taxes, and other	1,016	148	(172)	992
Total	$1,989	$148	$ (734)	$ 1,404

Expenses during the liquidation period are continually reviewed in order to insure that the overall cost structure during the wind down of the Company is reduced to minimal levels necessary to effectively manage the liquidation.

Example 2.13: Liquidation Is Not Imminent

Organization and Nature of Business As a result of the factors described below, the Company has no meaningful revenue-producing operations. Historically, the Company has operated an investment banking business, predominately fixed-income sales and trading and financial advisory services, through three principal business units: Investment Banking, Diamond Star Investments, and Credit Products. The Company also engaged in residential mortgage lending operations through Family Funding, Inc. ("Family Funding") until this business was discontinued, and the business sold to North Star Residential, Inc. ("North Star"), in February 20X3 (the "North Star Transaction").

The Company has disclosed previously various uncertainties that had adversely impacted counterparty relationships, employee turnover, and operating results. Those factors impacted the overall stability of the Company. During the second quarter of 20X3, the Company's Board of Directors approved plans to discontinue operations in its Diamond Star Investments (including Western Financial Services ["Western"]) and Homeland Products divisions (together, "Fixed Income" or the "Fixed Income businesses") as well as, later in the quarter, its Investment Banking division. Exiting these businesses impacted approximately 125 employees. As of December 14, 20X3, the Company had approximately 30 employees. Refer to Notes 20 and 21 herein for additional information.

The Company is evaluating several strategic alternatives in order to preserve and maximize stockholder value. These include:

- Pursuing a strategic transaction with a third party, such as a merger or sale of the Company;
- Reinvesting the Company's liquid assets in favorable opportunities; and
- Winding down the Company's remaining operations and distributing its net assets, after making appropriate reserves, to its stockholders.

The Company does not believe that discontinuing the businesses referenced above will have a significant near-term impact on its liquidity. The Company's liquidity needs will depend to a large extent on decisions it makes regarding the alternatives described above and its future business operations, generally. The Company's available liquidity, which consists primarily of cash, is currently anticipated to be sufficient to meet its ongoing financial obligations for a reasonable period of time.

Example 2.14: Going Concern—Substantial Doubt Remains—Contingent on Raising Capital

As shown in the accompanying consolidated financial statements the Company has incurred recurring losses of $688,217 and $709,913 for the years ended June 30, 20X8 and 20X7 respectively, and has incurred a cumulative loss of $4,075,605 since inception (November 14, 20X1). The Company is currently in the development stage and has spent a substantial portion of its time in the development of its technology.

There is no guarantee that the Company will be able to raise enough capital or generate revenues to sustain its operations. These conditions raise substantial doubt about the Company's ability to continue as a going concern.

Management believes that the Company's capital requirements will depend on many factors. These factors include the final phase of development and mass production being successful as well as product implementation and distribution.

The consolidated financial statements do not include any adjustments relating to the carrying amounts of recorded assets or the carrying amounts and classification of recorded liabilities that may be required should the Company be unable to continue as a going concern.

Example 2.15: Going Concern—Substantial Doubt Remains—Contingent on Obtaining Financing

The accompanying financial statements have been prepared on a going concern basis, which implies the Company will continue to realize its assets and discharge its liabilities in the normal course of business. The Company has not generated revenues since inception and has never paid dividends and is unlikely to pay dividends or generate earnings in the near future. The continuation of the Company as a going concern is dependent upon the ability of the Company to obtain necessary equity or debt financing to continue operations, the successful development of one or more alternative oil and gas properties, and the attainment of profitable operations. As of February 28, 20X4, the Company has not generated any revenues and has an accumulated loss of $1,889,899 since inception. These factors raise substantial doubt regarding the Company's ability to continue as a going concern. These financial statements do not include any adjustments to the recoverability and classification of recorded asset amounts and classification of liabilities that might be necessary should the Company be unable to continue as a going concern.

On May 15, 20X2, the Company modified an October 20X1 capital raising agreement with Emerald Capital Partners, LLP ("Emerald"), a corporate finance firm based in Dallas and regulated by the SEC. While the Company no longer pays a monthly fee to Emerald, it is obligated for a period of 18 months beginning May 1, 20X2 to pay Emerald a success fee for any transaction completed with any prospect previously introduced by Opal. Subsequent to the agreement modification, Emerald has introduced the Company to a very small number of further potential investors or joint venture partners. If the Company consummates a transaction with any of these, it generally expects to pay to this firm the stock success fee represented by 4,289,052 shares of the Company's common stock, which is subject to forfeiture, as originally agreed upon.

Example 2.16: Going Concern—Substantial Doubt—Management's Plans

The Company's consolidated financial statements have been prepared using accounting principles generally accepted in the United States. applicable to a going concern which contemplates the realization of assets and liquidation of liabilities in the normal course of business. The Company has a working capital deficit, recurring losses, and negative cash flows from operations. These matters raise substantial doubt about the Company's ability to continue as a going concern. The accompanying consolidated financial statements do not include any adjustments relating to the recoverability and classification of asset carrying amounts or the amount and classification of liabilities that might result from the outcome of this uncertainty.

At February 28, 20X1, the Company had an accumulated deficit of $4,891,093. Subsequent to February 28, 20X1 the Company has not received any cash proceeds from its stock subscriptions receivable, but the Company entered into stock purchase agreements and issued 1,283,500 restricted common shares at $0.26 per share, for total cash proceeds of $320,875. The Company anticipates that expected future proceeds from its stock subscriptions receivable, additional financing through the sale of its common stock or other equity-based securities, and additional sales of existing domain names will be sufficient to meet its working capital and capital expenditure needs through at least February 28, 20X2. In the event that the Company is unable to obtain additional capital in the future, it would be forced to further reduce operating expenses and/or cease operations altogether.

3 ASC 210 BALANCE SHEET

AUTHORITATIVE LITERATURE

Statements of financial positions (also commonly known as balance sheets or statements of financial condition) present information about assets, liabilities, and owners' equity and their relationships to each other. They reflect an entity's resources (assets) and its financing structure (liabilities and equity) in conformity with generally accepted accounting principles (GAAP). The statement of financial position reports the aggregate effect of transactions at a point in time, whereas the statements of income, retained earnings, comprehensive income, and cash flows all report the effect of transactions occurring during a specified period of time such as a month, quarter, or year.

It is common for the statement of financial position to be divided into classifications based on the length of the entity's operating cycle. Assets are classified as current if they are reasonably expected to be converted into cash, sold, or consumed either within one year or within one operating cycle, whichever is longer. Liabilities are classified as current if they are expected to be liquidated through the use of current assets or incurring other current liabilities. The excess or deficiency of current assets over or under current liabilities, which is referred to as networking capital, identifies, if positive, the relatively liquid portion of the entity's capital that is potentially available to serve as a buffer for meeting unexpected obligations arising within the ordinary operating cycle of the business.

Subtopics

ASC 210, *Balance Sheet*, is divided into two Subtopics:

- ASC 210-10, *Overall*, which focuses on the presentation of the balance sheet, particularly the operating cycle and the classification of current assets and liabilities, and
- ASC 210-20, *Offsetting*, which offers guidance on offsetting amounts for certain contracts and repurchase agreements accounted for as collateralized borrowings and reverse repurchase agreements accounted for as collateralized borrowings.

Scope and Scope Exceptions

ASC 210-10 The guidance in ASC 210-10 applies to all entities. However, the guidance related to classification of current assets and current liabilities does not apply if the entity does not present a classified balance sheet.

ASC 210-20 The guidance in ASC 210-20 does not apply to:

The derecognition or nonrecognition of assets and liabilities. Derecognition by sale of an asset or extinguishment of a liability results in removal of a recognized asset or liability and generally results in the recognition of gain or loss. Although conceptually different, offsetting that results in a net amount of zero and derecognition with no gain or loss are indistinguishable in their effects on the statement of financial position. Likewise, not recognizing assets and liabilities of the same amount in financial statements achieves similar reported results. (ASC 210-10-15-2)

Generally, right of setoff involves only two parties. Exceptions to this two-party principle are limited to the guidance in these Subtopics and paragraphs:

- ASC 840-30, paragraphs 32 through 52 (leveraged leases).
- Upon implementation of ASU 2016-02, *Leases*—ASC 842-50 (leveraged leases).
- ASC 715-30 (accounting for pension plan assets and liabilities).
- ASC 715-60 (accounting for plan assets and liabilities).
- ASC 740-10 (net tax asset or liability amounts reported).
- ASC 815, paragraphs 815-10-45-1 through 45-7 (derivative instruments with the right to reclaim cash collateral or the obligation to return cash collateral).
- ASC 940-320 (trade date accounting for trading portfolio positions) and 910-405 (advances received on construction contracts).
- ASC 942-210-45-3A.
  (ASC 210-20-15-3)

PRACTICE ALERT

Financial statement classification is a frequent topic of SEC comment letters. While SEC rules only apply to public entities, preparers of financial statements can benefit from the findings of SEC reviewers. The classifications of current and noncurrent assets and liabilities, including debt, have been a source of SEC staff comments. Preparers should look to the guidance in ASC 210-10-45 and the discussion in this chapter when preparing classified balance sheets to determine whether an item should be classified as current or noncurrent.

Another item that appears in SEC comments relates to the disaggregation of assets and liabilities. The SEC requires disclosure on the face of the financial statements or in the notes items in excess of 5% of total assets and total liabilities, respectively. Again, this is not required for non-SEC filers, but may be a benchmark for preparers to consider when deciding which items to disaggregate.

DISCLOSURE AND PRESENTATION REQUIREMENTS

ASC 210-10, *Overall*

Presenting one year of financial statements is acceptable under GAAP, but two years for nonpublic companies is desirable. It is common for the statement of financial position to be divided into classifications based on the length of the entity's operating cycle. Assets, liabilities, and shareholders' equity are separated in the statement of financial position so that important relationships can be shown and attention can be focused on significant subtotals. It is common for reporting entities to present the items in the order of liquidity.

Assets

Current Assets Current assets are cash and other assets that are reasonably expected to be realized in cash or sold or consumed during the normal operating cycle of the business (ASC 210-10-05-4). When the normal operating cycle is less than one year, a one-year period is used to distinguish current assets from noncurrent assets. When the operating cycle exceeds one year, the operating cycle will serve as the proper period for purposes of current asset classification. (ASC 210-10-45-3) When the operating cycle is very long, the usefulness of the concept of current assets diminishes. The following items are classified as current assets:

- *Cash and cash equivalents* include cash on hand consisting of coins, currency, undeposited checks; money orders and drafts; demand deposits in banks; and certain short- term, highly liquid investments. Any type of instrument accepted by a bank for deposit would be considered to be cash. Cash must be available for withdrawal on demand. Cash that is restricted as to withdrawal, such as certificates of deposit, would not be included with cash because of the time restrictions. Cash must be available for current use in order to be classified as a current asset. Cash that is restricted in use would not be included in cash unless its restrictions will expire within the operating cycle. Cash restricted for a noncurrent use, such as cash designated for the purchase of property or equipment, would not be included in current assets. (ASC 210-10-45-4) Cash equivalents include short-term, highly liquid investments that:
  - Are readily convertible to known amounts of cash, and
  - Are so near their maturity (maturities of three months or less from the date of purchase by the entity) that they present negligible risk of changes in value because of changes in interest rates.

    U.S. Treasury bills, commercial paper, and money market funds are all examples of cash equivalents. Only instruments with original maturity dates of three months or less qualify as cash equivalents. (ASC 205-10-45-1)
- Marketable securities representing the investment of cash available for current operations.
- *Receivables* include accounts and notes receivable, receivables from affiliated entities, and officer and employee receivables. The term "accounts receivable" is generally understood to represent amounts due from customers arising from transactions in the ordinary course of business (sometimes referred to as "trade receivables").

- *Inventories* are goods on hand and available-for-sale, raw materials, work in process, operating supplies, and ordinary maintenance materials and parts. The basis of valuation and the method of pricing are to be disclosed.
- *Prepaid expenses* are amounts paid in advance to secure the use of assets or the receipt of services at a future date. Prepaid expenses will not be converted to cash, but they are classified as current assets because, if not prepaid, they would have required the use of current assets during the coming year or operating cycle, if longer. (ASC 205-10- 45-2) Prepaid rent and prepaid insurance are the most common examples of prepaid expenses. (ASC 210-10-45-1)

Noncurrent Assets ASC 210-10-45-4 excludes the following from current assets:

- Cash and claims to cash that are:
  - Restricted as to withdrawal or use for other than current operations,
  - Designated for expenditure in the acquisition or construction of noncurrent assets, or
  - Segregated for the liquidation of long-term debts.

    Even though not actually set aside in special accounts, funds that are clearly to be used in the near future for the liquidation of long-term debts, payments to sinking funds, or for similar purposes shall also, under this concept, be excluded from current assets. However, if such funds are considered to offset maturing debt that has properly been set up as a current liability, they may be included within the current asset classification.
- Receivables arising from unusual transactions (such as the sale of capital assets, or loans or advances to affiliates, officers, or employees) that are not expected to be collected within 12 months.
- Investments that are intended to be held for an extended period of time (longer than one operating cycle). The following are the three major types of long-term investments:
  1. *Investments in securities*—stocks, bonds, and long-term notes receivable. Securities that are classified as available-for-sale or held-to-maturity investments are classified as long term if the entity intended to hold them for more than one year.
  2. *Tangible assets* not currently used in operations (e.g., land purchased as an investment and held for sale).
  3. *Investments held in special funds* (e.g., sinking funds, pension funds, amounts held for plant expansion, and cash surrender values of life insurance policies).
- Depreciable assets
  - *Property, plant, and equipment.* These are disclosed with related accumulated depreciation/depletion.
  - *Intangible assets* include legal and/or contractual rights that are expected to provide future economic benefits and purchased goodwill. Patents, copyrights, logos, and trademarks are examples of rights that are recognized as intangible assets.
  - *Other assets.* An all-inclusive heading that incorporates assets that do not fit neatly into any of the other asset categories (e.g., long-term prepaid expenses, deposits made to purchase equipment, deferred income tax assets (net of any required valuation allowance), bond issue costs, noncurrent receivables, and restricted cash).

Presenting significant amounts separately is good practice.

Liabilities Liabilities are displayed on the statement of financial position in the order of expected payment.

Current Liabilities Obligations are classified as current if their liquidation is reasonably expected to require the use of existing resources properly classifiable as current assets or to create other current obligations. (ASC 210-10-45-6) Current liabilities also includes obligations that are due on demand or that are callable at any time by the lender. These are classified as current regardless of the intent of the entity or lender. ASC 470-10-45 includes more guidance on those and on short-term debt expected to be refinanced. (ASC 205-10-45-7) The following items are classified as current liabilities:

1. Accounts payable
2. Trade notes payable
3. Current portion of obligations under leases
4. Accrued expenses
5. Income taxes
6. Derivative liabilities
7. Dividends payable
8. Advances and deposits
9. Agency collections and withholdings
10. Current portion of long-term debt
11. Other liabilities
    (ASC 210-10-45-8 and 45-9)

Noncurrent liabilities Obligations that are not expected to be liquidated within one year (or the current operating cycle, if longer) are classified as noncurrent. The following items would be classified as noncurrent:

1. Notes and bonds payable.
2. Lease obligations.
3. Written put options on the option writer's (issuer's) equity shares and forward contracts to purchase an issuer's equity shares that require physical or net cash settlement are classified as liabilities on the issuer's statement of financial position. The obligation is classified as noncurrent unless the date at which the contract will be settled is within the next year (or operating cycle, if longer).
4. Certain financial instruments that embody an unconditional obligation to issue a variable number of equity shares and financial instruments other than outstanding shares that embody a conditional obligation to issue a variable number of equity shares The obligation is classified as noncurrent unless the date at which the financial instrument will be settled is within the next year (or operating cycle, if longer).
5. Contingent obligations are recorded when it is probable that an obligation will occur as the result of a past event. The classification of a contingent liability as current or noncurrent depends on when the confirming event will occur and how soon afterward payment must be made.
6. Mandatorily redeemable shares are recorded as liabilities per ASC 480. A mandatory redemption clause requires common or preferred stock to be redeemed (retired) at a specific date(s) or upon occurrence of an event which is uncertain as to timing although ultimately certain to occur. The obligation is classified as noncurrent unless the date at which the shares must be redeemed is within the next year (or operating cycle, if longer).
7. Other noncurrent liabilities include defined benefit pension obligations, postemployment obligations, and postretirement obligations. Deferred income taxes are liabilities to pay income taxes in the future that result from differences between the carrying amounts of assets and liabilities for income tax and financial reporting purposes.

Stockholders' Equity

1. Nonredeemable preferred stock
2. Common stock
3. Treasury stock
4. Additional paid-in-capital
5. Accumulated other comprehensive income
6. Noncontrolling interests in consolidated subsidiaries

Form of the Statement of Financial Position

The format of a statement of financial position is not specified by any authoritative pronouncement. Instead, formats and titles have developed as a matter of tradition and, in some cases, through industry practice.

Two basic formats are used:

1. The balanced format, in which the sum of the amounts for liabilities and equity are added together on the face of the statement to illustrate that assets equal liabilities plus equity.
2. The less frequently presented equity format, which shows totals for assets, liabilities, and equity, but no sums illustrating that assets less liabilities equal equity.

Those two formats can take one of two forms:

1. The account form, presenting assets on the left-hand side of the page and liabilities and equity on the right-hand side.
2. The report form, which is a top-to-bottom or running presentation.

The three elements customarily displayed in the heading of a statement of financial position are:

1. The legal name of the entity whose financial position is being presented.
2. The title of the statement (e.g., statement of financial position or balance sheet).
3. The date of the statement (or statements, if multiple dates are presented for comparative purposes).

The entity's legal name appears in the heading exactly as specified in the document that created it (e.g., the certificate of incorporation, partnership agreement, LLC operating agreement, etc.). The legal form of the entity is often evident from its name when the name includes such designations as "incorporated," "LLP," or "LLC." Otherwise, the legal form is either captioned as part of the heading or disclosed in the notes to the financial statements. A few examples are as follows:

ABC Company
(a general partnership)

ABC Company
(a sole proprietorship)

ABC Company
(a division of DEF, Inc.)

The use of the titles "statement of financial position," "balance sheet," or "statement of financial condition" infers that the statement is presented using generally accepted accounting principles. If, instead, some other comprehensive basis of accounting, such as income tax basis or cash basis is used, the financial statement title must be revised to reflect this variation. The use of a title such as "Statements of Assets and Liabilities—Income Tax Basis" is necessary to differentiate the financial statement being presented from a GAAP statement of financial position.

The last day of the fiscal period is used as the statement date. Usually, this is a month-end date unless the entity uses a fiscal reporting period always ending on a particular day of the week such as Friday or Sunday. In these cases, the statement of financial position would be dated accordingly (i.e., December 26, October 1, etc.).

Statements of financial position generally are uniform in appearance from one period to the next with consistently followed form, terminology, captions, and patterns of combining insignificant items. If changes in the manner of presentation are made when comparative statements are presented, the prior year's information must be restated to conform to the current year's presentation.

The classification and presentation of information in a statement of financial position may be highly aggregated, highly detailed, or anywhere in between. In general, highly aggregated statements of financial position are used in annual reports and other presentations provided to the public. Highly detailed statements of financial position are used internally by the entity. The following highly aggregated statement of financial position includes only a few line items. The additional details required by GAAP are found in the notes to the financial statements.

ASC 210-20, *Offsetting*

Presentation In general, a debtor entity may offset assets and liabilities against each other if a right of setoff exists and certain specified criteria are met. (ASC 210-20-45-2) The Codification permits offsetting when *all* four criteria listed below are met:

1. Each of the two parties owes the other determinable amounts (although they may be in different currencies and bear different rates of interest).
2. The reporting party has the right to set off the amount it owes against the amount owed to it by the other party.
3. The reporting party intends to set off the two amounts.
4. The right of setoff is legally enforceable.
   (ASC 210-20-45-1)

Practice Pointer: If an entity has the ability to set off, but does not intend to use it, presenting the effect in the balance sheet is not representationally faithful. Criteria 3 requires judgment to discern the intent of the reporting entity. History may be an indicator of the entity's intent. (ASC 210-20-45-4 and 45-5)

When maturities differ, only the party with the nearest maturity can offset, because the party with the later maturity must settle in the manner determined by the party with the earlier maturity. (ASC 210-10-45-3)

Entitles must apply their choices to offset consistently. Net receivables arising from application of ASC 210-20 cannot be offset against net payables. (ASC 210-20-45-12)

Taxes Payable The offsetting of cash or other assets against a tax liability or other amounts due to governmental bodies is acceptable only under limited circumstances. (ASC 210-10-45-6) When it is clear that a purchase of securities is in substance an advance payment of taxes payable in the near future and the securities are acceptable for the payment of taxes, amounts may be offset. Primarily this occurs as an accommodation to governmental bodies that issue tax anticipation notes in order to accelerate the receipt of cash from future taxes. (ASC 210-10-45-7)

Bankruptcy In particular cases, state laws or bankruptcy laws may impose restrictions or prohibitions against the right of setoff. (ASC 210-10-45-8)

Repurchase agreements and reverse repurchase agreements ASC 210-20-45-11 permits the offset of amounts recognized as payables in repurchase agreements against amounts recognized as receivables in reverse repurchase agreements with the same counterparty. If certain conditions are met, an entity may, but is not required to, offset the amounts recognized. The additional conditions for offsetting repurchase agreements and reverse repurchase agreements are:

1. The agreements must have the same explicit settlement date.
2. The agreements must be executed in accordance with a master netting agreement.
3. The securities underlying the agreements exist in "book entry" form and can be transferred only by means of entries in the records of the transfer system operator or the security custodian
4. The agreements will be settled on a securities transfer system that transfers ownership of "book entry" securities, and banking arrangements are in place so that the entity must only keep cash on deposit sufficient to cover the net payable.
5. Cash settlements for securities transferred are made under established bank arrangements that provide that an entity to have cash on deposit for net amounts due at close of business. The entity uses the same account for cash inflows and outflows related to the settlement. (Also see ASC 210-20-45-14 through 17 for additional details.)

These conditions do not apply to amounts recognized for other types of repurchase and reverse repurchase agreements executed under a master netting arrangement. This does not mean that those amounts could not otherwise meet the conditions for a right of setoff. (ASC 210-20-45-13)

Disclosures The disclosures required by ASC 210-20 apply to:

- Recognized derivative instruments accounted for in accordance with ASC 815, including bifurcated embedded derivatives, repurchase agreements and reverse repurchase agreements, and securities borrowing and securities lending transactions that are offset in accordance with either ASC 210-20-45 or ASC 815-10-45
- Recognized derivative instruments accounted for in accordance with Topic 815, including bifurcated embedded derivatives, repurchase agreements and reverse repurchase agreements, and securities borrowing and securities lending transactions that are subject to an enforceable master netting arrangement or similar agreement, irrespective of whether they are offset in accordance with either ASC 210-20-45 or ASC 815-10-45. (ASC 210-20-50-1)

The FASB has made it clear in its Background Comments for ASU 2013-01 that the disclosure requirements do not apply to:

- Loan and customer deposits at the same financial institution.
- Financial instruments only subject to collateral agreement. The FASB views these as primarily credit enhancements.
- Trade receivables and payables with a counterparty to be netted in the event of default. The FASB views these as primarily credit enhancements. In addition, requiring these to be disclosed would cause an undue burden on financial statement preparers.
- Receivables and payables of brokers dealers resulting from unsettled regular-way trades.

Offsetting relates to presentation only. If an asset and liability are presented net, it does not mean that the entity no longer has a contractual right or obligation. Therefore, to adequately inform the users, the Codification requires entities to disaggregate the relevant information. The disclosures must include:

a. The gross amounts for those recognized assets and liabilities,
b. The amounts offset to determine the net amounts presented in the balance sheet,
c. The net amounts presented in the balance sheet,
d. Amounts subject to an enforceable netting arrangement not included in the statement of financial position, instruments that the entity makes an election not to offset, and the amounts related to financial collateral.
e. The net amount after deducting "d" from "c" above.
(ASC 210-20-50-3)

Unless another format is more appropriate, the disclosures above must be presented in tabular format, separately by assets and liabilities. (ASC 210-20-50-4)

In addition to the quantitative information, the entity must present a description of the rights of setoff for recognized assets and liabilities subject to an enforceable master netting or similar arrangement. (ASC 210-20-50-5)

PRESENTATION AND DISCLOSURE EXAMPLES

Example 3.1: Statement of Financial Position—Highly Aggregated

ABC Corporation
Statement of Financial Position
December 31, 20X1

Assets	
Current assets	xxx
Long-term investments	xxx
Property, plant, and equipment, net	xxx
Deferred income tax assets	xxx
Goodwill	xxx
Intangible and other assets	xxx
Total assets	xxx
Liabilities and Shareholders' Equity	
Current liabilities	xxx
Deferred income tax liabilities	xxx
Long-term debt	xxx
Total liabilities	xxx
Capital stock	xxx
Additional paid-in capital	xxx
Retained earnings	xxx
Accumulated other comprehensive income	xxx
Total shareholders' equity	xxx
Total liabilities and shareholders' equity	xxx

The following more comprehensive statement of financial position includes more line items (for details about specific assets and liabilities) than are found in most statements of financial position.

Example 3.2: Statement of Financial Position—Highly Detailed

ABC Corporation
Statement of Financial Position
December 31, 20X1

Assets

Current assets:

Cash and bank deposits:		
Restricted to current bond maturity	$xxx	
Unrestricted	<u>xxx</u>	$xxx
Short-term investments:		
Marketable equity securities (trading)		xxx
Marketable debt securities (available-for-sale)		xxx
Refundable income taxes		xxx
Receivables from affiliates		xxx
Accounts receivable	xxx	
Less allowance for uncollectible accounts	(xxx)	xxx
Notes receivable due in 20X2	xxx	
Less discounts on notes receivable	(xxx)	xxx
Installment notes receivable due in 20X2		xxx
Interest receivable		xxx
Creditors' accounts with debit balances		xxx
Advances to employees		xxx
Inventories (carried at the lower of cost or market using FIFO):		
Finished goods	xxx	
Work in process	xxx	
Raw materials	<u>xxx</u>	xxx
Deferred income taxes (net of valuation allowance of $xxx)		
Prepaid expenses:		
Prepaid rent	xxx	
Prepaid insurance	<u>xxx</u>	<u>xxx</u>
Total current assets		$xxx

Long-term investments:

Investments in equity securities (available-for-sale)		xxx
Investments in bonds (held-to-maturity)		xxx
Investments in equity securities (at cost, plus equity in undistributed net earnings since acquisition)		xxx
Investments in unused land and facilities		xxx
Cash surrender value of officers' life insurance policies		xxx
Sinking fund for bond retirement		xxx
Plant expansion fund		<u>xxx</u>
Total long-term investments		$xxx

Property, plant, and equipment:

Land	$xxx	
Buildings (including capitalized interest of $xxx)	xxx	
Machinery and equipment	xxx	
Furniture and fixtures	xxx	
Assets under leases	xxx	

Leasehold improvements	xxx	
Less accumulated depreciation and amortization	(xxx)	
Total property, plant, and equipment		xxx

Intangible assets net of amortization:

Goodwill of acquired businesses	$xxx	
Patents	xxx	
Trademarks	xxx	
Total intangible assets, net		xxx

Other assets:

Installment notes due after 20X2	$xxx	
Unamortized bond issue costs	xxx	
Deferred income taxes (net of valuation allowance of $xxx)		xxx
Total other noncurrent assets		xxx
Total assets		$xxx

Liabilities and Shareholders' Equity

Current liabilities:

Current maturities of long-term debt	$xxx	
Current maturities of lease obligations	xxx	
Commercial paper and other short-term notes payable	xxx	
Accounts payable	xxx	
Accrued salaries, wages, and commissions	xxx	
Payroll taxes withheld and accrued	xxx	
Employee 401(k) contributions withheld	xxx	
Accrued rent	xxx	
Income taxes payable	xxx	
Sales taxes payable	xxx	
Dividends payable	xxx	
Rent revenue collected in advance	xxx	
Other advances from customers	xxx	
Deferred income taxes	xxx	
Short-term portion of accrued warranty costs	xxx	
Other accrued liabilities	xxx	
Total current liabilities[1]		$xxx

Noncurrent liabilities:

Notes payable due after 20X2	$xxx		
Plus unamortized note premium	xxx	$xxx	
Long-term bonds:			
10% debentures due 20X8		xxx	
9 1/2% collateralized obligations maturing serially to 20X3		xxx	
8% convertible subordinated debentures due 20X9		xxx	
Less unamortized discounts net of premiums		(xxx)	xxx
Accrued pension cost			xxx
Lease obligations			xxx
Asset retirement obligations (net of accumulated accretion of $xxx)			xxx
Deferred income taxes			xxx
Long-term portion of accrued warranty costs			xxx
Total noncurrent liabilities			xxx
Total liabilities			$xxx

---

[1] Total of current liabilities is required. (ASC 210-10-45-5)

Shareholders' equity
Capital stock:

$12.50 convertible preferred stock, $100 stated value, 200,000 shares authorized, 175,000 outstanding	$xxx	
12% cumulative preferred stock, $100 stated value, callable at $115, 100,000 shares authorized and outstanding	xxx	
Common stock, $10 stated value, 500,000 shares authorized, 450,000 issued, 15,000 held in treasury	xxx	
Common stock subscribed 10,000 shares	xxx	
Less: Subscriptions receivable	(xxx)	$xxx

Additional paid-in capital:

From 12% cumulative preferred	xxx	
From common stock	xxx	
From treasury stock transactions	xxx	
From stock dividends	xxx	
From expiration of share options	xxx	
Warrants outstanding	xxx	xxx
Retained earnings		xxx
Accumulated other comprehensive income		(xxx)
Less: Treasury stock at cost		(xxx)
Total shareholders' equity		$xxx
Total liabilities and shareholders' equity		$xxx

Example 3.3: Disclosure by Type of Financial Instrument[2]

ABC Company has entered into transactions subject to an enforceable master netting arrangement or other similar agreement with the counterparties XYZ and QRS. The reporting entity has the following recognized financial assets and financial liabilities resulting from those transactions that meet the scope of the disclosure requirements in paragraph 210-20-50-1.

a. ABC has a derivative asset (fair value of $100 million) and a derivative liability (fair value of $80 million) with XYZ. Assume that the entity qualifies for and makes an accounting policy election to offset in accordance with Section 815-10-45. Cash collateral also has been received from XYZ for a portion of the net derivative asset ($10 million). The derivative liability and the cash collateral received are set off against the derivative asset in the statement of financial position, resulting in the presentation of a net derivative asset of $10 million.

b. Counterparty QRS (assume that the following two transactions are not offset):

   1. ABC had entered into a sale and repurchase agreement with QRS that is accounted for as a collateralized borrowing. The carrying value of the financial asset (bonds) used as collateral and held by the reporting entity for the transaction is $79 million, and their fair value is $85 million. The carrying value of the collateralized borrowing (repo payable) is $80 million.

   2. ABC also has entered into a reverse sale and repurchase agreement with QRS that is accounted for as a collateralized lending. The fair value of the asset (bonds) received as collateral (and not recognized in the statement of financial position) is $105 million. The carrying value of the secured lending (reverse repo receivable) is $90 million.

---

[2] Example based on example in ASC 210-20-55.

Offsetting of Financial Assets and Derivatives—As of December 31, 20X0
Gross Amounts Not Offset in the Statement of Financial Position

	Gross Amounts of Recognized Assets	Gross Amounts Offset in the Statement of Financial Position	Net Amounts of Assets Presented in the Statement of Financial Position	Gross Amounts Not Offset in the Statement of Financial Position		Net Amount
				Financial Instruments	Cash Collateral Received	
Derivatives	$100,000	$(90,000)	$10,000	$—	$—	$10,000
Reverse repurchase, securities borrowings, and similar arrangements	90,000		90,000	(90,000)		
Other financial instruments	–	–	–	–	–	–
Total	$190,000	$(90,000)	$100,000	$(90,000)	$—	$10,000

Offsetting of Financial Liabilities and Derivative Liabilities—As of December 31, 20X0

Description	Gross Amounts of Recognized Liabilities	Gross Amounts Offset in the Statement of Financial Position	Net Amounts of Liabilities Presented in the Statement of Financial Position	Gross Amounts Not Offset in the Statement of Financial Position		Net Amount
				Financial Instruments	Cash Collateral Pledged	
Derivatives	$80,000	$80,000	$–	$–	$–	$–
Repurchase, securities lending, and similar arrangements	$80,000	–	80,000	(80,000)	–	–
Other financial instruments	–	–	–	–	–	–
Total	$160,000	$(80,000)	$80,000	$(80,000)	$–	$–

Example 3.4: Disclosure by Type of Financial Instrument and Type of Counterparty[3]

The following table illustrates how an entity might provide the quantitative disclosure requirements in ASC 210-20-50-3 by type of instrument and by counterparty.

Offsetting of Financial Assets and Derivative Assets—As of December 31, 20X0

Description	Gross Amounts of Recognized Assets	Gross Amounts Offset in the Statement of Financial Position	Net Amounts of Assets Presented in the Statement of Financial Position
Derivatives	$100,000	$(90,000)	$10,000
Reverse repurchase, securities, borrowings, and similar arrangements	$90,000	–	$90,000
Other financial instruments	–	–	–
Total	$190,000	$(90,000)	$100,000

---

[3] Example based on example in ASC 210-20-55.

Financial Assets, Derivative Assets, and Collateral Held by Counterparty—As of December 31, 20X0

	Net Amounts of Assets Presented in the Statement of Financial Position	Gross Amounts Not Offset in the Statement of Financial Position		
		Financial Instruments	Cash Collateral Received	Net Amount
Counterparty A	$10,000	$ –	$ –	$ 10,000
Counterparty B	$90,000	(90,000)	–	–
Other	–	–	–	–
Total	$100,000	$(90,000)	$ –	$10,000

Offsetting of Financial Liabilities and Derivative Liabilities—As of December 31, 20X0

Description	Gross Amounts of Recognized Liabilities	Gross Amounts Offset in the Statement of Financial Position	Net Amounts of Liabilities Presented in the Statement of Financial Position
Derivatives	$80,000	$(80,000)	$ –
Repurchase, securities lending, and similar arrangements	80,000	–	80,000
Other financial instruments	–	–	–
Total	$160,000	$(80,000)	$80,000

Financial Liabilities, Derivative Liabilities, and Collateral Pledged by Counterparty—As of December 31, 20X0

	Net Amounts of Liabilities Presented in the Statement of Financial Position	Gross Amounts Not Offset in the Statement of Financial Position		
		Financial Instruments	Cash Collateral Pledged	Net Amount
Counterparty A	$ –	$ –	$ –	$ –
Counterparty B	80,000	(80,000)	–	–
Other	–	–	–	–
Total	$80,000	$(80,000)	$ –	$ –

> **Example 3.5: Sophisticated Entity Disclosure by Type of Financial Instrument and Type of Counterparty**[4]

The following table illustrates how a sophisticated entity that engages in significant derivative activity might provide the quantitative disclosure requirements in paragraph 210-20-50-3 by type of instrument and by type of counterparty. In this example, the entity further disaggregates the derivative line item into underlying risk, with further disaggregation based on how the derivative is transacted.

Offsetting of Financial Assets and Derivatives—As of December 31, 20X0

Description	Gross Amounts of Recognized Assets	Gross Amounts Offset in the Statement of Financial Position	Net Amounts of Assets Presented in the Statement of Financial Position
Derivatives:			
Interest rate contracts:			
Over the counter	$XX,XXX	XX,XXX	XX,XXX
Exchange traded	XX,XXX	XX,XXX	XX,XXX
Exchange cleared	XX,XXX	XX,XXX	XX,XXX
Foreign exchange contracts:			
Over the counter	XX,XXX	XX,XXX	XX,XXX
Exchange traded	XX,XXX	XX,XXX	XX,XXX
Exchange cleared	XX,XXX	XX,XXX	XX,XXX
Equity contracts:			
Over the counter	XX,XXX	XX,XXX	XX,XXX
Exchange traded	XX,XXX	XX,XXX	XX,XXX
Exchange cleared	XX,XXX	XX,XXX	XX,XXX
Commodity contracts:			
Over the counter	XX,XXX	XX,XXX	XX,XXX
Exchange traded	XX,XXX	XX,XXX	XX,XXX
Exchange cleared	XX,XXX	XX,XXX	XX,XXX
Credit contracts:			
Over the counter	XX,XXX	XX,XXX	XX,XXX
Exchange traded	XX,XXX	XX,XXX	XX,XXX
Exchange cleared	XX,XXX	XX,XXX	XX,XXX
Other contracts:			
Over the counter	XX,XXX	XX,XXX	XX,XXX
Exchange traded	XX,XXX	XX,XXX	XX,XXX
Exchange cleared	XX,XXX	XX,XXX	XX,XXX
Total derivatives, subject to a master netting arrangement or similar arrangement	XX,XXX	XX,XXX	XX,XXX
Total derivatives, not subject to a master netting arrangement or similar arrangement	XX,XXX	XX,XXX	XX,XXX
Total derivatives	XX,XXX	XX,XXX	XX,XXX

---

[4] Example based on example in ASC 210-20-55.

Reverse repurchase, securities borrowings, and similar arrangements	XX,XXX	XX,XXX	XX,XXX
Other financial instruments	XX,XXX	XX,XXX	XX,XXX
Total	$XX,XXX	$XX,XXX	$XX,XXX

Financial Assets, Derivative Assets, and Collateral Held by Counterparty—As of December 31, 20X0

	Net Amounts of Assets Presented in the Statement of Financial Position	Gross Amounts Not Offset in the Statement of Financial Position		Net Amount
		Financial Instruments	Cash Collateral Received	
Counterparty A	$XX,XXX	$XX,XXX	$XX,XXX	$XX,XXX
Counterparty B	XX,XXX	XX,XXX	XX,XXX	XX,XXX
Other	XX,XXX	XX,XXX	XX,XXX	XX,XXX
Total	$XX,XXX	$XX,XXX	$XX,XXX	$XX,XXX

The counterparty should present similar tables.

Example 3.6: Netting of Certain Balance Sheet Accounts

Certain risk management assets and liabilities and certain accrued gas sales and purchases are presented on a net basis in the balance sheet when all of the following exist: (i) Gas Storage Partners and the other party owe the other a determinable amount; (ii) the Company has the right to set off the amount owed with the amount owed by the other party; (iii) Gas Storage Partners intends to set off; and (iv) the right of setoff is enforceable by law.

4 ASC 215 STATEMENT OF SHAREHOLDER EQUITY

Authoritative Literature	**45**

AUTHORITATIVE LITERATURE

ASC 215, *Statement of Shareholder Equity*, contains one Subtopic:

- ASC 215-10, *Overall*

That Subtopic merely provides a referral to disclosure guidance in ASC 505, *Equity*.

5 ASC 220 INCOME STATEMENT—REPORTING COMPREHENSIVE INCOME

AUTHORITATIVE LITERATURE

In financial reporting, performance is primarily measured by net income and its components, which are presented in the income statement. A second performance measure—comprehensive income—is a more inclusive notion of performance than net income. It includes all recognized changes in equity that occur during a period except those resulting from investments by owners and distributions to owners.

Because comprehensive income includes the effects on an entity of economic events largely outside of management's control, some have said that net income is a measure of management's performance and comprehensive income is a measure of entity performance.

In contrast to the statement of financial position, which provides information about an entity at a point in time, an income statement provides information about a period of time. It reflects information about the transactions and other events occurring within the period. Most of the weaknesses of an income statement are a result of its periodic nature. Entities are continually creating and selling goods and services, and at any single point in time some of those processes will be incomplete.

Subtopics

ASC 220, *Income Statement—Reporting Comprehensive Income*, contains three Subtopics:

- ASC 220-10, *Overall*
- ASC 220-20, *Unusual Items or Infrequently Occurring Items*
- ASC 220-30, *Business Interruption Insurance*

The three Subtopics provide discrete information and are not interrelated. (ASC 220-10-05-1 through 05-5)

Scope

ASC 220 applies to all entities except it does *not* apply to the following:

- Those that do not have any items of comprehensive income.
- Those not-for-profit entities that are required to follow the guidance in ASC 958-205. (ASC 220-10-15-3)

It applies to general purpose financial statements that present results of operations according to GAAP. (ASC 220-10-15-5)

ASC 220 focuses on presentation and disclosure and does not address recognition and measurement requirements.

PRACTICE ALERT

Income statement classification is a frequent topic of SEC comment letters. While SEC rules only apply to public entities, preparers of financial statements can benefit from the findings of SEC reviewers. Topics for comment include:

- Omitting certain required line items.
- Disclosure of policies related to alternative permissible classifications under the guidance in ASC 235-10.
- Disaggregation of material amounts, especially in the "other expense" line item.
- Separation of product and service revenue if greater than 10%. See the section on aggregation later in this chapter for more information.
- Types of expenses in cost of sales. For example, do the amounts include depreciation and amortization?
- If the entity includes a subtotal for operating income, determine if items are properly included in the operating and nonoperating categories.

DISCLOSURE AND PRESENTATION REQUIREMENTS

ASC 220-10, *Overall*

Format of Statement of Income and Comprehensive Income In the period they are recognized, entities must present all items that meet the definition of comprehensive income:

- In a combined statement of income and comprehensive income, or
- In two separate, but consecutive statements.
  (ASC 220-10-45-1C)

Exhibit 5.1 Items Required to Be Displayed in Either Acceptable Format of the Statement of Comprehensive Income

Reporting Comprehensive Income	
Single Continuous Statement of Net Income and Comprehensive Income	**Two Separate but Consecutive Statements**
Show: • Components of net income • Total net income • Components of other comprehensive income • Total of other comprehensive income • Total comprehensive income	In the statement of net income show: • Components of net income • Total of net income In the statement of comprehensive income presented immediately after the statement of net income begin with net income and show: • Components of other comprehensive income • Total of other comprehensive income • Total of comprehensive income
(ASC 220-10-45-1A)	(ASC 220-10-45-1B and 45-1C)

Entities with an Outstanding Noncontrolling Interest In addition to presenting consolidated net income and comprehensive income, entities with an outstanding noncontrolling interest are required to report the following items in the financial statement in which net income and comprehensive income are presented:

- Amount of net income and comprehensive income attributable to the parent.
- Amount of net income and comprehensive income attributable to the noncontrolling interest in a less-than-wholly-owned subsidiary.
  (ASC 220-10-45-5)

The Order of Presentation and Headings The basic order of presentation of information in an income statement (or statement of income and comprehensive income) is defined by other accounting topics, as shown in Example 5.1 later in this chapter. Other than in the section "income from continuing operations," the display of revenues, expenses, gains, losses, and other comprehensive income is predetermined by the Codification guidance. Only within income from continuing operations do tradition and industry practice determine the presentation.

The three items that are shown in the heading of an income statement are:

1. The name of the entity whose results of operations is being presented.
2. The title of the statement.
3. The period of time covered by the statement.

Entity Name The entity's legal name should be used and supplemental information could be added to disclose the entity's legal form as a corporation, partnership, sole proprietorship, or other form if that information is not apparent from the entity's name.

Statement Titles The use of the titles "Income Statement," "Statement of Income and Comprehensive Income," "Statement of Operations," or "Statement of Earnings" denotes preparation in accordance with GAAP. If another comprehensive basis of accounting were used, such as the cash or income tax basis, the title of the statement would be modified accordingly. "Statement of Revenue and Expenses—Income Tax Basis" or "Statement of Revenue and Expenses—Modified Cash Basis" are examples of such titles.

Statement Date The date of an income statement must clearly identify the time period involved, such as "Year Ending March 31, 20X1." That dating informs the reader of the length of the period covered by the statement and both the starting and ending dates. Dating such as "The Period Ending March 31, 20X1" or "Through March 31, 20X1" is not useful because of the lack of precision in those titles. Income statements are rarely presented for periods in excess of one year but are frequently seen for shorter periods such as a month or a quarter. Entities whose operations form a natural cycle may have a reporting period end on a specific day (e.g., the last Friday of the month). These entities should head the income statement "For the 52 Weeks Ended March 29, 20X1" (each week containing seven days, beginning on a Saturday and ending on a Friday). Although that fiscal period includes only 364 days (except for leap years), it is still considered an annual reporting period.

Consistency of Form Income statements generally should be uniform in appearance from one period to the next. The form, terminology, captions, and pattern of combining insignificant items should be consistent. If comparative statements are presented, the prior year's information should be restated to conform to the current year's presentation if changes in presentation are made.

Aggregation The level of disaggregation is a matter of judgment. It should be efficient to give to readers meaningful information. Aggregation of items should not serve to conceal significant information, such as netting revenues against expenses or combining dissimilar types of revenues, expenses, gains, or losses. Although the Codification does not offer benchmarks for disaggregation of income items, the SEC's Division of Corporate Finance's Form and Content of and Requirements for Financial Statements, Regulation S-X 5-03(1) does require separate presentation for some items that exceed 10% of total revenue. Those items include net sales of tangible products, service revenue, rental income, operating revenue of public utilities or others, and other revenues. The SEC also requires the costs and expenses related to those items to be presented separately.[1] Non-SEC preparers may want to consider those thresholds when deciding which amounts to disaggregate. Any benchmarks used should be applied consistently.

The category "other or miscellaneous expense" should contain, at maximum, an immaterial total amount of aggregated insignificant items. Once this total approaches a material amount of total expenses, some other aggregations with explanatory titles should be selected.

Income from Continuing Operations The section "income from continuing operations" includes all revenues, expenses, gains, and losses that are not required to be reported in other sections of an income statement.

There are two generally accepted formats for the presentation of income from continuing operations:

- Single-step and
- Multiple-step

Single-Step Format In the single-step format, items are classified into two groups: revenues and expenses. The operating revenues and other revenues are itemized and summed to determine total revenues. The cost of goods sold, operating expenses, and other expenses are itemized and summed to determine total expenses. The total expenses (including income taxes) are deducted from the total revenues to arrive at income from continuing operations.

Multiple-Step Format In a multiple-step format, operating revenues and expenses are separated from nonoperating revenues and expenses to provide more information concerning the

---

[1] Application of Regulations S-X (17 CFR PART 210) can be found on the ecfr.gov website.

firm's primary activities. This format breaks the revenue and expense items into various inter-mediate income components so that important relationships can be shown and attention can be focused on significant subtotals. Some examples of common income components are as follows:

1. Gross profit (margin)
2. Operating income
3. Income before income taxes

Income from Continuing Operations The following items of revenue, expense, gains, and losses are included within income from continuing operations:

1. Sales or service revenues
2. Cost of goods sold
3. Operating expenses
4. Gains and losses
5. Other revenues and expenses
6. Unusual and/or infrequently occurring
7. Goodwill impairment losses
8. Exit or disposal activity costs
9. Income tax expense

Net Income The section ends in a subtotal that varies depending upon the existence of discontinued operations. Net income reflects all items of profit and loss recognized during the period, except for error corrections. (ASC 220-10-45-7A) The requirement that net income be presented as one amount does not apply to those entities that have statements different in format from commercial enterprises:

- Investment companies.
- Insurance entities.
- Certain not-for-profit entities (NFPs).
  (ASC 220-10-45-7A)

Items of Other Comprehensive Income ASC 220-10-45-10A lists the following as items currently within other comprehensive income:

- Foreign currency translation adjustments (see paragraph 830-30-45-12).
- Gains and losses on foreign currency transactions that are designated as, and are effec-tive as, economic hedges of a net investment in a foreign entity, commencing as of the designation date (see paragraph 830-20-35-3(a)).
- Gains and losses on intra-entity foreign currency transactions that are of a long-term investment nature (that is, settlement is not planned or anticipated in the foreseeable future), when the entities to the transaction are consolidated, combined, or accounted for by the equity method in the reporting entity's financial statements (see paragraph 830-20-35-3(b)).
- The difference between changes in fair value of the excluded components of derivatives designated in qualifying hedges and the initial value of the excluded components recog-nized in earnings under a systematic and rational method.[2]
- Gains and losses (effective portion) on derivative instruments that are designated as, and qualify as, cash flow hedges (see paragraph 815-20-35-1(c)).

---

[2] This bulleted item is effective upon implementation of ASU 2017-12.

- For derivatives that are designated in qualifying hedging relationships, the difference between changes in fair value of the excluded components and the initial value of the excluded components recognized in earnings under a systematic and rational method in accordance with ASC 815-20-25-83A.
- Unrealized holding gains and losses on available-for-sale debt securities (see paragraph 320-10-45-1).[3]
- Unrealized holding gains and losses that result from a debt security being transferred into the available-for-sale category from the held-to-maturity category (see paragraph 320-10-35-10(c)).
- Amounts recognized in other comprehensive income for debt securities classified as available-for-sale and held-to-maturity related to an other-than-temporary impairment recognized in accordance with Section 320-10-35 if a portion of the impairment was not recognized in earnings.[4]
- Subsequent decreases (if not an other-than-temporary impairment) or increases in the fair value of available-for-sale securities previously written down as impaired (see paragraph 320-10-35-18).[5]
- Gains or losses associated with pension or other postretirement benefits (that are not recognized immediately as a component of net periodic benefit cost) (see paragraph 715-20-50-1(j)).
- Prior service costs or credits associated with pension or other postretirement benefits (see paragraph 715-20-50-1(j)).
- Transition assets or obligations associated with pension or other postretirement benefits (that are not recognized immediately as a component of net periodic benefit cost) (see paragraph 715-20-50-1(j)).
- Changes in fair value attributable to instrument-specific credit risk of liabilities for which the fair value option is elected (see paragraph 825-10-45-5).
- Effects of changes in the discount rates used to measure traditional and limited-payment long-duration contracts[6] (see ASC 944-40-35-6A(b)(1)).
- Effects of changes in the fair value of a market risk benefit attributable to a change in the instrument-specific credit risk[7] (see ASC 944-40-35-6A(b)(1)).

The following items do not quality as comprehensive income:

- Changes in equity resulting from investment by and distributions to owners.
- Items that are required to be reported as direct adjustments to paid-in-capital, retained earnings, or other nonincome equity accounts.
  (ASC 220-10-45-10B)

Other comprehensive income is recognized and measured in accordance with the accounting pronouncement that deems it part of other comprehensive income.

---

[3] Upon implementation of ASU 2016-13, this reference will change to ASC 326-30-35-2.

[4] Upon implementation of ASU 2016-13, this bullet point is superseded.

[5] Ibid.

[6] This bulleted item is effective upon implementation of ASU 2018-02, *Financial Services—Insurance (Topic 944): Targeted Improvements to the Accounting for Long-Duration Contracts.*

[7] Ibid.

Income Tax Effects The items of other comprehensive income can be reported either:

- Net of related tax effects in the statement, or
- Gross with the tax effects related to all components reported on a single, separate line. (ASC 220-10-45-11)

The tax effects of each component of other comprehensive income must be presented in the statement in which those components are presented or in the notes of the financial statements. (ASC 220-10-45-12 and 50-4) If gross reporting is used, the notes to the financial statements must disclose the tax effects related to each component (if there is more than one component). Examples 5.5 and 5.6 later in this chapter illustrate the two presentations.

The Codification also has guidance on the reclassification of certain tax effects from AOCI. The guidance is intended to help entities address certain stranded income tax effects in accumulated other comprehensive income (AOCI) resulting from the Tax Cuts and Jobs Act. Under the guidance, entities have an option to reclassify stranded tax effects within AOCI to retained earnings in each period in which the effect of the change in the U.S. federal corporate income tax rate in the Tax Cuts and Jobs Act (or portion thereof) is recorded. If the entity elects to reclassify the income tax effects of the Tax Cuts and Jobs Act from AOCI to retained earnings, the reclassification includes:

a. The effects of the change in the U.S. federal corporate income tax rate as the gross defined tax amounts and related valuation allowances.
b. Other income tax effects that the entity elects to reclassify. (ASC 220-10-45-12A)

The guidance recommends financial statement preparers disclose:

- A description of the accounting policy for releasing income tax effects from AOCI.
- Whether they elect to reclassify the stranded income tax effects from the Tax Cuts and Jobs Act, and information about the other income tax effects that are reclassified. If the preparers elect not to reclassify the effects, they must disclose that fact in the period of adoption. (ASC 220-10-50-1 through 50-3)

  The guidance affects any organization that
  - Is required to apply the provisions of Topic 220, *Income Statement—Reporting Comprehensive Income*, and
  - Has items of other comprehensive income for which the related tax effects are presented in other comprehensive income as required by GAAP.

Accumulated Other Comprehensive Income At the end of the reporting period, that reporting period's total of other comprehensive income is transferred to a component of equity. It is presented separately from retained earnings and additional paid-in capital on the balance sheet. (ASC 220-10-45-14) On the face of the financial statements, or as a note, the entity must present:

- The changes in the accumulated balances of each component of other comprehensive income, and
- Current period reclassifications out of accumulated other comprehensive income and other amounts of other comprehensive income, either before-tax or net-of-tax. (ASC 220-10-45-14A and 50-5)

Reclassification Adjustments Some items impact other comprehensive income in one period and then affect net income in the same or a later period. Adjustments of that type are called reclassification adjustments. (ASC 220-10-45-15)[8] The process of including in net income an item previously reported in other comprehensive income is often referred to as "recycling." The entity determines the reclassification adjustments for each component of other comprehensive income. The sale of an investment in a foreign entity may trigger an adjustment for foreign currency items that had been included in other comprehensive income previously. In such a case, the requirement for a reclassification is limited to accumulated foreign currency translation gains or losses). An adjustment is also necessary upon the complete (or substantially complete) liquidation of an investment in a foreign entity. See ASC 830-30-40-1 through 40-1A for more information.

Amounts accumulated in other comprehensive income from cash flow hedges are reclassified into earnings in the same period(s) in which the hedged forecasted transactions (such as a forecasted sale) affect earnings. If it becomes probable that the forecasted transaction will not occur, the net gain or loss in accumulated other comprehensive income must be immediately reclassified. (ASC 815-30-35-38)

Reclassification adjustments required by other Topics can be presented by component of other comprehensive income, either:

- In a single note, or
- Parenthetically on the face of their annual financial statement.
  (ASC 220-10-45-17 and 50-6 describes the information requirements for disclosure in the notes)

If an entity chooses to present information for items reclassified out of AOCI on the face of the statement, the entity should present parenthetically:

- The effect of significant amounts reclassified from each component of AOCI based on its source, and
- The aggregate tax effect of those significant reclassifications on the line item for income tax expense or benefit.
  (ASC 220-10-45-17A)

If an entity uses a separate line item in the income statement to present pension or other posttretirement benefit cost components reclassified out of AOCI, the entity is not required to present those items parenthetically. (ASC 220-10-45-17A)

If an entity chooses or is required to place the information reclassified out of AOCI in the notes, it should provide:

- The significant amounts by each component of AOCI,
- A subtotal of each component of AOCI, and
- For those amounts required by other Topics to be reclassified to net income in their entirety in the same reporting period, the line items affected by the reclassification.

If a component is only partially reclassified to net income, entities must cross-reference to the related footnote for additional information. (ASC 220-10-50-6)

Interim Reporting For interim reporting, entities must present a total for comprehensive income but are *not* required to present the individual components of OCI. Entities that present two

---

[8] Life insurers should exclude from amounts reclassified out of accumulated other comprehensive income changes in unrealized gains and losses on available-for-sale debt securities associated with direct adjustments made to policy liabilities necessary to reflect these balances as if such unrealized gains and losses were realized. (ASC 220-10-55-15C)

statements in their annual financial reports have the option of using a single-statement approach in their condensed interim financial statements. Using one statement avoids the presentation of a separate statement of comprehensive income that contains only one line item for total comprehensive income. (ASC 220-10-45-18) Nonpublic entities are not required to meet the requirements for reclassifications in interim reporting. (ASC 220-10-45-18B)

ASC 220-20, *Unusual Items or Infrequently Occurring Items*

Items that are unusual or infrequent should be reported as a separate component of income from continuing operations or in the notes. The EPS effect of these items should *not* be reported on the face of the income statement. (ASC 220-20-45-1 and 50-1)

In addition, the entity should disclose the nature and financial effects of each event or transaction on the face of the income statement as a separate component of continuing operations, or alternatively, in notes to financial statements. (ASC 220-20-50-3 and 45-16)

ASC 220-30, *Business Interruption Insurance*

In general, proceeds from insurance claims are classified based on the nature of the loss and requires judgment. As long as it does not conflict with other guidance, entities should classify recoveries from business interruption insurance in the statement of operations. (ASC 220-30-45-1) In the notes to the financial statements, the entity should include:

- The nature of the event causing business interruption losses.
- Aggregate amount of interruption insurance recoveries and the line item where classified. (ASC 230-30-50-1)

The proceeds related to lost assets should not be recorded as reductions of the costs to rebuild or replace the insured asset.

DISCLOSURE AND PRESENTATION EXAMPLES

Example 5.1: Basic Order of Income Statement and Comprehensive Income Statement

Statement of Income
Income from continuing operations
Sales or service revenues
Costs of goods sold
Operating expenses
Remaining excess of fair value over cost of acquired net assets
in a business combination
Gains and losses
Other revenues and expenses
Items that are unusual or infrequent, gross
Income tax expense related to continuing operations
Results from discontinued operations
Income (loss) from operations of a discontinued component
Gain (loss) from disposal of a discontinued component
Net income
Earnings per share information

Other comprehensive income	
Foreign currency translation adjustments	
Unrealized gains (losses) on securities	
Adjustments related to pension liabilities or assets	
Gains/losses on cash-flow hedging items	
Gains/losses on hedges of forecasted foreign-currency-denominated transactions	
Reclassification adjustment (may be shown gross or net of tax, details may be disclosed in note)	
Income tax related to other comprehensive income (if components are not shown net of tax)	
Comprehensive income	
Earnings per share information	

Example 5.2: A Multiple-Step Format for Income from Continuing Operations

Sales:

Sales		$xxx	
Less: Sales discounts		$xxx	
Sales returns and allowances		<u>xxx</u>	<u>(xxx)</u>
Net sales			$xxx
Cost of goods sold			<u>xxx</u>
Gross profit			$xxx
Operating expenses:			
Selling expenses			
Sales salaries	$xxx		
Commissions	xxx		
Advertising expense	xxx		
Delivery expense	xxx		
Selling supplies expense	xxx		
Depreciation of store furniture and equipment	<u>xxx</u>	$xxx	
General and administrative expenses			
Officers' salaries	$xxx		
Office salaries	xxx		
Bad debts expense	xxx		
Office supplies expense	xxx		
Depreciation of office furniture and fixtures	xxx		
Depreciation of building	xxx		
Insurance expense	xxx		
Utilities expense	<u>xxx</u>	<u>xxx</u>	
Total operating expense		(xxx)	
Operating income			
Other revenues:			$xxx
Dividend income		$xxx	
Gain on business acquisition ("bargain purchase")		xxx	
Interest income		<u>xxx</u>	xxx
Other expenses:			
Interest expense			<u>(xxx)</u>
Income from continuing operations			<u>$xxx</u>

Example 5.3: A Single-Step Format for Income from Continuing Operations

Revenues:		
Sales (net of discounts and returns and allowances)	$xxx	
Gain on sale of equipment	xxx	
Interest income	xxx	
Dividend income	<u>xxx</u>	$xxx
Expenses:		
Cost of goods sold	$xxx	
Selling expenses	xxx	
General and administrative expenses	xxx	
Interest expense	<u>xxx</u>	xxx
Income from continuing operations		<u>xxx</u>

Example 5.4: Combined Statement of Income and Comprehensive Income with "Net of Tax" Presentation

Hypothetical Corporation
Statement of Comprehensive Income
for the Year Ended December 31, 20X1
($000 omitted)

Revenues		$395,400
Expenses		(251,220)
Other gains and losses		1,500
Income from operations before tax		<u>145,680</u>
Income tax expense		(62,430)
Net income		<u>83,250</u>
Earnings per share		
Basic and diluted 0.73		
Other comprehensive income		
Foreign currency translation adjustment, net of $5,100 tax		11,900
Unrealized gain on securities:		
Unrealized holding gains arising during period,	17,500	
net of $7,500 tax		
Less: Reclassification adjustment, net of $1,500 tax, for	<u>(3,500)</u>	14,000
gain included currently in net income		
Cash flow hedges		
Net derivative losses arising during the period,	(11,200)	
net of $4,800 tax		
Less: Reclassification adjustment for losses	<u>18,113</u>	6,913
included currently in net income, net of		
$7,762 tax		
Defined benefit pension plans:		
Prior service cost arising during period	(3,900)	
Net loss arising during period	(2,900)	
Less: Amortization of prior service cost	300	
included with net period pension cost		
Less: Tax effects	<u>1,950</u>	(4,550)
Other comprehensive income		(28,263)
Comprehensive income		<u>$111,513</u>

Example 5.5: Combined Statement of Income and Comprehensive Income with "Gross of Tax" Presentation

Hypothetical Corporation
Statement of Comprehensive Income
for the Year Ended December 31, 20X1
($000 omitted)

Sales		$395,400
Expenses		(251,220)
Other gains and losses		1,500
Income from operations before tax		145,680
Income tax expense		(62,430)
Net earnings		83,250
Earnings per share		
Basic and diluted 0.73		
Other comprehensive income		
Foreign currency translation adjustment		17,000
Unrealized gains on debt securities:		
Unrealized holding gains arising during period	25,000	
Less: Reclassification adjustment for gain included currently in net income	(5,000)	20,000
Cash flow hedges		
Net derivative losses arising during the period	(16,000)	
Less: Reclassification adjustment for losses included currently in net income	25,875	9,875
Defined benefit plans adjustment[9]		
Prior service cost arising during period	(3,900) (a)	
Net loss arising during period	(2,900) (a)	
Less: Amortization of prior service cost included with net period pension cost	300 (a)	(6,500)
		40,375
Other comprehensive income, before tax		(12,112)
Income tax expense related to items of other comprehensive income		28,263
Other comprehensive income, net of tax		
Comprehensive income		$111,513

These AOCI components are components of net periodic pension cost (see pension note for additional details).

If the "gross" approach illustrated above is used, it is also necessary to present in the notes to the financial statements details regarding the allocation of the tax effects to the several items included in other comprehensive income. An example of that note disclosure follows.

Example 5.6: Two Separate but Consecutive Statements of Income and Comprehensive Income—Net of Tax Presentation

Hypothetical Corporation
Statement of Income
for the Year Ended December 31, 20X1
($000 omitted)

Revenues, (includes $12,000 accumulated other comprehensive income reclassifications for net gains in cash flow hedges)	$395,400
Expenses, (includes ($10,000) accumulated other comprehensive income reclassifications for net loss in cash flow hedges)	(251,220)
Other gains and losses	1,500

---
[9] Ibid.

Income from operations before tax	145,680
Income tax expense	(62,430)
Net income	83,250
Earnings per share	
Basic and diluted 0.73	

Hypothetical Corporation
Statement of Comprehensive Income
for the Year Ended December 31, 20X1
($000 omitted)

Net income		83,250
Other comprehensive income		
Foreign currency translation adjustment, net of $5,100 tax		11,900
Unrealized gain on debt securities:		
Unrealized holding gains arising during period, net of $7,500 tax	17,500	
Less: Reclassification adjustment, net of $1,500 tax, for gain included currently in net income	(3,500)	14,000
Cash flow hedges		
Net derivative losses arising during the period, net of $4,800 tax		(11,200)
Less: Reclassification adjustment for losses included currently in net income, net of $7,762 tax	18,113	6,913
Defined benefit pension plans: tax[10]		
Prior service cost arising during period	(3,900) (a)	
Net loss arising during period	(2,900) (a)	
Less: Amortization of prior service cost included with net period pension cost	300 (a)	
Less: Tax effects	1,950	(4,550)
Other comprehensive income		28,263
Comprehensive income		$111,513

(a) These AOCI components are components of net periodic pension cost (see pension note for additional details).

Example 5.7: Note X: Income Taxes

The tax effects of items included in other comprehensive income for the year ended December 31, 20X1, are as follows:

	Before-Tax Amount	Tax Expense (Benefit)	Net-of-Tax Amount
Foreign currency translation adjustments	$17,000	$5,100	$11,900
Unrealized gains on debt securities:			
Unrealized holding gains arising during period	25,000	7,500	17,500
Less: Reclassification adjustment for gains realized in net income	(5,000)	(1,500)	(3,500)
Net unrealized holding gains	20,000	6,000	14,000
Cash flow hedges:			
Net derivative losses arising during the period	(16,000)	4,800	(11,200)
Plus: Reclassification adjustment for losses realized in net income	25,875	(6,913)	18,113
Net effects of cash flow hedges	9,875	(2,113)	6,913
Defined benefit plans:			
Prior service cost from plan amendment during the period	(5,800)	(1,640)	(4,200)

---

[10] Ibid.

	Before-Tax Amount	Tax Expense (Benefit)	Net-of-Tax Amount
Less: amortization of prior service cost included in net periodic pension cost	1,800	640	700
Net prior service cost during the period	(4,000)	(1,000)	(3,500)
Net loss arising during the period	(2,500)	(950)	(1,040)
Defined benefit plans, net	(6,500)	(1,950)	(4,540)
Other comprehensive income	$40,375	$12,112	$28,263

Note: An example of displaying unusual or infrequently occurring items on the balance sheet can be found in Exhibit 5.1.

Example 5.8: Unusual or Infrequently Occurring Item—Fire at Manufacturing Facility

In May 20X1, the Company experienced a fire that damaged certain inventory and machinery and equipment at the production facility in Raleigh, North Carolina. The fire occurred after business hours and was fully extinguished quickly, with no injuries. The plant was back in full operation shortly thereafter with no significant disruption in supply or service to customers. The Company maintains adequate insurance coverage for its operations.

The total amount of the loss related to assets and the related expenses was $2,690,000. The majority of the Company's insurance claim relates to the recovery of damaged inventory. Through payments received in May 20X2 and March 20X3, the Company has recorded approximately $2,397,000 as a partial payment on the claim. This resulted in no gain or loss being recognized. As of December 31, 20X3, the Company reflects a receivable from the insurance company relating to this claim of $285,000, net of $232,000, and represents additional proceeds to be received. The deductible charge was expenses in Fiscal Year 20X1, as a component of cost of goods sold in the statement of operations and comprehensive income.

Example 5.9: Unusual or Infrequently Occurring Items—Legal Settlement

In February 20X3, the Company received $8.3 million from Blake MedTech, Inc. to satisfy the May 20X0 jury award of damages for infringement of the Company's heart monitor. For further information, see Note X.

Example 5.10: Business Interruption and Insurance Recovery

On June 23, 20X1, an accidental gas explosion occurred at our manufacturing facility in Waco, Texas ("the Waco accident"). This facility was the primary production facility for the NutraBar brand. During fiscal 20X3, the Company settled its property and business interruption claims related to the Garner accident with our insurance providers. The total payments received from the insurers in fiscal 20X3 were $278.6 million and all previously deferred balances were immediately recognized upon settlement of the insurance claim in fiscal 20X3. The insurance recoveries recognized in fiscal 20X3, included in selling, general and administrative expenses totaled $132.6 million, representing $95 million in reimbursement for business interruption, a $32.4 million gain on involuntary conversion of property, plant and equipment and recovery of other expenses incurred of $5.2 million.

Example 5.11: Business Interruption and Insurance Recovery

A severe rainy season affected many parts of Mississippi in December 20X0 and caused the company to case manufacturing at its facility in Mississippi dues to a breach of a levy and flooding at the industrial park where the facility is located. The Company established temporary offices and worked with customers to meet critical needs through other manufacturing facilities. The facility re-established manufacturing operations on April 2, 20X1.

The Company maintains property and business interruption insurance policies. On February 4, 20X1, the Company filed a $5.0 million claim under one of its insurance policies to cover both the property damage and the business interruption. The policy had a $1.0 million deductible. In fiscal 20X1, the Company collected $4.0 million as settlement of the claim under the policy.

The Company included in Operating income (loss) for fiscal year 20X1 the $4.0 million of insurance proceeds related to recovery of certain losses recognized for property damage and business interruption experienced by the Company. Of the $4.0 million recorded for fiscal 20X1, $3.0 million were recorded in cost of goods sold and $1.0 million were recorded in Selling, general, and administrative expenses in order to offset the recognized losses.

6 ASC 230, STATEMENT OF CASH FLOWS

AUTHORITATIVE LITERATURE

Unlike other statements, the statement of cash flows is based on the cash basis of accounting rather than on the accrual basis. Therefore, all bank account debits and credits that are unrestricted demand deposits should be reported in the statement as inflows and outflows of cash. Reporting cash flows involves no estimated allocations and few judgments except regarding classification in the statement.

Cash flows are recognized in the statement of cash flows in the period they occur. However, entities must disclose in the statement noncash investing and financing activities. (FASB Concepts Statement [CON] No. 5)

Subtopic

ASC 230, *Statement of Cash Flows*, contains one Subtopic:

- ASC 230-10, *Overall*

Scope and Scope Exceptions

A statement of cash flows is a required part of a complete set of financial statements for business enterprises and not-for-profit organizations. The following are *not* required to present a statement of cash flows:

- Defined pension plans that present financial information under Topic 960.
- Other employee plans that present information similar to ASC 960. (ASC 962-205-45-9)
- A common trust fund, variable annuity account, or similar fund maintained by a bank, insurance entity, or other entity in its capacity as a trustee, administrator, or guardian for the collective investment and reinvestment of moneys.
- Investment companies within the scope of ASC 946 if the following conditions are met:
  - Substantially all of the entity's investments are highly liquid,
  - The entity's investments are carried at fair value and classified in accordance with ASC 820 as Level 1 or Level 2 or were measured using the practical expedient to determine fair value and are redeemable in the near term,
  - The entity has little or no debt, based on average debt outstanding during the period, in relation to average total assets, and
  - The entity provides a statement of changes in net assets.
  (ASC 230-10-15-4)

PRACTICE ALERT

The SEC offers suggestions for avoiding errors when preparing the statement of cash flow. While these suggestions apply to the statement of cash flows, they are equally valid when preparing other financial statement statements.

Information

- How are you collecting the financial data necessary to prepare the statement?
- What processes are in place to ensure this information is complete and accurate, especially to the extent new or nonrecurring transactions have occurred?
- Are there manual processes that are ad hoc that could be standardized or automated?

People

- Do those individuals preparing the statement of cash flows understand the principles in ASC 230?
- Are there ways you can provide them with better training to perform their job?
- Do those individuals reviewing the statement of cash flows have enough expertise to identify and prevent misstatements in their review process?

Timing

- Are there ways to prepare and review the statement of cash flows earlier in the financial statement closing process?
  (Source: https://www.sec.gov/news/speech/2014-spch120814tkc)

PRESENTATION AND DISCLOSURE REQUIREMENTS

Objective

The primary purpose of the statement of cash flows is to provide information about the entity's operations, investing transactions, and financing activities during the period. (ASC 230-10-45-1) The statement includes inflows and outflows of cash and cash equivalents. The statement must also present a reconciliation of net income and net cash from operating activities. (ASC 230-10-45-2) Operating activities are particularly useful to investors because they show the entity's ability to act as a going concern.

Cash flow per share may *not* be displayed in the financial statements of a reporting entity. (ASC 230-10-45-3)

Cash and Cash Equivalents

Entities must explain the changes in the total of cash and cash equivalents and amounts described as restricted cash or restricted cash equivalents. Entities must combine restricted cash with unrestricted cash and cash equivalents in the statement of cash flows. If those amounts are presented in more than one line item in the statement of financial position, the entity must disclose:

- The line items
- Amounts of cash described as restricted cash or restricted cash equivalents

The disaggregated amounts must equal the total shown in the statement of cash flows. This information may be presented on the face of the statement or in the notes in narrative or tabular format. (ASC 230-10-45-4 and 50-8)

Entities commonly invest excess cash on hand in short-term, highly liquid investments, and those amounts are substantively the cash the entity owns. Therefore, it makes sense for the statement of cash flows to focus on the aggregate amount of those accounts. Cash purchases and sales of cash equivalents are part of the entity's cash management activities, and those transactions need not be reported in the statement of cash flows. Entities should not present transfers between cash and cash equivalents and restricted cash and restricted cash equivalents. (ASC 230-10-45-5)

Cash equivalents generally include any short-term, highly liquid investments used as a temporary investment of idle cash. The entity must, however, have a policy as to which investments that meet the definition are treated as cash equivalents and that policy should be disclosed in the notes. (ASC 230-10-45-6 and 50-1)

Restrictions on Cash and Cash Equivalents

While the ASC does not provide a formal definition of unrestricted cash, it does require entities to disclose information about the nature of the restriction on its cash, cash equivalents, and amounts described as restricted cash or restricted cash equivalents. (ASC 230-10-50-7) Companies generally present restricted cash separately from cash and cash equivalents. However, the line item may not be titled restricted cash.

Gross versus Net Basis

The emphasis in the statement of cash flows is on gross cash receipts and payments, and, with limited exceptions, most investing and financing activities must be presented gross. For instance, reporting the net change in bonds payable would obscure the financing activities of the entity by not disclosing separately cash inflows from issuing bonds and cash outflows from retiring bonds.

In a few circumstances, netting of cash flows is allowed. The items must have these characteristics:

- Quick turnovers,
- Large amounts, and
- Short maturities (maturities of three months or less).
  (ASC 230-10-45-8)

Net reporting for the following assets and liabilities is allowed provided the original maturity is three months or less:

1. Investments (other than cash equivalents),
2. Loans receivable, and
3. Debts.

For this purpose, due on demand amounts are considered to have maturities three months or less. Also, credit card receivables of financial services operations are considered loans with maturities of three months or less when at the cardholders option:

- The amount charged may be paid in full when first billed,
- The payment is usually due within one month without interest, and
- The charges are not from the entity's sale of goods or services.
  (ASC 230-10-45-9)

Classification of Cash Receipts and Disbursements The statement of cash flows requires classification of cash receipts and cash disbursements into three categories:

1. Investing activities
2. Financing activities
3. Operating activities
   (ASC 230-10-45-10)

These classifications allow users to evaluate significant relationships and among the activities and to understand the cash flow effects of major activities and to identify trends. (ASC 230-10-10-2) These classifications mirror the order of the statement of cash flows. That is, the operating activities section appears first with the investing and financing activities following.

Operating Activities Operating activities include all transactions and other events that are not defined as investing or financing activities. Operating activities generally involve producing and delivering goods and providing services. (ASC 230-10-20)

Investing Activities Investing activities include making and collecting loans and acquiring and disposing of debt or equity instruments and property, plant, and equipment and other productive assets, that is, assets held for or used in the production of goods or services by the entity (other than materials that are part of the entity's inventory). Investing activities exclude acquiring and disposing of certain loans or other debt or equity instruments that are acquired specifically for resale. (ASC 230-10-20)

Financing Activities Financing activities include obtaining resources from owners and providing them with a return on, and a return of, their investment; receiving restricted resources that by donor stipulation must be used for long-term purposes; borrowing money and repaying amounts borrowed, or otherwise settling the obligation; and obtaining and paying for other resources obtained from creditors on long-term credit. (ASC 230-10-20)

Following is a list of the classifications of cash inflows and outflows within the statement of cash flows.

Operating Activities—Cash Inflows

- Receipts from sale of goods or services.
- Returns on loans, other debt instruments of other entities, and equity securities (interest and dividends).
- All other cash receipts not from inventory or financing activities.
  (ASC 230-10-45-16)
- Receipts from sales of other securities and other assets if acquired for resale and carried at fair value in a trading account.
  (ASC 230-10-45-20)
- Receipts from acquisitions and sales of loans acquired specifically for resale and carried at fair value at the lower of amortized cost basis or fair value. (ASC 230-10-45-21)
- Not-for-profits' sale of donated financial assets that on receipt had no donor-imposed limitations on sale and were converted immediately into cash.
  (ASC 230-10-45-21A)
- For lessors—cash receipts from lease payments from leases classified as sales-type, direct financing, or operating leases.
  (ASC 842-30-45-5 and 45-7)

Operating Activities—Cash Outflows

- Payments for inventory.
- Payments to employees and other suppliers for goods and services.
- Payments to government for taxes, duties, fines, and other fees or penalties.
- Payments of interest, including interest portion of settlement of zero coupon debt instruments and those with relatively insignificant interest rates.
- Payments of asset retirement obligations.
- Cash payments, not made soon after the acquisition date of a business combination by an acquirer to settle a contingent consideration liability that exceed the amount of the contingent consideration liability recognized at the acquisition date, less any amounts paid soon after the acquisition date to settle the contingent consideration liability.
- All other cash payments that do not stem from transactions defined as investing or financing activities, such as payments to settle lawsuits, cash contributions to charities, and cash refunds to customers.
  (ASC 230-10-45-17)
- Cash payments for purchase of other securities and assets acquired specifically for resale carried at fair value in a trading account.
  (ASC 230-10-45-20)
- Cash payments for loans acquired specifically for resale and carried at fair value or at the lower of amortized cost basis or fair value.
  (ASC 230-10-45-21)

- For lessees:
  - Payments for the interest portion of the lease liability from a finance lease.
  - Payments from operating leases, except to the extent that those payments represent costs to bring another asset for its intended use.
  - Variable lease payments and short-term payments not included in the lease liability. (ASC 842-20-45-5b-d)

Investing Activities—Cash Inflows

- Cash flows from purchases, sales, and maturities of available-for-sale debt securities, reported gross. (ASC 230-10-45-11)
- Receipts from collections or sales of loans and sales of other entities' debt instruments except, for cash equivalents and certain debt instruments acquired specifically for resale, and donated debt instruments received by not-for-profit entities per ASC 230-10-45-21A.
- Receipts from collections on a transferor's beneficial interest in the securitization of the transferor's trade receivables.
- Receipts from sales of equity instruments, held in available-for-sale or held-to-maturity portfolios, of other enterprises and from returns on investments on those instruments.
- Receipts from donated debt instruments received from NFPs and from returns of investment in those instruments.
- Receipts from sales of property, plant, and equipment and other productive assets, including directly related proceeds from insurance settlements.
- Receipts from sales of loans not specifically acquired for resale, including specifically acquired for directly related proceeds from insurance settlements.
- Receipts from proceeds of insurance settlements directly related to the sale or disposal of loans, debt or equity investments, or property, plant, or equipment. (ASC 230-10-45-12)
- Cash received as proceeds from the settlement of corporate-owned life insurance policies (COLI), including bank-owned life insurance (BOLI). (ASC 230-10-45-21C)

Investing Activities—Cash Outflows

- Payments for loans made.
- Payments for acquisitions of other entities' debt instruments other than cash equivalents and certain debt instruments acquired for resale.
- Payments to purchase equity of other enterprises instruments, other than certain instruments carried in a trading account.
- Payments at the time of purchase, or soon before or after, of property, plant, and equipment and other productive assets, including interest capitalized as part of the cost of those assets.
- Contingent consideration payments by an acquirer made soon after an acquisition's consummation date in a business combination. (ASC 230-10-45-13)

Financing Activities—Cash Inflows

- Proceeds from issuing equity instruments.
- Proceeds from issuing debt (short-term or long-term), including bonds, mortgages, and notes.
- Not-for-profits' cash receipts contributions and investment income that are donor-restricted for long-term purposes or for increasing a donor-restricted endowment fund.

- Proceeds from derivative instruments that include, at inception, financing elements. The proceeds may be received at inception or over the term of the instrument. Not included are a financing element inherently included in an at-the-market derivative instrument. (ASC 230-10-45-14)
- Cash receipts from the sale of donated financial assets restricted to a long-term purchase. (ASC 230-10-45-21A)

Financing Activities—Cash Outflows

- Payment of dividends or other distributions to owners, including for repurchase of entity's stock.
- Cash paid to a tax authority when a grantor is withholding shares from a grantee's award for tax-withholding purposes is considered an outlay to reacquire the entity's equity instruments.
- Repayment of debt principal, including payment of principle of zero coupon or relatively insignificant interest rate debt instruments.
- Other payments to creditors for long-term credit.
- Distributions, to counterparties of derivative instruments that include financing elements at inception. These may be received at inception or over the term of the instrument. Not included are a financing element inherently included in an at-the-market derivative instrument with no prepayments.
- Payments for debt issue costs.
- Contingent payments up to the amount of the original contingent consideration liability by an acquirer made after three months an acquisition's consummation date in a business combination.
- Payments from debt prepayment.
- Payments from debt extinguishment costs. (ASC 230-10-45-15)
- For lessee: repayments for the principal portion of the lease liability from a financing lease. (ASC 842-20-45-5a)

Other Issues Related to Classification of Cash Flows

Acquisition and Sales of Trading Debt Securities Cash receipts and payments from purchases and sales of securities that are classified in the statement of financial position as trading debt securities in accordance with Topic 320 and equity securities accounted for in accordance with Topic 321 are classified in the statement of cash flows based on the nature and purpose for which the securities were acquired. (ASC 230-10-45-19)

Insurance Proceeds and Payments Proceeds from the settlement of insurance claims are classified based on the nature of each component of the loss. (ASC 230-10-45-21B)

Cash payments for premiums on corporate-owned life insurance policies (COLI), including bank-owned life insurance (BOLI), are classified as outflows for investing or operating activities or a combination of investing or operating activities. (ASC 230-10-45-21C)

Distributions Received from Equity Method Investees Upon applying the equity method, the entity must make an accounting policy election regarding the classification of distributions received from equity method investees choosing one of two approaches:

1. **The cumulative earnings approach.** In this approach, the investor compares the distribution received with its cumulative equity method earnings since inception. Distributions received up to the amount of cumulative earnings are a return on investment classified in operating activities. Excess distributions are considered a return on interest, classified as investing activities.

2. **Nature of distribution approach.** The entity classifies distributions based on the nature of the investee's activates that generated the distribution. If the information necessary to implement this approach is not available, the investor should use the cumulative earnings approach and report a change in accounting principle. (ASC 230-10-45-21D)

More Than One Class of Cash Flows If a cash receipt or payment has aspects of more than one class of cash flows, entities should apply the guidance in ASC 230 and any other relevant Topic. If there is no specific guidance, classify separately each cash source or use based on the nature of the underlying cash flow. (ASC 230-10-45-22) When a cash receipt or payment has aspects of more than one cash flow category that cannot be separated, it should be in the category that is likely to be the predominant source of cash flows. (ASC 230-10-45-22A)

Discontinued Operations The disclosure requirements relevant to discontinued operations and related cash flows can be found in ASC 205-20-50-5B(c). (ASC 230-10-45-24A)

Noncash Investing and Financing Activities The effects of investing and financing investing or operating activities that do not result in receipts or payments of cash should be reported in a separate schedule immediately following the statement of cash flows or in the notes to the financial statements in narrative or tabular format. (ASC 230-10-50-3) This is to preserve the statement's primary focus on cash flows from operating, investing, and financing activities. Examples of noncash investing and financing activities include:

- Converting debt to equity.
- Acquiring assets by assuming liabilities, such as buying a building by incurring a mortgage to the seller.
- Obtaining a right-of-use asset in exchange for a lease liability.
- Obtaining an asset by receiving a gift.
- Exchanging noncash assets or liabilities for other noncash assets or liabilities. (ASC 230-10-50-4)

If a transaction is part cash and part noncash, only the cash portion is reported in the body of the statement of cash flows. (ASC 230-10-50-5) If the entity has only a few noncash transaction, they may be included on the same page as the statement of cash flows. If not, the transactions may be reported elsewhere in the financial statements with a clear reference to the statement of cash flows. (ASC 230-10-50-6)

Reporting Hedging Transactions The cash flows resulting from derivative instruments that are accounted for as fair value hedges or cash flow hedges may be classified as the same type of cash flows as the hedged items provided that the accounting policy is disclosed. There is an exception for hedges considered to have a financing element at inception. If the derivative instrument used to hedge includes at inception an other-than-insignificant financing element, all cash inflows and outflows associated with the derivative instrument are reported by the borrower as cash flows from financing activities. A derivative that at inception includes off-market terms, or requires up-front cash payment, or both, often contains a financing element. A derivative instrument is viewed as including a financing element if its contractual terms have been structured to ensure that net payments will be made by one party in the earlier periods of the derivative's term and subsequently returned by the counterparty in the later periods (other than elements that are inherent in at-the-money derivative instruments with no prepayments). If for any reason hedge accounting for an instrument is discontinued, then any cash flows subsequent to the date of discontinuance are classified consistent with the nature of the instrument. (ASC 230-10-45-27)

Other Topics with Cash Flow Subtopics Some other Topics in the Codification have Subtopics on cash flows. Those should be reviewed for additional guidance and include:

- ASC 830-230, *Foreign Currency Matters*
- ASC 926-230, *Entertainment—Films*
- ASC 942-230, *Financial Services—Depository and Lending*
- ASC 946-230, *Financial Services—Investment Companies*
- ASC 958-230, *Not-for-Profit Entities*
- ASC 970-230 *Real Estate—General*
- ASC 978-230 *Real Estate—Time-Sharing Activities*
  (ASC 230-10-05-03)

Format of the Statement of Cash Flows

The statement may be prepared using either the direct or the indirect method of presenting net cash from operating activities.

- Direct method—presents major classes of gross cash receipts and payments and their sum.
- Indirect method—reconciles net income and net cash flow from operating activities

The FASB has long expressed a preference for the direct method. Conversely, the indirect method has always been vastly preferred by preparers.

The Direct Method The direct method shows the items that affected cash flow during the reporting period. Cash received and cash paid are presented, as opposed to converting accrual-basis income to cash flow information. At a minimum, entities using the direct method are required to report separately the following classes of operating cash receipts and payments:

1. Cash collected from customers, including leases, licensees, and the like
2. Interest and dividends received
3. Other operating cash receipts
4. Cash paid to employees and other suppliers
5. Interest paid, including the portion of the payments made to settle zero-coupon debt instruments attributed to accreted interest related to the debt discount
6. Income taxes paid
7. Other operating cash payments
   (ASC 230-10-45-25)

Entities are encouraged to make further breakdowns that would be useful to financial statement users. For example, disaggregating number 4 above, "cash paid to employees and suppliers," might reveal useful information.

The direct method portrays the amounts of cash both provided by and used in the reporting entity's operations, instead of presenting net income and reconciling items. The direct method reports only the items that affect cash flow (inflows/outflows of cash) and ignores items that do not affect cash flow (depreciation, gains, etc.) as in the indirect method described below. The general formats of both the direct method and the indirect method are shown below.

The direct method allows the user to clarify the relationship between the company's net income and its cash flows. For example, payments of expenses are shown as cash disbursements and are deducted from cash receipts. In this way, the user is able to understand the cash receipts and cash payments for the period. The information needed to prepare the operating activities section using the direct method can often be obtained by converting information already appearing in the statement of financial position and income statement. Formulas for conversion of various income statement amounts for the direct method of presentation from the accrual basis to the cash basis are summarized below.

The Indirect Method The indirect method is the most widely used presentation of cash from operating activities, because it is easier to prepare. It focuses on the differences between net income and cash flows. The indirect format begins with net income, which is obtained directly from the income statement. An entity using the indirect method to provide information about major classes of operating cash receipts and payments must report the same amount of net cash flow from operating activities indirectly. This is done with an adjustment to net income to reconcile it to net cash from operating activities by removing:

- The effects of all deferrals of past operating activities, and
- All items included in net income that do not affect cash provided for or used for operating activities.
  (ASC 230-10-45-28)

Thus, the statement of cash flows prepared using the indirect method emphasizes changes in the components of most current asset and current liability accounts. Changes in inventory, accounts receivable, and other current accounts are used to determine the cash flow from operating activities. Preparers calculate the change in accounts receivable using the balances net of the allowance account in order to ensure that write-offs of uncollectible accounts are treated properly. Other adjustments under the indirect method include changes in the account balances of deferred income taxes and the income (loss) from investments reported using the equity method. However, short-term borrowing used to purchase equipment is classified as a financing activity.

The major drawback to the indirect method involves the user's difficulty in comprehending the information presented. This method does not show the sources or uses of cash. Only adjustments to accrual-basis net income are shown. In some cases, the adjustments can be confusing. For instance, the sale of equipment resulting in an accrual-basis loss would require that the loss be added to net income to arrive at net cash from operating activities. (The loss was deducted in the computation of net income, but because the sale will be shown as an investing activity, the loss must be added back to net income.)

Reconciliation of Net Income and Net Cash Flow from Operating Activities When the direct method is used, a schedule reconciling net income to net cash flows from operating activities must also be provided. That reconciliation must be presented in a separate schedule. (ASC 230-10-45-30) That schedule reports the same information as the operating activities section prepared using the indirect method. Therefore, a firm must prepare and present both the direct and indirect methods when using the direct method for reporting cash from operating activities.

Reconciliation of Net Income to Net Cash Flow from Operating Activities		
Type of Entity	*Method*	*Presentation*
Business	Direct	A separate schedule
	Indirect	Within the statement of cash flows or in a separate schedule.*
Not-for-profit	Direct	Not required, see ASC 953-320-45-29)
	Indirect	Same as above for business entities.
ASC 230-10-45-29 through 45-32D		

---

* If presented separately, the statement of cash flow reports only the net cash flow from operating activities. If the reconciliation is presented in the statement of cash flows, adjustments to net income to determine net cash flow from operating activities must be identified as reconciling items. (ASC 230-10-45-31 and 45-32)

PRESENTATION AND DISCLOSURE EXAMPLES

Example 6.1: Statement of Cash Flows (without Details of Operating Activities)

The following exhibit demonstrates the classification of cash receipts and disbursements in the investing and financing activities of a statement of cash flows (though without detail of the required operating activities section).

Liquid Corporation
Statement of Cash Flows
For the Year Ended December 31, 20X1

Net cash flows from operating activities		$ xxx
Cash flows from investing activities:		
Purchase of property, plant, and equipment	$(xxx)	
Proceeds from sales of investments	Xxx	
Purchases of investments	(xxx)	
Sale of equipment	Xx	
Collection of notes receivable	<u>Xx</u>	
Net cash provided by (used in) investing activities		(xx)
Cash flows from financing activities:		
Dividend payments	(xxx)	
Payment of contingent consideration	(xxx)	
Sale of common stock	Xxx	
Repayment of long-term debt	(xx)	
Reduction of notes payable	(xx)	
Proceeds from debt	Xxx	
Payment of debt issue costs	(xx)	
Principal payments under lease obligations	<u>(xxx)</u>	
Net cash provided by financing activities		xx
Effect of exchange rate changes on cash, cash equivalents, and restricted cash		<u>xx</u>
Cash, cash equivalents, and restricted cash		
Net increase (decrease) in cash, cash equivalents, and restricted cash and		xxx
restricted cash equivalents		
Cash, cash equivalents, and restricted cash at beginning of year		<u>xxx</u>
Cash, cash equivalents, and restricted cash at end of year		$ <u>xxx</u>
Supplemental disclosure of cash flow information		
Cash paid for interest, net of amounts capitalized		($xxx)
Cash paid for income taxes, net of refunds		($xxx)
Schedule of noncash financing and investing activities:		
Conversion of bonds into common stock		$ xxx
Right-to-use property acquired in exchange for a lease liability		$ xxx
Dividends declared, not paid		$ xxx

Operating Activities Presentation　The operating activities section of the statement of cash flows can be presented under the direct method or the indirect method.

Exhibit—Converting Income Statement Amounts from the Accrual Basis to the Cash Basis—Direct Method

Accrual Basis		Additions		Deductions		Cash Basis
Net sales	+	Beginning A/R	–	Ending A/R	=	Cash received from customers
Cost of goods sold	+	Ending inventory Beginning A/P	–	Manufacturing depreciation and amortization Beginning inventory Ending A/P	=	Cash paid to suppliers
Operating expenses	+	Ending prepaid expenses Beginning accrued expenses	–	Sales and administrative depreciation and amortization Beginning prepaid expenses Ending accrued expenses payable Bad debts expense	=	Cash paid for operating expenses

Example 6.2: Operating Activities: Formats for Direct and Indirect Methods

Direct Method

Cash flows from operating activities:

Cash received from sale of goods	$xxx	
Cash interest received	xxx	
Cash dividends received	xxx	
Cash provided by operating activities		$xxx
Cash paid to suppliers	(xxx)	
Cash paid for operating expenses	(xxx)	
Cash interest paid	(xxx)	
Cash paid for taxes	(xxx)	
Cash disbursed for operating activities		(xxx)
Net cash flows from operating activities		$xxx

Indirect Method

Cash flows from operating activities:

Net income	$ xx
Add/deduct items not affecting cash:	
Decrease (increase) in accounts receivable	(xx)
Depreciation and amortization expense	xx
Increase (decrease) in accounts payable	xx
Decrease (increase) in inventories	xx
Loss on sale of equipment	
Net cash flows from operating activities	$ xx

Example 6.3: Statement of Cash Consolidated Entities

A consolidated statement of cash flows must be presented when a complete set of consolidated financial statements is issued. The consolidated statement of cash flows would be the last statement to be prepared, as the information to prepare it will come from the other consolidated statements (consolidated statement of financial position, income statement, and statement of retained earnings). The preparation of a consolidated statement of cash flows involves the same analysis and procedures as the statement for an individual entity with a few additional items. When the indirect method is used, the additional noncash transactions relating to the business combination, such as the differential amortization, must also be reversed, and all transfers to affiliates must be eliminated, as they do not represent cash inflows or outflows of the consolidated entity.

All unrealized intercompany profits should have been eliminated in preparation of the other statements. Any income or loss allocated to noncontrolling parties would need to be added back, as it would have been eliminated in computing consolidated net income but does not represent a true cash outflow or inflow. Finally, only dividend payments that are not intercompany should be recorded as cash outflows in the financing activities section.

In preparing the operating activities section of the statement by the indirect method following a purchase business combination, the changes in assets and liabilities related to operations since acquisition should be derived by comparing the consolidated statement of financial position as of the date of acquisition with the year-end consolidated statement of financial position. These changes will be combined with those for the acquiring company up to the date of acquisition as adjustments to net income. The effects due to the acquisition of these assets and liabilities are reported under investing activities.

Example 6.4: Cash and Cash Equivalents—Accounting Policy

The company considers all investments with original maturities of three months or less when purchased to be cash equivalents.

Example 6.5: Accounting Policy for Cash and Cash Equivalents, Including Details

Cash and cash equivalents consist of cash on hand and other highly liquid investments that are unrestricted as to withdrawal or use, and which have an original maturity of three months or less when purchased. The Company maintains cash and cash equivalents with various financial institutions in the United States. As of June 30, 2018, and 2017, a cash balance of $84,865 and $46,279, respectively, was maintained at U.S. financial institutions and were insured by the Federal Deposit Insurance Corporation or other programs subject to certain limitations.

Example 6.6: Amount of Interest and Income Taxes Paid and Noncash Investing and Financing Activities

Supplemental Cash Flow Information		
Cash paid for interest, net of amount capitalized	$39,213	$41,954
Noncash Investing and Financing Activities		
Equipment acquired with notes payable—equipment	—	$82,229
Equipment acquired with obligation under capital lease	—	165,816
Accounts payable paid with exchange of equity	—	63,000
Equipment note revised through repossession of equipment	$87,912	

Example 6.7: Amount of Interest and Income Taxes Paid and Noncash Investing and Financing Activities

Supplemental Cash Flow Information	
Cash paid for interest	$23,700
Cash paid for income taxes	$35,700
Noncash investing and financing transactions	
Derivative liability of convertible secured promissory note	$75,957
Common stock issueds for debt inducement	$36,720

Example 6.8: Nature of Restrictions on Cash and Cash Equivalents

Restricted Cash At June 30, 20X8, Best Foods had on deposit approximately $20,000 securing a lease bond for one of its properties. The cash securing the bond is restricted from access or withdrawal so long as the bend remains in place.

Example 6.9: Nature of Restrictions on Cash and Cash Equivalents with Internal Reference

Restricted Cash Restricted cash includes cash balances that are legally or contractually restricted to use. The Company's restricted cash as of July 31, 20X6, included proceeds that were placed in escrow in connection with the sale of a restaurant. See Note 3.

Example 6.10: Disclosure in Tabular Format—Restricted Cash Presented in More Than One Line Item on the Balance Sheet

The following table provides a reconciliation of cash, cash equivalents, and restricted cash reported within the consolidated balance sheets that sum to the total of the same amounts shown in the consolidated statements of cash flows.

Current Presentation	**July 31, 20X8**	**July 31, 20X7**	**July 31, 20X6**
Cash and cash equivalents	$24,436	$20,708	$12,428
Restricted cash	—	—	1,000
Total cash, cash equivalents, and restricted cash	$24,436	$20,708	$13,428

7 ASC 235 NOTES TO FINANCIAL STATEMENTS

AUTHORITATIVE LITERATURE

Subtopic

ASC 235, *Notes to Financial Statements*, contains one Subtopic:

- ASC 235-10, *Overall*, which addresses "the content and usefulness of the accounting policies judged by management to be most appropriate to fairly present the entity's financial statement."

Scope

- ASC 235 applies to all entities and has no scope exceptions.

Disclosure Techniques

When preparing disclosure notes, entities should consider the purpose of the disclosure—to provide users with information that assists them in assessing the entity's performance and cash flow. The notes should enhance the information presented on the face of the financial statements, provide clarity, and be organized in a logical manner. Entities should also word notes in plain English, consider tabular formats, and cross references.

The following five disclosure techniques are used in varying degrees in contemporary financial statements:

1. Parenthetical explanations
2. Notes to the financial statements
3. Cross-references
4. Valuation allowances (sometimes referred to as "contra" amounts)
5. Supporting schedules.

Parenthetical Explanations

Information is sometimes disclosed by means of parenthetical explanations appended to the appropriate statement of financial position caption. Parenthetical explanations have an advantage over both notes to the financial statements and supporting schedules. Parenthetical explanations place the disclosure prominently in the body of the statement instead of in a note or schedule where it is more likely to be overlooked. For example:

Example—Parenthetical Explanations

Common stock ($10 par value, 200,000 shares authorized, 150,000 issued) $1,500,000

Notes to Financial Statements

If the information cannot be disclosed in a relatively short and concise parenthetical explanation, a note disclosure is used. For example, see the following.

Example—Internal Reference to Note

Inventories (see note 1) $2,550,000

The notes to the financial statements would contain the following:

Note 1: Inventories are stated at the lower of cost or market. Cost is determined using the first-in, first-out (FIFO) method.

Cross-References

Cross-referencing is used when there is a direct relationship between two accounts on the statement of financial position. For example, among the current assets, the following might be shown if $1,500,000 of accounts receivable were pledged as collateral for a $1,200,000 bank loan.

Example—Cross-References to Other Line Items

Accounts receivable pledged as collateral on bank loan payable $1,500,000

Included in the current liabilities would be the following:

Bank loan payable—collateralized by accounts receivable $1,200,000

Valuation Allowances or Contra Accounts

Valuation allowances are used to reduce or increase the carrying amounts of certain assets and liabilities. Accumulated depreciation reduces the carrying value of property, plant, and equipment, and a bond premium (discount) increases (decreases) the face value of a bond payable as shown in the following illustration.

Example—Valuation Allowances or Contra Accounts

Equipment	$18,000,000	
Less accumulated depreciation	(1,625,000)	$16,375,000
Bonds payable	$20,000,000	
Less discount on bonds payable	(1,300,000)	$18,700,000
Bonds payable	$20,000,000	
Add premium on bonds payable	1,300,000	$21,300,000

PRACTICE ALERT

Disclosures have drawn the attention of both the FASB and the SEC. As the disclosure requirements have accumulated over the years, there has been a growing concern about information overload and whether more is necessarily better. Both the FASB and the SEC have initiatives to improve disclosures.

FASB Initiative

The FASB currently has projects on:

- Income taxes
- Interim reporting
- Inventory
- Government assistance
- Disaggregation of performance information
- Not-for-profit reporting of gifts-in-kind
- Segment reporting
- Simplifying the balance sheet classification of deb t

The most recent information on the FASB initiative can be found in this volume in the chapter on ASC 105.

SEC Initiative

In August 2018, the SEC as part of its Disclosure Simplification Initiative published a rule reducing the public company's disclosure requirements and asked the FASB to review its corresponding disclosure rules. For more information, see SEC Release No. 33-10110 on sec.gov.

In December 2015, the Fixing America's Surface Transportation (FAST) Act directed the SEC to modernize and simplify form S-K requirements. The SEC is reviewing specific sections of regulations S-K and S-X, with a goal of updating requirements and eliminating duplicate disclosures. The Commission also wants to continue to provide material information and reduce cost burdens on companies. As part of the project, the SEC amended its rules in August 2018 and March 2019. In January 2020, the SEC, in response to a study mandated by the Jumpstart Our Business Startups Act, proposed amendments to modernize, simplify, and enhance certain financial disclosures required by Regulation S-K. These proposed changes are designed to eliminate duplicative disclosures and modernize and enhance Management's Discussion and Analysis disclosures. Those interested in the SEC's disclosure project should visit sec.gov.

Suggestions for Improving Disclosure Effectiveness

In an April 2014 speech by Keith Higgins, SEC Division of Corporation Finance Director, Mr. Higgins suggested some ways that all entities can use to improve disclosure effectiveness. The highlights can be found below, and the full speech is available on sec.gov.

- ***Reduce Repetition:***
  - Think twice before repeating something.
  - Consider using cross references.

- ***Focus Your Disclosure:***
  - Do not simply follow what others have done.
  - Do not include a disclosure because it is a "hot button" issue. Consider whether it applies to the company.

- ***Eliminate Outdated Information:*** Disclosure should evolve over time. In a survey of 122 public companies, 74% said that once they include disclosure in a public filing in response to an SEC comment, it is rarely, if ever, removed.[1]

---

[1] See KPMG LLP and Financial Executives Research Foundation, Inc., Disclosure overload and complexity: hidden in plain sight. Available at: http://www.kpmg.com/US.

   ◦ Companies and their representatives should regularly evaluate their disclosures to determine whether they are material to investors. If they are not material, and they are not required, take them out.

   ◦ Remove a disclosure when it is immaterial or outdated even if it was included in a prior filing in response to a staff comment. If it remains material, keep it in.

The full speech is available on sec.gov.

DISCLOSURE REQUIREMENTS[2]

The entity is responsible for adopting and adhering to the highest quality accounting policies possible. In discharging this responsibility, the entity must adopt accounting principles and methods of applying them that are the most appropriate in the circumstances to present fairly in accordance with generally accepted accounting principles (GAAP):

- Financial position,
- Cash flows, and
- Results of operations.
  (ASC 235-10-50-1)

To achieve this goal, the entity must:

- Identify and describe significant accounting principles followed and methods of applying them that materially affect statements; disclosures should include principles and methods that involve:
  ◦ Selection from acceptable alternatives.
  ◦ Principles and methods peculiar to the entity's industry.
  ◦ Unusual or innovative applications of GAAP.
    (ASC 235-10-50-1 and 3)

Among others, common accounting policies are:

a. Basis of consolidation
b. Depreciation methods
c. Amortization of intangibles
d. Inventory pricing
e. Recognition of revenue from contracts with customers
f. Recognition of revenue from leasing operations
   (ASC 235-10-50-4)

Accounting policies disclosures should not duplicate details presented elsewhere. It may be appropriate to refer to related details presented elsewhere in the financial statements. (ASC 235-10-50-5) While recognizing the need for flexibility, the Codification notes that it is preferable to disclose significant accounting policies in a separate summary preceding the notes to financial statements, or as the initial note, under the same or a similar title. (FASB ASC 235-10-50-6)

---

[2] Note: This Codification Topic does not include a Subtopic 45 on presentation requirements.

DISCLOSURE EXAMPLES

Accounting Period

Example 7.1: Fiscal Period The Company's fiscal year ends on the Sunday closest to January 31 of the following year, typically resulting in a 52-week year, but occasionally giving rise to an additional week, resulting in a 53-week year. Fiscal 20X8 was a 53-week year. Fiscal 20X7 and fiscal 20X6 were each 52-week years. Fiscal 20X8, 20X7, and 20X6 ended on February 3, 20X9, January 28, 20X8, and January 29, 20X7, respectively.

Example 7.2: Change in Fiscal Year-End In January 20X2, the Board of Directors of the Company approved a change in the Company's fiscal year from that of a calendar year-end beginning on January 1 and ending on December 31 of each year to a fiscal year beginning on July 1 of each year and ending on June 30 of the following calendar year. This change to the fiscal year reporting cycle began July 1, 20X2. As a result of the change, the Company had a six-month transition period from January 1, 20X2 to June 30, 20X2 (the "transition period ended June 30, 20X18"). Accordingly, the Company is reporting its audited financial results as of and for the fiscal year ended June 30, 20X3, the transition period ended June 30, 20X2, and the calendar year ended December 31, 20X1, in this Annual Report.

Accounts Receivable

Example 7.3: Receivables and Allowances for Doubtful Accounts and Composition of Other Receivables Accounts receivable are presented at net realizable value. The Company maintains allowances for doubtful accounts and for estimated losses. The Company reviews the accounts receivable on a periodic basis and makes general and specific allowances when there is doubt as to the collectability of individual receivable balances. In evaluating the collectability of individual receivable balances, the Company considers many factors, including the age of the balances, customers' historical payment history, their current credit-worthiness, and current economic trends. Receivables are considered past due after 180 days. Accounts Receivable are written off against the allowances only after exhaustive collection efforts.

Other receivables represent mainly prepaid employee insurance and welfare benefits, which will be subsequently deducted from the employee payroll, and guarantee deposits on behalf of shipowners as well as office lease deposits.

Example 7.4: Accounts Receivable, Including Amounts of Allowance Accounts Accounts receivable are recorded, net of allowance for doubtful accounts and sales returns. Management reviews the composition of accounts receivable and analyzes historical bad debts, customer concentration, customer credit worthiness, current economic trends, and changes in customer payment patterns to determine if the allowance for doubtful accounts is adequate. An estimate for doubtful accounts is made when collection of the full amount is no longer probable. Delinquent account balances are written off after management has determined that the likelihood of collection is not probable and known bad debts are written off against the allowance for doubtful accounts when identified. As of August 31, 20X2 and 20X1, the allowance for uncollectible accounts receivable was $829,054, and $1,015,282, respectively.

Advertising

Example 7.5: Marketing and Advertising Expenses Marketing and advertising expenditures are expensed in the annual period in which the expenditure is incurred.

Example 7.6: Advertising Expenses and Promotional Costs Advertising and promotional costs are generally expensed at first showing. Advertising and promotional costs and cooperative advertising allowances were as follows:

	20X3	20X2	20X1
	(In millions)		
Gross advertising and promotional costs	$1,358	$1,397	$1,547
Cooperative advertising allowances	196	289	394
Advertising and promotional costs, net of cooperative advertising allowances	$1,162	$1,108	$1,153
Net sales	$24,971	$24,939	$25,908
Advertising and promotional costs, net of cooperative advertising allowances, as a percent to net sales	4.7%	4.4%	4.5%

Cash Equivalents

Example 7.7: Cash Equivalents For the purpose of the statement of cash flows, cash equivalents include time deposits, certificate of deposits, and all highly liquid debt instruments with original maturities of three months or less.

Example 7.8: Cash Equivalents—No Cash Equivalents Cash and cash equivalents include cash on hand and on deposit at banking institutions as well as all highly liquid short-term investments with original maturities of 90 days or less. The Company did not have cash equivalents as of December 31, 20X2 and 20X1.

Comprehensive Income

Example 7.9: Comprehensive Income (Loss) The Company reports comprehensive income (loss) in accordance with the FASB issued authoritative guidance which establishes standards for reporting comprehensive income (loss) and its component in financial statements. Comprehensive income (loss), as defined, includes all changes in equity during a period from nonowner sources.

Concentrations of Risk

Example 7.10: Concentration of Risk Financial instruments that potentially subject the Company to concentrations of credit risk consist principally of cash. The Company places its cash with high quality banking institutions. The Company had cash balances in excess of the Federal Deposit Insurance Corporation limit as of December 31, 20X1.

Example 7.11: Concentration of Risk Accounts receivable are primarily from wholesale accounts, for landlord lease inducements, and from license and supply arrangements. The Company does not require collateral to support the accounts receivable; however, in certain circumstances, the Company may require parties to provide payment for goods prior to delivery of the goods. The accounts receivable are net of an allowance for doubtful accounts, which is established based on management's assessment of the credit risk of the underlying accounts.

Cash and cash equivalents are held with high-quality financial institutions. The amount of cash and cash equivalents held with certain financial institutions exceeds government-insured limits. The Company is also exposed to credit-related losses in the event of nonperformance by the counterparties to the forward currency contracts. The credit risk amount is the Company's unrealized gains on its derivative instruments, based on foreign currency rates at the time of nonperformance. The Company has not experienced any losses related to these items, and it believes credit risk to be minimal. The Company seeks to minimize its credit risk by entering into transactions with credit-worthy and reputable financial institutions and by monitoring the credit standing of the financial institutions with whom it transacts. It seeks to limit the amount exposure with any one counterparty.

The Company's derivative contracts contain certain credit risk-related contingent features. Under certain circumstances, including an event of default, bankruptcy, termination, and cross-default under the Company's revolving credit facility, the Company may be required to make immediate payment for outstanding liabilities under its derivative contracts.

Consolidation Policy

Example 7.12: Basis of Presentation and Basis of Consolidation: Combined Note The accompanying consolidated financial statements have been prepared in accordance with generally accepted accounting principles in the United States of America (U.S. GAAP). The consolidated financial statements include the accounts of all directly and indirectly owned subsidiaries and variable interest entity. All intercompany transactions and balances have been eliminated in consolidation.

Example 7.13: Basis of Consolidation with Detail The accompanying consolidated financial statements include the accounts of the Company and its wholly owned subsidiaries: NSHL, New Star Peak Health Inc., New Star Healthnet Rehab Limited, Blake Assessments Inc., an 80% interest in New Star Healthnet Rockville Centre, Inc., a Recovery Physical Therapy and Health Centre clinic operated by NSHL, and a 50% stake in a joint venture with the Joseph Coffey Dental Hygiene Professional Corporation operated as New Star Dental. All of the Company's subsidiaries are incorporated under the laws of the Province of Victoria, Australia. All intercompany transactions have been eliminated.

Example 7.14: Basis of Consolidation, Including a VIE The consolidated financial statements include the accounts of the Company, its subsidiaries, and its affiliates. All significant intercompany transactions and balances are eliminated in consolidation. Global Shipping ("Global"), a People's Republic of China (PRC) corporation, is considered a variable interest entity ("VIE"), with the Company as the primary beneficiary. The Company, through Guangzhou Seaway, entered into certain agreements with Global, pursuant to which the Company receives 90% of Global's net income. The Company does not receive any payments from Global unless Global recognizes net income during its fiscal year. These agreements do not entitle the Company to any consideration if Global incurs a net loss during its fiscal year. If Global incurs a net loss during its fiscal year, the Company is not required to absorb such net loss.

As a VIE, Global's revenues are included in the Company's total revenues, and any loss from operations is consolidated with that of the Company. Because of contractual arrangements between the Company and Global, the Company has a pecuniary interest in Global that requires consolidation of the financial statements of the Company and Global.

The Company has consolidated Global's operating results because the entities are under common control in accordance with ASC 805-10, *Business Combinations*. The agency relationship between the Company and Global and its branches is governed by a series of contractual arrangements pursuant to which the Company has substantial control over Global. Management makes ongoing reassessments of whether the Company remains the primary beneficiary of Global.

Example 7.15: Noncontrolling Interest The Company follows FASB ASC Topic 810, *Consolidation,* which governs the accounting for and reporting of noncontrolling interests ("NCIs") in partially owned consolidated subsidiaries and the loss of control of subsidiaries. Certain provisions of this standard indicate, among other things, that NCIs be treated as a separate component of equity, not as a liability, that increases and decreases in the parent's ownership interest that leave control intact be treated as equity transactions rather than as step acquisitions or dilution gains or losses, and that losses of a partially owned consolidated subsidiary be allocated to the NCI even when such allocation might result in a deficit balance.

The net income (loss) attributed to the NCI is separately designated in the accompanying consolidated statements of operations and other comprehensive income (loss).

Contingencies

Example 7.16: Contingencies In the ordinary course of business, the Company is involved in legal proceedings regarding contractual and employment relationships and a variety of other matters. The Company records contingent liabilities resulting from claims against us, when a loss is assessed to be probable and the amount of the loss is reasonably estimable.

Derivatives

Example 7.17: Convertible Notes Payable and Derivative Instruments The Company has adopted the provisions of ASU 2017-11 to account for the down-round features of warrants issued with private placements effective as of January 1, 2017. In doing so, warrants with a down-round feature previously treated as derivative liabilities in the consolidated balance sheet and measured at fair value are henceforth treated as equity, with no adjustment for changes in fair value at each reporting period. The Company accounted for conversion options embedded in convertible notes in accordance with ASC 815. ASC 815 generally requires companies to bifurcate conversion options embedded in convertible notes from their host instruments and to account for them as free-standing derivative financial instruments. ASC 815 provides for an exception to this rule when convertible notes, as host instruments, are deemed to be conventional, as defined by ASC 815-40. The Company accounts for convertible notes deemed conventional and conversion options embedded in nonconventional convertible notes which qualify as equity under ASC 815, in accordance with the provisions of ASC 470-20, which provides guidance on accounting for convertible securities with beneficial conversion features. Accordingly, the Company records, as a discount to convertible notes, the intrinsic value of such conversion options based upon the differences between the fair value of the underlying common stock at the commitment date of the note transaction and the effective conversion price embedded in the note. Debt discounts under these arrangements are amortized over the term of the related debt.

Earnings Per Share

Example 7.18: Earnings (Loss) Per Share Basic earnings (loss) per share is computed by dividing net income (loss) attributable to holders of common shares of the Company by the weighted average number of common shares of the Company outstanding during the applicable period. Diluted earnings per share reflect the potential dilution that could occur if securities or other contracts to issue common shares of the Company were exercised or converted into common shares of the Company. Common share equivalents are excluded from the computation of diluted earnings per share if their effects would be anti-dilutive.

For the year ended June 30, 20X2 and 20X1, the effect of potential shares of common stock of the Company was dilutive since the exercise prices for options and warrants were lower than the average market price for the related periods. As a result, a total of 321,231 and 18,200 of unexercised options and warrants were dilutive for the year ended June 30, 20X2 and 20X1, respectively, and were included in the computation of diluted EPS.

Example 7.19: Loss per Common Share Basic loss per common share excludes dilution and is computed by dividing net loss by the weighted average number of common shares outstanding during the period. Diluted loss per common share reflect the potential dilution that could occur if securities or other contracts to issue common stock were exercised or converted into common stock or resulted in the issuance of common stock that then shared in the loss of the entity. Convertible promissory notes as at December 31, 20X2 are likely to be converted into shares, however, due to losses, their effect would be antidilutive. As of December 31, 20X2, convertible notes outstanding could be converted into 91,250 shares of common stock.

Use of Estimates

Example 7.20: Use of Estimates and Assumptions The preparation of consolidated financial statements in conformity with U.S. GAAP requires management to make estimates and assumptions that affect the reported amounts of assets and liabilities and disclosure of contingent assets and liabilities at the date of the consolidated financial statements and the reported amounts of revenues and expenses during the reporting period. The Company regularly evaluates estimates and assumptions. The Company bases its estimates and assumptions on current facts, historical experience and various other factors that it believes to be reasonable under the circumstances, the results of which form the basis for making judgments about the carrying values of assets and liabilities and the accrual of costs and expenses that are not readily apparent from other sources. The actual results experienced by the Company may differ materially and adversely from the Company's estimates. To the extent there are material differences between the estimates and the actual results, future results of operations will be affected.

Financial Instruments

Example 7.21: Fair Value of Financial Instruments For certain of the Company's financial instruments, including cash and equivalents, restricted cash, accounts receivable, advances to suppliers, accounts payable, accrued liabilities and short-term debt, the carrying amounts approximate their fair values due to their short maturities.

FASB ASC Topic 820, *Fair Value Measurements and Disclosures*, requires disclosure of the fair value of financial instruments held by the Company. FASB ASC Topic 825, *Financial Instruments*, defines fair value, and establishes a three-level valuation hierarchy for disclosures of fair value measurement that enhances disclosure requirements for fair value measures. The carrying amounts reported in the consolidated balance sheets for receivables and current liabilities each qualify as financial instruments and are a reasonable estimate of their fair values because of the short period of time between the origination of such instruments and their expected realization and their current market rate of interest. The three levels of valuation hierarchy are defined as follows:

- Level 1 inputs to the valuation methodology are quoted prices for identical assets or liabilities in active markets.

- Level 2 inputs to the valuation methodology include quoted prices for similar assets and liabilities in active markets, quoted prices for identical or similar assets in inactive markets, and inputs that are observable for the asset or liability, either directly or indirectly, for substantially the full term of the financial instrument.
- Level 3 inputs to the valuation methodology us one or more unobservable inputs which are significant to the fair value measurement.

The Company analyzes all financial instruments with features of both liabilities and equity under FASB ASC Topic 480, *Distinguishing Liabilities from Equity*, and FASB ASC Topic 815, *Derivatives and Hedging*.

As of August 31, 20X8 and 20X7, respectively, the Company did not identify any assets and liabilities required to be presented on the balance sheet at fair value.

Example 7.22: Derivative Financial Instruments The Company uses derivative financial instruments to manage its exposure to certain foreign currency exchange rate risks.

Net investment hedges. The Company enters into certain forward currency contracts that are designated as net investment hedges. The effective portions of the hedges are reported in accumulated other comprehensive income or loss, net of tax, and will subsequently be reclassified to net earnings in the period in which the hedged investment is either sold or substantially liquidated. Hedge effectiveness is measured using a method based on changes in forward exchange rates. The Company classifies the cash flows at settlement of its net investment hedges within investing activities in the consolidated statements of cash flows.

Derivatives not designated as hedging instruments. The Company also enters into certain forward currency contracts that are not designated as net investment hedges. They are designed to economically hedge the foreign exchange revaluation gains and losses of certain monetary assets and liabilities. The Company has not applied hedge accounting to these instruments and the change in fair value of these derivatives is recorded within selling, general and administrative expenses. The Company classifies the cash flows at settlement of its forward currency contracts which are not designated in hedging relationships within operating activities in the consolidated statements of cash flows.

The Company presents its derivative assets and derivative liabilities at their gross fair values within other prepaid expenses and other current assets and other current liabilities on the consolidated balance sheets. However, the Company's Master International Swap Dealers Association, Inc., Agreements and other similar arrangements allow net settlements under certain conditions.

The Company does not enter into derivative contracts for speculative or trading purposes. Additional information on the Company's derivative financial instruments is included in Notes 14 and 15 of these consolidated financial statements.

Foreign Currency Transactions

Example 7.23: Foreign Currency Transactions and Comprehensive Income GAAP generally requires recognized revenue, expenses, gains and losses be included in net income. Certain statements, however, require entities to report specific changes in assets and liabilities, such as gain or loss on foreign currency translation, as a separate component of the equity section of the balance sheet. Such items, along with net income, are components of comprehensive income. The functional currency of the Company's Australian subsidiaries is the Australian dollar. Translation gains of $605,430 and $616,738 for the years ended August 31, 20X2 and 20X1, respectively, are classified as an item of other comprehensive income in the stockholders' equity section of the balance sheet.

Income Taxes

Example 7.24: Taxation, Including Tax Cuts and Jobs Act Disclosure The Company uses the liability method of accounting for income taxes in accordance with U.S. Generally Accepted Accounting Principles ("U.S. GAAP"). Deferred taxes, if any, are recognized for the future tax consequences of temporary differences between the tax basis of assets and liabilities and their reported amounts in the consolidated financial statements. A valuation allowance is provided against deferred tax assets if it is more likely than not that the asset will not be utilized in the future.

The Company recognizes the tax benefit from an uncertain tax position only if it is more likely than not that the tax position will be sustained on examination by the taxing authorities, based on the technical merits of the position. The Company recognizes interest and penalties, if any, related to unrecognized tax benefits as income tax expense. The Company had no uncertain tax positions as of June 30, 20X8 and 20X7, respectively.

Income tax returns for the years prior to 20X4 are no longer subject to examination by U.S. tax authorities.

On December 22, 2017, the "Tax Cuts and Jobs Act" (the "Act") was enacted. Under the provisions of the Act, the U.S. corporate tax rate decreased rom 35% to 21%. As the Company has a June 30 fiscal year-end, the lower corporate income tax rate will be phased in, resulting in a U.S. statutory federal rate of approximately 28% for our fiscal year ending June 30, 2018, and 21% for subsequent fiscal years. Additionally, the Tax Act imposes a one-time transition tax on deemed repatriation of historical earnings of foreign subsidiaries, and future foreign earnings are subject to U.S. taxation. The change in rate has caused the Company to remeasure all U.S. deferred income tax assets and liabilities for temporary differences and net operating loss ("NOL") carryforwards and recorded a one-time transition tax expense.

Example 7.25: Taxation The Company accounts for income taxes in accordance with ASC Topic 740, *Income Taxes.* ASC 740 requires a company to use the asset and liability method of accounting for income taxes, whereby deferred tax assets are recognized for deductible temporary differences, and deferred tax liabilities are recognized for taxable temporary differences. Temporary differences are the differences between the reported amounts of assets and liabilities and their tax bases. Deferred tax assets are reduced by a valuation allowance when, in the opinion of management, it is more likely than not that some portion, or all of, the deferred tax assets will not be realized. Deferred tax assets and liabilities are adjusted for the effects of changes in tax laws and rates on the date of enactment.

Under ASC 740, a tax position is recognized as a benefit only if it is "more likely than not" that the tax position would be sustained in a tax examination, with a tax examination being presumed to occur. The amount recognized is the largest amount of tax benefit that is greater than 50% likely of being realized on examination. For tax positions not meeting the "more likely than not" test, no tax benefit is recorded. The Company has no material uncertain tax positions for any of the reporting periods presented.

Intangible Assets

Example 7.26: Intangible Assets, Net Intangible assets are recorded at cost less accumulated amortization. Amortization is calculated on a straight-line basis over the following estimated useful lives:

Logistics platform—three years

The Company evaluates intangible assets for impairment whenever events or changes in circumstances indicate that the assets might be impaired. There was no such impairment as of June 30, 20X8.

Example 7.27: Goodwill Goodwill represents the excess of purchase price over the underlying net assets of businesses acquired. Under accounting requirements, goodwill is not amortized but is subject to annual impairment tests. At August 31, 20X8, the Company recorded goodwill of $150,618 and $92,989, respectively, related to its acquisition of Blake Health, Inc. during the fiscal year ended August 31, 20X7 and Global Fitness Leaders during the fiscal year ended August 31, 20X8. As of August 31, 20X8 and 20X7, the Company performed the required impairment reviews. Based on its reviews at August 31, 20X8 and 20X7, the Company believes there was no impairment of its goodwill.

Example 7.28: Goodwill and Intangible Assets Goodwill and other identifiable intangible assets with indefinite lives that are not being amortized, such as trade names, are tested at least annually for impairment and are written down if impaired. Identifiable intangible assets with finite lives are amortized over their estimated useful lives and are reviewed for impairment whenever facts and circumstances indicate that their carrying values may not be fully recoverable. The intangible assets with definite lives are being amortized over its estimated useful lives of 5 years using the straight-line method.

The Company operated an online gaming site featuring sophisticated playing zones, game broadcasts with software analyses and top analysts' commentaries, education and other chess oriented resources. Intangible assets represented the amount incurred by the Company related to the development of the online chess gaming website.

Under ASC 985-20, there are two main stages of software development. These stages are defined as:

(A) When the technological feasibility is established, and

(B) When the product is available for general release to customers.

Costs incurred by the Company up to stage A have been expensed while costs incurred to move from stage A to stage B have been capitalized.

The Company evaluates the recoverability of the infinite-lived intangible assets for possible impairment whenever events or circumstances indicate that the carrying amount of such assets may not be recoverable. Recoverability of these assets is measured by a comparison of the carrying amounts to the future undiscounted cash flows the assets are expected to generate. If such review indicates that the carrying amount of intangible assets is not recoverable, the carrying amount of such assets is reduced to fair value.

During the year ended December 31, 20X7, the intangible asset was written off based on management's review and evaluation of its recoverability. With respect to goodwill, during the year ended December 31, 20X8, the Company has identified no circumstances which would call for further evaluation of goodwill impairment.

Example 7.29: Software Development Costs The costs incurred in the preliminary stages of development are expensed as incurred. Once an application has reached the development stage, internal and external costs, if direct and incremental, are capitalized until the application is substantially complete and ready for its intended use. These costs are amortized using the straight-line method over the estimated economic useful life of 5 years starting from when the application is substantially complete and ready for its intended use.

Inventories

Example 7.30: Inventories and Cost Method Inventories, consisting of finished goods, inventories in transit, and raw materials, are stated at the lower of cost and net realizable value. Cost is determined using weighted-average costs, and includes all costs incurred to deliver inventory to the Company's distribution centers including freight, nonrefundable taxes, duty, and other landing costs.

The Company makes provisions as necessary to appropriately value goods that are obsolete, have quality issues, or are damaged. The amount of the provision is equal to the difference between the cost of the inventory and its estimated net realizable value based upon assumptions about future demand, selling prices and market conditions. In addition, the Company provides for inventory shrinkage based on historical trends from actual physical inventory counts. Inventory shrinkage estimates are made to reduce the inventory value for lost or stolen items. The Company performs physical inventory counts and cycle counts throughout the year and adjusts the shrink reserve accordingly.

Example 7.40: Inventories—Merchandise Inventories Merchandise inventories are valued at lower of cost or market using the last-in, first-out (LIFO) retail inventory method. Under the retail inventory method, inventory is segregated into departments of merchandise having similar characteristics, and is stated at its current retail selling value. Inventory retail values are converted to a cost basis by applying specific average cost factors for each merchandise department. Cost factors represent the average cost-to-retail ratio for each merchandise department based on beginning inventory and the annual purchase activity. At January 2, 20X3 and January 3, 20X2, merchandise inventories valued at LIFO, including adjustments as necessary to record inventory at the lower of cost or market, approximated the cost of such inventories using the first-in, first-out (FIFO) retail inventory method. The application of the LIFO retail inventory method did not result in the recognition of any LIFO charges or credits affecting cost of sales for 20X3, 20X2 or 20X1. The retail inventory method inherently requires management judgments and estimates, such as the amount and timing of permanent markdowns to clear unproductive or slow-moving inventory, which may impact the ending inventory valuation as well as gross margins.

Permanent markdowns designated for clearance activity are recorded when the utility of the inventory has diminished. Factors considered in the determination of permanent markdowns include current and anticipated demand, customer preferences, age of the merchandise and fashion trends. When a decision is made to permanently markdown merchandise, the resulting gross margin reduction is recognized in the period the markdown is recorded.

Physical inventories are generally taken within each merchandise department annually, and inventory records are adjusted accordingly, resulting in the recording of actual shrinkage. Physical inventories are taken at all store locations for substantially all merchandise categories approximately three weeks before the end of the year. Shrinkage is estimated as a percentage of sales at interim periods and for this approximate three-week period, based on historical shrinkage rates. While it is not possible to quantify the impact from each cause of shrinkage, the Company has loss prevention programs and policies that are intended to minimize shrinkage, including the use of radio frequency identification cycle counts and interim inventories to keep the Company's merchandise files accurate.

Property and Equipment and Depreciation Methods

Example 7.41: Property and Equipment, Net, Straight-Line Depreciation Method and Impairment Policy Net property and equipment are stated at historical cost less accumulated depreciation. Historical cost comprises its purchase price and any directly attributable costs of bringing the assets to its working condition and location for its intended use. Depreciation is calculated on a straight-line basis over the following estimated useful lives:

Buildings	20 years
Motor vehicles	5–10 years
Furniture and office equipment	3–5 years
Leasehold improvements	Shorter of lease term or useful lives

The carrying value of a long-lived asset is considered impaired by the Company when the anticipated undiscounted cash flows from such asset is less than its carrying value. If impairment is identified, a loss is recognized based on the amount by which the carrying value exceeds the fair value of the long-lived asset. Fair value is determined primarily using the anticipated cash flows discounted at a rate commensurate with the risk involved or based on independent appraisals. Management has determined that there were no impairments at the balance sheet dates.

Example 7.42: Property and Equipment, Net, Declining Balance Depreciation Method Property and equipment are stated at cost. Expenditures for maintenance and repairs are charged to earnings as incurred; additions, renewals and betterments are capitalized. When property and equipment are retired or otherwise disposed of, the related cost and accumulated depreciation are removed from the respective accounts, and any gain or loss is included in operations. Depreciation of property and equipment is provided using the declining balance method for substantially all assets with estimated lives as follows:

Leasehold improvements	5 years
Clinical equipment	5 years
Computer equipment	3 years
Office equipment	5 years
Furniture and fixtures	5 years

Example 7.43: Long-lived Assets—Impairment or Disposal The Company applies the provisions of ASC Topic 360, *Property, Plant, and Equipment*, which addresses financial accounting and reporting for the impairment or disposal of long-lived assets. ASC 360 requires impairment losses to be recorded on long-lived assets used in operations when indicators of impairment are present and the discounted cash flows estimated to be generated by those assets are less than the assets' carrying amounts. In that event, a loss is recognized based on the amount by which the carrying amount exceeds the fair value of the long-lived assets. Loss on long-lived assets to be disposed of is determined in a similar manner, except that fair values are reduced for the cost of disposal. Based on its review at August 31, 20X2 and 20X1, the Company believes there was no impairment of its long-lived assets.

Nature of Operations

Example 7.44: Nature of Operations RJ, Inc. and subsidiaries (the "Company") is an omnichannel retail organization operating stores, websites and mobile applications under three brands (TJ's, Chelsea's and bluestar) that sell a wide range of merchandise, including apparel and accessories (men's, women's, and children's), cosmetics, home furnishings and other consumer goods. The Company has stores in 34 states, the District of Columbia and Puerto Rico. As of February 2, 20X3, the Company's operations and operating segments were conducted through RJ's, TJ's, Chelsea's, RJ's Off Rack, and bluestar, which are aggregated into one reporting segment in accordance with the Financial Accounting Standards Board ("FASB") Accounting Standards Codification ("ASC") Topic 280, *Segment Reporting*. The metrics used by management to assess the performance of the Company's operating divisions include sales trends, gross margin rates, expense rates, and rates of earnings before interest and taxes ("EBIT") and earnings before interest, taxes, depreciation and amortization ("EBITDA"). The Company's operating divisions have historically had similar economic characteristics and are expected to have similar economic characteristics and long-term financial performance in future periods.

Revenue

Example 7.45: Revenue Recognition under ASC 606 with Effects of Adoption of ASU 2014-09 ASU 2014-09, *Revenue from Contracts with Customers* ("Topic 606"), became effective for the Company on March 1, 2018. The Company's revenue recognition disclosure reflects its updated accounting policies that are affected by this new standard. The Company applied the "modified retrospective" transition method for open contracts for the implementation of Topic 606. As sales are and have been primarily from providing eyecare services, and the Company has no significant post-delivery obligations, this new standard did not result in a material recognition of revenue on the Company's accompanying consolidated financial statements for the cumulative impact of applying this new standard. The Company made no adjustments to its previously reported total revenues, as those periods continue to be presented in accordance with its historical accounting practices under Topic 605, *Revenue Recognition.*

Revenue from providing eyecare services are recognized under Topic 606 in a manner that reasonably reflects the delivery of its services to customers in return for expected consideration and includes the following five elements:

1. Executed contracts with the Company's customers that it believes are legally enforceable;
2. Identification of performance obligations in the respective contract;
3. Determination of the transaction price for each performance obligation in the respective contract;
4. Allocation the transaction price to each performance obligation; and
5. Recognition of revenue only when the Company satisfies each performance obligation.

These five elements, as applied to the Company's revenue category, are summarized below:

- Eyecare services—gross service revenue is recorded in the accounting records at the time the services is provided on an accrual basis at the provider's established rates, regardless of whether the provider expects to collect that amount. The Company reserves a provision for contractual adjustment and discounts that are deducted from gross service revenue. The Company reports revenues net of any sales taxes.

Example 7.46: Revenue Recognition under ASC 606, Including Policies Regarding Performance Obligations, Estimated Returns, Shipping Fees, and Gift Cards Net revenue is comprised of company-operated store net revenue, direct to consumer net revenue through websites and mobile apps, including mobile apps on in-store devices that allow demand to be fulfilled via the Company's distribution centers, and other net revenue, which includes revenue from outlets, temporary locations, sales to wholesale accounts, showrooms, warehouse sales, and license and supply arrangement net revenue, which consists of royalties as well as sales of the Company's products to licensees. All revenue is reported net of sales taxes collected from customers on behalf of taxing authorities.

Revenue is recognized when performance obligations are satisfied through the transfer of control of promised goods to the Company's customers. Control transfers once a customer has the ability to direct the use of, and obtain substantially all of the benefits from, the product. This includes the transfer of legal title, physical possession, the risks and rewards of ownership, and customer acceptance. Revenue from company-operated stores and other retail locations is recognized at the point of sale. Direct to consumer revenue and sales to wholesale accounts are recognized upon receipt by the customer. In certain arrangements the Company receives payment before the customer receives the promised good. These payments are initially recorded as deferred revenue, and recognized as revenue in the period when control is transferred to the customer.

Revenue is presented net of an allowance for estimated returns, which is based on historic experience. The Company's liability for sales return refunds is recognized within other current liabilities, and an asset for the value of inventory which is expected to be returned is recognized within other prepaid expenses and other current assets on the consolidated balance sheets.

Shipping fees billed to customers are recorded as revenue, and shipping costs are recognized within selling, general, and administrative expenses in the same period the related revenue is recognized.

Proceeds from the sale of gift cards are initially deferred and recognized within unredeemed gift card liability on the consolidated balance sheets, and are recognized as revenue when tendered for payment. Based on historical experience, and to the extent there is no requirement to remit unclaimed card balances to government agencies, an estimate of the gift card balances that will never be redeemed is recognized as revenue in proportion to gift cards which have been redeemed.

While the Company will continue to honor all gift cards presented for payment, management may determine the likelihood of redemption to be remote for certain card balances due to, among other things, long periods of inactivity. In these circumstances, to the extent management determines there is no requirement for remitting card balances to government agencies under unclaimed property laws, the portion of card balances not expected to be redeemed are recognized in net revenue in proportion to the gift cards which have been redeemed, under the redemption recognition method.

Recent Accounting Pronouncements

Example 7.47: Recent Accounting Pronouncements In February 2016, the FASB issued ASU No. 2016-02, *Leases (Topic 842)* (ASU 2016-2) that revises accounting for operating leases by a lessee, among other changes, and requires a lessee to recognize a liability to make lease payments and an asset representing its right to use the underlying asset for the lease term in the balance sheet. This update will be effective for nonpublic business entities for fiscal years beginning after December 15, 2020, including interim periods within those fiscal years. In July 2018, the FASB issued ASU 2018-10, *Codification Improvements to Topic 842, Leases,* to clarify how to apply certain aspects of the new leases standard. The amendments address the rate implicit in the lease, impairment of the net investment in the lease, lessee reassessment of lease classification, lessor reassessment of lease term and purchase options, variable payments that depend on an index or rate and certain transition adjustments, among other issues. In addition, in July 2018, the FASB issued ASU 2018-11, *Leases (Topic 842): Targeted Improvements,* which provides an additional (and optional) transition method to adopt the new leases standard. Under the new transition method, a reporting entity would initially apply the new lease requirements at the effective date and recognize a cumulative-effect adjustment to the opening balance of retained earnings in the period of adoption, continue to report comparative periods presented in the financial statements in the period of adoption in accordance with current U.S. GAAP (i.e., ASC 840, *Leases*) and provide the required disclosures under ASC 840 for all periods presented under current U.S. GAAP. A modified retrospective transition approach is required for lessees for capital and operating leases existing at, or entered into after, the beginning of the earliest comparative period presented in the financial statements, with certain practical expedients available. The Company plans to adopt these new guidance in the first quarter of fiscal year 2010 and is still evaluating the effect that this guidance will have on the Company's financial statements and related disclosures.

In July 2017, the FASB issued ASU 2017-11, *Earnings Per Share (Topic 260); Distinguishing Liabilities from Equity (Topic 480); Derivatives and Hedging (Topic 815)*. The amendments in Part I of this Update change the classification analysis of certain equity-linked financial instruments (or embedded features) with down-round features. When determining whether certain financial instruments should be classified as liabilities or equity instruments, a down-round feature no longer precludes equity classification when assessing whether the instrument is indexed to an entity's own stock. The amendments also clarify existing disclosure requirements for equity-classified instruments. The amendments in Part II of this Update recharacterize the indefinite deferral of certain provisions of Topic 480 that now are presented as pending content in the Codification, to a scope exception. Those amendments do not have an accounting effect. For public business entities, the amendments in Part I of this Update are effective for fiscal years, and interim periods within those fiscal years, beginning after December 15, 2018. Early adoption is permitted for all entities, including adoption in an interim period. If an entity early adopts the amendments in an interim period, any adjustments should be reflected as of the beginning of the fiscal year that includes that interim period. The Company does not expect that the adoption of this guidance will have a material impact on its consolidated financial statements.

In March 2018, the FASB issued ASU 2018-05, *Income Taxes (Topic 740): Amendments to SEC Paragraphs Pursuant to SEC Staff Accounting Bulletin No. 118* ("ASU 2018-05"), which amends the FASB Accounting Standards Codification and XBRL Taxonomy based on the Tax Cuts and Jobs Act (the "Act") that was signed into law on December 22, 2017 and Staff Accounting Bulletin No. 118 ("SAB 118") that was released by the Securities and Exchange Commission. The Act changes numerous provisions that impact U.S. corporate tax rates, business-related exclusions, and deductions and credits, and may additionally have international tax consequences for many companies that operate internationally. The Company has evaluated the impact of the Act as well as the guidance of SAB 118 and incorporated the changes into the determination of a reasonable estimate of its deferred tax liability and appropriate disclosures in the notes to its consolidated financial statements (see Note 9).

In June 2018, the FASB issued ASU 2018-07, *Compensation-Stock Compensation (Topic 718): Improvements to Nonemployee Share-Based Payment Accounting*. The guidance largely aligns the accounting for share-based payment awards issued to employees and nonemployees, whereby the existing employee guidance will apply to nonemployee share-based transactions (as long as the transaction is not effectively a form of financing), with the exception of specific guidance related to the attribution of compensation cost. The cost of nonemployee awards will continue to be recorded as if the grantor had paid cash for the goods or services. In addition, the contractual term will be able to be used in lieu of an expected term in the option-pricing model for nonemployee awards. The ASU is effective for fiscal years beginning after December 15, 2020, including interim periods within that fiscal year. The ASU is required to be applied on a prospective basis to all new awards granted after the date of adoption. The Company is still evaluating the effect that this guidance but does not expect the standard to have a material impact on its consolidated financial statements.

The Company does not believe other recently issued but not yet effective accounting standards, if currently adopted, would have a material effect on the Company's consolidated financial statements.

Example 7.48: Recent Accounting Pronouncements In February 2016, the FASB issued ASU 2016-02, *Leases (Topic 842)*. ASU 2016-02 requires lessees to recognize lease assets and lease liabilities on the balance sheet and requires expanded disclosures about leasing arrangements. ASU 2016-02 is effective for fiscal years beginning after December 15, 2020, for nonpublic business entities, with early adoption permitted. The Company is in the process of evaluating the impact of this ASU on its financial statements.

Management does not believe that any recently issued, but not yet effective, accounting standards could have a material effect on the accompanying financial statements. As new accounting pronouncements are issued, we will adopt those that are applicable under the circumstances.

Example 7.49: Recently Adopted Accounting Pronouncements In May 2014, the Financial Accounting Standards Board ("FASB") issued Accounting Standards Update ("ASU") 2014-09, *Revenue from Contracts with Customers* ("ASC 606"), which supersedes the revenue recognition requirements in ASC 605, *Revenue Recognition*. This ASU requires that an entity recognize revenue to depict the transfer of promised goods or services to customers in an amount that reflects the consideration to which the entity expects to be entitled in exchange for those goods or services.

The Company adopted ASC 606 on January 29, 2018, on a modified retrospective basis. There were no changes to the consolidated statement of operations as a result of the adoption, and the timing and amount of its revenue recognition remained substantially unchanged under this new guidance. Under the provisions of ASC 606, the Company is now required to present its provision for sales returns on a gross basis, rather than a net basis. The Company's liability for sales return refunds is recognized within other current liabilities, and the Company now presents an asset for the value of inventory which is expected to be returned within other prepaid expenses and other current assets on the consolidated balance sheets. Under the modified retrospective approach, the comparative prior period information has not been restated for this change.

The effect of adoption of ASC 606 on the Company's consolidated balance sheet as of February 3, 2019, was as follows:

	As Reported	*Adjustment for ASC 606*	*Balances without Adoption of ASC 606*
Other prepaid expenses and other current assets	$57,949	$(3,719)	$54,230
Current assets	1,429,282	(3,719)	1,425,563
Total assets	2,084,711	(3,719)	2,080,992
Other current liabilities	112,698	3,719	116,417
Current liabilities	500,477	3,719	504,196
Total liabilities	638,736	3,719	642,455

In May 2017, the FASB amended ASC 718, *Stock Compensation*, to reduce diversity in practice and to clarify when a change to the terms or conditions of a share-based payment award must be accounted for as a modification and will result in fewer changes to the terms of an award being accounted for as modifications. The new guidance was effective beginning in the first quarter of fiscal 2018 and will apply on a prospective basis. The adoption does not have a material impact on the Company's consolidated financial statements.

In January 2018, the FASB released guidance on the accounting for the global intangible low-taxed income ("GILTI") provisions of the tax bill H.R.1, commonly known as the U.S. Tax Cuts and Jobs Act ("U.S. tax reform"). The GILTI provisions impose a tax on foreign subsidiary earnings in excess of a deemed return on the foreign subsidiary's tangible assets. The Company has made an accounting policy election to treat the GILTI tax as an in period tax, which is consistent with the treatment prior to the accounting policy election.

In February 2018, the FASB amended ASC 220, *Income Statement—Reporting Comprehensive Income*. ASC 740, *Income Taxes*, requires that the effect of a change in tax laws or rates on deferred tax assets and liabilities be included in income from continuing operations. In situations in which the tax effects of a transaction were initially recognized directly in other comprehensive income, this results in "stranded" amounts in accumulated other comprehensive income related to the income tax rate differential. The amendments to ASC 220 allow a reclassification from accumulated other comprehensive income to retained earnings for stranded tax effects resulting from the enactment of U.S. tax reform. As permitted by the ASU the Company early adopted the amendments to ASC 220, and made the policy election to not reclassify "stranded" amounts from accumulated other comprehensive income to retained earnings.

Example 7.50: Recently Issued Adopted Pronouncements In February 2016, the FASB issued ASC 842, *Leases* ("ASC 842") to increase transparency and comparability among organizations by recognizing lease assets and lease liabilities on the balance sheet and disclosing key information about leasing arrangements. Under the new guidance, lessees are required to recognize a lease liability, which represents the discounted obligation to make future minimum lease payments, and a corresponding right-of-use asset on the balance sheet. This guidance is effective for the Company beginning in its first quarter of fiscal 2019. The new guidance can be applied using a modified retrospective approach at the beginning of the earliest period presented, or at the beginning of the period in which it is adopted.

The Company adopted ASC 842 on February 4, 2019 using the modified retrospective approach and will not be restating comparative periods.

The Company has chosen to apply the transition package of three practical expedients that allow companies not to reassess whether agreements contain leases, the classification of leases, and the capitalization of initial direct costs. The Company has also made an accounting policy election to recognize lease expense for leases with a term of 12 months or less on a straight-line basis over the lease term and will not recognize any right of use assets or lease liabilities for those leases.

The Company has completed the implementation of new lease accounting software, and updated its internal controls to address the requirements of the new standard.

The primary financial statement impact upon adoption will be the recognition, on a discounted basis, of the Company's minimum commitments under noncancellable operating leases as right of use assets and obligations on the consolidated balance sheets. The adoption of ASC 842 results in the recognition of lease-related assets and liabilities of approximately $620.0 million and $650.0 million, respectively. Preexisting net lease-related assets and liabilities of approximately $30.0 million have been reclassified as part of the adoption of the new standard, and there is no adjustment to opening retained earnings. The standard is not expected to have a material impact on the Company's net income or cash flows.

Risks and Uncertainties

Example 7.51: Risks and Uncertainties The Company's business, financial position, and results of operations may be influenced by the political, economic, and legal environments in the People's Republic of China (PRC), as well as by the general state of the PRC economy. The Company's operations in the PRC are subject to special considerations and significant risks not typically associated with companies in North America and Western Europe. These include risks associated with, among others, the political, economic and legal environment and foreign currency exchange. The Company's results may be adversely affected by changes in the political, regulatory and social conditions in the PRC, and by changes in governmental policies or interpretations with respect to laws and regulations, anti-inflationary measures, currency conversion, remittances abroad, and rates and methods of taxation, among other things. Moreover, the Company's ability to grow its business and maintain its profitability could be negatively affected by the nature and extent of services provided to its major customers, Guangzhou Investment Group Co., and Maoming Northwest Mining Co.

Stock-Based Compensation

Example 7.52: Stock-Based Compensation Valuations are based upon highly subjective assumptions about the future, including stock price volatility and exercise patterns. The fair value of share- based payment awards was estimated using the Black-Scholes option pricing model. Expected volatilities are based on the historical volatility of the Company's stock. The Company uses historical data to estimate option exercise and employee terminations. The expected term of options granted represents the period of time that options granted are expected to be outstanding. The risk-free rate for periods within the expected life of the option is based on the U.S. Treasury yield curve in effect at the time of the grant.

Example 7.53: Stock-Based Compensation The Company accounts for stock-based payments in accordance with the provision of ASC 718, which requires that all share-based payments issued to acquire goods or services, including grants of employee stock options, be recognized in the statement of operations based on their fair values, net of estimated forfeitures. ASC 718 requires forfeitures to be estimated at the time of grant and revised, if necessary, in subsequent periods if actual forfeitures differ from those estimates. Compensation expense related to share-based awards is recognized over the requisite service period, which is generally the vesting period.

The Company accounts for stock-based compensation awards issued to nonemployees for services, as prescribed by ASC 718-10, at either the fair value of the services rendered or the instruments issued in exchange for such services, whichever is more readily determinable, using the guidelines in ASC 505-50. The Company issues compensatory shares for services including, but not limited to, executive, management, accounting, operations, corporate communication, financial and administrative consulting services.

8 ASC 250 ACCOUNTING CHANGES AND ERROR CORRECTIONS

AUTHORITATIVE LITERATURE

Subtopic

ASC 250, *Accounting Changes and Error Corrections*, contains one Subtopic:

- ASC 250-10, *Overall*

Changes in accounting for given transactions can have a profound influence on investing and operational decisions. ASC 250 contains the underlying presumption that in preparing financial statements, an accounting principle, once adopted, should not be changed when accounting for events and transactions of a similar type. This consistent use of accounting principles is intended to enhance the utility of financial statements. The presumption that a reporting entity should not change an accounting principle may be overcome only if the entity justifies the use of an alternative acceptable accounting principle on the basis that it is actually preferable.

Scope

ASC 250 applies to all entities' financial statements and summaries of information that reflect an accounting period affected by an accounting change or error. (ASC 250-10-15-2)

Reasons for Accounting Changes

There are generally three scenarios that result in an accounting change:

1. Change in accounting principle
2. Change in estimate
3. Change in reporting entity

To apply the proper accounting guidance, preparers must be able to determine the reasons for the change.

ASC 250 provides guidance for accounting and reporting on the changes above. In addition, although technically not an "accounting change" as defined in GAAP literature, ASC 250 also provides guidance for corrections of errors made in previously issued financial statements.

It is important for the reporting entity to adequately inform financial statement users when one or more of these changes are made, and to provide sufficient information to enable the reader to distinguish the effects of the change from other factors affecting results of operations.

PRACTICE ALERT

While SEC comments pertain to public entities, their comments can provide valuable practice pointers for nonpublic entity financial statement preparers. In the areas covered in this Topic, the SEC has commented in recent years that preparers should consider carefully:

- When correcting an accounting error, management should carefully reassess the implications for its ICFR and disclosure controls and procedures.
- The quantitative and qualitative factors they considered when they assessed the materiality of error corrections. This is especially important If an entity concludes that a large error was immaterial and should not be treated as a restatement of previously published financial statements.
- For a change in accounting principle, document the conclusion as to the new method's preferability.
- Document the analysis that led to the conclusion that there was or was not a change in reporting entity based on the criteria in ASC 250-10.

DISCLOSURE AND PRESENTATION REQUIREMENTS

Change in Accounting Principle

Presentation of Changes in Accounting Principle   An entity is permitted to change from one generally accepted accounting principle to another only when:

1. It voluntarily decides to do so and can justify the use of the alternative accounting principle as being preferable to the principle currently being followed, or

2. It is required to make the change as a result of a newly issued accounting pronouncement. (ASC 250-10-45-2)

The following are *not* considered a change in accounting principle:

- Initial adoption of an accounting principle.
- Adoption or modification of an accounting principle for transactions or events substantially different from previous transactions.
  (ASC 250-45-1)

According to ASC 250, the term *accounting principle* includes not only the accounting principles and practices used by the reporting entity, but also its methods of applying them. A change in the components used to cost a firm's inventory is considered a change in accounting principle and, therefore, is permitted only when the new inventory costing method is preferable to the former method.

Accounting Standards Updates include specific provisions regarding transitioning to the new accounting principles. Adopting entities must follow these provisions. The default method is retrospective restatement. Updates may provide for adoption using cumulative effect or catch-up adjustments, if FASB believes that is the most beneficial method of transition. (ASC 250-10-45-3)

There are two methods for reporting changes in accounting principles:

1. Retrospective application—restating the financial statements to apply the new principle as if the new principle had always been used:
   a. Adjust the carrying amounts of assets and liabilities for the cumulative effect of the change in periods prior to those presented in the financial statements.
   b. Offset the effects of the adjustment in step "a" above by adjusting the opening balance of retained earnings or other appropriate component of equity.
   c. Adjust the financial statements for period-specific effects of accounting change for each period presented, if practicable.
   (ASC 250-10-45-5 and 45-6)
2. Prospective application:
   ○ Reflects the change in current and future financial statements without restating prior years.

Entities must apply all voluntary changes in accounting principles retrospectively to prior period financial statements unless it is impracticable to do so or guidance mandates another approach. If it is impracticable to determine the cumulative effect on any prior period, the entity should apply the new principle as if the change was made prospectively as of the earliest date practicable. (ASC 250-10-45-7) Prospectively reflects the change in current and future financial statements without restating prior years.

Inability to determine period-specific effects If the entity is able to determine the adjustment to beginning retained earnings for the cumulative effect of applying the new accounting principle to periods prior to those presented in the financial statements, but is unable to determine the period-specific effects of the change on all of the prior periods presented in the financial statements, the entity must follow these steps to adopt the new accounting principle:

1. Adjust the carrying amounts of the assets and liabilities for the cumulative effect of applying the new accounting principle at the beginning of the earliest period presented for which it is practicable to make the computation.
2. Any offsetting adjustment required by applying Step 1 is made to beginning retained earnings (or other applicable components of equity or net assets) of that period.
   (ASC 250-10-45-6)

Inability to determine effects on any prior periods If it is impracticable to determine the cumulative effect of adoption of the new accounting principle on any prior periods, the entity must apply the new principle prospectively as of the earliest date that it is practicable to do so. (ASC 250-10-45-7) The most common example of this occurs when the entity of a reporting entity decides to change its inventory costing assumption from first-in, first-out (FIFO) to last-in, first-out (LIFO).

Direct and Indirect Effects Changing accounting principles sometimes results in indirect effects from legal or contractual obligations of the reporting entity, such as profit sharing or royalty arrangements that contain monetary formulas based on amounts in the financial statements. ASC 250 specifies that irrespective of whether the indirect effects arise from an explicit requirement in the agreement or are discretionary, if incurred, they are to be recognized in the period in which the reporting entity makes the accounting change.

Effect of the change in accounting principles should be treated as follows:

- Direct effects, including any related income tax effects—include in the retrospective application.
- Indirect effects:
  - That would have been recognized in prior periods—do not include in the retrospective application.
  - Actually incurred and recognized—report in the period in which the accounting change is made.
  (ASC 250-10-45-8)

Impracticability Exception All prior periods presented in the financial statements are required to be adjusted for the retroactive application of the newly adopted accounting principle, unless it is impracticable to do so. (ASC 250-10-45-9) The Codification recognizes that there are certain circumstances when there is a change in accounting principle when it will not be feasible to compute:

- The retroactive adjustment to the prior periods affected, or
- The period-specific adjustments relative to periods presented in the financial statements.

Preferability Assessment The entity is only permitted to voluntarily change the reporting entity's accounting principles when the newly employed principle is *preferable* to the principle it is replacing. The preferability assessment should be made from the perspective of financial reporting, and not solely from an income tax perspective. Thus, favorable income tax consequences alone do not justify making a change in financial reporting practices. (ASC 250-10-45-12) ASC 250 does not provide a definition of preferability or criteria by which to make such assessments, so this remains a matter of professional judgment. What is preferable for one industry or company is not necessarily considered preferable for another.

Disclosures for Change in Accounting Principle For the period in which the change in accounting principle is made, entities must disclose:

- The nature of and reasons for making the change.
- The reason the new principle is preferable.
- Descriptions of prior period items that have been retrospectively restated.
- The effects of the change for both current period and prior period(s) being presented, including specific quantification of the effects on:
  - Income from continuing operations;
  - Net income;
  - Any other financial statement caption materially affected; and
  - Corresponding per-share amounts for each.

- As of the beginning of the earliest statement presented, the cumulative effect of the change in retained earnings or other components of equity or net assets in the statement of financial position.
- If the requirement to restate prior periods is impracticable,
  - The reason, and
  - Details regarding the alternative method of accounting applied.

When indirect effects of change in accounting principle are included,

- A description of these effects.
- The amounts recognized in the current reporting period, together with:
  - The per-share amounts.
  - The amount of indirect effects of the change in each of the prior periods being presented, if practicable.
  (FASB ASC 250-10-50-1)
- For interim reports after the date of adoption of a new accounting principle:
  - The effect of the change on income from continuing operations.
  - Net income.
  - Related per-share amounts for those post-change interim periods.
  (FASB ASC 250-10-50-3)

Reclassifications

Occasionally, a company will choose to change the way it applies an accounting principle, resulting in a change in the way that a particular financial statement caption is displayed or in the individual general ledger accounts that comprise a caption. These reclassifications may occur for a variety of reasons, including:

1. In the entity's judgment, the revised methodology more accurately reflects the economics of a type or class of transaction.
2. An amount that was immaterial in previous periods and combined with another number has become material and warrants presentation as a separately captioned line item.
3. Due to changes in the business or the manner in which the financial statements are used to make decisions, the entity deems a different form of presentation to be more useful or informative.

To maintain comparability of financial statements when such changes are made, the financial statements of all periods presented must be reclassified to conform to the new presentation.

Such reclassifications, which usually affect only the statement of income, do not affect reported net income or retained earnings for any period since they result in simply recasting amounts that were previously reported. Normally, a reclassification will result in an increase in one or more reported numbers with a corresponding decrease in one or more other numbers. In addition, these changes reflect changes in the application of accounting principles either for which there are multiple alternative treatments or for which GAAP is silent, and thus the entity has discretion in presentation.

Reclassifications are not explicitly dealt with in GAAP, but as mentioned in the chapter on ASC 205, the Codification emphasizes the need for comparability (ASC 205-10-45-3) and reclassifications do commonly occur in practice.

Change in Accounting Estimate

The preparation of financial statements requires frequent use of estimates for such items as asset service lives, salvage values, asset impairments, collectability of accounts receivable, loan losses or bad debts, estimated liabilities for warranties, obsolete and excess inventory, pension costs, and the like. Future conditions and events that affect these estimates cannot be estimated with certainty. Therefore, changes in estimates will be inevitable as new information and more experience is obtained.

Presentation Requirements for Change in Accounting Estimate Changes in estimates must be recognized currently and prospectively. (ASC 250-10-45-17) The effect of the change in accounting estimate is accounted for prospectively in:

- The period of change if the change affects that period only, *or*
- The period of change and future periods if the change affects both.

The reporting entity is precluded from retrospective application, restatement of prior periods, or presentation of pro forma amounts as a result of a change in accounting estimate.

Disclosure Requirements for Change in Accounting Estimate Entities must make the following disclosures:

- If the change affects several future periods, the effect on:
  - Income from continuing operations;
  - Net income of current period; and
  - Related per-share amounts.
- For a change in estimate not having material effect in the current period, but which is deemed likely to have material effects on later periods, a description of the change. (FASB ASC 250-10-50-4)

Change in Accounting Estimate Effected by a Change in Accounting Principle

To change certain accounting estimates, the entity must adopt a new accounting principle or change the method it uses to apply an accounting principle. In contemplating such a change, the entity would not be able to separately determine the effects of changing the accounting principle from the effects of changing its estimate. The change in estimate is accomplished by changing the method.

A change in accounting estimate that is affected by a change in accounting principle is accounted for in the same manner as a change in accounting estimate, that is, currently and prospectively in the current and future periods affected. However, because the entity is changing the company's accounting principle or method of applying it, the new accounting principle, as previously discussed, must be preferable to the accounting principle being superseded. (ASC 250-10-45-18)

The entity may decide, for example, to change its depreciation method for certain types of assets from straight-line to an accelerated method, such as double-declining balance to recognize the fact that those assets are more productive in their earlier years of service because they require less downtime and do not require repairs as frequently. Such a change is permitted only if the entity justifies it based on the fact that using the new method is preferable to the old one, in this case because it more accurately matches the costs of production to periods in which the units are produced. (ASC 250-10-45-19)

Practice Pointer: Guidance makes a distinction for entities that elect to apply a depreciation method that results in accelerated depreciation until the point during the useful life of the depreciable asset when it is useful to change to straight-line depreciation in order to fully depreciate the asset over the remaining term. At this point, the remaining carrying value (net book value) is depreciated using the straight-line method over its remaining useful life. If this method is consistently followed by the reporting entity, the changeover to straight-line depreciation is not considered to be an accounting change. (ASC 250-10-45-20)

Change in Reporting Entity

A change in reporting entity is a special type of change in accounting principle. Changes in reporting entity include:

- Consolidated or combined financial statements in place of individual entities' statements.
- A change in the members of the group of subsidiaries that comprise the consolidated financial statements.
- A change in the companies included in combined financial statements.

Specifically *excluded* from qualifying as a change in reporting entity are:

- A business combination accounted under ASC 805, and
- Consolidation of a variable interest entity accounted for under the acquisition method in ASC 810.

Presentation Requirements An accounting change resulting in financial statements that are, in effect, of a different reporting entity than previously reported on, is retrospectively applied to the financial statements of all prior periods presented in order to show financial information for the new reporting entity for all periods (ASC 250-10-45-21). One exception is that interest cost previously capitalized under ASC 835-20 is not changed when retrospectively applying the change to prior periods. The change is also retrospectively applied to previously issued interim financial information.

Disclosure Requirements Entities reporting a change in entity must disclose:

- The nature of the change.
- The reason for the change.
- For all periods presented, the effect of the change on:
  - Income from continuing operations
  - Net income
  - Other comprehensive income
  - Per-share amounts
- For a change in entity not having material effect currently but anticipated to have such effect in later periods, in the period of the change:
  - The nature of the change, and
  - The reason the change was made.
    (FASB ASC 250-10-50-6)

Error Corrections

Errors are sometimes discovered after financial statements have been issued. Errors result from mathematical mistakes, mistakes in the application of GAAP, or the oversight or misuse of facts known or available to the accountant at the time the financial statements were prepared. Errors can occur in recognition, measurement, presentation, or disclosure. A change from an unacceptable (or incorrect) accounting principle to a correct principle is also considered a correction of an error and not a change in accounting principle. Such a change should not be confused with the preferability determination discussed earlier that involves two or more acceptable principles. An error correction pertains to the recognition that a previously used method was not an acceptable method at the time it was employed.

Presentation Requirements for Error Corrections The essential distinction between a change in estimate and the correction of an error depends upon the availability of information. An estimate requires revision because by its nature it is based upon incomplete information. Later data will either confirm or contradict the estimate and any contradiction will require revision of the estimate. An error results from the misuse of existing information available at the time which is discovered at a later date. However, this discovery is not as a result of additional information or subsequent developments.

When considering if an error meets the materiality threshold for reporting a correction of an error, the entity should compare the magnitude of the error with estimated annual income and the effects on earnings trends. (ASC 250-10-45-27 and 50-12)

If the entity presents historical summaries for several periods, the entity should restate net income and other affected items for the affected periods. Disclosure should be made in the first summary after the correction. (ASC 250-10-50-7A)

Correction of a material misstatement is done through the entity issuing corrected financial statements that have been restated. If comparative financial statements are soon to be issued, the entity may reflect the correction of the error in those statements, indicating that the prior period has been restated. Users of the previously issued financial statements must be notified to no longer rely on those financial statements. If only a single period is presented, the entity makes an adjustment to beginning retained earnings for the cumulative effect of the error.

ASC 250 specifies that, when correcting an error in prior period financial statements, the term "restatement" should be used. That term is exclusively reserved for this purpose so as to effectively communicate to users of the financial statements the reason for a particular change in previously issued financial statements.

Restatement consists of the following steps:

Step 1	Adjust the carrying amounts of assets and liabilities at the beginning of the first period presented in the financial statements for the cumulative effect of correcting the error on periods prior to those presented in the financial statements.

Step 2	Offset the effect of the adjustment in Step 1 (if any) by adjusting the opening balance of retained earnings (or other components of equity or net assets, as applicable to the reporting entity) for that period.

Step 3	Adjust the financial statements of each individual prior period presented for the effects of correcting the error on that specific period (referred to as the period-specific effects of the error).
(ASC 250-10-45-23)

Disclosure Requirements for Error Corrections Entities must make the following disclosures:

- That the previously issued statements have been restated and:
  - The nature of the error in previously issued statements.
  - The effect of its correction on each financial statement line item (only in period of discovery and correction), with per-share equivalents.
  - The cumulative effect on retained earnings.
  (FASB ASC 250-10-50-7)
  - "If restated, historical, statistical-type summaries of financial data for error corrections" (FASB ASC 250-10-50-27A)

- The effects (both gross and net of applicable income tax) of prior period adjustments on the net income of prior periods in:
  - The annual report for the year in which the adjustments are made.
  - Interim reports issued during that year after the date of recording the adjustments. (FASB ASC 250-10-50-8)
- For single period only financial statements, the effects of such restatement on:
  - The balance of retained earnings at the beginning of the period, and
  - The net income of the immediately preceding period.
- For financial statements with more than one period presented:
  - The effects for each of the periods included in the statements.
  - Include the amounts of income tax applicable to the prior period adjustments. (FASB ASC 250-10-50-9)

Requirements of FASB ASC 250-10-50-7 through 50-9 are not repeated in subsequent periods. (ASC 250-10-50-10)

Interim Reporting Considerations

Changes that are material in the interim period, but not to estimated income for the fiscal year or the trend in earnings should be disclosed separately in the interim statements. (FASB ASC 250-10-50-12)

For interim reporting considerations regarding changes in accounting principles, accounting estimates and reporting entities and corrections of errors, also see the chapter on ASC 270. (ASC 250-10-50-10)

EXAMPLE DISCLOSURES

Example 8.1: Change in Accounting Principle—Note A: Change in Method of Accounting for Inventories

During 20X3, management changed the company's method of accounting for all of its inventories from first-in, first-out (FIFO) to last-in, first-out (LIFO). The change was made because management believes that the LIFO method provides a better matching of costs and revenues. In addition, with the adoption of LIFO, the company's inventory pricing method is consistent with the method predominant in the industry. The change and its effect on net income ($000 omitted except for per-share amounts) and earnings per share for 20X3 are as follows:

	Net Income	Earnings Per Share
Net income before the change	$4,800	$4.80
Reduction of net income due to the change	2,200	2.20
Net income as adjusted	$2,600	$2.60

Management has not retrospectively applied this change to prior years' financial statements because beginning inventory on January 1, 20X3, using LIFO is the same as the amount reported on a FIFO basis at December 31, 20X2. As a result of this change, the current period's financial statements are not comparable with those of any prior periods. The FIFO cost of inventories exceeds the carrying amount valued using LIFO by $2, 200,000 at December 31, 20X3.

Example 8.2: Change in Accounting Principle—Retrospective Application of a Change in Accounting Principle

In 20X1, upon the incorporation of Newburger Company, its management elected to recognize advertising air time costs as incurred. Newburger has been consistently following that policy in its financial statements. In 20X8, Newburger's management reviewed its accounting policies and concluded that application of its current policy was resulting in substantial media air time costs associated being recognized in financial reporting periods that preceded the periods in which the related media aired. Consequently, management decided to change Newburger's policy from expensing advertising costs when incurred to expensing costs when the media first aired. This approach is permitted by ASC 720-35-25-5. Additional assumptions follow:

1. As has been its policy in the past, Newburger plans to issue comparative financial statements presenting two years, 20X8 and 20X7.
2. Newburger does not engage in direct-response advertising activities.
   A combined federal and state income tax rate of 40% was in effect for all relevant periods.
3. Prior to the change in accounting principle, there were no temporary differences or loss carryforwards and, thus, there were no deferred income tax assets or liabilities.

Advertising costs are deductible for income tax purposes when incurred and, therefore, upon adoption of the new accounting policy, Newburger will have a temporary difference between the book and income tax bases of its asset, deferred advertising costs. These advertising costs that are being recognized in the financial statements in the year after they are deducted on Newburger's income tax return represent a future taxable temporary difference that will give rise to a deferred income tax liability.

The financial statements originally issued as of and for the years ended December 31, 20X7 and 20X6, prior to the adoption of the new accounting principle, are presented below with advertising-related captions shown separately for illustrative purposes.

Newburger Company
Statements of Income and Retained Earnings
Prior to Change in Accounting Principle
Years Ended December 31, 20X7 and 20X6

	20X7	*20X6*
Sales	$ 2,300,000	$ 2,000,000
Cost of sales	(850,000)	(750,000)
Gross profit	1,450,000	1,250,000
Advertising expense	65,000	55,000
Other selling, general, and administrative expenses	385,000	445,000
	450,000	500,000
Income from operations	1,000,000	750,000
Other income (expense)	11,000	10,000
Income before income taxes	1,011,000	760,000
Income taxes	(404,000)	(304,000)
Net income	607,000	456,000
Retained earnings, beginning of year	13,756,000	14,500,000
Dividends	(1,400,000)	(1,200,000)
Retained earnings, end of year	$12,963,000	$13,756,000

Newburger Company
Statements of Financial Position
Prior to Change in Accounting Principle
December 31, 20X7 and 20X6

	20X7	20X6
Assets		
Current assets		
Cash and cash equivalents	$ 2,200,000	$ 2,400,000
Deferred advertising cost	–	–
Prepaid expenses	125,000	120,000
Other current assets	22,000	20,000
Total current assets	2,347,000	2,540,000
Property and equipment	10,729,000	11,311,000
Total assets	$13,076,000	$13,851,000
Liabilities and stockholders' equity		
Current liabilities		
Other current liabilities	35,000	12,000
Total current liabilities	35,000	12,000
Noncurrent liabilities	65,000	70,000
Deferred income taxes	$ –	$ –
Total liabilities	100,000	82,000
Stockholders' equity		
Common stock	13,000	13,000
Retained earnings	12,963,00	13,756,000
Total stockholders' equity	12,976,000	13,769,000
Total liabilities and stockholders' equity	$13,076,000	$ 13,851,000

Newburger Company
Statements of Cash Flows
Prior to Change in Accounting Principle
Years Ended December 31, 20X7 and 20X6

	20X7	20X6
Operating activities		
Net income	$ 607,000	$ 456,000
Depreciation	715,000	715,000
Deferred income taxes	–	–
Gain on sale of property and equipment	–	–
Changes in		
Deferred advertising costs	–	–
Prepaid expenses	(5,000)	1,000
Other current assets	(2,000)	1,500
Other current liabilities	23,000	900
Net cash provided by operating activities	1,338,000	1,174,400

Newburger Company
Statements of Cash Flows
Prior to Change in Accounting Principle
Years Ended December 31, 20X7 and 20X6

	20X7	*20X6*
Investing activities		
Property and equipment		
Acquisition	(133,000)	(120,000)
Proceeds from sale	–	–
Net cash used for investing activities	(133,000)	(120,000)
Financing activities		
Dividends paid to stockholders	(1,400,000)	(1,200,000)
Long-term debt		
Borrowed	–	–
Repaid	(5,000)	(5,000)
Net cash used for financing activities	(1,405,000)	(1,205,000)
Decrease in cash and cash equivalents	(200,000)	(150,600)
Cash and cash equivalents, beginning of year	2,400,000	2,550,600
Cash and cash equivalents, end of year	$2,200,000	$2,400,000

Newberger applies Step 1 in the exhibit above and adjusts the carrying amounts of assets and liabilities at the beginning of the first period presented in the financial statements (January 1, 20X7) for the cumulative effect of changing to the new accounting principle on periods prior to those presented in the financial statements.

Newberger refers to the previously issued 20X7 financial statements presented above. Assume the following data regarding advertising costs at December 31, 20X6/January 1, 20X7:

Costs incurred during 20X6 for advertising that will not take place for the first time until 20X7	$25,000
Deferred income tax liability that would have been recognized at December 31, 20X6, computed at 40% of the temporary difference	(10,000)
Net adjustment to beginning assets and liabilities	$ 15,000

Newberger applies Step 2 in the Exhibit above and offsets the effect of the adjustment in Step 1 by adjusting the opening balance of retained earnings for 20X7 (or other components of equity or net assets, as applicable to the reporting entity).

The $15,000 net effect of the adjustment in Step 1 is presented in the statement of income and retained earnings as an adjustment to the January 1, 20X7, retained earnings as previously reported at December 31, 20X6.

In Step 3, Newberger adjusts the financial statements of each individual prior period presented for the effects of applying the new accounting principle to that specific period.

In this case, the following adjustments are necessary to adjust the 20X7 financial statements for the period-specific effects of the change in accounting principle:

Cost Incurred in Year the Advertising
Was First Aired

20X6	20X7	$ 25,000
20X7	20X8	(45,000)
Pretax, period-specific adjustment to advertising costs at 12/31/X6	(20,000)	
× 40% income tax effect		8,000
Effect on 20X7 net income		$(12,000)

Adjustments to the 20X7 financial statements for the period-specific effects of retrospective application of the new accounting principle are:

	Deferred Advertising Costs	Deferred Income Tax Liability	Advertising Expense	Income Tax Expense
Balance at 12/31/X7 prior to adjustment	$ –	$ –	$65,000	$404,000
Adjustment to opening balances from retrospective application to 20X7	25,000	10,000	–	–
Advertising costs incurred in 20X6, first aired in 20X7	(25,000)	–	25,000	–
Advertising costs incurred in 20X7, first aired in 20X8	45,000	–	(45,000) (20,000)	–
Income tax effect of net adjustment to	8,000	–	–	–
20X7 advertising expense (40%)	8,000	–	–	–
Adjusted amounts for 20X7 financial statements	$45,000	$18,000	$45,000	$412,000

The adjusted comparative financial statements, reflecting the retrospective application of the new accounting principle, follow.

Newburger Company
Statements of Income and Retained Earnings
Reflecting Retrospective Application of Change in Accounting Principle
Years Ended December 31, 20X8 and 20X7

	20X8	20X7 as Adjusted
Sales	$ 2,700,000	$ 2,300,000
Cost of sales	995,000	850,000
Gross profit	1,705,000	1,450,000
Advertising expense	66,000	45,000
Other selling, general, and administrative expenses	423,000	385,000
	489,000	430,000
Income from operations	1,216,000	1,020,000
Other income (expense)	9,000	11,000

Newburger Company
Statements of Income and Retained Earnings
Reflecting Retrospective Application of Change in Accounting Principle
Years Ended December 31, 20X8 and 20X7

	20X8	*20X7*
Income before income taxes	1,225,000	1,031,000
Income taxes	490,400	412,000
Net income	734,600	619,000
Retained earnings, beginning of year, as originally reported		13,756,000
Adjustment for retrospective application of new accounting principle (Note X)		15,000
Retained earnings, beginning of year, as adjusted	12,990,000	13,771,000
Dividends	1,600,000	1,400,000
Retained earnings, end of year	$12,124,600	$12,990,000

Newburger Company
Statements of Financial Position
Reflecting Retrospective Application of Change in Accounting Principle
Years Ended December 31, 20X8 and 20X7

Assets	*20X8*	*20X7* *as Adjusted*
Current assets		
Cash and cash equivalents	$ 2,382,000	$ 2,200,000
Deferred advertising costs	16,000	45,000
Prepaid expenses	123,000	125,000
Other current assets	21,000	22,000
Total current assets	2,542,000	2,392,000
Property and equipment	9,800,000	10,729,000
Total assets	$12,342,000	$13,121,000
Liabilities and stockholders' equity		
Other current liabilities	$ 36,000	$ 35,000
Total current liabilities	36,000	35,000
Deferred income taxes	$ 6,000	$ 18,000
Other noncurrent liabilities	162,000	65,000
Total noncurrent liabilities	$ 168,000	$ 83,000
Total liabilities	204,400	118,000
Stockholders' equity		
Common stock	13,000	13,000
Retained earnings	12,124,600	12,990,000
Total stockholders' equity	12,137,600	13,003,000
Total liabilities and stockholders' equity	$12,342,000	$13,121,000

Newburger Company
Statements of Cash Flows
Reflecting Retrospective Application of Change in Accounting Principle
Years Ended December 31, 20X8 and 20X7

Operating activities	20X8	20X7 as Adjusted
Net income	$ 734,600	$ 619,000
Depreciation	725,000	715,000
Deferred income taxes	(11,600)	8,000
Gain on sale of property and equipment	(1,200,000)	–
Changes in		
Deferred advertising costs	29,000	(20,000)
Prepaid expenses	2,000	(5,000)
Other current assets	1,000	(2,000)
Other current liabilities	1,000	23,000
Net cash provided by operating activities	$281,000	$1,338,000
Investing activities		
Property and equipment		
Acquisition	(1,096,000)	(133,000)
Proceeds from sale	2,500,000	–
Net cash provided by (used for) investing activities	1,404,000	(133,000)
Financing activities		
Dividends paid to stockholders	(1,600,000)	(1,400,000)
Long-term debt		
Borrowed	105,000	–
Repaid	(8,000)	(5,000)
Net cash used for financing activities	(1,503,000)	(1,405,000)
Increase (decrease) in cash and cash equivalents	182,000	(200,000)
Cash and cash equivalents, beginning of year	2,200,000	2,400,000
Cash and cash equivalents, end of year	$ 2,382,000	$ 2,200,000

Practice Pointer: It is important to note that, in presenting the previously issued financial statements for 20X7, the caption "as adjusted" is included in the column heading. ASC 250 explicitly defines a restatement as a revision to previously issued financial statements to correct an error. Therefore, to avoid misleading the financial statement reader, use of the terms restatement or restated are limited to prior period adjustments to correct errors.

Indirect effects. The example above only reflects the direct effects of the change in account-ing principle, net of the effect of income taxes. Changing accounting principles sometimes results in indirect effects from legal or contractual obligations of the reporting entity, such as profit sharing or royalty arrangements that contain monetary formulas based on amounts in the financial statements. In the preceding example, if Newburger Company had an incentive com-pensation plan that required it to contribute 15% of its pretax income to a pool to be distributed to its employees, the adoption of the new accounting policy would potentially require Newburger to provide additional contributions to the pool computed as:

Effect of	*Contractual Retroactive Application*	*Pretax Indirect Rate*	*Effect*
Prior to 20X7	$25,000	15%	$3,750
20X7	(20,000)	15%	(3,000)
			$ 750

Contracts and agreements are often silent regarding how such a change might affect amounts that were computed (and distributed) in prior years. Management of Newburger Company might have discretion over whether to make the additional contributions. Further, it would probably consider it undesirable to reduce the 20X7 incentive compensation pool because of an account-ing change of this nature, and it might thus decide for valid business reasons not to reduce the pool under these circumstances.

ASC 250 specifies that irrespective of whether the indirect effects arise from an explicit requirement in the agreement or are discretionary, if incurred they are to be recognized in the period in which the reporting entity makes the accounting change, which is 20X8 in the example above.

Example 8.3: Change in Accounting Principle—Adoption of a New Accounting Principle—Retrospective Application

In April 2015, the Financial Accounting Standards Board (FASB) issued guidance that requires debt issuance costs related to term debt to be presented in the balance sheet as a direct reduction from the associated debt liability. This standard requires retrospective application and is effective for annual reporting periods beginning after December 15, 20X5. This change in accounting principle is preferable because it allows both debt issuance costs and debt discounts to be presented similarly in the consolidated balance sheets as a direct reduction from the face amount of our debt balances. A retrospective change to our consolidated balance sheet as of December 31, 2015, as previously pre-sented, is required pursuant to the guidance. The retrospective adjustment to the December 31, 2015, consolidated balance sheet is shown below.

	As Previously Reported	*December 31, 2015 Adjustment Effect ($ in millions)*	*As Adjusted*
Other long-term assets	$ 666	$ (86)	$ 580
Long-term debt, net	$ 20,708	$ (86)	$ 20,622

In addition, certain revisions have been made to the fair value of debt table included in Note 3 to conform to the presentation used for our 2016 disclosure. The 8.00% Senior Secured Second Lien Notes due 2022 were previously classified as Level 1 and should have been classified as Level 2, as these senior notes are not exchange-traded. The following table reflects the revisions made.

	As Previously Reported		December 31, 2015 Adjustment Effect		As Revised	
	Carrying Amount	*Estimated Fair Value*	*Carrying Amount*	*Estimated Fair Value ($ in millions)*	*Carrying Amount*	*Estimated Fair Value*
Short-term debt (Level 1)	$ 762	$ 732	$ —	$ —	$ 762	$ 732
Long-term debt (Level 1)*	$ 20,694	$ 7,470	$ (7,254)	$ (2,378)	$ 13,440	$ 5,092
Long-term debt (Level 2)	$ —	$ —	$ 7,168	$ 2,378	$ 7,168	$ 2,378

---

* The difference in the carrying amount is due to the debt issuance costs retrospective change noted above.

Example 8.4: Reclassifications—Reclassification of Intellectual Property Income, Gains, and Losses

Effective January 1, 20X3, the company removed the impact of intellectual property income, gains and losses on sales, and other-than-temporary declines in market value of certain investments, realized gains and losses on certain real estate activity, and foreign currency transaction gains and losses from the caption "Selling, General, and Administrative Expenses" in the consolidated statement of income. Custom development income was also removed from the "Research, Development, and Engineering" caption on the consolidated statement of income. Intellectual property and custom development income are now presented in a separate caption in the consolidated statement of income. The other items listed above are now included as part of "Other Income and Expense." Results of prior periods have been reclassified to conform to the current year presentation.

Example 8.5: Reclassifications—Reclassification of Expenses

Effective January 1, 20X3, management has elected to reclassify certain expenses in its consolidated statements of income. Costs of the order entry function and certain accounting and information technology services have been reclassified from cost of sales to selling, general, and administrative expense. Costs related to order fulfillment have been reclassified from selling, general, and administrative expense to cost of sales. These reclassifications resulted in a decrease to cost of sales and an increase to selling, general, and administrative expense of $31.8 million, and $36.2 million for the years ended December 31, 20X2 and 20X1, respectively.

Example 8.6: Change in Accounting Estimate Effected by a Change in Accounting Principle—Change in Amortization Method of Fixed Maturity Securities

The cost of fixed maturity securities classified as available-for-sale is adjusted for amortization of premiums and accretion of discounts, which are included in net investment income on the consolidated statements of operations. The amortization of premium and accretion of discount for fixed maturity securities takes into consideration call and maturity dates that produce the lowest yield. This represents a change from prior reporting periods as previously the amortization of premiums was to maturity. This change in estimate effected by a change in accounting principle will result in a better reflection of the yield on fixed maturity securities with call provisions. This change, which was adopted in the fourth quarter of 20X5, decreased Net investment income and the amortized cost of fixed maturity securities by $43 million in the consolidated statement of operations for the year ended December 31, 20X5, and the consolidated balance sheet as of December 31, 20X5, respectively. This adjustment decreased basic and diluted earnings per share by $0.08 for the year ended December 31, 20X5.

Example 8.7: Change in Accounting Estimate—Change in Depreciable Life of Equipment

During 20X6, management assessed its estimates of the useful lives and residual values of the company's machinery and equipment. Management revised its original estimates and currently estimates that its production equipment acquired in 20X1 and originally estimated to have a 10-year useful life and a residual value of $1,000 will have a 15-year useful life and a residual value of $800. The effects of reflecting this change in accounting estimate on the 20X6 financial statements are as follows:

Increase in	
Income from continuing operations and net income	$430.00
Earnings per share (for public companies)*	$ 0.02

---

* Assuming 25,000 shares were outstanding for al1 1 of 20X8.

Example 8.8: Correction of Error—Example of a Correction of an Error in Previously Issued Financial Statements

Assume that Truesdell Company had overstated its depreciation expense by $50,000 in 20X0 and $40,000 in 20X2. Both overstatements are the result of mathematical mistakes. The errors affected both the financial statements and the income tax returns in 20X1 and 20X2 and are discovered in 20X3.

Truesdell's statements of financial position and statements of income and retained earnings as of and for the year ended December 31, 20X2, prior to the restatement were as follows:

Truesdell Company
Statement of Income and Retained Earnings
Prior to Restatement
Year Ended December 31, 20X2

	20X2
Sales	$ 2,000,000
Cost of sales	
Depreciation	750,000
Other	390,000
	1,140,000
Gross profit	860,000
Selling, general, and administrative expenses	450,000
Income from operations	410,000
Other income (expense)	10,000
Income before income taxes	420,000
Income taxes	168,000
Net income	252,000
Retained earnings, beginning of year	6,463,000
Dividends	(1,200,000)
Retained earnings, end of year	$ 5,515,000

Truesdell Company
Statement of Financial Position
Prior to Restatement
December 31, 20X2

	20X2
Assets	
Current assets	$ 2,540,000
Property and equipment	
Cost	3,500,000
Accumulated depreciation and amortization	(430,000)
	3,070,000
Total assets	$ 5,610,000
Liabilities and stockholders' equity	
Income taxes payable	$ –
Other current liabilities	12,000
Total current liabilities	12,000
Noncurrent liabilities	70,000
Total liabilities	82,000
Stockholders' equity	
Common stock	13,000
Retained earnings	5,515,000
Total stockholders' equity	5,528,000
Total liabilities and stockholders' equity	$ 5,610,000

The following steps are followed to restate Truesdell's prior period financial statements:

Step 1   Adjust the carrying amounts of assets and liabilities at the beginning of the first period presented in the financial statements for the cumulative effect of correcting the error on periods prior to those presented in the financial statements.

The first period presented in the 20X3 financial report is 20X2. At the beginning of that year, $50,000 of the mistakes had been made and reflected on both the income tax return and financial statements. Assuming a flat 40% income tax rate and ignoring the effects of penalties and interest that would be assessed on the amended income tax returns, the following adjustment would be made to assets and liabilities at January 1, 20X2:

Decrease in accumulated depreciation	$50,000
Increase in income taxes payable	(20,000)
	$30,000

Step 2   Offset the effect of the adjustment in Step 1 by adjusting the opening balance of retained earnings (or other components of equity or net assets, as applicable to the reporting entity) for that period.

Retained earnings at the beginning of 20X2 will increase by $30,000 as the offsetting entry resulting from Step 1.

Step 3   Adjust the financial statements of each individual prior period presented for the effects of correcting the error on that specific period (referred to as the period-specific effects of the error).

The 20X2 prior period financial statements will be corrected for the period-specific effects of the restatement as follows:

Decrease in depreciation expense and accumulated depreciation	$40,000
Increase in income tax expense and income taxes payable	(16,000)
Increase 20X2 net income	$24,000

The restated financial statements are presented below.

Truesdell Company
Statements of Income and Retained Earnings
As Restated
Years Ended December 31, 20X3 and 20X2

	20X3	20X2 Restated
Sales	$2,100,000	$2,000,000
Cost of sales		
Depreciation	740,000	710,000
Other	410,000	390,000
	1,150,000	1,100,000
Gross profit	950,000	900,000
Selling, general, and administrative expenses	460,000	450,000
Income from operations	490,000	450,000
Other income (expense)	(5,000)	10,000

Truesdell Company
Statements of Income and Retained Earnings
As Restated
Years Ended December 31, 20X3 and 20X2

	20X3	*20X2 Restated*
Income before income taxes	485,000	460,000
Income taxes	200,000	184,000
Net income	285,000	276,000
Retained earnings, beginning of year, as originally reported	5,569,000	6,463,000
Restatement to reflect correction of depreciation (Note X)	–	30,000
Retained earnings, beginning of year, as restated	5,569,000	6,493,000
Dividends	(800,000)	(1,200,000)
Retained earnings, end of year	$5,054,000	$5,569,000

Truesdell Company
Statements of Financial Position
As Restated
December 31, 20X3 and 20X2

	20X3	*20X2 Restates*
Assets		
Current assets	$ 2,840,000	$ 2,540,000
Property and equipment		
Cost	3,750,000	3,500,000
Accumulated depreciation and amortization	(1,050,000)	(340,000)
	2,700,000	3,160,000
Total assets	$ 5,540,000	$ 5,700,000
Liabilities and stockholders' equity		
Income taxes payable	$50,000	$35,000
Other current liabilities	110,000	12,000
Total current liabilities	160,000	48,000
Noncurrent liabilities	313,000	70,000
Total liabilities	473,000	118,000
Stockholders' equity		
Common stock	13,000	13,000
Retained earnings	5,054,000	5,569,000
Total stockholders' equity	5,067,000	5,582,000
Total liabilities and stockholders' equity	$ 5,540,000	$ 5,700,000

For disclosures related to restatements of financial statements previously issued, see the *Disclosure and Presentation Checklist for Commercial Businesses* at www.wiley.com/go/FSDM2021. The disclosures need not be repeated in subsequent periods. The correction of an error in the financial statements of a prior period discovered subsequent to their issuance is reported as a prior period adjustment in the financial statements of the subsequent period.

Example 8.9: Correction of Error—Correction of Immaterial Error

During the quarter ended July 2, 20X6, the Company identified an immaterial error in previously issued financial statements related to an overstatement of a rent liability in the amount of $350,000 ($275,000 net of tax or $0.08 per basic and $0.05 per diluted share for the 13 and 39 weeks ended July 2, 20X6). The Company reviewed this accounting error and determined the impact of the error to be immaterial to any prior period's presentation. The accompanying financial statements as of October 1, 20X6, reflect the correction of the aforementioned immaterial error.

Example 8.10: Correction of Error

During the first quarter of fiscal year 20X6, the Company identified errors in the consolidated financial statements for the fiscal year ended August 31, 20X5, and for fiscal years previous to 20X3. The errors related to incorrect (i) accounting for the 20X1 merger described above which impacted the translation of Property and equipment, net from foreign currencies to U.S. dollars and the related offset to Accumulated other comprehensive loss; and (ii) the translation of Property and equipment, net from foreign currencies to U.S. dollars and the related offset to Accumulated other comprehensive loss. The correction of these errors would have decreased comprehensive income by $3.2 million in fiscal year 20X1 and increased comprehensive income by $2 million in fiscal year 20X5. The total of these corrections, which was recorded in the first quarter of fiscal 20X6 as a charge to comprehensive income was approximately $2.1 million. The Company decreased property and equipment, net and increased Accumulated other comprehensive loss by the same amount.

The Company analyzed the impact of these items and concluded that neither error would be material to any individual period. Management evaluated the materiality of errors from a quantitative and qualitative perspective. Based on such evaluation, the Company concluded that correcting the cumulative errors, which decreased comprehensive income by approximately $2.1 million for the three-month period ended November 30, 20X5, was immaterial to the expected full-year results for fiscal 20X6 and financial position as presented on the consolidated balance sheet. Correcting the error would not have had a material impact on any individual prior period presented in the 20X5 financial statements, nor would it have affected the trend of financial results. Therefore the error correction did not require the restatement of the consolidated financial statements for prior periods.

9 ASC 255 CHANGING PRICES

AUTHORITATIVE LITERATURE

Subtopic

ASC 255, *Changing Prices*, contains one Subtopic:

- ASC 255-10, *Overall*, which provides guidance on reporting the effects of changing prices or inflation.

Scope The Topic applies to business entities that prepare U.S. GAAP financial statements and "foreign entities that prepare financial statements in the currency for which the operations and that operate in countries with hyperinflationary economies."

The ASC disclosures are *encouraged*, but not required.

DISCLOSURE AND PRESENTATION REQUIREMENTS

Presentation

The degree of inflation in an economy may become so great as to render conventional financial statements worthless. General price-level statements may be more meaningful. ASC 255 permits the application of price-level adjusted financial statements to the extent that it is consistent with historical accounting.

In presenting the basic foreign currency financial statements of entities operating in countries with highly inflationary economics, if the statements are intended for U.S. readers, the presentation must be consistent with guidance regarding historical cost-constant purchasing power accounting. (ASC 255-10-45-3) ASC 255 guidance applies only to statements prepared in the currency in which the operations are conducted. Only conventional statements of foreign subsidiaries can be used to prepare historical-dollar consolidated statements. (ASC 255-10-45-4)

Elective Disclosures

Business entities are encouraged, but not required, to present supplementary information on the effects of changing prices. ASC 255-10-50-3 contains a list of items that should be disclosed in a five-year summary of financial data:

- Net sales and other operating revenues.
- Income from continuing operations on a current cost basis.
- Purchasing power gain or loss on net monetary items.
- Increase or decrease in the current cost or lower recoverable amount of inventory and property, plant, and equipment, net of inflation.
- The aggregate foreign currency translation adjustment on a current cost basis, if applicable.
- Net assets at year-end on a current cost basis.
- Income per common share from continuing operations on a current cost basis.
- Cash dividends declared per common share.
- Market price per common share at year-end.

In addition to the disclosures above, if income from continuing operations on a current cost-constant purchasing power basis would differ significantly from income from continuing operations in the primary financial statements, an entity should provide the following information (ASC 255-10-50-11 through 16):

- Components of income from continuing operations for the current year on a current cost basis, applying the same constant purchasing power option used for presentation of the five-year summary.
- Separate amounts for the current cost or lower recoverable amount at the end of the current year of inventory and property, plant, and equipment.
- Increase or decrease in current cost or lower recoverable amount before and after adjusting for the effects of inflation of inventory and property, plant, and equipment for the current year.
- Any differences between (1) the depreciation methods, estimates of useful lives, and salvage values of assets used for calculations of current cost-constant purchasing power and (2) the methods and estimates used for calculations of depreciation in the primary financial statements.

ASC 255 includes other elective disclosures related to entities with mineral resource assets. Entities that have elected to make ASC 255 disclosures should refer to the Codification for additional guidance.

EXAMPLE PRESENTATION AND DISCLOSURE

Example 9.1: Statement of Income from Operations in a Statement of Annual Information

Statement of Income from Continuing Operations Adjusted for Changing Prices*
for the Year Ended December 31, 20X1
In Thousands of Dollars

	As Reported in the Primary Statements	As Adjusted for Specific Prices
Net sales and other operating revenues	$ 110,200	$ 110,200
Cost of goods sold	78,800	82,163
Depreciation expenses	4,110	8,009
Other operating expense	5,874	5,874
Interest expense	3,020	3,020
Income tax expense	9,198	9,198
	101,002	108,264
Income from continuing operations	$ 9,198	$ 1,936
Gain from decline in purchasing of net amounts owed		980
Increase in specific prices (current cost) of inventory and property, plant, and equipment in the current year		10,338
Effect of increase in general price level		2,155
Excess of increases in specific prices over increase in the general price level		8,183
Foreign currency translation adjustment	$ (118)	$ (250)

---

*   Adapted from ASC 255-10-55-18.

The Company is voluntarily presenting the information in the table above. The table contains historical cost, constant dollar information, indicating the changes in the general price level on certain items that appear in the primary financial statements based on dollar values determined as of the dates the transactions occurred. *The presentation of this financial information is not intended to be considered in isolation or as a substitute for, or with greater prominence to, the financial information prepared and presented in accordance with GAAP. A reconciliation of the non-GAAP financial measures follows, which includes more detail on the GAAP financial measure that is most directly comparable to each non-GAAP financial measure, and the related reconciliations between these financial measures.*

Current cost amounts for foreign operations are measured in their functional currencies, translated into dollar equivalents using the average exchange rate for the year, and restated into constant units of purchasing power using the Consumer Price Index for All Urban Consumers. Essentially, the foreign currency translation adjustment is the effect of changes in exchange rates during the year on shareholders' equity. The negative translation adjustment indicates that, overall, the dollar rate increased in value relative to the functional currencies used to measure the foreign operations of the entity.

10 ASC 260 EARNINGS PER SHARE

AUTHORITATIVE LITERATURE

Subtopic

ASC 260, *Earnings Per Share*, consists of one Subtopic:

- ASC 260-10, *Overall*, which provides the guidance for computation, presentation, and disclosure for earnings per share (EPS) for entities with publicly held common stock or potential common stock.
- This Subtopic also offers guidance on EPS and recognition and measurement of the effect of a down-round feature when it is triggered.
  (ASC 260-10-05-1 and 05-1A)

- This Subtopic includes master limited partnership subsections that clarify the application to master limited partnership of the Other Presentation Matters subsection.
  (ASC 260-10-05-1 and 05-1A)

Scope and Scope Exceptions

ASC 260 applies to entities:

- Whose common stock or potential common stock is traded in a public market, or
- Who have made a filing or are in the process of making a filing to trade their stock publicly.
  (ASC 260-10-15-2)

The guidance does not apply to investment companies who comply with ASC 946 or in statements of wholly owned subsidiaries.

Practice Pointer: Notice that nonpublic companies are not required to report earnings per share. If an entity not required to report under ASC 260 chooses to provide EPS information, the entity must comply with the ASC 260 guidance. (ASC 260-10-15-3 and 45-5)

Introduction

Earnings per share (EPS) is an indicator widely used by investors to gauge the profitability of a corporation. Its purpose is to indicate how effective an enterprise has been in using the resources provided by its common stockholders.

In its simplest form, EPS is net income (loss) divided by the weighted-average number of shares of outstanding common stock. (ASC 260-10-45-2)

Basic EPS Calculation

$$\text{EPS} = \frac{\text{Net income-preferred dividends (income available to common stockholders)}}{\text{Weighted-average number of shares outstanding}}$$

Shares are weighted for the portion of the fiscal period for which there were outstanding. (ASC 260-10-45-40)

The EPS computation becomes more complex with the existence of securities that are not common stock but have the potential of causing additional shares of common stock to be issued and, therefore, to dilute EPS upon conversion or exercise (e.g., convertible preferred stock, convertible debt, options, and warrants). Diluted EPS (DEPS) includes the potential dilution that could occur from other financial instruments that would increase the total number of outstanding shares of common stock. An EPS number that does not take into account the potential dilutive effects of such securities would be misleading. In addition, a lack of standardization in the way in which these securities are included in such an EPS computation would make comparability among corporations extremely difficult.

A complex capital structure is one that includes securities that grant rights with the potential to be exercised and reduce EPS, that is, dilutive securities. The denominator is increased to include the number of additional shares that would have been outstanding had the dilutive shares been issued. The numerator is also adjusted for any change in income or loss that would have resulted from the conversion. Any antidilutive securities (those that increase EPS) are not included in the computation of EPS. If basic and diluted EPS are the same, dual presentation can be shown in one line on the income statement. (ASC 260-10-4-7) The common stock outstanding and all other dilutive securities are used to compute DEPS.

Note that a complex capital structure requires dual presentation of basic EPS and DEPS.

DEPS represents the earnings attributable to each share of common stock after giving effect to all potentially dilutive securities which were outstanding during the period. The computation of DEPS requires the entity to:

1. Identify all potentially dilutive securities.
2. Compute dilution, the effects that the other dilutive securities have on net income and common shares outstanding.

Presentation of DEPS DEPS is a pro forma presentation that reflects the dilution of EPS that would have occurred if all contingent issuances of common stock that would individually reduce EPS had taken place at the beginning of the period (or the date actually issued, if later). The presentation of the concept of EPS and DEPS provides the reader with factually supportable EPS that range from no dilution to the maximum potential dilution. DEPS assumes that all issuances that have the legal right to become common stock exercise that right (unless the exercise would be antidilutive), and therefore anticipates and measures all potential dilution. The underlying basis for the computation is that of conservatism. The DEPS considers all other potentially dilutive securities, but uses only those securities that are dilutive. Thus, in most cases, the DEPS is less than the basic EPS. DEPS can never be greater than the basic EPS, but it could potentially be the same if all of the convertible securities were antidilutive.

PRACTICE ALERT

While SEC rules only apply to public entities, preparers of financial statements can benefit from the findings of SEC reviewers. Topics for comment include:

- **Effect of an error on EPS.** Explain in further detail the nature of the error you identified related to the classification of foreign currency adjustments associated with the European noncontrolling redeemable equity. Please quantify for us the amount by which each financial statement line item including EPS was impacted in the period ended June 30, 20X8.
- **Effect of a reorganization on EPS.** The earnings per share information presented is based on the 6.0 million shares actually outstanding as reflected in the historical financial statements of your predecessor instead of the 38.9 million shares to be issued to existing shareholders in your reorganization. Indicate how this per share and other per share or share information presented on a pre-reorganization basis provides investors with meaningful information when it is inconsistent with the capital structure going forward. Include in the explanation, your consideration for providing pro forma share and per share information throughout your statements that is consistent with your post-reorganization capital structure.
- **Subsequent event occurring after year end.** A description of a subsequent event that occurs after the end of the most recent balance sheet, but before issuance of the financial statements, that will materially change capitalization should be described. The SEC has commented, for example, since you expect material changes in capitalization to occur after the latest balance sheet date and those changes will result in a material reduction to earnings per share, please revise the historic per share data to reflect the pro forma effects of this 100-for-1 stock split.

PRESENTATION AND DISCLOSURE REQUIREMENTS

Note: Subtopic ASC 260-45 contains many provisions related to the measurement of earnings per share. Details on the measurement requirements can be found in *Wiley GAAP*. The information below details the requirements and methods for presenting those measurements. In addition, see the *Disclosure and Presentation Checklist for Commercial Businesses* at www.wiley.com/go/FSDM2021 to get a complete list of disclosure and presentation items.

The reason for the differentiation between simple and complex capital structures is that ASC 260 requires different financial statement presentations for each. ASC 260 mandates that EPS be shown on the face of the income statement for each of the following items (when applicable):

- Income from continuing operations
- Net income
  (ASC 260-10-45-2)

These requirements must be fulfilled regardless of whether the capital structure is simple or complex. The difference in the two structures is that a simple capital structure requires presentation of only a single EPS number for each item, while a complex structure requires the dual presentation of basic EPS and DEPS for each item.

An entity that reports a discontinued operation or the cumulative effect of a change in accounting principle presents basic and diluted EPS amounts for these line items either on the face of the income statement or in the notes to the financial statements. (ASC 260-10-45-3)

Note that cash flow per share is expressly forbidden. (ASC 260-10-45-3)

EPS data must be presented for all periods for which an income statement or summary of earnings is presented. If DEPS is reported for at least one period, it must be reported for all periods presented, regardless of whether or not DEPS differs from basic EPS. (ASC 260-10-45-7) However, if basic and diluted EPS are the same amounts for all periods presented, dual presentation may be accomplished in one line on the face of the income statement.

For each period for which an income statement is presented, an entity must disclose:

- A reconciliation of the numerators and the denominators of the basic and diluted per-share computations for income from continuing operations, including the individual income and share amount effects of all securities that affect earnings per share. Entities are cross reference to pertinent information about securities included in the EPS computations provided elsewhere in the financial statements.
- The effect given to preferred dividends in arriving at income available to common stockholders in computing basic EPS.
- The terms and conditions of securities that could potentially dilute basic EPS in the future that were not included in the computation of diluted EPS because to do so would have been antidilutive for the period presented. These include securities issuable pursuant to contingent stock agreements.

COMPREHENSIVE EXAMPLE

Assume the following facts concerning the capital structure of a company:

- Income from continuing operations and net income are both $50,000. Income from continuing operations is not displayed on the firm's income statement.
- The weighted-average number of common shares outstanding is 10,000 shares.
- The income tax rate is a flat 40%.
- Options to purchase 1,000 shares of common stock at $8 per share were outstanding all year.
- Options to purchase 2,000 shares of common stock at $13 per share were outstanding all year.
- The average market price of common stock during the year was $10.

- 200 7% convertible bonds, each convertible into 40 common shares, were outstanding the entire year. The bonds were issued at par value ($1,000 per bond) and no bonds were converted during the year.
- 4% convertible, cumulative preferred stock, par value of $100 per share, 1,000 shares issued and outstanding the entire year. Each preferred share is convertible into one common share. The preferred stock was issued at par value and no shares were converted during the year.

Note that reference is made below to some of the tables included in the body of the chapter because the facts above represent a combination of the facts used for the examples in the chapter. To determine both basic EPS and DEPS, the following procedures must be performed:

1. Calculate basic EPS as if the capital structure were simple.
2. Identify other potentially dilutive securities.
3. Calculate the per-share effects of assuming issuance or conversion of each potentially dilutive security on an individual basis.
4. Rank the per-share effects from smallest to largest.
5. Recalculate EPS (Step 1 above) adding the potentially dilutive securities one at a time in order, beginning with the security with the *smallest* per-share effect.
6. Continue adding potentially dilutive securities to each successive calculation until all have been added or until the addition of a security increases EPS (antidilution) from its previous level.

Applying these procedures to the facts above:

1. Basic EPS

$$\frac{\text{Net income} - \text{Preferred dividends}}{\text{Weighted-average number of common shares outstanding}} = \frac{\$50,000 - \$4,000}{10,000\,\text{shares}} = \$4.60$$

2. Identification of other potentially dilutive securities:

   a. Options (two types).
   b. 7% convertible bonds
   c. 4% convertible cumulative preferred stock.

Diluted EPS (DEPS)

3. Per-share effects of conversion or issuance of other potentially dilutive securities calculated individually:

   a. Options—Only the options to purchase 1,000 shares at $8.00 per share are potentially dilutive. The options to purchase 2,000 shares of common stock are antidilutive because the exercise price is greater than the average market price. Thus, they are not included in the computation.

   Proceeds if options exercised:

   $$1,000\,\text{shares} \times \$8\,\text{per share} = \underline{\underline{8,000}}$$

Shares that could be acquired:

$$\$8,000 \div \$10 = \underline{800}$$

$$\text{Dilutive shares: } 1,000 - 800 = \underline{\underline{200}}$$

$$\frac{\text{Increase/decrease in net income}}{\text{Increase in weighted-average number of common shares outstanding}} = \frac{\$0}{200 \text{ shares}} = \$0$$

b. 7% convertible bonds.

$$\frac{\text{Increase/decrease in net income}}{\text{Increase in weighted-average number of common shares outstanding}} = \frac{\$8,400}{8,000 \text{ shares}}$$
$$= \$1.05$$

c. 4% convertible cumulative preferred stock—the outstanding common shares increase by 1,000 when all shares are converted. This results in total dividends of $4,000 not being paid.

$$\frac{\text{Increase/decrease in net income}}{\text{Increase in weighted-average number of common shares outstanding}} = \frac{\$4,000}{1,000 \text{ shares}}$$
$$= \$4.00$$

4. Rank the per-share effects from smallest to largest:

a. Options $ 0
b. 7% convertible bonds   1.05
c. 4% convertible cumulative preferred stock   4.00

5. Recalculate the EPS in rank order starting from the security with the smallest per-share dilution and adding one potentially dilutive security at a time:

a. DEPS—options added:

$$\frac{\text{Net income} - \text{Preferred dividends}}{\substack{\text{Weighted-average number of common shares outstanding} + \text{Shares not acquired with} \\ \text{proceeds of options}}}$$

$$= \frac{\$50,000 - \$4,000}{10,000 + 200 \text{ shares}} = \$4.51$$

b. DEPS—options and 7% convertible bonds added:

$$\frac{\text{Net income} - \text{Preferred dividends} + \text{Interest expense (net of tax)}}{\substack{\text{Weighted-average number of common shares outstanding} + \text{Shares not acquired with} \\ \text{proceeds of options} + \text{Shares issued upon conversion of bonds}}}$$

$$= \frac{\$50,000 - \$4,000 + \$8,400}{10,000 + 200 + 8,000 \text{ shares}} = \$2.99$$

c. DEPS—options, 7% convertible bonds, and 4% convertible cumulative preferred stock added:

$$\frac{\text{Net income} + \text{Interest expense (net of tax)}}{\substack{\text{Weighted-average number of common shares outstanding} + \text{Shares not acquired with} \\ \text{proceeds of options} + \text{Shares issued upon conversion of bonds and} \\ \text{preferred stock}}}$$

$$= \frac{\$50,000 + \$8,400}{10,000 + 200 + 8,000 + 1,000 \text{ share}} = \$3.04$$

DEPS = $2.99

Since the addition of the 4% convertible cumulative preferred stock raises DEPS from $2.99 to $3.04, the preferred stock is antidilutive and is therefore excluded from the computation of DEPS.

A dual presentation of basic EPS and DEPS is required. The dual presentation on the face of the income statement would appear as follows:

Net income	$50,000
Earnings per common share* (Note X)	$ 4.60
Earnings per common share, assuming dilution* (Note X)	$ 2.99

* The captions "Basic EPS" and "Diluted EPS" may be substituted, respectively.

Note X: Earnings Per Share (Illustrative Disclosure Based on Facts from the Example)

The following adjustments were made to the numerators and denominators of the basic and diluted EPS computations:

	Income (Numerator)	*Year Ended December 31, 20X1 Weighted-Average Number of Outstanding Shares (Denominator)*	*Amount per Share*
Net income	$50,000		
Less: Preferred stock dividends	(4,000)		
Basic EPS			
Income available to common stockholders	46,000	10,000	$4.60
Effects of dilutive securities			

	Income (Numerator)	Year Ended December 31, 20X1 Weighted- Average Number of Outstanding Shares (Denominator)	Amount per Share
Options to purchase common stock		200	
7% convertible bonds	8,400	8,000	
Diluted EPS			
Income available to common stockholders adjusted for the effects of assumed exercise of options and conversion of bonds	$54,400	18,200	$2.99

There were 1,000 shares of $100 par value, 4% convertible, cumulative preferred stock issued and outstanding during the year ended December 31, 20X1, that were not included in the above computation because their conversion would not have resulted in a dilution of EPS.

Example of the Presentation and Computation of Earnings Per Share

Assume that 100,000 shares were outstanding throughout the year.

ABC Company
Income Statement
for the Year Ended December 31, 20X1

Sales		$2,000,000
Cost of goods sold		750,000
Gross profit		$1,250,000
Selling and administrative expenses		500,000
Income from operations		$ 750,000
Other revenues and expense		
Interest income	$40,000	
Interest expense	(30,000)	10,000
Income before unusual or infrequent items and income taxes		$ 760,000
Unusual or infrequent items:		
Loss from permanent impairment of value of manufacturing facilities		(10,000)
Income from continuing operations before income taxes		$ 750,000
Income taxes		300,000
Income from continuing operations		$ 450,000
Discontinued operations:		
Loss from operations of Division X, including loss on disposal of $100,000 and income tax benefit of $58,000		$ 102,000
Net income		$ 348,000

ABC Company
Income Statement
for the Year Ended December 31, 20X1

Basic EPS computation

Income from continuing operations ($450,000/100,000)	$ 4.50
Discontinued operations* ($30,000/100,000)	(0.30)
Net income available for common stockholders	$ 4.20

---

* *May instead be shown in the notes to the financial statements.*

PRESENTATION AND DISCLOSURE EXAMPLES

Example 10.1: Earnings (Loss) Per Share Attributable to Common Stockholders

Note 15. Basic and diluted net income (loss) per share attributable to common stockholders is presented in conformity with the two-class method required for participating securities. We consider convertible preferred stock and early exercised share options to be participating securities. In connection with our IPO, we established two classes of authorized common stock: Class A common stock and Class B common stock. As a result, all then-outstanding shares of common stock were converted into shares of Class B common stock upon effectiveness of our IPO. The rights of the holders of Class A and Class B common stock are identical, except with respect to voting, conversion, and transfer rights. Each share of Class A common stock is entitled to one vote per share, and each share of Class B common stock is entitled to ten votes per share. Each share of Class B common stock is convertible at any time at the option of the stockholder into one share of Class A common stock.

Undistributed earnings allocated to participating securities are subtracted from net income (loss) in determining net income (loss) attributable to common stockholders. Basic earnings per share ("EPS") attributable to common stockholders is computed by dividing the net income (loss) attributable to common stockholders by the weighted-average number of common shares outstanding during the period. All participating securities are excluded from basic weighted-average common shares outstanding.

For the calculation of diluted earnings per share, net income (loss) attributable to common stockholders for basic EPS is adjusted by the effect of dilutive securities. Diluted net income (loss) per share attributable to common stockholders is computed by dividing the net income (loss) attributable to common stockholders by the weighted-average number of common shares outstanding, including all potentially dilutive common shares. The undistributed earnings are allocated based on the contractual participation rights of the Class A and Class B common shares as if the earnings for the year have been distributed. As the liquidation and dividend rights are identical, the undistributed earnings are allocated on a proportionate basis. The computation of the diluted net income (loss) per share of Class A common stock assumes the conversion of Class B common stock, while diluted net income (loss) per share of Class B common stock does not assume the conversion of Class A common stock as Class A common stock is not convertible into Class B common stock.

A reconciliation of the numerator and denominator used in the calculation of the basic and diluted EPS attributable to common stockholders is as follows (in thousands except share and per share amounts).

(in thousands except share and per share amounts)	December 31, 20X3		December 31, 20X2		December 31, 20X1
	Class A	Class B	Class A	Class B	Class B
Numerator:					
Net income (loss)	$ 8,302	$ 10,139	$ 3,825	$ 18,625	$ (297)
Less: noncumulative dividends to preferred stockholders	—	—	(66)	(319)	—
Less: undistributed earnings to participating securities	(4)	(5)	(731)	(3,564)	—
Net income (loss) attributable to common stockholders—basic	8,298	10,134	3,028	14,763	(297)
Less: change in fair value of preferred stock warrant liability (net of tax)	—	—	(5,343)	(5,343)	—
Add: adjustments to undistributed earnings to participating securities	1	—	1,215	1,008	—
Reallocation of undistributed earnings as a result of conversion of Class B to Class A shares	10,134	—	14,743	—	—
Reallocation of undistributed earnings to Class B shares	—	151	—	1,061	—
Net income (loss) attributable to common stockholders—diluted	$ 18,432	$ 11,285	$ 13643	$ 11,469	$ (29)
Denominator:					
Weighted-average shares of common stock—basic	22,513,476	27,493,055	6,470,297	33,503,583	12,486,966
Conversion of Class B to Class A common shares outstanding	27,493,055	—	31,503,583	—	—
Effect of dilutive stock options and restricted stock units	1,820,182	1,414,869	2,510,846	2,505,856	—
Effect of potentially dilutive preferred stock warrants	—	—	159,484	159,484	—
Weighted-average shares of common stock—diluted	51,868,813	28,917,924	40,644,209	34,168,923	12,486,966
Earnings (loss) per share attributable to common stockholders:					
Basic	$ 0.37	$ 0.37	$ 0.47	$ 0.47	$ (0.02)
Diluted	$ 0.36	$ 0.36	$ 0.34	$ 0.34	$ (0.02)

The following common stock equivalents were excluded from the computation of diluted earnings (loss) per share for the periods presented because including them would have been antidilutive:

	December 31, 20X9	*December 31, 20X8*	*December 31, 20X7*
Convertible preferred stock	—	—	29,555,528
Preferred stock warrants	—	—	533,113
Restricted stock units	1,457,315	1,138,497	—
Stock options to purchase Class A common stock	773,248	635,576	—
Stock options to purchase Class B common stock	484,589.5	1,844,684.5	2,837,723
Total	2,715,652	3,618,758	33,126,364

Example 10.2: Exclusion of Shares with Antidilutive Effects

Basic and Diluted Earnings Per Share Basic earnings per share (BEPS) is computed by dividing the net income by the weighted average number of common shares outstanding for the period. Diluted earnings per share (DEPS) is computed giving effect to all dilutive potential common shares outstanding during the period. Dilutive potential common shares consist of incremental shares issuable upon the exercise of stock options and warrants using the "treasury stock" method. The computation of DEPS does not assume conversion, exercise or contingent exercise of securities that would have an antidilutive effect on earnings. For the years ended June 30, 20X9 and 20X8, there were common share equivalents of 23,010 and 22,650, respectively, included in the computation of the DEPS. For the years ended June 30, 20X9 and 20X8, 136,000 and 180,071 shares of common stock, respectively, vest based on the market price of the Company's common stock and were excluded from the computation of DEPS because the shares have not vested, but no stock options were excluded from the computation of DEPS.

The following is a reconciliation of the numerators and denominators of the basic and diluted earnings per share computations for the years ended June 30 (in thousands, except for per share amounts):

	For the Years Ended	
	20X9	*20X8*
Numerator:		
Net income	$1,485	$1,284
Denominator:		
Basic weighted-average shares outstanding	4,860	4,740
Effect of dilutive securities	23	22
Diluted weighted-average diluted shares	$4,883	4,762
Earnings per share attributed to common stockholders—basic	$0.31	$0.27
Earnings per share attributed to common stockholders—diluted	$0.30	$0.27

Example 10.3: Discontinued Operations

Blake Medical Equipment, Inc., and Subsidiaries
Consolidated Statements of Operation
(In thousands, except for per share data)

	December 31, 20X9	December 31, 20X8	December 31, 20X7
Net sales	$10,693,534	$5,113,341.5	4,637,236
Cost of sales	9,301,029	4,351,958	3,922,775
Gross profit	1,392,505	761,383.5	714,460.5
Operating expenses	1,314,857	637,281	598,016
Goodwill and asset impairment charges	146,385	5,621	—
Restructuring, acquisition and integration related expenses	77,769	4,869	3,432
Operating (loss) income	(145,506)	113,613	113,013
Other expense (income):			
Net periodic benefit income, excluding service cost	(17,363)	—	—
Interest expense, net	89,981.5	8,013	8,377
Other, net	(479)	(773)	(2,576)
Total other expense, net	72,140	7,240	5,801
(Loss) income from continuing operations before income taxes	(217,646)	106,373	107,211.5
(Benefit) provision for income taxes	(42,304.5)	23,538	42,134
Net (loss) income from continuing operations	(175,341.5)	82,835	65,078
Income from discontinued operations, net of tax	32,900	—	—
Net (loss) income including noncontrolling interests	(142,442)	82,835	65,077.5
Less net (income) loss attributable to noncontrolling interests	(54)	—	—
Net (loss) income attributable to United Natural Foods, Inc.	$ (142,496)	$ 82,835	$ 65,078
Basic (loss) earnings per share:			
Continuing operations	$ 3.42	$ 1.64	$ 1.29
Discontinued operations	$ .64	$ —	$ —
Basic (loss) income per share	$ (2.78)	$ 1.64	$ 1.29
Diluted (loss) earnings per share:			
Continuing operations	$ (3.42)	$ 1.63	$ 1.28
Discontinued operations	$ .64	$ —	$ —
Diluted (loss) income per share	$ (2.78)	$ 1.63	$ 1.28
Weighted average shares outstanding:			
Basic	51,245	50,530	50,570
Diluted	51,237	50,837	50,778

Example 10.4: Beneficial Conversion

The Company computes net loss per share in accordance with ASC 260, "Earnings Per Share." Basic net loss per share of common stock is computed by dividing the Company's net loss attributable to Lawson, Inc., common stockholders by the weighted-average number of shares of common stock outstanding during the period. Diluted net loss per share of common stock is computed by giving effect to all potentially dilutive securities, including stock options, restricted stock units, convertible preferred stock, convertible promissory notes and common stock warrants, using the Treasury stock method or the as-converted method, as applicable. For the years ended December 31, 20X8 and 20X7, basic net loss per share was the same as diluted net loss per share because the inclusion of all potentially dilutive securities outstanding was antidilutive. As such, the numerator and the denominator used in computing both basic and diluted net loss were the same for those years.

The Company follows the two-class method when computing net loss per common share when shares are issued that meet the definition of participating securities. The two-class method requires income available to common stockholders for the period to be allocated between common stock and participating securities based upon their respective rights to receive dividends as if all income for the period had been distributed. The two-class method also requires losses for the period to be allocated between common stock and participating securities based on their respective rights if the participating security contractually participates in losses. The Company's convertible preferred stock are participating securities as they contractually entitle the holders of such shares to participate in dividends and contractually require the holders of such shares to participate in the Company's losses.

The following table presents the calculation of basic and diluted net loss per share of common stock attributable to Lawson, Inc. common stockholders:

Years Ended December 31, *(In Thousands, Except Shares and per Share Amounts)*	*20X8*	*20X7*
		(As Restated, Note 2)
Net loss attributable to Lawson, Inc.	(172,676)	(116,987)
Less deemed dividend related to beneficial conversion feature on Series A preferred stock	—	(422)
Less deemed dividend related to beneficial conversion feature on Series B preferred stock	—	(476)
Less deemed dividend related to beneficial conversion feature on Series D preferred stock	—	(4,318)
Less deemed dividend upon settlement of make-whole provision on Series A preferred stock	—	(7,879)
Less deemed dividend upon settlement of make-whole provision on Series B preferred stock	—	(16,974)
Less deemed dividend related to the recognition of discounts on Series A preferred stock upon conversion	—	(16,184)
Less deemed dividend related to the recognition of discounts on Series B preferred stock upon conversion	—	(18,275)
Less deemed dividend related to proceeds discount upon conversion of Series D preferred stock	(5,139)	—
Add: losses allocated to participating securities	10,493	30,119
Net loss attributable to Lawson, Inc., common stockholders, basic	$(167,322)	$(151,393)
Adjustment for losses allocated to participating securities	(10,493)	(30,119)
Net loss attributable to Lawson, Inc., common stockholders, diluted	$(177,815)	$(181,512)

Years Ended December 31, *(In Thousands, Except Shares and per Share Amounts)*	*20X8*	*20X7*
Denominator:		
Weighted-average shares of common stock outstanding used in computing net loss per share of common stock, basic and diluted	45,304,433	24,190,178
Basic and diluted loss per share	$ (3.69)	$ (6.26)

The following outstanding shares of potentially dilutive securities were excluded from the computation of diluted net loss per share of common stock for the periods presented because including them would have been antidilutive:

Years Ended December 31	*20X8*	*20X7*
	(As Restated, Note 2)	
Period-end common stock warrants	19,489,778	22,441,383
Convertible promissory notes[*]	10,277,372	6,152,866
Period-end stock options to purchase common stock	4,044,202	1,003,775
Period-end restricted stock units	3,971,136	513,755
Period-end preferred shares on an as-converted basis	2,216,799	3,378,159
Total potentially dilutive securities excluded from computation of diluted net loss per share	39,999,287	44,653,251

[*] The potentially dilutive effect of convertible promissory notes was computed based on conversion ratios in effect at the respective year-end. A portion of the convertible promissory notes issued carries a provision for a reduction in conversion price under certain circumstances, which could potentially increase the dilutive shares outstanding. Another portion of the convertible promissory notes issued carries a provision for an increase in the conversion rate under certain circumstances, which could also potentially increase the dilutive shares outstanding.

11 ASC 270 INTERIM REPORTING

AUTHORITATIVE LITERATURE

The term "interim reporting" refers to financial reporting for periods of less than a year. The Codification does not mandate interim reporting. However, the SEC requires public companies to file quarterly summarized interim financial data on its Form 10-Q. The level of detail of the information required in those interim reports is substantially less than is specified under the Codification for annual financial statements.

The objective of interim reporting is to provide current information regarding enterprise performance to existing and prospective investors, lenders, and other financial statement users. This enables users to act upon relevant information in making informed decisions in a timely manner. The demand for timely information means that interim data will often be more heavily impacted by estimates and assumptions.

Subtopic

ASC 270, *Interim Reporting*, contains one Subtopic:

- ASC 270-10, *Overall*, which provides guidance on:
  - Accounting and disclosure issues for reporting on periods less than one year, and
  - Minimum disclosure requirements for interim reporting for publicly traded companies.

Scope and Scope Exceptions

ASC 260 applies to all entities:

- Whose common stock or potential common stock is traded in a public market, or
- Who have made a filing or are in the process of making a filing to trade their stock publicly.

Notice that nonpublic companies are not required to report earnings per share. The guidance also does not apply to investment companies who comply with ASC 946 or in statements of wholly owned subsidiaries. If an entity not required to report under ASC 260 chooses to provide EPS information, the entity must comply with the ASC 260 guidance. (ASC 260-10-45-5)

Integral Approach

Historically, there have been two competing views of interim reporting. Under the *integral* view, the interim period is considered an integral part of the annual accounting period. It thus follows that annual operating expenses are to be estimated and allocated to the interim periods based on forecasted annual activity levels such as sales volume. The results of subsequent interim periods are adjusted to reflect the effect of estimation errors in earlier interim periods of the same fiscal year. ASC 270-10-45-1 prefers the integral view.

Discrete Approach

Under the *discrete* view, each interim period is considered a discrete accounting period. Thus, estimations and allocations are made using the same methods used for annual reporting. It follows that the same expense recognition rules apply as under annual reporting, and no special interim accruals or deferrals would be necessary or permissible. Annual operating expenses are recognized in the interim period incurred, irrespective of the number of interim periods benefited (i.e., no special deferral rules would apply to interim periods).

PRESENTATION AND DISCLOSURE REQUIREMENTS

The explanations and interpretations in this chapter have been divided into two sections. The first part discusses issues applicable to *both* public and nonpublic reporting entities (including, where applicable, not-for-profit organizations). The second part discusses issues applicable *only* to publicly traded companies.

The usefulness of interim reports rests on the relationship to annual reports. Therefore, ASC 270-10-45-1 states that "each interim period should be viewed primarily as an integral part of an annual period," and the accounting should be based on the principles and practices used in the entity's annual reporting. The exception to this is if the entity has adopted a change in accounting in the interim period. Certain principles and practices may also have to be modified so that the interim reporting better relates to the annual results. The modifications are detailed in ASC 270-10-45-4 through 45-11 and are discussed in the following sections.

REQUIREMENTS APPLICABLE TO ALL REPORTING ENTITIES

Revenues

Revenues are recognized as earned during an interim period using the same principles followed in annual reports, that is, "as the entity satisfies a performance obligation by transferring a promised good or service to a customer." (ASC 270-10-45-3) This rule applies to both product sales and service revenues. For example, product sales cutoff procedures are applied at the end of each interim period in the same manner that they are applied at year-end, and revenue from long-term construction contracts is recognized at interim dates using the same method used at year-end.

Product Costs and Direct Costs

Product costs and costs directly associated with service revenues are treated in interim reports in the same manner as in annual reports. (ASC 270-20-45-5) The Codification provides four integral view exceptions:

1. The gross profit or other method that is not the method used at annual dates may be used to estimate cost of goods sold and ending inventory for interim periods. The method used must be disclosed.
2. When inventory consists of LIFO layers, and a portion of the base period layer is liquidated at an interim date, and it is expected that this inventory will be replaced by year-end, the anticipated cost of replacing the liquidated inventory is included in cost of sales of the interim period.
3. Inventory losses from the application of subsequent measurement guidance in ASC 330-10 should not be deferred beyond the interim period. Recoveries from such losses on the same inventory are recognized as a gain in the subsequent interim period. Recognition of this gain in the later interim period is limited to the extent of loss previously recognized. If the entity reasonably expects to restore the market value or net realizable value, it does not have to recognize that temporary decline in the interim financial statements.
4. Entities using standard cost accounting systems ordinarily report purchase price, wage rate, and usage or efficiency variances in the same manner as year-end. Planned purchase price and volume or capacity cost variances, are deferred if expected to be absorbed by year-end. (ASC 270-10-45-6)

The first exception above eliminates the need for a physical inventory count at the interim date. The other three exceptions attempt to synchronize the quarterly financial statements with the annual report. For example, consider the LIFO liquidation exception. Without this exception, interim cost of goods sold could include low earlier year or base-period costs, while annual cost of goods sold would include only current year costs.

Other Costs and Expenses

The integral view is evident in how the Codification treats costs incurred in interim periods. Most costs and expenses are recognized in interim periods as incurred. However, a cost that clearly benefits more than one interim period (e.g., annual repairs or property taxes) is allocated among the periods benefited. (ASC 270-10-45-8) The allocation is based on:

- Estimates of time expired,
- Benefit received, or
- Activity related to the specific periods.

Allocation procedures are to be consistent with those used at year-end reporting dates. However, if a cost incurred during an interim period cannot be readily associated with other interim periods, it is not arbitrarily assigned to those periods. The following parameters (ASC 270-45-10-9) are used in interim periods to account for certain types of expenses incurred in those periods:

- Costs that benefit two or more interim periods (e.g., annual major repairs) are assigned to interim periods through the use of deferrals or accruals.
- Quantity discounts given to customers based on annual sales volume are allocated to interim periods on the basis of sales to customers during the interim period relative to estimated annual sales.
- Property taxes (and like costs) are deferred or accrued at a year-end date to reflect a full year's charge to operations. Charges to interim periods follow similar procedures.

- Advertising costs are permitted to be deferred to subsequent interim periods within the same fiscal year if the costs clearly benefit those later periods. Prior to actually receiving advertising services, advertising costs may be accrued and allocated to interim periods on the basis of sales if the sales arrangement implicitly includes the advertising program.

Costs and expenses subject to year-end determination, such as discretionary bonuses and profit-sharing contributions, are assigned to interim periods in a reasonable and consistent manner to the extent they can be reasonably estimated. (ASC 270-10-45-10)

Seasonality

The operations of many businesses are subject to recurring material seasonal variations. Such businesses are required to disclose the seasonality of their activities to avoid the possibility of misleading interim reports. ASC 270-10-45-11 also recommends that such businesses present results of operations for 12-month periods ending at the interim date of the current and preceding year.

Fair Value of Financial Instruments

ASC 825-10-50 requires disclosures about the fair value of financial instruments in interim reporting periods, as well as in annual financial statements. Those requirements can be found in the disclosure checklist at www.wiley.com/go/FSDM2021.

Unusual or Infrequent Items and Disposals of Components

The effects of the disposal of a component of the entity and unusual or infrequently occurring transactions or events that are material to operating results of the interim period are reported separately in the interim period in which they occur. (ASC 270-10-45-11A) The same treatment is given to other unusual or infrequently occurring events. No attempt is made to allocate the effects of these items over the entire fiscal year in which they occur.

Note that classification as an unusual or infrequently occurring item is based on facts and circumstances, given the requirement under the Codification that the event be infrequent in occurrence or unusual in nature. If a plant was located in Kansas, for example, and tornado damage did not qualify under both criteria given its location, then this would not have been presented as an unusual or infrequently occurring item.

Contingencies

In general, contingencies and uncertainties that exist at an interim date are accrued or disclosed in the same manner required for annual financial statements. For example, contingent liabilities that are probable and subject to reasonable estimation are to be accrued. The materiality of the contingency is evaluated in relation to the expected annual results. Disclosures regarding material contingencies and uncertainties are to be repeated in all interim and annual financial statements until they have been settled, adjudicated, transferred, or judged to be immaterial.

The following adjustments or settlements are accorded special treatment in interim reports if they relate to prior interim periods of the current fiscal year:

- Litigation or similar claims.
- Income taxes (except for the effects of retroactive tax legislation enacted during an interim period).

- Renegotiation proceedings associated with government contracts.
- Utility revenue under rate-making processes.

If the item is material, directly related to prior interim periods of the current fiscal year in full or in part, and becomes reasonably estimable in the current interim period, it is reported as follows:

- The portion directly related to the current interim period is included in that period.
- Prior interim periods are restated to reflect the portions directly related to those periods.
- The portion directly related to prior years is recognized in the restated first interim period of the current year.

Accounting Changes

The Codification recommends making a change in accounting principle in the first interim report of a fiscal year wherever possible. (ASC 270-10-45-15)

Change in Accounting Principle Entities must disclose in interim financial statements any changes in accounting principles or the methods of applying them from those that were followed in:

- The prior fiscal year,
- The comparable interim period of the prior fiscal year, and
- The preceding interim periods of the current fiscal year.
  (ASC 270-10-45-12)

The information to be included in these disclosures is the same as is required to be included in annual financial statements and is to be provided in the interim period in which the change occurs, subsequent interim periods of that same fiscal year, and the annual financial statements that include the interim period of change.

ASC 250 requires changes in accounting principles to be adopted through retrospective application to all prior periods presented. This accounting treatment is the same in both interim and annual financial statements. The entity is precluded from using the impracticability exception to avoid retrospective application to pre-change interim periods of the same fiscal year in which the change is made. Thus, if it is impracticable to apply the change to those pre-change interim periods, the change can be made as of the beginning of the following fiscal year. (ASC 250-10-45-14) The FASB believes this situation will rarely occur in practice.

Change in Accounting Estimate A change in accounting estimate is accounted for in the period of change. ASC 250 requires that changes in accounting estimate be accounted for currently and prospectively. Retroactive restatement and presentation of pro forma amounts are not permitted. This accounting is the same whether the change occurs at the end of a year or during an interim reporting period. (ASC 270-10-45-14)

Change in Reporting Entity When an accounting change results in the financial statements presenting a different reporting entity than was presented in the past, all prior periods presented in the new financial statements, including all previously issued interim financial information, are to be retroactively restated to present the financial statements of the new reporting entity. In restating the previously issued information, however, interest previously capitalized under ASC 835, with respect to equity-method investees that have not yet commenced their planned principal operations, is not to be changed.

Corrections of Errors Adjustments related to prior interim periods of the current year arise from:

- Settlement of litigation or similar claims.
- Income taxes.

- Renegotiation procedures.
- Utility revenue governed by rate-making processes.
  (ASC 250-10-45-25)

The term "restatement" is used to describe a correction of an error from a prior period. When a restatement is made, the financial statements of each individual prior period presented (whether interim or annual) must be adjusted to reflect correction of the effects of the error that relate to that period. Full disclosure of the restatement must be provided in the financial statements of the:

- Interim period in which the restatement is first made,
- Subsequent interim periods during the same fiscal year that includes the interim period in which the restatement is first made, and
- Annual period that includes the interim period in which the restatement is first made.

If the item occurs after the first interim period and affects prior interim periods of the current year, the entity:

- Restates prior interim periods.
- For portions of the item affecting prior years, includes in the determination of net income of the first interim period of the current year.
  (ASC 270-10-45-18)

REQUIREMENTS APPLICABLE TO PUBLIC REPORTING ENTITIES

Quarterly Reporting to the SEC

Summarized Interim Financial Data The SEC does not require registrants to file complete sets of quarterly financial statements. Rather, on a quarterly basis, condensed (summarized) unaudited interim financial statements are required to be filed with the SEC on its Form 10-Q (Regulation S-X, Rule 10-01—ASC 270-10-S99-1). There are minimum captions and disclosures required to be included in these financial statements. For detailed guidance, entities should look to ASC 270-10-S99 SEC Materials and Regulation S-X Rule 10-02, Interim Financial Statements.

PRESENTATION AND DISCLOSURE EXAMPLES

Example 11.1: Consolidated Statement of Income and Comprehensive Income

Consolidated Statements of Operations and Comprehensive Income (Loss)
(Unaudited)
(in thousands, except per share amounts)

	Three Months Ended		Nine Months Ended	
	December 31, 20X9	*December 31, 20X8*	*December 31, 20X9*	*December 31, 20X8*
Net sales	$56,466	$66,616	$133,222	$155,130
Cost of sales	41,473	49,884	99,816	121,234
Gross profit	14,933	16,732	33,406	34,896
Selling, general, and administrative expenses	10,827	14,359	32,570	42,998

Restructuring expenses	302	525	1,700	1,589
Impairment of goodwill				695
Operating income (loss)	3,864	1,848	(864)	(10,386)
Interest expense (income), net	399	392	1,224	740
Other expense (income), net	(325)	(72)	(863)	(218)
Income (loss) before income taxes	3,790	1,528	(1,225)	(10,908)
Income tax expense	170	4,918	538	4,171
Net income (loss)	3,620	(3,390)	(1,763)	(15,079)
Net income (loss) per common share:				
Basic	.82	(.77)	(.40)	(3.35)
Diluted	.81	(.77)	(.40)	(3.35)
Weighted average shares outstanding:				
Basic	4,440	4,423	4,438	4,504
Diluted	4,451	423	4,438	4,504
Net income (loss)	$ 3,620	(3,390)	(1,763)	(15.079)
Other comprehensive income (loss), net:				
Currency translation adjustments:				
Total currency translation gain (loss)	225	(92)	(35)	(575)
Pension and postretirement benefits:				
Net income arising from pension and postretirement benefits, net of tax $9 for the three and nine months ended December 31, 2019	14		14	
Interest rate swap agreement:				
Fair value adjustment, net of tax $(185) for the three months, and $(87) for the nine months ended December 31, 2018		(293)		(55)
Other comprehensive income (loss), net	369	(385)	(27)	(630)
Comprehensive income (loss)	3,859	(3,775)	(184)	(15,709)

See accompanying notes to consolidated financial sttatements.

Example 11.2: Seasonal Nature of Business

The seasonal nature of Phillips' business has historically resulted in lower sales levels and operating losses in the first and fourth quarters and comparatively higher sales levels and operating profits in the second and third quarters of the Company's fiscal year, thereby causing significant fluctuations in the quarterly results of operations of the Company.

Example 11.3: Inventories Measured Using LIFO

Inventories consist of:	December 31, 20X9	September 30, 20X9
Raw materials and supplies	$2,694	$2,256
Work-in-process	1,804	1,365
Finished goods	2,121	1,638
Total inventories	**$6,619**	**$5,259**

For a portion of the Company's inventory, cost is determined using the last-in, first-out ("LIFO") method. Approximately 32% and 28% of the Company's inventories at December 31, 20X9, and September 30, 20X9, respectively, use the LIFO method to value its inventories. An actual valuation of inventory under the LIFO method is made at the end of each fiscal year based on the inventory levels and costs existing at that time. Accordingly, interim LIFO calculations must be based on management's estimates of expected year-end inventory levels and costs. Because the actual results may vary from these estimates, calculations are subject to many factors beyond management's control, annual results may differ from interim results as they are subject to adjustments based on the differences between the estimates and the actual results. The first-in, first-out ("FIFO") method is used for the remainder of the inventories, which are stated at the lower of cost or net realizable value. If the FIFO method had been used for the inventories for which cost is determined using the LIFO method, inventories would have been $4,159 and $4,148 higher than reported at December 31, 20X9, and September 30, 20X9, respectively.

Example 11.4: Business Restructuring

In the first quarter of fiscal 20X9, the Company announced a restructuring plan to combine its operations in the United Kingdom and Australia, respectively. This restructuring was undertaken in order to improve profitability and efficiency through the elimination of (i) redundant back office functions, (ii) certain staffing positions, and (iii) excess distribution and warehouse capacity, and was substantially completed in the second quarter of fiscal 20X9. Commencing in the second quarter of fiscal 20X9, the Company recorded an initial restructuring reserve, subsequent adjustments, and has made cash payments as part of this restructuring plan. Also, in connection with this restructuring plan, the Company recorded an impairment of property, plant, and equipment at one of the affected facilities in the United Kingdom of $696,000, which is included in restructuring expenses. As of December 31, 20X9 and 20X8, the remaining liability of $3,500 and $138,000, respectively, was classified in accrued other expenses in the accompanying consolidated balance sheets.

Example 11.5: Impairment—Property, Plant, and Equipment

Long-lived assets (including property, plant, and equipment), except for indefinite lived intangible assets, are reviewed for impairment when events or circumstances indicate the carrying value of an asset group may not be recoverable. Recoverability of assets to be held and used is measured by a comparison of the carrying amount of the asset group to future net cash flows estimated by the Company to be generated by such assets. If such asset group is considered to be impaired, the impairment to be recognized is the amount by which the carrying amount of the asset group exceeds the fair value of the asset group. Assets to be disposed of are recorded at the lower of their carrying value or estimated net realizable value.

There were no triggering events identified during the nine months ended December 31, 20X9, that required interim impairment testing for long-lived assets. The Company recorded an impairment of property, plant, and equipment of $699,000 in the nine months ended December 31, 20X8, related to a restructuring plan to combine its operations in the United Kingdom.

Example 11.6: Recurring Fair Value Measurements

The Company historically used certain derivative financial instruments as part of its risk management strategy to reduce interest rate and foreign currency risk. The Company recognized all derivatives on the consolidated balance sheets at fair value based on quotes obtained from financial institutions. As of March 31, 20X9, the interest rate swap agreement was discontinued and the fair value of the interest rate swap agreement as of March 31, 20X9, of $260,000 was reclassified into earnings with a realized loss included in other expense (income), net in the consolidated statement of operations and comprehensive income (loss). There was no interest rate swap agreement as of December 31, 20X9. There were no foreign currency contracts outstanding as of December 31, 20X9, and March 31, 20X9.

The Company maintains a nonqualified deferred compensation plan (the "Deferred Comp Plan") for qualified employees. The Deferred Comp Plan provides eligible key employees with the opportunity to elect to defer up to 50% of their eligible compensation under the Deferred Comp Plan. The Company may make matching or discretionary contributions, at the discretion of the Board. All compensation deferred under the Deferred Comp Plan is held by the Company. The Company maintains separate accounts for each participant to reflect deferred contribution amounts and the related gains or losses on such deferred amounts. A participant's account is notionally invested in one or more investment funds and the value of the account is determined with respect to such investment allocations. The related liability is recorded as deferred compensation and included in other long-term obligations in the consolidated balance sheets as of December 31, 20X9 and March 31, 20X9.

In connection with the acquisition of BeesKnees in fiscal 20X9, the Company may pay up to an additional $5,250,000 of contingent earn-out consideration, in cash, if net sales of certain products meet or exceed five different thresholds during the period from the acquisition date through March 31, 20X3. The estimated fair value of the contingent earn-out consideration is determined using a Monte Carlo simulation discounted to a present value which is accreted over the earn-out period. The contingent consideration liability is included in accrued other expenses in the consolidated balance sheets as of March 31, 20X9. As of September 30, 20X9, the estimated fair value of the contingent earn-out consideration was reduced to zero, and it remains unchanged as of December 31, 20X9, as the projected sales for the certain products that qualify for the earn-out are less than the required thresholds.

Example 11.7: Income Taxes

Income taxes are accounted for under the asset and liability method. Deferred tax assets and liabilities are recognized for the future tax consequences attributable to differences between the financial statement carrying amounts of existing assets and liabilities and their respective tax bases and operating loss and credit carryforwards. Deferred tax assets and liabilities are measured using enacted tax rates expected to apply to taxable income in the years in which those temporary differences and carryforwards are expected to be recovered or settled. The effect on deferred tax assets and liabilities of a change in tax rates is recognized in income in the period that includes the enactment date.

The Company records a valuation allowance to reduce deferred tax assets to the amount that is more likely than not to be realized. Management assesses all available positive and negative evidence to estimate whether sufficient future taxable income will be generated to realize existing deferred tax assets. A significant piece of objective negative evidence evaluated in fiscal 20X9 was the cumulative U.S. pretax loss incurred over the then-most-recent three-year period. Such objective evidence limits the ability to consider other subjective evidence, such as projections for future taxable income. On the basis of that evaluation, as of December 31, 20X8, a full valuation allowance was recorded to fully offset the U.S. net deferred tax assets, as they more likely than not will not be realized. Management updated this assessment as of December 31, 20X9, and concluded that the full valuation allowance for U.S. net deferred tax assets is still required.

The Company recognizes the impact of an uncertain tax position if it is more likely than not that such position will be sustained on audit, based solely on the technical merits of the position.

The income tax provision for interim periods is comprised of tax on ordinary income (loss) provided at the most recent estimated annual effective tax rate, adjusted for the tax effect of discrete items. Management estimates the annual effective tax rate quarterly based on the forecasted pretax income (loss) results of its U.S. and non-U.S. jurisdictions. Items unrelated to current fiscal year ordinary income (loss) are recognized entirely in the period identified as a discrete item of tax. These discrete items generally relate to changes in tax laws, adjustments to the actual liability determined upon filing tax returns, and adjustments to previously recorded reserves for uncertain tax positions.

12 ASC 272 LIMITED LIABILITY ENTITIES

AUTHORITATIVE LITERATURE

Subtopic

ASC 272, *Limited Liability Entities*, contains one Subtopic:

- ASC 272-10, *Overall*, which contains guidance for limited liability entities organized in the United States that prepare financial statements under U.S. GAAP.

Scope

ASC 272 applies to all entities structured as limited liability entities. (ASC 272-10-15-2)

DISCLOSURE AND PRESENTATION REQUIREMENTS

Presentation

Complete Set of Financial Statements A complete set of financial statements includes:

- A statement of financial position.
- A statement of operations.
- A statement of cash flows.
- Changes in members' equity:
  - As a separate statement.
  - Combined with the statement of operations.
  - In the notes.
- Notes to the financial statements.
  (ASC 274-10-45-1)

Headings of Financial Statements The headings of each statement must identify the entity as being a limited liability entity. (ASC 272-10-45-2) This alerts the user to certain anomalies, such as (most commonly) an absence of income tax expense and a related liability, and the use of somewhat distinctive captions in the equity section of the statement of financial position.

Members' Equity A limited liability company (LLC) presents its equity using the caption "members' equity." The equity attributable to each class of member should be separately stated on the face of the statement of financial position or disclosed in the notes to the financial statements. (ASC 272-10-45-3)

A deficit, if one exists, should be reported in the members' equity account(s), even if there is limited liability for the members. (ASC 272-10-45-4) This is consistent with the "going concern" assumption that underlies GAAP. There is no requirement to disaggregate members' equity into separate components (undistributed earnings, unallocated capital, etc.) on the face of the statement of financial position or in the notes, although this is of course permissible. Amounts due from members for capital contributions, if any remain unpaid at the date of the statement of financial position, should be shown as deductions from members' equity. This is entirely consistent with practice for unpaid stock subscriptions receivable. (ASC 272-10-45-5)

Comparative Statements GAAP presumes that comparative financial statements are more useful than those for a single period. For such financial statements to be meaningful, the information for the earlier period must be truly comparable to that of the more recent period. (ASC 272-10-45-6) See FASB ASC 272-10-50-2 If the formation of the limited liability entity results in a new reporting entity being created, the guidance of ASC 250 dealing with changes in accounting entities should be consulted. (ASC 272-10-45-7)

Disclosures

ASC 272 requires certain disclosures to be made in the financial statements of limited liability companies.

- The equity of each class of member, if not presented in the financial statements.
- If separate accounts for components of members' equity are maintained and not disclosed in the financial statements, those amounts in the notes.
  (ASC 2372-10-50-1)
- Any inconsistencies in periods presented.
  (ASC 272-10-50-2)
- A description of any limitations on members' equity.
- A description of the different *classes* of members' interests and the respective rights, preferences, and privileges of each class and amounts thereof.
- If the entity will cease to exist at a stipulated date, this must be disclosed.
  (ASC 2372-10-50-3)
- If subject to income taxes in any jurisdiction, the disclosures required by ASC 740-10-50.
  (ASC 2372-10-50-4)

DISCLOSURE EXAMPLES

Example 12.1: Member's Equity

Future Energy LLC (the Company) was established as a Delaware limited liability company in July 20X6. Sullivan Investments, Inc. (Sullivan), and Reserve Corporation (Reserve) have formed Future Energy LLC as a joint venture to invest in oil and natural gas exploration opportunities within the onshore U.S. market. Sullivan and Reserve each committed $500 million in equity.

Operations of the Company commenced in 20X7. Additional equity commitments were made by certain members of Future Energy management and the Company's board of representatives (the Members). The Company is authorized to issue one class of units to be designated as "Common Units." The Units are not represented by certificates. All Common Units are issued at a price equal to $1,000 per unit.

Example 12.2: Income Taxes

The Company is a limited liability company treated as a partnership for federal and state income tax purposes with all income tax liabilities and/or benefits of the Company being passed through to the member. As such, no recognition of federal or state income taxes for the Company or its subsidiaries that are organized as limited liability companies have been provided for in the accompanying consolidated financial statements. Any uncertain tax position taken by the member is not an uncertain position of the Company.

13 ASC 274 PERSONAL FINANCIAL STATEMENTS

AUTHORITATIVE LITERATURE

Subtopics

ASC 274, *Personal Financial Statements*, consists of one Subtopic:

- ASC 274-10, *Overall*, which addresses the preparation and presentation of financial statements of individuals or groups of related individuals (i.e., families).

Scope

ASC 274 applies to individuals and groups of related individuals (ASC 274-10-15-2)

DISCLOSURE AND PRESENTATION REQUIREMENTS

Presentation

Personal financial statements can be prepared for an individual, jointly for a husband and wife, or collectively for a family.

Personal financial statements consist of:

1. *Statement of financial condition*—The only required financial statement, the statement of financial condition, presents the estimated current values of assets and the estimated current amounts of liabilities. A liability is recognized for estimated income taxes on the difference between the asset and liability amounts set forth in the statement of financial condition and their respective income tax bases. Naturally, the residual amount after deducting the liabilities (including the estimated income tax liability) from the assets is presented as net worth at that date.
2. *Statement of changes in net worth*—An optional statement that presents the primary sources of increases and decreases in net worth over a period of time. (ASC 274-10-45-4)

3. *Comparative financial statements*—The inclusion of a comparison of the current period's financial statements with one or more previous period's financial statements is optional. (ASC 274-10-45-5)

The presentation of personal financial statements does not require the classification of assets and liabilities as current and noncurrent. Instead, assets and liabilities are presented in order of liquidity and maturity. (ASC 274-10-45-7)

Disclosures

The following disclosures are typically made in either the body of the financial statements or in the accompanying notes.

1. A clear identification of the individuals covered by the financial statements.
2. That assets are presented at their estimated current values and liabilities are presented at their estimated current amounts.
3. The methods used in determining the estimated current values of major assets and the estimated current amounts of major liabilities or major categories of assets and liabilities.
4. Changes in methods used in (3) from one period to the next.
5. If assets held jointly by the person and by others are included in the statements, the nature of the joint ownership.
6. If the person's investment portfolio is material in relation to his or her other assets and is concentrated in one or a few companies or industries, the names of the companies or industries and the estimated current values of the securities.
7. If the person has a material investment in a closely held business:
   a. The name of the company.
   b. The person's percentage of ownership.
   c. The nature of the business.
   d. Summarized financial information about assets, liabilities, and results of operations for the most recent year based on the businesses' own financial statements as well as the basis of presentation (e.g., GAAP, cash basis, income tax basis, etc.), and any significant loss contingencies.
8. Description of intangible assets and their estimated useful lives.
9. The face amount of life insurance the individual owns.
10. Certain nonforfeitable rights, such as pensions based on life expectancy.
11. The methods and assumptions used to calculate estimated income taxes on the differences between the estimated current values of assets and the estimated current amounts of liabilities and their tax bases as well as a statement that the provision will probably differ from the amounts eventually paid as the timing and method of disposal as well as changes in the tax laws and regulations will affect the actual taxes to be paid.
12. Unused operating loss and capital loss carryforwards and any other unused deductions or credits and, if applicable, the tax year in which they expire (under the current income tax code, there will frequently be unused alternative minimum tax credit carryforwards).
13. The differences between the estimated current values of major assets and the estimated current amounts of major liabilities or categories of assets and liabilities and their tax bases.
14. Maturities, interest rates, collateral, and other pertinent details relating to receivables and debt.
15. Certain noncancellable commitments.
    (ASC 274-10-50-2)

PRESENTATION AND DISCLOSURE EXAMPLE

Example 13.1: Hypothetical Set of Personal Financial Statements

Luke and Jean Blake
Statements of Financial Condition
December 31, 20X2 and 20X1

Assets	*20X2*	*20X1*
Cash	$ 762,874	$ 415,242
Certificate of deposit	40,000	20,000
Securities		
Marketable (Note 2)	257,574	520,970
Tax-exempt bonds (Note 3)	3,780,444	1,972,556
Loans receivable (Note 4)	525,754	725,754
Partnership and joint venture interests (Note 5)	1,870,000	1,876,000
Real estate interests (Note 6)	1,780,000	5,000,000
Matilda Corporation (Note 7)	5,501,374	5,200,554
Cash surrender value of life insurance (Note 8)	776,000	530,000
Personal residences (Note 9)	4,774,458	4,760,458
Deferred losses from partnerships	137,140	121,660
Vested interest in Matilda Corporation benefit plan	1,091,920	1,061,920
Personal jewelry and furnishings (Note 10)	1,026,000	13,400
Total assets	$22,323,718	$22,218,514
Liabilities		
Mortgage payable (Note 11)	$ 508,000	$ 534,000
Security deposits—rentals		11,400
Income taxes payable—current year balance	19,600	21,360
Total liabilities	$ 527,600	$ 566,760
Estimated income taxes on difference between estimated current values of assets and estimated current amounts of liabilities and their tax bases (Note 12)	$ 1,110,800	$ 1,462,000
Net Worth	$20,685,318	$20,189,754
Total liabilities and net worth	$22,323,718	$22,218,514

Luke and Jean Blake
Statement of Changes in Net Worth
for the Years Ended December 31, 20X2 and 20X1

	20X2	*20X1*
Realized increases in net worth		
Salary and bonus	$ 400,000	$ 350,000
Dividends and interest income	$ 368,520	$ 170,000
Distribution from limited partnerships	$ 560,000	$ 520,000
Gain on sales of marketable securities	$ 116,480	$ 285,600
	$ 1,445,000	$ 1,325,600
Realized decreases in net worth	$ 0	$ 0
Income taxes	$ 360,000	$ 280,000
Interest expense	$ 50,000	$ 52,000
Real estate taxes	$ 42,000	$ 36,000
Personal expenditures	$ 485,072	$ 800,000
	$ 937,072	$ 1,168,000
Net realized increase in net worth	$ 507,928	$ 157,600
	$ 0	$ 0
Unrealized increases in net worth	$ 0	$ 0
Marketable securities (net of realized gains on securities sold)	$ 74,920	$ 60,540
Benefit plan—Matilda Corporation	$ 30,000	$ 28,000
Personal jewelry and furnishings	$ 40,000	$ 36,000
	$ 144,920	$ 124,540
Unrealized decreases in net worth	$ 0	$ 0
Estimated income taxes on the difference between the estimated current values of assets and the estimated current amounts of liabilities and their tax bases	$ 157,464	$ 128,236
Net unrealized decrease in net worth	($12,544)	($3,696)
Net increase in net worth	$ 495,384	$ 153,904
Net worth at the beginning of year	$20,189,754	$20,035,850
Net worth at the end of year	$20,685,138	$20,189,754

Luke and Jean Blake
Notes to Financial Statements

Note 1: The accompanying financial statements include the assets and liabilities of Luke and Jean Blake. Assets are stated at their estimated current values, and liabilities at their estimated current amounts.

Note 2: The estimated values of marketable securities are either (1) their quoted closing prices or (2) for securities not traded on the financial statement date, amounts that fall within the range of quoted bid and asked prices.

Marketable securities consist of the following:

Stocks	Number of Shares	Estimated Current Values 12/31/20X2	Number of Shares	Estimated Current Values 12/31/20X1
Alice Harvey, Inc.			2000	$244,000
Lawson Robotics Corp.	500	$103,854	2000	240,970
M.A.L. Corporation	300	41,400	200	10,000
Daniel & Mattie Corp.	300	41,400	400	10,000
L.R.B. Corporation	200	70,920	400	16,000
		$257,574		$520,970

Note 3: The interest income from state and municipal bonds is generally not subject to federal income taxes but is, except in certain cases, subject to state income tax and federal alternative minimum tax.

Note 4: The loan receivable from Carol Parker, Inc., matures January 20X3 and bears interest at the prime rate.

Note 5: Partnership and joint venture interests consist of the following:

	Percent Owned	Cost	Estimated Current Value 12/31/20X2	Estimated Current Value 12/31/20X1
East Sydney Partnership	50.0%	$100,000	$200,000	200,000
1958 Ballarat Joint Venture	20.0	20,000	70,000	76,000
27 Radcliffe Partnership	22.5	20,000	80,000	100,000
Collins Partnership	10.0	80,000	120,000	100,000
Chapman Joint Venture	30.0	200,000	1,200,000	1,200,000
Jean Beazley Group	20.0	40,000	200,000	200,000
45 Phillips Joint Venture	50.0	−22,000	—	—
			$1,870,000	$1,876,000

Note 6: Mr. and Mrs. Blake own a one-half interest in an apartment building in Schaumberg, Illinois. The estimated current value was determined by Mr. and Mrs. Blake. Their income tax basis in the apartment building was $2,000,000 for both 20X2 and 20X1.

Note 7: Jean Blake owns 75% of the common stock of the Matilda Corporation. A condensed statement of assets, liabilities, and stockholders' equity (income tax basis) of Matilda Corporation as of December 31, 20X2 and 20X1, is summarized below.

	20X2	*20X1*
Current assets	$5,950,000	$6,294,000
Investments	400,000	$ 400,000
Property and equipment (net)	290,000	$ 330,000
Loans receivable	220,000	$ 240,000
Total assets	$6,860,000	$7,264,000
Current liabilities	$4,060,000	$4,314,000
Other liabilities	$900,000	$ 800,000
Total liabilities	4,960,000	$5,114,000
Stockholders' equity	1,900,000	$2,150,000
Total liabilities and stockholders' equity	$6,860,000	$7,264,000

Note 8: At December 31, 20X2 and 20X1, Luke Blake owned a $1,000,000 whole life insurance policy. Mrs. Blake is the sole beneficiary under the policy.

Note 9: The estimated current values of the personal residences are their appraisal value based on an estimate of selling price, net of estimated selling costs obtained from an independent real estate agent familiar with similar properties in similar locations. Both residences were purchased in 20X0.

Note 10: The estimated current values of personal effects and jewelry are the appraised values of those assets, determined by an independent appraiser for insurance purposes.

Note 11: The mortgage (collateralized by the residence) is payable in monthly installments of $4,958, including interest at an annual rate of 6% through 20X9.

Note 12: The estimated current amounts of liabilities at December 31, 20X2, and December 31, 20X1, equaled their income tax bases. Estimated income taxes have been provided on the excess of the estimated current values of assets over their tax bases as if the estimated current values of the assets had been realized on the dates of the statements of financial condition, using applicable income tax laws and regulations. The provision will probably differ from the amounts of income taxes that eventually will be paid because those amounts are determined by the timing and the method of disposal or realization and the income tax laws and regulations in effect at the time of disposal or realization.

The excess of estimated current values of major assets over their income tax bases are:

	December 31	
	20X2	*20X1*
Investment in Matilda Corporation	$2,800,000	$2,700,000
Vested interest in benefit plan	700,000	600,000
Investment in marketable securities	200,000	240,600
	$3,700,000	$3,540,600

14 ASC 275 RISKS AND UNCERTAINTIES

AUTHORITATIVE LITERATURE

Subtopic

ASU 275, *Risks and Uncertainties,* contains one Subtopic:

- ASU 275-10, *Overall,* which provides guidance on disclosures of risks and uncertainties inherent in entity's operations and activities in cases where principal operations have not begun.

Scope and Scope Exceptions

The guidance applies to all GAAP financial statements, interim and annual, but not to condensed or summarized financial statements. The guidance does not apply to risks and uncertainties associated with:

- Management or key personnel.
- Proposed changes in accounting principles.
- Deficiencies in the internal control structure.
- The possible effects of acts of God, war, or sudden catastrophes.
  (ASC 275-10-15-4)

The Codification points out that there is overlap between this Topic and the requirements of the SEC and other Codification Topics, particularly ASC 450. The guidance in ASC 275 does not alter any of those requirements.

Key Terms

ASC 275, *Risks and Uncertainties,* is focused on disclosures. It does not contain a Subtopic 45—*Presentation*, but does contain a robust Subtopic 50—*Disclosures* that contains detailed guidance on disclosures of risks and uncertainties existing as of the date of the financial statements that could significantly affect the amounts reported in the near term. These requirements are meant to provide users with early warning about potential issues with key information. It looks at risks and uncertainties arising internally as well as those arising from changes in the industry and economic environment. When applying the guidance in ASC 275, it is important to understand several key terms used in this Subtopic that provide threshold levels for disclosure:

Near Term A period of time not to exceed one year from the date of the financial statements.

Reasonably Possible The chance of the future event or events occurring is more than remote but less than likely.

Severe Impact (Used in reference to current vulnerability due to certain concentrations.) A significant financially disruptive effect on the normal functioning of an entity. Severe impact is a higher threshold than material. Matters that are important enough to influence a user's decisions are deemed to be material, yet they may not be so significant as to disrupt the normal functioning of the entity. Some events are material to an investor because they might affect the price of an entity's capital stock or its debt securities, but they would not necessarily have a severe impact on (disrupt) the entity itself. The concept of severe impact, however, includes matters that are less than catastrophic. Matters that are catastrophic include, for example, those that would result in bankruptcy.

PRACTICE ALERT

While SEC comments pertain to public entities, their comments can often provide valuable practice pointers for preparers of nonpublic entities. In the area of risks and uncertainties, the SEC has commented in recent years that:

- Entities need to provide sufficient information—both qualitative and quantitative—to allow a financial statement user to evaluate the effect those risks may have on results of operations.
- The risk disclosures should not be vague, but enable readers to understand which aspect of the business is exposed to those risks.
- The entity must identify the actual risks.
- The disclosures should avoid generic risks factors that could apply to any entity and avoid boilerplate language.
- The disclosures should include material risks that currently affect the entity, including cybersecurity risks.
- Entities should be mindful of disclosing risks associated with business activities in areas identified by the U.S. State Department as state sponsors of terrorism.

Specific areas of vulnerability the SEC has identified include:

- Business combinations and estimates related to valuations of intangible assets and goodwill
- Impairment of assets

- Fair value of goodwill
- Estimates of contingencies
- Why an entity is unable to estimate contingencies
- Valuation allowance for income taxes

DISCLOSURE REQUIREMENTS

The four areas of disclosure required by ASC 275-10-50 are risks and uncertainties relating to

1. The nature of the entity's operations, even if principal operations have not begun,
2. Use of estimates in the preparation of financial statements,
3. Certain significant estimates, and
4. Vulnerability due to certain concentrations.

These areas are not mutually exclusive and may overlap with other requirements. The disclosures may be

- Grouped together,
- Placed in other parts of the financial statements, or
- Made as part of the disclosures required by other ASC Topics.
  (ASC 275-10-50-1)

It is also important to note that for comparative statements, ASC 275 applies only to the current period.

Nature of Operations

ASC 275-10-50-2 requires that entitles that have commenced planned principal operations disclose:

- The major products or services that they sell or provide,
- The principal markets that they serve, and
- The location of those markets.

Quantification is not required in disclosures about the nature of operations.
An entity operating in more than one industry must disclose:

- All industries it is operating within.
- The relative importance of each industry. (This does not have to presented quantitatively but can be conveyed by the use of words such as "predominantly," "about equally," or "major.")
- The basis for determining the relative importance of each industry (assets, revenue, or earnings).

Not-for-profit entities should disclose the nature of their principal services and the revenue sources for those services.

If an entity has not commenced principal operations, it should also disclose what activities are being planned. (ASC 275-10-50-2A)

Use of Estimates in the Preparation of Financial Statements

Users must be clearly alerted to the pervasiveness of estimates. Therefore, financial statements must include an explanation that the preparation of financial statements in accordance with GAAP requires the use of estimates by management. (ASC 275-10-50-4) Often, this information is presented in a basis of presentation note.

Certain Significant Estimates

ASC 275-10-50-6 and 50-7 require disclosures regarding estimates used in valuing assets, liabilities, or gain or loss contingencies if known at the time the financial statements are issued or available to be issued and both of the following criteria are met:

1. It is at least *reasonably possible* that the estimate of the effect on the financial statements of a condition, situation, or set of circumstances that existed at the date of the financial statements will change in the *near term* due to one or more future confirming events.
2. The effect of the change would be *material* to the financial statements. In this case, materiality is measured against the effect of using a different estimate.

Entities must also disclose information regarding an estimate when:

- It is at least reasonably possible that the effect on the financial statements of a condition or situation existing at the statement of financial position date for which an estimate has been made will change in the near term due to one or more future confirming events.
- The effect of the change would be material to the financial statements.
  (FASB ASC 275-10-50-8)

In assessing the criteria, management should factor in its risk-related activities. If management concludes that such activities would make the change in estimate immaterial, no disclosure is needed. (ASC 275-10-50-10) Management should consider all information available when the financial statements are issued or available to be issued. This assessment is separate from that required by ASC 855.

The disclosure must indicate:

- The nature of the uncertainty, and
- That it is reasonably possible that the estimate will change in the near term.

ASC 275-10-50 is separate from and does not change ASC 450, *Contingencies*. If an estimate is covered under ASC 450 as a loss contingency, the disclosure must include an estimate of the possible range of loss or state that an estimate cannot be made. Disclosure of any factors that would make an estimate sensitive to change is encouraged but not required. (ASC 275-10-50-9) For loss contingencies meeting the ASC 450 and ASC 275-10-50-8 criteria above, entities must disclose that it is at least reasonably possible that the confirmation of the loss or a change in the estimate amount of the low future events will occur in the near term. So, too, entities with long-term operating assets and profitable long-term contracts may meet the criteria in ASC 275-10-50-8 and, therefore, should disclose the nature of the estimate and indicate that it is at least reasonably possible that a change in the estimate may occur in the near term. (ASC 275-10-50-11)

Exhibit—Examples of Items That May Be Based on Estimates That Are Particularly Sensitive to Change in the Near Term (ASC 275-10-50-15)

Inventory subject to rapid technological obsolescence
Specialized equipment subject to technological obsolescence
Valuation allowances for deferred income tax assets based on future taxable income
Capitalized motion picture film production costs
Capitalized computer software costs

Deferred policy acquisition costs of insurance entities
Valuation allowances for commercial and real estate loans
Environmental remediation-related obligations
Litigation-related obligations
Contingent liabilities for guarantees of other entities' obligations
Amounts reported for long-term obligations, such as amounts reported for pensions and postemployment benefits
Net proceeds recoverable, the provisions for expected loss to be incurred, or both, on disposition of a business or assets
Amounts reported for long-term contracts

ASC 275 clarified that when assessing whether a disclosure about estimated useful life of an intangible asset is needed, management should consider the change material if it would result in a change in the:

- Useful life of the intangible asset.
- Expected likelihood of renewal or existence.
  (ASC 275-10-50-15A)

Vulnerability Due to Concentrations Vulnerability from concentrations occurs when entities fail to diversify in order to mitigate risk. Financial statements must disclose such concentrations if management knows prior to issuance of the financial statements that *all* of the following conditions exist (ASC 275-10-50-16):

1. The concentration exists at the date of the financial statements.
2. The concentration makes the entity vulnerable to the risk of a near-term severe impact.
3. It is at least reasonably possible that the events that could cause the severe impact will occur in the near term.

The potential for severe impact can occur as the result of the total or partial loss of a business relationship, price or demand changes, loss of patent protection, changes in the availability of a resource or right, or the disruption of operations in a market or geographic area. For purposes of this Topic, it is always considered reasonably possible in the near term that any customer, grantor, or contributor will be lost and that operations located outside an entity's home country will be disrupted.

Exhibit—Examples of Concentrations That Require Disclosure (ASC 275-10-50-18)

Concentrations in:
• The volume of business transacted with a particular customer, supplier, lender, grantor, or contributor.
• Revenue from particular products, services, or fundraising events.
• The available sources of supply of materials, labor, services, or of licenses or other rights used in the entity's operations.
• The market or geographic area in which an entity conducts its operations.

In addition to the above, the following disclosures related to concentrations of labor are required (ASC 275-10-50-20):

- For labor subject to collective bargaining agreements,
  - Both the percentage of the labor force covered by collective bargaining agreements, and
  - The percentage of the labor force covered by collective bargaining agreements that will expire within one year.
- For operations located outside the entity's home country,
  - The carrying amounts of net assets, and
  - The geographic areas in which they are located.

DISCLOSURE EXAMPLES

Example 14.1: Nature of Operations—Business Subject to Regulatory Delays

Our pipeline of products in development may be subject to regulatory delays at the FDA. Delays in key products could have material adverse effects on our business, financial position, and results of operations.

Our future revenue growth and profitability are dependent upon our ability to develop and introduce new products on a timely basis in relation to our competitors' product introductions. Our failure to do so successfully could have a material adverse effect on our financial position and results of operations.

Many products require FDA approval prior to being marketed. The process of obtaining FDA approval to manufacture and market new and generic pharmaceutical products is rigorous, time-consuming, costly, and largely unpredictable. We may be unable to obtain requisite FDA approvals on a timely basis for new generic products that we may develop. The Company has experienced delays on non-material products from time to time, and has on occasion withdrawn Abbreviated New Drug Applications (ANDAs) when the Company determined that approval was not likely.

The ANDA process often results in the FDA granting final approval to a number of ANDAs for a given product. We may face immediate competition when we introduce a generic product into the market. These circumstances could result in significantly lower prices, as well as reduced margins, for generic products compared to brand products. New generic market entrants generally cause continued price and margin erosion over the generic product life cycle.

Example 14.2: Nature of Operations—Highly Competitive Business

The cosmetic categories in which we participate are very competitive, and if we are not able to compete effectively, our results of operations could be adversely affected. Our principal competitors in these categories all have substantial financial, marketing, and other resources. In most product categories, we compete not only with other widely advertised branded products, but also with generic and private label products that are generally sold at lower prices. Competition in our product categories is based on product innovation, product quality, price, brand recognition and loyalty, effectiveness of marketing, promotional activity, and the ability to identify and satisfy consumer preferences. If our large competitors were to seek an advantage through pricing or promotional changes, we could choose to do the same, which could adversely affect our margins and profitability. If we did not do the same, our revenues and market share could be adversely affected. Our market share and revenue growth could also be adversely impacted if we are not successful in introducing innovative products in response to changing consumer demands or by new product introductions of our competitors. If we are unable to build and sustain brand equity by offering recognizably superior product quality, we may be unable to maintain premium pricing over generic and private label products.

Example 14.3: Nature of Operations—Raw Materials and Supplies

We obtain our raw materials from domestic and international sources. We currently obtain a majority of our walnuts from growers located in California who have entered into supply contracts with us. We also purchase walnuts from time to time from other growers and walnut processors on the open market. We purchase other nuts from domestic and international processors on the open market. For example, during fiscal 20X3, all of the walnuts, peanuts and almonds we obtained were grown in the United States, most of our supply of hazelnuts came from the United States, and our supply of pecans were sourced from the United States and Mexico. With respect to nut types sourced primarily from abroad, we import Brazil nuts from the Amazon Basin, cashew nuts from India, Africa, Brazil, and Southeast Asia, macadamia nuts from Australia and South Africa, and pine nuts from China and Turkey. The popcorn we source comes from our primary third party co-packer in the United States, with additional sourcing capabilities, if needed, from Argentina. We obtain potatoes from the United States and the United Kingdom, with additional sourcing capabilities, if needed, from Europe.

The availability and cost of walnut raw materials are subject to supply contract renewals, crop size, quality, yield fluctuations, and changes in governmental regulation, as well as other factors. We purchase all other supplies used in our business from third parties. Those supplies include, for example, roasting oils, seasonings, plastic containers, flexible packaging, labels, and other packaging materials. We believe that each of these supplies is available from multiple sources and that our business is not materially dependent upon any individual supplier relationship.

Example 14.4: Use of Estimates

The preparation of financial statements in conformity with GAAP requires management to make estimates and assumptions that affect the reported amounts of assets and liabilities and disclosure of contingent assets and liabilities at the date of the financial statements and the reported amounts of revenues and expenses during the reporting period. Actual results could differ from those estimates.

Example 14.5: Other Significant Estimates—Valuation Allowances for Deferred Income Tax Assets Based on Future Taxable Income

We could be subject to adverse changes in tax laws, regulations, and interpretations or challenges to our tax positions. We compute our income tax provision based on enacted tax rates in the jurisdictions in which we operate. As the tax rates vary among jurisdictions, a change in earnings attributable to the various jurisdictions in which we operate could result in an unfavorable change in our overall tax provision. From time to time, legislative initiatives are proposed that could adversely affect our tax positions, effective tax rate, tax payments, or financial condition. In addition, tax laws are complex and subject to varying interpretations. Any change in enacted tax laws, rules or regulatory or judicial interpretations, any adverse outcome in connection with tax audits in any jurisdiction or any change in the pronouncements relating to accounting for income taxes could adversely affect our effective tax rate, tax payments, and results of operations.

Example 14.6: Concentration of Volume of Business with One Customer

During fiscal 20X1, National Box Stores, Inc. accounted for 22% of our consolidated net sales and 32% of our net sales in the U.S. retail segment. No other customer accounted for 10% or more of our consolidated net sales. National Box Stores also represented 7% of our net sales in the International segment and 8% of our net sales in the OTC drug segment. The five largest customers in our U.S. retail segment accounted for 55% of its net sales for fiscal 20X1, the five largest customers in our International segment accounted for 25% of its net sales for fiscal 20X1, and the five largest customers in our OTC drug segment accounted for 42% of its net sales for fiscal 20X1. The loss of any large customer for an extended length of time could adversely affect our sales and profits. In addition, large retail customers may seek to use their position to improve their profitability through improved efficiency, lower pricing, increased reliance on their own brand name products, increased emphasis on generic and other economy brands, and increased promotional programs. If we are unable to use our scale, marketing expertise, product innovation, knowledge of consumers' needs, and category leadership positions to respond to these demands, our profitability or volume growth could be negatively impacted.

Example 14.7: Customer Concentration

One customer, ABC Company, a mass merchant, accounted for approximately 14% of our sales in 20X1 and approximately 8% of our sales in 20X2. No other customer was more than 10 percent of our sales during the periods presented. During 20X2, sales to our top ten customers accounted for 17% percent of our sales and our top 20 customers accounted for 21% percent of our sales. We do not make a material amount of sales in foreign countries.

Example 14.8: Product Concentration

We do not have any single class of products that accounts for more than 10% of our sales. However, sales of our floor-covering products may be classified by significant end-user markets into which we sell, and such information for the past three years is summarized as follows:

	20X2	*20X1*	*20X0*
Residential floor-covering products	76%	73%	72%
Commercial floor-covering products	24%	27%	28%

Example 14.9: Concentration of Risk—Major Customers

The Company is exposed to concentrations of risk from major customers. For the years ended March 31, 20X2 and 20X1, the customers who account for 10% or more of the Company's revenues and its outstanding accounts receivable at year-end date, are presented as follows:

	Year Ended March 31, 20X2		**March 31, 20X2**
	Revenues	*Percentage of Revenues*	*Accounts Receivable*
Customer A	$3,305,248	58%	$ 439,478
Customer B (Vendor A)	1,250,412	22%	1,893,254
Total	$4,555,600	80%	$2,332,732

	Year Ended March 31, 20X1		March 31, 20X1
	Revenues	*Percentage of Revenues*	*Accounts Receivable*
Customer A	$3,830,430	57%	$246,304
Customer B	1,175,641	18%	1,768,258
Total	$5,006,071	75%	$2,014,562

Example 14.10: Concentration of Volume with Suppliers

The Company is exposed to concentrations of risk from major suppliers. For the years ended March 31, 20X2 and 20X1, the suppliers who account for 10% or more of the Company's purchases and its outstanding accounts payable at year-end date, are presented as follows:

	Year Ended March 31, 20X2		March 31, 20X2
	Purchases	*Percentage of Purchases*	*Accounts Payable*
Vendor A	$1,271,482	17%	$—
Vendor B	902,144	12%	41,612
Vendor C	881,285	12%	96,405
Total	$3,054,911	41%	$138,017

	Year Ended March 31, 20X1		March 31, 20X1
	Purchases	*Percentage of Purchases*	*Accounts Payable*
Vendor A	$2,225,871	25%	$—
Vendor B	852,685	10%	—
Total	$3,078,556	35%	$—

Example 14.11: Geographic Concentration

A segment of the Group's operations are conducted in Hong Kong and the People's Republic of China (PRC). Accordingly, the Group's business, financial condition and results of operations may be influenced by the political, economic, and legal environment in the PRC, and by the general state of the PRC economy.

The Group's operations in the PRC are subject to special considerations and significant risks not typically associated with companies in North America and Western Europe. These include risks associated with, among others, the political, economic, and legal environment and foreign currency exchange. The Group's results may be adversely affected by changes in the political and social conditions in the PRC, and by changes in governmental policies with respect to laws and regulations, anti-inflationary measures, currency conversion, remittances abroad, and rates and methods of taxation, among other things.

Example 14.12: Concentration of Credit Risks

The Corporation sells primarily to customers in the retail trade, primarily those in mass merchandising, which is comprised of three distinct channels: mass merchandisers (including discount retailers), chain drug stores and supermarkets. In addition, the Corporation sells its products through a variety of other distribution channels, including card and gift shops, department stores, military post exchanges, variety stores and combo stores (stores combining food, general merchandise, and drug items) as well as through its recently acquired retail operations in the UK. The Corporation also sells paper greeting cards through its website, and, from time to time, the Corporation sells its products to independent, third-party distributors. These customers are located throughout the United States, Canada, the United Kingdom, Australia, and New Zealand. Net sales to the Corporation's five largest customers accounted for approximately 41%, 39%, and 42% of total revenue in 20X3, 20X2, and 20X1, respectively. Net sales to Discount Retail Giant Stores, Inc. and its subsidiaries accounted for approximately 15%, 13%, and 16% of total revenue in 20X3, 20X2, and 20X1, respectively. Net sales to Retail Corporation accounted for approximately 14%, 15%, and 15% of total revenue in 20X3, 20X2, and 20X1, respectively.

15 ASC 280 SEGMENT REPORTING

AUTHORITATIVE LITERATURE

With many companies organized as conglomerates, the presentation of basic consolidated financial statements on an aggregated basis does not provide users with sufficient information for decision-making purposes. The primary benefit of segment reporting is the release of "hidden data" from consolidated financial information. Different segments may possess different levels of profitability, risk, and growth. Assessing future cash flows and their associated risks can be aided by segment data. For example, knowledge of the level of reporting entity operations in growing or declining product lines can help in the prediction of cash flow, while knowledge of the scope of reporting entity operations in an unstable geographic area can help in the assessment of risk. In general, information about the nature and relative size of an enterprise's various business operations is considered useful by decision makers.

Subtopic

ASC 280, *Segment Reporting*, has one Subtopic:

- ASC 280-10, *Overall*, which provides guidance to public business entities on how to report certain information about:
  - ○ Operating segments in complete sets of financial statements, and in
  - ○ Condensed financial statements of interim periods issued to shareholders.

Scope

ASC 280 applies to *public entities*. The statement does not mandate application to not-for-profit organizations or to nonpublic entities—which are, nevertheless, encouraged to voluntarily provide the segment disclosures prescribed by ASC 280. It also does not apply to "parent entities, subsidiaries, joint ventures, or investees accounted for by the equity method if those entities' separate company statements also are consolidated or combined in a complete set of financial statements and both the separate company statements and the consolidated or combined statements are included in the same financial report." However, ASC 280 does apply to those entities if they are public entities, whose financial statements are issued separately. (ASC 28010-15-2 and 3)

Management Approach

The disaggregation approach adopted by ASC 280-10-05-03 and 04 is the "management approach," meaning it is based on the way management organizes segments internally to make operating decisions and assess performance. The management approach, in general, provides that external financial reporting will closely conform to internal reporting, thus giving financial statement users the ability to view the reporting entity's segments in the same manner as internal decision makers.

Financial information can be segmented in several ways:

- By types of products or services,
- By geography, by legal entity, or
- By type of customer.

The Codification does not limit segment reporting to purely financial information. It also requires a description of the company's rationale or methods employed in determining the composition of the segments. This description includes

- The products or services produced by each segment,
- Differences in measurement practices between segments and the consolidated entity, and
- Differences in the segments' measurement practices between periods.

Operating Segments

An operating segment is a component of a public entity that:

- Engages in business activities from which it may recognize revenue and incur expenses.
- Has its operating results regularly reviewed by its chief operating decision maker (CODM) for the purpose of allocating resources and assessing the segment's performance.
- Has available discrete financial information.
  (ASC 280-10-50-1)

Operating segments may be components of a public entity that sell primarily to the entity's other segment. (ASC 280-10-50-2) Additionally, an operating segment may not be revenue generating from its inception, because it may be in a start-up phase. (ASC 280-10-50-3)

Practice Tip: Not all activities that occur within the reporting entity are allocable to its operating segments. Activities that are non-revenue-producing or that are incidental to the reporting entity, such as corporate headquarters or certain service or support departments, should not be attributed to operating segments. ASC 280 specifies that the reporting entity's pension and other postretirement benefit plans are not considered to be operating segments. (ASC 280-10-50-4)

Operating segments frequently have a segment manager function that communicates on an ongoing basis with the reporting entity's CODM. The segment manager is not necessarily a single individual but rather the segment management responsibility can vest functionally in a committee or group of designated individuals. (ASC 280-10-50-7)

Reportable Segments

An operating segment is considered to be a reportable segment if it meets the description above and is significant to the enterprise as a whole because it satisfies one of the three quantitative 10% tests described below. If a segment does not meet any of the tests below, but management believes the information may be useful, the operating segment may be reportable.

Revenue Test Segment revenue (unaffiliated and intersegment) is at least 10% of the combined revenue (unaffiliated and intersegment) of all operating segments. (ASC 280-10-50-12a)

Profit and Loss Test The absolute amount of segment profit or loss is at least 10% of the greater, in absolute amount, of:

1. Combined profits of all operating segments reporting a profit.
2. Combined losses of all operating segments reporting a loss.
   (ASC 280-10-50-12b)

Assets Test Segment assets are at least 10% of the combined assets of all operating segments. (ASC 280-10-50-12c) Segment assets include those assets used exclusively by the segment and the allocated portion of assets shared by two or more segments. Assets held for general corporate purposes are not assigned to segments.

Comparability Interperiod comparability should be considered in conjunction with the results of the 10% tests. If a segment fails to meet the tests in the current reporting period but has satisfied the tests in the past and is expected to in the future, it is considered as being reportable in the current year for the sake of comparability. Similarly, if a segment which rarely passes the tests does so in the current year as the result of an unusual event, that segment may be excluded to preserve comparability.

75% Test After the 10% tests are completed, a 75% test must be performed. (ASC 280-10-50-14) The combined external revenue of all reportable segments must be at least 75% of the combined unaffiliated revenue of all operating segments. If the 75% test is not satisfied, additional segments must be designated as reportable until the test is satisfied. The purpose of this test is to ensure that reportable segments account for a substantial portion of the entity's operations.

Aggregating Segments Certain other factors must be considered when identifying reportable segments. Management may consider aggregating two or more operating segments if:

1. They have similar economic characteristics,
2. Aggregation is consistent with the objective and basic principles of ASC 280, and
3. The segments are similar in all of the following areas:
   a. The nature of the products and services
   b. The nature of the production processes
   c. The type of customer for their products and services
   d. The methods used to distribute their products or provide their services
   e. The nature of the regulatory environment.
      (ASC 280-10-50-11)

At the discretion of management, this aggregation can occur prior to performing the 10% tests.

Management may *optionally* combine information on operating segments that do not meet any of the 10% tests to produce a reportable segment, but only if the segments being combined have similar economic characteristics and also share a majority of the five aggregation criteria listed above. (ASC 280-10-50-13)

Note that information about operating segments that do not meet any of the 10% thresholds may still be disclosed separately. (ASC 280-10-50-15) By utilizing the aggregation criteria and quantitative thresholds (10% tests) for determining reportable segments, ASC 280 uses what should be considered a modified management approach.

The number of reportable segments should not be so great as to decrease the usefulness of segment reporting. As a rule of thumb, FASB suggests that if the number of reportable segments exceeds ten, segment information may become too detailed. In this situation, the most closely related operating segments should be combined into broader reportable segments, again, however, subject to the objectives inherent in ASC 280's requirements. (ASC 280-10-50-18)

Practice Alert

Segment reporting is a frequent topic of SEC comment letters. While SEC rules only apply to public entities, preparers of financial statements can benefit from the findings of SEC reviewers. For segment reporting, these are some of the areas commented on by the SEC:

- How operating segments were identified.
- The basis of aggregation of operating segments.
- Confirmation that prior periods were revised so that information is consistent.
- Lack of quantitative disclosure about products and services.
- Lack of disclosure about geographic information.

DISCLOSURE AND PRESENTATION REQUIREMENTS

Presentation

The ASC 280-10-45 Subtopic provides limited guidance. It points out that the ASC 280 does not require an entity to present cash flows, although certain requirements may lead to disclosure of cash flow items. The Subtopic also points out that a public entity may provide additional segment information not specifically required by ASC 280. (ASC 280-10-45-1 and 45-2)

Segment Disclosure Requirements

ASC 280 requires disclosures regarding the reporting entity's reportable segments. Those disclosures can be found in the *Disclosure Checklist for Commercial Businesses* at www.wiley.com/go/FSDM2021.

Restatement of Previously Reported Segment Information

ASC 280-10-50-34 requires segment reporting on a comparative basis when the associated financial statements are comparative. Therefore, restate the information to preserve comparability whenever the reporting entity has changed the structure of its internal organization in a manner that causes a change to its reportable segments. Management must explicitly disclose that it has restated the segment information of earlier periods.

Entity-Wide Disclosure Requirements

In addition to segment data, ASC 280-10-50-38 through 42 mandates that certain entity-wide disclosures be made, but only on an annual basis. Those disclosures are listed in the *Disclosure Checklist for Commercial Businesses* at www.wiley.com/go/FSDM2021, and are explained in detail below. The entity-wide disclosures are required for all reporting entities subject to ASC 280, even those that have only a single reportable segment. (ASC 280-10-50-38 and 50-39)

Products and Services Revenue from external customers for each product and service or each group of similar products and services must be reported by the reporting entity unless impracticable. If deemed to be impracticable, disclose that fact. If the company's reportable segments have been organized around products and services, then this disclosure will generally not be required. (ASC 280-10-50-40)

Geographic Areas A reporting entity separately discloses revenues from external customers and long-lived assets attributable to its domestic operations and foreign operations. If the reportable segments have been organized around geographic areas, then these disclosures will generally not be required because they would be duplicative. (ASC 280-10-50-41)

Domestic operations are those operations located in the reporting entity's home country that generate either unaffiliated or intersegment revenues. Foreign operations are similar operations located outside of the home country of the reporting entity. For the purposes of these disclosures, U.S. reporting entities' operations in Puerto Rico are not considered to be foreign operations, although management is not precluded from voluntary disclosure regarding Puerto Rican operations. (ASC 280-10-55)

If the reporting entity functions in two or more foreign geographic areas, to the extent revenues or assets of an individual foreign geographic area are material, then separately disclose these amounts. In addition, disclosure is required of the basis for attributing revenue to different geographic areas. A geographic area is defined as an individual country. If providing this information is impracticable, disclose that fact.

Major Customers If the reporting entity earns 10% or more of its revenue on sales to a single external customer, disclose that fact and the amount of revenue from each such customer. Also, disclose the segment making these sales. This disclosure provides information on concentrations of risk. For the purpose of this disclosure, a group of customers under common control, such as subsidiaries of a common parent, is regarded as a single customer. Similarly the various agencies of a government are considered to be a single customer. An insuring entity (such as Blue Cross) is not considered to be the customer unless that entity (rather than the patient) controls the decision as to the doctor, type of service, etc.

EXAMPLE PRESENTATIONS AND DISCLOSURES

Example 15.1: Summary of Significant Accounting Policies—Segments

The consolidated financial statements include the accounts of Blake Medical, Inc. and its wholly owned subsidiaries (together, the "Company"). All significant intercompany accounts and transactions have been eliminated.

Blake Medical manufactures, distributes and sells residential and commercial furniture. Products are sold primarily through furniture dealers throughout the United States and Canada. The Company's operations comprise a single business segment and all the Company's long-lived assets are located within the United States.

Example 15.2: Business Segment and Geographic Information

We operate in the organic consumer foods industry. We have three operating segments by type of customer and geographic region as follows: U.S. Retail, 72% of our fiscal 20X3 consolidated net sales; International, 18% of our fiscal 20X3 consolidated net sales; and Bakeries and Foodservice, 10% of our fiscal 20X3 consolidated net sales.

Our U.S. Retail segment reflects business with a variety of specialty grocery stores, membership stores, and natural food chains operating throughout the United States. Our product categories in this business segment include ready-to-eat cereals, refrigerated yogurt, ready-to-serve soup, dry dinners, frozen vegetables, gluten free dessert and baking mixes, frozen pizza and pizza snacks, and grain, fruit, and savory snacks.

Our International segment consists of retail and foodservice businesses outside of the United States. In Canada, our product categories include ready-to-eat cereals, shelf-stable and frozen vegetables, dry dinners, refrigerated and frozen dough products, dessert and baking mixes, frozen pizza snacks, refrigerated yogurt, and grain and fruit snacks. In markets outside North America, our product categories include organic almond and rice ice cream and frozen desserts, refrigerated yogurt, snacks, shelf-stable and frozen vegetables, and frozen dinners. Our International segment also includes products manufactured in the United States for export, mainly to Caribbean and Latin American markets, as well as products we manufacture for sale to our international joint ventures. Revenues from export activities and franchise fees are reported in the region or country where the end customer is located.

In our Bakeries and Foodservice segment our product categories include ready-to-eat cereals, refrigerated yogurt, ready-to-serve soup, dry dinners, frozen vegetables, gluten free dessert and baking mixes, frozen pizza and pizza snacks, and grain, fruit, and savory snacks, baking mixes, and flour. Many products we sell are branded to the consumer and nearly all are branded to our customers. We sell to distributors and operators in many customer channels including foodservice, specialty stores, vending, and supermarket bakeries. Substantially all of this segment's operations are located in the United States.

Operating profit for these segments excludes unallocated corporate items and restructuring, impairment, and other exit costs. Unallocated corporate items include corporate overhead expenses, variances to planned domestic employee benefits and incentives, contributions to the Organic Foods Foundation, and other items that are not part of our measurement of segment operating performance. These include gains and losses arising from the revaluation of certain grain inventories and gains and losses from mark-to-market valuation of certain commodity positions until passed back to our operating segments. These items affecting operating profit are centrally managed at the corporate level and are excluded from the measure of segment profitability reviewed by executive management. Under our supply chain organization, our manufacturing, warehouse, and distribution activities are substantially integrated across our operations in order to maximize efficiency and productivity. As a result, fixed assets and depreciation and amortization expenses are neither maintained nor available by operating segment.

Example 15.3: Segments Based on Services

Consistent with the Company's strategy to focus on the growth of its skilled nursing segment and the sale of the majority of its assisted living facilities beginning in the fourth quarter of 20X2, the Company evaluates operating performance of its 35 skilled nursing facilities (SNFs), the three remaining assisted living facilities (ALFs) and the one independent living facility on a combined basis. Through the fourth quarter of 2012, the Company reported its operations under three segments: SNF, Assisted Living Facilities ("ALF"), and Corporate and Other.

With the execution of an agreement to sell six of its assisted living facilities located in Indiana occurring during the fourth quarter of 20X2, the Company has provided segment reporting herein for 20X2 and 20X1 based on its prior three operating segments. The SNF and ALF segments provide services to individuals needing long-term care in a nursing home or assisted living setting and management of those facilities. The Corporate and Other segment engages in the management of facilities and accounting and IT services. The Company previously evaluated operating performance and allocated resources primarily based upon segment operating income (loss). Segment operating results exclude interest expense and other nonoperating income and expenses. The table below contains continuing operations segment information for the years ended December 31, 20X2 and 20X1, based on the Company's former operating segments. The revenue, expenses, and income/(loss) of all facilities reflected in discontinued operations (see Note 3) are excluded. Assets of disposal group are included in Corporate and Other below.

Year Ended December 31, 20X2

Amounts in (000's)

	SNF	ALF	Corporate and Other	Eliminations	Total
Total revenues	$78,073	$1,728	$ 4,878	$(4,015)	$80,664
Cost of services	69,656	1,490	152	(4,015)	67,283
General and administrative	—	—	6,802	—	6,802
Facility rent expense	3,000	—	76	—	3,076
Depreciation and amortization	2,111	161	450	—	2,722
Salary retirement and continuation costs	—	—	17	—	17
Operating income/(loss)	$ 3,306	$77	$(2,619)	$ —	$ 763
Total assets	$58,464	$5,162	$34,270	$(4,116)	$93,780
Capital spending	$ 1,711	$ 82	$580	$ —	$ 2,311

Year Ended December 31, 20X1

	SNF	ALF	Corporate and Other	Eliminations	Total
Total revenue	$54,055	$ 582	$ 3,797	$(3,149)	$55,285
Cost of services	47,288	586	2	3,149	44,727
General and administrative	—	—	5,312	—	5,312
Facility rent expense	2,834	—	42	—	2,877
Depreciation and amortization	1,178	68	97	—	1,344
Salary retirement and continuation costs	—	—	580	—	580
Operating income/(loss)	$ 2,755	$ (72)	$(2,236)	$ —	$447
Total assets	$43,872	$2,791	$ 20,797	$(3,819)	$63,641
Capital spending	$ 818	$31	$ 848	$ —	$ 1,697

Example 15.4: Single Business Segment—Prior Years Restated—Sales Disclosed by Marketing Category

We are a single business segment. The following table summarizes retail sales by major merchandise category:

	20X3	*20X2* Restated	*20X1* Restated
Ladies' apparel and accessories	$373,508	$365,726	$373,443
Men's apparel and accessories	133,389	127,984	129,508
Home	75,174	67,561	68,853
Other	24,469	18,176	19,644
Owned department sales	606,340	579,426	591,448
Leased department commissions	9,844	9,550	9,093
Net sales	$616,183	$588,976	$600,541

Example 15.5: Segment Information—Three Segments Based on Products

The Company operates in three reportable business segments: generic computer tablets (referred to as "Hi-Tech Generic"), OTC branded tablets (referred to as "OTC Tech Products," or "TP") and branded tablets (referred to as "BT"). Branded products are marketed under brand names through marketing programs that are designed to generate IT officers and consumer loyalty. Generic tablet products are the technologic equivalents of corresponding brand tablets. Our Chief Operating Decision Maker is our Chief Executive Officer.

The business segments were determined based on management's reporting and decision-making requirements in accordance with FASB ASC 280-10 Segment Reporting. The generic products represent a single operating segment because the demand for these products is mainly driven by consumers seeking a lower cost alternative to brand-name drugs. Certain of our expenses, such as the direct sales force and other sales and marketing expenses and specific research and development expenses, are charged directly to the respective segments. Other expenses, such as general and administrative expenses, are included under the Corporate and Other cost center.

16 ASC 310 RECEIVABLES

TECHNICAL ALERTS

ASU 2019-10

Guidance Regarding Effective Dates In November 2019, The FASB issued ASU 2019-10, *Financial Instruments—Credit Losses (Topic 326), Derivatives and Hedging (Topic 815), and Leases (Topic 842): Effective Dates*. The ASU grants private companies, not-for-profit organizations, and certain small public company SEC filers additional time to implement recent FASB standards on current expected credit losses (CECL).

ASU 2019-10 Effective Dates		
Topic	Public business entities that meet *the definition of SEC Filers,* except Smaller Reporting Companies (SRCs) as defined by the SEC	All Other Entities
CECL (ASC 326)	Fiscal years beginning after December 15, 2019	Fiscal years beginning after December 15, 2022

* Includes Employee Benefit Plans and NFP Conduit Bond Obligors that file with the SEC or furnish financial statements to the SEC.

ASU 2016-13

In June 2016, the FASB issued ASU 2016-13, *Financial Instruments—Credit Losses (Topic 326): Measurement of Credit Losses on Financial Instruments*. This ASU makes changes to several topics, and adds a new Topic—ASC 326.

Note: The section in ASC 310-35 on subsequent measurement of specific types of receivables remains in effect, with some changes, after implementation of ASU 2016-13. The guidance in ASC 310 on impairment of loans and receivables is superseded upon implementation of ASU 2016-13, including paragraphs ASC 310-10-35-1 through 35-43. Those paragraphs apply to:

- Loan impairments,
- Credit losses for loans and trade receivables,
- Credit losses for certain standby letters of credit and certain loan commitments, and
- Subsequent measurement of specific types of receivables.
  (ASC 310-10-35-1)

The superseded guidance addresses the impairment concepts related to:

- All receivables and points to the guidance in ASC 450-20, and
- Loans identified for evaluation and are individually deemed to be impaired.
  (ASC 310-10-35-3)

The information on subsequent measurement that follows reflects the guidance in effect before the implementation of ASU 2016-13, with references to the ASU 2016-13 changes. For more information, see the chapter on ASC 326.

Effective Dates See information above on ASU 2019-10 for changes in effective dates. Early adoption is allowed for all entities for fiscal years beginning after December 15, 2018, including interim periods therein. (ASC 326-10-65-1)

Guidance The new guidance affects several topics. Readers should look to those topics for more information. This chapter will outline how ASU 2016-13 affects ASC 310.

ASU 2016-13 changes the accounting for credit impairments for trade and other receivables and purchased-credit impaired (PCD) financial assets. The guidance on the latter is being deleted from ASC 310-30 and moved to ASC 326. Further information on accounting for PCDs under the ASU 2016-13 amendments can be found in the chapter on ASC 326.

Under the new guidance, ASC 326's current expected credit loss (CECL) model replaces the expected loss model in ASC 310-10. Under the CECL model, entities will have to estimate expected credit losses for trade receivables and other financing receivables. Currently, an allowance or loss is recognized when it is probable. Under the new model, an allowance or loss will be recognized upon initial recognition of the asset and will reflect all future events that will lead to a recognized loss, regardless of whether it is probable that future event will occur. The extant guidance looks at past events and current conditions, whereas the new guidance is forward looking and requires estimates for future expectations.

To assess credit risk, the new guidance allows entities to continue to pool assets with similar characteristics. However, entities will want to take a second look at the receivables in a pool and make sure they have similar risk characteristics.

If an entity is not able to develop a reasonable and supportable forecast for the full remaining life of a financial asset, it should go back to using historical loss information.

AUTHORITATIVE LITERATURE

Subtopics

ASC 310, *Receivables,* consists of four subtopics:

- ASC 310-10, *Overall*
- ASC 310-20, *Nonrefundable Fees and Other Costs*
- ASC 310-30, *Loans and Debt Securities Acquired with Deteriorated Credit Quality*
- ASC 310-40, *Troubled Debt Restructurings by Creditors*

ASC 310-10, *Overall*

Receivables exist in nearly every entity. They come from credit sales, loans, or other transactions and may be in the form of loans, notes, or other type of financial instruments. (ASC 310-10-05-4)

Scope ASC 310-10-15-3 lists two exceptions to the guidance in the General Subsections of ASC 310-10:

- Mortgage banking activities and
- Contracts accounted for as derivative instruments under ASC 815-10.

ASC 310-10-15-5 states that the Acquisition, Development, and Construction Subsections' guidance applies to all entities, but not all arrangements. It applies only to those acquisition, development, and construction arrangements in which the lender participates in expected residual profit.

Types of Receivables Financing receivables are contractual rights to receive cash either on demand or on fixed or determinable dates. They are recognized as assets on the statement of financial position. Financing receivables include:

- Trade accounts receivable.
- Loans.
- Lease receivables arising from sales-type leases or direct financing leases. (This bullet is added by ASU 2016-02 on *Leases.*)
- Credit cards.

- Notes receivable.
- Receivables relating to a lessor's right to payments from a lease other than an operating lease that should be recognized as assets.[1]
  (ASC 310-10-55-14)

The following are not financing receivables:

- Debt securities in the scope of ASC 320.
- Unconditional promises to give recognized in accordance with ASC 958-605-25-7 through 25-15.
- A transferor's interest in securitization transactions accounted for as sales in ASC 860.
- Purchased beneficial interest in securitized financial assets within the scope of ASC 325-40.
  (ASC 310-10-55-15)

Loan Origination Fees These fees should be deferred and recognized over the life of the loan as an adjustment of interest income. (ASC 310-20-25-2) If there are any related direct loan origination costs, the origination fees and origination costs should be netted, and only the net amount should be deferred and amortized via the interest method. Origination costs include those incremental costs such as credit checks and security arrangements, among others, pertaining to a specific loan.

The only exception to the foregoing rule would be in the instance of certain loans that also qualify as debt instruments under ASC 320. For those carried in the "trading securities" portfolio, related loan origination fees should be charged to expense when incurred; the requirement that these be carried at fair value would make adding these costs to the asset carrying amounts a useless exercise.

Lending and Financing Activities, Including Trade Receivables—Receivables Generally Arise from Extending Credit to Others If the reporting entity has the intent and ability to hold trade receivables or loans for the foreseeable future or until maturity or payoff, those receivables are reported in the statement of financial position at their outstanding principal (face) amounts less any write-offs and allowance for uncollectible receivables or at fair value. Loans originated by the reporting entity are reported net of deferred fees or costs of originating them, and purchased loans are reported net of any unamortized premium or discount. If a decision has been made to sell loans, those loans are transferred to a held-for-sale category on the statement of financial position and reported at the lower of cost or fair value. Any amount by which cost exceeds fair value is accounted for as a valuation allowance.

When a trade receivable or loan is deemed uncollectible, the balance is written off against the allowance for uncollectible receivables. Recoveries of loans and trade receivables that were previously written off are recorded when received—either by a credit directly to earnings or by a credit to the allowance for uncollectible receivables.

ASC 310-10-25 also includes standards for recognizing fees related to receivables. Delinquency fees are recognized when chargeable, provided that collectibility is reasonably assured. Prepayment fees are not recognized until prepayments have occurred. Rebates of finance charges

---

[1] Upon implementation of ASU 2016-02, *Leases*, this bullet point will change to "Receivables relating to a lessor's right to payments from a leveraged lease that should be recognized in accordance with ASC 842-10-65-1(z)."

due because payments are made earlier than required are recognized when the receivables are prepaid and are accounted for as adjustments to interest income. (ASC 310-10-25-11 through 25-13)

Imputed Interest The proper valuation of a receivable is the present value of future payments to be received, determined by using an interest rate commensurate with the risks involved at the date of the receivable's creation. (ASC 310-10-30-3)

Valuation Allowance for Uncollectible Amounts[2] The recording of a valuation allowance for anticipated uncollectible amounts is almost always necessary. Proper matching, which remains a valid financial reporting objective, can only be achieved if bad debts are recorded in the same fiscal period as the revenues to which they are related. Since the amount of uncollectible accounts is not known with certainty, an estimate must generally be made.

Pledging, Assigning, and Factoring Receivables An organization can alter the timing of cash flows resulting from sales to its customers by using its accounts receivable as collateral for borrowings or by selling the receivables outright. The most common arrangements are pledging, assignment, and factoring.

ASC 310-20, *Nonrefundable Fees and Other Costs*

Scope and Scope Exceptions
Transactions The following transactions are included in ASC 315-20:

- Recognition and the balance sheet classification of nonrefundable fees and costs associated with lending activities,
- Accounting for discounts, premiums, and commitment fees associated with the purchase of loans and other debt securities, and
- Loans designated as a hedged item in a fair value hedge, ASC 815.
  (ASC 310-20-15-2)

Specifically excluded from ASC 310-20 guidance are:

- Loan origination or commitment fees that are refundable; however, the guidance does apply when such fees subsequently become nonrefundable.
- Costs that are incurred by the lender in transactions with independent third parties if the lender bills those costs directly to the borrower.
- Nonrefundable fees and costs associated with originating or acquiring loans that are carried at fair value if the changes in fair value are included in earnings of a business entity or change in net assets of a not-for-profit entity (NFP). The exclusion provided in this paragraph and the preceding paragraph applies to nonrefundable fees and costs associated with originating loans that are reported at fair value and premiums or discounts associated with acquiring loans that are reported at fair value. Loans that are reported at cost or the lower of cost[3] or fair value, loans or debt securities reported at fair value with changes in fair value reported in other comprehensive income (includes financial assets subject to prepayment as defined in paragraph 860-20-35-2, and debt securities classified as available-for-sale under Topic 320), and loans that have a market interest rate, or adjust to a market interest rate, are not considered to be loans carried at fair value.

---

[2] See the Technical Alert on ASU 2016-13 at the beginning of this chapter for updated information.
[3] Upon implementation of ASU 2016-13, "cost" becomes "amortized cost basis."

- Fees and costs related to a commitment to originate, sell, or purchase loans that is accounted for as a derivative instrument under Subtopic 815-10.
- Fees and costs related to a standby commitment to purchase loans if the settlement date of that commitment is not within a reasonable period or the entity does not have the intent and ability to accept delivery without selling assets. For guidance on fees and costs related to such a commitment, see paragraph 310-10-30-7.
(ASC 310-20-15-3)

Transactions   The following table outlines the applicability of this Subtopic to various types of assets.

Types of Assets	Basis of Accounting	Does ASC 310-20 Apply?
Loans or debt securities held in an investment portfolio	Historical or amortized cost basis	Yes
Loans held for sale	Lower of cost or when ASC 2016-13 is implemented amortized cost basis o/r fair value	Yes
Loans or debt securities held in trading securities by certain financial institutions	Fair value, changes in value are included in earnings	No
Loans or debt securities, available for sale	Fair value, changes in value reported in OCI	Yes
ASC 310-20-15-4)		

Commitment Fees and Costs   Often fees are received in advance in exchange for a commitment to originate or purchase a loan. These fees should be deferred and recognized upon exercise of the commitment as an adjustment of interest income over the life of the loan (ASC 310-20-35-2). If a commitment expires unexercised, the fees should be recognized as income upon expiration. (ASC 310-20-35-3)

As with loan origination fees and costs, if both commitment fees are received and commitment costs are incurred relating to a commitment to originate or purchase a loan, the net amount of fees or costs should be deferred and recognized over the life of the loan. (ASC 310-20-25-12)

ASC 310-30, *Certain Loans and Debt Securities Acquired with Deteriorated Credit Quality*[4]

Scope and Scope Exceptions   This Subtopic applies to loans acquired by completion of a transfer for which it is probable at the time of acquisition that the new investor will not be able to collect all the contractually required payments. The loans have evidence of deterioration of credit quality since their origination. ASC 310-30-15-2 excludes the following transactions from ASC 310-30 guidance:

---

[4] ASC 310-30 is superseded upon implementation of ASU 2016-13. Financial assets for which this guidance has been applied currently should look to the new guidance in ASU 2016-13 on PCD asset.

- Loans that are measured at fair value if all changes in fair value are included in earnings or, for an NFP, loans that are measured at fair value if all changes in fair value are included in the statement of activities and included in the performance indicator if a performance indicator is presented. Examples include those loans classified as trading securities under Topic 320 and Subtopic 948-310.
- Mortgage loans classified as held for sale under paragraph 948-310-35-1.
- Leases as defined in Topic 840. Only contracts that are classified by the purchaser as leases under that topic meet this exclusion. The distinction between purchasing a lease and purchasing a stream of cash flows must be drawn to determine applicability of this Section. (This bullet is superseded by ASU 2016-02.)
- Loans acquired in a business combination accounted for at historical cost, including business combinations of two or more NFPs, the acquisition of a for-profit business entity by an NFP, and combinations of two or more mutual entities.
- Loans held by liquidating banks (financial reporting by liquidating banks is discussed in Topic 942).
- Revolving credit agreements, such as credit cards and home equity loans, if at the acquisition date the borrower has revolving privileges.
- Loans that are a transferor's interests (see Subtopic 325-40).

ASC 310-30-15-4 further excludes the following transactions and activities:

- Loans that are derivative instruments subject to the requirements of Topic 815. If a loan would otherwise be in the scope of this paragraph of this Section and has within it an embedded derivative that is subject to that Topic, the host instrument (as described in that Topic) remains within the scope of this paragraph of this Section if it satisfies the conditions in this paragraph.
- Loans for which it is possible, but not probable, that the investor will be unable to collect all amounts due according to the contractual terms of the loan.
- Situations in which credit is still being offered, and the entire relationship is excluded if, at the acquisition date, the borrower has revolving privileges. This scope exclusion is appropriate because lenders generally will not continue to make credit available to borrowers from whom it is probable that the lender will not collect all contractually required payments receivable.

Overview ASC 310-30 requires the preparer to differentiate between securities investments acquired directly from the issuer and those obtained on the secondary market. It imposes accounting requirements for debt instruments acquired in transfers when the purchase price reflects a change in the debtor's credit standing since the original issuance of the instrument. This guidance is applicable to all acquirers of loans or debt securities (bonds, securitized loans, etc.), not merely financial institutions, although fewer commercial or industrial entities would tend to be making such purchases.

In applying ASC 310-30, entities must:

- Refer to the price at which the loan or security has been transferred, in relation to its "par" or original issuance price, and
- Examine whether there is information to suggest that there has been a change in the issuer's credit quality since inception of the obligation.

ASC 310-30 applies only if there has been a change in the issuer's credit quality since the inception of the debt.

Loans acquired by transfer (i.e., in the secondary market) are recorded initially at acquisition cost. If the acquisition price differs from the par or face amount (i.e., there is a premium or a discount), the effective yield has to be computed and used to accrete the discount (or, if a premium, amortize it) over the expected term of the instrument.

Subsequent Measurement—Loans Not Accounted for as a Debt Security At the date of transfer, if there is evidence of a decline in creditworthiness since the instrument's inception, such that the full amount of contractual cash flows will not be received, the provisions of ASC 310-30 must be applied. In this context, the loan is considered impaired for purposes of applying ASC 450 or, if applicable, ASC 310-10. To apply the guidance in ASC 310-10-35-10 through 35-11, the investor must meet certain criteria. It must be unable to collect all cash flows expected to be collected by the investor plus any additional cash flows expected to collected arising from a change in estimate after acquisition.

In such cases, the investor must estimate cash flows to be received, and accrete the initial carrying amount to that amount, rather than to the gross amount of future contractual cash flows. An uncertainty regarding future cash flows that suggests only a possible shortfall versus contractual amounts owed would not qualify for the accounting in Subtopic ASC 310-30. In such a situation, there would be disclosure of reasonably possible contingent losses, and if at a later date the loss is deemed to have become probable, a loss accrual would be recognized per ASC 450 as a change in estimate. (ASC 310-30-35-10)

ASC 310-40, *Troubled Debt Restructurings by Creditors*

A TDR occurs under specific circumstances: when a creditor "for economic or legal reasons related to the debtor's financial difficulties grants a concession to the debtor that it would not otherwise consider." Therefore, a TDR does not apply to restructurings that merely reflect general economic conditions that may lead to a reduction in interest rates. It also does not apply if a debt is refunded with new debt having an effective interest rate that approximates that of similar debt issued by nontroubled debtors.

ASC 310-40 focuses on the substance of debt modifications—their effect on future cash receipts or payments. Timing, interest, or principal may be modified under a TDR. These all affect cash flows and a creditor's total return on the receivable. Evaluating whether a modification of debt terms is in substance a TDR is critical to determining whether ASC 310-40 applies. Therefore, the scope and scope exceptions of this subtopic take on added significance.

Scope ASC 310-40 applies to all troubled debt restructurings by creditors. Accounting by debtors is found in ASC 470-60.

TDRs may include, but are not limited to, one or a combination of two basic transaction types:

1. Settling the debt for less than its recorded investment in the receivable through:
   - Transfer from the debtor to the creditor of receivables from third parties, real estate, or other assets to satisfy fully or partially a debt.
   - Granting of an equity interest to the creditor by the debtor to satisfy fully or partially a debt. This does not apply if the equity interest is granted pursuant to existing terms for converting the debt into an equity interest. (ASC 310-40-15-6b)

2. Continuing to carry the debt, but modifying the terms through, for instance,
   ○ Reduction of the stated interest rate, accrued interest, face amount of the debt, or maturity amount of the debt.
   ○ Extension of the maturity date at a stated interest rate lower than the current market rate.
   (ASC 310-40-15-9)

The following are *excluded* for consideration under the TDR guidance:

- Lease modifications
- Changes in employment-related agreements
- Unless they involve an agreement between debtor and creditor to restructure:
  ○ Debtors' failures to pay trade accounts according to their terms, or
  ○ Creditors' delays in taking legal action to collect overdue amounts of interest and principal
- Modifications of loans within a pool accounted for as impaired loans[5]
- Changes in expected cash flows of a pool of loans accounted for as impaired loans resulting from the modification of one or more loans within the pool.[6]
  (ASC 310-40-15-11)

Even if a debtor is experiencing some financial difficulties, a debt restructuring may not be a troubled debt restructuring for the purposes of ASC 310-40. None of the following situations are considered TDRs:

- The fair value of assets or equity accepted by a creditor from a debtor in full satisfaction of its receivable at least equals the creditor's amortized cost basis in the receivable.
- The fair value of assets or equity transferred by a debtor to a creditor in full settlement of its payable at least equals the debtor's carrying amount of the payable.
- The creditor reduces the effective interest rate on the debt primarily to reflect a decrease in market interest rates in general or a decrease in the risk so as to maintain a relationship with a debtor that can readily obtain funds from other sources at the current market interest rate.
- The debtor issues, in exchange for its debt, new marketable debt having an effective interest rate based on its market price that is at or near the current market interest rates of debt with similar maturity dates and stated interest rates issued by nontroubled debtors.
  (ASC 310-40-15-12)

PRACTICE ALERT

Financial statement classification is a frequent topic of SEC comment letters. While SEC rules only apply to public entities, preparers of financial statements can benefit from the findings of SEC reviewers. Recent SEC comments related to ASC 310 include:

- **Impaired loan identification in factoring portfolio:** Please tell us all the facts and circumstances related to the material weakness in the identification of impaired loans within the factoring portfolio and its impact on financial reporting during the periods presented in your financial statements.

---

[5] This bullet is superseded by ASU 2016-03.
[6] Ibid.

- **Related party note receivable:** In regards to the modification on June 29, 20X4, explain further how the reduction of the interest rate did not cause the loan to be considered a troubled debt restructuring. Specifically, your response indicates that the John Jackson (related party) stock pledge of 4,400,000 shares served as adequate compensation for the decrease in interest rate and extension of the loan repayment. However, it is unclear how the stock pledge compensates the Company for the substantial reduction in interest rate for the modified contractual period. Provide your analysis for determining that the collateral served as adequate compensation, particularly since Jackson had already provided guaranties on the loan prior to the modification. Additionally, provide your analysis as to whether you believe the modified interest rate resulted in a market rate of interest for the loan.
- **Imputation of interest:** Please tell us the authoritative accounting literature management relied upon to account for the option sale proceeds as a loan discount that will be recognized as interest income over the term of the loan.

PRESENTATION AND DISCLOSURE REQUIREMENTS

Presentation

The codification permits loans and trade receivables to be reported in the aggregate. However, major categories must be presented separately on the balance sheet or in the notes. Those held for sale must be reported separately on the balance sheet. Allowances for doubtful accounts should be shown as reductions of the related receivables, as should unearned discounts (except for cash or quantity discounts), finance charges, and prepaid interest.

Receivables should be reported as part of the related loan balance. The unamortized balance of loan origination, commitment, and other fees and costs and purchase premiums and discounts recognized as an adjustment of yield should be reported on the balance sheet as part of the loan balance to which it relates. (FASB ASC 310-20-45-1)

Amounts of loan origination, commitment, and other fees and costs recognized as an adjustment to yield should be reported as part of interest income. Amortization of other fees being amortized on a straight-line basis over the commitment period or included in income when the commitment expires should be reported as service fee income. (FASB ASC 310-20-45-3)

Disclosures

For loans and trade receivables, he summary of significant accounting policies should include:

- The basis for accounting.
- The method used in determining lower of amortized cost or fair value of nonmortgage loans held for sale.
- The classification and method of accounting for interest-only strips, loans, other receivables, or retained interest in securitizations that can be contractually prepaid or otherwise settled in a way that the holder would not recover substantially all of its recorded investment.
- The method for recognizing interest income on loan and trade receivables, including a statement about the entity's policy for treatment of related fees and costs, including the method of amortizing net deferred fees or cost.
  (ASC 310-10-50-2)

ASC 310 contains many other detailed presentation and disclosure requirements. For complete presentation and disclosure requirements for the guidance covered in this chapter, see the *Disclosure and Presentation Checklist for Commercial Businesses* at www.wiley.com/go/FSDM2021.

PRESENTATION AND DISCLOSURE EXAMPLES

Example 16.1: Summary of Significant Accounting Policies—Accounts Receivable and Allowance for Doubtful Accounts

We review our accounts receivable balance routinely to identify any specific customers with collectability issues. In circumstances where we are aware of a specific customer's inability to meet its financial obligation to us, we record a specific allowance for doubtful accounts (with the offsetting expense charged to selling and distribution expenses in our Consolidated Statements of Operations) against the amounts due, reducing the net recognized receivable to the amount we estimate will be collected.

Example 16.2: Significant Accounting Policies—Accounts Receivable

Substantially all of our trade accounts receivable is due from customers located within the United States. We maintain an allowance for doubtful accounts for estimated losses resulting from the inability of our customers to make required payments. The allowance for doubtful accounts is based on a review of specifically identified accounts in addition to an overall aging analysis. Judgments are made with respect to the collectibility of accounts receivable based on historical experience and current economic trends. Actual losses could differ from those estimates.

Example 16.3: Allowance for Doubtful Accounts—Accounting Policies and Estimates

We maintain an allowance for doubtful accounts for estimated losses resulting from the inability of our customers to make required payments. Our accounts receivable reserves were $423 and $351 at December 31, 20X9 and December 31, 20X8, respectively, representing 4.7% and 4.8% of our gross accounts receivable balances at those dates, respectively. The allowance for doubtful accounts is based on a review of specifically identified customer accounts in addition to an overall aging analysis. We evaluate the collectability of our receivables from our licensees and other customers on a quarterly basis based on factors such as their financial condition, our collateral position, potential future plans with licensees and other similar factors. Our allowance for doubtful accounts represents our best estimate of potential losses on our accounts and notes receivable and is adjusted accordingly based on historical experience, current developments, and present economic conditions and trends. Although actual losses have not differed materially from our previous estimates, future losses could differ from our current estimates. Unforeseen events such as a licensee or customer bankruptcy filing could have a material impact on our results of operations.

Example 16.4: Concentrations of Credit Risk and Major Customers

Financial instruments that subject us to credit risk consists primarily of investments, accounts and notes receivable and financial guarantees. Investments are managed within established guidelines to mitigate risks. Accounts and notes receivable and financial guarantees subject us to credit risk partially due to the concentration of amounts due from and guaranteed on behalf of independent licensee customers. At December 31, 20X9 and December 31, 20X8, our aggregate exposure from receivables and guarantees related to customers consisted of the following:

	20X9	*20X8*
Accounts receivable, net of allowances (Note 5)	$10,689	$9,527.5
Contingent obligations under lease and loan guarantees, less amounts recognized (Note 16)	875.5	997.5
Other	84	—
Total credit risk exposure related to customers	$11,648.5	$10,525

At December 31, 20X9 and December 31, 20X8, approximately 28% and 33%, respectively, of the aggregate risk exposure, net of reserves, shown above was attributable to five customers. In fiscal 20X9, 20X8, and 20X7, no customer accounted for more than 10% of total consolidated net sales. However, two customers accounted for approximately 44%, 40%, and 47% of our consolidated revenue from logistical services during 20X9, 20X8, and 20X7, respectively.

Example 16.5: Sale of Receivables Program

Iconic has an arrangement with three financial institutions to sell certain customer receivables without recourse on a revolving basis. The sale of such receivables is completed using a bankruptcy remote special purpose entity, which is a consolidated subsidiary of Iconic. This arrangement provides up to a maximum funding of $400 for receivables sold. Iconic maintains a beneficial interest, or a right to collect cash, on the sold receivables that have not been funded (deferred purchase program). On March 30, 20X2, Iconic initially sold $304 of customer receivables in exchange for $50 in cash and $254 of deferred purchase program under the arrangement. Iconic has received additional net cash funding of $300 ($3,558 in draws and $3,258 in repayments) since the program's inception, including net cash draws totaling $0 ($600 in draws and $600 in repayments) in 20X9 and net cash draws totaling $0 ($600 in draws and $600 in repayments) in 20X8.

As of December 31, 20X9 and 20X8, the deferred purchase program receivable was $246 and $234, respectively, which was included in other receivables on the accompanying consolidated balance sheet. The deferred purchase program receivable is reduced as collections of the underlying receivables occur; however, as this is a revolving program, the sale of new receivables will result in an increase in the deferred purchase program receivable. The gross amount of receivables sold and total cash collected under this program since its inception was $48,383 and $47,787, respectively. Iconic services the customer receivables for the financial institutions at market rates; therefore, no servicing asset or liability was recorded. In 20X9 and 20X8, the gross cash outflows and inflows associated with the deferred purchase program receivable were $6,599 and $6,586, respectively, and $6,375 and $6,328, respectively.

Cash receipts from customer payments on sold receivables (which are cash receipts on the underlying trade receivables that have been previously sold in this program) as well as cash receipts and cash disbursements from draws and repayments under the program are presented as cash receipts from sold receivables within investing activities in the statement of consolidated cash flows.

On January 2, 20X0, the Company entered into an amendment to remove subsidiaries of the GRP business from the sale of receivables program in preparation for the planned Separation of Iconic and repurchased the remaining $282 unpaid receivables of GRP customers in a noncash transaction by reducing the amount of the deferred purchase program receivable.

Allowance for Doubtful Accounts The following table details the changes in the allowance for doubtful accounts related to customer receivables and other receivables:

	Customer Receivables			Other Receivables		
	20X9	*20X8*	*20X7*	*20X9*	*20X8*	*20X7*
Balance at beginning of year	$4	$8	$13	$31	$34	$32
Provision for doubtful accounts	3	2	1	13	7	9
Write-off of uncollectible accounts	(2)	(2)	(5)	(2)	(2)	(1)
Recoveries of prior write-offs	—	—	—	(5)	(3)	(3)
Other	(2)	(4)	(1)	(4)	(5)	(3)
Balance at end of year	$3	$4	$8	$33	$31	$34

Example 16.6: Accounts Receivable Detail

Accounts receivable consists of the following:

	December 31, 20X9	*December 31, 20X8*
Gross accounts receivable	$ 11,100	$ 9,400
Allowance for doubtful accounts	(410)	(750)
Net accounts receivable	$ 10,490	$ 8,650

(In thousands, except share and per share data)

Activity in the allowance for doubtful accounts was as follows:

	20X9	*20X8*
Balance, beginning of the year	$375	$308
Acquired allowance on accounts receivable (Note 3)	—	25
Additions charged to expense	30	170
Reductions to allowance, net	—	(252)
Balance, end of the year	$405	$377

We believe that the carrying value of our net accounts receivable approximates fair value. The inputs into these fair value estimates reflect our market assumptions and are not observable. Consequently, the inputs are considered to be Level 3 as specified in the fair value hierarchy in ASC Topic 820, *Fair Value Measurements and Disclosures*. See Note 4.

Example 16.7: Schedule of Trade and Other Accounts Receivables

The components of ToolKit's trade and other accounts receivable as of 20X9 and 20X8 year-end are as follows:

(Amounts in millions)	*20X9*	*20X8*
Trade and other accounts receivable	$357.75	$355.05
Less: Allowances for doubtful accounts	(10.45)	(8.75)
Total trade and other accounts receivable—net	$347.3	$346.3

Example 16.8: Finance and Contract Receivables

The components of Toolkit's current finance and contract receivables as of 20X9 and 20X8 year-end are as follows:

(Amounts in millions)	*20X9*	*20X8*
Finance installment receivables	$255.95	$249.5
Finance lease receivables, net of unearned finance charges of $11.7 million and $11.4 million, respectively	18.95	19.55
Total finance receivables	$274.9	$269.05
Contract installment receivables	$25.4	$24.45
Contract lease receivables, net of unearned finance charges of $18.2 million and $18.4 million, respectively	25.7	25.3
Total contract receivables	51.1	49.75
Total	$326.0	$318.8
Allowances for doubtful accounts:		
Finance installment receivables	$(9.6)	$(9.5)
Finance lease receivables	(0.25)	(0.3)
Total finance allowance for doubtful accounts	(9.85)	(9.8)
Contract installment receivables	(0.25)	(0.2)
Contract lease receivables	(0.5)	(0.4)
Total contract allowance for doubtful accounts	$(0.75)	$(0.6)
Total allowance for doubtful accounts	(10.6)	(10.4)
Total current finance and contract receivables—net	315.4	308.4
Finance receivables—net	$265.05	$259.25
Contract receivables—net	50.35	49.15
Total current finance and contract receivables—net	$315.4	$308.4

Example 16.9: Noncurrent Receivables

The components of ToolKit's finance and contract receivables with payment terms beyond one year as of 20X9 and 20X8 year-end are as follows:

(Amounts in millions)	*20X9*	*20X8*
Finance installment receivables	$ 553.0	$540.05
Finance lease receivables, net of unearned finance charges of $8.2 million and $6.7 million, respectively	19.85	18.05
Total finance receivables	572.85	558.1
Contract installment receivables	$97.75	$95.3
Contract lease receivables, net of unearned finance charges of $29.4 million and $27.8 million, respectively	84.35	78.7
Total contract receivables	171.1	174.0
Total finance and contract receivables	754.95	732.1
Allowances for doubtful accounts:		
Finance installment receivables	(20.8)	(20.65)
Finance lease receivables	(0.3)	(0.25)
Total finance allowance for doubtful accounts	(21.1)	(20.9)
Contract installment receivables	(0.9)	(0.75)

Contract lease receivables	(1.15)	(0.8)
Total contract allowance for doubtful accounts	(2.05)	(1.55)
Total allowance for doubtful accounts	(23.15)	(22.45)
Total current finance and contract receivables—net	$731.8	$709.65
Finance receivables—net	$551.75	$537.2
Contract receivables—net	180.05	172.45
Total current finance and contract receivables—net	$731.8	$709.65

Example 16.10: Schedule of Long-Term Finance and Contract Receivables

Long-term finance and contract receivables installments, net of unearned finance charges, as of end are scheduled as follows:

	20X9		20X8	
(Amounts in millions)	**Finance Receivables**	**Contract Receivables**	**Finance Receivables**	**Contract Receivables**
Due in Months:				
13–24	$219.55	$43.2	$214.35	$41.1
25–36	$176.2	$38.45	$172.5	$36.25
37–48	$119.0	$32.8	$116.4	$30.25
49–60	$58.1	$25.65	$54.85	$24.4
Thereafter	—	$42.0	—	$42.0
Total	$572.85	$182.1	$558.1	$174.0

Example 16.11: Financing Receivable, Past Due

The aging of Finance and contract receivables as of 20X9 and 20X8 year-end is as follows:

(Amounts in millions)	**30–59 Days Past Due**	**60–90 Days Past Due**	**Greater Than 90 Days Past Due**	**Total Past Due**	**Total Not Past Due**	**Total**	**Greater Than 90 Days Past Due and Accruing**
20X9 year-end:							
Finance receivables	$9.85	$6.0	$10.7	$26.55	$821.2	$847.75	$8.6
Contract receivables	0.75	0.45	0.75	1.95	231.25	233.2	0.25
20X8 year-end:							
Finance receivables	$9.4	$6.05	$10.15	$25.9	$801.25	$827.15	7.95
Contract receivables	0.85	0.6	2.6	4.05	219.7	233.75	0.1

Example 16.12: Financing Receivable Credit Quality Indicators

The amount of performing and nonperforming finance and contract receivables based on payment activity as of year-end as follows:

(Amounts in millions)	*Finance Receivables*	*Contract Receivables*	*Finance Receivables*	*Contract Receivables*
Performing	$833.05	$231.85	$813.2	$220.75
Nonperforming	14.7	1.38	13.95	3.0
Total	$847.75	$233.2	$827.55	$223.75

Example 16.13: Financing Receivable, Nonaccrual

The amount of finance and contract receivables on nonaccrual status as of year-end is as follows:

(Amounts in millions)		
Finance receivables	$6.1	$6.0
Contract receivables	1.1	2.9

Example 16.14: Financing Receivable, Allowance for Credit Loss

The following is a roll-forward of the allowances for doubtful accounts for finance and contract receivables for 20X9 and 20X8:

	20X9		*20X8*	
Amounts in millions	*Finance Receivables*	*Contract Receivables*	*Finance Receivables*	*Contract Receivables*
Allowances for doubtful accounts				
Beginning of year	$ 30.7	$ 2.15	$ 28.25	$ 2.3
Provisions	24.95	(2.35)	(28.75)	(1)
Charge-offs	(28.55)	(1.96)	(29.2)	(1.25)
Recoveries	3.85	.25	3.55	.2
Currency translation	—	—	(.15)	(.1)
End of year	$ 30.95	$ 2.8	$ 30.7	$ 2.15

Example 16.15: Roll-forward of Combined Allowances for Doubtful Accounts Related to Trade and Other Accounts Receivable

The following is a roll-forward of the combined allowances for doubtful accounts related to trade and other accounts receivable as well as finance and contract receivables for 20X9, 20X8, and 20X7:

(Amounts in millions)	Balance at Beginning of Year	Expenses	Deductions*	Balance at End of Year
Allowances for doubtful accounts				
20X9	$41.6	$34.1	$(31.5)	$44.2
20X8	37.85	35.15	(31.4)	41.6
20X7	33.25	32.55	(27.95)	37.85

* Represents write-offs of bad debts, net of recoveries, and the net impact of currency translation.

Example 16.16: Accounting Policy—Troubled Debt Restructuring

A restructuring of debt is considered a TDR when (i) the borrower is experiencing financial difficulties and (ii) the creditor grants a concession, such as forgiveness of principal, reduction of the interest rate, changes in payments, or extension of the maturity, that it would not otherwise consider. Loans are not classified as TDRs when the modification is short-term or results in only an insignificant delay or shortfall in the payments to be received. The Company's TDRs are determined on a case-by-case basis in connection with ongoing loan collection processes.

The Company does not accrue interest on any TDRs unless it believes collection of all principal and interest under the modified terms is reasonably assured. For TDRs to accrue interest, the borrower must demonstrate both some level of past performance and the capacity to perform under the modified terms. Generally, six months of consecutive payment performance by the borrower under the restructured terms is required before TDRs are returned to accrual status. However, the period could vary depending on the individual facts and circumstances of the loan. An evaluation of the borrower's current creditworthiness is used to assess whether the borrower has the capacity to repay the loan under the modified terms. This evaluation includes an estimate of expected cash flows, evidence of strong financial position, and estimates of the value of collateral, if applicable.

Example 16.17: Accounting Policy—Troubled Debt Restructuring with Details

Troubled debt restructurings include loans with respect to which concessions have been granted to borrowers that generally would not have otherwise been considered had the borrowers not been experiencing financial difficulty. The concessions granted may include payment schedule modifications, interest rate reductions, maturity date extensions, modifications of note structure, principal balance reductions or some combination of these concessions. There were no loans modified with concessions granted during the years ended December 31, 20X9 or 20X8. Restructured loans may involve loans remaining on nonaccrual, moving to nonaccrual or continuing on accrual status, depending on the individual facts and circumstances of the borrower. Nonaccrual restructured loans are included with all other nonaccrual loans. In addition, all accruing restructured loans are reported as troubled debt restructurings. Generally, restructured loans remain on nonaccrual until the customer has attained a sustained period of repayment performance under the modified loan terms (generally a minimum of six months). However, performance prior to the restructuring, or significant events that coincide with the restructuring, are considered in assessing whether the borrower can meet the new terms and whether the loan should be returned to or maintained on nonaccrual status. If the borrower's ability to meet the revised payment schedule is not reasonably assured, then the loan remains on nonaccrual. As of December 31, 20X9 and 20X8, the Company had $16 thousand and $65 thousand, respectively, of nonaccruing loans that were previously restructured and that remained on nonaccrual status. For both of the years ended December 31, 20X9 and 20X8, the Company had no loans that were restored to accrual status based on a sustained period of repayment performance.

The following table provides, as of December 31, 20X9 and 20X8, the number of loans remaining in each loan category that the Bank had previously modified in a troubled debt restructuring, as well as the pre- and post-modification principal balance as of each date.

	December 31, 20X9			December 31, 20X8		
		Pre-Modification Outstanding	*Post-Modification*		*Pre-Modification Outstanding*	*Post-Modification*
	Number of Loans	*Principal Balance*	*Principal Balance*	*Number of Loans*	*Principal Balance*	*Principal Balance*
	(Dollars in Thousands)					
Loans secured by real estate:						
Construction, land development and other land loans	1	$107	$62	1	$107	$73
Secured by 1–4 family residential properties	2	59	14	3	318	118
Secured by nonfarm, nonresidential properties	–	–	–	1	53	34
Commercial loans	2	116	60	2	116	72
Total	5	$282	$136	7	$594	$297

As of December 31, 20X9 and 20X8, no loans that previously had been modified in a troubled debt restructuring had defaulted subsequent to modification.

Restructured loan modifications primarily included maturity date extensions and payment schedule modifications. There were no modifications to principal balances of the loans that were restructured. Accordingly, there was no impact on the Company's allowance for loan losses resulting from the modifications.

All loans with a principal balance of $0.5 million or more that have been modified in a troubled debt restructuring are considered impaired and evaluated individually for impairment. The nature and extent of impairment of restructured loans, including those that have experienced a subsequent payment default, are considered in the determination of an appropriate level of allowance for loan losses. This evaluation resulted in an allowance for loan losses attributable to such restructured loans of $1,000 and $2,000 as of December 31, 20X9 and 20X8, respectively.

17 ASC 320 INVESTMENTS—DEBT SECURITIES

TECHNICAL ALERTS

The FASB has an ongoing financial instruments project. As part of this project, the FASB issued the following updates:

- ASU 2016-13, *Financial Instruments—Credit Losses (Topic 326): Measurement of Credit Losses on Financial Instruments*
- ASU 2018-09, *Codification Improvements to Topic 326, Financial Instruments— Credit Losses*
- ASU 2019-04, *Codification Improvements to Topic 326, Financial Instruments— Credit Losses, Topic 815, Derivatives and Hedging, and Topic 825, Financial Instruments* and
- ASU 2019-05, *Financial Instruments—Credit Losses (Topic 326): Targeted Transition Relief*

- ASU 2019-10, *Financial Instruments—Credit Losses (Topic 326), Derivatives and Hedging (Topic 815), and Leases (Topic 842): Effective Dates.*

These are discussed below.

ASU 2019-10

Guidance Regarding Effective Dates In November 2019, The FASB issued ASU 2019-10, *Financial Instruments—Credit Losses (Topic 326), Derivatives and Hedging (Topic 815), and Leases (Topic 842: Effective Dates.* The ASU grants private companies, not-for-profit organizations, and certain small public company SEC filers additional time to implement recent FASB standards on current expected credit losses (CECL).

ASU 2019-10 Effective Dates		
Topic	*Public Business Entities That Meet the Definition of SEC Filers, Except Smaller Reporting Companies (SRCs) as Defined by the SEC**	*All Other Entities*
CECL (ASC 326)	Fiscal years beginning after December 15, 2019	Fiscal years beginning after December 15, 2022

* *Includes Employee Benefit Plans and NFP Conduit Bond Obligors that file with the SEC or furnish financial statements to the SEC.*

The ASUs in this chapter that are affected are:

- ASU 2016-13, *Financial Instruments—Credit Losses (Topic 326): Measurement of Credit Losses on Financial Instruments,*
- ASU 2018-19, *Codification Improvements to Topic 326, Financial Instruments—Credit Losses,*
- ASU 2019-04, *Codification Improvements to Topic 326, Financial Instruments—Credit Losses, Topic 815, Derivatives and Hedging, and Topic 825, Financial Instruments,* and
- ASU 2019-05, *Financial Instruments—Credit Losses (Topic 326): Targeted Transition Relief*

ASU 2016-13

In June 2016, the FASB issued ASU 2016-13, *Financial Instruments—Credit Losses (Topic 326): Measurement of Credit Losses on Financial Instruments.* This ASU makes changes to several topics, and adds a new topic—ASC 326. The primary coverage can be found in the chapter on ASC 326. This Technical Alert covers the changes related to ASC 320.

Guidance Related to ASC 320 The ASU created a current expected credit loss (CECL) model in ASC 326-20 that replaces the impairment guidance in ASC 310-10. However, the FASB decided that the CECL model should not apply to available-for-sale (AFS) debt securities. The ASU instead made targeted amendments to the current AFS debt security impairment model and placed the new guidance in a new subtopic, ASC 326-30. This will result in entities using different impairment models for AFS debt securities and those that are classified as held to maturity.

The amendments do not apply to an AFS debt security that the entity intends to sell or will likely be required to sell before the recovery of the amortized cost basis. In those cases, the entity would write down the debt security's amortized cost to the debt security's fair value as required under existing GAAP.

AFS Debt Securities		
Item	*Existing Guidance*	*New, ASU 2016-13 Guidance*
Credit losses	Recognize impairment as a reduction of the cost basis of the investment.	Recognize an allowance for credit losses. The allowance is limited by the amount that the fair value is less than the amortized cost basis.
Improvements in estimated credit losses	Recognize improvements in earnings as a reduction in the allowance and credit loss expense.	Prospectively recognize as interest income over time.

In addition, the ASU eliminates "other-than-temporary" impairment (OTTI). The new guidance focuses on determining whether unrealized losses are credit losses or whether they are caused by other factors. Therefore, the entity cannot use the length of time a security has been in an unrealized loss position as a factor to conclude that a credit loss does not exist. Also, when assessing whether a credit loss exists, the entity may not consider recoveries in fair value after the balance sheet date.

Disclosures The ASU retains the existing AFS debt security disclosure requirements, but amends them to reflect the use of an allowance for credit losses and the elimination of the OTTI concept. The new guidance also requires some new disclosures. Entities will have to disclose a tabular roll forward of the allowance account and to disclose their accounting policy for recognizing write-offs.

Effective Date See the information in ASU 2019-10 above.

Early adoption is allowed for all entities for fiscal years beginning after December 15, 2018, including interim periods therein. (ASC 326-10-65-1)

Also, please see the information below on ASU 2019-05.

Transition Method Except where noted in the following table, entities should use a modified-retrospective approach and record a cumulative-effect adjustment to retained earnings as of the beginning of the first reporting period that the entity adopts the guidance. For example, a calendar-year private company that adopts the standard in 2022 records the cumulative effect adjustment on January 1, 2022. The transition adjustment includes those adjustments made as a result of an entity amending its accounting policy if it adopts the amendments in ASU 2019-04 related to determining when accrued interest receivables are deemed uncollectible and written off. Also, see the information below on ASU 2019-05 for an option to select the fair value option.

Prospective Transition Approach Required	
Circumstance	*Accounting Treatment*
Debt securities for which an OTTI was recognized before the adoption date	If amounts relate to improvements in cash flows expected to be collected, continue to accrete into income over the remaining life of the asset. If cash flows improve because of improvements in credit after the adoption date, record in the income statement in the period received. If cash flows are expected to decrease because of deterioration in credit expectations, record an allowance.
Assets previously accounted for as PCD (purchased financial assets with credit deterioration)	Adjust the amortized cost basis on adoption to reflect the addition of the allowance for credit losses on the transition date. Continue to accrete or amortize, at the effective interest rate at the adoption date, the remaining noncredit discount or premium. Apply the same transition requirements to beneficial interests that previously applied the PCD model or have a significant difference between contractual cash flows and expected cash flows.
(ASC 326-10-65-1)	

ASU 2018-19

In November 2018, the FASB issued ASU 2018-19, *Codification Improvements to Topic 326, Financial Instruments—Credit Losses*. ASU 2018-19 affects this chapter by changing the effective date of ASU 2016-13 for nonpublic entities. Those changes are reflected in the effective dates above. Also, for an option to use the fair value option, see the information on ASU 2019-05 below.

ASU 2019-04

In April 2019, the FASB issued *Codification Improvements to Topic 326, Financial Instruments— Credit Losses, Topic 815, Derivatives and Hedging, and Topic 825, Financial Instruments*. Issue 1B of the ASU provides revised guidance on how an entity should account for transfer of debt securities between categories. The changes require that an entity:

- Reverse in earnings any allowance for credit losses or valuation allowances that had been previously measured on a debt security category,
- Reclassify and transfer the debt security to the new category, and
- Apply the applicable measurement guidance in accordance with the new category.

ASU 2019-04 has the same effective dates as ASU 2016-13 explained above. The ASC 320 amendments in ASU 2019-04 are noted in this chapter.

ASU 2019-05

In May 2019, the FASB issued ASU 2019-05, *Financial Instruments—Credit Losses (Topic 326): Targeted Transition Relief.*

Guidance This Update provides an option to irrevocably elect the fair value option for certain financial assets previously measured at amortized cost basis. The FASB expects this amendment to increase comparability because it aligns measurement methodologies for similar financial assets. This option is available to reporting entities within the scope of ASC 326. The new option may be applied on an instrument-by-instrument basis for eligible instruments. Note that this option *does not* apply to held-to-maturity debt securities. An entity that applies the fair value option should then apply the guidance in ASC 820-10 and ASC 825-10. (ASC 326-10-65-3)

For entities that have not yet adopted ASU 2016-13, provisions of ASU 2019-04 related to ASC 320 have the same effective dates as ASU 2016-13. For those entities that have adopted ASU 2016-13, the provisions one effective for fiscal years beginning after December 15, 2019, including interim periods within those fiscal years. Early adoption is permitted in any interim period if the entity has adopted ASU 2016-13.

Transition For entities that have not yet implemented ASU 2016-13, the effective date and transition methodology in ASU 2019-05 are the same as ASU 2016-13. For entities that have adopted ASU 2016-13, ASU 2019-05 is effective for fiscal years beginning after December 15, 2019, including interim periods within those fiscal years. Those entities may early adopt in any of the interim periods.

Entities should adopt the changes using a modified-retrospective basis by means of a cumulative-effect adjustment to the opening balance of retained earnings balance as of the date the entity adopted ASU 2016-13.

AUTHORITATIVE LITERATURE

ASC 320, *Investments—Debt Securities*, contains one Subtopic:

- ASC 320-10, *Overall*, which contains guidance for all investments in debt securities. (ASC 320-10-05-1)

ASC 320 classifies debt securities into one of three categories:

1. Held-to-maturity,
2. Trading, or
3. Available-for-sale.

Classification of Debt Securities

Classification is made and documented at the time of the initial acquisition of each investment. (ASC 320-10-25-1 and 2) The appropriateness of classification is reassessed at each reporting date. (ASC 320-10-35-5) ASC 320 requires all debt securities to be placed into one of three categories. Their characteristics and accounting and reporting requirements are summarized in the exhibit below and the discussion that follows.

Exhibit—Classification and Measurement of Debt Securities

Category	Characteristics	Reported Subsequently on Statement of Financial Position	Reported in Income
Held-to-maturity	Positive intent and ability to hold until maturity	Amortized cost	Interest and dividends, including amortization of premiums and discounts arising at acquisition. Realized gains and losses. (Unrealized gains and losses are not recognized.) A transaction gain or loss on a foreign-currency-denominated held-to-maturity security is accounted for according to ASC 830-20.
Trading	Bought and held principally to sell short-term.	Fair value.	Interest and dividends, including amortization of premium and discount arising at acquisition. Realized gains and losses. Unrealized gains and losses when realized. Changes in fair value.
Available-for-sale	Neither held-to-maturity nor trading securities. Have readily determinable fair value.	Fair value as current assets. Unrealized gains and losses in accumulated other comprehensive income as a component of equity. If designated as a fair value hedge, all or a portion of the unrealized gain or loss should be recognized in earnings.	Interest and dividends, including amortization of premium and discount arising at acquisition. Realized gains and losses. Unrealized holding gains and losses in OCI, except for those designated as a hedged in a fair value ledge.

Source: ASC 320-10-25-4, 35-1, and 35-4.

Transfers between Categories ASC 320 includes provisions intended to curtail management manipulation of income through careful selection of portfolio securities to be sold, a practice commonly known as "gains trading" and primarily used by financial institutions.

Exhibit—Transfers of Debt Securities between Categories: Accounting Treatment for Unrealized Holding Gains or Losses—Before Implementation of ASU 2019-04

From	To	Accounting Treatment for Unrealized Holding Gains or Losses
Trading	AFS or HTM	Fair value at date of transfer. Do not reverse unrealized gain or loss already recognized.
AFS or HTM	Trading	Recognize in income those not already recognized. Transfers into or from the trading category should be rare.
HTM	AFS	Recognize in OCI per ASC 320-10-35-10c Few transfers are expected from the HTM category.
AFS	HTM	Continue to report in a separate component of shareholders' equity, such as AOCI, but amortize over the remaining life of the security as an adjustment of yield.
(ASC 320-10-35-10)		

Exhibit—Transfers of Debt Securities between Categories After Implementation of ASU 2019-04

From	To	Accounting Treatment
Trading	AFS or HTM	Fair value at date of transfer. Do not reverse unrealized gain or loss already recognized.
AFS or HTM	Trading	Recognize in earnings any unrealized gain or loss not previously recognized in earnings.
HTM	AFS	Reverse in earnings any allowance for credit losses on the HTM security previously recorded. Transfer at amortized port. Determine if an allowance for credit losses is necessary under ASC 326-30. Report in OCI any unrealized gain or loss on the AFS security, excluding the amount recorded for credit losses. Consider whether the transfer calls into question management's intent to hold to maturity the remaining securities.
AFS	HTM	Reverse in earnings any allowance for credit losses previously recorded on the AFS security. Transfer the AFS security at amortized cost basis net of any unrealized gain or loss reported in AOCI. Determine if an allowance for credit losses is necessary under ASC 326-30. Continue to report the holding gain or loss in a separate component of stockholders' equity such as AOCI. Amortize unrealized holding gain or loss over the life of the security as arrangements of yield.
(ASC 320-10-35-10, 10A, 35-10B)		

PRACTICE ALERT

While SEC rules only apply to public entities, preparers of financial statements can benefit from the findings of SEC reviewers. Investments are a frequent topic of SEC comment letters. Determining when an investment is other-than-temporarily-impaired requires significant judgment. Neither the SEC nor the FASB offer definitive guidelines. The SEC commonly requests:

- Support for the preparer's conclusion that unrealized losses are temporary.
- Information on how the preparer determined which period to report the impairment.
- More transparent disclosures
- Basis for determining that unrealized losses are recoverable.
- How entities separate their OTTI losses on debt securities between credit and noncredit components.

Entities would be prudent to document how their conclusions were reached.

When certain areas of the world economy experience volatility, the SEC has focused on disclosures related to holdings of sovereign debt issued by countries experiencing financial difficulty. Debt securities issued in those areas experiencing economic volatility need a careful evaluation.

PRESENTATION AND DISCLOSURE REQUIREMENTS

Presention Requirements

Balance Sheet Entities should report financial assets separately by measurement category and form of financial asset. (ASC 825-10-45-1A) Assets measured at fair value should be presented separately from similar assets measured at amortized cost. (ASC 320-10-45-1) Therefore, the entity should present either:

- The aggregate amounts in the same line item with parenthetical disclosure of the fair value amount in the aggregate amount, or
- The fair value and non–fair value amounts in two separate time items.

Entities should report debt securities categorized as trading or AFS as current or as noncurrent based on their maturities or whether they represent investments available for current operations. HTM debt securities are classified as current or noncurrent based on their current maturity or call dates. Excluded from the definition of current assets are investments made for the purposes of control, affiliation, or other continuing business advantage. (ASC 210-10-45-4)

Generally, activity in cash equivalents may be reported as a net change. However, if the cash equivalent is a security, it is subject to the guidance in ASC 320. If they are disclosed in the notes, individual amounts for the three categories of investments do *not* have to be presented on the face of the statement of financial position. So, for example, entities that report some debt securities as cash equivalents in accordance with ASC 210 may do so as long as the notes reconcile the reporting classifications. (ASC 320-10-45-13)

Income Statement Income statement presentation can be found in the exhibit "Classification and Measurement of Debt Securities" earlier in this chapter.

Statement of Cash Flows The table below summarizes the cash flow presentation of debt and equity securities as detailed in ASC 320-10-45-11.

Classification of Security	Transaction	Cash Flow Statement Presentation
AFS, HTM	Purchases, sales, and maturities	Investing activity Gross for each security classification
Trading	Purchases, sales, and maturities	Based on the nature and purpose for which the securities were acquired

Disclosure Requirements

AFS Securities The disclosures for investments in debt and equity securities are required for all interim and annual periods. (ASC 320-10-50-1A) ASC 320 requires entities to consider whether securities should be disaggregated based on characteristics such as geographic concentrations, credit quality, or economic characteristics. (ASC 320-10-50-1B)

For AFS debit securities, the entity should disclose by major security types:

- Amortized cost basis.
- Aggregate fair value.
- Upon implementation of ASU 2016-13, total allowance for credit losses.
- Total OTTI recognized in AOCI.
- Total gains for securities with net gains in AOCI.
- Total losses for securities with net losses in AOCI.

The checklist at www.wiley.com/go/FSDM2021 contains detailed presentation and disclosure requirements on the above and other areas, such as reclassifications, HTM securities, securities by maturity date, impairments, credit losses, sales, transfers, etc.

HTM Securities For securities classified as held-to-maturity, the entity must disclose by major security type as of each date for which a statement of financial position is presented:

- Amortized cost basis.
- Upon implementation of ASU 2106-13, total allowance for credit losses.
- Net carrying amount.
- Gross gains and losses in AOCI for any derivatives that hedged the forecasted acquisition of the held-to-maturity securities.
- Information about the contractual maturities of those securities as of the date of the statement of financial position presented. (Maturity information may be combined in appropriate groupings.)
  (FASB ASC 320-10-50-5)

Impairment of Securities For all investments for which there is an unrealized loss where OTTI has not been recognized in earnings, the entity must disclose:

a. Quantitative information in tabular form and aggregated by category of investment under ASC 320, as of the date of each statement of financial position presented.
   1. The aggregate related fair value of investments with unrealized losses.
   2. The aggregate amount of unrealized losses.

Note: The disclosures in (1) and (2) above should be segregated by those investments that have been in a continuous unrealized loss position for less than 12 months and those that have been in a continuous unrealized loss position for 12 months or longer.

---

b. A narrative as of the date of the most recent statement of financial position that provides information that enables the reader of the financial statements to understand the disclosures in a. above, as well as both the positive and negative information that the investor considered in reaching the conclusion that the impairment is not other than temporary.

Note: These disclosures may be aggregated by investment category; however, individually significant unrealized losses should not be aggregated.

---

c. Other evidence considered by the investor in concluding that the impairment is not other than temporary (e.g., reports from industry analysts, sector credit ratings, volatility data regarding the fair value of the security, and/or any other relevant information that the investor considered).
(ASC 320-10-50-6 and 7)[1]

For each period in which an OTTI of a debt security is recognized and only the amount related to a credit loss was recognized in earnings, the entity must disclose by major security type, the methodology and significant inputs used to measure the amount related to credit loss. Examples of significant inputs include, but are not limited to, all of the following:

- Performance indicators of the underlying assets in the security, including all of the following:
  ○ Default rates.
  ○ Delinquency rates.
  ○ Percentage of nonperforming assets.
- Loan-to-collateral-value ratios.
- Third-party guarantees.
- Current levels of subordination.
- Vintage.
- Geographic concentration.
- Credit ratings.
(FASB ASC 320-10-5-8A)[2]

For each period presented, the entity must present in the notes a tabular roll forward of the amount related to credit losses recognized in earnings in accordance with paragraph 320-10-35-34D, which include at a minimum:

- The beginning balance of the amount related to credit losses on debt securities held by the entity at the beginning of the period for which a portion of an other-than-temporary impairment was recognized in other comprehensive income.
- Additions for the amount related to the credit loss for which an other-than-temporary impairment was not previously recognized.
- Reductions for securities sold during the period.
- Reductions for securities for which the amount previously recognized in other comprehensive income was recognized in earnings because the entity intends to sell the security or more likely than not will be required to sell the security before recovery of its amortized cost basis.

---

[1] Upon implementation of ASU 2016-13, these paragraphs are superseded.
[2] Ibid.

- If the entity does not intend to sell the security and it is not more likely than not that the entity will be required to sell the security before recovery of its amortized cost basis, additional increases to the amount related to the credit loss for which an other-than-temporary impairment was previously recognized.
- Reductions for increases in cash flows expected to be collected that are recognized over the remaining life of the security (see paragraph 320-10-35-35).
- The ending balance of the amount related to credit losses on debt securities held by the entity at the end of the period for which a portion of an other-than-temporary impairment was recognized in other comprehensive income.
  (FASB ASC 320-10-50-8B)[3]

PRESENTATION AND DISCLOSURE EXAMPLES

Example 17.1: Recent Accounting Pronouncements

In June 2016, the FASB issued ASU 2016-13, *Financial Instruments—Credit Losses (Topic 326): Measurement of Credit Losses on Financial Instruments*, which creates a new credit impairment standard for financial assets measured at amortized cost and available-for-sale debt securities. The ASU requires financial assets measured at amortized cost (including loans, trade receivables and held-to-maturity debt securities) to be presented at the net amount expected to be collected, through an allowance for credit losses that are expected to occur over the remaining life of the asset, rather than incurred losses. The ASU requires that credit losses on available-for-sale debt securities be presented as an allowance rather than as a direct write-down. The measurement of credit losses for newly recognized financial assets (other than certain purchased assets) and subsequent changes in the allowance for credit losses are recorded in the statement of income as the amounts expected to be collected change. The ASU is effective for public entities for fiscal years beginning after December 15, 2019 [and for all other entities for fiscal years beginning after December 15, 2022]. The Company is currently evaluating the impact of adopting this new guidance on its consolidated financial statements and does not expect the impact to be significant.

Example 17.2: Accounting Policy—Investment in Debt Securities

Investment in Debt Securities. The Company classifies its investments in debt securities as either held-to-maturity or available-for-sale in accordance with Statement of Financial Accounting Standards (SFAS) No. 115, *Accounting for Certain Investments in Debt and Equity Securities,* which was codified into ASC 320. Securities classified as held-to-maturity are recorded at cost or amortized cost. Available-for-sale securities are carried at fair value. Fair value calculations are based on quoted market prices when such prices are available. If quoted market prices are not available, estimates of fair value are computed using a variety of techniques, including extrapolation from the quoted prices of similar instruments or recent trades for thinly traded securities, fundamental analysis, or through obtaining purchase quotes. Due to the subjective nature of the valuation process, it is possible that the actual fair values of these investments could differ from the estimated amounts, thereby affecting the financial position, results of operations and cash flows of the Company. If the estimated value of investments is less than the cost or amortized cost, the Company evaluates whether an event or change in circumstances has occurred that may have a significant adverse effect on the fair value of

---

[3] Ibid.

the investment. If such an event or change has occurred and the Company determines that the impairment is other-than-temporary, a further determination is made as to the portion of impairment that is related to credit loss. The impairment of the investment that is related to the credit loss is expensed in the period in which the event or change occurred. The remainder of the impairment is recorded in other comprehensive income.

Example 17.3: Accounting Policy—Marketable Securities

Marketable securities include available-for-sale debt securities and are recorded at fair value. Cost of securities sold use the first-in, first-out (FIFO) method. The classification of marketable securities as current or non-current is based on the availability for use in current operations. ABC reviews impairments associated with its marketable securities in accordance with the measurement guidance provided by ASC 320, *Investments—Debt Securities*, when determining the classification of the impairment as "temporary" or "other-than-temporary." A temporary impairment charge results in an unrealized loss being recorded in accumulated other comprehensive income as a component of shareholders' equity. Such an unrealized loss does not reduce net income for the applicable accounting period because the loss is not viewed as other-than-temporary. The factors evaluated to differentiate between temporary and other-than-temporary include the projected future cash flows, credit ratings actions, and assessment of the credit quality of the underlying collateral, as well as other factors. Amounts are reclassified out of accumulated other comprehensive income and into earnings upon sale or "other-than-temporary" impairment.

Example 17.4: Accounting Policy—Other Than Temporary Investment

Upon acquisition of a security, the Company determines whether it is within the scope of the accounting guidance for investments in debt and equity securities or whether it must be evaluated for impairment under the accounting guidance for beneficial interests in securitized financial assets.

Example 17.5: Credit Losses

Credit Losses Recognized on Investments The Company's investments in trust preferred securities experienced fair value deterioration due to credit losses but were not otherwise other-than-temporarily impaired. The following table provides information about those trust preferred securities for which only a credit loss was recognized in income and other losses were recorded in other comprehensive income (loss) for the years ended December 31, 20X9, 20X8, and 20X7 (in thousands).

	20X9	*20X8*	*20X7*
Credit losses on trust preferred securities held:			
Beginning of period	$ —	$ 1,111	$ 1,111
Additions related to OTTI losses not previously recognized	—	—	—
Reductions due to sales/ (recoveries)	—	(1,111)	—
Reductions due to change in intent or likelihood of sale	—	—	—
Additions related to increases in previously recognized OTTI losses	—	—	—
Reductions due to increase in expected cash flows	—	—	—
End of period	$ —	$ —	$ 1,111

Example 17.6: Maturities of Investment Securities

Maturities of investment securities were as follows at December 31, 20X9 (in thousands):

Available-for-sale	*Amortized Cost*	*Estimated Fair Value*
Due in 1 year or less	$128,892	$129,656
Due after 1–5 years	78,637	80,882
Due after 5–10 years	74,167	77,953
Due after 10 years	1,220	1,431
	282,916	289,922
Mortgage-backed securities: GSE residential	391,307	396,126
Total available-for-sale	674,223	686,048
Held-to-maturity		
Due in 1 year or less	64,511	64,501
Due after 1–5 years	5,031	5,071
Total held-to-maturity	$69,542	$69,572

18 ASC 321 INVESTMENTS— EQUITY SECURITIES

AUTHORITATIVE LITERATURE

An equity security represents:

- An ownership interest in an entity. This may take the form of common, preferred, or other capital stock.
- The right to acquire an ownership interest, for instance, warrants, rights, and call options.
- The right to dispose of an ownership interest at fixed or determinable prices. This includes put options and forward sale contracts.
  (ASC 321-10-20-20)

Subtopic

ASC 321, *Investments—Equity Securities*, contains one Subtopic:

- ASC 321-10, *Overall*, which provides accounting and reporting guidance for investments in equity securities.
  (ASC 321-10-05-2)

Scope and Scope Exceptions

Scope—Entities The guidance in ASC 321 applies to all entities, including entities that are not deemed specialized industries for purposes of this Topic:

- Cooperatives and mutual entities, such as credit unions and mutual insurance entities.
- Trusts that do not report substantially all of their securities at fair value.
  (ASC 321-10-15-2)

Note: The disclosures required by ASC 321-10-50-4 are not required for entities within the scope of ASC 958 on not-for-profit entities.

The guidance does *not* apply to entities in specialized industries that account for substantially all investments at fair value, with changes in value recognized in earnings (income) or in the change in net assets. Examples of those entities are:

- Brokers and dealers in securities (Topic 940).
- Defined benefit pension, other postretirement plans, and health and welfare plans (Topics 960, 962, and 965).
- Investment companies (Topic 946).
  (ASC 321-10-15-3)

Scope—Instruments Included in the scope, as if the ownership interests are equity securities, are ownership interests in an entity, including:

- Investments in partnerships,
- Unincorporated joint ventures, and
- Limited liability corporations.
  (ASC 321-10-15-4)

It also applies to forwards and purchased options to acquire and dispose of ownership interests that are not treated as derivatives in ASC 815, but are accounted for under ASC 321. ASC 815-10-15-141A offers guidance on applying the guidance in ASC 815-10-15-141, to forward contracts and purchased options to purchase securities in ASC 321's scope. (ASC 321-10-15-6)

ASC 321 does *not* apply to any of the following items:

- Derivative instruments subject to the requirements of ASC 815, including those that have been separated from a host contract as required by ASC 815-15-25.
- Investments accounted for under the equity method. (ASC 323)
- Investments in consolidated subsidiaries.
- An ownership interest in an exchange, usually held by broker-dealers and by depository and lending institutions.
- Federal Home Loan Bank Stock. (ASC 942-325)
- Federal Reserve Bank Stock. (ASC 942-325)
  (ASC 321-10-15-5)

Initial Measurement—Investments That No Longer Qualify for the Equity Method

There may be circumstances where the investor's share of the investment no longer qualifies for the equity method. For instance, the level of investment may decline. In those cases, the security's initial basis becomes the carrying value. Any losses accrued remain as part of the carrying value and those related to the investment account are not adjusted retroactively. If the equity method is discontinued, the equity security is remeasured following the guidance in ASC 321-10-35-1 or 35-2. In applying ASC 321-10-35-2 to the investment retained, if the investor identifies observable price changes in transactions for the same or a similar investment by the same issuer that results in the entity discontinuing the equity method, the entity remeasures the retained investment at fair value once it no longer applies ASC 323. (ASC 323-10-30-1)

Subsequent Measurement

Equity Securities with Readily Determinable Fair Value Because, unlike debt securities, equity securities do not have a maturity date, the entity primarily realizes the value of an equity investment through a sale. So, fair value is the most appropriate measure. All equity investments in the scope of ASC 321, with readily determinable fair value, are measured at fair value, using the guidance in ASC 820, with changes in fair value reflected in income. (ASC 321-10-35-1)

Equity Securities without Readily Determinable Fair Values—ASC 820-20 Practical Expedient Some investments that do not have readily determinable fair value as defined in ASC 820-20 may qualify for a practical expedient under ASC 820-10-35-59. If so, they are measured at net asset value, that is, cost minus impairment, plus or minus observable price changes in an orderly transaction for an identical or similar instrument from the same issuer.

This expedient is available to:

- Investment companies within the scope of ASC 946, or
- Real estate funds that use measurement principles consistent with those in ASC 946; if the investment meets those qualifications, the entity may value them at net asset value per share, that is, the amount of net assets attributable to each share of common stock. (ASC 820-10-35-59)

Equity Securities without Readily Determinable Fair Values—ASC 321 Measurement Alternative Fair value through current income is ASC 321's default accounting for equity investments not accounted for using the equity method. However, ASC 321 offers a measurement exception for equity investments without readily determinable fair values. ASC 321 allows some entities to elect the cost method. This method is intended to reflect the fair value of the security as of the date that the observable transaction took place.

Entities following specialized accounting models, such as investment companies and broker-dealers, do not have that option. All others may elect to record these investments at cost, less impairment, adjusted for subsequent price changes. Entities that elect the cost-method option must make changes in the carrying value of the equity investment as of the date that observable price changes occurred:

- In orderly transactions.
- For the identical or similar investment.
- Of the same issuer.
  (ASC 321-10-35-2)

Entities are required to make a reasonable effort to identify reasonably knowable price changes. (ASC 321-10-55-8) This approach eliminates the need for entities to get a valuation every reporting period for equity investments without readily determinable fair values. However, in making its measurement election, the entity should also consider the effort required to identify known or reasonably knowable observable transactions, determine whether those transactions were orderly, and determine if those transactions were for similar investments.

The entity should adjust the observable price of the similar security as of the date the observable transaction took place. Determining whether an equity security is similar requires significant judgment. When making the determination, entities should consider differences in rights and obligations of the securities, such as voting rights, distribution rights and preferences, and conversion features. Differences may indicate either that:

- The observable price should not be used to adjust the value of the security, or
- The observable price should be adjusted to reflect the differences. (ASC 321-10-55-9)

An entity elects the measurement exception on an investment by investment basis. Once elected, it should be applied to an investment consistently as long as the investment meets the qualifying criteria. Each reporting period, the entity must reassess whether an equity investment qualifies for the measurement alternative. (ASC 321-10-35-2) For example, if an investee goes public and there is a readily determinable fair value, the investment must be measured prospectively at fair value using the guidance in ASC 820.

The application of the measurement exception requires professional judgment. Entities would be prudent to document their assessments.

Changes in Measurement Approach An entity that measures an equity security without readily determinable fair value using the ASC 321 measurement exception may change to the ASC 820 expedient through an election. That election is irrevocable and the entity must measure all future purchases of identical or similar investments of the same issuer using the ASC 820 fair value expedient. (ASC 321-10-35-2) To avoid manipulation, the Board believes that just because of difference in purchase dates an entity should not measure the same equity in different ways.

Impairment Model for Equity Securities without Readily Determinable Fair Values An entity must follow the impairment guidance in ASC 321 for an investment without readily determinable fair value if:

- The investment does not qualify for the practical expedient in ASC 820-10-35-59, and
- The entity uses the ASC 321 measurement exception to measure the investment. (ASC 321-10-35-3)

ASC 321 has a single-step, impairment model for equity investments without readily determinable fair values. The single-step model requires the entity to perform a qualitative assessment of impairment each reporting period. If the entity determines impairment exists, it then turns to a quantitative assessment and estimates the fair value of the investment the loss is the difference between the carrying value and the fair value of the investment and is recognized in net income. (ASC 321-10-35-4) Using the single-step model, the entity does not have to predict whether the investment will recover its value.

Impairment Indicators ASC 321 includes the following impairment indicators:

- A significant deterioration in the investee's:
  - Earnings performance,
  - Credit rating,
  - Asset quality, or
  - Business prospects.
- A significant adverse change in the investee's:
  - Regulatory,
  - Economic, or
  - Technological environment.

- A significant adverse change in the general market condition of either the geographical area or the industry in which the investee operates.
- For an amount less than the carrying amount of that investment:
  ○ A bona fide offer to purchase,
  ○ An offer by the investee to sell, or
  ○ A completed auction process for the same or similar investment.
- Factors that raise significant concerns about the investee's ability to continue as a going concern, such as negative cash flows from operations, working capital deficiencies, or noncompliance with statutory capital requirements or debt covenants.
  (ASC 323-10-35-3)

The guidance does not assign a probability threshold to the indicators. The presence of any one of these or other indicators does not mean impairment exists. It does mean that the entity needs a quantitative valuation of the investment.

Dividend Income Dividend income from investments in equity securities is included in income of the investor. (ASC 321-10-35-6)

PRESENTATION AND DISCLOSURE REQUIREMENTS

For ASC 321 detailed presentation and disclosure requirements, see the *Disclosure and Presentation Checklist for Commercial Businesses* at www.wiley.com/go/FSDM2021.

Presentation

Statement of Financial Position Entities should present, separately in the statement of financial position or in the notes, financial assets, and financial liabilities by:

- Measurement category and
- Form of financial asset
  (ASC 825-10-45-1A)

Marketable equity securities representing cash available for current operations should be included in current assets.

Cash Flows Cash flows from purchases and sales should be classified based on the nature and purpose for which they were acquired. (ASC 321-10-45-1)

Disclosures

For an equity investment measured using the measurement alternative, the entity should disclose:

- Carrying amount.
- Amount of impairment and downward adjustments recognized during the annual period and cumulative.
- Amount of upward adjustments recognized during both the annual period and cumulative.
- In narrative form, the information that management considered to determine the amount of impairment and downward or upward adjustments.
  (ASC 321-10-50-3)

For each period presented and for equity securities held at the reporting date, the entity should disclose unrealized gains and losses related to equity securities. (ASC 321-10-50-4)

PRESENTATION AND DISCLOSURE EXAMPLES

Example 18.1: Accounting Policy—Investments

All equity securities that do not result in consolidation and are not accounted for under the equity method are measured at fair value with changes therein reflected in net income. ABC utilizes the measurement alternative for equity investments that do not have readily determinable fair values and measures these investments at cost less impairment plus or minus observable price changes in orderly transactions. The balance of these securities is disclosed in Note X.

Example 18.2: Recent Pronouncements

In January 2020, the FASB issued ASU 2020-01, *Clarifying the Interactions between Topic 321, Investments—Equity Securities, Topic 323, Investments—Equity Method and Joint Ventures, and Topic 815, Derivatives and Hedging.* This ASU clarifies that when accounting for certain equity securities, a Company should consider observable transactions before applying or upon discontinuing the equity method of accounting for the purposes of applying the measurement alternative. Further, this ASU notes when determining the accounting for certain derivatives, a Company should not consider if the underlying securities would be accounted for under the equity method or fair value option. The transition requirements are prospective and the effective date for ABC is January 1, 2021, with early adoption permitted. As ABC does not currently have a material amount of equity securities and equity method investments or relevant derivatives, ABC does not expect this ASU to have a material impact on its consolidated results of operations and financial condition, but will apply such guidance, where applicable, to future circumstances.

Example 18.3: Gains and Losses Recognized on Equity Securities

Net gains and losses recognized during the period on equity securities	$1,000,000
Less: Net gains and losses recognized during the period on equity securities sold during the period	800,000
Unrealized gains and losses recognized during the reporting period on equity securities still held at the reporting date	$ 200,000

Example 18.4: Equity Securities—Upward and Downward Adjustments

The following table presents the carrying value of the Company's strategic investments in publicly traded and privately held companies as of the dates indicated:

January 31, 20X2				January 31, 20X1			
Cost	Unrealized Gain	Unrealized (Loss)	Current Value	Cost	Unrealized Gain	Unrealized (Loss)	Current Value
$783	$116	$(35)	$864	$638	$539	$(172)	$1,005
In thousands (000s)							

For the fiscal year ended January 31, 20X2, the equity and other securities without readily determinable fair values of $852,000 increased by $110,000 due to upward adjustments for observable price changes, offset by $150,000 of downward adjustments that were primarily attributable to impairments. For the fiscal year ended January 31, 20X1, the equity and other securities without readily determinable fair values increased by $233,000 due to upward adjustments for observable price changes, offset by $80,000 of downward adjustments that were primarily attributable to impairments. The remainder of equity and other securities consisted of publicly traded investments that are measured at fair value on a recurring basis for both the fiscal years ended January 31, 20X2 and January 31, 20X1.

19 ASC 323 INVESTMENTS— EQUITY METHOD AND JOINT VENTURES

TECHNICAL ALERT

ASU 2020-01

In January 2020, the FASB's EITF issued ASU 2020-01, *Investments—Equity Securities (Topic 321), Investment Equity Method and Joint Ventures (Topic 323),* and *Derivatives and Hedging (Topic 815).* The purpose of the ASU is to clarify the interactions between Topics 321, 323, and 815.

Guidance Issue 1 of the ASU addresses what happens when an entity applies or discontinues the equity method of accounting. The changes are noted in this chapter.

Issue 2 addresses whether to apply the guidance in ASC 321 or 815 to forward contracts and purchased options to buy securities that, upon settlement of the forward contract or exercise of the purchased option, should be accounted for under the equity method in ASC 323 or under ASC 321. The investments under question are not derivatives or in-substance common stock in the scope of ASC 323. The Emerging Issues Task Force (EITF) decided that:

- For the purpose of applying ASC 815-10-15-141(a), entities should not consider whether, upon the settlement of the forward contract or service of the purchased option either individually or with existing investments, the underlying securities should be accounted for under ASC 323 or the fair value option in ASC 825.
- Entities should evaluate the remaining ASC 815-10-15-141 characteristics to determine how to account for the forward contracts and purchased options.

Effective Date The ASU is effective:

- For public business entities—fiscal years beginning after December 15, 2020, and interim periods within those fiscal years.
- For all other entities—fiscal years beginning after December 15, 2020, and interim periods within those fiscal years.

Early adoption is permitted.

Transition The ASU should be applied prospectively.

AUTHORITATIVE LITERATURE

Subtopics

ASC 323, *Investments—Equity Method and Joint Ventures*, contains three Subtopics:

- ASC 323-10, *Overall,* which addresses the application of the equity method to entities within its scope,
- ASC 323-30, *Partnerships, Joint Ventures, and Limited Liability Entities*, which provides guidance on applying the equity method to partnerships, joint ventures, and limited liability entities, and
- ASC 323-740, *Income Taxes,* which provides stand-alone guidance on a specific type of real estate investment, Qualified Affordable Housing Project Subsections. (ASC 323-10-05-2)

Scope and Scope Exceptions

ASC 323 applies to all entities and their investments in common stock or in-substance common stock, including common stock of corporate joint ventures. (ASC 323-10-15-3)

The guidance in ASC 323 guidance does not apply to an investment:

- Accounted for in accordance with ASC 815-10, *Derivatives and Hedging—Overall.*
- In common stock held by a nonbusiness entity, such as an estate, trust, or individual.
- In common stock within the scope of ASC 810, *Consolidation.*
- Held by an investment company within the scope of ASC 946, except as discussed in paragraph 946-323-45-2, an entity that provides services to the investment company. (ASC 323-10-15-4)

ASC 323-10 does not apply to an investment in a partnership or unincorporated joint venture (covered in ASC 323-30) or an investment in a limited liability company that maintains specific ownership accounts for each investor (discussed in ASC 272). (ASC 323-10-15-5)

ASC 323-30 follows the same scope and scope exceptions as ASC 323-10, providing guidance specifically on:

- Partnerships
- Unincorporated joint ventures
- Limited liability companies

ASC 323-740 follows the same scope and scope exceptions as ASC 323-10 and the guidance applies to investments in limited partnerships that operate qualified affordable housing projects.

ASC 323-10 Investments in the stock of joint ventures and other noncontrolled entities are usually accounted for by either:

- The recognition and measurement guidance in ASC 321, or
- The equity method in this Topic.
  (ASC 323-10-05-4)

When an investor has significant influence over an investee, the investor is no longer considered to be a passive investor, and the equity method is an appropriate way to reflect that fact and to account for the investment. If an investor has the ability to exert significant influence over the operations and financial policies of an investee, it is appropriate for the investor to reflect that responsibility in the investor's financial statements. The advantages of the equity method are that it:

- Recognizes changes to the underlying economic resources.
- More closely meets the objectives of accrual accounting than the cost method.
- Best enables investors in corporate joint ventures to reflect their investment in those ventures.

The equity method of accounting has been referred to as a "one-line consolidation," because the net result of applying ASC 323 on reported net income and on net worth should be identical to what would have occurred had full consolidation been applied. However, rather than include its share of each component (e.g., sales, cost of sales, operating expenses, etc.) in its financial statements, the investor only includes its share of the investee's net income as a separate line item in its income. (Note that there is an exception to this one-line rule for prior period adjustments.) It should be noted that the final bottom-line impact on the investor's financial statements is identical whether the equity method or full consolidation is employed; only the amount of detail presented within the financial statements differs.

The equity method recognizes a substantive economic relationship between the investor and investee. The equity method is not, however, a substitute for consolidation. It is employed where the investor has significant influence over the operations of the investee but lacks control. In general, significant influence is inferred when the investor owns between 20% and 50% of the investee's voting common stock. Any ownership percentage over 50% presumably gives the investor actual voting control, making full consolidation of financial statements necessary. Indications of significant influence are:

- Representation on the board of directors.
- Participation in policy-making processes.
- Material intraentity transactions.
- Interchange of managerial personnel.
- Technological dependency.
- Extent of ownership in relation to other investors.
  (ASC 323-10-15-6)

The 20% threshold stipulated in ASC 323 is presumptive, but not absolute. Circumstances may suggest that significant influence exists even though the investor's level of ownership is less than 20% or, conversely, that it is absent despite a level of ownership above 20%. (ASC 323-10-15-7 and 15-8)

Whether sufficient contrary evidence exists to negate the presumption of significant influence is a matter of judgment. Judgment requires a careful evaluation of all pertinent facts and circumstances, and significant influence may change over time. For more information, see the section later on "Change in Ownership Level or Influence."

In determining whether significant influence may not exist, the entity should consider the following factors:

- Opposition by the investee.
- Agreements, such as standstill agreements, under which the investor surrenders shareholder rights.
- Majority ownership by a small group of shareholders.
- Inability to obtain desired information from the investee.
- Inability to obtain representation on investee board of directors, etc. (ASC 323-10-15-10)

As a practical matter, absence of control by the parent is the only remaining reason to not consolidate a majority-owned investee. (ASC 323-10-15-11)

ASC 323-30 This subtopic includes guidance on investments in partnerships, joint ventures, and limited liability entities that follow the equity method of accounting. The guidance is generally the same as that in ASC 323-10. Exceptions or additions are found in this section.

A wide variety of noncorporate entities and structures are used to:

- Operate businesses,
- Hold investments in real estate or in other entities, or
- Undertake discrete projects as joint ventures.

These include:

- Partnerships, for example, limited partnerships, general partnerships, limited liability partnerships, and
- Limited liability companies (LLC).

Practice questions persistently arise regarding whether directly or by analogy, authoritative GAAP literature that applies to corporate structures is also applicable to investors in noncorporate entities.

By analogy to ASC 323-10, investors with controlling interests in unincorporated entities, such as partnerships and other unincorporated joint ventures, generally should account for their investments using the equity method. (ASC 323-30-25-1)

General Partnerships There is a rebuttable presumption that a general partner that has a majority voting interest is in control of the partnership. If voting rights are indeterminate under the provisions of the partnership agreement or applicable law, the general partner with a majority of the financial interests in the partnership's profits or losses would be presumed to have control. If this presumption is not overcome, the general partner with voting control or the majority financial interest would consolidate the partnership in its financial statements and the other noncontrolling general partners would use the equity method. (ASC 323-30-35-7)

Limited Liability Companies A limited liability company may maintain a specific ownership account for each investor—similar to a partnership capital account structure. In that case, the investment in the limited liability company is viewed as similar to an investment in a limited partnership for purposes of determining whether a noncontrolling investment in a limited liability company is accounted for in using the guidance in ASC 321 or the equity method. (ASC 323-30-35-3)

ASC 323-740 ASC 323-740 provides guidance on a specific U.S. tax issue—investments in a Qualified Affordable Housing Project. Created under the Tax Reform Act of 1986, this federal program gives incentives for the utilization of private equity in the development of afford-able housing for low-income Americans. The Revenue Reconciliation Act of 1993 retroactively extended and made permanent the affordable housing credit. Corporations eligible for the credits generally purchase an interest in a limited partnership that operates the qualified affordable hous-ing projects. So, the guidance in ASC 323-740 applies to investments in limited partnerships that operate qualified affordable housing projects.

These investments are accounted for using:

- Effective yield method, or
- The guidance in ASC 970-323, *Real Estate General—Investments—Equity Method and Joint Ventures.*

The cost method may be appropriate and the guidance in ASC 323-740-25-3 through 25-5 that are not related to the proportional method may be applied. (ASC 323-740-25-2A)

The Proportional Amortization Method Election The Codification includes an election available to qualified affordable housing projects. The election allows a "proportional amortiza-tion method" that can be used to amortize the investment basis of investments that meet certain conditions. If elected, the method is required for all eligible investments in qualified affordable housing projects and must be applied consistently. It replaces the effective yield method. Under the proportional method, an investor amortizes the costs of its investment, in proportion to the tax credits and other tax benefits it receives, to income tax expense.

To elect the proportional method, all of the following conditions must be met:

- It is probable that the tax credits allocable to the investor will be available.
- The investor does not have the ability to exercise significant influence over the operating and financial policies of the limited liability entity.
- Substantially all of the projected benefits are from tax credits and other tax benefits (for example, tax benefits generated from the operating losses of the investment).
- The investor's projected yield is based solely on the cash flows from the tax credits and other tax benefits is positive.
- The investor is a limited liability investor in the limited liability entity for both legal and tax purposes, and the investor's liability is limited to its capital investment.
  (ASC 323-740-25-1)

The decision to use the proportional amortization method is an accounting policy decision that must be applied consistently to individual qualifying investments. (ASC 323-740-25-4)

Equity Method Investors that do not qualify for the proportional amortization presenta-tion must continue to account for their investments under the equity method or cost method, which results in losses recognized in pretax income and tax benefits recognized in income taxes ("gross" presentation of investment results).

Recognition The investor should recognize a liability for:

- Delayed equity contributions that are unconditional and legally binding.
- Equity contributions that are contingent upon a future event when that event becomes probable. (ASC 323-740-25-3)

An investor should not recognize credits before their inclusion in the investor's tax return. (ASC 323-740-25-5)

Subsequent Measurement Under the proportional allocation method, investors amortize the initial cost of the investment to recognize an effective yield in proportion to the tax credit and other tax benefits allocated to the investor. (ASC 323-740-35-2) Investors include in earnings any cash received from operations of the limited partnership. (ASC 323-740-35-5)

Practice Alert

While SEC comments pertain to public entities, their comments can often provide valuable practice pointers for preparers of nonpublic entities. Following are pointers from the SEC comments:

- Significant judgment is required to determine whether a measure meets the test to proportionately consolidate equity method investees. Entities should document their rationales for choosing the equity method.
- The financial statement requirements are based on whether certain thresholds or criteria are met and have specific requirements about which financial statements or additional information needs to be included in financial statements. The SEC staff frequently questions whether registrants have appropriately applied the requirements in their annual reports.
- The SEC staff also asks questions about recently acquired businesses when reviewing an annual report.
- When performing the significance tests, registrants should ensure that they:
  - Document the tests each period. This is particularly important since the significance of an equity method investee may change each period. For example, in some cases, such as a near-break-even year for the investor or a large income or loss at the investee level, the current year's significance may change, making the equity method investee significant for the first time.
  - Update the tests each period. For example, registrants should update and assess the significance tests for all appropriate periods after they report a retrospective change for the classification of a component as a discontinued operation.

PRESENTATION AND DISCLOSURE REQUIREMENTS

Note: Additional detail is included in the Disclosure and Presentation Checklist for Commercial Businesses at www.wiley.com/go/FSDM2021.

Presentation

The following table summarizes the presentation of equity method investments.

Equity Method Investments	
Balance Sheet	*Income Statement*
Presented as a single amount	Classified separately
Classify separately the investee's share of accounting changes.	Other comprehensive amounts may be combined with the investor's own comprehensive income amounts and shown in the aggregate.
(ASC 323-10-45-1 through 45-3)	

For entities following the guidance in ASC 323-740 for the proportional amortization method, the investor recognizes the amortization of the investment in the income statement as a component of income tax expense or benefit. The current portion of the expense or benefit is accounted for under the requirements of ASC 740. (ASC 323-740-45-2)

Disclosure

When determining the extent of disclosure related to an equity investment, the investor should consider:

- the significance of the investment relative to the investor's financial position and
- results of operations.

The investor may choose to combine disclosures for equity investments. (ASC 323-10-50-2)

Generally, the investor should disclose, in the notes or parenthetically on the face of the statements:

- Name of each investee and the percentage of ownership of common stock.
- Accounting policies with respect to each of the investments.
- If the investor holds more than 20% of the voting stock of an investee, but does not account for it using the equity method, the investor should disclose:
  - The names of any significant investee.
  - The reasons why the equity method is not appropriate.
- Conversely, if the investor holds less than 20% of the existing stock of an investee, but uses the equity method, the investor should disclose:
  - The name of a significant investee.
  - The reason why the equity method is appropriate.
- The difference between the carrying amount for each investment and its underlying equity in the investee's net assets and the accounting treatment of the difference between these amounts.
- For those investments which have a quoted market price, the aggregate value based on market price of each investment.
- For material investments in corporate joint ventures or other investments accounted for under the equity method, summarized data for the investor's assets, liabilities, and results of operations, disclosed in groups or individually.
- If potential conversion of convertible securities and exercise of options and warrants would have material effects on the investor's percentage of the investee.
  (ASC 323-10-50-3)

An investor in a qualified affordable housing project must disclose information that enables the users of its financial statements to understand:

- The nature of the investment.
- The effect of the measurement of those investments and the related tax audits on its financial position and results of operations.
  (ASC 323-740-50-1)

PRESENTATION AND DISCLOSURE EXAMPLES

Example 19.1: Accounting Policy—Equity Method

The Company accounts for investments in unconsolidated entities where it exercises significant influence, but does not have control, using the equity method. Under the equity method of accounting, the Company recognizes its share of the investee's net income or loss. Losses are only recognized to the extent the Company has positive carrying value related to the investee. Carrying values are only reduced below zero if the Company has an obligation to provide funding to the investee. The Company's share of net income or loss of unconsolidated entities from which the Company purchases merchandise or merchandise components is included in Costs of Goods Sold, Buying, and Occupancy in the Consolidated Statements of Income (Loss). The Company's share of net income or loss of all other unconsolidated entities is included in Other Income (Loss) in the Consolidated Statements of Income (Loss). The Company's equity method investments are required to be reviewed for impairment when it is determined there may be an other than temporary loss in value.

Example 19.2: Investment Securities, Including Equity Securities and Unrealized Gains and Losses on Securities

The amortized cost and approximate fair values, together with gross unrealized gains and losses, of securities are as follows:

		20X2		
	Amortized Cost	Gross Unrealized Gains	Gross Unrealized Losses	Fair Value
Available for sale				
U.S. treasury securities	$ 2,997	$ —	$ 6	$ 2,991
SBA Pools	14,497	—	114	14,383
Federal agencies	21,765	—	119	21,646
State and municipal obligations	45,635	357	152	45,840
Mortgage-backed securities:				
Government-sponsored enterprises (GSE) residential	117,769	111	969	116,911
Equity securities	13	—	—	13
	202,676	468	1,360	201,784
Held to maturity				
State and municipal obligations	$ 15,917	$244	$ 5	$ 16,156
	15,917	244	5	16,156
Total investment securities	$218,593	$712	$1,365	$217,940

| | *20X1* | | | |
	Amortized Cost	*Gross Unrealized Gains*	*Gross Unrealized Losses*	*Fair Value*
Available for sale				
Federal agencies	$ 40,812	$ —	$2,802	$ 38,010
State and municipal obligations	30,531	34	776	29,789
Mortgage-backed securities:				
Government-sponsored enterprises (GSE) residential	56,945	11	2,286	54,670
Equity securities	13	—	—	13
	128,301	45	5,864	122,482
Held to maturity				
State and municipal obligations	18,580	70	107	18,543
Corporate obligations	2,500	2,610	—	5,110
	21,080	2,680	107	23,653
Total investment securities	$149,381	$2,725	$5,971	$146,135

Example 19.3: Amortized Cost and Fair Value of Securities

The amortized cost and fair value of securities at December 31, 20X2, by contractual maturity, are shown below. Expected maturities will differ from contractual maturities because issuers may have the right to call or prepay obligations with or without call or prepayment penalties.

| | *20X2* | | | |
| | *Available for Sale* | | *Held to Maturity* | |
	Amortized Cost	*Fair Value*	*Amortized Cost*	*Fair Value*
Within one year	$ 308	$ 309	$ 2,427	$ 2,430
One to five years	16,405	16,463	9,653	9,767
Five to ten years	35,716	35,729	2,777	2,877
After ten years	32,465	32,359	1,060	1,082
	84,894	84,860	15,917	16,156
Mortgage-backed securities:				
GSE residential	117,769	116,911	—	—
Equity securities	13	13	—	—
Totals	$ 202,676	$ 201,784	$ 15,917	$ 16,156

Securities with a carrying value of $114,907,000 and $86,267,000 were pledged at December 31, 20X2 and 20X1, respectively, to secure certain deposits and for other purposes as permitted or required by law.

Proceeds from sales of securities available for sale during year ended December 31, 20X2 and 20X1 were $65,892,348 and $5,871,002, respectively. Gross gains of $184,000 and $15,000 resulting from sales of available-for-sale securities were realized for the years ended December 31, 20X2 and 20X1, respectively. Gross losses of $86,000 and $0 were realized from sales of available-for-sale securities for the years ended December 31, 20X2 and 20X1, respectively.

Certain investments in debt securities are reported in the consolidated financial statements and notes at an amount less than their historical cost. Total fair value of these investments at December 31,

20X2 and 20X1 was $138, 391,000 and $126,736,000, which is approximately 63% and 88%, respectively, of the Company's available-for-sale and held-to-maturity investment portfolio.

Based on evaluation of available evidence, including recent changes in market interest rates, credit rating information and information obtained from regulatory filings, management believes the declines in fair value for these securities are temporary.

Should the impairment of any other securities become other-than-temporary, the cost basis of the investment will be reduced and the resulting loss recognized in net income in the period the other-than-temporary impairment is identified.

Example 19.4: Gross Unrealized Losses and Fair Value

The following tables show the Company's investments' gross unrealized losses and fair value, aggregated by investment category and length of time that individual securities have been in a continuous unrealized loss position at December 31, 20X2 and 20X1:

20X9

Description of Securities	Less Than 12 Months Fair Value	Unrealized Losses	12 Months or More Fair Value	Unrealized Losses	Total Fair Value	Unrealized Losses
Available-for-sale						
U.S. Treasury securities	2,991	6	—	—	2,991	6
SBA Pools	14,262	114	—	—	14,262	114
Federal agencies	9,657	109	2,990	10	12,647	119
State and municipal obligations	12,606	130	2,948	22	15,554	152
Mortgage-backed securities:						
GSE residential	57,928	464	34,344	505	92,272	969
Total available-for-sale	97,444	823	40,282	537	137,726	1,360
Held-to-maturity						
State and municipal obligations	665	5	—	—	665	5
Total temporarily impaired securities	98,109	828	40,282	537	138,391	1,365

20X8

Description of Securities	Less Than 12 Months Fair Value	Unrealized Losses	12 Months or More Fair Value	Unrealized Losses	Total Fair Value	Unrealized Losses
Available-for-sale						
Federal agencies	—	—	38,010	2,802	38,010	2,802
State and municipal obligations	4,516	26	21,529	750	26,045	776
Mortgage-backed securities:						
GSE residential	5,872	30	45,676	2,256	51,548	2,286
Total available-for-sale	10,388	56	105,215	5,808	115,603	5,864
Held-to-maturity						
State and municipal obligations	3,271	11	7,862	96	11,133	107
Total temporarily impaired securities	13,659	67	113,077	5,904	126,736	5,971

Example 19.5: Equity Method Investment—Summarized Financial Information

The Company has land and other investments in Garden City, a planned community in Indianapolis, Indiana that integrates office, hotel, retail, residential and recreational space. These investments, totaling $118 million as of February 1, 20X3 and $89 million as of February 2, 20X2, are recorded in Other Assets on the Consolidated Balance Sheets.

Included in the Company's Garden City investments are equity interests in Garden City Town Center, LLC ("GCTC") and Garden City Gateway, LLC ("GCG"), entities that own and develop commercial entertainment and shopping centers. The Company's investments in GCTC and GCG are accounted for using the equity method of accounting. The Company has a majority financial interest in GCTC and GCG, but another unaffiliated member manages them, and certain significant decisions regarding GCTC and GCG require the consent of unaffiliated members in addition to the Company.

The Company received cash distributions of $7 million, $16 million and $29 million during 20X2, 20X1, and 20X0, respectively, from certain of its Easton investments, which are included as return of capital within Investing Activities of the Consolidated Statements of Cash Flows. As a result of these distributions, the Company recognized pre-tax gains totaling $5 million, $8 million, and $20 million during 20X2, 20X1, and 20X0, respectively, which are included in Other Income (Loss) in the Consolidated Statements of Income (Loss).

Example 19.6: Equity Investments in Unconsolidated Joint Ventures

The following tables present the Company's investments in unconsolidated ventures as of December 31, 20X9 and 20X8, and activity for the years ended December 31, 20X9 and 20X8 (dollars in thousands):

			Carrying Value	
			December 31,	*December 31,*
	Acquisition		*20X9*[1]	*20X8*[1]
Portfolio	*Date*	*Ownership*		
Eclipse	May-20X4	5.6%	$ 9,483	$ 11,765
Envoy[2]	Sep-20X4	11.4%	399	4,717
Griffin-American	Dec-20X4	14.3%	125,597	113,982
Espresso[3]	Jul-20X5	36.7%	—	—
Trilogy[4]	Dec-20X5	23.2%	133,361	133,764
Subtotal			$268,840	$264,228
Operator Platform[5]	Jul-20X7	20.0%	54	91
Total			$288,894	$264,319

(1) *Includes $1.3 million, $13.4 million, $7.6 million, and $9.8 million of capitalized acquisition costs for the Company's investments in the Eclipse, Griffin-American, Espresso and Trilogy joint ventures, respectively.*

(2) *In March 20X9, the Envoy joint venture completed the sale of its remaining 11 properties for a sales price of $118.0 million, which generated net proceeds to the Company totaling $4.3 million.*

(3) *As a result of impairments and other noncash reserves recorded by the joint venture, the Company's carrying value of its Espresso unconsolidated investment was reduced to zero in the fourth quarter of 20X8. The Company has recorded the excess equity in losses related to its unconsolidated venture as a reduction to the carrying value of its mezzanine loan, which was originated to a subsidiary of the Espresso joint venture.*

(4) *In October 20X8, the Company sold 20.0% of its ownership interest in the Trilogy joint venture, which generated gross proceeds of $48.0 million and reduced the Company's ownership interest in the joint venture from approximately 29% to 23%.*

(5) *Represents investment in Solstice Senior Living, LLC ("Solstice"). In November 20X7, the Company began the transition of operations of the Winterfell portfolio from the former manager, an affiliate of Holiday Retirement, to a new manager, Solstice, a joint venture between affiliates of Integral Senior Living, LLC ("ISL"), a management company of ILF, ALF, and MCF founded in 20X0, which owns 80.0%, and the Company, which owns 20.0%.*

Portfolio	Equity in Earnings (Losses)	Year Ended December 31, 20X9 Select Revenues and (Expenses), net[1]	Cash Distributions	Equity in Earnings (Losses)	Year Ended December 31, 20X8 Select Revenues and (Expenses), net[1]	Cash Distributions
Eclipse[2]	$ 435	$ (987)	$ 2,717	$ (624)	$ (2,280)	$ (754)
Envoy	20	(892)	4,339	(37)	(301)	(283)
Griffin - American[3]	(4,540)	(16,359)	23,061	(12,717)	(24,780)	5,553
Espresso	(2,426)	(8,530)	—	(21,460)	(26,906)	—
Trilogy	3,003	(13,797)	5,805	1,153	(14,810)	5,977
Subtotal	$ (3,508)	$ (40,565)	$ 35,922	$ (33,685)	$ (69,077)	$ 12,567
Operator Platform[4]	(37)	—	—	168	—	107
Total	$ (3,545)	$ (40,565)	$ 35,922	$ (33,517)	$ (69,077)	$ 12,674

(1) Represents the net amount of the Company's proportionate share of select revenues and expenses, including: straight-line rental income (expense), (above-)/below-market lease and in-place lease amortization, (above-)/below-market debt and deferred financing costs amortization, depreciation and amortization expense, acquisition fees and transaction costs, loan loss reserves, liability extinguishment gains, debt extinguishment losses, impairment, as well as unrealized and realized gain (loss) from sales of real estate and investments.

(2) Equity in earnings for the year ended December 31, 2019, includes a gain on the sale of nine properties within the portfolio. The Company's proportionate share of the net proceeds generated from the sale totaled approximately $2.1 million.

(3) Equity in losses for the year ended December 31, 2019, includes a gain on the sale of three properties within the portfolio. The Company's proportionate share of the net proceeds generated from the sale totaled approximately $16.9 million.

(4) Represents the Company's investment in Solstice.

Example 19.7: Summarized Financial Data

The combined balance sheets as of December 31, 20X9 and 20X8 and combined statements of operations for the years ended December 31, 20X9, 20X8, and 20X7 for the Company's unconsolidated ventures are as follows (dollars in thousands):

Assets	December 31, 20X9	December 31, 20X8		Year Ending December 31, 20X9	20X8	20X7
Operating real estate, net	$4,821,757	$5,016,977	Total revenues	$1,575,774	$1,514,098	$1,457,208
Other assets	1,199,552	$1,003,614	Net income (loss)	$(17,689)	$(150,170)	$(158,445)
Total assets	$6,021,309	$6,020,591				
Liabilities and equity						
Total liabilities	$4,578,905	$4,565,451				
Equity	1,442,404	1,455,140				
Total liabilities and equity	$6,021,309	$6,020,591				

The following table indicates the Company's investments for which Colony Capital is also an equity partner in the joint venture. Each investment was approved by the Company's board of directors, including all of its independent directors.

Portfolio	Partner(s)	Acquisition Date	Ownership
Eclipse	Colony Capital/Formation Capital, LLC	May 2014	5.6%
Griffin-American	Colony Capital	December 2014	14.3%

Example 19.8: Qualified Affordable Housing Project Investments

The Company began investing in qualified affordable housing projects in 20X6. At December 31, 20X9 and December 31, 20X8, the balance of the investment for qualified affordable housing projects was $8.6 million and $9.5 million, respectively. This balance is reflected in the accrued interest and other assets line on the consolidated balance sheets. Total unfunded commitments related to the investments in qualified affordable housing projects totaled $4.2 million and $6.8 million at December 31, 20X9 and December 31, 20X8. The Company expects to fulfill these commitments between 20Y0 and 20Y7.

During the years ending December 31, 20X9, 20X8, and 20X7, the Company recognized amortization expense of $900,000, $644,000 and $316,000, respectively, which was included within income tax expense on the consolidated statements of income.

During the years ended December 31, 20X9, 20X8, and 20X7, the Company recognized tax credits from its investment in affordable housing tax credits of $1.1 million, $573,000, and $275,000, respectively. The Company had no impairment losses during the years ended December 31, 20X9, 20X8, and 20X7.

20 ASC 325 INVESTMENTS—OTHER

TECHNICAL ALERT

This Topic is affected by ASU 2016-13. For more information about the ASU, see the chapter on ASC 326.

AUTHORITATIVE LITERATURE

Subtopics

ASC 325 provides guidance for investments not within the scope of other Topics: investments in insurance contracts and in securitized financial assets.

ASC 325 contains three Subtopics:

- ASC 325-10, *Overall*, which merely identifies the other three topics.
- ASC 325-30, *Investments in Insurance Contracts*, which provides guidance on investments, life insurance contracts in general, and life settlement contracts.
- ASC 325-40, *Beneficial Interests in Securitized Financial Assets*, which provides guidance on accounting for a transferor's interest in securitized transactions accounted for as sales and purchased beneficial interests.

Scope

ASC 325-10

Note: This Subtopic does not contain a scope section.

ASC 325-30 ASC 325-30 applies to all entities and transactions for entities that purchase life insurance where the entity is either the owner or beneficiary of the contract. Life insurance purchased by retirement plans and subject to ASC 960 are not in the scope of ASC 325-30. (ASC 325-30-15-1 through 15-3) The Subtopic's guidance on life settlement contracts applies to all entities.

ASC 325-40 ASC 325-40 applies to:

- A transferor's interests in securitization transactions that are accounted for as sales under Topic 860, and
- Purchased beneficial interests in securitized financial assets. (ASC 325-40-15-2)

The guidance applies to beneficial interests that have *all* of the following characteristics:

a. Are either debt securities under Subtopic 320-10 or required to be accounted for like debt securities under that subtopic per ASC 860-20-35-2.
b. Involve securitized financial assets that have contractual cash flows.
c. Do not result in consolidation of the entity issuing the beneficial interest by the holder of the beneficial interests.
d. Are not within the scope of ASC 310-30.[1]
e. Are not beneficial interests in securitized financial assets that have both of the following characteristics:
    ○ Are of high credit quality.
    ○ Cannot contractually be prepaid or otherwise settled in a way that the holder would not recover substantially all of its recorded investment.
    (ASC 325-40-15-3)

For guidance on the recognition of interest income on beneficial interest for items with the characteristics in "e" above, entities should refer to the guidance in ASC 320-10. Guidance on other-than-temporary impairment can be found in ASC 320-10-35-17 through 35-34 or when ASU 2016-13 is implemented in ASC 326.[2] (ASC 325-40-15-4)

Note that a beneficial interest in securitized financial assets that is in equity form may meet the definition of a debt security. These beneficial interests would be within the scope of this Topic and ASC 320 because ASC 320 requires them to be accounted for as debt securities:

- If the beneficial interests issued in the form of equity:
    ○ Represent solely a right to receive a stream of future cash flows to be collected under preset terms and conditions, or
    ○ According to the terms of the special-purpose entity, must be redeemed by the issuing entity or must be redeemable at the option of the investor.
    (ASC 325-40-15-5)

---

[1] This item is superseded upon implementation of ASU 2016-13.
[2] Upon implementation of ASU 2016-13, this sentence changes to: "For guidance on determining the allowance for credit losses on beneficial interests with the characteristics in 'e' above, other than trading debt securities, see ASC 326."

If beneficial interests are issued in the form of equity but do not meet the criteria in ASC 325-40-15-5, those interests should be accounted for under ASC 323-10, ASC 320-10, ASC 810-10, or ASC 321-10. (ASC 325-40-15-6)

ASC 325-40 does not apply to hybrid beneficial interests measured at fair value pursuant to paragraphs 815-15-25-4 through 25-6 for which the transferor does not report interest income as a separate item in its income statements. (ASC 325-40-15-9)

ASC 325-10, *Overall*

ASC 325-10 merely lists the investment topics and the ASC 325-10 Subtopics and other sources. It does not have recognition, subsequent measurement, presentation, or disclosure guidance.

ASC 325-30, *Investments in Insurance Contracts*

Overview ASC 325-30 provides guidance on investments in insurance contracts and is divided between general guidance and guidance for life settlement contracts.

General Guidance

Exchange of Mutual Membership Interests for Stock in a Demutualization Entities should measure stock received in a demutualization at fair value. (ASC 325-30-1AA) A gain on exchange of mutual membership interests is recognized in income from continuing operations. (ASC 325-30-40-1)

Guidance for Investments in Life Settlement Contracts For a life settlement contract, the investor must elect to account for these investments using either the investment method or the fair value method. (ASC 325-30-25-2) This irrevocable election is made in one of two ways:

1. On an instrument-by-instrument basis supported by documentation prepared concurrently with acquisition of the investment, or
2. Based on a preestablished, documented policy that automatically applies to all such investments.

The Investment Method If the investor elects this method, the investor recognizes the initial investment at the transaction price plus all initial direct external costs. (ASC 325-30-30-1C) Continuing costs (payments of policy premiums and direct external costs, if any) necessary to keep the policy in force are capitalized. (ASC 325-30-35-8) Gain recognition is deferred until the death of the insured. (ASC 325-30-35-9) At that time the investor recognizes in net income (or other applicable performance indicator) the difference between the carrying amount of the investment and the policy proceeds. (ASC 325-30-40-1A)

The investor is required to test the investment for impairment upon the availability of new or updated information that indicates that, upon the death of the insured, the expected proceeds from the insurance policy may not be sufficient for the investor to recover the carrying amount of the investment plus anticipated gross future premiums (undiscounted for the time value of money) and capitalizable external direct costs, if any. (ASC 325-30-35-10)

The Fair Value Method If the investor elects the fair value method for life settlement contracts, the initial investment is recorded at the transaction price. (ASC 325-30-30-2) Each subsequent reporting period, the investor remeasures the investment at fair value and recognizes changes in fair value in current period net income (or other relevant performance indicators for reporting entities that do not report net income). (ASC 325-30-35-12)

Cash payments for policy premiums and receipts for policy proceeds are included in the same financial statement line item as the changes in fair value are reported.

ASC 325-40, *Beneficial Interests in Securitized Financial Assets*

Overview A beneficial interest is the right to receive all or a percentage of specified cash inflows. For instance, when a reporting entity sells a portion of an asset that it owns, the portion retained becomes an asset separate from the portion sold and separate from the assets obtained in exchange. This is the situation when financial assets such as loans are securitized with certain interests being retained (e.g., a defined portion of the contractual cash flows).

Initial Recognition and Measurement The reporting entity must allocate the previous carrying amount of the assets sold based on the relative fair values of each component at the date of sale or upon implementation of ASU 2016-13, the fair value of the beneficial interest at the date of transfer following the guidance in ASC 860-20-30-1. (ASC 325-40-30-1) In most cases, the initial carrying amount (i.e., the allocated cost) of the retained interest will be different from the fair value of the instrument. Furthermore, cash flows from those instruments may be delayed depending on the contractual provisions of the entire structure (for example, cash may be retained in a trust to fund a cash collateral account).

Upon implementation of ASU 2016-13, entities with purchased financial assets with credit deterioration should follow the guidance in ASC 326-20 for a beneficial interests classified as available for sale if

- There is a significant difference between contractual cash flow and expected cash flow at the date of recognition, or
- The beneficial interests meet the definition of purchased assets with credit deterioration. (ASC 325-40-30-1A)

Subsequent Measurement

Accretable Yield The holder recognizes accretable yield as interest income using the effective yield method. The holder is required to update the estimate of cash flows over the life of the beneficial interest. (ASC 325-40-35-1) The method used for recognizing and measuring the amount of interest income is the same for each classification of change in GAAP chapter's beneficial interest. (ASC 325-40-35-2) Note upon implementation of ASU 2016-13, ASC 325-40-35-2 is superseded, and entities should to the guidance in ASC 326.

Credit Losses[3]

Note: For credit losses on beneficial interests held to maturity and available for sale entities should apply the guidance in ASC 326. (ASC 325-40-6A)

Credit losses should be measured using the present value of expected future cash flows. If the original estimate of present value is less than the current estimate, the change is favorable. Conversely, if the previous estimate is greater than the current one, the change is adverse. (ASC 325-40-35-7)

Entities should look to the guidance on credit losses in ASC 326 and unless that guidance points to a credit loss, changes in an interest rate generally would not result in the recognition of a credit loss. (ASC 325-40-35-9)

Entities should not assume that a credit loss has occurred simply because not all the scheduled payments have been received. So, too, not every decline in fair value is a credit loss. The entity must analyze the situation further and exercise judgment to assess the decline. (ASC 325-40-35-10A)

---

[3] The paragraphs below in this section reflect the guidance in ASU 2016-13.

PRESENTATION AND DISCLOSURE REQUIREMENTS

Note: For detailed information on presentation and disclosure related to ASC 325, see www.wiley.com/go/ FSDM2021.

325-30, *Investments in Insurance Contracts*

Presentation In the statement of financial position, ASC 325-30 requires that investments remeasured at fair value be presented separately from those accounted for under the investment method. The investments should be shown by separate line items or aggregated with parenthetical disclosure of the amount accounted for under the fair value method. (ASC 325-30-45-1)

In the income statement, the investor should classify in earnings the amount recognized upon the death of insured. (ASC 325-30-45-2) Investment income from contracts remeasured at fair value on the income statement should be presented separately from those accounted for under the investment method:

- Through separate line items, or
- Aggregated with parenthetical disclosure of amount accounted for under the fair value method.
  (ASC 325-30-45-3)

If the fair value method is applied, premiums paid and life insurance proceeds received, should be shown on the same line as the changes in fair value. (FASB ASC 325-30-45-4)

In the statement of cash flows, cash receipts and payments classified as current or noncurrent based on the nature and purpose for which the life settlements were acquired. (FASB ASC 325-30-45-5)

Disclosure Investors in insurance contracts should disclose contractual restrictions on the ability to surrender a policy. (ASC 325-30-50-1)

Investors in life settlement contracts should disclose their accounting policy, including the classification of cash receipts and cash disbursements in statement of cash flows. (FASB ASC 325-30-50-2) Those investors should also disclose all of the following for those contracts accounted for under the investment method based on the remaining life expectancy for each of the first five succeeding years from the date of the statement of financial position and thereafter, as well as in the aggregate:

- The number of life settlement contracts, and
- Their carrying value and the face value of underlying life insurance policies.
- As of the date of the most recent statement of financial position, the life insurance premiums anticipated to be paid for each of the five succeeding fiscal years in order to keep the life settlement contracts in force.
  (ASC 325-30-50-4 and 50-5)

If the investor has changed its expectations on the timing of the realization of investments in life settlement contract proceeds, it should disclose:

- The nature of the new or updated information, and
- The related effect on the timing of the realization of proceeds from the life settlement contracts.
  (ASC 325-30-50-6)

Those investors using the fair value method should disclose the method and significant assumptions used by the investor to estimate the fair value of investments in life settlement contracts, including any mortality assumptions. (FASB ASC 325-30-50-7) Additional disclosures include the remaining life expectancy for each of the first five succeeding years from the date of the statement of financial position, as well as in the aggregate:

- The number and carrying value of life settlement contracts, and
- The face value (death benefits) of the life insurance policies underlying the contracts. (ASC 325-30-50-8)

If the investor changes its expectations of the timing of the realization of the investments in life settlement contracts, the investor should disclose the reasons for those changes. (ASC 325-30-50-9)

Investors should report for each reporting period presented in the investor's income statement:

- The gains or losses recognized during the period on investments sold during the period, and
- The unrealized gains or losses recognized during the period on investments held at the date of the statement of financial position. (ASC 325-30-50-10)

ASC 325-40, *Beneficial Interests in Securitized Financial Assets*

Presentation   Note that investors should bear in mind that the amount of accretable yield is *not* displayed in the balance sheet. (ASC 325-40-45-1)

PRESENTATION AND DISCLOSURE EXAMPLES

Example 20.1: Accounting Policy—Insurance Contracts

Our investments in life insurance policies are valued based on unobservable inputs that are significant to their overall fair value. Changes in the fair value of these policies, net of premiums paid, are recorded in gain (loss) on life insurance policies, net in our consolidated statements of operations. Fair value is determined on a discounted cash flow basis that incorporates life expectancy assumptions generally derived from reports obtained from widely accepted life expectancy providers (other than insured lives covered under small face-amount policies—those with $1 million in face value benefits or less—which utilize either a single fully underwritten, or simplified report based on self-reported medical interview), assumptions relating to cost-of-insurance (premium) rates and other assumptions. The discount rate we apply incorporates current information about the discount rates observed in the life insurance secondary market through competitive bidding observations (which have recently declined for us as a result of our decreased purchase activity) and other means, fixed income market interest rates, the estimated credit exposure to the insurance companies that issued the life insurance policies and management's estimate of the operational risk yield premium a purchaser would require to receive the future cash flows derived from our portfolio as a whole. Management has significant discretion regarding the combination of these and other factors when determining the discount rate. As a result of management's analysis, a discount rate of 8.25% was applied to our portfolio as of both December 31, 20X9 and 20X8.

Example 20.2: Portfolio of Insurance Contracts

Our portfolio of life insurance policies, owned by our subsidiaries as of December 31, 20X9, is summarized below.

Investment in Life Insurance Policies (Details) $ in Thousands	12 Months Ended December 31, 20X9
Total life insurance portfolio face value of policy benefits (in thousands)	$ 2,020,973
Average face value per policy (in thousands)	1,756
Average face value per insured life (in thousands)	$ 1,883
Average age of insured (years)*	82.4
Average life expectancy estimate (years)*	7.2
Total number of policies ⎸ Policies	1,151
Number of unique lives ⎸ Lives	1,073
Demographics	74% Male; 26% Female
Number of smokers ⎸ Smokers	48
Largest policy as % of total portfolio face value	0.70%
Average policy as % of total portfolio face value	0.10%
Average annual premium as % of face value	3.30%

* Averages presented in the table are weighted averages by face amount of policy benefits.

Example 20.3: Life Insurance Contracts—Summary of Policies According to Estimated Life Expectancy Data, Grouped by Year

A summary of our policies organized according to their estimated life expectancy dates, grouped by year, as of the reporting date, is as follows:

Years Ending December 31,	As of December 31, 20X2			As of December 31, 20X1		
	Number of Policies	Estimated Fair Value (in thousands)	Face Value (in thousands)	Number of Policies	Estimated Fair Value (in thousands)	Face Value (in thousands)
20X9	—	$ —	$ —	9	$ 6,380	$ 7,305
20X0	8	5,869	6,342	41	46,338	59,939
20X1	55	62,061	79,879	81	68,836	108,191
20X2	90	89,074	138,723	104	97,231	177,980
20X3	128	123,352	222,369	109	93,196	185,575
20X4	109	103,111	217,053	107	84,150	211,241
20X5	113	74,223	171,961	124	77,718	210,781
Thereafter	648	338,349	1,184,646	579	274,074	1,086,980
Totals	**1,151**	**$ 796,039**	**$ 2,020,973**	**1,154**	**$ 747,923**	**$ 2,047,992**

Example 20.4: Life Insurance Contracts—Fair Value Method—Reconciliation of Gain and Loss

We recognized life insurance benefits of $125.1 million and $71.1 million during the years ended December 31, 20X9 and 20X8, respectively, related to policies with a carrying value of $33.2 million and $20.8 million, respectively, and as a result recorded realized gains of $91.9 million and $50.3 million. A reconciliation of gain (loss) on life insurance policies is as follows (in thousands):

		12 Months Ended	
Investment in Life Insurance Policies (Details 2)		*Dec. 31, 20X9*	*Dec. 31, 20X8*
Change in estimated probabilistic cash flows	(1)	$ 67,186	$ 75,444
Unrealized gain on acquisitions	(2)	6,921	28,017
Premiums and other annual fees		(65,577)	(54,087)
Change in discount rates	(3)		
Change in life expectancy evaluation	(4)	(2,332)	(4,890)
Change in life expectancy evaluation methodology	(5)		(87,100)
Face value of matured policies		125,148	71,090
Fair value of matured policies		(56,026)	(42,579)
Gain (loss) on life insurance policies, net		$ 75,320	$ (14,105)

[1] Change in fair value of expected future cash flows relating to our investment in life insurance policies that are not specifically attributable to changes in life expectancy, discount rate changes or policy maturity events.
[2] Gain resulting from fair value in excess of the purchase price for life insurance policies acquired during the reporting period.
[3] The discount rate applied to estimate the fair value of the portfolio of life insurance policies we own was 8.25% at December 31, 20X9 and 20X8.
[4] The change in fair value due to updating life expectancy estimates on certain life insurance policies in our portfolio.
[5] The change in fair value due to the adoption of the Longest Life Expectancy methodology on life policies in our portfolio, partially offset by the impact of a decrease in the discount rate associated thereto.

Example 20.5: Change in Fair Value of Investment in Life Insurance Policies

Change in Fair Value of the Investment in Life Insurance Policies (in thousands)

	Change in Life Expectancy Estimates			
	Minus 8 Months	*Minus 4 Months*	*Plus 4 Months*	*Plus 8 Months*
December 31, 20X9	$ 113,812	$ 57,753	$ (55,905)	$ (111,340)
December 31, 20X8	$ 113,410	$ 57,611	$ (55,470)	$ (110,473)

	Change in Discount Rate			
	Minus 2%	*Minus 1%*	*Plus 1%*	*Plus 2%*
December 31, 20X9	$ 91,890	$ 43,713	$ (39,790)	$ (76,118)
December 31, 20X8	$ 95,747	$ 45,440	$ (41,179)	$ (78,615)

21 ASC 326 FINANCIAL INSTRUMENTS—CREDIT LOSSES

TECHNICAL ALERTS

ASU 2019-10

Guidance Regarding Effective Dates In November 2019, the FASB issued ASU 2019-10, *Financial Instruments—Credit Losses (Topic 326), Derivatives and Hedging (Topic 815), and Leases (Topic 842): Effective Dates*. The ASU grants private companies, not-for-profit organizations, and certain small public company SEC filers additional time to implement recent FASB standards on current expected credit losses (CECL).

ASU 2019-10 Effective Dates		
Topic	**Public Business Entities That Meet the Definition of SEC Filers, Except Smaller Reporting Companies (SRCs) as Determined by the SEC as of November 15, 2019**	**All Other Entities**
CECL (ASC 326)	Fiscal years beginning after December 15, 2019	Fiscal years beginning after December 15, 2022

ASU 2016-13

In June 2016, the FASB issued ASU 2016-13, *Financial Instruments—Credit Losses (Topic 326): Measurement of Credit Losses on Financial Instruments.* This ASU makes changes to several topics and adds a new topic—ASC 326. ASU 2016-13 marks a significant change in practice, requiring the immediate recognition of estimated credit losses expected to occur over the remaining life of many financial assets.

Effective Date Early adoption is allowed for all entities for fiscal years beginning after December 15, 2018, including interim periods therein. (ASC 326-10-65-1)

See the information on effective dates in the technical alert on ASU 2019-10 at the beginning of this chapter.

See the information below on ASU 2019-05.

Transition Except where noted in the table below, entities should use a modified-retrospective approach and record a cumulative-effect adjustment to retained earnings as of the beginning of the first reporting period that the entity adopts the guidance. (ASC 326-10-65-1) For example, a calendar-year private company that adopts the standard in 2022 records the cumulative effect adjustment on January 1, 2022. The transition adjustment includes those adjustments made as a result of an entity amending its accounting policy if it adopts the amendments in ASU 2019-04 related to determining when accrued interest receivables are deemed uncollectible and written off. Also, see the information below on ASU 2019-05 for an option to select the fair value option.

Prospective Transition Approach Required	
Circumstance	*Accounting Treatment*
Debt securities for which an OTTI was recognized before the adoption date	If amounts relate to improvements in cash flows expected to be collected, continue to accrete into income over the remaining life of the asset. If cash flows improve because of improvements in credit after the adoption date, record in the income statement in the period received. If cash flows are expected to decrease because of deterioration in credit expectations, record an allowance.
Assets previously accounted for as PCD (purchased financial assets with credit deterioration)	Adjust the amortized cost basis on adoption to reflect the addition of the allowance for credit losses on the transition date. Continue to accrete or amortize, at the effective interest rate at the adoption date, the remaining noncredit discount or premium. Apply the same transition requirements to beneficial interests that previously applied the PCD model or have a significant difference between contractual cash flows and expected cash flows.
(ASC 326-10-65-1)	

ASU 2018-19

In November 2018, the FASB issued *Codification Improvements to Topic 326, Financial Instruments—Credit Losses.* This update changes the effective date for nonpublic entities and clarifies ASC 326's scope related to leases. Those changes are reflected in the effective dates above and in the scope guidance in this chapter. Also, for the fair value option, see the information on ASU 2019-05 below.

ASU 2019-04

In April 2019, the FASB issued ASU 2019-04, *Codification Improvements to Topic 326, Financial Instruments—Credit Losses, Topic 815, Derivatives and Hedging,* and *Topic 825, Financial Instruments.* The ASU addresses four issues:

1. Scope,
2. Held-to-maturity disclosures,
3. Measurements alternative, and
4. Remeasurement of equity securities.

The ASC 326 amendments in ASU 2019-04 are incorporated in this chapter and relate to:

- Accrued interest:
  - ○ Provisions to measure, present, and disclose the allowance for credit losses separately.
  - ○ An accounting policy election to write off accrued interest through interest income, credit loss expense, or a combination of both.
  - ○ An accounting policy election to record no accrued credit loss if accrued interest is remeasured on a timely basis.
- Transfers from HFS (held-to-investment) to HFI (held-for-investment) loans, AFS (available-for-sale) to held-to-maturity (HTM) debt securities:
  - ○ Guidance on how the CECL model should be applied to an HFS loan transferred to HFI or credit-impaired AFS security transferred to HTM.
- Recoveries:
  - ○ Expected recoveries required to be considered when measuring a credit loss.
  - ○ Permits a negative allowance, but only up to the amount previously written off.
- Consideration of prepayment in determining the EIR (effective interest rate):
  - ○ Policy election to adjust the EIR for expected prepayments when using a DCF (discounted cash flow) method.
- Projections of interest rate environments for variable rate financial instruments:
  - ○ Policy election to project future interest rate environments when using a DCF method on variable-rate financial instruments.
  - ○ If above is elected, entity must also elect to adjust the effective interest rate for expected prepayments.
  - ○ Vintage disclosure:
    - ○ Lines of credit that are converted to term loans
- Consider contractual extensions and renewals of a financial asset:
  - ○ Contractual extensions and renewals that are in the original or modified contract at the reporting date and are not unconditionally cancelable by the entity.

ASU 2019-05

In May 2019, the FASB issued ASU 2019-05, *Financial Instruments—Credit Losses (Topic 326): Targeted Transition Relief.*

Guidance This Update provides an option to irrevocably elect the fair value option for certain financial assets previously measured at amortized cost basis. The FASB expects this amendment to increase comparability because it aligns measurement methodologies for similar financial assets. This option is available to reporting entities within the scope of ASC 326. The new option may be applied on an instrument-by-instrument basis for eligible instruments. Note that this option *does not* apply to held-to-maturity debt securities. An entity that applies the fair value option should then apply the guidance in ASC 825-10. (ASC 326-10-65-1)

Effective Date See the information on effective dates in the technical alert on ASU 2019-10 at the beginning of this chapter.

Transition Entities should adopt the changes using a modified-retrospective basis by means of a cumulative-effect adjustment to the opening balance of retained earnings balance as of the date the entity adopted ASU 2016-13.

ASU 2019-11

In November 2019, the FASB issued ASU 2019-11, *Codification Improvements to Topic 326, Financial Instruments—Credit Losses*. The purpose of the update is to clarify certain aspects of ASC 326.

The guidance is incorporated in this chapter and the effective dates are the same as those for ASU 2016-13 included in the information on ASU 2019-10 at the beginning of this chapter.

AUTHORITATIVE LITERATURE

ASC 326 changes the impairment model for most financial assets currently measured at amortized cost and certain other instruments. The model changes from an incurred loss model to an expected loss model, referred to as the current expected credit loss model (CECL).

The CECL model's underlying principle is that a reporting entity holding financial assets is exposed to credit risk throughout the holding period, that is, from origination until settlement or disposal. The CECL model, based on an expected loss approach, should result in entities recognizing losses on a timely basis.

Subtopic

ASC 326 contains three Subtopics:

- ASC 326-10, *Overall*, which contains scope, definitions, and effective date information
- ASC 326-20, *Financial Instruments—Credit Losses—Measured at Amortized Cost*, which provides guidance on how entities measure expected credit losses on
  - Financial instruments measured at amortized cost, and
  - Leases.
- ASC 326-30, *Financial Instruments—Credit Losses—Available-for-Sale Debt Securities*

Scope The guidance in ASC 326-10 applies to all entities.
ASC 326-20 applies to all entities and the following items:

- Financial assets measured at amortized cost, such as financing receivables, HTM debt securities, receivables recorded under ASC 606 and ASC 610, and receivables related to repurchase agreements and securities lending agreements under ASC 860,
- Net investments in leases,
- Off-balance-sheet credit exposures not accounted for as insurance, and

- Reinsurance recoverables from insurance transactions within the scope of ASC 944. (ASC 326-20-15-1 and 15-2)

The Subtopic *does not* apply to:

a. Financial assets measured at fair value through net income,
b. Available-for-sale debt securities (see ASC 326-30),
c. Loans made to participants by defined contribution employee benefit plans,
d. Policy loan receivables of an insurance entity,
e. Promises to give (pledges receivable) of a not-for-profit, entity,
f. Loans and receivables between entities under common control, and
g. Receivables resulting from operating leases accounted for under ASC 842. (ASC 326-20-15-3)

The FASB decided that the measurement attribute for AFS debt securities requires a separate credit loss model. ASC 326-30 applies to all entities and debt securities classified as available-for-sale securities, including loans that meet the definition of debt securities and are classified as available-for-sale securities. (ASC 326-30-15-1 and 15-2) Therefore, the credit loss model to use under the new standard depends on the classification of the debt security. This is a change from existing practice.

ASC 326 also requires recording available-for-sale (AFS) debt securities' credit losses through an allowance account.

It is anticipated that entities will recognize losses earlier under the new model.

ASC 326-10, *Overall*

This Subtopic contains scope, definitions, and transition guidance. It does not contain recognition, measurement, presentation, or disclosure guidance.

ASC 326-20, *Measured at Amortized Cost*

Estimating Expected Credit Losses The allowance for credit losses should reflect the portion of the amortized cost basis of a financial asset that the entity does not expect to collect. Entities record the expected credit loss as an allowance deducted from or added to the amortized cost basis of the financial asset. A related credit loss expense is recorded in net income. The allowance account includes:

- Recoveries of amounts previously written off and
- Amounts expected to be written off.

However, these amounts must not exceed amounts previously written off and expected to be written off. The estimate for expected credit losses is updated at each reporting date. (ASC 326-20-30-1)

CECL model inputs include:

1. Historical Loss Information. Entities should measure expected credit losses on a pool basis, that is, aggregate financial assets that have similar risk characteristics. A financial asset may only be measured individually if it does not share similar risk characteristics with other financial assets. A financial asset should be included in a pool or on an individual basis, but not both. (ASC 326-20-30-2 and 55-5)

2. Current Conditions.
3. Reasonable and Supportable Forecasts.

Subsequent Measurement At each reporting date, entities should compare their current estimate of expected credit losses with the estimate recorded. (ASC 326-20-35-1) The amount needed to adjust the allowance for credit losses is reported in net income as a:

- Credit loss expense, or
- A reversal of a credit loss expense

Generally, an entity would want to use the same estimation method applied consistently over time. (ASC 326-20-35-2)

Off-balance-sheet exposures must be evaluated and reported in the same way. (ASC 326-20-35-3)

ASC 326-30, *Available-for-Sale Debt Securities*

The CECL model in ASC 326-20 replaces the impairment guidance in ASC 310-10. However, the FASB decided that the CECL model should not apply to available-for-sale (AFS) debt securities. The FASB instead made targeted amendments to the current AFS debt security impairment model and places the new guidance in a new subtopic, ASC 326-30. This will result in entities using different impairment models for AFS debt securities than those that are classified as held to maturity.

The ASU eliminates "other-than-temporary" impairment (OTTI). The new guidance focuses on determining whether unrealized losses are credit losses or whether they are caused by other factors. (ASC 326-30-35-2) Also, when assessing whether a credit loss exists, the entity may not consider recoveries in fair value after the balance sheet date.

For purchased financial assets with credit deterioration, if the indicators of a credit loss described in ASC 326-30-55-1 (see Factors to Consider When Determining Impairment below) exist, the purchased AFS debt security is considered a purchased financial asset with credit deterioration. Entities should measure the allowance for credit losses at the individual security level as discussed in ASC 326-30-35-3 through 35-10. (ASC 326-30-30-2)

To determine if a credit loss exists, the entity compares the present value of cash flows expected with the amortized cost basis of the security. If the present value is less than the amortized cost basis, a credit loss exists. (ASC 326-30-35-1) The entity records the difference in an allowance for credit losses up to the fair value of the security. (ASC 326-30-35-2)

If the fair value of a debt security does not exceed its amortized cost after a credit loss has been recognized in earnings, but the credit quality of the debt security improves, the credit loss is reversed for an amount that reflects the improved credit quality. However, the entity cannot reverse a previously recorded allowance for credit losses to an amount below zero. (ASC 326-30-35-12)

Factors to Consider When Determining Impairment The entity can no longer use the length of time a security has been in an unrealized loss position as a factor to conclude that a credit loss does not exist. However, it can consider the following:

- The extent to which fair value is less than the amortized cost basis.
- Adverse conditions related to the security, an industry, or geographical area.
- The payment structure of the debt security.
- Failure of the issuer to make scheduled interest or principal payments.
- Changes to the rating of the security by a rating agency.
  (ASC 326-30-55-1)

- Information relevant to the collectability of the security, such as remaining payment terms, prepayment speeds, financial condition of the issuer, expected defaults, value of collateral
- Industry analyst reports, credit ratings, other relevant market data.
- How other credit enhancements affect the expected performance of the security. (ASC 326-30-55-2 through 55-4)

PRESENTATION AND DISCLOSURE REQUIREMENTS

Note: See www.wiley.com/go/FSDM2021 for detailed information on presentation and disclosure.

Under ASC 326, CECLs are presented as an allowance against the amortized cost basis of the asset. Entities have to present narrative disclosures that help users understand:

- The entity's methods for developing the allowance.
- The information used.
- The changes in estimates within the period.

Entities must also present a roll forward of the allowance for each period. Note that this requirement includes accounts receivables from sales under ASC 606 with a contractual maturity date of one year or less. It also applies to net investments in leases.

Regarding AFS debt securities, ASC 326 requires entities to make the disclosures included in ASC 320, updated to reflect the use of an allowance account and the elimination of other than temporary impairment. Entities are required to include a tabular roll forward of the allowance at the date of each statement of financial position. Entities are also required to disclose their accounting policy for write-offs.

PRESENTATION AND DISCLOSURE EXAMPLES

Example 21.1: Accounting Policy—Adoption of ASU 2016-13

In June 2016, the FASB issued ASU No. 2016-13, *Financial Instruments—Credit Losses (Topic 326): Measurement of Credit Losses on Financial Instruments*. This update changes the impairment model from the currently used incurred loss methodology to an expected loss methodology, which will result in the more timely recognition of losses. The ASU is scheduled to be effective in 2023 for smaller reporting companies. The Company is currently assessing the impact of this ASU on its consolidated financial statements.

Example 21.2: Recently Issued Accounting Standards—Not Yet Effective

In June 2016, the FASB issued ASU No. 2016-13, *Credit Losses (Topic 326)* ("ASU 2016-13"). The core principle of ASU 2016-13 is that all assets measured at amortized cost basis should be presented at the net amount expected to be collected using historical experience, current conditions, and reasonable and supportable forecasts as a basis for credit loss estimates, instead of the probable initial recognition threshold used under current GAAP. In November 2018, FASB issued ASU No. 2018-19, *Codification Improvements to Topic 326, Financial Instruments—Credit Losses* ("ASU 2018-09"), which clarified that receivables arising from operating leases are not within the scope of Accounting Standards Codification ("ASC") 326-20, *Financial Instruments—Credit Losses— Measured at Amortized Cost,* and should be accounted for in accordance with ASC 842, *Leases.* In April 2019, FASB issued ASU No. 2019-04, *Codification Improvements to Topic 326, Financial Instruments—Credit Losses, Topic 815, Derivatives and Hedging,* and *Topic 825, Financial Instruments* ("ASU 2019-04"), which includes clarifications to the amendments issued in ASU 2016-13. In May 2019, FASB issued ASU No. 2019-05, *Financial Instruments—Credit Losses (Topic 326),* which provides entities that have certain instruments within the scope of ASC 326-20 with an option to irrevocably elect the fair value option in ASC 825, *Financial Instruments,* upon adoption of ASU 2016-13. In November 2019, FASB issued ASU No. 2019-10, *Financial Instruments—Credit Losses (Topic 326), Derivatives and Hedging (Topic 815),* and *Leases (Topic 842)* ("ASU 2019-10"), which modifies the effective dates for ASU 2016-13, ASU 2017-12, and ASU 2016-02 to reflect the FASB's new policy of staggering effective dates between larger public companies and all other companies. With the issuance of ASU 2019-10, the Company's effective date for adopting all amendments related to the new credit loss standard has been extended to January 1, 2023. In November 2019, FASB also issued ASU No. 2019-11, *Codification Improvements to Topic 326, Financial Instruments—Credit Losses* ("ASU 2019-11"), which includes clarifications to and addresses specific stakeholders' issues concerning the amendments issued in ASU 2016-13. The Company plans to adopt the requirements of these amendments upon their effective date of January 1, 2023, using the modified-retrospective method and is evaluating the potential impact of the adoption on its financial position, results of operations and related disclosures.

Example 21.3: Credit Quality Disclosures (Source: ASC 326-20-55-79)

Term Loans
Amortized Cost Basis by Origination Year

As of December 31, 20X5	20X5	20X4	20X3	20X2	20X1	Prior	Revolving Loans Amortized Cost Basis	Revolving Loans Converted to Term Loans Amortized Cost Basis	Total
Residential mortgage:									
Risk rating									
1–2 internal grade	$ —	$ —	$ —	$ —	$ —	$ —	$ —	$ —	$ —
3–4 internal grade	—	—	—	—	—	—	—	—	—
5 internal grade	—	—	—	—	—	—	—	—	—
6 internal grade	—	—	—	—	—	—	—	—	—
7 internal grade	—	—	—	—	—	—	—	—	—
Total residential mortgage loans	$ —	$ —	$ —	$ —	$ —	$ —	$ —	$ —	$ —
Residential mortgage loans:									
Current-period gross writeoffs	$ —	$ —	$ —	$ —	$ —	$ —	$ —	$ —	$ —
Current-period recoveries	—	—	—	—	—	—	—	—	—
Current-period net writeoffs	$ —	$ —	$ —	$ —	$ —	$ —	$ —	$ —	$ —

Consumer:

Risk rating:

1–2 internal grade	$ —	$ —	$ —	$ —	$ —	$ —	$ —	$ —	$ —
3–4 internal grade	—	—	—	—	—	—	—	—	—
5 internal grade	—	—	—	—	—	—	—	—	—
6 internal grade	—	—	—	—	—	—	—	—	—
7 internal grade	—	—	—	—	—	—	—	—	—
Total consumer	$ —	$ —	$ —	$ —	$ —	$ —	$ —	$ —	$ —

Consumer loans:

Current-period gross writeoffs	$ —	$ —	$ —	$ —	$ —	$ —	$ —	$ —	$ —
Current-period recoveries	—	—	—	—	—	—	—	—	—
Current-period net writeoffs	$ —	$ —	$ —	$ —	$ —	$ —	$ —	$ —	$ —

Commercial business:

Risk rating

1–2 internal grade	$ —	$ —	$ —	$ —	$ —	$ —	$ —	$ —	$ —
3–4 internal grade	—	—	—	—	—	—	—	—	—
5 internal grade	—	—	—	—	—	—	—	—	—
6 internal grade	—	—	—	—	—	—	—	—	—
7 internal grade	—	—	—	—	—	—	—	—	—
Total commercial business	$ —	$ —	$ —	$ —	$ —	$ —	$ —	$ —	$ —

Commercial business loans:

Current-period gross writeoffs	$ —	$ —	$ —	$ —	$ —	$ —	$ —	$ —	$ —
Current-period recoveries	—	—	—	—	—	—	—	—	—
Current-period net writeoffs	$ —	$ —	$ —	$ —	$ —	$ —	$ —	$ —	$ —

Commercial mortgage:

Risk rating

1–2 internal grade	$ —	$ —	$ —	$ —	$ —	c	$ —	$ —	$ —
3–4 internal grade	—	—	—	—	—		—	—	—
5 internal grade	—	—	—	—	—		—	—	—
6 internal grade	—	—	—	—	—		—	—	—
7 internal grade	—	—	—	—	—		—	—	—
Total commercial mortgage	$ —	$ —	$ —	$ —	$ —	$ —	$ —	$ —	$ —

Commercial mortgage loans:

Current-period gross writeoffs	$ —	$ —	$ —	$ —	$ —	$ —	$ —	$ —	$ —
Current-period recoveries	—	—	—	—	—	—	—	—	—
Current-period net writeoffs	$ —	$ —	$ —	$ —	$ —	$ —	$ —	$ —	$ —

Example 21.4: Schedule of Past Due Loans

Loans are considered past due if the required principal and interest payments have not been received as of the date such payments were due. The Company's past due loans are as follows:

(In thousands)	30–89 Days Past Due	90 Days or More Past Due	Total Past Due	Total Current	Total Loans	Total 90 Days Past Due Still Accruing
December 31, 20X9						
Commercial and industrial	$ 571	$ —	$ 571	$ 84,905	$ 85,476	—
Consumer installment	—	—	—	3,409	3,409	—
Real estate— residential	—	—	—	5,232	5,232	—
Real estate— commercial	521	—	521	46,460	46,981	—
Real estate— construction and land	—	—	—	7,865	7,865	—
SBA	—	5,931	5,931	133,755	139,686	—
USDA	—	—	—	2,430	2,430	—
Other	—	—	—	—	—	—
Total	$ 1,092	$ 5,931	$ 7,023	$ 284,056	$ 291,079	$ —
December 31, 20X8						
Commercial and industrial	$ 614	$ —	$ 614	$ 88,301	$ 88,915	$ —
Consumer installment	—	—	—	3,636	3,636	—
Real estate— residential	—	—	—	7,488	7,488	—
Real estate— commercial	—	—	—	35,221	35,221	—
Real estate— construction and land	—	—	—	4,653	4,653	—
SBA	1,431	1,114	2,545	89,065	91,610	—
USDA	—	—	—	3,367	3,367	—
Other	—	—	—	17	17	—
Total	$ 2,045	$ 1,114	$ 3,159	$ 231,748	$ 234,907	$ —

As part of the ongoing monitoring of the credit quality of the Company's loan portfolio, management tracks certain credit quality indicators including internal credit risk based on past experiences as well as external statistics and factors. Loans are graded in one of six categories: (i) pass,

(ii) pass-watch, (iii) special mention, (iv) substandard, (v) doubtful, or (vi) loss. Loans graded as loss are charged off.

The classifications of loans reflect a judgment about the risks of default and loss associated with the loan. The Company reviews the ratings on credits quarterly. No significant changes were made to the loan risk-grading system definitions and allowance for loan loss methodology during the past year. Ratings are adjusted to reflect the degree of risk and loss that is felt to be inherent in each credit. The Company's methodology is structured so that specific allocations are increased in accordance with deterioration in credit quality (and a corresponding increase in risk and loss) or decreased in accordance with improvement in credit quality (and a corresponding decrease in risk and loss).

Credits rated pass are acceptable loans, appropriately underwritten, bearing an ordinary risk of loss to the Company. Loans in this category are loans to highly credit worthy borrowers with financial statements presenting a good primary source as well as an adequate secondary source of repayment.

Credits rated pass-watch loans have been determined to require enhanced monitoring for potential weaknesses which require further investigation. They have no significant delinquency in the past twelve months. This rating causes the loan to be actively monitored with greater frequency than pass loans and allows appropriate downgrade transition if verifiable adverse events are confirmed. This category may also include loans that have improved in credit quality from special mention but are not yet considered pass loans.

Credits rated special mention show clear signs of financial weaknesses or deterioration in credit worthiness; however, such concerns are not so pronounced that the Company generally expects to experience significant loss within the short-term. Such credits typically maintain the ability to perform within standard credit terms and credit exposure is not as prominent as credits rated more harshly.

Credits rated substandard are those in which the normal repayment of principal and interest may be, or has been, jeopardized by reason of adverse trends or developments of a financial, managerial, economic, or political nature, or important weaknesses exist in collateral. A protracted workout on these credits is a distinct possibility. Prompt corrective action is therefore required to strengthen the Company's position, and/or to reduce exposure and to assure that adequate remedial measures are taken by the borrower. Credit exposure becomes more likely in such credits and a serious evaluation of the secondary support to the credit is performed. Guaranteed portions of SBA loans graded substandard are generally on nonaccrual due to the limited amount of interest covered by the guarantee, usually 60 days maximum. However, there typically will be no exposure to loss on the principal amount of these guaranteed portions of the loan.

Credits rated doubtful are those in which full collection of principal appears highly questionable, and which some degree of loss is anticipated, even though the ultimate amount of loss may not yet be certain and/or other factors exist which could affect collection of debt. Based upon available information, positive action by the Company is required to avert or minimize loss.

Loans classified as loss are considered uncollectible and of such little value that their continuance as bankable assets is not warranted. This classification does not mean that the loan has absolutely no recovery or salvage value, but rather that it is not practical or desirable to defer writing off this asset even though partial recovery may be affected in the future.

22 ASC 330 INVENTORY

TECHNICAL ALERT

The FASB has a current project on inventory disclosures. Preparers are encouraged to monitor that project at fasb.org.

AUTHORITATIVE LITERATURE

Subtopic

ASC 330, *Inventory*, consists of one Subtopic:

- ASC 330-10, *Overall*, which provides guidance on the accounting and reporting practices on inventory. ASC 330, *Inventory*, discusses the definition, valuation, and classification of inventory.

Scope ASC 330 applies to all entities but is not necessarily applicable to:

- Not-for-profit entities
- Regulated utilities
  (ASC 330-10-15-2 and 15-3)

Classification There are two types of entities for which the accounting for inventories is relevant:

1. Merchandising
2. Manufacturing

The merchandising entity normally purchases ready-to-use inventory for resale to its customers, and only one inventory account is needed. Manufacturers, on the other hand, may have raw goods, work-in-process, and finished goods inventory classifications. The manufacturer buys raw materials and processes those raw materials, using labor and equipment, into finished goods that are then sold to its customers.

In the case of either type of entity, entities are concerned with answering the same basic questions:

- At what point in time should the items be included in inventory (ownership)?
- What costs incurred should be included in the valuation of inventories?
- What cost flow assumption should be used?
- At what value should inventories be reported?

Accounting for Inventories

A major objective of accounting for inventories is the matching of appropriate costs to the period in which the related revenues are earned in order to properly compute gross profit, also referred to as gross margin. Inventories are recorded in the accounting records using either a periodic or perpetual system.

Control of Goods Generally, in order to obtain an accurate measurement of inventory quantity, it is necessary to determine when control passes from seller to buyer. Generally, entities consider inventory is the buyer's when it is released. The exception to this general rule arises from situations when the buyer assumes the significant risks of ownership of the goods prior to taking title and/or physical possession of the goods. Substance over form in this case would dictate that the inventory is an asset of the buyer and not the seller, and that a purchase and sale of the goods should be recognized by the parties irrespective of the party that holds legal title. See the chapter on ASC 606 for more information on when control passes from seller to buyer.

Costs Included in Inventory The primary basis of accounting for inventories is cost. Cost is defined as the sum of the applicable expenditures and charges directly or indirectly incurred in bringing an article to its existing condition and location. (ASC 330-10-30-1)

Cost Flow Assumptions The most common cost flow assumptions used are specified in ASC 330-10-30-9:

- Average,
- First-in, first-out (FIFO),
- Last-in, first-out (LIFO), and
- Retail inventory method.

Additionally, there are variations in the application of each of these assumptions, which are commonly used in practice. ASC 330-10-30-9 points out that:

The major objective in selecting a method should be to choose the one which, under the circumstances, most clearly reflects periodic income.

Valuation Issues Inventory can lose value for a variety of reasons including damage, spoilage, obsolescence, changes in market prices, and the like. The Codification essentially divides valuation methods into two sections:

1. Lower of cost or net realizable value, and
2. Lower of cost or market.

The lower of cost or market (LCM) method is applicable to LIFO and retail methods, and all other methods use the lower of cost or net realizable value method. (ASC 330-10-35-1A)

Lower of Cost or Net Realizable Value (NRV) NRV is selling price in the ordinary course of business less reasonably estimable costs of completion, disposal, and transportation. If NRV is less than cost because of, for example, damage, physical deterioration, obsolescence, changes in price level, or other cause, entities must recognize the difference as a loss in the period it occurs. (ASC 330-10-35-1B)

Lower of Cost or Market (LCM)

Note: LCM applies only to inventories using LIFO or retail inventory cost-flow methods.

The term "market" means current replacement cost not to exceed a ceiling of net realizable value (selling price in the ordinary course of business less reasonably estimable costs of completion, disposal, and transportation) or be less than a floor of net realizable value adjusted for a normal profit margin.

For income tax purposes, LCM is not applied in conjunction with the LIFO method of inventory valuation. However, it is important to note that LCM/LIFO is applied for financial reporting purposes. Such application gives rise to a temporary difference in the carrying value of inventory between financial statements and income tax returns.

Retail Inventory Method The retail inventory method is used by retailers to estimate the cost of their ending inventory. The retailer can either take a physical inventory at retail prices or estimate ending retail inventory and then use a computed cost-to-retail ratio to convert the ending inventory priced at retail to its estimated cost. This method eliminates the process of going back to original vendor invoices or other documents in order to determine the original cost for *each* inventoriable item. To apply this method, the retailer must record:

- The total cost of retail value of:
  - Purchased goods
  - Goods available for sale
  - Sales for the period

The retail method can be used under any of the three cost flow assumptions discussed earlier: average cost, FIFO, or LIFO.

LIFO Retail Inventory Method As with other LIFO methods, Treasury regulations are the governing force behind the LIFO retail inventory method. The regulations differentiate between a "variety" store, which is required to use an internally computed index, and a "department" store, which is permitted to use a price index published by the Bureau of Labor Statistics. The computation of an internal index involves applying the double-extension method to a representative sample of the ending inventory. Selection of an externally published index must be in accordance with the Treasury regulations.

Standard Costs Standard costs are predetermined unit costs used by manufacturing firms for planning and control purposes. Standard costs are often used to develop approximations of

GAAP inventories for financial reporting purposes. The use of standard cost approximations in financial reporting is acceptable only if adjustments to the standards are made at reasonable intervals to reflect current conditions and if their use approximates the results that would be obtained by directly applying one of the recognized cost flow assumptions. (ASC 330-10-30-12)

PRACTICE ALERT

While SEC comments do not pertain to nonpublic entities, their comments can often provide valuable guidance. In the area of inventory, the SEC has commented on:

- The selection and disclosure of valuation methods,
- How spoilage is estimated,
- Cost capitalized in inventory, and
- Disclosure of adjustments.

Preparers should pay close attention to the accounting and disclosures in those areas.

PRESENTATION AND DISCLOSURE REQUIREMENTS

Presentation

ASC 310 has no presentation requirements, however, the SEC has presentation requirements that private companies may want to consider.[1] In the case of a manufacturing concern, supplies, raw materials, work in process, and finished goods should be stated separately on the statement of financial position or disclosed in the notes to the financial statements. Customarily, the components of manufacturing inventories are stated in order of their readiness for sale and ultimate conversion to cash—that is, finished goods are ready for sale, work in process is closer to being finished than raw materials and, of course, raw materials have not yet been placed into production. A sample form of presentation is:

Inventories:	
Finished goods	$xxx
Work in process	xxx
Raw materials	xxx
	$xxx

Inventory markdowns attributed to restructuring activity, other than an activity accounted for as discontinued should be classified as a component of cost of goods sold.

Disclosure

The basis of valuation and the method of pricing must be disclosed, for example, lower of cost or net realizable value. Entities must also disclose the method used to remove costs from inventory, such as average cost, FIFO, LIFO, or estimated average cost per unit. LFO requires additional disclosures. (ASC 330-10-50-1)

One form of presentation is as follows:

Inventories—at the lower of cost or market (specific identification) $xxx

---

[1] Source: ASC 210-10-S99-1, Regulation S-X Rule 5-02.6.

In the case of a manufacturing concern, supplies, raw materials, work in process, and finished goods should be stated separately on the statement of financial position or disclosed in the notes to the financial statements. Customarily, the components of manufacturing inventories are stated in order of their readiness for sale and ultimate conversion to cash—that is, finished goods are ready for sale, work in process is closer to being finished than raw materials and, of course, raw materials have not yet been placed into production. The disclosures must also include the basis upon which the amounts are stated and where practical the method of determining cost. A sample form of presentation is as follows:

Inventories:	
Finished goods	$xxx
Work in process	xxx
Raw materials	xxx
	$xxx

Additional disclosure requirements include:

- A change in the measurement basis. This is a change in accounting principle and entities must justify and disclose the change and explain why it's preferable, as well as any material effects. Entities must disclose any material effect on the income in the statements presented currently and also in subsequent years if there is an inconsistency among the financial statements presented. (See the chapter on ASC 250.) (ASC 330-10-50-1)
- Substantial and unusual losses that result from the subsequent measurement of inventory. (ASC 330-10-50-2)
- Goods stated above cost. (ASC 330-10-50-3)
- If inventories are stated at sales price, the use of that basis. (ASC 330-10-50-4)
- Amount of net losses on firm purchase commitments accrued under 330-10-35-17. (ASC 330-10-50-5)
- Significant estimates applicable to inventories as required by ASC 275-10-50. (ASC 330-10-50-6)

PRESENTATION AND DISCLOSURE EXAMPLES

Example 22.1: Inventory Accounting Policy, Including Basis of Valuations, Method of Determining Cost, Shrinkage, Reserves, and Vendor Payments

Inventory The Company's inventory is stated at the lower of cost or net realizable value, net of reserves and allowances, with cost determined using the average cost method, with average cost approximating current cost. Inventory cost consists of the direct cost of merchandise including freight. The carrying value of our inventory is affected by reserves for shrinkage, damages, and obsolescence.

The Company incurs various types of warehousing, transportation, and delivery costs in connection with inventory purchases and distribution. Such costs are included as a component of the overall cost of inventories and recognized as a component of cost of sales as the related inventory is sold. As of February 1, 20X2 and February 2, 20X1, there were $5.9 million and $6.1 million, respectively, of distribution center costs included in inventory.

The Company estimates as a percentage of sales the amount of inventory shrinkage that has occurred between the most recently completed store physical count and the end of the financial reporting period based upon historical physical inventory count results. The Company adjusts these estimates based on changes, if any, in the trends yielded by its physical inventory counts, which occur throughout the fiscal year. The reserve for estimated inventory shrinkage was $1.3 million at both February 1, 20X2 and February 2, 20X1.

The Company estimates a reserve for unknown damaged inventory based on historical damage data. Management adjusts these estimates based on any changes in actual damage results. The reserve for estimated damaged inventory was $1.1 million and $1.0 million as of February 1, 20X2 and February 2, 20X1, respectively.

The Company also evaluates the cost of inventory by category and class of merchandise in relation to the estimated sales price. This evaluation is performed to ensure that inventory is not carried at a value in excess of the amount expected to be realized upon the sale of the merchandise. As of February 1, 20X2 and February 2, 20X1, our reserve for excess and obsolescence was approximately $745,000 and $255,000, respectively.

The Company receives various payments and allowances from vendors, including rebates and other credits. The amounts received are subject to the terms of vendor agreements, which generally do not state an expiration date, but are subject to ongoing negotiations that may be impacted in the future based on changes in market conditions and changes in the profitability, quality, or sell-through of the related merchandise. For all such vendor allowances, the Company records the vendor funds as a reduction of inventories. As the related inventory is sold, such allowances and credits are recognized as a reduction to cost of sales.

Example 22.2: Accounting Policy, Merchandise Inventory, Valued Using the LIFO Retail Inventory Method, Including Major Components of Inventory and Change in Basis

All of the Company's inventories are valued at the lower of cost or market using the last-in, first-out ("LIFO") inventory method. Approximately 97% of the Company's inventories are valued using the LIFO retail inventory method. Under the retail inventory method, the valuation of inventories at cost and the resulting gross margins are calculated by applying a cost to retail ratio to the retail value of inventories. The retail inventory method is an averaging method that is widely used in the retail industry due to its practicality. Inherent in the retail inventory method calculation are certain significant management judgments including, among others, merchandise mark-on, markups, and markdowns, which significantly impact the ending inventory valuation at cost as well as the resulting gross margins. During periods of deflation, inventory values on the first-in, first-out ("FIFO") retail inventory method may be lower than the LIFO retail inventory method. Additionally, inventory values at LIFO cost may be in excess of net realizable value. At February 1, 20X2 and February 2, 20X1, merchandise inventories valued at LIFO, including adjustments as necessary to record inventory at the lower of cost or market, approximated the cost of such inventories using the FIFO retail inventory method. The application of the LIFO retail inventory method did not result in the recognition of any LIFO charges or credits affecting cost of sales for fiscal 20X9, 20X8, or 20X7.

The Company regularly records a provision for estimated shrinkage, thereby reducing the carrying value of merchandise inventory. Complete physical inventories of all of the Company's stores and warehouses are performed no less frequently than annually, with the recorded amount of merchandise inventory being adjusted to coincide with these physical counts. The differences between the estimated amounts of shrinkage and the actual amounts realized during the past three years have not been material.

Example 22.3: Inventory Detail Disclosed in the Notes with Change in Basis Note

December 31,	*20X2*	*20X1*
Finished goods	$305	$346
Work-in-process	282	189
Purchased raw materials	453	529
Operating supplies	158	146

As of January 1, 20X1, the Company changed its method for valuing certain of its inventories held in the United States and Canada to the average cost method of accounting from the LIFO method. Inventories held by other subsidiaries of the parent company were previously, and continue to be, valued principally using the average cost method. Management believes that the change in accounting is preferable as it results in a consistent method to value inventory across all regions of the business, it improves comparability with industry peers, and it more closely resembles the physical flow of inventory.

Example 22.4: Effect of Change in Basis of Stating Inventory

The following table compares the amounts that would have been reported under LIFO with the amounts recorded under the average cost method in the consolidated financial statements as of December 31, 20X9 and for the year then ended:

Statement of Consolidated Operations for the year ended December 31, 20X9:	*As Computed under LIFO*	*As Reported under Average Cost*	*Effect of Change*
Cost of goods sold	$ 8,528	$ 8,537	$ 9
Provision for income taxes	400	415	15
Net loss	(829)	(853)	(24)
Net income attributable to noncontrolling interest	246	272	26
Net loss attributable to corporation parent	(1,075)	(1,125)	(50)
Earnings per share attributable to parent corporation common shareholders:			
Basic	$(5.80)	$(6.07)	$(.27)
Diluted	$(5.80)	$(6.07)	$(.27)

Example 22.5: Manufacturing Inventories Showing Adjustment Due to Change in Cost Basis

Inventories at December 31, 20X9 and 20X8 were as follows (in millions):

	20X9	*20X8*
Raw materials and supplies:	$164.9	$191.5
Work-in-process	899.6	914.1
Finished goods	161.3	191.1
Total inventories at current cost	1,225.8	1,296.7
Adjustment from current cost to LIFO cost basis	33.6	2.9
Inventory valuation reserves	(104.1)	(88.5)

Inventories determined on the LIFO method were $776.1 million at December 31, 20X9, and $794.3 million at December 31, 20X8. The remainder of the inventory was determined using the FIFO and average cost methods, and these inventory values do not differ materially from current cost. Due to deflationary impacts primarily related to raw materials, the carrying value of the Company's inventory as valued on LIFO exceeds current replacement cost, and based on a lower of cost or market value analysis, the Company maintains net realizable value (NRV) inventory valuation reserves to adjust carrying value of LIFO inventory to current replacement cost. These NRV reserves were $33.6 million and $8.0 million at December 31, 20X9 and 20X8, respectively. In applying the lower of cost or market principle, market means current replacement cost, subject to a ceiling (market value shall not exceed net realizable value) and a floor (market shall not exceed net realizable value reduced by an allowance for a normal profit margin).

Impacts to cost of sales for changes in the LIFO costing methodology and associated NRV inventory reserves were as follows (in millions):

	Fiscal Year Ended December 31,		
	20X9	*20X8*	*20X7*
LIFO benefit (charge)	$25.5	$28.6	$(54.2)
NRV benefit (charge)	(25.6)	27.9	54.0
Net cost of sales impact	$(0.1)	$(0.7)	(0.2)

Example 22.6: Reserve for Obsolete Inventory

The Company's inventories include the following at December 31, 20X9 and December 31, 20X8:

	December 31, 20X9	*December 31, 20X8*
Raw Material	$6,375,032	$527,456
Packaging and Miscellaneous	4,887,970	2,511,769
Work in Process	10,394,590	5,231,630
Finished Goods	26,408,762	4,088,209
Reserve for Obsolete Inventory	(2,031,873)	—
Total Inventories	$46,034,481	$12,359,064

The reserve for obsolete inventory primarily relates to packaging (raw materials) for certain products that the Company has rebranded during 20X9 of otherwise determined to be unsuitable.

Example 22.7: LIFO Inventory Liquidation

Inventories are summarized as follows:

	20X9	*20X8*
Raw materials	$ 32,377	$ 36,875
Work-in-process	18,642	20,274
Finished goods	64,978	67,085
Supplies and other	260	190
LIFO reserve	(20,748)	(19,229)
Inventories, net	$ 95,509	$ 105,195

In March 20X9, the Company incurred an inventory liquidation due to a consignment agreement with a primary vendor of raw materials. The former inventory levels are not expected to be reinstated. The Company recognized the effect within 20X9, which resulted in liquidations of LIFO inventories carried at prevailing costs established in prior years and reduced cost of sales by $281.

Example 22.8: Purchase Commitment

On January 31, 20X1, as part of Asset Purchase Agreement to acquire products from ABC, we assumed a Collaborative License, Exclusive Manufacture and Global Supply Agreement with XYZ Pharmaceuticals, Inc. (the "Supply Agreement") for the manufacture and supply of lavender oil to DCC for commercial distribution in the United States. We are obligated to purchase all of our requirements for lavender oil from XYZ Pharmaceuticals, Inc., and are required to meet minimum purchase requirements for the calendar years 20X1 and 20X2. The term of the Supply Agreement extends through July 31, 20X5, and there are no minimum requirements in any of the other subsequent years.

Example 22.9: Provision for Inventory Losses

As of December 31, 20X9, Green held inventory valued at approximately $340,000. The Company renegotiated the selling price of the finished goods as of December 31, 20X9, resulting in a $240,000 reduction in the original cost as well as a provision for inventory losses of $163,800 related to writing down inventory to its net realizable value.

23 ASC 340 OTHER ASSETS AND DEFERRED COSTS

AUTHORITATIVE LITERATURE

Subtopics

ASC 340, *Other Assets and Deferred Costs*, contains four Subtopics:

- ASC 340-10, *Overall*, which provides guidance on certain deferred costs and prepaid expenses.
- ASC 340-30, *Insurance Contracts That Do Not Transfer Insurance Risk*, which provides guidance on how to apply the deposit method of accounting when it is required for insurance and reinsurance contracts that do not transfer risk.
- ASC 340-40, *Contracts with Customers*, provides guidance on costs incurred related to a contract with a customer. It also covers amortization of assets arising from costs to obtain or fulfill a contract, and impairment of assets arising from costs to obtain or fulfill a contract.

The specific guidance for many other deferred costs is included in various other areas of the Codification.

Scope and Scope Exceptions

ASC 340-10 The guidance in Topic 340 applies to all entities and to all subtopics of ASC 340 unless specifically excepted.

ASC 340-30 The guidance in the Subtopic includes the following transactions:

- Short-duration insurance and reinsurance contracts that do not transfer insurance risk as described in paragraph 720-20-25-1 and, for reinsurance contracts, as described in Section 944-20-15.
- Multiple-year insurance and reinsurance contracts that do not transfer insurance risk or for which insurance risk transfer is not determinable.
  (ASC 340-30-15-3)

The guidance in ASC 340-30 does not apply to the following transactions and activities:

- Long-duration life and health insurance contracts that do not indemnify against mortality or morbidity risk. These are accounted for as investment contracts under Topic 944.
  (ASC 340-30-15-4)

ASC 340-40 ASC 340-40 applies to the following costs of obtaining a contract with a customer within the scope of ASC 606:

- Incremental costs of obtaining a contract with a customer.
- Costs of fulfilling a contract with a customer.

The guidance on costs incurred in fulfilling a contract does not apply to costs included in:

- ASC 330 on inventory.
- ASC 340–10–25-1 through 25-4 on preproduction costs related to long-term supply arrangements.
- ASC 350-40 on internal-use software.
- ASC 360 on property, plant, and equipment.
- ASC 985-20 on cost of software to be sold leased or otherwise marketed.
  (ASC 340-40-15-3)

ASC 340-10, *Overall*

The guidance in ASC 340-10 is limited to a discussion of the nature of prepaid expenses and guidance for preproduction costs related to long-term supply arrangements. Prepaid expenses are amounts paid to secure the use of assets or the receipt of services at a future date or continuously over one or more future periods. Prepaid expenses will not be converted to cash, but they are classified as current assets because, if they were not prepaid, they would have required the use of current assets during the coming year (or operating cycle, if longer).

Preproduction Costs Related to Long-Term Supply Arrangements Manufacturers often incur preproduction costs related to products and services they will supply to their customers under long-term arrangements. ASC 340-10-25 states the following with respect to these costs:

- Costs of design and development of products to be sold under long-term supply arrangements are expensed as incurred. (ASC 340-10-25-1)
- Costs of design and development of molds, dies, and other tools that the supplier will own and that will be used in producing the products under the long-term supply arrangement are capitalized as part of the molds, dies, and other tools (subject to an ASC 360 recoverability

assessment when one or more impairment indicators is present). There is an exception, however, for molds, dies, and other tools involving new technology, which are expensed as incurred as research and development costs under ASC 730. (ASC 340-10-25-2)

- If the molds, dies, and other tools described in the bullet point immediately above are *not to be owned* by the supplier, then their costs are expensed as incurred unless the supply arrangement provides the supplier the noncancellable right (as long as the supplier is performing under the terms of the supply arrangement) to use the molds, dies, and other tools during the term of the supply arrangement. (ASC 340-10-25-2)
- If there is a legally enforceable contractual guarantee for reimbursement of design and development costs that would otherwise be expensed under these rules, the costs are recognized as an asset as incurred. Such a guarantee must contain reimbursement provisions that are objectively measurable and verifiable. The ASC provides examples illustrating this provision. (ASC 340-10-25-3)

It is important to note that the above provisions do not apply to assets acquired in a business combination that are used in research and development activities. Instead, such assets are accounted for in accordance with ASC 805, which permits recognition of in-process research and development assets.

ASC 340-30, *Insurance Contracts That Do Not Transfer Insurance Risk*

Insurance risk is comprised of both timing risk and underwriting risk, and in certain circumstances one or both of these may not be transferred to the insurer or entity in the case of reinsurance. For example, many workers' compensation policies provide for *experience adjustments*, which have the effect of keeping the underwriting risk with the insured, rather than transferring it to the insurer; in such instances, deposit accounting would be prescribed.

Deposit method is a revenue recognition method under which premiums are not recognized as revenue and claim costs are not charged to expense until the ultimate premium is reasonably estimable, and recognition of income is postponed until that time. (ASC Master Glossary)

This Subtopic offers guidance for applying the deposit method of accounting when it is required for insurance and reinsurance contracts. If insurance risk is not transferred, there are four possible categories for deposit arrangements:

1. Only significant timing risk is transferred.
2. Neither significant timing nor underwriting risk is transferred.
3. Only significant underwriting risk is transferred.
4. The insurance contract has an indeterminate risk.
   (ASC 340-30-05-2)

For insurance contracts with indeterminate risk, the procedures set forth in ASC 944-605 (the open-year method) should be applied. (ASC 340-40-05-8)

ASC 340-40, *Contracts with Customers*

Entities should recognize as an asset incremental costs of obtaining a contract if the entity expects to recover that cost.

Incremental Costs of Obtaining a Contract Incremental costs are those that an entity would not have incurred if the contract had not been obtained. (ASC 340-40-25-2) An example of this type of cost is a sales commission. Such incremental costs should be recognized as assets if the entity expects to recover those costs. This is in line with the definition of an asset.

Recoverable amounts are an asset, provided the entity's right to reimbursement is unconditional. Recovery may be:

- Direct, through explicit reimbursement under the contract, or
- Indirect through the margin in a contract.

Recoverability of costs is assessed on a contract-by-contract basis or for a group of contracts if the costs in question are associated with a group of contracts.

Generally, costs that are not incremental, that would have been incurred trying to obtain a contract regardless of whether the contract was obtained, for example bid, proposal, selling, and marketing, including the advertising costs mentioned previously, costs, should be expensed as incurred. However, those costs should be capitalized if they:

- Can clearly be identified as related directly to a specific contract, and
- Are explicitly chargeable to the customer regardless of whether a contract is obtained. (ASC 340-40-25-3)

Fixed salaries for sales personnel, unlike sales commissions mentioned above, are not considered incremental.

A practical expedient offers relief to entities with short-duration contracts without expectation of renewal. If the amortization period of capitalizable incremental contract costs of obtaining a contract is one year or less, the entity may recognize it as an expense. (ASC 340-40-25-4) When determining the amortization period, the entity should take into account renewals, amendments, and follow-on contracts.

Costs of Fulfilling a Contract Before transferring goods or services, an entity often incurs costs to fulfill the contract's performance obligations. An entity may also incur such costs in anticipation of obtaining a specifically identified contract. Those costs can be capitalized.

To address how to recognize fulfillment costs, the entity must first determine whether those costs are addressed by other guidance. Cost to fulfill a contract required to be expensed by other standards cannot be capitalized under ASC 340-40. That is, entities should first refer to the out-of-scope guidance listed at the beginning of this chapter and then use ASC 340-40's guidance to determine whether costs need to be capitalized. If the other standards preclude capitalization of a cost, then it cannot be capitalized under ASC 340-40.

Entities are required to recognize assets for costs of fulfilling a contract, if not addressed by other standards, and if all of the following three criteria are met:

1. The costs relate directly to a contract or to an anticipated contract that the entity can specifically identify.
2. The costs generate or enhance resources of the entity that will be used in satisfying (or in continuing to satisfy) performance obligations in the future.
3. The costs are expected to be recovered.
   (ASC 340-10-25-5)

ASC 340-40 divides contract fulfillment costs into two categories: costs to be capitalized and costs to be expensed as incurred. ASC 340-40 includes specific guidance on each type of contract-related costs.

The costs capitalized in connection with contracts with customers must be amortized. The amortization method selected must result in a systematic basis consistent with the contract's transfer of goods or services to the customer. (ASC 340-10-35-1)

Assets must be tested for impairment at the end of each reporting period. Before recognizing an impairment loss related to contract costs, the entity should recognize impairment losses on contract assets in accordance with other guidance.

Entities should perform impairment testing in the following order:

- Assets not within the scope of AC 340, ASC 350, or ASC 360 (e.g., investors subject to ASC 330).
- Assets within the scope of ASC 340.
- Asset groups and reporting units within the scope of ASC 360 or ASC 350. (ASC 340-40-35-5)

PRACTICE ALERT

While SEC comments do not pertain to nonpublic entities, their comments can often provide valuable guidance. SEC comments on ASC 340-40 focus on area where the entity exercises substantial judgment, for example, determining the amortization period of capitalized contract costs. The entity should exercise its judgment and consider facts and circumstances, such as customer retention and changes in the entity's services and products. Judgments should be documented, including:

- Costs to obtain a contract, including how renewal sales commissions are factored into the amortization period.
- Amount of costs to be capitalized.
- Whether sales commissions paid upon renewal of a contract align with the initial commission.
- How expected renewals are considered when determining the amortization period.
- Amortization method chosen.

PRESENTATION AND DISCLOSURE REQUIREMENTS

Presentation

Prepaid Expenses The chapter on ASC 210 contains a discussion of prepaid expenses and the classification of current and noncurrent assets. When deciding which items of prepaid expenses to disclose separately, preparers may want to consider the SEC guidance in Articles of Regulation, Article 5, S-X-5-02(8) calling for entities to disclose separately on the face of the balance sheet or in a note any amounts in excess of 5% of total current assets.

Disclosures

Insurance Contracts That Do Not Transfer Insurance Risk Unless the right of offset exists, deposit assets and liabilities are presented on a gross basis. (ASC 340-30-45-1) Changes in the deposit's carrying amount are presented as interest income or expense. (ASC 340-30-45-2) Changes in the deposit arising from the present value measure are reported:

- In the insured's income statement as an offset against the loss to be reimbursed.
- In the insurer's income statement as an incurred loss. (ASC 340-30-45-3)

The reduction due to amortization of the deposit is reported as an adjustment to incurred losses by the insurer. (ASC 340-30-45-4)

Entities other than insurance entities should present the reduction in the deposit related to the expired portion of the coverage provided as an expense. (ASC 340-30-45-5)

Disclosures

Note: ASC 340-10 does not have disclosure requirements.

The following disclosures are required for insurance contracts that do not transfer insurance risk.

- A description of the contracts accounted for as deposits and the separate amounts of total deposit assets and total deposit liabilities reported in the statement of financial position. (ASC 340-30-50-1)
- Insurance entities: for the changes in the recorded amount of the deposit arising from an insurance or reinsurance contract that transfers only significant underwriting risk:
  - Present values of initial expected recoveries that will be reimbursed under the insurance or reinsurance contracts recorded as an adjustment to incurred losses,
  - Adjustment of amounts initially recognized for expected recoveries, and
  - Amortization expense related to the expiration of coverage.
  (ASC 340-30-50-2)

Disclosures
Assets Recognized from the Costs to Obtain or Fulfill a Contract with a Customer

Note: Entities other than public entities as defined by ASC 606 may elect not to disclose the items below in ASC 340-40-50-2 and 50-3. (ASC 340-40-50-4)

- Description of judgments made in determining the amount of the costs incurred to obtain or fulfill a contract with a customer.
- The method used to determine amortization of fulfillment costs.
  (ASC 340-40-50-2)
- By main category of asset, the closing balances of assets recognized from the costs incurred to obtain or fulfill a contract with a customer.
- Amortization amount
- Impairment losses recognized in the reporting period.
  (ASC 340-40-50-3)

Practical Expedients Entities that are using the practical expedient in ASC 340-40-25-4 on the incremental costs of obtaining a contract must disclose that use. (ASC 340-40-50-5) Entities other than public entities as defined by ASC 606 may elect not to disclose the use of the practical expedient. (ASC 340-40-50-6)

PRESENTATION AND DISCLOSURE EXAMPLES

Example 23.1: Accounting Policy—Use of Deposit Accounting for Insurance Contracts

If the Company determines that a reinsurance agreement does not expose the reinsurer to a reasonable possibility of a significant loss from insurance risk, the Company records the agreement using the deposit method of accounting. Deposits received are included in Other liabilities, and deposits made are included in Other assets on the consolidated balance sheets. As amounts are paid or received, consistent with the underlying contracts, the deposit assets or liabilities are adjusted. Interest on such deposits is recorded as Other revenues or Operating expenses in the consolidated statements of operations, as appropriate. Periodically, the Company evaluates the adequacy of the expected payments or recoveries and adjusts the deposit asset or liability through Other revenues or Other expenses, as appropriate.

Accounting for reinsurance requires use of assumptions and estimates, particularly related to the future performance of the underlying business and the potential impact of counterparty credit risks. The Company periodically reviews actual and anticipated experience compared to the assumptions used to establish assets and liabilities relating to ceded and assumed reinsurance. The Company also evaluates the financial strength of potential reinsurers and continually monitors the financial condition of reinsurers.

Only those reinsurance recoverable balances deemed probable of recovery are recognized as assets on the Company's consolidated balance sheets and are stated net of allowances for uncollectible reinsurance. Amounts currently recoverable and payable under reinsurance agreements are included in Premiums receivable and reinsurance recoverable and Other liabilities, respectively. Such assets and liabilities relating to reinsurance agreements with the same reinsurer are recorded net on the consolidated balance sheets if a right of offset exists within the reinsurance agreement. Premiums, fee income and interest credited and other benefits to contract owners/policyholders are reported net of reinsurance ceded. Amounts received from reinsurers for policy administration are reported in Other revenue.

The Company utilizes reinsurance agreements, accounted for under the deposit method, to manage reserve and capital requirements in connection with a portion of its deferred annuities business. The agreements contain embedded derivatives for which carrying value is estimated based on the change in the fair value of the assets supporting the funds withheld under the agreements.

Example 23.2: Accounting Policy—Deferred Sales Commissions

The adoption of Topic 606 resulted in a significant change to the method in which the Company accounts for commission expenses. The Company now capitalizes sales commission expenses and associated payroll taxes paid to internal sales personnel that are incremental to obtaining customer contracts. These costs are deferred and then amortized over the expected period of benefit, which is estimated to be five years. The Company has determined the period of benefit taking into consideration several factors including the expected subscription term and expected renewals of its customer contracts, the duration of its relationships with its customers, and the life of its technology. Amortization expense is included in Sales and marketing in the accompanying consolidated statements of comprehensive loss.

Example 23.3: Accounting Policy—Costs Incurred to Obtain a Contract and the Use of the Practical Expedient

In connection with the adoption of ASC Topic 606, an entity is required to capitalize, and subsequently amortize into expense, certain incremental costs of obtaining a contract with a customer if these costs are expected to be recovered. The incremental costs of obtaining a contract are those costs that an entity incurs to obtain a contract with a customer that it would not have incurred if the contract had not been obtained (for example, sales commission). The Company utilizes the practical expedient which allows entities to immediately expense contract acquisition costs when the asset that would have resulted from capitalizing these costs would have been amortized in one year or less. The Company did not capitalize any contract acquisition cost during the years ended December 31, 20X9 or 20X8.

24 ASC 350 INTANGIBLES—GOODWILL AND OTHER

TECHNICAL ALERT

ASU 2017-04, *Intangibles—Goodwill and Other (Topic 350): Simplifying the Test for Goodwill Impairment*

To simplify the accounting for goodwill impairment, in January 2017, the FASB issued ASU 2017-04. The new guidance eliminates the need to determine the fair value of individual assets and liabilities of a reporting unit in order to measure goodwill impairment.

Guidance

Impairment Step 2 Eliminated This new guidance simplifies accounting for goodwill impairment by eliminating Step 2 of the current goodwill impairment test. The need to determine the fair value of a reporting unit's assets and liabilities will no longer be needed. Under the new guidance, the existence of impairment and the amount of impairment charges are based on Step 1 in the current guidance. Impairment charges will be based on the excess of a reporting unit's carrying amount over its fair value. The amount of impairment is limited to the reporting unit's goodwill. In addition, entities will no longer be able to record a preliminary impairment in the one period and determine the final amount in a later period.

Tax-Deductible Goodwill In some tax jurisdictions goodwill is deductible. In those cases a goodwill impairment charge either increases a deferred tax asset or decreases a tax liability. Such charges result in the reporting units carrying value exceeding its fair value that would require another impairment charge. The new guidance addresses that problem by requiring an entity to calculate the impairment charge and a deferred tax effect using the simultaneous equation method. This method is similar to the measurement of goodwill and related deferred tax assets in a business combination. (ASC 350-20-35-8B)

Reporting Units with Zero or Negative Carrying Amendment With the deletion of ASC 350-20-35-8A, entities with reporting units with zero or negative carrying amounts will not be required to perform the qualitative assessment and will be expected to pass only the simplified impairment test. Entities will be required to identify those units and disclose which reportable segments include those reporting units.

Implementation Entities should apply this update on a prospective basis. This is considered a change in accounting principle, and entities must disclose the nature of and reason for the change in accounting principle upon transition.

Effective Dates[1] The effective dates are as follows:

- For public business entities that are SEC filers, excluding entities eligible to be smaller reporting entities. The one-time determination of whether an entity is eligible to be a smaller reporting company shall be based on an entity's most recent determination as of November 15, 2019.
- For annual or any interim goodwill impairment tests in fiscal years beginning after December 15, 2019.
- All other entities, including not-for-profit entities:
  - For annual or any interim goodwill impairment tests in fiscal years beginning after December 15, 2022.

---

[1] This section is updated for changes made by ASU 2019-10, *Financial Instruments—Credit Losses (Topic 326), Derivatives and Hedging (Topic 815),* and *Leases (Topic 842).* The change in effective dates maintains the alignment of the mandatory effective dates of goodwill with those for credit losses.

Early adoption is permitted for interim or annual goodwill impairment tests performed on testing dates after January 1, 2017.

ASC 2019-06, Intangibles—Goodwill and Other (Topic 350) and Not-for-Profits (Topic 958): Extending the Private Company Accounting Alternatives on Goodwill and Certain Identifiable Assets to Not-for-Profit Entities

Guidance The guidance extends two private company alternatives discussed later in this chapter to not-for-profit entities. Instead of testing goodwill for impairment annually at the reporting unit level, a not-for-profit entity that elects the accounting alternative will be able to:

- Amortize goodwill over ten years or less, on a straight-line basis,
- Test for impairment on a triggering event, and
- Have the option to elect to test for impairment at the entity level.

A not-for-profit entity now has the option to subsume certain customer-related intangible assets and all noncompete agreements into goodwill and subsequently amortize it.

Effective Date The guidance is effective upon issuance.

Implementation If a not-for-profit entity elects the accounting alternative, it should apply the alternative prospectively for existing goodwill and for all new goodwill generated through an acquisition. If the not-for-profit elects the accounting alternative in ASC 805, it should adopt it prospectively upon the occurrence of the first transaction in the scope of the alternative.

ASU 2018-15, Intangibles—Goodwill and Other—Internal-Use Software (Subtopic 350-40): Customer's Accounting for Implementation Costs Incurred in a Cloud Computing Arrangement That Is a Service Contract

The goal of this ASU is to clarify the guidance and align the requirements for customer's accounting for implementation, setup, and other upfront costs incurred in a cloud computing arrangement (CCA) hosted by the vendor, that is a service contract with those incurred to develop or obtain internal-use software and hosting arrangements that include an internal-use software license.

Guidance The FASB widened the definition of a hosting arrangement to include an arrangement where the customer accesses or uses software but does not take possession of software.

Regarding implementation costs, the ASU requires capitalizing:

- Those costs incurred in a hosted CCA that is a service contract.
- Those costs incurred in developing or obtaining an internal-use software license and hosting arrangements that include an internal-use software license.

The guidance in the latter bullet requires the entity to capitalize or expense costs depending on:

- The nature of the cost, and
- The project stage when they occurred.

Implementation The customer in a CCA that is a service contract should follow the internal-use software guidance in ASC 350-40 to determine which costs to capitalize and which costs to expense as incurred. The changes should be applied to all implementation costs incurred after the date of the adoption either:

- Retrospectively, or
- Prospectively.

Effective Dates The effective dates are as follows:

- For public business entities that are SEC filers
- For annual or any interim periods in fiscal years beginning after December 15, 2019.
- All other entities
  - For annual periods in fiscal years beginning after December 15, 2020.
  - For interim periods within annual periods beginning after December 15, 2021.

Early adoption is permitted.

AUTHORITATIVE LITERATURE

Intangible assets are defined as both current and noncurrent assets that lack physical substance. Specifically excluded, however, are financial instruments and deferred income tax assets. The value of intangible assets is based on the rights or privileges to which they entitle the reporting entity. Most of the accounting issues associated with intangible assets involve their characteristics, valuation, and amortization.

Subtopics

ASC 350, *Intangibles—Goodwill and Other*, consists of five Subtopics:

- ASC 350-10, *Overall*, which provides an overview of the other subtopics and the overall scope of the topic.
- ASC 350-20, *Goodwill*, which provides guidance on the measurement of goodwill subsequent to acquisition and for the derecognition of goodwill allocated to a reporting unit. It also provides guidance on the accounting alternative for private companies. It also provides presentation and measurement guidance.
- ASC 350-30, *General Intangibles Other Than Goodwill*, which provides guidance on initial accounting and reporting for intangible assets, other than goodwill, acquired individually or with a group of other assets acquired in a transaction that is not a business combination or an acquisition by a not-for-profit entity or are internally generated.
- ASC 350-40, *Internal-Use Software*, which provides guidance on accounting for the costs of software developed or obtained for internal use and hosting arrangements obtained for internal use. ASU 2018-15 adds two Subsections to the Sections in this Subtopic:
  - General, and
  - Implementation Costs of a Hosting Arrangement That Is a Service Contract.
- ASC 350-50, *Website Development Costs*, which provides guidance on accounting for costs associated with the development of a website, including costs incurred:
  - In the planning, application development, infrastructure development, and operating stages.
  - To develop graphics and content.
    (ASC 350-10-05-3)

For guidance on goodwill or intangible assets acquired in a business combination or acquisition by a not-for-profit entity guidance, see ASC 805 or 958-805. (ASC 350-10-05-3A)

ASC 350-10, *Overall*

Scope and Scope Exceptions The guidance in ASC 350 applies to all entities.

All of the Subtopics in this Topic adopt the following scope limitations of ASC 350-10. The guidance does *not* apply to:

- Accounting at acquisition for goodwill acquired in a business combination (see ASC 805-30) or in an acquisition by a not-for-profit entity (see ASC 958-805).
- Accounting at acquisition for intangible assets other than goodwill acquired in a business combination or in an acquisition by a not-for-profit entity (see ASC 805-20 and ASC 958-805).
  (ASC 350-10-15-3)

ASC 350-10-15-4 goes on to list Codification locations that are *not* affected by the guidance in ASC 350:

- Research and development costs under Subtopic 730-10.
- Extractive activities under Topic 932.
- Entertainment and media, including records and music under Topic 928.
- Financial services industry under Topic 950.
- Entertainment and media, including broadcasters under Topic 920.
- Regulatory operations under paragraphs 980-350-35-1 through 35-2.
- Software under Topic 985.
- Income taxes under Topic 740.
- Transfers and servicing under Topic 860.

Derecognition In addition to the Scope section discussed above, ASC 350-10 contains an overview of the other Subtopics and a derecognition section: ASC 350-10-40. The guidance in the derecognition section explains that:

- Derecognition of a nonfinancial asset that falls under the scope of ASC 350 should be accounted for under the guidance in ASC 610, unless that asset meets a scope exception in ASC 610. (ASC 350-10-40-1)
- Derecognition of a subsidiary or group of assets that qualifies as a business or not-for-profit activity should be accounted for under the guidance in ASC 810-10. (ASC 350-10-40-2)

If a nonfinancial asset is transferred under ASC 350-10-40-1 the transfer should meet the requirements in ASC 606-10-25-1. (See the "Five Contract Criteria" section in the chapter on ASC 606.) If the transfer does not meet the requirements, the entity should account for it as follows until it does:

- Continue to report it in the financial statements.
- Report related amortization currently in the income statement.
- Account for impairments according to the guidance in ASC 350-30-35.
  (ASC 350-10-40-3)

ASC 350-20, *Goodwill*

Scope All of the ASC 350 subtopics follow the scope guidance in ASC 350-10. In addition, ASC 350-20 applies to:

- Goodwill recognized in a business combination after it has been initially recognized and measured.
- The costs of internally developed goodwill.
- Amounts recognized as goodwill in applying the equity method of accounting and to the excess reorganization value recognized by entities that adopt the fresh-start reporting guidance in ASC 852.
  (ASC 350-20-15-2)

The accounting alternative policy election for a private company or not-for-profit entity follows the same scope guidance as above, except it does not apply to the costs of internally developed goodwill. (ASC 350-20-15-4)

Goodwill is an intangible asset; however, in this subtopic "intangible asset" is used to refer to intangible assets other than goodwill. (ASC 350-20-15-3)

Goodwill is not considered an identifiable intangible asset, and accordingly, under ASC 350-20, it is accounted for differently from identifiable intangibles. The lack of identifiability is the critical element in the definition of goodwill.

Goodwill is considered to have an indefinite life and, therefore, is not amortized. (See the "Goodwill—Accounting Alternative" section for a different approach to amortization for private companies and not-for-profit entities.) Goodwill is, however, subject to impairment testing. ASU 2017-04 requires impairment testing at the reporting unit level at least annually. (ASC 350-20-35-1) Goodwill is impaired when its *implied* fair value is less than its carrying amount. (AC 350-20-35-2) The fair value of goodwill cannot be measured directly; it can only be "implied," that is, measured as a residual.[2] (Also see the Technical Alert section at the beginning of this chapter for updated information on ASU 2017-04 and tax deductible goodwill.)

Performing the Impairment Test In what is referred to as Step 0, entities determine whether it is more likely than not that the fair value of the reporting unit is less than the carrying amount. Step 0 gives entities the option of performing a qualitative assessment before performing the entities calculations of fair value in Step 1. In Step 1, entities compare the fair value of the reporting unit as a whole to its carrying amount, including goodwill. (ASC 350-20-35-4) In Step 2, entities measure the impairment loss by comparing the implied fair value of reporting unit goodwill with the carrying amount of that goodwill. (ASC 350-20-35-9)[3]

For the purpose of computing the fair value of a reporting unit's goodwill, assumptions must be made as to the income tax bases of the reporting unit's assets and liabilities in order to compute any relevant deferred income taxes. If the computation of the reporting unit's fair value in Step 1 of the goodwill impairment test assumed that the reporting unit was structured as a taxable transaction, then new income tax bases are used. If not, the existing income tax bases are used. (ASC 350-20-35-20)

Timing of Testing The annual goodwill impairment test may be performed at any time during the fiscal year as long as it is done consistently at the same time each year. Each reporting unit is permitted to establish its own annual testing date. (ASC 350-20-35-28)

ASC 350-20-35-30 indicates that additional impairment tests are required between annual impairment tests if:

1. They are warranted by a change in events and circumstances, and
2. It is more likely than not that the fair value of the reporting unit is below its carrying amount.

The factors that indicate impairment testing should be done between annual tests are the same as those that should be considered when performing Step 0. (ASC 350-20-35-30) That list is not intended to be all-inclusive. Other indicators may come to the attention of management

---

[2] Upon implementation of ASU 2017-04, "implied fair value" in ASC 350-20-35-2 changes to "fair value" and impairment recognition is described as follows: "A goodwill impairment loss is recognized for the amount that the carrying amount of a recording unit, including goodwill, exceeds its fair value, limited to the total amount of goodwill allocated to that reporting unit. However, an entity shall consider the related income tax effect from any tax deductible goodwill, if applicable, in accordance with paragraph 350-20-35-8B."

[3] Upon implementation of ASU 2017-04, Step 2 is eliminated and this paragraph is superseded.

that would indicate that goodwill impairment testing should be performed between annual tests. Goodwill must also be tested for impairment if a portion of goodwill is allocated to a business to be disposed of.

If goodwill is tested for impairment at the same time as tangible long-lived assets or amortizable intangibles, the other assets are tested/evaluated first and any impairment loss is recognized prior to testing goodwill for impairment. (ASC 350-20-35-31)

Reporting Unit The impairment test for goodwill is performed at the level of the reporting unit. A reporting unit, as detailed in ASC 350-20-35-33 through 46, is an operating segment or one level below an operating segment.

Determination of reporting units is largely dependent on how the business is managed and its structure for reporting and management accountability. An entity may have only one reporting unit, which would, of course, result in the goodwill impairment test being performed at the entity level. This can occur when the entity has acquired a business that it has integrated with its existing business in such a manner that the acquired business is not separately distinguishable as a reporting unit.

Goodwill—Accounting Alternative[4]

Scope Public companies and employee benefit plans within the scope of Topics 960 through 965 on plan accounting are outside the scope of this alternative. Entities electing this alternative are subject to its related subsequent measurement, derecognition, other presentation, and disclosure requirements. Once an entity elects the alternative, it must apply it to existing goodwill and additional goodwill recognized in the future. (ASC 350- 20-15-5)

Amortization of Goodwill Companies within scope are allowed to amortize goodwill, including equity method goodwill:

- Existing at the beginning of the period of adoption
- Prospectively
- On a straight-line basis over a period of no more than ten years

A period of less than ten years is allowed if a shorter life is more appropriate. (ASC 350-20-35-63)

Goodwill Impairment

Testing Level Entities electing this alternative must make an accounting policy decision to test goodwill for impairment at either the reporting-unit level or the entity level.

Timing of Testing Under this alternative impairment model, goodwill should be tested when a triggering event occurs, rather than once a year as required for other entities. A triggering event is one that indicates that the fair value of the reporting unit or the company may be below its carrying value. (ASC 350-20-35-66)

Measurement In addition, for companies electing the alternative, step two of the existing impairment model is eliminated. Once impairment is indicated, no further testing is necessary. The entity measures the amount of goodwill impairment to recognize by determining the fair value of the entity or reporting unit and comparing it to the carrying amount. The impairment loss should not exceed the entity's or reporting unit's carrying amount of goodwill. (ASC 350-20-35-71 through 35-73) Upon implementation of ASU 2017-04, the entity should also consider

---

[4] See the Technical Alerts on ASU 2017-04 and ASU 2019-06 at the beginning of this chapter for important updates on goodwill impairment testing.

the income tax effect from any tax deductible goodwill on the carrying amount of the entity or reporting unit when measuring the goodwill impairment loss. Also see the guidance in ASC 350-20-35-73 cited previously. (ASC 350-20-35-73)

Authoritative Literature—ASC 350-30, General Intangibles Other Than Goodwill

Scope All of the ASC 350 subtopics follow the scope guidance in ASC 350-10. In addition, the guidance in ASC 350-30 applies to:

- Intangible assets acquired individually or with a group of other assets
- Intangible assets (other than goodwill) after initial recognition and measurement that an entity recognizes in accordance with the guidance in ASC 805-20 or ASC 985-805
- Internally developed identifiable intangible assets
  (ASC 350-30-15-3)

The guidance does not apply to:

- Capitalized software costs, except as noted above
- Intangible assets recognized for acquired insurance contracts[5]
  (ASC 350-30-15-4)

Intangible assets, other than goodwill, fall into two categories:

1. Those with *finite* useful lives, which are amortized and subject to impairment testing
2. Those with *indefinite* lives, which are not amortized, but are subject to impairment testing

Intangibles acquired individually or with a group of other assets[6] are initially recognized and measured based on their fair values. Fair value, consistent with ASC 820, *Fair Value Measurements,* is determined based on the assumptions that market participants would use in pricing the asset. Even if the reporting entity does not intend to use an intangible asset in a manner that is its highest and best use, the intangible is nevertheless measured at its fair value.

The aggregate amount assigned to a group of assets acquired in other than a business combination should be allocated to the individual assets acquired based on their relative fair values. Goodwill is prohibited from being recognized in such an asset acquisition. (ASC 350-30-25-2)

Although a reporting entity can purchase intangibles that were developed by others, the Codification has a strict prohibition against capitalizing costs of internally developing, maintaining, or restoring intangibles, including goodwill. (ASC 350-30-25-3) Exceptions to this general rule are software developed for internal use and website development costs. Both are discussed later in this chapter.

An income approach is commonly used to measure the fair value of an intangible asset. The period of expected cash flows used to measure fair value of the intangible, adjusted for applicable entity-specific factors should be considered by management in determining the useful life of the intangible for amortization purposes.

Identifiable intangible assets, such as franchise rights, customer lists, trademarks, patents and copyrights, and licenses should be amortized over their expected useful economic life with required impairment reviews of their recoverability when necessitated by changes in facts and circumstances in the same manner as set forth in ASC 360 for tangible long-lived assets.

---

[5] Upon implementation of ASU 2018-12 for financial statements issued after December 15, 2020 (public entities) and December 15, 2021 (nonpublic entities), this bullet adds: "Disclosures required by ASC 946-805-50-1."

[6] See discussion in the chapter on ASC 805, *Business Combinations.*

Identifiable intangible assets having indefinite useful economic lives supported by clearly identifiable cash flows are not subject to regular periodic amortization. (ASC 350-30-35-15) Instead, the carrying amount of the intangible asset is tested for impairment annually, and again between annual tests if events or circumstances warrant such a test. (ASC 350-30-35-18) An impairment loss is recognized if the carrying amount exceeds the fair value. Furthermore, amortization of the asset commences when evidence suggests that its useful economic life is no longer deemed indefinite. (ASC 350-30-35-18A)

Authoritative Literature—ASC 350-40, Internal-Use Software

Scope All of the ASC 350 Subtopics follow the scope guidance in ASC 350-10. (ASC 350-10-15-1) In addition, the General Subsections[7] in ASC 350-40 apply to:

- Internal-use software
- The proceeds of computer software developed or obtained for internal use that is marketed
- New internal-use software that replaces previously existing internal-use software
- Computer software that consists of more than one component or module
  (ASC 350-40-15-2)

Software must meet two criteria to be accounted for as internal-use software:

1. The software is acquired, internally developed, or modified *solely* to meet the reporting entity's *internal* needs.
2. During the period in which the software is being developed or modified, there can be *no plan or intent to market* the software externally.
   (ASC 350-40-15-2A)

The guidance in this Subtopic does *not* apply to:

- Software to be sold, leased, or otherwise marketed as a separate product or as part of a product or process, subject to Subtopic 985-20.
- Software to be used in research and development, subject to Subtopic 730-10.
- Software developed for others under a contractual arrangement, subject to contract accounting standards.
- Accounting for costs of reengineering activities, which often are associated with new or upgraded software applications.
- Software that a customer obtains access to in a hosting arrangement that does not meet the criteria in paragraph 350-40-15-4A. (Upon implementation of ASU 2018-15, this bullet is superseded.)
  (ASC 350-40-15-4)

The guidance in the General Subsections of this Topic applies to internal-use software that a customer obtains access to in a hosting arrangement only if *both* of the following criteria are met:

1. The customer has the contractual right to take possession of the software at any time during the hosting period without significant penalty. Indicators that there is not significant penalty would be the ability to:

---

[7] Upon implementation of ASU 2018-15, these sections are divided into two subsections: General and Implementation Costs of a Hosting Arrangement That Is a Service Contract.

    a. Take delivery of the underlying software without significant cost.

    b. Use that software separately without a significant reduction in the value. (ASC 350-40-15-4B)

2. It is feasible for the customer to either run the software on its own hardware or contract with another party unrelated to the vendor to host the software.
(ASC 350-40-15-4A)

If both those provisions are *not* met, the hosting arrangement is treated as service contract, and separate accounting for a license is not permitted. (ASC 350-40-15-4C)

Upon implementation of ASU 2018-15, if implementation costs of a hosting arrangement do *not* meet the criteria above, they should be accounted for under the provisions for implementation costs of a hosting arrangement that is a service contract. (ASC 350-40-15-4D)

ASC 350-40 offers guidance on whether the costs of computer software developed for internal use can be capitalized and whether costs relating to cloud computing arrangements (CCAs) can be capitalized or treated as service contracts. ASU 2018-15 requires a customer in a CCA that is a service contract to capitalize implementation costs as though the CCA was an internal-use project.

It is important to note that some costs of internal-use computer software are research and development costs and treated under ASC 730-10. The Codification provides guidance in ASC 985-20 on the accounting treatment for software to be sold, leased, or otherwise marketed as a separate product or as part of a product or process whether internally developed and produced or purchased. (ASC 350-40-15-5 and ASC 985-20-05-1)

Customer's Accounting for Fees Paid in a Cloud Computing Arrangement In cloud computing arrangements, the customer never takes possession of a physical product. Instead, the software resides on a vendor's or third party's hosting site, which the customer accesses remotely. Customers will essentially use the same criteria as vendors in determining whether the arrangement contains a software license or is solely a service contract. See paragraphs ASC 350-40-15-4A through 15-4C in the "Scope" section at the beginning of this chapter.

Recognition and Measurement

Cost Recognition—General Subsection[8] To justify capitalization of related costs, it is necessary for management to conclude that it is probable that the project will be completed and that the software will be used as intended. Absent that level of expectation, costs must be expensed currently as research and development costs. Entities that engage in both research and development of software for internal use and for sale to others must carefully identify costs with one or the other activity, since the former is (if all conditions are met) subject to capitalization, while the latter is expensed as research and development costs until technological feasibility is demonstrated, per ASC 985-20.

Software projects can be divided into three phases:

1. Preliminary Project Stage
2. Application Development Stage
3. Post Implementation-Operation Stage

Cost capitalization commences when an entity has completed the conceptual formulation, design, and testing of possible project alternatives, including the process of vendor selection for

---

[8] Upon implementation of ASU 2018-15 the General subsection should be applied as though a hosting arrangement that meets the qualifications for a service contract were an internal-use computer software project. (ASC 350-40-25-18 and 30-5)

purchased software, if any. These early-phase costs (referred to as "preliminary project stage" in ASC 350-40) are analogous to research and development costs and must be expensed as incurred. (ASC 350-40-25-1) These cannot be later restored as assets if the development proves to be successful.

License from a Third Party If an entity licenses internal-use software from a third party and the license is in the scope of ASC 350-40, the license is accounted for as an intangible asset and a liability to the extent that all or a portion of the licensing fees are not paid on or before the acquisition date. (ASC 350-40-25-17) The asset is recognized and measured at cost. Cost includes the present value of the license obligation if the license is paid over time.

Costs Expensed General and administrative costs, overhead costs, and training costs are expensed as incurred. (ASC 350-40-30-3) Even though these may be costs associated with the internal development or acquisition of software for internal use, under the Codification those costs relate to the period in which they are incurred. The issue of training costs is particularly important, since internal-use computer software purchased from third parties often includes, as part of the purchase price, training for the software (and often fees for routine maintenance as well). When the amount of training or maintenance fees is not specified in the contract, entities are required to allocate the cost among training, maintenance, and amounts representing the capitalizable cost of computer software. Training costs are recognized as expense as incurred. (ASC 350-40-25-4) Maintenance fees are recognized as expense ratably over the maintenance period.

Multiple-Element Arrangements Entities may enter into a CCA where the customer pays the vendor or another third party to provide services, such as training employees to use the software, maintenance, data conversion, reengineering of hardware and business processes, and rights to future upgrades and enhancements. Current guidance requires these costs to be allocated on objective evidence of the fair value of the elements of the contract. ASU 2018-15 changes this and upon implementation, these costs must be allocated to each element based on the relevant standalone price of the contract for each element. (ASC 350-40-30-4)

Subsequent Measurement—General Subsection

Impairment—General Subsection Impairment of capitalized internal-use software is recognized and measured in accordance with the provisions of ASC 360 in the same manner as tangible long-lived assets and other amortizable intangible assets.

Amortization—General Subsection The cost of computer software developed or obtained for internal use should be amortized on a straight-line basis unless another systematic and rational manner better represents its use. (ASC 350-40-35-4) The intangible nature of the asset contributes to the difficulty of developing a meaningful estimate, however. Among the factors to be weighed are the effects of obsolescence, new technology, and competition. The entity especially needs to consider if rapid changes are occurring in the development of software products, software operating systems, or computer hardware, and whether it intends to replace any technologically obsolete software or hardware. (ASC 350-40-35-5)

Amortization commences for each module or component of a software project when the software is ready for its intended use, without regard to whether the software is to be placed in service in planned stages that might extend beyond a single reporting period. Computer software is deemed ready for its intended use after substantially all testing has been completed. (ASC 350-40-35-6)

Internal-Use Software Subsequently Marketed In some cases internal-use software is later sold or licensed to third parties, notwithstanding the original intention of management that the software was acquired or developed solely for internal use. In such cases, any proceeds received are to be applied first as a reduction of the carrying amount of the software. (ASC 350-40-35-7) No profit is recognized until the aggregate net proceeds from licenses and amortization have reduced the carrying amount of the software to zero. After the carrying value is fully recovered, any subsequent proceeds are recognized as revenue or gain, depending on whether the contract is with a customer. (ASC 350-40-35-8)

If during the development, management decides to market internal-use software, the entity should follow the guidance in ASC 985-20. (ASC 350-40-35-9)

Impairment—Costs of a Hosting Arrangement That Is a Service Contract Subsection

---

Note: The guidance in this section is effective upon implementation of ASU 2018-15.

ASC 360-10-35 requires that assets be grouped at the lowest level for which identifiable cash flows are largely independent of cash flows from other groups. (ASC 360-10-35-23) For example, that guidance applies to the hosting arrangement when the following events or changes occur:

- The arrangement is not expected to provide substantial service potential
- A significant change occurs in the extent or manner of the use or expected use of the hosting arrangement
- A significant change is made or will be made to the hosting arrangement
  (ASC 350-40-35-11)

The ASC 360-40 impairment guidance is applied to the capitalized implementation costs as if the costs were long-lived assets. On abandonment, the related capitalized implementations costs are also subject to the guidance in ASC 360-10-35. An asset is considered abandoned when it ceases to be used. Each implementation cost should be evaluated separately. (ASC 350-40-35-12)

Amortization—Costs of a Hosting Arrangement That Is a Service Contract Subsection Customer entities are required to expense the capitalized implementation costs of a hosting arrangement that is a service contract over the term of the arrangement. The capitalized implementation costs should be amortized on a straight-line basis unless another systematic and rational manner better represents its use. (ASC 350-40-35-13) Periodically, the customer entity should reassess the estimated term of the arrangement. Any change should be accounted for as a change in accounting estimate under ASC 250. (ASC 350-40-35-15)

Under ASU 2018-15, the term includes the noncancellable period of the arrangement plus periods covered by:

- An option to extend the arrangement provided the customer is reasonably certain to exercise the option,
- An option to terminate the arrangement if the customer is reasonably certain not to exercise the termination option, and
- An option to extend or not to terminate the arrangement where exercise of the option is in the control of the vendor.
  (ASC 350-40-35-14)

When considering and reassessing the terms of the hosting arrangement, the entity should weigh the effects of:

- Obsolescence,
- New technology,
- Competition,

- Other economic factors,
- Rapid changes, and
- Significant implementation costs when the option to extend or terminate becomes exercisable. (ASC 350-40-35-16)

Amortization should begin when the module or components are ready for its intended use, regardless of whether the overall CCA has been placed in service. This occurs when all substantial testing is complete. (ASC 350-40-35-17)

Authoritative Literature—ASC 350-50, *Website Development Costs*

Scope All of the ASC 350 subtopics follow the scope guidance in ASC 350-10. In addition, the guidance in ASC 350-50 applies to costs incurred to develop a website, but does not apply to the cost of hardware and acquisition of servers and related hardware transactions. (ASC 350-50-15-2 and 15-3)

Capitalization of Costs The costs of developing a website, including the costs of developing services that are offered to site visitors (e.g., chat rooms, search engines, blogs, social networking, e-mail, calendars, and so forth), are often quite significant. The SEC staff had expressed the opinion that a large portion of those costs should be accounted for in accordance with ASC 350-50, which sets forth certain conditions that must be met before costs may be capitalized.

Here is the accounting treatment for website development costs:

- Costs incurred in the planning stage must be expensed as incurred. (ASC 350-50-25-2)
- The cost of software used to operate a website must be accounted for consistent with ASC 350-40, unless a plan exists to market the software externally, in which case ASC 985-20, *Software—Costs of Software to Be Sold, Leased, or Marketed*, governs, and costs should be expensed until the entity establishes the software's technological feasibility.
- Costs incurred to develop graphics (broadly defined as the "look and feel" of the web page) are included in software costs, and thus accounted for under ASC 350-40 or ASC 985-20. (ASC 350-50-25-4)
- Costs of hosting websites are generally expensed over the benefit period. (ASC 350-50- 25-5)

ASC 350-50-55 includes a detailed list stipulating how a variety of specific costs are to be accounted for under its requirements.

PRACTICE ALERT

While SEC comments pertain to public entities, those comments can often provide valuable practice pointers for preparers of nonpublic entity financial statements. In the area of goodwill the SEC has commented in recent years that entities should:

- Disclose the accounting policy for goodwill impairment.
- Consider reporting units that may be at risk of impairment and disclose:
  - Identity of the reporting unit.
  - The goodwill amount.
  - The method and key assumptions used to determine fair value.
  - The percentage by which fair value exceeds the carrying value
  - How the entity determined the key assumptions.
  - The timing of impairment losses.

- Consider potential events that could have a negative effect on goodwill.
- Document the judgments made when determining that the fair value is not significantly more than the carrying value and, therefore, putting the goodwill at risk.
- Document the timing of a goodwill impairment change to establish that the change should not have been made in a previous period.
- Document the reasons for and results of goodwill impairment tests, and, if no goodwill impairment loss was recognized, why not.

In the area of intangible assets, other than goodwill, the SEC has commented in recent years that entities should:

- Provide an explanation of how the entity determined the useful lives of finite-lived assets.
- Include information about how the amortization method for intangible assets was selected.
- Consider the useful life of a finite lived intangible asset, considering especially the underlying assumptions.
- Document how the useful life of an intangible asset with an indefinite life was determined.
- Consider how the period over which the intangible asset is expected to contribute to cash flows.

PRESENTATION AND DISCLOSURE REQUIREMENTS

Detailed presentation and disclosure requirements can be found at www.wiley.com/go/FSDM2021.

Note: ASC 350-10 has no presentation or disclosure requirements.

Goodwill

Presentation Entities must present:

- On the balance sheet, the aggregate amount of goodwill on the balance sheet.
- For a goodwill impairment loss not associated with a discontinued operation, the aggregate amount of goodwill impairment losses presented as a separate line item in the income statement before the substantial income from continuing operations.
- Included net-of-tax within the results of discontinued operations, goodwill impairment loss associated with discontinued operations.
  (ASC 350-20-45-1-43-3)

Private Company Alternative On the balance sheet, entities should present the aggregate amount of goodwill, net of accumulated amortization and impairment. (ASC 350-20-45-5) On the income statement, within continuing operations, the entity should present the amortization and aggregate amount of goodwill impairment if not associated with a discontinued operation. (ASC 350-20-45-6) If associated with a discontinued operation, the amortization and impairment should be shown net of tax within the results of discontinued operations. (ASC 350-20-45-7)

Disclosure For goodwill, entities should include a reconciliation of changes in the carrying amount during the period, showing separately:

- The gross amount and accumulated impairment losses at the beginning of the period.
- Additional goodwill recognized during the period, except goodwill that is included in a disposal group that, upon acquisition, meets the criteria in ASC 360 to be classified as held for sale.

- Adjustments resulting from the subsequent recognition of deferred tax assets during the period in accordance with ASC 805-740.
- Goodwill included in a disposal group classified as held for sale in accordance with 360-10-45-9 and goodwill derecognized during the period without having previously been reported in a disposal group classified as held for sale.
- Impairment losses recognized during the period.
- Net foreign exchange differences arising during the period.
- Any other changes in carrying amounts during the period.
- The gross amount and accumulated impairment losses at the end of the period.

Note: For entities that report segment information in accordance with Topic 280, provide the above information about goodwill in total and for each reportable segment and disclose any significant changes in the allocation of goodwill by reportable segment. If any portion of goodwill has not yet been allocated to a reporting unit at the date the financial statements are issued, disclose that unallocated amount and the reasons for not allocating that amount. (ASC 350-20-50-1)

For entities with reporting units with zero or negative carrying amounts of net assets, the following should be disclosed:

- Those reporting units with allocated goodwill,
- The amount of goodwill, and
- Reportable segment where unit appears.
  (ASC 350-20-50-1A)

Disclosure for goodwill impairment losses recognized during the period include:

- The facts and circumstances causing the impairment.
- The amount of the impairment loss and the method of determining fair value of the associated reporting unit (whether based on quoted market prices; prices of comparable businesses; or present value or other valuation techniques; or a combination of these methods).
- If the amount recognized is an estimate that has not yet been finalized, that fact and the reasons why the estimate is not yet complete.[9]
  (ASC 350-20-50-2)

Private Company Alternative Private companies that choose the accounting alternative are required to disclose in the notes:

- For any addition to goodwill for each period for which a statement of financial position is presented:
  - Amount assigned to goodwill in total by major business combination or by reorganization event that results in fresh-start reporting.
  - The weighted average amortization period in total and by major business combination or by reorganization event that results in fresh-start reporting.
    (ASC 350-20-50-4)
- For each period for which a statement of financial position is presented:
  - The gross carrying amount of:
    - Goodwill.

---

[9] This item is superseded upon implementation of ASU 2017-04.

- Accumulated amortization.
- Accumulated impairment loss.
- Aggregate amortization expense.
- Goodwill in a disposal group classified as held for sale.
- Goodwill recognized during the period without having previously been reported in a disposal group classified as held for sale.
  (ASC 350-20-50-5)
- For each goodwill impairment loss:
  - Description of the facts and circumstances leading to the impairment.
  - Amount of the loss and how the fair value of the entity or reporting unit was determined.
  - Where the impairment loss is included in the income statement amount.
  - Method used to allocate the loss to the individual amortizable units of goodwill.
    (ASC 350-20-50-6)
- Quantitative disclosures about significant unobservable inputs used in fair value measurements categorized in Level 3 required by ASC 820-10-50-2 (bbb) are not required for fair value measurements related to the financial accounting and reporting for goodwill after its initial recognition in a business combination.
  (ASC 350-20-50-7)

Intangible Assets

Presentation Intangible assets should be presented separately in the balance sheet. (ASC 350-30-45-1) Entities may want to consider the SEC benchmark of 5% of total assets when determining if a class of intangible assets should be presented separately.

Amortization expense and impairment losses for intangible assets should be presented in line items in the continuing operations section of the income statement. (ASC 350-30-45-2)

Disclosure In the year of acquisition, entities must disclose:

- The amount of research and development costs acquired in other than a business combination or acquisition,
- The amount written off, and
- The line item that contains the amounts written off.
  (ASC 350-30-50-1)

For each period for which a statement of financial position is presented, entities should disclose:

- For tangible assets subject to amortization:
  - Gross carrying amount and accumulated amortization, in total and by major class of intangible asset.
  - Amortization expense for the period.
  - Estimated aggregate amortization expenses for each of the five succeeding fiscal years as of the date of the latest statement of financial position presented.
- For intangible assets not subject to amortization, the total carrying amount and the carrying amount for each major intangible asset class.
- The entity's accounting policy on the treatment of costs incurred to renew or extend the term of a recognized intangible asset.
- If intangible assets have been renewed or extended in the period for which the statement of financial position is presented:

- ○ If capitalized, the total amount of costs incurred to renew or extend the term of a recognized intangible asset, by major intangible asset class.
- ○ Weighted-average period before the next renewal or extension, by major intangible asset class.
  (ASC 350-30-50-2)

For impairment losses, entities must disclose:

- ○ A description of the impaired asset.
- ○ The facts and circumstances leading to the impairment.
- ○ The amount of the loss.
- ○ The method for determining fair value.
- ○ The line item where the loss is aggregated.
- ○ The segment in which the impaired intangible asset is reported.
  (ASC 350-30-50-3)

The entity may be able to extend or renew that asset's legal or contracted life. Entities must disclose management's intent and/or ability to do so and its effect on cash flows. (ASC 350-30-50-4)

Internal Software—Cloud Computing Arrangements

Presentation

Balance Sheet Capitalized implementation costs should be classified in the same line item as amounts prepaid for the hosted CCA service, usually as an other asset. Licensed internal-use software is classified as an intangible asset. (ASC 350-40-45-2)

Income Statement Amortization of capitalized implementation costs should be presented in the same line item as the fees for the hosted CCA service and not included with property, plant, and equipment or intangible assets. (ASC 350-40-45-1)

Cash Flows Entities should present cash flows related to capitalized implementation costs in a manner consistent with the fees related to the hosted CCA service. This is generally in cash flows from operations. (ASC 350-40-45-3)

Disclosure Entities must disclose the nature of the entity's hosting arrangements that are service contracts with material capitalized implementation costs. (ASC 350-40-50-2 and 50-3)

PRESENTATION AND DISCLOSURE EXAMPLES

Example 24.1: Accounting Policy, Goodwill

Goodwill is the excess of cost of an acquired entity over the amounts assigned to assets acquired and liabilities assumed in a business combination. Goodwill is not amortized. Goodwill is tested for impairment annually in the fourth quarter of each year, and is tested for impairment between annual tests if an event occurs or circumstances change that would indicate the carrying amount may be impaired. Impairment testing for goodwill is done at a reporting unit level, with all goodwill assigned to a reporting unit. Reporting units are one level below the business segment level, but are required to be combined when reporting units within the same segment have similar economic characteristics. ABC did not combine any of its reporting units for impairment testing. The impairment loss is measured as the amount by which the carrying value of the reporting unit's net assets exceeds its estimated fair value, not to exceed the carrying value of the reporting unit's goodwill. The estimated fair value of a reporting unit is determined using earnings for the reporting unit multiplied by a price/earnings ratio for comparable industry groups or by using a discounted cash flow analysis. Companies have the option to first assess qualitative factors to determine whether the fair value of a reporting unit is not "more likely than not" less than its carrying amount, which is commonly referred to as "Step 0." ABC has chosen not to apply Step 0 for its annual goodwill assessments.

Example 24.2: Accounting Policy for Timing of Tests of Goodwill Impairment

Accounting standards require that goodwill be tested for impairment annually and between annual tests in certain circumstances such as a change in reporting units or the testing of recoverability of a significant asset group within a reporting unit. At ABC, reporting units correspond to a division.

Example 24.3: Adoption of ASU 2017-04

In January 2017, the FASB issued ASU 2017-04, *Intangibles—Goodwill and Other (Topic 350): Simplifying the Test for Goodwill Impairment*. Topic 350, *Intangibles—Goodwill and Other (Topic 350)*, currently requires an entity that has not elected the private company alternative for goodwill to perform a two-step test to determine the amount, if any, of goodwill impairment. In Step 1, an entity compares the fair value of a reporting unit with its carrying amount, including goodwill. If the carrying amount of the reporting unit exceeds its fair value, the entity performs Step 2 and compares the implied fair value of goodwill with the carrying amount of the goodwill for that reporting unit. An impairment charge equal to the amount by which the carrying amount of goodwill for the reporting unit exceeds the implied fair value of that goodwill is recorded, limited to the amount of goodwill allocated to that reporting unit. To address concerns over the cost and complexity of the two-step goodwill impairment test, the amendments in this ASU remove the second step of the test. An entity will now apply a one-step quantitative test and record the amount of goodwill impairment as the excess of a reporting unit's carrying amount over its fair value, not to exceed the total amount of goodwill allocated to the reporting unit. The new guidance does not amend the optional qualitative assessment of goodwill impairment. The Company elected to early adopt ASU 2017-04 effective March 31, 2017.

Goodwill impairment is tested at least annually (October 1st) or when factors indicate potential impairment using a two-step process that begins with a qualitative evaluation of each reporting unit. If such test indicates potential for impairment, a one-step quantitative test is performed and if there is excess of a reporting unit's carrying amount over its fair value, impairment is recorded, not to exceed the total amount of goodwill allocated to the reporting unit.

Estimating the fair value of a reporting unit requires various assumptions including projections of future cash flows, perpetual growth rates and discount rates. The assumptions about future cash flows and growth rates are based on the Company's assessment of a number of factors, including the reporting unit's recent performance against budget, performance in the market that the reporting unit serves, and industry and general economic data from third-party sources. Discount rate assumptions are based on an assessment of the risk inherent in those future cash flows. Changes to the underlying businesses could affect the future cash flows, which in turn could affect the fair value of the reporting unit.

Example 24.4: Roll-forward of Goodwill by Business Segment

Goodwill from acquisitions total $3.5 million in 20X9, none of which is deductible for tax purposes. There were no acquisitions that closed during 20X8. The acquisition activity in the following table also includes the net impact of adjustments to the preliminary allocation of purchase price within the one year measurement-period following prior acquisitions, which increased goodwill by $700,000 during 20X8. The amounts in the "Translation and other" columns in the following table primarily relate to changes in foreign currency exchange rates. The goodwill balance by business segment follows:

(Thousands)	*Hardware*	*Software*	*Services*	*Financing*	*Total Company*
Balance as of					
December 31, 20X7	$ 5,077	$ 1,886	$ 3,317	$ 233	$ 10,513
Acquisition activity	7	—	—	—	7
Divestiture activity	(268)	—	(4)	—	(272)
Translation and other	(100)	(29)	(65)	(3)	(197)
Balance as of					
December 31, 20X8	4,716	1,857	3,248	230	10,051
Acquisition activity	—	—	**3,469**	—	**3,469**
Divestiture activity	**(49)**	—	—	—	**(49)**
Translation and other	(46)	(27)	22	24	(27)
Balance as of					
December 31, 20X9	$ 4,621	$ 1,830	$ 6,739	$ 254	$ 13,444

Example 24.5: Assessment of Effect of Changes in Segment Reporting on Goodwill

Effective in the second quarter of 20X9, the Company realigned its former five business segments into four to enable the Company to better serve global customers and markets. In addition, effective in the first quarter of 20X9, the Company changed its business segment reporting in its continuing effort to improve the alignment of its businesses around markets and customers. For any product changes that resulted in reporting unit changes, the Company applied the relative fair value method to determine the impact on goodwill of the associated reporting units. Goodwill balances reported above reflect these business segment reporting changes in the earliest period presented. During the first and second quarters of 20X9, the Company completed its assessment of any potential goodwill impairment for reporting units impacted by this new structure and determined that no impairment existed. The Company also completed its annual goodwill impairment test in the fourth quarter of 20X9 for all reporting units and determined that no impairment existed. In addition, the Company had no impairments of goodwill in 20X8 or 20X7.

Example 24.6: Accounting Policy, Intangible Assets

Intangible asset types include customer related, patents, other technology-based, tradenames and other intangible assets acquired from an independent party. Intangible assets with a definite life are amortized over a period ranging from four to twenty years on a systematic and rational basis (generally straight line) that is representative of the asset's use. The estimated useful lives vary by category, with customer-related largely between twelve and nineteen years, patents largely between six and seventeen years, other technology-based largely between six and fifteen years, definite lived tradenames largely between six and twenty years, and other intangibles largely between five and thirteen years.

Intangible assets are removed from their respective gross asset and accumulated amortization accounts when they are no longer in use. Costs related to internally developed intangible assets, such as patents, are expensed as incurred, within "Research, development and related expenses."

Intangible assets with a definite life are tested for impairment whenever events or circumstances indicate that the carrying amount of an asset (asset group) may not be recoverable. An impairment loss is recognized when the carrying amount exceeds the estimated undiscounted cash flows from the asset's or asset group's ongoing use and eventual disposition. If an impairment is identified, the amount of the impairment loss recorded is calculated by the excess of the asset's carrying value over its fair value. Fair value is generally determined using a discounted cash flow analysis.

Intangible assets with an indefinite life, namely certain tradenames, are not amortized. Indefinite-lived intangible assets are tested for impairment annually, and are tested for impairment between annual tests if an event occurs or circumstances change that would indicate that the carrying amount may be impaired. An impairment loss would be recognized when the fair value is less than the carrying value of the indefinite-lived intangible asset.

Example 24.7: Accounting Policy for Tradenames with Indefinite Lives

Certain tradenames acquired by ABC are not amortized because they have been in existence for over 55 years, have a history of leading-market share positions, have been and are intended to be continuously renewed, and the associated products of which are expected to generate cash flows for 3M for an indefinite period of time.

Example 24.8: Disclosure of Gross Carrying Amount of Intangible Assets and Accumulated Amortization

The carrying amount and accumulated amortization of acquired finite-lived intangible assets, in addition to the balance of nonamortizable intangible assets, as of December 31, follow:

(In thousands)	*December 31, 20X9*	*December 31, 20X8*
Customer-related intangible assets	$ 4,316	$ 2,291
Patents	538	542
Other technology-based intangible assets	2,124	576
Definite-lived tradenames	1,158	664
Other amortizable intangible assets	125	125
Total gross carrying amount	$ 8,261	$ 4,198
Accumulated amortization—customer related	(1,180)	(998)
Accumulated amortization—patents	(499)	(487)
Accumulated amortization—other technology-based	(435)	(333)
Accumulated amortization—definite-lived tradenames	(316)	(276)
Accumulated amortization—other	(90)	(88)
Total accumulated amortization	$ (2,520)	$ (2,182)
Total finite-lived intangible assets—net	$ 5,741	$ 2,016
Nonamortizable intangible assets (primarily tradenames)	638	641
Total intangible assets—net	$ 6,379	$ 2,657

Example 24.9: Roll-forward of Carrying Amount of Identifiable Intangible Assets with Narrative

The following table summarizes identifiable intangible assets of the Company as of December 31, 20X3 and 20X2:

December 31, 20X3	Useful Lives (In Years)	Gross Carrying Amount	Accumulated Amortization	Net Carrying Amount
Amortized:				
Customer relationships	9–12	$ 19,299	$ (1,108)	$ 18,191
Trademark and tradename	3–15	7,553	(488)	7,065
Patents	7–11	2,117	(1,436)	681
Technology	7	10,911	(634)	10,277
Favorable contract interest	4	388	(234)	154
Covenant not to compete	5	208	(102)	106
		40,476	(4,002)	36,474
Unamortized:				
Customer list		104	—	104
Trademark and tradename		61	—	61
		165	—	165
Total		$ 40,641	$ (4,002)	$ 36,639

December 31, 20X2	Useful Lives (in Years)	Gross Carrying Amount	Accumulated Amortization	Net Carrying Amount
Amortized:				
Customer relationships	10	$ 3,123	$ (442)	$ 2,681
Trademark and tradename	10–15	1,367	(178)	1,189
Patents	11	1,489	(1,218)	271
Favorable contract interest	5	388	(137)	251
Covenant not to compete	5	208	(60)	148
		6,575	(2,035)	4,540
Unamortized:				
Customer list		104	—	104
Trademark and tradename		61	—	61
		165	—	165
Total		$ 6,740	$ (2,035)	$ 4,705

The Company tests the goodwill and other indefinite lives intangible assets on an annual basis in the fourth quarter or more frequently if the Company believes indicators of impairment exist. As of December 31, 20X2 and 20X3, the Company determined that no impairment existed to the goodwill, customer list and trademark and trade name of its acquired intangibles.

The Company also determined that the use of indefinite lives for the customer list and remaining trademark and trade name remains applicable at December 31, 20X2 and 20X3, as the Company expects to continue to derive future benefits from these intangible assets.

At December 31, 20X3, the weighted-average amortization period for the intangible assets was 9.0 years. At December 31, 20X3, the weighted-average amortization periods for customer relationships, trademarks and trade names, patents, favorable contract interests, and covenant not to compete were 11.9, 4.5, 7.5, 4.0, and 5.0 years, respectively.

Amortization expense for the years ended December 31, 20X1, 20X2, and 20X3 was $375, $712 and $1,967, respectively. Estimated future amortization expense for each of the five succeeding fiscal years for these intangible assets is as follows:

Year ending December 31	
20X4	$ 5,329
20X5	5,153
20X6	4,479
20X7	4,434
20X8	4,431
Thereafter	12,648
	$ 36,474

The change in goodwill from January 1, 20X3 to December 31, 20X3 is as follows:

Balance as of January 1, 20X3	$ 7,318
Blake acquisition	78,642
Lauren acquisitions	3,108
Balance as of December 31, 20X3	$ 89,068

Example 24.10: Accounting Policy, Internal-Use Software

The Company capitalizes direct costs of services used in the development of, and external software acquired for use as, internal-use software. Amounts capitalized are amortized over a period of three to seven years, generally on a straight-line basis, unless another systematic and rational basis is more representative of the software's use. Amounts are reported as a component of either machinery and equipment or finance leases within property, plant, and equipment. Fully depreciated internal-use software assets are removed from property, plant, and equipment and accumulated depreciation accounts.

25 ASC 360 PROPERTY, PLANT, AND EQUIPMENT

ACCOUNTING REQUIREMENTS

Subtopics

ASC 360, *Property, Plant, and Equipment*, consists of two Subtopics:

- ASC 360-10, *Overall*, which is further divided into two Subsections:
  - *General*, which provides guidance on accounting and reporting on property, plant, and equipment, including accumulated depreciation.
  - *Impairment or disposal of long-lived assets*, which contains guidance for:
    - Recognizing impairment of long-lived assets to be held and used,
    - Long-lived assets to be disposed of by sale, and
    - Disclosures for the implementation and disposals of individually significant components of an entity.
- ASC 360-20, *Real Estate Sales—Sale Leaseback Accounting*, which provides guidance to determine if a sale of real estate has occurred for purposes of applying sale-leaseback accounting. This subtopic is superseded upon adoption of ASU 2016-02, *Leases*.

AUTHORITATIVE LITERATURE

ASC 360-10, *Overall*

Scope and Scope Exceptions The guidance in the ASC 360-10, *General*, Subsection applies to all entities.

The guidance in the ASC 360-10, *Impairment or Disposal of Long-Lived Assets*, Subsection applies to:

- Capital leases of lessees or when ASU 2016-02 is implemented, right-of-use assets of lessees,
- Long-lived assets of lessors subject to operating leases,
- Proved oil and gas properties accounted for using the successful-efforts method of accounting, and
- Long-term prepaid assets.
  (ASC 360-10-15-4)

The guidance in both these Subsections does *not* apply to the following transactions and activities:

- Goodwill.
- Intangible assets not being amortized that are to be held and used.
- Servicing assets.
- Financial instruments, including investments in equity securities accounted for under the cost or equity method.
- Deferred policy acquisition costs.
- Deferred tax assets.
- Unproved oil and gas properties that are being accounted for using the successful-efforts method of accounting.
- Oil and gas properties that are accounted for using the full-cost method of accounting as prescribed by the Securities and Exchange Commission (SEC) (see Regulation S-X, Rule 4-10, Financial Accounting and Reporting for Oil and Gas Producing Activities Pursuant to the Federal Securities Laws and the Energy Policy and Conservation Act of 1975).
- Certain other long-lived assets for which the accounting is prescribed elsewhere in the standards. See:
  - ASC 928, *Entertainment—Music*
  - ASC 920, *Entertainment—Broadcasters*
  - ASC 985-20, *Software*
  - ASC 980-360, *Regulated Operations*
    (ASC 360-10-15-5)

Entities holding collections should look to the guidance in ASC 958-360. (ASC 360-10-15-6)

Recognition and Measurement Entities use historical cost to value property, plant, and equipment. Upon acquisition, the reporting entity measures and capitalizes all the historical costs necessary to deliver the asset to its intended location and prepare it for its productive use, including any encumbrances, such as tax liens. (ASC 360-10-30-1) Interest costs incurred during the period of time necessary to ready the asset for use are also part of its cost. (ASC 835-20-05-1)

All direct costs (labor, materials, payroll, and related benefit costs) of constructing an entity's own tangible fixed assets are capitalized. However, a degree of judgment is involved in allocating costs between indirect costs—a reasonable portion of which are allocable to construction costs—and general and administrative costs, which are treated as period costs.

An interest in the residual value of a leased asset is recorded as an asset at the date the right is acquired. (ASC 360-10-25-4) The asset is recorded initially at:

- The amount of cash disbursed,
- The fair value of other consideration, and
- The present value of liabilities assumed.
  (ASC 360-10-30-3)

To measure cost, entities may use the fair value of the interest acquired if it is more evident than the fair value of assets or services surrendered or liabilities assumed. (ASC 360-10-30-4)

It is important to differentiate the acquisition of assets in a group from those acquired in a business combination. If the assets acquired and liabilities assumed constitute a "business," the transaction is a business combination, and it is accounted for under the guidance in ASC 805. Otherwise, it is accounted for as an asset acquisition. For guidance related to assets acquired in a business combination, see the chapter on ASC 805.

Assets acquired in an asset acquisition are initially recognized at their cost to the acquirer, including related transaction costs. The costs of assets acquired as a group are allocated to the individual assets acquired or liabilities assumed based on their relative fair values. Goodwill is recognized in a transaction of this nature.

The proper accounting treatment postacquisition depends on a careful analysis of whether the cost is expected to provide future benefits to the reporting entity and, if so, the nature of those expected benefits. Costs incurred that bring greater future benefit should generally be capitalized. There are two major categories of such costs:

1. Costs that increase the value of the asset by increasing capacity or operating efficiency. In effect, a new asset has been created that is subject to the same capitalization considerations applied in recognizing the original asset. When the cost is significant, the cost is capitalized and the depreciation for future periods is revised based on the new book value of the asset.
2. Costs that increase the useful life of the asset.

The costs of property, plant, and equipment are allocated to the periods of their expected useful life through depreciation or depletion. (ASC 360-10-35-4) The method of depreciation or depletion chosen is that which results in a systematic and rational allocation of the cost of the asset (less its residual or salvage value) over the asset's expected useful life, the periods over which the entity will benefit. (ASC 360-10-35-4)

The impairment provisions of ASC 360-10 are generally split between:

- Long-lived assets classified as held and used, and
- Long-lived assets classified as held for sale.

Note that the Codification rules for measuring and recording impairment of assets are not uniform for all assets or for all industries, and preparers should review the applicable industry guidance.

Impairment losses for long-lived assets to be held and used are only recognized when the carrying amount of the impaired asset (or asset group) is not recoverable and exceeds its fair value. Recoverability is determined by comparing the carrying amount of the asset (or asset group) on the date it is being evaluated for recoverability to the sum of the undiscounted cash flows expected to result from its use and eventual disposition. It is important to note that, as opposed to the measure used in recoverability testing, the impairment loss to be recorded is measured by the amount by which the carrying amount exceeds its fair value. If the carrying value is recoverable from expected future cash flows from its use and disposition, as defined, no impairment loss is recognized. (ASC 360-10-35-17)

Long-lived assets (disposal groups) classified as held-for-sale are measured at the lower of their carrying amount or fair value less cost to sell. (ASC 360-10-35-43) A loss is recognized for any initial or subsequent write-down to fair value less cost to sell. A gain is recognized for any subsequent increase in fair value less cost to sell, but recognized gains may not exceed the cumulative losses previously recognized.

Long-lived assets (disposal groups) being held for sale are not depreciated (amortized) while being presented under the held-for-sale classification. Interest and other expenses related to the liabilities of a held-for-sale disposal group are accrued as incurred.

Impairment losses from long-lived assets to be held and used, gains or losses recognized on long-lived assets to be sold, and other costs associated with exit or disposal activities (as defined in ASC 420) should be accounted for consistently. Therefore, if the entity reports income from operations, these amounts are reported in operations unless they qualify as discontinued operations.

Upon removal of an individual asset or liability from a disposal group classified as held-for-sale, the remaining part of the group should be evaluated to determine if it still meets the criteria to be classified as held-for-sale. If all of the criteria are still met, then the remaining assets and liabilities will continue to be measured and accounted for as a group. If not all of the criteria are met, then the remaining long-lived assets are to be measured individually at the lower of their carrying amounts or fair value less cost to sell at that date. (ASC 360-10-35-45) Any assets that will not be sold are reclassified as held-and-used as described above. (ASC 360-10-35-44)

If the entity commits to a plan to abandon an asset before the end of its previously estimated useful life, the depreciable life is revised in accordance with the rules governing a change in estimate under ASC 250 and depreciation of the asset continues until the end of its shortened useful life. (ASC 360-10-35-47) Abandoned assets are considered disposed of when they cease to be used. Temporary idling of an asset, however, is not considered abandonment. (ASC 360-10-35-49)

At the time an asset is abandoned, its carrying value should be adjusted to its salvage value, if any, but not less than zero (i.e., a liability cannot be recorded upon abandonment). (ASC 360-10-35-48) If an acquired asset meets the criteria to be considered a defensive intangible asset, it is prohibited from being considered abandoned upon its acquisition.

Authoritative Literature—ASC 360-20, *Real Estate Sales—Sale Leaseback Accounting*

Note: Upon implementation of ASU 2016-02, Leases, this Subtopic is superseded. See the chapter on ASC 842 for more information.

Entities must determine under what circumstances a transaction is an in-substance sale of real estate. To make that determination, ASC 360-20 suggests the preparer consider the nature of the entire component being sold, that is

- The land,
- The property improvements, and
- The integral equipment.

Further, when making that determination, entities should not consider whether the operations in which the assets are involved are traditional or nontraditional real estate activities. For example, if a ski resort is sold and the lodge and ski lifts are considered to be affixed to the land (that is, they cannot be removed and used separately without incurring significant cost), then it would appear that the sale is in substance the sale of real estate and that the entire sale transaction would be subject to the provisions of ASC 360-20. For purposes of determining profit recognition involving the sale of underlying land (or the sale of the property improvements or integral equipment subject to a lease of the underlying land), the transactions should not be bifurcated into a real estate component (the sale of the underlying land) and a non–real estate component (the sale of the lodge and lifts). (ASC 360-20-15-2)

In addition, the following assets that are part of a sale-leaseback transaction are included in ASC 360-20 guidance.

1. Real estate, including real estate with property improvements or integral equipment. The terms *property improvements* and *integral equipment* as they are used in this Subtopic refer to any physical structure or equipment attached to the real estate that cannot be removed and used separately without incurring significant cost. Examples include an office building, a manufacturing facility, a power plant, and a refinery.
2. Property improvements or integral equipment subject to an existing lease of the underlying land should be accounted for in accordance with paragraphs 360-20-40-56 through 40-59.
3. An investment in the form of a financial asset that is in substance real estate.
4. Timberlands or farms (that is, land with trees or crops attached to it).
   (ASC 360-20-15-3)

ASC 360-20-15 *excludes* the following transactions and activities:

- The sale of only property improvements or integral equipment without a concurrent (or contemplated) sale of the underlying land. However, ASC 360-20 does apply to sales of property improvements or integral equipment with the concurrent lease (whether explicit or implicit in the transaction) of the underlying land to the buyer.
- The sale of the stock or net assets of a subsidiary or a segment of a business if the assets of that subsidiary or that segment contain real estate. If such a transaction is, in substance, the sale of real estate, ASC 360-20 does apply.
- Exchanges of real estate for other real estate. See the accounting for nonmonetary transactions in ASC 845.
- The sale of debt and equity securities accounted for under ASC 320 or ASC 321. See ASC 860 for guidance on sales of such assets.
- Retail land sales.
- Natural assets such as those that have been extracted from the land (for example, oil, gas, coal, and gold). See ASC 932.
  (ASC 360-20-15-10)

Profit Recognition In some transactions the seller, rather than an independent third party, finances the buyer, while in others, the seller may be required to guarantee a minimum return to the buyer or continue to operate the property for a specified period of time. In many of these complex transactions, the seller still has some association with the property even after the property has been sold. The question that must be answered in these transactions is: At what point does the seller become disassociated enough from the property that profit may be recognized on the transaction?

Profit from real estate sales is recognized in full, provided the following:

- The profit is determinable (i.e., the collectability of the sales price is reasonably assured or the amount that will not be collectible can be estimated), and
- The earnings process is virtually complete, that is, the seller is not obliged to perform significant activities after the sale to earn the profit.
(ASC 360-20-40-3)

When both of these conditions are satisfied, the method used to recognize profits on real estate sales is referred to as the full accrual method. If both of these conditions are not satisfied, recognition of all or part of the profit is postponed.

The profit is recognized by the full accrual method when all of the following criteria are met (ASC 360-20-40-5):

1. A sale is consummated.
2. The buyer's initial and continuing investments are adequate to demonstrate a commitment to pay for the property.
3. The seller's receivable is not subject to future subordination.
4. The seller has transferred to the buyer the usual risks and rewards of ownership in a transaction that is in substance a sale, and the seller does not have a substantial continuing involvement in the property.

If all of the criteria have not been met, the seller records the transaction by one of the following methods as indicated by ASC 360-20-40-21 through 40-64:

- Deposit
- Cost recovery
- Installment
- Reduced profit
- Percentage-of-completion

PRACTICE ALERT

While SEC comments do not pertain to nonpublic entities, their comments can often provide valuable guidance. SEC questions on property, plant, and equipment related to the following areas:

- How an entity valued acquired property, plant, and equipment.
- The presentation of property, plant, and equipment in the statement of cash flows, recommending presenting the cash flows gross rather than net.
- The impairment analysis, requesting indicators of impairment lost for recoverability, and measurement of impairment.
- Whether the criteria listed in ASC 360-10-45-9 were met for a disposal group to be classified as held for sale. Among the items the SEC has questioned is management approval, for instance, if a majority of the company stockholders, where necessary had approved the sale.

PRESENTATION AND DISCLOSURE REQUIREMENTS

Presentation

Long-Lived Assets Classified as Held and Used Impairment loss is recognized for a long-lived asset (asset group) to be held and used:

- In income from continuing operations before income taxes.
- Include in income from operations subtotal if presented.
  (ASC 360-10-45-4)

Gain or loss, recognized on the sale of a long-lived asset (disposal group) that is not a discontinued operation is included:

- In income from continuing operations before income taxes.
- In income from operations subtotal if presented.
  (ASC 360-10-45-5)

Long-lived assets no longer classified as held for sale should be reclassified as held and used. (ASC 360-10-45-6) The adjustment required to the carrying amount of an asset (disposal group) being reclassified from held-for-sale to held-and-used is included in income from continuing operations in the period that the decision is made not to sell. (ASC 360-10-45-7)

Long-Lived Assets Classified as Held for Sale

The Six Held-for-Sale Criteria Long-lived assets (or disposal groups) are classified as held-for-sale in the period in which *all* of the following six criteria are met:

1. Management possesses the necessary authority commits to a plan to sell.
2. The asset (disposal group) is immediately available for sale on an "as is" basis (i.e., in its present condition subject only to usual and customary terms for the sale of such assets).
3. An active program to find a buyer and other actions required to execute the plan to sell the asset (disposal group) have commenced.
4. An assessment of management plans indicates that it is unlikely that significant changes will be made to the plan or that the plan will be withdrawn.
5. Sale is probable, as that term is used in the context of ASC 450-20 (i.e., likely to occur), and transfer of the asset (disposal group) is expected to qualify for recognition as a completed sale within one year.
6. The asset (disposal group) is being actively marketed for sale at a price that is reasonable in relation to its current fair value.
   (ASC 360-10-45-9)

When the criteria are no longer met, the asset is reclassified as held and used. (ASC 360-10-45-10) It is possible that events beyond the entity's control may extend the period required to complete the sale. The Codification provides an exception to the one-year rule in number 5 above if:

- The entity, at the date committed to a plan to sell, reasonably expects that entities other than the buyer, will impose conditions and the transfer that will extend the period to sell and a firm purchase commitment must be obtained within one year.
- The entity has a firm purchase commitment and the buyers impose conditions that will extend the period and the actions needed to meet those conditions have or will be initiated timely and a favorable resolution is expected.
- Circumstances previously considered unlikely arise and the entity has initiated the necessary response, the asset is being actively marketed as a reasonable price, and the criteria above from ASC 360-10-45-9 are met.
  (ASC 360-10-45-11)

For a long-lived asset (disposal group) that has been newly acquired in a business combination to be classified as held for sale at the acquisition date, it must:

- Meet criterion 5 above (subject to the same exceptions noted in 5), and
- Any other of the required criteria that are not met at the date of acquisition are judged to be probable of being met within a short period (approximately three months or less) of acquisition. (ASC 360-10-45-12)

If the criteria are met after the date of the statement of financial position but prior to issuance of the entity's financial statements, the long-lived asset continues to be classified as held-and-used at the date of the statement of financial position. (ASC 360-10-45-13) Appropriate subsequent events disclosures would be included in the financial statements in accordance with ASC 855, *Subsequent Events*.

If, at any time after meeting the criteria to be classified as held-for-sale, the asset (disposal group) no longer meets those criteria, the long-lived asset (disposal group) should be reclassified from held-for-sale to held-and-used (ASC 360-10-45-10), measured at the *lower of*:

- Carrying amount prior to classification as held-for-sale, adjusted for any depreciation (amortization) that would have been recognized had the asset (disposal group) continued to be classified as held-and-used, or
- Fair value at the date of the subsequent decision not to sell the asset (disposal group). (ASC 360-10-35-44)

Long-Lived Assets to Be Disposed of Other Than by Sale Long-lived assets may be abandoned, exchanged, or distributed to owners in a spin-off. Until the actual disposal occurs, the assets continue to be classified on the statement of financial position as "held and used." (ASC 360-10-45-15)

Disclosure

Entities must disclose the balance of major classes of depreciable assets, accumulated depreciation, by major or in total, depreciation expenses. The entity also must describe the depreciation method used. (ASC 360-10-50-1)

Impairment of Long-Lived Assets Classified as Held and Used In the period in which an impairment loss is incurred disclosures should include:

- A description of the impaired long-lived asset (asset group) and the facts and circumstances leading to the impairment.
- If not separately presented on the face of the statement, the amount of the impairment loss and the caption in the income statement or the statement of activities that includes that loss.
- The method or methods for determining fair value (whether based on a quoted market price, prices for similar assets, or another valuation technique).
- If applicable, the segment in which the impaired long-lived asset (asset group) is reported under Topic 280.
  (ASC 360-10-50-2)

Long-Lived Assets Classified as Held for Sale or Disposed Of For the period in which a long-lived asset has been disposed of or classified as held for sale, the disclosures should include:

- The facts and circumstances leading to the disposal or expected disposal.
- Manner and timing of disposal.
- Gain or loss recognized.

- If not separately presented, the caption that includes the gain or loss.
- If not separately presented, carrying amounts of the major classes of assets and liabilities included as part of a disposal group classified as held for sale.
- The segment in which the long-lived asset is reported.
(ASC 360-10-50-3)

If a long-lived asset includes an individually significant component of an entity that either has been disposed of or is classified as held for sale and does not qualify for presentation as a discontinued operation, the entity should make these disclosures:

- For public entities and a not-for-profit entity that has issued, or is conduit bond obligor for, securities that are traded, listed, or quoted on an exchange or an over-the-counter market:
  - Pretax profit or loss or change in net assets of the individually significant component of an entity for the period in which it is disposed of or classified as held for sale and prior periods presented.
  - If a noncontrolling interest is included, the pretax profit or loss or change in net assets attributable to the parent for the period in which it is disposed of or classified as held for sale and prior periods presented.
- For all other entities:
  - The pretax profit or loss of change and assets of the individual individually significant component of an entity for the period in which it is disposed of is classified as held for sale and for all prior periods presented.
  - If the individually significant component of an entity includes a noncontrolling interest, the pretax profit or loss or change in net assets attributable to the parent for the period in which it is disposed of or is classified as held for sale.
(ASC 360-10-50-3A)

PRESENTATION AND DISCLOSURE EXAMPLES

Example 25.1: Policy for Maintenance and Repairs

XYZ invests in renewal and maintenance programs, which pertain to cost reduction, cycle time, maintaining and renewing current capacity, eliminating pollution, and compliance. Costs related to maintenance, ordinary repairs, and certain other items are expensed.

Example 25.2: Estimated Service Lives

The Company's property and equipment are recorded at cost and depreciation is computed on a straight-line basis using the following depreciable life ranges:

Category of Property and Equipment	*Depreciable Life Range*
Software, including software developed for internal use	3–5 years
Store-related assets	3–10 years
Leasehold improvements	Shorter of lease term or 10 years
Non-store-related building and site improvements	10–15 years
Other property and equipment	20 years
Buildings	30 years

Example 25.3: Accounting Policy for Disposal of Property and Equipment

When a decision has been made to dispose of property and equipment prior to the end of the previously estimated useful life, depreciation estimates are revised to reflect the use of the asset over the shortened estimated useful life. The Company's cost of assets sold or retired and the related accumulated depreciation are removed from the accounts with any resulting gain or loss included in net income (loss). Maintenance and repairs are charged to expense as incurred. Major renewals and betterments that extend useful lives are capitalized.

Example 25.4: Accounting Policy for Review for Impairment

Long-lived store assets, which include leasehold improvements, store-related assets, and operating lease assets (subsequent to the adoption of ASC 842, *Leases*), are reviewed for impairment whenever events or changes in circumstances indicate that the carrying amount of the assets may not be recoverable. Store assets are grouped at the lowest level for which they are largely independent of other assets or asset groups. If the estimated undiscounted future cash flows related to the asset group are less than the carrying value, the Company recognizes a loss equal to the difference between the carrying value and the estimated fair value, determined by the estimated discounted future cash flows of the asset group. For operating lease assets, the Company determines the fair value of the assets by comparing the contractual rent payments to estimated market rental rates. An individual asset within an asset group is not impaired below its estimated fair value. The fair value of long-lived store assets is determined using Level 3 inputs within the fair value hierarchy.

Example 25.5: Components of Property and Equipment

Property and equipment (which are carried at cost) as of 20X9 and 20X8 year-end are as follows:

(Amounts in thousands)	20X9	20X8
Land	$ 31.9	$ 31.7
Buildings and improvements	405.1	368.6
Machinery, equipment, and computer software	988.0	944.4
Property and equipment—gross	1,425.0	1,344.7
Accumulated depreciation and amortization	(903.5)	(849.6)
Property and equipment—net	$ 521.5	$ 495.1

Example 25.6: Estimated Service Lives and Depreciation Expense

The estimated service lives of property and equipment are principally as follows:

Buildings and improvements	3 to 50 years
Machinery, equipment, and computer software	2 to 15 years

Depreciation expense was $70.1 thousand, $68.8 thousand, and $65.6 thousand in 20X9, 20X8, and 20X7, respectively.

Example 25.7: Cash Flows from Investing Activity, Including Property, Plant, and Equipment

Cash Flows from Investing Activities:

	Years ended December 31		
(Millions)	*20X9*	*20X8*	*20X7*
Purchases of property, plant, and equipment (PP&E)	$ (1,699)	$ (1,577)	$ (1,373)
Proceeds from sale of PP&E and other assets	123	262	49
Acquisitions, net of cash acquired	(4,984)	13	(2,023)
Purchases and proceeds from maturities and sale of marketable securities and investments, net	(192)	669	(798)
Proceeds from sale of businesses, net of cash sold	236	846	1,065
Other—net	72	9	(6)
Net cash provided by (used in) investing activities	$ (6,444)	$ 222	$ (3,086)

26 ASC 405 LIABILITIES

AUTHORITATIVE LITERATURE

Subtopics

ASC 405, *Liabilities*, consists of four Subtopics:

- ASC 405-10, *Overall*, which merely points to other areas of the Codification that contain guidance on liabilities.
- ASC 405-20, *Extinguishments of Liabilities*, which provides guidance on when an entity should consider a liability settled.
- ASC 405-30, *Insurance-Related Assessments*, which provides guidance on items such as assessments for state guaranty funds and workers' compensation second-injury funds.
- ASC 405-40, *Obligations Resulting from Joint and Several Liabilities*, which provides guidance on arrangements where the total amount of the obligation is fixed at the reporting date.

Overview

ASC 405 provides accounting and reporting guidance related to short-term liabilities and certain guidance that may apply broadly to any liability.

Although measurement of liabilities is generally straightforward, some liabilities are difficult to measure because of uncertainties. Uncertainties can impact whether, when, and for how much an obligation will be recognized in the financial statements.

Most entities continue to measure their current liabilities at their settlement value, which is the amount of cash (or its equivalent amount of other assets) that will be paid to the creditor to liquidate the obligation during the current operating cycle. Accounts payable, dividends payable, salaries payable, and other current obligations are measured at settlement value because they require the entity to pay a determinable amount of cash within a relatively short period of time. If a current liability is near its payment date, there will be only an insignificant risk of changes in fair value because of changes in market conditions or the entity's credit standing, and settlement value and fair value will be essentially the same.

Other current liabilities are measured as the proceeds received when the obligation arose. Liabilities that are measured in this manner generally require the entity to discharge the obligation by providing goods or services rather than by paying cash. Deposits payable, or rents paid in advance on the statement of financial position of a lessor, are examples of current liabilities measured by reference to proceeds received.

ASC 405-10, *Overall*

ASC 405-10 contains no guidance. Its purpose is to point to guidance in other areas of the Codification. ASC 410-10-05-02 points to the following Codification topics, which contain guidance on accounting and reporting on liabilities:

- *Asset Retirement and Environmental Obligations*—ASC 410
- *Exit or Disposal Cost Obligations and Contract Liabilities (added by ASU 2014-09)*— ASC 420
- *Deferred Revenue and Contract Liabilities*—ASC 430
- *Commitments*—ASC 440
- *Contingencies*—ASC 450
- *Guarantees*—ASC 460
- *Debt*—ASC 470
- *Distinguishing Liabilities from Equity*—Topic 480

ASC 405-20, *Extinguishments of Liabilities*

ASC 405-20 applies to:

- All entities with the covered transactions, and
- Extinguishments of both financial and nonfinancial liabilities unless addressed by another topic.
  (ASC 405-20-15-2)

Unless addressed by other guidance, the entity recognizes extinguishment of a liability when:

- The debtor pays the creditor.
- The debtor is legally given relief from the liability.
  (ASC 405-20-40-1)

If the entity becomes a guarantor on the debt, the entity applies the guidance in ASC 460. (ASC 405-20-40-2)

ASC 405-30, *Insurance-Related Assessments*

ASC 405-30 applies to entities:

- Subject to guaranty-forward assessments.
- Subject to other insurance-related assessments.
  (ASC 405-30-15-1)

The guidance also applies to assessments mandated by statue or regulatory authority related directly or indirectly to underwriting activities, such as self-insurance. (ASC 405-30-30-15-2)

ASC 405-30 does *not* apply to the following:

- Amounts payable or paid as a result of reinsurance contracts or arrangements that are in substance reinsurance, including assumed reinsurance activities and certain involuntary pools that are covered by Topic 944.
- Assessments of depository institutions related to bank insurance and similar funds.
- The annual fee imposed on health insurers by the Patient Protection and Affordable Care Act as amended by the Health Care and Education Reconciliation Act (the Acts). The accounting for the Acts' fee is addressed in Subtopic 720-50.
(ASC 405-30-15-3)

ASC 405-30 also does not apply to assessments related to income taxes and premium taxes. Entities that self-insure, as well as insurance entities, are subject to assessments related to insurance activities. However, note that the annual fee imposed on health insurers by the Patient Protection and Affordable Care Act is not considered an insurance-related assessment. The accounting for that fee falls under the guidance in ASC 720-50. (ASC 405-30-05-1)

Entities that are subject to assessment recognize liabilities when all of the following conditions are met:

- It is probable, before the financial statements are issued or available to be issued, an assessment will be imposed.
- The events obligating the entity to pay has occurred on or before the date of the financial statements.
- The entity can reasonably estimate the assessment.
(ASC 405-30-25-1)

ASC 405-30-40 requires issuers to derecognize financial liabilities related to breakage amounts in either of the following two ways:

- If the entity expects to have a related breakage amount, derecognize the liability:
  - In amounts proportionate to the pattern of rights expected to be exercised by the holder of the product,
  - To the extent that a significant reversal of the breakage amount will not subsequently occur, or
  - If the entity does not expect to be entitled to a breakage amount, the entity derecognizes the liability when the likelihood of the exercise of rights becomes remote.
(ASC 405-20-40-4)

Entities must reassess their breakage estimates each reporting period. Changes in estimates are accounted for as a change in accounting estimate under the guidance in ASC 250-10-45-17 through 45-20.

ASC 405-40, *Obligations Resulting from Joint and Several Liabilities*

ASC 405-40 applies to all entities and obligations such as debt arrangements, other contractual obligations, and settled litigation and judicial rulings. The guidance does *not* apply to obligations accounted for under the following topics:

- ASC 410, *Asset Retirement and Environmental Obligations*
- ASC 450, *Contingencies*
- ASC 460, *Guarantees*

- ASC 715, *Compensation—Retirement Benefits*
- ASC 740, *Income Taxes*
  (ASC 405-40-15-1)

To be within the scope of this subtopic, the total amount of the entity's and its co-obligors' obligation must be fixed at the reporting date. However, the amount the entity expects to pay on behalf of its co-obligors may be uncertain. (ASC 405-40-15-2)

ASC 405-40 requires an entity to measure obligations resulting from joint and several liability arrangements for which the total amount of the obligation within the scope of the guidance is fixed at the reporting date as the sum of:

- The amount the reporting entity agreed to pay on the basis of its arrangement among its obligors, and
- Any additional amount the entity expects to pay on behalf of its co-obligors.
  (ASC 405-40-30-1)

The corresponding entry depends on the particular facts and circumstances. (ASC 405-40-30-2)

PRESENTATION AND DISCLOSURE REQUIREMENTS

405-20, *Extinguishment of Liabilities*

Disclosure

- Methodology used to recognize breakage.
- Judgment used in applying methodology.
  (ASC 405-20-50-2)

405-30, *Insurance-Related Assessments*

Disclosure

- For discounted loss contingencies:
  - The undiscounted amounts,
  - Related asset for premium tax offsets or policy surcharges, and
  - The discount rate used.
- For undiscounted loss contingencies:
  - Amount of the liability,
  - Related asset for premium tax offsets or policy surcharges,
  - Periods during which the assessments are expected to be paid, and
  - Period during which the recorded premium tax offsets or policy surcharges are expected to be realized.
    (ASC 405-30-50-1)

405-40, *Obligations Resulting from Joint and Several Liability Arrangements*

Disclosure

- About each obligation, or each group of similar obligations, resulting from joint and several liability arrangements for which the total amount under the arrangement is fixed at the reporting date:
  - The nature of the arrangement.
  - How the liability arose.

- ○ The relationship with other co-obligors.
- ○ Terms and conditions of the arrangement.
- ○ The total outstanding amount under the arrangement (not reduced by the effect of any amounts that may be recoverable from other entities.
- ○ The carrying amount of the liability and the carrying amount of any receivable recognized.
- ○ The nature of any recourse provisions that would enable recovery from other entities of the amounts paid, including any limitations on the amounts that might be recovered.
- ○ In the period the liability is initially recognized and measured or in a period the measurement changes significantly:
  - ○ The corresponding entry, and
  - ○ Where the entry was recorded in the financial statements.
    (ASC 405-40-50-1)

PRESENTATION AND DISCLOSURE EXAMPLES

Example 26.1: Stored-Value Cards

Gift Card and Other Deferred Revenue We defer revenue when cash payments are received in advance of satisfying performance obligations, primarily associated with our stored-value cards, merchandise sales, customer loyalty programs, and incentives received from credit card issuers.

We issue stored-value cards that may be redeemed on future merchandise purchases at our stores or through our e-commerce channel. Our stored-value cards have no expiration dates. Revenue from stored-value cards is recognized at a point in time upon redemption of the card and as control of the merchandise is transferred to the customer. Revenue from estimated unredeemed stored-value cards (breakage) is recognized in a manner consistent with our historical redemption patterns over the estimated period of redemption of our cards of approximately four years, the majority of which is recognized within one year of the card's issuance. Breakage revenue is not material to our consolidated financial statements.

Example 26.2: Liability for Insurance-Related Assessments, Not Discounted

Liabilities for guaranty fund and other insurance-related assessments are accrued when an assessment is probable, when it can be reasonably estimated and when the event obligating the entity to pay an imposed or probable assessment has occurred. Liabilities for guaranty funds and other insurance-related assessments are not discounted and are included as part of Other liabilities on the Consolidated Balance Sheets.

Example 26.3: Joint and Several Liability

Heritage LP's 20X9 Senior Notes were issued in a private offering on December 4, 20X2. The 20X9 Senior Notes were guaranteed by Heritage LP's 100% owned subsidiary. Heritage Reserves Operating GP LLC The guarantee by the Subsidiary is full and unconditional, except for customary release provisions. The guarantees by the Parent Guarantor were full and unconditional, except for customary release provisions. The guarantee constitutes joint and several obligations of the Guarantor and Parent Guarantor.

27 ASC 410 ASSET RETIREMENT AND ENVIRONMENTAL OBLIGATIONS

AUTHORITATIVE LITERATURE

Overview

An asset retirement obligation (ARO) is a legal obligation:

- Established between two or more parties,
- Imposed by the government, or
- Arisen because of a promissory estoppel.

Activities that may result in an ARO because of legal obligations include:

- Removal of asbestos when the related asset is retired,
- Removal of transmission assets, such as transformers and wires,
- Cleanup of landfill contamination, or
- Removal of lessee's leasehold improvements

Subtopics

ASC 410, *Asset Retirement and Environmental Obligations*, consists of three Subtopics. The sole purpose of ASC 410-10 is to explain the difference between the other two Subtopics.

Subtopic	Accounting and Financial Reporting of:
ASC 410-20, *Asset Retirement Obligations*	• A liability associated with the retirement of a long-lived asset (ARO) and the associated capitalized asset retirement cost (ARC). • The obligation is unavoidable. • An environmental remediation liability resulting from the acquisition, construction, or development and/or *normal* operation of a long-lived asset.

ASC 410-30, *Environmental Obligations*	• Environmental remediation liabilities that relate to
	  ○ Pollution from some past action generally as a result of:
	    • Provisions of the Superfund Act,
	    • The corrective provisions of the Recourse Conservation Recovery Act, or
	    • Analogous state and non-U.S. laws and regulations.
	
	(ASC 410-30-10-1)

(ASC 410-10-05-2)	

Another way to distinguish AROs from environmental obligations is the timing. If immediate remediation is required, it may be because of the improper operation of an asset, for example, in an oil spill.

The Scope and Scope Exceptions paragraphs provide details of the transactions covered by each subtopic.

ASC 410-20, *Asset Retirement Obligations*

Scope and Scope Exceptions ASC 410-20 applies to all entities and the following events and transactions.

    a. Legal obligations associated with the retirement of a tangible long-lived asset result from the acquisition, construction or development, and/or the normal operation of a long-lived asset.

    b. An environmental liability that results from the normal operation of a long-lived asset and that is associated with the retirement of that asset.

    c. A conditional obligation to perform a retirement activity.

    d. Obligations of a lessor in connection with leased property meeting the provisions in "a" above. (Upon adoption of ASU 2016-02, this language will change to: Obligations of a lessor in connection with an underlying asset that meet the provisions in "a" above.)

    e. The costs associated with the retirement of specified assets that qualifies as historical waste equipment defined by EU Directive 2002/96/EC.
    (ASC 410-20-15-1 and 15-2)

It does *not* apply to these transactions:

- Obligations that arise solely from a plan to sell or otherwise dispose of a long-lived asset.
- An environmental remediation liability that results from the improper operation of a long-lived asset.
- Activities necessary to prepare an asset for an alternative use as they are not associated with the retirement of the asset.
- Historical waste held by private households.
- Obligations of a lessee in connection with leased property, whether imposed by a lease agreement or by a party other than the lessor, that meet the definition of either minimum lease payments or contingent rentals in paragraphs. (Upon adoption of ASU 2016-02 on leases, this wording will change to: Obligations of a lessee in connection with an underlying asset, whether imposed by a lease or by a party other than the lessor, that meet the definition of either lease payments or variable lease payments in ASC 842-10.)
- An obligation for asbestos removal resulting from the other-than-normal operation of an asset.
- Costs associated with complying with funding or assurance provisions.
- Obligations associated with maintenance, rather than retirement, of a long-lived asset.
- The cost of a replacement part that is a component of a long-lived asset. (ASC 410-20-15-3)

Recognition Upon initial recognition of a liability for an asset retirement obligation, the entity records an increase to the carrying amount of the related long-lived asset and an offsetting liability. (ASC 410-20-25-5) Asset retirement obligations are initially measured at fair value. The ARO may be incurred in one or more of the entity's reporting periods. Each period's incremental liability incurred is recognized as a separate liability and is estimated using these principles based on market and interest rate assumptions existing in the period of recognition. The table below summarizes the accounting treatment and is explained in detail in the information that follows.

Circumstance	Accounting Treatment		
	Statement of Financial Position	*Income Statement*	*Statement of Cash Flows*
Initial Recognition in the Period Incurred or When a Reasonable Estimate Can Be Made	Record the ARO liability at fair value of legal obligation. Capitalize the ARC by increasing the carrying amount of the related asset for the same amount as the ARO.	No impact	No impact
Changes in the Liability— Passage of Time	Increase ARO through periodic accretion expense.	Accretion expense recorded as part of operating expenses.	Classify accretion and depreciation expenses as noncash adjustments to net income in operating cash flows.
	Allocate ARC expense using a systematic and rational method over its useful life.	ARC expense recorded as depreciation.	

Circumstance	Accounting Treatment		
	Statement of Financial Position	*Income Statement*	*Statement of Cash Flows*
Subsequent Measurement— Change in Expected Cash Flows: PV Increases	Increase the carrying amount of the related ARC and ARO using the current credit-adjusted risk-free rate.	No effect at time of change, but will affect future amortization and accretion expense.	
Subsequent Measurement— Change in Expected Cash Flows: PV Decreases	Decrease the carrying amount of the related ARC and ARO using the current credit-adjusted risk-free rate that existed at the time the ARO was originally recorded.	No effect at time of change, but will affect future amortization and accretion expense.	
Retirement	Derecognize ARO as costs are incurred	Record a gain or loss for the difference between the recorded ARO and the cost of settling the liability.	Classify cash outflows for settlement of the ARO in operating cash flows. Settlement difference is presented as a noncash adjustment to net income within operating cash flows.
	Derecognize unamortized ARC	Record a loss for any unamortized ARC.	

An ARO is required to be recognized when incurred (or acquired), even if uncertainty exists regarding the timing and/or method of eventually settling the obligation. (ASC 410-20-25-7) In effect, ASC 410-20 distinguishes between a contingency and an uncertainty. If the obligation to perform the retirement activities is unconditional, the fact that uncertainty exists regarding the timing and/or method of retirement does not relieve the reporting entity of the requirement to estimate and record the obligation if, in fact, it is reasonably estimable. The assumptions regarding the probabilities of the various outcomes used in the computation are to take into account that uncertainty. An ARO is considered reasonably estimable if:

- It is evident that the obligation's fair value is included in an asset's acquisition price,
- An active market exists for the transfer of the obligation, or
- Sufficient information is available to enable the use of the CON 7 expected present value technique to estimate the obligation.
  (ASC 410-20-25-6)

Sufficient information is considered to be available to reasonably estimate the obligation if either:

- The settlement date and method of settlement have been specified by others (e.g., the end of a lease term or the end of a statutory period), or
- Information is available to reasonably estimate:
    ○ The settlement date or range of potential settlement dates.
    ○ The settlement method or potential settlement methods.
    ○ The probabilities of occurrence of the dates and methods in a and b.
    (ASC 410-20-25-8)

If management concludes that sufficient information to record the obligation at inception is not available, management is expected to continuously consider whether this remains true in future accounting periods, and to recognize the obligation in the first period when sufficient information becomes available to enable the fair value estimate. (ASC 410-20-25-10)

The information necessary to make these estimates can be based on the reporting entity's own historical experience, industry statistics or customary practices, management's own intent, or estimates of the asset's economic useful life. (ASC 410-20-25-11)

Funding and Assurance Provisions Factors such as laws, regulations, public policy, the entity's creditworthiness, or the sheer magnitude of the future obligation may cause an entity to be required to provide third parties with assurance that the entity will be able to satisfy its ARO in the future. Such assurance is provided using instruments such as surety bonds, insurance policies, letters of credit, guarantees by other entities, establishment of trust funds, or by custodial arrangements segregating other assets dedicated to satisfying the ARO. Although providing such means of assurance does not satisfy the underlying obligation, the credit-adjusted interest rate used in calculating the expected present value is adjusted for the effect on the entity's credit standing of employing one or more of these techniques. (ASC 410-20-35-9)

ASC 410-30, *Environmental Obligations*

Scope ASC 410-30 applies to all entities. It applies to accounting for environmental remediation liabilities and is written in the context of operations taking place in the United States, however, it is applicable to all the operations of an entity. The guidance should be applied on a site-by-site basis. (ASC 410-30-15-1 and 15-2)

It does *not* apply to these transactions:

- Environmental contamination incurred in the normal operation of a long-lived asset.
- Pollution control costs with respect to current operations or on accounting for costs of future site restoration or closure that are required upon the cessation of operations or sale of facilities, as such current and future costs and obligations represent a class of accounting issues different from environmental remediation liabilities.
- Environmental remediation actions that are undertaken at the sole discretion of management and that are not induced by the threat, by governments or other parties, of litigation or of assertion of a claim or an assessment.
- Recognizing liabilities of insurance entities for unpaid claims.
- Natural resource damages and toxic torts.
- Asset impairment issues.
(ASC 410-30-15-3)

Environmental remediation costs, the costs of cleaning up environmental contamination, are generally expensed as incurred as operating expenses. (ASC 410-30-25-16) The exceptions to this general rule that result in capitalizing these costs are as follows:

- If the costs result from legal obligations associated with the eventual retirement of an asset or group of assets they will be capitalized as an ARO, as discussed and illustrated in the previous section of this chapter on ASC 410-20.
- If the costs do not qualify as ARO, but they meet one of the following criteria, they may be capitalized subject to reduction for impairment, if warranted:
  - The costs extend the life, increase the capacity, or improve the safety or efficiency of property owned by the reporting entity.
  - The costs mitigate or prevent future environmental contamination while also improving the property compared with its condition when originally constructed or acquired by the reporting entity.
  - The costs are incurred in preparing for sale a property that is currently held for sale (the application of this criterion must be balanced with the limitation in ASC 360 regarding assets held for sale being carried at the lower of carrying value or fair value less cost to sell).

  (ASC 410-30-25-17)

Environmental costs associated with the improper operation or use of an asset (e.g., penalties and fines) are specifically excluded from the accounting guidance with respect to ARO and, should they be incurred, under ASC 410-30, they would most likely not qualify to be capitalized under GAAP.

Environmental Remediation Liabilities ASC 430-30 contains the principal rules with respect to accounting for environmental obligations (e.g., determining the threshold for accrual of a liability, etc.) and it sets "benchmarks" for liability recognition. The benchmarks for the accrual and evaluation of the estimated liability (i.e., the stages which are deemed to be important to ascertaining the existence and amount of the liability) are:

- The identification and verification of an entity as a potentially responsible party (PRP), since ASC 410-30 stipulates that accrual is to be based on the premise that expected costs will be borne by only the "participating potentially responsible parties" and that the "recalcitrant, unproven, and unidentified" PRP will not contribute to costs of remediation.
- The receipt of a "unilateral administrative order."
- Participation, as a PRP, in the remedial investigation/feasibility study (RI/FS).
- Completion of the feasibility study.
- Issuance of the Record of Decision (RoD).
- The remedial design through operation and maintenance, including postremediation monitoring.

  (ASC 410-30-25-15)

The amount of the liability to be accrued is affected by the entity's allocable share of liability for a specific site and by its share of the amounts related to the site that will not be paid by the other PRP or the government. The categories of costs to be included in the accrued liability include incremental direct costs of the remediation effort itself, as well as the costs of compensation and benefits for employees directly involved in the remediation effort. (ASC 410-30-30-10) Costs should be estimated based on existing laws. (ASC 410-30-30-15)

Potential recoveries cannot be offset against the estimated liability, and further notes that any recovery recognized as an asset is to be reflected at fair value, which implies that only the present value of future recoveries can be recorded. It is presumed that the costs are operating in nature and thus cannot normally be included in the "other income and expense" category of the income statement, either. Disclosure of accounting policies regarding recognition of the liability and of any related asset (for recoveries from third parties) is also needed, where pertinent.

PRACTICE ALERT

While SEC comments relate to registrants, other preparers may benefit from its remarks. Regarding asset retirement obligations, the SEC has questioned preparers about:

- An entity's consideration of recording asset retirement obligations connected to future, anticipated events.
- Whether an entity should consider additional accounting policy disclosures allowing the users to assess the probability, magnitude, and timing of future changes.
- Suggesting an entity describe specific events or circumstances that could be depicted to result in early retirement or shutdown of assets.

PRESENTATION AND DISCLOSURE REQUIREMENTS

Presentation

ASC 410-20 Accretion expense appears as an operating expense with a description that conveys the nature of the expense. (ASC 410-20-45-1) Presentation in the statement of cash flows can be found in ASC 230-10-45-7. Cash payments for AROs are classified as operating items and a cash payment to settle an ARO is a cash outflow for operating activities. (ASC 410-20-45-2 and 45-3)

ASC 410-30 An entity may present on the balance sheet several assets related to environmental obligations, including:

- Receivables from other potentially responsible parties.
- Anticipated insurance resources.
- Anticipated recoveries from previous events.
  (ASC 410-30-45-1)

If environmental remediation liabilities relate to a discontinued operation that is accounted for as such, the liabilities should be classified as discontinued operations. (ASC 410-30-45-5)

Disclosure

ASC 410-20

- General description of asset retirement obligations and the related long-lived assets.
- Fair value of assets legally restricted to satisfy the liability.
- Reconciliation of the beginning and ending aggregate carrying amount of the liability separately, whenever there is a significant change in any of these components during the reporting period, showing the changes resulting from:
  - Liabilities incurred during the current period.
  - Settlements of liabilities during the current period.
  - Accretion expense.
  - Revisions in estimated cash flows.
    (ASC 410-20-50-1)

- If the fair value of an asset retirement obligation cannot be reasonably estimated, that fact and the reasons therefor.
  (ASC 410-20-50-2)

ASC 410-30   ASC 410-30-50 is divided between disclosures that are required and disclosures that are encouraged, but not required. (ASC 410-30-50-2) The following disclosures are required:
- Whether the accrual is measured on a discounted basis and if the entity uses a discounted rate in the present value determination, the undiscounted amount and the discount rate used.
- The disclosures required by ASC 275-10 in *Risks and Uncertainties*.
- The disclosures required by ASC 450-20 on *Contingencies*.
  (ASC 410-30-50-4 through 50-7)

The following disclosures are encouraged, but not required.

- Accrual benchmarks for remediation obligations, such as the event, situation, or set of circumstances that generally triggers recognition of loss contingencies, for example, during or upon completion of the feasibility study.
- The policy concerning the timing of recognition of recoveries.
  (ASC 410-30-50-8)
- Because uncertainties associated with environmental remediation loss contingencies are pervasive and often result in wide ranges of reasonably possible losses with respect to such contingencies and often occur over a span of many years, additional specific disclosures with respect to environmental remediation loss contingencies that would be useful to further users' understanding of the entity's financial statements.
  (ASC 410-30-50-9)

The following:

- The estimated time frame of disbursements for recorded amounts if expenditures are expected to continue over the long term.
- The estimated time frame for realization of recognized probable recoveries, if realization is not expected in the near term.
- If an estimate of the probable or reasonably possible loss or range of loss cannot be made, the reasons why it cannot be made.
- If information about the reasonably possible loss or the recognized and additional reasonably possible loss for an environmental remediation obligation related to an individual site is relevant to an understanding of the financial position, cash flows, or results of operations of the entity, the following with respect to the site:
  - The total amount accrued for the site.
  - The nature of any reasonably possible loss contingency or additional loss, and an estimate of the possible loss or the fact that an estimate cannot be made and the reasons why it cannot be made.
  - Whether other potentially responsible parties are involved and the entity's estimated share of the obligation.
  - The status of regulatory proceedings.
  - The estimated time frame for resolution of the contingency.
    (ASC 410-30-50-10)

- The estimated time frame for resolution of the uncertainty as to the amount of the loss (see paragraph 410-30-55-17).
  (ASC 410-30-50-11)
- The amount of environmental remediation costs recognized in the income statement in the following detail:
  - The amount recognized for environmental remediation loss contingencies in each period.
  - Any recovery from third parties that is credited to environmental remediation costs in each period.
  - The income statement caption in which environmental remediation costs and credits are included.
  (ASC 410-30-50-12)

The guidance cautions that when an entity is required by existing laws and regulations to report the release of hazardous substances and to begin a remediation study or where an assertion of a claim is deemed probable, the matter represents a loss contingency subject to the disclosure provisions of paragraphs 450-20-50-3 through 50-4. (ASC 410-30-50-13)

PRESENTATION AND DISCLOSURE EXAMPLES

Example 27.1: Accounting Policy, Asset Retirement Obligation

Conditional asset retirement obligations: A liability is initially recorded at fair value for an asset retirement obligation associated with the retirement of tangible long-lived assets in the period in which it is incurred if a reasonable estimate of fair value can be made. Conditional asset retirement obligations exist for certain long-term assets of the Company. The obligation is initially measured at fair value using expected present value techniques. Over time the liabilities are accreted for the change in their present value and the initial capitalized costs are depreciated over the remaining useful lives of the related assets. The asset retirement obligation liability was $137 million and $122 million at December 31, 20X9 and 20X8, respectively.

Example 27.2: Reconciliation of Beginning and Ending Carrying Amounts of Asset Retirement Obligations, Using a Discounted Basis

The Company's asset retirement obligations are principally for costs to close its surface mines and reclaim the land it has disturbed as a result of its normal mining activities as well as for costs to dismantle certain mining equipment at the end of the life of the mine. The Company determined the amounts of these obligations based on cost estimates, adjusted for inflation, projected to the estimated closure dates, and then discounted using a credit-adjusted risk-free interest rate. The accretion of the liability is being recognized over the estimated life of each individual asset retirement obligation and is recorded in the line "Cost of sales" in the accompanying consolidated statements of operations. The associated asset is recorded in "Property, Plant, and Equipment, net" in the accompanying consolidated balance sheets. The depreciation of the asset is recorded in the line "Cost of sales" in the accompanying consolidated statements of operations.

Ballarat is a nonoperating subsidiary of the Company with legacy liabilities relating to closed mining operations, primarily former Eastern U.S. underground coal mining operations. These legacy liabilities include obligations for water treatment and other environmental remediation that arose as part of the normal course of closing these underground mining operations. The Company determined the amounts of these obligations based on cost estimates, adjusted for inflation, and then discounted the amounts using a credit-adjusted risk-free interest rate. The accretion of the liability is recognized over the estimated life of the asset retirement obligation and is recorded in the line "Closed mine obligations" in the accompanying consolidated statements of operations. Since Ballarat properties are no longer active operations, no associated asset has been capitalized.

A reconciliation of the Company's beginning and ending aggregate carrying amount of the asset retirement obligations are as follows:

	Coal Mining	Other Mining	Unallocated Items	MineCo Consolidated
Balance at January 1, 20X8	$ 22,589	$ 1,085	$ 16,423	$ 40,097
Liabilities incurred during the period	—	189	—	189
Liabilities settled during the period	(920)	—	(747)	(1,667)
Accretion expense	1,504	31	1,044	2,579
Revision of estimated cash flows	(2,777)	(820)	102	(3,495)
Balance at December 31, 20X8	$ 20,396	$ 485	$ 16,822	$ 37,703
Liabilities incurred during the period	—	91	—	91
Liabilities settled during the period	(8,265)	—	(752)	(9,017)
Accretion expense	1,260	28	1,323	2,611
Revision of estimated cash flows at TXMC	3,145	—	—	3,145
Revision of estimated cash flows at Adelaide	2,479	—	(153)	2,326
Balance at December 31, 20X9	$ 19,015	$ 604	$ 17,240	$ 36,859

During 20X9, the Company transferred the mine permits for certain Adelaide mines to an unrelated third party. As a result of these transfers, the Company was relieved of the associated mine reclamation obligations and recorded a $5.4 million reduction to Adelaide's asset retirement obligation, included in "Liabilities settled during the current period" in the table above. As part of these transactions, the Company transferred a $3.4 million escrow account and paid $2.4 million of cash, resulting in a net loss on the transactions of $0.4 million recognized within cost of sales in the Consolidated Statement of Operations and reflected on the line "Revision of estimated cash flows at Adelaide" in the table above. The reduction to the asset retirement obligation related to these transfers was offset by a $2.0 million increase to the asset retirement obligation related to updated costs estimates for the remaining Adelaide asset retirement obligations recognized within cost of sales in the consolidated statement of operations and reflected on the line "Revision of estimated cash flows at Adelaide" in the table above.

Due to updated cost estimates and changes in timing of the asset retirement obligation for TXMC, the Company recognized a $3.1 million increase to the asset retirement obligation in 20X9 within cost of sales in the consolidated statement of operations and reflected on the line "Revision of estimated cash flows at TXMC" in the table above.

Prior to 20X8, Ballarat established a $5.0 million Mine Water Treatment Trust to provide a financial assurance mechanism in order to assure the long-term treatment of post-mining discharges. The fair value of the Mine Water Treatment assets, which are recognized as a component of "Other Noncurrent Assets" on the Consolidated Balance Sheets, are $10.1 million at December 31, 20X9, and are legally restricted for purposes of settling the Ballarat asset retirement obligation.

Example 27.3: Environmental Expense Policy and Liability

Environmental expenditures relating to existing conditions caused by past operations that do not contribute to current or future revenues are expensed. Reserves for liabilities related to anticipated remediation costs are recorded on an undiscounted basis when they are probable and reasonably estimable, generally no later than the completion of feasibility studies, the Company's commitment to a plan of action, or approval by regulatory agencies. Environmental expenditures for capital projects that contribute to current or future operations generally are capitalized and depreciated over their estimated useful lives.

Example 27.4: Environmental Obligations, Changes in the Carrying Value of Environmental Remediation Liabilities—Optional Disclosures

Metal Corporation participates in environmental assessments and cleanups at several locations. These include owned or operating facilities and adjoining properties, previously owned or operating facilities and adjoining properties, and waste sites, including Superfund (Comprehensive Environmental Response, Compensation and Liability Act (CERCLA)) sites.

The following table details the changes in the carrying value of recorded environmental remediation reserves:

Balance at December 31, 20X0	$ 324
Liabilities incurred	11
Cash payments	(48)
Reversals of previously recorded liabilities	(10)
Foreign currency translation and other	17
Balance at December 31, 20X1	294
Liabilities incurred	19
Cash payments	(25)
Reversals of previously recorded liabilities	(3)
Foreign currency translation and other	(5)
Balance at December 31, 20X2	280
Liabilities incurred	73
Cash payments	(17)
Reversals of previously recorded liabilities	(1)
Balance at December 31, 20X3	$ 335

At December 31, 20X3 and 20X2, the current portion of the remediation reserve balance was $39 and $44, respectively.

In 20X9, the Company incurred liabilities of $73, which was primarily related to the closure of the Point Hewlett metalworks refinery that was recorded in Restructuring and other charges, net, on the accompanying statement of consolidated operations. The remaining amount was recorded to Cost of goods sold.

In 20X2 and 20X1, changes to the liability were the result of ongoing remediation work at various sites. The additional accruals were recorded to Cost of goods sold except for $2 and $8 in 20X2 and 20X1, respectively, that were recorded to Restructuring and other charges, net, on the accompanying statement of consolidated operations.

The estimated timing of cash outflows on the environmental remediation reserve at December 31, 20X3 is as follows:

20X4	$ 39
20X5–20X9	187
Thereafter	109
Total	$ 335

Reserve balances at December 31, 20X3 and 20X2, associated with significant sites with active remediation underway or for future remediation were $274 and $214, respectively. In management's judgment, the Company's reserves are sufficient to satisfy the provisions of the respective action plans.

Example 27.5: Company Records Liabilities for Environmental Remediation Cost on an Undiscounted Basis

As of December 31, 20X9, the Company had recorded liabilities of $1 million for estimated "environmental remediation" costs to clean up, treat, or remove hazardous substances at current or former ABC manufacturing or third-party sites. The Company evaluates available facts with respect to each individual site each quarter and records liabilities for remediation costs on an undiscounted basis when they are probable and reasonably estimable, generally no later than the completion of feasibility studies or the Company's commitment to a plan of action. Liabilities for estimated costs of environmental remediation, depending on the site, are based primarily upon internal or third-party environmental studies, and estimates as to the number, participation level and financial viability of any other potentially responsible parties, the extent of the contamination and the nature of required remedial actions. The Company adjusts recorded liabilities as further information develops or circumstances change. The Company expects that it will pay the amounts recorded over the periods of remediation for the applicable sites, currently ranging up to 20 years.

Example 27.6: Company Has Been Designated as a Potentially Responsible Party, But Does Not Expect to Incur Material Costs

We are subject to a variety of federal, state, local, and foreign laws and regulations relating to the discharge of materials into the environment, or otherwise relating to the protection of the environment ("Environmental Laws"). We believe our operations are in substantial compliance with all Environmental Laws. We do not believe existing Environmental Laws have had or will have any material effects upon our capital expenditures, earnings, or competitive position.

Under certain Environmental Laws, we could be held liable, without regard to fault, for the costs of remediation associated with our existing or historical operations. We could also be held responsible for third-party property and personal injury claims or for violations of Environmental Laws relating to contamination. We are a party to, or otherwise involved in, proceedings relating to several contaminated properties being investigated and remediated under Environmental Laws, including as a potentially responsible party in several Superfund site cleanups. Based on our information regarding the nature and volume of wastes allegedly disposed of or released at these properties, the total estimated cleanup costs and other financially viable potentially responsible parties, we do not believe the costs to us associated with these properties will be material, either individually or in the aggregate. We have established reserves that we believe are adequate to cover our anticipated remediation costs. However, certain events could cause our actual costs to vary from the established reserves. These events include, but are not limited to: a change in governmental regulations or cleanup standards or requirements; undiscovered information regarding the nature and volume of wastes allegedly disposed of or released at these properties; the loss of other potentially responsible parties that are financially capable of contributing toward cleanup costs and other factors increasing the cost of remediation.

28 ASC 420 EXIT OR DISPOSAL COST OBLIGATIONS

AUTHORITATIVE LITERATURE

Subtopic

ASC 420, *Exit or Disposal Cost Activities*, consists of one Subtopic:

- ASC 420-10, *Overall*, which provides guidance on the definition, reporting, and disclosure of such costs.

Scope and Scope Exceptions

The guidance in ASC 420 applies to:

- Termination benefits for current employees involuntarily terminated under the terms of a benefit arrangement that is not an ongoing benefit arrangement or individual deferred compensation contract.
- Costs related to:
  - A contract that is not a lease.
  - Consolidation of facilities or relocation of employees.

- ◦ A disposal activity under ASC 205-20.
- ◦ An exit activity.
  (ASC 420-10-15-3)

ASC 420 applies to all entities. It does *not* apply to:

- Costs associated with the retirement of a long-lived asset covered by ASC 410-20.
- Impairment of an unrecognized asset while it is being used.
  (ASC 420-10-15-5)

ASC 420-10-15-4 clarifies that an exit activity includes, but is not limited to:

- A restructuring
- The sale or termination of a line of business
- The closure of business activities in a particular location
- The relocation of business activities
- Changes in management structure
- A fundamental reorganization that affects the nature and focus of operation

Exit or Disposal Costs—General

When to Recognize a Liability Except for employee termination benefits discussed below, an entity should recognize exit or disposal costs in the same period it incurs the liability. If the fair value cannot be estimated initially, the cost should be recognized in the first period that it can be estimated. This should be a rare occurrence. (ASC 420-10-25-1)

Measurement Exit or disposal costs should be measured at fair value. Often, quoted market values are not available for those costs. A present value technique may be the best option. However, in some situations the use of estimates may not be materially different from present value techniques and those are acceptable if consistent with a fair value measurement objective. (ASC 420-10-30-1 through 3)

Subsequent Measurement Entities should measure changes in the initial measurement using the credit-adjusted risk-free rate used for the initial measurement. (ASC 420-10-35-1) The table below summarizes how to account for various changes.

Change	Recognition
Cumulative effect of a change resulting from a revision to the timing or the estimated amount of cash flows.	As an adjustment in the period of change.
Employees that were expected to be terminated within the minimum retention period are retained beyond that period.	Adjust the liability in the period of change.
Changes due to the passage of time.	As an increase in the carrying amount of the liability and as an expense.
(ASC 420-10-35-2 through 35-4)	

Exit or Disposal Costs—One-Time Employee Termination Benefits

ASC 420, *Exit or Disposal Cost Obligations*, applies to termination benefits provided to current employees that are involuntarily terminated under the terms of a benefit arrangement that applies to a specified termination event or for a specified future period. Those benefits are referred to as onetime termination benefits. If an entity has a history of providing similar benefits to employees involuntarily terminated in earlier events, the benefits are presumed to be part of an ongoing benefit arrangement (rather than a onetime benefit arrangement) unless there is evidence to the contrary.

A onetime benefit arrangement first exists at the date the plan of termination meets *all* of the following criteria:

- Management approves and commits to the termination plan.
- The termination plan specifies the number of employees to be terminated, their job classifications or functions, and their locations, as well as the expected completion date.
- The termination plan establishes the terms of the benefit arrangement in sufficient detail that employees are able to determine the type and amount of benefits that they will receive if they are involuntarily terminated.
- Actions required to complete the plan indicate that significant changes to the plan are unlikely.
(ASC 460-10-25-4)

Communicating the plan to employees creates a liability at the communication date. (ASC 420-10-25-5)

Timing The timing of recognition of the liability for onetime termination benefits depends on whether the employees are required to render service beyond a minimum retention period. (ASC 420-10-25-6) The minimum retention period is the notification period that an entity is required to provide to employees in advance of a termination event as a result of law, statute, or contract, or in the absence of a legal notification period, the minimum retention period cannot exceed 60 days. (ASC 420-10-25-7)

If employees are entitled to receive the termination benefits regardless of when they leave or if employees will not be retained to render service beyond the minimum retention period, the liability for the termination benefits is recognized and measured at its fair value at the communication date. (ASC 420-10-25-8)

If employees are required to render service until they are terminated in order to receive the termination benefit and will be retained beyond the minimum retention period, the liability for the termination benefits is measured at its fair value at the communication date and recognized ratably over the service period. (ASC 420-10-25-9)

Subsequent Measurement If subsequent to the communication date there are changes in either the timing or amount of the expected termination benefit cash flows, the cumulative effect of the change should be computed and reported in the same line item(s) in the income statement in which the costs were initially reported. If present value techniques were used to measure the initial liability, the same credit-adjusted risk-free rate should be used to remeasure the liability.

Changes in the liability due to the passage of time (accretion) are recognized as accretion expense in the income statement. (ASC 420-10-35-4) If employees are not required to provide services or are required to provide services only during the minimum retention period, accretion expense is charged for the passage of time after the communication date. If employees are required to provide services beyond the minimum retention period, accretion expense is charged for the passage of time after the termination date. Accretion expense should not be titled interest expense or be considered interest costs subject to capitalization. (ASC 420-10-45-5)

According to ASC 420-10-55, if newly offered benefits represent a revision to an ongoing arrangement that is not limited to a specified termination event or to a specified future period, the benefits represent an enhancement to an ongoing benefit arrangement.

If a plan of termination changes and employees that were expected to be terminated within the minimum retention period are retained to render service beyond that period, the liability amount should be recomputed as though it had been known at the initial communication date that those employees would be required to render services beyond the minimum retention period. (ASC 420-10-35-3) The cumulative effect of the change is recognized as a change in the liability and reported in the same line item(s) in the income statement in which the costs were initially reported. The remainder of the liability is recognized ratably from the date of change to the termination date.

Plan Includes Voluntary and Involuntary Benefits If a plan of termination includes both voluntary and involuntary termination benefits, a liability for the involuntary benefits is recognized as described above. A liability for the incremental voluntary benefits (the excess of the voluntary benefit amount over the involuntary benefit amount) is recognized in accordance with ASC 712-10-25-1 through 25-3. That is, if the benefits are special termination benefits offered only for a short period of time, the liability is recognized when the employees accept the offer and the amount can be reasonably estimated. If, instead, the voluntary termination benefits are contractual termination benefits (for example, required by a union contract or a pension contract) the liability is recognized when it is probable that employees will be entitled to benefits and the amount can be reasonably estimated.

Exit or Disposal Costs—Contract Termination Costs

In addition to employee termination costs, an entity may incur contract termination costs, relocation costs, plant consolidation costs, and other costs associated with the exit or disposal activity. ASC 420 offers the following guidance for recognition. Note that upon implementation of ASU 2016-02, *Leases,* leases within the scope of ASC 842 are excluded from this guidance. (ASC 420-10-25-11)

Recognition A liability for the costs to terminate a contract before the end of its term is recognized and measured at its fair value when the entity actually terminates the contract in accordance with the contractual term (e.g., by written notice). (ASC 420-10-25-12) A liability for the costs that will continue to be incurred under a contract for its remaining term without economic benefit to the entity is recognized at its cease-use date. (ASC 420-10-25-13)

Measurement If an entity terminates a contract according to the terms of the contract, the entity should record a liability for the termination costs measured at fair value at the time of termination. (ASC 420-10-30-7)

An entity may continue to incur costs without realizing any economic benefit. In that case, the entity should record a liability at its fair value at the cease-use date (ASC 420-10-30-9)

If the contract is an operating lease, the fair value of the liability should be determined based on the remaining lease rentals, reduced by estimated sublease rentals, even if the entity does not intend to find a sublease. However, remaining operating lease payments should not be reduced to an amount less than zero by the estimated sublease payments. (ASC 420-10-30-8)

Other Associated Costs to Exit an Activity

Recognition Other associated costs are items such as employee relocation costs and costs associated with facility closings or consolidations (ASC 420-10-25-14). A liability for other costs associated with the exit or disposal activity should be recognized when the liability is incurred, which is generally when the goods or services associated with the activity are received.

The liability should not be recognized before it is incurred even if the costs are incremental and a direct result of the exit or disposal plan. (ASC 420-10-25-15)

Measurement The liability should be measured at fair value in the period when the liability is incurred. This is usually when goods or services associated with the activity are received. (ASC 420-10-30-10)

PRACTICE ALERT

While SEC comments do not pertain to private companies, the recommendations may be useful practice pointers for preparers of private company financial statements. The SEC has commented:

- Include in the notes the information required by ASC 420-20-50-1, that is, for the period in which an exit or disposal cost is initiated and any subsequent period until the exit or disposal activity is completed:
  ○ A description of the activity.
  ○ The expected completion date.
  ○ The income statement line items that contain the costs.
  ○ Quantitative information by major category of cost and by segment.
- If the entity cannot determine fair value, that fact should be disclosed.
- Where exit and involuntary termination costs have been aggregated, disaggregate and be precise in the labelling in the income statement and in footnotes.
- Evaluate restructuring liabilities at each balance sheet date to ensure that unnecessary amounts are reversed in the proper period.
- Exit costs should be charged to the accrual only to the extent the costs were included in the original accrual. Otherwise, the costs should be expensed in the period in which they occurred.

PRESENTATION AND DISCLOSURE REQUIREMENTS

Presentation and disclosure requirements can be found at www.wiley.com/go/FSDM2021.

Presentation

Exit or disposal costs associated with a discontinued operative should be included in the results of discontinued operations. (ASC 420-10-45-2) Other exit or disposal costs are included in income from continuing operations before income taxes, with separate presentations permitted. (ASC 420-10-45-3) Accretion expense associated with exit costs or disposals and mentioned earlier in this chapter should not be classified with interest expense. (ASC 420-10-45-5)

Disclosure

ASC 420 requires comprehensive disclosures in the notes beginning in the period in which an exit or disposal activity is initiated and continuing until the activity is completed. All of the following should be disclosed:

a. A description of the exit or disposal activity, including the facts and circumstances leading to the expected activity and the expected completion date.
b. For each major type of cost associated with the activity, both of the following:

- ○ The total amount expected to be incurred in connection with the activity, the amount incurred in the period, and the cumulative amount incurred to date.
  - ○ A reconciliation of the beginning and ending liability balances showing separately the changes during the period attributable to costs incurred and charged to expense, costs paid or otherwise settled, and any adjustments to the liability with an explanation of the reason(s) why.
  c. Line item(s) in the income statement or the statement of activities in which the costs in b. are aggregated.
  d. For each reportable segment:
  - ○ The total amount of costs expected to be incurred in connection with the activity,
  - ○ The amount incurred in the period, and
  - ○ The cumulative amount incurred to date, net of adjustments to the liability with an explanation of the reason.
  e. If a liability for a cost associated with the activity is not recognized because fair value cannot be reasonably estimated, that fact and the reasons why.
  (ASC 420-10-50-1)

The reconciliation mentioned above informs users and enhances comparability over time.

PRESENTATION AND DISCLOSURE EXAMPLES

Example 28.1: Accounting Policy—Exit or Disposal Costs

The Company accounts for exit or disposal of activities in accordance with ASC 420, *Exit or Disposal Cost Obligations*. The Company defines a business restructuring as an exit or disposal activity that includes but is not limited to a program which is planned and controlled by management and materially changes either the scope of a business or the manner in which that business is conducted. Business restructuring charges may include (i) contract termination costs and (ii) other related costs associated with exit or disposal activities.

Contract termination costs include costs to terminate a contract or costs that will continue to be incurred under the contract without benefit to the Company. A liability is recognized and measured at its fair value when the Company either terminates the contract or ceases using the rights conveyed by the contract.

Example 28.2: Accounting Policy—One-Time Termination Benefits

Benefits related to the relocation of employees and certain other termination benefits are accounted for under ASC 420, "Exit or Disposal Cost Obligations," and are expensed over the required service period.

Example 28.3: Effect of Adopting ASU 2016-02 on Lease Termination Charges

As of March 2, 20X8, the Company had $124,046 in closed store and lease exit liabilities under Topic 420 Liabilities. Under transition to Topic 842, existing Topic 420 liabilities were eliminated by recording a reduction to the right of use asset balance. However, in certain cases the Company had larger existing Topic 420 liabilities than the right of use asset balances. This excess amount of $9,333 continues to be recorded as a liability and will reduce lease expense over the remaining lease term of the affected stores. In addition, upon transition, the Company reclassified deferred rent, including unamortized tenant income allowances, prepaid rent, and favorable and unfavorable lease balances resulting from prior acquisition accounting to the ROU asset.

Example 28.4: Lease Termination Charges after Adoption of ASU 2016-02

Upon adoption of ASU 2016-02, *Leases* (Topic 842), we recorded a future lease liability for every real estate lease and therefore, we no longer record a lease termination charge. Post adoption, we record ancillary costs in connection with store closings. Prior to the adoption of ASU 2016-02, charges to close a store, which principally consist of continuing lease obligations associated with ancillary costs, are recorded at the time the store is closed and all inventory is liquidated, pursuant to the guidance set forth in ASC 420, *Exit or Disposal Cost Obligations*. We calculate our liability for closed stores on a store-by-store basis. The calculation for stores where remaining lease term exceeds one year includes the ancillary costs from the date of closure to the end of the remaining lease term. We evaluate these assumptions each quarter and adjust the liability accordingly. As part of our ongoing business activities, we assess stores and distribution centers for potential closure and relocation. Decisions to close or relocate stores or distribution centers in future periods would result in lease termination charges for lease exit costs and liquidation of inventory, as well as impairment of assets at these locations.

In fiscal 20X9, 20X8, and 20X7, we recorded lease termination charges of $2.9 million, $44.5 million, and $20.9 million, respectively. We have no plans to close a significant number of stores in future periods.

Example 28.5: Workforce Reduction Expenses Determining Accounting Guidance

On November 29, 20X1, following the completion of a strategic review of its business, the Company's Board of Directors approved a workforce reduction plan, or the Workforce Reduction, to reduce its workforce headcount by approximately 38%. The Company evaluated the related employee severance and other benefits to employees in connection with the Workforce Reduction to determine whether the benefits were within the scope ASC 712, *Compensation—Nonretirement Postemployment Benefits*, or within the scope of ASC 420, *Exit or Disposal Cost Obligations,* depending on the nature of the benefit and whether it is part of an ongoing benefit arrangement under ASC 712 or a one-time termination benefit unique to the Workforce Reduction. The Company recorded restructuring expense of $0.6 million at the time of the Workforce Reduction, pursuant to ASC 420 as the Company did not have an on-going benefit arrangement under ASC 712. The Workforce Reduction was complete as of December 31, 20X1.

Example 28.6: Schedule of Restructuring Charges Accounted for under ASC 420

The following table outlines the components of the restructuring charges during the year ended December 31, 20X1, included in the consolidated statement of operations, and ending liability recorded in the balance sheet as at December 31, 20X1 (in thousands):

	Charges Incurred during the Year Ended December 31, 20X1	*Amount Paid through December 31, 20X1*	*Remaining Liability at December 31, 20X1*
Employee severance, bonus and other	$605	$(232)	$373
Total restructuring charges	$605	$(232)	$373

29 ASC 430 DEFERRED REVENUE AND CONTRACT LIABILITIES

This Topic merely provides a link to deferred revenue *and* contract liabilities. See the Chapter on ASC 606 for guidance.

30 ASC 440 COMMITMENTS

AUTHORITATIVE LITERATURE

The FASB codification has three related Topics:

- ASC 440, *Commitments*,
- ASC 450, *Contingencies*, and
- ASC 460, *Guarantees*

Subtopics

ASC 440, *Commitments*, contains only one Subtopic:

- ASC 440-10, *Overall*, which provides general guidance on financial accounting and reporting for certain commitments.

The Subtopic has two Subsections:

1. *General*
2. *Unconditional Purchase Obligations*

The *General* Subsection provides guidance for:

- Unused letters of credit,
- Preferred stock dividends in arrears,
- Commitments such as those for plant acquisitions, and
- Obligations to reduce debts, maintain working capital, or restrict dividends. (ASC 440-10-05-2)

The *Unconditional Purchase Obligation* Subsection provides guidance for unconditional purchase obligations, such as throughput and take-or-pay contracts. (ASC 440-10-05-3)

Scope and Scope Exceptions

ASC 440 applies to all entities and to all relevant transactions. (ASC 440-10-15-1 through 15-3) However, for guidance on product financing arrangements, the preparer should look to ASC 470-40-15 and repurchase agreements within the scope of ASC 606-10-55-66 through 55-78.

Unconditional Purchase Obligations

An unconditional purchase obligation may be subject to:

- ASC 840 (or ASC 842 upon implementation of ASU 2016-02, *Leases*), or
- ASC 815, or
- Neither.
  (ASC 440-10-25-1)

To determine the appropriate guidance, entities should determine first if an obligation is subject to the guidance on leases. (ASC 440-10-25-2) Then, the entity should apply the guidance in ASC 815 to determine if any portion of the obligation that is not a lease is subject to 815 and whether the lease portion contains an embedded derivative. (ASC 440-10-25-3)

Throughput and take-or-pay contracts are sometimes used to help a supplier pay for new facilities, machines, or other expenditures. They are negotiated as a way of arranging financing for the facilities that will produce the goods or provide the services desired by a purchaser. Some of these contracts are reported on the statement of financial position as an asset and a liability. Others are not reported.

Losses on unconditional purchase obligations for goods or inventory should be recognized under the provisions contained in ASC 330-10-35. (ASC 440-10-25-4)

The disclosure requirements for ASC 440 can be found at www.wiley.com/go/FSDM2021.

PRACTICE ALERT

While SEC comments pertain to public entities, their comments can often provide valuable practice pointers for preparers of nonpublic entities. In the area of commitments, the SEC has commented in recent years that:

- Specific information contained in disclosures regarding a contingency
- Information about why an estimate could not be made
- Detail about how assumptions were made and judgments formed
- Disclosure of accounting policy related to legal costs
- Amount accrued
- Information about possible loss
- Details about range of loss

DISCLOSURE REQUIREMENTS

Note: ASC 440 does not contain a "45" Subtopic on presentations.
ASC 440-10-50 delineates two categories for commitments:

- General commitments, and
- Unconditional purchase obligations.

General Commitments

The notes must include disclosure of the following:

- Unused letters of credit.
- Leases.

- Assets pledged as security for loans.
- Pension plans.
- The existence of cumulative preferred stock dividends in arrears.
- Commitments, including:
  - a commitment for plant acquisition,
  - obligations to reduce debts,
  - obligations to maintain working capital, and
  - obligations to restrict dividends.
  (ASC 440-10-50-1)

Unconditional Purchase Obligations

Specific disclosures are required for unconditional purchase obligations, such as take-or-pay contracts and through-put contracts. If an unconditional purchase obligation has *all* of the following criteria, it must be disclosed. Unconditional purchase obligations in accordance with ASC 440-10-50-4 (if not recorded on the statement of financial position) or ASC 440-10-50-6 (if recorded on the statement of financial position), if all the following criteria are met:

- It is noncancellable, or cancellable only:
  - Upon the occurrence of some remote contingency.
  - With the permission of the other party.
  - If a replacement agreement is signed between the same parties.
  - Upon payment of a penalty in an amount such that continuation of the agreement appears reasonably assured.
- It is negotiated as part of a supplier's product financing arrangement for the facilities that will provide the contracted goods or services or for costs related to those goods or services (e.g., carrying costs for contracted goods).
- It has a remaining term in excess of one year.
  (ASC 440-10-50-2)

Future lease payments that constitute an unconditional purchase obligation are not required to be disclosed as long as the required disclosures for leases are made under ASC 840 or under ASC 842 upon implementation of ASU 2016-02, *Leases.* (ASC 440-10-50-3)

If the obligation meets the criteria of ASC 440-10-50-2 above and is not recorded on the statement of financial position, then the following must be disclosed:

- The nature and term of the obligation(s).
- The amount of the fixed and determinable portion of the obligation(s) at the statement of financial position date in the aggregate and for each of the next five years, if determinable.
- The nature of any variable components of the obligation(s).
- The amounts purchased under the obligation for each period for which an income statement is presented.

Note: The disclosures above may be omitted only if the aggregate commitment is immaterial.
(ASC 440-10-50-4)

In addition to the items above, entities are encouraged to disclose the amount of imputed interest necessary to reduce the unconditional purchase obligations to present value. If known, the discount rate used should be the same as the effective interest rate used initially for the borrowings that financed the facility providing the goods or services. If the discount rate is not known, the entity should use its incremental borrowing rate when the commitment originated. (ASC 440-10-50-5)

For each of the five years following the most recent balance sheet, entities should disclose the aggregate payments for unconditional purchase obligations that meet the criteria in ASC 440-10-50-2 above. (ASC 440-10-50-6)

PRESENTATION AND DISCLOSURE EXAMPLES

Example 30.1: Minimum Guaranteed Payments

The Company's contracts with some licensors include minimum guaranteed royalty payments, which are payable regardless of the ultimate revenue generated from end users. In accordance with Accounting Standard Codification 440-10, *Commitments* ("ASC 440-10"), the Company recorded a minimum guaranteed royalty liability of $40,150 and $7,304 as of December 31, 20X9 and 20X8, respectively. The balance is included in accrued royalties and long-term accrued royalties on the Company's consolidated balance sheet. When no significant performance remains with the licensor, the Company initially records each of these guarantees as an asset and as a liability at the contractual amount. When significant performance remains with the licensor, the Company records royalty payments as an asset when actually paid and as a liability when incurred, rather than upon execution of the contract. The classification of minimum royalty payment obligations between long-term and short-term is determined based on the expected timing of recoupment of earned royalties calculated on projected revenue for the licensed IP games.

Example 30.2: Accounting for Minimum Guaranteed Royalty Payments, Accounting Methods

The Company's royalty expenses consist of fees that it pays to content owners for the use of their brands, properties and other licensed content, including trademarks and copyrights, in the development of the Company's games. Royalty-based obligations are either paid in advance and capitalized on the balance sheet as prepaid royalties or accrued as incurred and subsequently paid. These royalty-based obligations are expensed to cost of revenue at the greater of the revenue derived from the relevant game multiplied by the applicable contractual rate or an effective royalty rate based on expected net product sales.

The Company's contracts with some licensors include minimum guaranteed royalty payments, which are payable regardless of the ultimate revenue generated from end users. In accordance with Accounting Standard Codification 440-10, *Commitments* ("ASC 440-10"), the Company recorded a minimum guaranteed royalty liability of $40,150 and $7,304 as of December 31, 20X9 and 20X8, respectively. The balance is included in accrued royalties and long-term accrued royalties on the Company's consolidated balance sheet. When no significant performance remains with the licensor, the Company initially records each of these guarantees as an asset and as a liability at the contractual amount. When significant performance remains with the licensor, the Company records royalty payments as an asset when actually paid and as a liability when incurred, rather than upon execution of the contract. The classification of minimum royalty payment obligations between long-term and short-term is determined based on the expected timing of recoupment of earned royalties calculated on projected revenue for the licensed IP games.

Each quarter, the Company evaluates the realization of its prepaid royalties as well as any recognized guarantees not yet paid to determine amounts that it deems unlikely to be realized through product sales. The Company uses estimates of revenue, cash flows, and net margins to evaluate the future realization of prepaid royalties, license fees, and guarantees. This evaluation considers multiple factors such as the term of the agreement, forecasted demand, game life cycle status, game development plans, and current and anticipated sales levels, as well as other qualitative factors such as the success of similar games and similar genres on mobile devices published by the Company and its competitors and/or other game platforms (e.g., consoles and personal computers) utilizing the intellectual property. To the extent that this evaluation indicates that the remaining prepaid and guaranteed royalty payments are not recoverable, the Company records an impairment charge to cost of revenue in the period in which impairment is indicated. The Company recorded impairment charges to cost of revenue of $457, $711, and $27,323 related to prepaid guaranteed royalties for certain of its celebrity license agreements, and certain other prepaid royalties during the years ended December 31, 20X9, 20X8, and 20X7, respectively.

31 ASC 450 CONTINGENCIES

AUTHORITATIVE LITERATURE

Subtopics

ASC 450, *Contingencies*, contains guidance for reporting and disclosure of gain and loss contingencies and has three Subtopics:

- ASC 450-10, *Overall*, which, along with ASC 450-20 and 450-30, provides guidance on accounting and disclosures for contingencies.
- ASC 450-20, *Loss Contingencies*, which describes accounting for potential liabilities in circumstances involving uncertainties.
- ASC 450-30, *Gain Contingencies*, which describes accounting and disclosure requirements for gain contingencies.

Scope and Scope Exceptions

ASC 450-10 applies to all entities. Not all uncertainties are contingencies. ASC 450-10-55 points out several common estimates that do not fall under the contingency guidance:

- Depreciation
- Estimates used in accruals
- Changes in tax law

ASC 450 guidance does *not* apply to the recognition and initial measurement of:

- Assets or liabilities arising from contingencies that are measured at fair value, or
- Assets arising from contingencies measured at an amount other than fair value on the acquisition date in a business combination, or
- An acquisition by a not-for-profit entity under the requirements of Subtopic 805-20 or 958-805.
  (ASC 450-10-15-2A)

The following transactions are excluded from the guidance in ASC 450-20 because for them guidance is elsewhere in the Codification:

- Stock issued to employees. (ASC 718)
- Employment-related costs, including deferred compensation contracts. (ASC 710, 712, and 715) However, certain postemployment benefits are included in the scope of this ASC 450-20 by reference in 712-10-25-4 through 25-5.
- Uncertainty in income taxes. (ASC 740-10-25)
- Accounting and reporting by insurance entities. (ASC 944)
  (ASC 450-20-15-2)

ASC 450-30 follows the same scope guidance as ASC 450-10.

ASC 450-10, *Overall*

ASC 450 defines a contingency as an existing condition, situation, or set of circumstances involving uncertainty as to possible gain or loss and that will result in the acquisition of an asset, the reduction of a liability, the loss or impairment of an asset, or the incurrence of a liability. (ASC 450-10-05-5) The uncertainty will ultimately be resolved when one or more future events occur or fail to occur.

ASC 450-20, *Loss Contingencies*

Loss contingencies are common and include those related to product warranties and litigation.

Recognition Loss contingencies are recognized only if there is an impairment of an asset or the incurrence of a liability as of the date of the statement of financial position. A loss must be accrued if *both* of the following conditions are met:

a. It is *probable* that an asset has been impaired or a liability has been incurred at the date of the financial statements.
b. The amount of loss can be *reasonably estimated.*
   (ASC 450-20-25-2)

For example, estimated settlement amounts for ongoing lawsuits are recognized prior to a court's decision if it is probable that the outcome will be unfavorable. Further, difficulty in measuring an obligation is not, by itself, a reason for not recording a liability if the amount can be estimated. For example, warranty obligations are commonly recognized as liabilities even though the number of claims and the amount of each claim are unknown at the time of the sale of the item covered by the warranty. Although future events will eventually resolve the uncertainties (the warranty claims will be paid and the lawsuit will be adjudicated or settled), the liabilities are required to be recognized before all of the uncertainties are resolved so that relevant information is provided on a timely basis.

Levels of Probability ASC defines the different levels of probability as to whether or not future events will confirm the existence of a loss as follows:

- *Probable*—The future event or events are likely to occur.
- *Reasonably possible*—The chance of the future event or events occurring is more than remote but less than likely.
- *Remote*—The chance of the future event or events occurring is slight.
  (ASC 450-20-20)

Professional judgment is required to classify the likelihood of the future events occurring. All relevant information that can be acquired concerning the uncertain set of circumstances needs to be obtained and used to determine the classification.

Estimating the Loss When estimating the fair value of the loss, it is not necessary that a single amount be identified. A range of amounts is sufficient to indicate that some amount of loss has been incurred and is required to be accrued. (ASC 450-20-25-5) The amount accrued is the amount within the range that appears to be the best estimate. If there is no best estimate, the minimum amount in the range is accrued, since it is probable that the loss will be at least that amount. (ASC 450-20) The maximum amount of loss is required to be disclosed. (ASC 450-20-30-1) If future events indicate that the minimum loss originally accrued is inadequate, an additional loss should be accrued in the period when this fact becomes known.

ASC 450-30, *Gain Contingencies*

The guidance in ASC 450-30 states simply that a "contingency that might result in a gain usually should not be reflected in the financial statements because to do so might be to recognize revenue before its realization." (ASC 450-30-25-1)

PRACTICE ALERT

Loss contingencies are an area of frequent SEC comments and focus on disclosure about reasonably possible losses and the timeliness of disclosures. The SEC has raised the following questions and made suggestions:

- There is a reasonable possibility of a loss for more than the amount accrued. Explain why a higher amount has not been accrued.
- Explain how the entity determined that an estimate of a reasonably possible loss or range of losses cannot be made.
- Use clear language in the disclosure, consistent with the language of ASC 450, that is remote, reasonably possible, or probable, when discussing the likelihood of occurrence.
- As time goes on and the circumstances clarify, the disclosures are expected to include more quantitative details. Please add more specific quantitative information.
- Provide specific information regarding the matter.
- Quantify accruals.
- Include sufficient detail for the financial statement users to make meaningful judgments about assumptions underlying significant accruals.

PRESENTATION AND DISCLOSURE REQUIREMENTS

Presentation

ASC 450 does not include a "45" Section on presentation.

Disclosure

Note: ASC 450-10 does not contain any disclosure requirements.

ASC 450-20, *Loss Contingencies* Because contingency accruals are estimates, guidance recommends entities use terms such as "estimated liability" or "a liability of an estimated amount" when describing the accrual. The term "reserve" should not be used. (ASC 450-20-50-1)

The table below summarizes the three possible outcomes related to loss contingencies and disclosure requirements.

Material Loss Contingency Is:	Action
Probable* and reasonably estimable	Accrue a loss
Probable* but not reasonably estimable	Disclose the nature of the contingency and the fact that an estimate cannot be made
Possible but not probable*	Disclose the nature of the contingency and an estimate of the range of loss or the fact that an estimate cannot be made
Remote	No accrual or disclosure required[1]
(ASC 450-10-25-2 and 50-1 through 50-5)	

* *Probable is generally understood as a 75% threshold.*

Unasserted Claims or Assessments It is not necessary to disclose loss contingencies for an unasserted claim or assessment where there has been no manifestation of an awareness of possible claim or assessment by a potential claimant unless it is deemed probable that a claim will be asserted and a reasonable possibility of an unfavorable outcome exists. (ASC 450-20-50-6) Under the provisions of ASC 450, general or unspecified business risks are not loss contingencies and therefore no accrual is necessary. Disclosure of these business risks may be required under ASC 275. (ASC 450-20-50-8)

Events Subsequent to Balance Sheet Date It is important for the entity to distinguish between events that provide additional information about circumstances that existed at the balance sheet date and those related to conditions that did not exist at the balance sheet date. An accrual is not appropriate but disclosures should be considered. Events that occur after the date of the statement of financial position, for example, bankruptcy or expropriation, but before issuance of the financial statements that give rise to loss contingencies may require disclosure so that statement users are not misled. If, however, the information relates to an impairment of an asset or liability incurred that did not exist at the date of the statement of financial position, the conditions for accrual are not present. (ASC 450-20-50-9) Evaluation of whether accruals are necessary should be based on the principles found in ASC 855 on subsequent events.

---

[1] Note that ASC 460 contains an exception to the "no disclosure for remotely possible loss contingencies."

Litigation The most difficult area of contingencies is litigation. Accountants must rely on attorneys' assessments concerning the likelihood of such events. Unless the attorney indicates that the risk of loss is remote or slight, or that the loss if it occurs would be immaterial to the company, disclosure in financial statements is necessary and an accrual may also be necessary. In practice, attorneys are loathe to state that the risk of loss is remote, as that term is defined by ASC 450, although the likelihood of obtaining a definitive response to lawyers' letters under AU-C Section 501 is improved if the auditors explicitly cite a materiality threshold. In cases where judgments have been entered against the reporting entity or where the attorney gives a range of expected losses or other amounts and indicates that an unfavorable outcome is probable, accruals of loss contingencies for at least the minimum point of the range must be made. In determining whether an accrual or disclosure is required, the entity should consider:

- The period in which the underlying cause takes place.
- The degree of probability of an unfavorable outcome.
- The ability to make a reasonable return of the loss.
  (ASC 450-20-55-10)

In most cases, however, an estimate of the contingency is unknown and the contingency is reflected only in footnotes.

Accruals for contingencies, including those arising in connection with litigation, are limited under GAAP to expected losses resulting from events occurring prior to the date of the statement of financial position. (ASC 450-20-25-6) One unresolved issue is whether expected legal costs to be incurred in connection with a loss contingency that is being accrued should be accrued as well. Apparently, GAAP would permit such an accrual, but practice is varied. Preparers may want to refer to the SEC staff views. The SEC staff expects consistency and the decision to accrue legal costs should be disclosed in the financial statements and applied consistently. (ASC 450-20-S99)

The Codification states that entities may consider disclosing a gain contingency as long as the disclosure is adequate and is not misleading. (ASC 450-30-50-1) Preparers should refer to the guidance in ASC 220-30 on business interruption insurance and the ASC 210 Subtopic 20 on offsetting.

ASC 450-30, *Gain Contingencies* The ASC 450-30-50 Subtopic contains only one paragraph and that offers a caution to preparers to include adequate disclosure and not to mislead readers about the likelihood of realization.

PRESENTATION AND DISCLOSURE EXAMPLES

Example 31.1: Assessment of Lawsuits and Claims

Assessments of lawsuits and claims can involve a series of complex judgments about future events and can rely heavily on estimates and assumptions. The Company accrues an estimated liability for legal proceeding claims that are both probable and estimable in accordance with Accounting Standard Codification (ASC) 450, *Contingencies*. Please refer to the example below entitled "Process for Disclosure and Recording of Liabilities Related to Legal Proceedings" for additional information about such estimates.

Example 31.2: Process for Disclosure and Recording of Liabilities Related to Legal Proceedings

Management records liabilities for legal proceedings in those instances where it can reasonably estimate the amount of the loss and when the liability is probable. Where the reasonable estimate of the probable loss is a range, management records the most likely estimate of the loss, or the low end of the range if there is no one best estimate. Management either discloses the amount of a possible loss or range of loss in excess of established accruals if estimable, or states that such an estimate cannot be made. Management discloses significant legal proceedings even where liability is not probable or the amount of the liability is not estimable, or both, if management believes there is at least a reasonable possibility that a loss may be incurred.

The principal considerations for our determination that performing procedures relating to legal proceedings contingencies is a critical audit matter are there was significant judgment by management when assessing the likelihood of a loss being incurred and when estimating the loss or range of loss for each claim, which in turn led to significant auditor judgment, subjectivity, and effort in performing procedures and evaluating management's assessment of the liabilities and disclosures associated with legal proceedings.

Addressing the matter involved performing procedures and evaluating audit evidence in connection with forming our overall opinion on the consolidated financial statements. These procedures included testing the effectiveness of controls relating to management's evaluation of the liability related to legal proceedings, including controls over determining the likelihood of a loss and whether the amount of loss can be reasonably estimated, as well as financial statement disclosures. These procedures also included, among others, obtaining and evaluating the letters of audit inquiry with internal and external legal counsel, evaluating the reasonableness of management's assessment regarding whether an unfavorable outcome is reasonably possible or probable and reasonably estimable, and evaluating the sufficiency of the Company's disclosures related to legal proceedings.

Example 31.3: Unconditional Purchase Obligations

Unconditional purchase obligations are defined as an agreement to purchase goods or services that is enforceable and legally binding (noncancellable, or cancellable only in certain circumstances). The Company estimates its total unconditional purchase obligation commitment (for those contracts with terms in excess of one year) as of December 31, 20X1, at $983 million. Payments by year are estimated as follows: 20X2 ($306 million), 20X3 ($278 million), 20X4 ($156 million), 20X5 ($184 million), 20X6 ($42 million), and after 20X6 ($17 million). Many of these commitments relate to take or pay contracts, in which LRB guarantees payment to ensure availability of products or services that are sold to customers. The Company expects to receive consideration (products or services) for these unconditional purchase obligations. The purchase obligation amounts do not represent the entire anticipated purchases in the future, but represent only those items for which the Company is contractually obligated. The majority of LRB's products and services are purchased as needed, with no unconditional commitment. For this reason, these amounts will not provide an indication of the Company's expected future cash outflows related to purchases.

Example 31.4: Product Warranties

JMB's accrued product warranty liabilities, recorded on the Consolidated Balance Sheet as part of current and long-term liabilities, are estimated at approximately $51 million at December 31, 20X2, and $48 million at December 31, 20X1. Further information on product warranties are not disclosed, as the Company considers the balance immaterial to its consolidated results of operations and financial condition. The fair value of JMB's guarantees of loans with third parties and other guarantee arrangements are not material.

Example 31.5: Accounting Policy—Contingencies Related to Lawsuits and Claims

Many lawsuits and claims involve highly complex issues relating to causation, scientific evidence, and alleged actual damages, all of which are otherwise subject to substantial uncertainties. Assessments of lawsuits and claims can involve a series of complex judgments about future events and can rely heavily on estimates and assumptions. When making determinations about recording liabilities related to legal proceedings, the Company complies with the requirements of ASC 450, *Contingencies*, and related guidance, and records liabilities in those instances where it can reasonably estimate the amount of the loss and when liability is probable. Where the reasonable estimate of the probable loss is a range, the Company records as an accrual in its financial statements the most likely estimate of the loss, or the low end of the range if there is no one best estimate. The Company either discloses the amount of a possible loss or range of loss in excess of established accruals if estimable, or states that such an estimate cannot be made. The Company discloses significant legal proceedings even where liability is not probable or the amount of the liability is not estimable, or both, if the Company believes there is at least a reasonable possibility that a loss may be incurred.

Because litigation is subject to inherent uncertainties, and unfavorable rulings or developments could occur, there can be no certainty that the Company may not ultimately incur charges in excess of presently recorded liabilities. Many of the matters described are at preliminary stages or seek an indeterminate amount of damages. It is not uncommon for claims to be resolved over many years. A future adverse ruling, settlement, unfavorable development, or increase in accruals for one or more of these matters could result in future charges that could have a material adverse effect on the Company's results of operations or cash flows in the period in which they are recorded. Although the Company cannot estimate its exposure to all legal proceedings, the Company currently believes that the ultimate outcome of legal proceedings or future charges, if any, would not have a material adverse effect on the consolidated financial position of the Company. Based on experience and developments, the Company reexamines its estimates of probable liabilities and associated expenses and receivables each period, and whether it is able to estimate a liability previously determined to be not estimable and/or not probable. Where appropriate, the Company makes additions to or adjustments of its estimated liabilities. As a result, the current estimates of the potential impact on the Company's consolidated financial position, results of operations and cash flows for the legal proceedings and claims pending against the Company could change in the future.

Example 31.6: Accounting Policy—Insurance Recoveries

The Company carries liability insurance to mitigate its exposure to certain losses, including those relating to property damage and business interruption. The Company records the estimated amount of expected insurance proceeds for property damage and other losses incurred as an asset (typically a receivable from the insurer) and income up to the amount of the losses incurred when receipt of insurance proceeds is deemed probable. Any amount of insurance recovery in excess of the amount of the losses incurred is considered a gain contingency and is not recorded in fee and other income until the proceeds are received. Insurance recoveries for business interruption for lost revenue or profit are accounted for as gain contingencies in their entirety, and therefore are not recorded in income until the proceeds are received.

Example 31.7: Intellectual Property Rights Litigation—No Contingency Accrued

Market participants rely on patented and nonpatented proprietary information relating to product development and other core competencies of their business. Protection of intellectual property is important. Therefore, steps such as patent applications, confidentiality and nondisclosure agreements, as well as other security measures are generally taken. The Company has not created a litigation reserve for intellectual property rights litigation. As a business judgment, the Company does not patent or copyright or trademark all intellectual property due to a combination of factors, including, in part, the cost of registration and maintenance of registration, odds and cost of successful defense of the registration and commercial value of the intellectual property rights. To enforce or protect intellectual property rights, litigation or threatened litigation is common. The Company has not sued any third parties over intellectual property rights.

Example 31.8: Business Acquisition—Contingent Compensation Recorded as Deferred Compensation

On May 29, 20X2, the Company purchased a 51% membership interest in Ballarat Entertainment LLC, a talent management and television/film production company. A portion of the purchase price, up to $38.3 million, may be recoupable for a five-year period commencing on the acquisition date of May 29, 20X2, contingent upon the continued employment of certain employees, or the achievement of certain EBITDA targets, as defined in the Ballarat Entertainment acquisition and related agreements. Accordingly, $38.3 million was initially recorded as a deferred compensation arrangement within other current and noncurrent assets and is being amortized in general and administrative expenses over a five-year period.

The acquired finite-lived intangible assets primarily represent customer relationships and are being amortized over a weighted average estimated useful life of 12 years. The Company incurred approximately $1.3 million of acquisition-related costs that were expensed in restructuring and other expenses during the fiscal year ended March 31, 20X3.

The Company used discounted cash flows ("DCF") analyses, which represent Level 3 fair value measurements, to assess certain components of its purchase price allocation, including acquired intangible assets and the redeemable noncontrolling interest. The acquisition goodwill arises from the opportunity for synergies of the combined companies to grow and strengthen the Company's television operations by expanding the Company's talent relationships, and improving the Company's television production capabilities. The goodwill recorded as part of this acquisition is included in the Television Production segment. The goodwill is not amortized for financial reporting purposes, but is deductible for federal tax purposes.

Example 31.9: Accounting Policy—Insurance Recoveries

The Company carries liability insurance to mitigate its exposure to certain losses, including those relating to property damage and business interruption. The Company records the estimated amount of expected insurance proceeds for property damage and other losses incurred as an asset (typically a receivable from the insurer) and income up to the amount of the losses incurred when receipt of insurance proceeds is deemed probable. Any amount of insurance recovery in excess of the amount of the losses incurred is considered a gain contingency and is not recorded in fee and other income until the proceeds are received. Insurance recoveries for business interruption for lost revenue or profit are accounted for as gain contingencies in their entirety, and therefore are not recorded in income until the proceeds are received.

Example 31.10: Deferred Payment Obligation

Pursuant to an Agreement and Plan of Merger, or the Merger Agreement, dated as of May 15, 2008, and subsequently amended, The Carlyle Group indirectly acquired all of the issued and outstanding stock of the Company. In connection with this transaction, on July 31, 2008 the Company established a deferred payment obligation, or DPO, of $158.0 million, payable 8.5 years after the closing date, or until settlement of all outstanding claims, less any settled claims. Pursuant to the merger agreement, $78.0 million of the $158.0 million DPO was required to be paid in full to the selling stockholders. On December 11, 2009, in connection with a recapitalization transaction, $100.4 million was paid to the selling stockholders, of which $78.0 million was the repayment of that portion of the DPO, with approximately $22.4 million representing accrued interest.

The remaining $80.0 million balance, which was recorded in other current liabilities, was available to indemnify the Company for certain pre-acquisition tax contingencies, related interest and penalties, and other matters pursuant to the Merger Agreement. All remaining potential claims outstanding that were able to be indemnified under the DPO related to former officers and stockholders' lawsuits, which were all settled as of December 31, 2019. See Note X to the accompanying consolidated financial statements. Any amounts remaining after the settlement of all claims were to be paid out to the selling stockholders. On December 18, 2019, the Company paid approximately $83.0 million to the selling stockholders, of which $80.0 million was the repayment of the remaining DPO balance, with $3.0 million representing accrued interest.

32 ASC 460 GUARANTEES

AUTHORITATIVE LITERATURE

Overview

Guarantees embody two separate obligations:

1. The contingent obligation to make future payments under the guarantee in the event of nonperformance by the party whose obligation is guaranteed, and
2. An obligation to be ready to perform, referred to as a standby obligation, during the period that the guarantee is in effect.

As a result of this bifurcation of the obligation, many guarantees are now required to be recognized as liabilities on the statement of financial position.

Subtopic

ASC 460, *Guarantees*, consists of one Subtopic:

- ASC 460-10, *Overall*, which provides requirements to be met by a guarantor for certain guarantees issued and outstanding.

ASC 460-10 has two Subsections:

1. *General,* which discusses the guarantor's recognition and disclosure of a liability at the inception of a guarantee.

2. *Product Warranties.*
   (ASC 460-10-05-1)

Additional sources of guidance are listed in the "Other Sources" section at the end of this chapter.

Scope and Scope Exceptions

General ASC 460 applies to all entities. (ASC 460-10-15-1) ASC 460 applies to:

a. Guarantee contracts that contingently require the guarantor to make payments to the guaranteed party as described in "b" below based on changes to an underlying related to an asset, a liability, or an equity security of the guaranteed party.
b. Contracts that contingently require a guarantor to make payments based on another entity's failure to perform under an obligating agreement. For example, the provisions apply to a performance standby letter of credit, which obligates the guarantor to make a payment if the specified entity fails to perform its nonfinancial obligation. (ASC 460-10-55-12)
c. The occurrence of a specified event or circumstance in an indemnification agreement that requires the indemnifying party to pay an indemnified party based on changes in underlying related to an asset, a liability, or an equity security of the indemnified party. Examples are an adverse judgment in a lawsuit or the imposition of additional taxes due to either a change in the tax law or an adverse interpretation of the tax law, provided that the guarantor is an entity other than an insurance or reinsurance company. (ASC 460-10-55-13)
d. Indirect guarantee of the indebtedness of others even though the payment may not be based on changes to an underlying related to an asset, liability or equity security of the guaranteed party.
   (ASC 460-10-15-4)

The following are examples of the types of contracts referred to in ASC 460-10-15-4(b) above:

- A financial standby letter of credit.
- A market value guarantee on either securities (including the common stock of the guaranteed party) or a nonfinancial asset owned by the guaranteed party.
- A guarantee of the market price of the common stock of the guaranteed party.
- A guarantee of the collection of the scheduled contractual cash flows from individual financial assets held by a variable interest entity (VIE).
- A guarantee granted to a business or its owners that the revenue received by the business will equal or exceed some stated amount.
  (ASC 460-10-55-2, with reference to ASC 460-10-15-4(a))

ASC 460 does *not* apply to:

- A guarantee or an indemnification that is excluded from the scope of Topic 450, *Contingencies*, primarily employment-related guarantees.
- A lessee's guarantee of the residual value of leased property if the lessee accounts for the lease as a capital lease.[1]
- Contingent rents.[2]

---

[1] Upon implementation of ASU 2016-02, *Leases,* this bullet will read: "A lessee's guarantee of the residual value of the underlying asset at the expiration of the lease term under Topic 8842."
[2] Upon implementation of ASU 2016-02, this bullet will change to "A contract that is accounted for as Variable lease payments."

- A guarantee contract or an indemnification agreement, accounted for under ASC 944, that is issued by either an insurance or a reinsurance company.
- Vendor rebates (by the guarantor) based on either the sales revenues of or the number of units sold by the guaranteed party.
- Vendor rebates (by the guarantor) based on the volume of purchases by the buyer (because the underlying relates to an asset of the seller not the buyer who receives the rebate).
- Guarantees that prevent the guarantor from recognizing either the sale of the asset underlying the guarantee or the profits from that sale.
- A registration payment arrangement within the scope of ASC 825-20-15, *Financial Instruments, Registration Payment Arrangements.*
- A guarantee or an indemnification of an entity's own future performance.
- A guarantee accounted for as a credit derivative instrument at fair value under ASC 815-10-50-4 J through 4 L.
- A sales incentive program where a manufacturer guarantees to recognize the equipment at a specified time or place.
(ASC 460-10-15-7)

Product Warranties The guidance in the Product Warranties subsections applies only to product warranties, which include all of the following:

- Product warranties issued by the guarantor, regardless of whether the guarantor is required to make payment in services or cash.
- Separately priced extended warranty or product maintenance contracts and (per ASC 606) "warranties that provide a customer with a service in addition to the assurance that product complies with agreed-upon specifications."
- Warranty obligations that are incurred in connection with the sale of the product, that is, obligations in which the customer does not have the option to purchase the warranty separately and that do not provide the customer with a service in addition to the assurance that the product complies with agreed-upon specifications.
(ASC 460-10-15-9)

ASC 460's requirement to recognize an initial liability does *not* apply to the following types of guarantees. However, these guarantees are subject only to ASC 460's disclosure requirements:

- A guarantee that is accounted for as a derivative instrument at fair value under ASC 815.
- A contract that guarantees the functionality of nonfinancial assets that are owned by the guaranteed party (product warranties).
- Contingent consideration in a business combination or an acquisition of a business or nonprofit activity by a not-for-profit entity.
- A guarantee that requires the guarantor to issue its own equity shares.
- A guarantee by an original lessee that has become secondarily liable under a new lease that relieved the original lessee of the primary obligation under the original lease.
- A guarantee issued between parents and their subsidiaries or between corporations under common control.
- A parent's guarantee of a subsidiary's debt to a third party (irrespective of whether the parent is a corporation or an individual).
- A subsidiary's guarantee of a parent's debt to a third party or the debt of another subsidiary of the parent.
(ASC 460-10-25-1)

Guarantees ASC 460:

- Requires that the fair value of guarantees be recognized as a liability, and
- Establishes the notion that a guarantee actually consists of two distinct components.

These two components have quite different accounting implications:

1. *Noncontingent obligation.* The first of these components is a noncontingent obligation, namely, the obligation to stand ready to perform over the term of the guarantee in the event that the specified triggering events or conditions occur. This stand-ready obligation is unconditional and thus is not considered a contingent obligation.
2. *Contingent obligation.* The second component, which is a contingent obligation, is the obligation to make future payments if those triggering events or conditions occur. (ASC 460-10-25-2)

Note that ASC 460 does not require bifurcation or separate accounting for the contingent and noncontingent assets of the guarantee. Upon implementation of ASC 2016-13, that will be true only for guarantees not within the scope of ASC 326-20. For those within the scope of ASC 326-20, the contingent aspect should be measured and accounted for in addition to and separately from the fair value of the noncontingent aspect. (ASC 460-10-25-2)

Even though it is not probable that payments will be required, a guarantor may recognize a liability for a guarantee. (ASC 460-10-25-3)

Initial Recognition At the inception of a guarantee, the guarantor recognizes a liability for both the noncontingent and contingent obligations at their fair values. (ASC 460-10-25-4) However, in the unusual circumstance that a liability is recognized under ASC 450-20 for the contingent obligation (i.e., because it is deemed probable of occurrence and reasonable of estimation that the guarantor will pay), the liability initially recognized for the noncontingent obligation would be only the portion, if any, of the guarantee's fair value not already recognized to comply with ASC 450-20. (ASC 460-10-25-3)

It is important to stress that this does not mean that the guarantor records the entire face amount of the guarantee; rather, it is the fair value of the stand-ready obligation that is recognized. When a guarantee is issued in a stand-alone, arm's-length transaction with an unrelated party, the fair value of the guarantee (and thus the amount to be recognized as a liability) is the premium received by the guarantor. When a guarantee is issued as part of another transaction (such as the sale or lease of an asset) or as a contribution to an unrelated party, the fair value of the liability is measured by the premium that would be required by the guarantor to issue the same guarantee in a stand-alone, arm's-length transaction with an unrelated party.

In practice, if the likelihood that the guarantor will have to perform is judged to be only "reasonably possible" or "remote," the only amount recorded is the fair value of the noncontingent obligation to stand ready to perform. If, however, the contingency is probable of occurrence and can be reasonably estimated under ASC 450-20, that amount must be recognized and the liability under the guarantee arrangement will be the greater of:

- The fair value computed as explained above, or
- The amount computed in accordance with ASC 450-20's provisions. (ASC 460-10-30-3)

Upon implementation of ASU 2016-13, at the inception of a guarantee on financial instruments measured at amortized costs, the guarantor should recognize as liabilities:

- The amount that satisfies the fair value obligation in ASC 460-10-30-2 described above, and
- The contingent liability related to the expected credit loss measured according to ASC 326-20.
  (ASC 460-10-30-5)

When initially issued, the guidance on computing guarantees where no market information is available made reference to CON 7. In so doing, FASB endorsed the use of the discounted, probability-weighted cash flow method for estimating the stand-ready obligation.

Since, in the author's opinion, in the absence of other, better input data, such as the pricing of insurance to assume the risk of performing on the guarantee, the probability-weighted present value of possible future cash flows could serve as useful input to determining the fair value of guarantees made, the following example is presented.

Subsequent Measurement After initial recognition, the liability is adjusted as the guarantor is either released from risk or is subject to increased risk. If the guarantor is subsequently released from risk, logically that could be recognized in one of three ways:

1. The liability could simply be written off at its expiration or settlement.
2. The liability could be amortized systematically over the guarantee period.
3. The liability might be adjusted to reflect changing fair value, which presumably declines over time as the risk of having to perform decreases.

ASC 460 does not prescribe the accounting for guarantees subsequent to initial recognition, and there is no requirement to reassess the fair value of the guarantee after inception. Fair value should be used only in subsequent accounting for the guarantee if the use of that method can be justified under other authoritative guidance. (ASC 460-10-35-2)

This guidance does not address the recognition and subsequent accounting of the contingent liability related to the contingent loss for the guarantee. That should be accounted for using the guidance in:

- ASC 450-20 unless the guarantee is:
  - Accounted for as a derivative under the provisions of ASC 815, or
  - Within the scope of ASC 326-20, when implemented.
    (ASC 460-10-35-4)

Product Warranties Product warranties providing for repair or replacement of defective products may be sold separately or may be included in the sale price of the product. ASC 460-10-25-5 points out that "because of the uncertainty surrounding claims that may be made under warranties, warranty obligation falls within the definition of a contingency" and losses are accrued if the conditions in ASC 450-20-25 are met:

- If it is *probable* that an obligation has been incurred because of a transaction or event that occurred on or before the date of the financial statements, and
- If the amount of the obligation can be *reasonably estimated*.

These conditions may be made for individual elements or groups of items and the particular parties making claims may not be identified at the time of the accrual. (ASC 460-10-25-7)

For information on extended warranty contracts, product maintenance contracts, and warranties that provide a service in addition to the assurance that the product complied with the specifications, see the chapter on ASC 606. (ASC 460-10-25-8)

PRESENTATION AND DISCLOSURE REQUIREMENTS

Presentation An accrual for a credit loss on a financial instrument with off-balance-sheet risk is recorded as a liability separate from a valuation account related to a recognized financial instrument. This requirement includes financial standby letters of credit.

Disclosure An entity must disclose certain loss contingencies even though the possibility of loss may be remote. The common characteristic of those contingencies is a guarantee that provides a right to proceed against an outside party in the event that the guarantor is called on to satisfy the guarantee. Examples include the following:

- Guarantees of indebtedness of others, including indirect guarantees of indebtedness of others.
- Obligations of commercial banks under standby letters of credit.
- Guarantees to repurchase receivables (or, in some cases, to repurchase the related property) that have been sold or otherwise assigned.
- Other agreements that have in substance the same guarantee characteristics.
  (ASC 460-10-50-2)

The guarantor must disclose the following for each guarantee or group of similar guarantees:

1. The nature of the guarantee including:
   a. Approximate term.
   b. How it originated.
   c. Events and circumstances that would require performance.
   d. Current status, as of the balance sheet date, of the payment/performance risk.
   e. If a reporting entity uses internal groupings for "d," it must disclose how such groupings are determined and used for managing risk.

2. The maximum potential amount of future payments (undiscounted) that the guarantor could be required to make under the guarantee. With regard to this disclosure:
   a. The amount of undiscounted potential future payments, not reduced by any potential recoveries under collateralization or recourse provisions in the guarantee.
   b. If there is no limitation, based on the terms of the guarantee, to the maximum potential future payments, then this fact must be disclosed.
   c. If the guarantor cannot estimate the amount of the maximum estimated future payments under the guarantee, the guarantor must disclose the reasons why an estimate cannot be determined.
   d. The current carrying amount of any guarantor's obligations under the guarantee (including any amount recognized under the contingency guidance within ASC 450 or, when ASU 2016-13 is implemented ASC 326 on financial instruments measured at amortized cost). This disclosure is required regardless of whether the guarantee is freestanding or embedded in another contract.
   e. The nature of any recourse provisions that would allow the guarantor to recover amounts paid under the guarantee.
   f. The nature of any assets held either by third parties or as collateral that the guarantor could obtain to recover amounts paid under the guarantee.

g. The approximate extent to which the proceeds from the liquidation of assets held either by third parties or as collateral would cover the maximum potential future payments under the guarantee, if the amount is estimable.

The information outlined above is required to be disclosed even when there is a remote probability of the guarantor making any payments under the guarantee or group of guarantees. (ASC 460-10-50-4)

Guarantees issued by a reporting entity to benefit related parties, such as equity method investees and joint ventures, require incremental disclosures pursuant to ASC 850, *Related Party Disclosures*. (ASC 460-10-50-6)

PRESENTATION AND DISCLOSURE EXAMPLES

Example 32.1: Accounting Policy—Warranties, Claims Are Immaterial

The Company's products come with a standard assurance type warranty which cannot be purchased separately and accounted for pursuant to ASC 460, *Guarantees*. As historical warranty claims have been immaterial, the Company has recognized expenses in cost of goods sold as incurred. The Company will recognize an estimated reserve, when material, based on its analysis of historical experience.

Example 32.2: Product Warranties—No Disclosure because Amounts Are Immaterial

JMB's accrued product warranty liabilities, recorded on the Consolidated Balance Sheet as part of current and long-term liabilities, are estimated at approximately $51 million at December 31, 20X2, and $48 million at December 31, 20X1. Further information on product warranties are not disclosed, as the Company considers the balance immaterial to its consolidated results of operations and financial condition. The fair value of 3M guarantees of loans with third parties and other guarantee arrangements are not material at approximately $51 million at December 31, 20X2, and $48 million at December 31, 20X1. Further information on product warranties are not disclosed, as the Company considers the balance immaterial to its consolidated results of operations and financial condition. The fair value of JMB's guarantees of loans with third parties and other guarantee arrangements are not material.

Example 32.3: Guarantees

The Company has applied the disclosure provisions of ASC 460, *Guarantees*, to its agreements that contain guarantee or indemnification clauses. These disclosure provisions expand those required by ASC 440, *Commitments*, and ASC 450, *Contingencies*, by requiring a guarantor to disclose certain types of guarantees, even if the likelihood of requiring the guarantor's performance is remote. The following is a description of arrangements in which the Company is the guarantor or indemnifies a party.

In the normal course of business, the Company has made certain guarantees and indemnities, under which it may be required to make payments to a guaranteed or indemnified party, in relation to certain transactions. The Company indemnifies other parties, including customers, lessors, and parties to other transactions with the Company, with respect to certain matters. The Company has agreed to hold the other party harmless against losses arising from certain events as defined within the particular contract, which may include, for example, litigation or claims arising from a breach of representations or covenants. In addition, the Company has entered into indemnification agreements with its executive officers and directors and the Company's bylaws contain similar indemnification obligations. Under these arrangements, the Company is obligated to indemnify, to the fullest extent permitted under applicable law, its current or former officers and directors for various amounts incurred with respect to actions, suits, or proceedings in which they were made, or threatened to be made, a party as a result of acting as an officer or director.

It is not possible to determine the maximum potential amount under these indemnification agreements due to the limited history of prior indemnification claims and the unique facts and circumstances involved in each particular agreement. Historically, payments made related to these indemnifications have been immaterial. At December 31, 2016, the Company has determined that no liability is necessary related to these guarantees and indemnities.

Example 32.4: Product Warranty Costs, Accrual Policy, and Schedule with Changes

As required by FASB ASC 460, Guarantees, the Company is including the following disclosure applicable to its product warranties.

The Company accrues for warranty costs based on the expected material and labor costs to provide warranty replacement products. The methodology used in determining the liability for warranty cost is based upon historical information and experience. The Company's warranty reserve is calculated as the gross sales multiplied by the historical warranty expense return rate.

The following table shows the changes in the aggregate product warranty liability for the year ended December 31, 20X2 and December 31, 20X1, respectively:

	20X2	*20X1*
Balance as of beginning of year	$20,500	$20,000
Less: Payments made	4,500	7,500
Add: Provision for current years warranty	8,000	8,000
Balance as of end of year	$24,000	$20,500

Example 32.5: Guarantees and Indemnifications

MTL and its subsidiaries enter into various contracts that include indemnification and guarantee provisions as a routine part of the Company's business activities. Examples of these contracts include asset purchases and sale agreements, commodity sale and purchase agreements, retail contracts, joint venture agreements, EPC (Engineering, Procurement, Consulting) agreements, operation and maintenance agreements, service agreements, settlement agreements, and other types of contractual agreements with vendors and other third parties, as well as affiliates. These contracts generally indemnify the counterparty for tax, environmental liability, litigation and other matters, as well as breaches of representations, warranties and covenants set forth in these agreements. The Company is obligated with respect to customer deposits associated with the Company's retail businesses. In some cases, MTL's maximum potential liability cannot be estimated, since the underlying agreements contain no limits on potential liability.

Example 32.6: Schedule of Maximum Potential Amount of Future Payments for Guarantees

The following table summarizes the maximum potential exposures that can be estimated for MTL's guarantees by maturity:

(In millions)	*By Remaining Maturity at December 31, 20X2*					
Guarantees	*Under One Year*	*One to Three Years*	*Three to Five Years*	*Over Five Years*	*Total*	*20X1 Total*
Letters of credit and surety bonds(a)	$ 878	$ 115	$ 31	$ —	$ 1,024	$ 1,253
Asset sales guarantee obligations	4	490	—	204	698	793
Other guarantees	77	5	—	206	288	721
Total guarantees	$ 959	$ 610	$ 31	$ 410	$ 2,010	$ 2,767

Example 32.7: Letters of Credit

As of December 31, 20X2, MTL and its consolidated subsidiaries were contingently obligated for a total of $1.0 billion under letters of credit and surety bonds. Most of these letters of credit and surety bonds are issued in support of the Company's obligations to perform under commodity agreements and obligations associated with future closure and maintenance of ash sites, as well as for financing or other arrangements. A majority of these letters of credit and surety bonds expire within one year of issuance, and it is typical for the Company to renew them on similar terms.

33 ASC 470 DEBT

AUTHORITATIVE LITERATURE

Debt remains on the books of the debtor until it is extinguished. In many cases, a debt is extinguished at maturity when the required principal and interest payments have been made and the debtor has no further obligation to the creditor. In other cases, the debtor may extinguish the debt before its maturity. For example, if market interest rates are falling, a debtor may choose to issue debt at the new lower rate and use the proceeds to retire older higher-interest-rate debt. A debt is extinguished if either of two conditions is met:

1. The debtor pays the creditor and is relieved of its obligation for the liability.
2. The debtor is legally released from being the primary obligor under the liability, either judicially or by the creditor.
   (ASC 405-20-40-1)

If a debtor experiences financial difficulties before the debt is repaid and for economic or legal reasons related to the debtor's financial difficulties, the creditor grants the debtor concessions that would not otherwise have been granted, the debtor must determine how to recognize the effects of the troubled debt restructuring. (ASC 470-60)

Some debt is issued with terms that allow it to be converted to an equity instrument (common or, less often, preferred stock) at a future date. These issuances can create complex accounting issues. In certain situations, a debtor will modify the conversion privileges after issuance of the debt in order to induce prompt conversion of the debt into equity, in which case the debtor must recognize an expense for this consideration. (ASC 470-20-40-16)

Debt can also be issued with stock warrants, which allow the holder to purchase a stated number of common shares at a certain price within a defined time period. If debt is issued with detachable warrants, the proceeds of issuance are allocated between the two financial instruments. (ASC 470-20-05)

Subtopics

ASC 470, *Debt*, consists of six Subtopics:

- ASC 470-10, *Overall*, which provides guidance on classification of obligations, such as:
  ○ Short-term debt expected to be refinanced on a long-term basis,
  ○ Due-on-demand loans,
  ○ Callable debt,
  ○ Sales of future revenue,
  ○ Increasing rate debt, debt with covenants,
  ○ Revolving credit agreements subject to lockbox arrangements and subjective acceleration clauses, and
  ○ Indexed debt.
  (ASC 470-10-05-5)
- ASC 470-20, *Debt with Conversion and Other Options*, which provides guidance on debt and certain preferred stock with specific conversion features:
  ○ Debt instruments with detachable warrants,
  ○ Convertible debt instruments,
  ○ Interest forfeiture,
  ○ Induced conversions,
  ○ Conversion upon issuer's exercise of call option, and
  ○ Own-share lending arrangements issued in contemplation of convertible debt issuance or other financing.
  (ASC 470-20-05-1)
- ASC 470-30, *Participating Mortgage Loans*, which provides guidance on the borrower's accounting for a participating mortgage loan if the lender is entitled to participate in appreciation in the fair value of the mortgaged real estate project or the results of operations of the mortgaged real estate project.
- ASC 470-40, *Product Financing Arrangements*, which provides guidance for determining whether an arrangement involving the sale of inventory is in substance a financing arrangement.
- ASC 470-50, *Modifications and Extinguishments*, which provides guidance on all debt instruments extinguishment, except for debt extinguished in a troubled debt restructuring.
- ASC 470-60, *Troubled Debt Restructurings by Debtors*, which addresses measuring and recognition from the debtor's perspective.

Scope and Scope Exceptions

ASC 470-20 ASC 470-20 is divided into two Subsections:

1. General
2. Cash conversion

General Subsections The guidance in the General Subsections' paragraphs does not apply to those instruments within the scope of the Cash Conversion Subsections. The guidance on own-share lending arrangements applies to an equity-classified share-lending arrangement on an entity's own shares when executed in contemplation of a convertible debt offering or other financing. (ASC 470-20-15-2)

It is important to note that the guidance in this Subsection should be considered after consideration of the guidance in Subtopic 815-15 on bifurcation of embedded derivatives, as applicable (see paragraph 815-15-55-76A).

Cash Conversion Subsections The guidance in the Cash Conversion subsections applies only to convertible debt instruments that may be settled in cash (or other assets) upon conversion, unless the embedded conversion option is required to be separately accounted for as a derivative instrument under Subtopic 815-15. (ASC 470-20-15-4)

The Cash Conversion subsections do *not* apply to any of the following instruments:

- A convertible preferred share that is classified in equity or temporary equity.
- A convertible debt instrument that requires or permits settlement in cash (or other assets) upon conversion only in specific circumstances in which the holders of the underlying shares also would receive the same form of consideration in exchange for their shares.
- A convertible debt instrument that requires an issuer's obligation to provide consideration for a fractional share upon conversion to be settled in cash but that does not otherwise require or permit settlement in cash (or other assets) upon conversion. (ASC 470-20-15-5)

For purposes of determining whether an instrument is within the scope of the Cash Conversion Subsections, a convertible preferred share should be considered a convertible debt instrument if it is:

- A mandatorily redeemable financial instrument, and
- Classified as a liability under Subtopic 480-10. (ASC 470-20-15-6)

ASC 470-30 ASC 470-30 does *not* apply to creditors in participating mortgage loan arrangements and to the following transactions:

- Participating leases.
- Debt convertible at the option of the lender into equity ownership of the property.
- Participating loans resulting from troubled debt restructurings. (ASC 470-30-15-2 and 15-3)

ASC 470-40 The guidance in ASC 470-40 applies to product financing arrangements for products that were purchased by another entity on behalf of the sponsor. The arrangement must have the following characteristics:

- The financing arrangement requires the sponsor to purchase the product, a substantially identical product, or processed goods of which the product is a component at specified prices. The specified prices are not subject to change except for fluctuations due to finance and holding costs. This characteristic of predetermined prices also is present if any of the following circumstances exist:

- ○ The specified prices in the financing arrangement are in the form of resale price guarantees under which the sponsor agrees to make up any difference between the specified price and the resale price for products sold to third parties.
- ○ The sponsor is not required to purchase the product but has an option to purchase the product, the economic effect of which compels the sponsor to purchase the product; for example, an option arrangement that provides for a significant penalty if the sponsor does not exercise the option to purchase.
- ○ The sponsor is not required by the agreement to purchase the product but the other entity has an option whereby it can require the sponsor to purchase the product.
- • The payments that the other entity will receive on the transaction are established by the financing arrangement, and the amounts to be paid by the sponsor will be adjusted, as necessary, to cover substantially all fluctuations in costs incurred by the other entity in purchasing and holding the product (including interest). This characteristic ordinarily is not present in purchase commitments or contractor-subcontractor relationships. (ASC 470-40-15-2)

ASC 470-40 does *not* apply to the following transactions and activities:

- • Ordinary purchase commitments in which control of goods or services are retained by the seller (for example, a manufacturer or other supplier) until the goods or services are transferred to a purchaser.
- • Typical contractor-subcontractor relationships in which the contractor is not in substance the owner of product held by the subcontractor and the obligation of the contractor is contingent on substantial performance on the part of the subcontractor.
- • Long-term unconditional purchase obligations (for example, take-or-pay contracts) specified by Subtopic 440-10. At the time a take-or-pay contract is entered into, which is an unconditional purchase obligation, either the product does not yet exist (for example, electricity) or the product exists in a form unsuitable to the purchaser (for example, unmined coal); the purchaser has a right to receive future product but is not the substantive owner of existing product.
- • Unmined or unharvested natural resources and financial instruments.
- • Transactions for which sales revenue is recognized currently in accordance with the provisions of ASC 606.
- • Typical purchases by a subcontractor on behalf of a contractor. In a typical contractor-subcontractor relationship, the purchase of product by a subcontractor on behalf of a contractor ordinarily leaves a significant portion of the subcontractor's obligation unfulfilled.
- • The subcontractor has the risks of ownership of the product until it has met all the terms of a contract. Accordingly, the typical contractor-subcontractor relationship shall not be considered a product financing arrangement. (ASC 470-40-15-3)

ASC 470-50 The general guidance for extinguishment of liabilities can be found in the chapter on ASC 405. The guidance in ASC 470-50 applies in part to extinguishments of debt effected by issuance of common or preferred stock that do not represent the exercise of a conversion right contained in the debt. (ASC 470-50-15-2)

ASC 470-50 does *not* apply to the following transactions and activities:

- Conversions of debt into equity securities of the debtor pursuant to conversion privileges provided in the terms of the debt at issuance. Additionally, the guidance in this Subtopic does not apply to conversions of convertible debt instruments pursuant to terms that reflect changes made by the debtor to the conversion privileges provided in the debt at issuance (including changes that involve the payment of consideration) for the purpose of inducing conversion. Guidance on conversions of debt instruments (including induced conversions) is contained in paragraphs 470-20-40-13 and 470-20-40-15.
- Extinguishments of debt through a troubled debt restructuring. (See information later in this chapter on Section 470 for guidance on determining whether a modification or exchange of debt instruments is a troubled debt restructuring. If it is determined that the modification or exchange does not result in a troubled debt restructuring, the guidance in ASC 470-50 should be applied.)
- Transactions entered into between a debtor or a debtor's agent and a third party that is not the creditor.
(ASC 470-50-15-3)

ASC 470-60 The guidance in ASC 470-60 applies to all debtors and all troubled debt restructurings (TDRs) by debtors. (ASC 470-60-15-1 and 15-2) Note that the creditor's accounting for a TDR may differ if the debtor's carrying amount and the creditor's amortized cost basis differ. Also, a debtor may have a TDR under ASC 470-60, but the related creditor may not have a TDR under the tests in ASC 310-40. That is, the tests established by the two topics are not symmetrical. (ASC 470-60-15-3) In this Topic, debt whether a receivable or a payable represents a contractual right to receive money or a contractual obligation to pay money on demand or on fixed or determinable dates that is already included as an asset or a liability in the creditor's or debtor's balance sheet at the time of the restructuring. (ASC 470-60-15-4A) Troubled debt restructurings under ASC 470-60 include situations in which the creditor, for economic or legal reasons related to the debtor's financial difficulties, grants the debtor a concession that would not otherwise be granted. (ASC 470-60-15-5)

The objective of the creditor in a TDR is to protect as much of its investment as possible. To accomplish that a creditor may restructure the terms to alleviate the burden or accept assets or an equity interest in satisfaction of the debt at a value less than the amount of the debt. TDRs include debt that is fully satisfied by foreclosure, repossession, or other transfer of assets or by grant of equity securities. (ASC 470-60-15-6)

If a debtor can obtain funds from other than existing creditors at or near market interest rates for nontroubled debt, the debtor is not involved in a TDR. A debtor in a TDR can only obtain funds at interest rates that are so high that the debtor cannot afford them. (ASC 470-60-15-8)

A TDR may include:

- Transfer from the debtor to the creditor assets to fully or partially satisfy a debt.
- Granting of an equity interest.
- Modification of terms of a debt, such as through:
  - Reduction of the stated interest rate.
  - Extension of the maturity date at a lower interest rate.
  - Reduction of the face amount of the debt.
  - Reduction of the accrued interest.
(ASC 470-60-15-9)

ASC 470-60 does not apply to debtors in bankruptcy unless the restructuring does not result from a general restatement of the debtor's liabilities in bankruptcy proceedings. That is, ASC 470-60 applies only if the debt restructuring is isolated to the creditor. (ASC 470-60-15-10)

None of the following are considered TDRs under ASC 470-60:

- Lease modifications.
- Change in employment-related agreements.
- Unless they involve an agreement between debtor and creditor to restructure, neither:
  - Debtor's failure to pay trade accounts according to their terms, nor
  - Creditor delays in taking legal action to collect overdue amounts of interest and principal. (ASC 470-60-15-11)

In any of the following four situations, a concession granted by the creditor does *not automatically* qualify as a restructuring:

- The fair value of the assets or equity interest accepted by a creditor from a debtor in full satisfaction of its receivable is at least equal to the creditor's amortized cost basis in the receivable.
- The fair value of the assets or equity interest transferred by a debtor to a creditor in full settlement of its payable is at least equal to the carrying value of the payable.
- The creditor reduces the effective interest rate to reflect a decrease in current interest rates or a decrease in the risk, in order to maintain the relationship.
- The debtor, in exchange for old debt, issues new marketable debt with an interest rate that reflects current market rates. (ASC 470-60-15-12)

PRACTICE ALERT

While SEC comments are not binding for private companies, they serve as reminders of good practice. SEC comments on ASC 470 have focused on:

- Whether debt refinancing transactions should be accounted for as debt extinguishments under ASC 470-50.
- Disclosures about the significant components of gains or losses recorded as extinguishments.
- How those gains or losses were calculated.
- Specific terms of debt covenants where a limited waiver was obtained subsequent to the fiscal year end.
- The classification of debt with clauses that may accelerate the maturity of the debt, such as due on demand or callable by the creditor and subjective acceleration clauses that hasten the schedule of maturities if certain events occur that are not objectively determinable.
- Which debt agreements have subjective acceleration clauses.
- Quantifying the amount of debt obligations classified as long term that have subjective acceleration agreements.
- The nature of waivers or modifications of debt covenants and how long those waivers apply.
- The likelihood of insolating financial covenants.

PRESENTATION AND DISCLOSURE REQUIREMENTS

Presentation

ASC 470-10, *Overall*

Debt with Covenants Most commercial debt agreements contain a range of financial covenants. These covenants legally bind the borrower to comply with their requirements as a condition of the lender extending credit. The failure by the borrower to comply with these conditions often provides the lender with the contractual right to accelerate the due date, commonly to declare the full amount of the debt due and payable on demand. Unless a properly worded waiver is obtained by the borrower in such a situation, its statement of financial position would have to reflect the debt, that which would otherwise be classified as long-term, as a current liability. This in turn might create or complicate issues for management with respect to the assessment of whether there is substantial doubt about the ability of the reporting entity to continue as a going concern.

Under these circumstances, management of the borrower/reporting entity considers whether both of the following conditions exist under the specific circumstances:

- A violation of one or more covenants that gives the lender the right to call the debt (declare it payable on demand) has occurred at the statement of financial position date, or would have occurred absent a modification of the loan, and
- It is probable that, at measurement dates occurring during the next 12 months, the borrower will be unable to cure the default (i.e., comply with the covenant).
  (ASC 470-10-45-1)

If both of these conditions are present, the borrower is required to classify the debt as a current liability; otherwise, it can continue to classify the debt as noncurrent.

Subjective Acceleration Clauses Long-term obligations that contain subjective acceleration clauses are classified as current liabilities if circumstances (such as recurring losses or liquidity problems) indicate that it is probable that the lender will exercise its rights under the clause and demand repayment within one year (or one operating cycle, if longer). If, on the other hand, the likelihood of the acceleration of the due date is remote, the obligation continues to be classified as long-term debt on the statement of financial position. Situations between the probable and remote thresholds (i.e., it is deemed reasonably possible that the lender would demand repayment) require disclosure of the existence of the provision of the agreement. (ASC 470-10-45-2)

Revolving Credit Agreements Borrowings outstanding under a revolving credit agreement sometimes include both a subjective acceleration clause (as discussed above) and a requirement to maintain a lockbox into which the borrower's customers send remittances that are then used to reduce the debt outstanding. These borrowings are short-term obligations and are classified as current liabilities unless the entity has the intent and ability to refinance the revolving credit agreement on a long-term basis (i.e., the conditions in ASC 470-10-45-14, as discussed below, are met). (ASC 470-10-45-5) However, if the lockbox is a springing lockbox, which is a lockbox agreement in which remittances from the borrower's customers are forwarded to its general bank account and do not reduce the debt outstanding unless the lender exercises the subjective acceleration clause, the obligations are still considered to be long term since the remittances do not automatically reduce the debt outstanding if the acceleration clause has not been exercised. (ASC 470-10-45-6)

Increasing-Rate Debt Arrangements commonly referred to as "increasing-rate notes" are debt instruments that mature at a defined, near-term date, but which can be continually extended (renewed) by the borrower for a defined longer period of time with predefined increases in the interest rate as extensions are elected. (ASC 470-10-35-1)

The borrower entity estimates the effective outstanding term of the debt after considering its plans, ability, and intent to service the debt. Based upon this estimated term, the borrower's periodic interest rate is determined using the interest method. Thus, a constant yield is computed over the estimated term resulting in the accrual of additional interest during the earlier portions of the term. Debt interest costs are amortized over the estimated outstanding term of the debt using the interest method. Any excess accrued interest resulting from repaying the debt prior to the estimated maturity date is an adjustment of interest expense in the period of repayment. (ASC 470-10-35-2)

The classification of the debt as current or noncurrent is based on the expected source of repayment. Thus, this classification need not be consistent with the period used to determine the periodic interest cost. (ASC 470-10-45-7) For example, the time frame used for the estimated outstanding term of the debt could be a year or less, but because of a planned long-term refinancing agreement the noncurrent classification could be used.

Furthermore, the term-extending provisions of the debt instrument are evaluated to ascertain whether they constitute a derivative financial instrument under ASC 815. (ASC 470-10-35-2) If so, the derivative element of the instrument is, in all likelihood, not considered "clearly and closely related" to the host instrument (the debt), and thus would have to be reported separately at fair value, with changes in fair value reported in net income each period.

Due on Demand Loans Obligations that, by their terms, are due on demand or will be due on demand within one year, or one operating cycle if longer, from the statement of financial position date, even if liquidation is not expected to occur within that period, are required to be classified as current liabilities. (ASC 470-10- 45-10)

Demand Notes with Scheduled Repayment Terms In some instances, a demand loan will include a repayment schedule calling for scheduled principal reductions. The loan agreement may contain language such as:

> This term note shall mature in monthly installments as set forth herein, or on demand, whichever is earlier.
>
> Principal and interest are due on demand, or if demand is not made, in quarterly installments commencing on.

An obligation containing such terms is considered due on demand even though the debt agreement specifies repayment terms. (ASC 470-10-45-9) The creditor, at its sole discretion, can demand full repayment at any time. This situation is distinguished from a subjective acceleration clause, which is addressed separately below.

Callable Debt Even noncurrent debt may be due on demand under certain circumstances. Long-term obligations that contain creditor call provisions should be classified as current liabilities, if as of the statement of financial position date the debtor is in violation of the agreement and either:

- That violation makes the obligation callable, or
- Unless cured within a grace period specified in the agreement, that violation will make the obligation callable.

If either of the two conditions above exist, the long-term obligation is required to be classified as a current liability unless either:

- The creditor has waived the right to call the obligation caused by the debtor's violation or the creditor has subsequently lost the right to demand repayment for more than one year (or one operating cycle, if longer) from the statement of financial position date, or
- The obligation contains a grace period for remedying the violation, and it is probable that the violation will be cured within the grace period.
  (ASC 470-10-45-11)

If either of these situations applies, management is required to disclose the circumstances in the financial statements.

While a complete waiver, effectively a promise by the lender that it will not exercise its rights under the financial covenants for at least one year from the statement of financial position date, makes it possible to continue presenting the debt as noncurrent, great care must be exercised in interpreting the substance of such an agreement. (ASC 470-10-45-11)

In practice, many waivers are not effective and cannot form the basis for continued accounting for the debt as noncurrent. For example, a waiver "as of" the current statement of financial position date provides no real comfort, since the lender is entitled to assert its rights as soon as the very next day. Likewise, a waiver pending (i.e., conditioned on) compliance with the covenants at the next scheduled submission of a borrower's covenant compliance letter (generally quarterly, possibly monthly) offers no assurance that the borrower will successfully meet its obligations, and hence also affords no basis for presentation of the debt as noncurrent.

A loan covenant may require that compliance determinations be made at quarterly or semiannual intervals. A borrower may be in violation of the covenant at the end of its fiscal year and obtain a waiver from the lender, for a period greater than one year, of the lender's right to demand repayment arising from that specific year-end violation. Often, however, the lender will include language in the waiver document that reserves its right to demand repayment should another violation occur at a subsequent measurement date, including those dates that occur during the ensuing year.

Short-Term Obligations Expected to Be Refinanced Short-term obligations that arise in the normal course of business and are due under customary trade terms are classified as current liabilities. Under certain circumstances, however, the reporting entity is permitted to exclude all or a portion of these obligations from current liabilities. To qualify for this treatment, management must have both the intent and ability to refinance the obligation on a long-term basis. Management's intent should be supported by *either* of the following:

- **Post-statement of financial position date issuance of a long-term obligation or equity securities.** After the date of the entity's statement of financial position, but before that statement of financial position is issued, a long-term obligation is incurred or equity securities are issued for the purpose of refinancing the short-term obligations on a long-term basis.
- **Financing agreement.** Before the statement of financial position is issued, the entity has entered into a financing agreement that clearly enables the entity to refinance its short-term obligation on a long-term basis on readily determinable terms that meet *all* of the following requirements:
  a. The agreement is noncancellable by the lender (or prospective lender) or investor and will not expire within one year (or one operating cycle, if longer) of the statement of financial position date.

    b. The replacement debt will not be callable during that period except for violation of a provision of the financing agreement with which compliance is objectively determinable or measurable.

    c. At the date of the statement of financial position, the reporting entity is not in violation of the terms of the financing agreement and there is no information that a violation occurred subsequent to the statement of financial position and before issuance of the financial statements, unless such a violation was waived by the lender.

    d. The lender (prospective lender) or investor is expected to be financially capable of honoring the financing agreement.
       (ASC 470-10-45-14)

A violation should not be disregarded for this purpose, even if the agreement contains a grace period to cure it and/or if the lender is required to give the borrower notice. The requirement that compliance be objectively determinable or measurable precludes commitments that include subjective acceleration clauses (discussed below) from being considered qualified financing agreements. (ASC 470-10-45-14)

The above scenario is based on an assumption that the refinancing takes place subsequent to the date of the statement of financial position. However, prior to the date of the statement of financial position, the reporting entity may receive cash proceeds from long-term financing intended to be used to repay a short-term obligation after the date of the statement of financial position. In that case, the cash received is classified on the statement of financial position in noncurrent assets if the short-term obligation to be settled with that cash is classified in noncurrent liabilities.

The amount of short-term debt to be reclassified should not exceed:

- The amount raised by the replacement debt or equity issuance or
- The amount specified in the financing agreement.

If the amount specified in the financing agreement can fluctuate, then the maximum amount of short-term debt that can be reclassified is equal to a reasonable estimate of the minimum amount expected to be available on any date from the due date of the maturing short-term obligation to the end of the succeeding fiscal year. If no estimate can be made of the minimum amount available under the financing agreement, none of the short-term debt can be reclassified as long term. (ASC 470-10-45-19)

If the short-term debt is refinanced by issuing equity instruments, the portion excluded from current liabilities should be classified under noncurrent liabilities. Under no circumstances should the reclassified debt be shown in the equity section of the statement of financial position.

Other agreements may limit the ability of the reporting entity to fully utilize the proceeds of the refinancing agreement. This may happen, for example, if a clause in another debt agreement sets a maximum debt-to-equity ratio. In such a case, only the amount that can be borrowed without violating the limitations expressed in those other agreements can be reclassified as long term. (ASC 470-10-45-18)

If an entity uses current assets after the statement of financial position date to repay a current obligation, and then replaces those current assets by issuing either equity securities or long-term debt before the issuance of the statement of financial position, the currently maturing debt must continue to be classified as a current liability at the date of the statement of financial position. (ASC 470-10-45-15)

ASC 470-20, *Debt with Conversion and Other Options*

Presentation For own-share lending arrangements issued in contemplation of convertible debt issuance, the financial statements should exclude loaned shares from EPS unless default of the share-lending occurs. If default occurs, the loaned shares are included in the EPS calculation. (ASC 470-20-45-2A)

ASC 470-30, *Participating Mortgage Loans*

Presentation Amortization of debt discount relating to the participation liability should be included in interest expense. (ASC 470-30-45-1) Debt extinguishment gain or loss should be reported currently in income as a separate item if the participating mortgage loan is extinguished before its due date. (ASC 470-30-45-2)

ASC 470-40, *Product Financing Arrangements*

Note: This Subtopic does not have a "45" Section.

ASC 470-60, *Troubled Debt Restructurings by Debtors*

Note: For this Subtopic, it is particularly important to consider the scope and scope exceptions information at the beginning of this chapter.

A troubled debt restructuring can occur in one of two ways:

- A settlement of the debt at less than the carrying amount.
- A continuation of the debt with a modification of terms.

Disclosures

ASC 470-10, *Overall* ASC 470's disclosure requirements depend on the nature of the debt. The guidance in ASC 470-10-50 provides the following general disclosure requirements for all long-term borrowings.

Disclosures of Long-Term Obligations The combined aggregate amount of maturities and sinking fund requirements for each of the five years following the date of the latest balance sheet must be disclosed. (ASC 470-10-50-1)

The entity must also disclose the circumstances surrounding any obligations that have a covenant violation at the balance sheet date and are classified as noncurrent. (ASC 470-10-50-2)

Subjective Acceleration Clauses Subjective acceleration clauses required under ASC 470-10-45-2 discussed in the presentation section above must be disclosed. If the likelihood of acceleration is remote, neither reclassification nor disclosure are required. (ASC 470-10-50-3)

Short-Term Obligations Expecting to Be Refinanced If a short-term obligation is excluded from current liabilities because it is expected to be refinanced under conditions specified in this Topic, the entity must disclose a general description of the financing agreement and the terms of any new obligation incurred, or expected to be incurred, or equity securities issued, or expected to be issued as part of the refinancing.

(ASC 470-10-50-4)

Securities Outstanding The entity must disclose the following for securities outstanding:

- Explanation of the pertinent rights and privileges of various securities outstanding, such as:
  - Information regarding participation rights.
  - Call price and dates.

- ○ Conversion exercise prices or rates and pertinent dates.
- ○ Number of shares issued upon conversion, exercise, or satisfaction of required conditions during at least the most recent annual period and any subsequent interim period presented. (ASC 470-10-50-5 and ASC 505-10-50-3)

ASC 470-20, *Debt with Conversion and Other Features*

Own-share Lending Arrangements—Convertible Debt Issuance A reporting entity that enters into a share-lending arrangement on its own shares in contemplation of a convertible debt offering or other financing should disclose:

- A description of any outstanding share-lending arrangements on its own stock.
- Significant terms including:
  - ○ Number of shares,
  - ○ Term,
  - ○ Circumstances under which cash settlement would be required, and
  - ○ Other significant terms.
- Requirements for the counterparty to provide collateral.
- Reason for entering into the arrangement.
- Fair value of the outstanding loaned shares as of the balance sheet date.
- Treatment for the purposes of calculating earnings per share.
- Unamortized amount and classification of the issuance costs.
- Classification of issuance costs associated with the share-lending arrangement at the balance sheet date.
- Amount of interest cost recognized relating to the amortization of the issuance cost associated with the share-lending arrangement for the reporting period.
- Any amounts of dividends paid related to the loaned shares that will not be reimbursed. (ASC 470-20-50-2A)

A reporting entity that enters into a share-lending arrangement on its own shares in contemplation of a convertible debt offering or other financing is also required to comply with the disclosure requirements of ASC 505-10-50.

In the period in which a counterparty defaults or a reporting entity concludes it is probable that the counterparty to its share-lending arrangement will default, the reporting entity should disclose:

- The amount of expense reported in the income statement related to the default.
- In subsequent periods, any material changes in the amount of expense recorded due to changes in fair value of the reporting entity's shares or probable recoveries.
- If the default is probable but has not yet occurred, the number of shares related to the share- lending arrangement that will be reflected in basic and diluted earnings per share when the counterparty defaults. (ASC 470-20-50-2C)

Debt with Cash Conversion Features If convertible debt instruments fall within the scope of the cash conversion guidance in ASC 470-20-15-4 through ASC 470-20-15-5, the following disclosures should be made as of each balance sheet presented for those instruments:

- The carrying amount of the equity component.
- For the liability component, the principal amount, the unamortized discount, and the net carrying amount for the liability component. (ASC 470-20-50-4)

As of the most recent balance sheet date, the reporting entity should disclose the following terms:

- The remaining period over which any discount on the liability component will be amortized.
- The conversion price and the number of shares issued upon conversion.
- For public entities only, the amount by which the instrument's if-converted value exceeds its principal amount, regardless of whether the instrument is currently convertible (for public entities only).
  (ASC 470-20-50-5a through 5c)

If any derivatives are executed in connection with these convertible debt instruments, the reporting entity should disclose the following related to the derivatives, regardless of whether the derivatives are accounted for as assets, liabilities, or equity instruments:

- The derivative transactions' terms.
- How those derivative transactions relate to the instruments.
- The number of shares underlying the derivative transactions.
- The reasons for entering into those derivative transactions.
  (ASC 470-20-50-5c)

For each period for which an income statement is presented, a reporting entity should disclose both of the following related to the liability component:

- The effective interest rate, and
- The amount of interest cost recognized relating to both the contractual interest coupon and amortization of the discount.
  (ASC 470-20-50-6)

ASC 470-30, *Participating Mortgage Loans* Issuers of participating mortgages must disclose:
- The aggregate amount of participating mortgage obligations.
- The aggregate amount of gross participation liabilities and the related debt discount.
- The lender's participation terms related to either or both:
  - The increase in the fair value of the mortgaged real estate.
  - The operations of the mortgaged real estate.
    (ASC 470-30-50-1)

ASC 470-40, *Product Financing Arrangements* This Subtopic has no disclosure requirements.

ASC 470-50, *Modifications and Extinguishments* If any debt was considered to be extinguished by in-substance defeasance under FASB Statement No. 76, before the effective date of FASB Statement No. 125, the entity should disclose a general description of the transaction and the amount of debt considered extinguished at the end of each period the debt is outstanding. (ASC 470-50-50-1)

ASC 470-60, *Troubled Debt Restructurings by Debtors* A troubled borrower must disclose the following, either in the financial statements or the footnotes:

- A description of the principal changes in terms, major features of settlement, or both.
- Aggregate gain on restructuring of payables.
- Aggregate net gain or loss on transfers of assets recognized during the period.
- Per-share amount of the aggregate gain on restructuring of payables.
  (ASC 470-60-50-1)

Either in the notes or in the body of the financial statements:

- A description of the changes in terms and/or major features of the settlement.
- The aggregate gain on restructuring and the related tax effect.
- The aggregate net gain or loss on the transfer of assets recognized during the period.
- The per share amount of the aggregate gain or loss.
  (ASC 470-60-50-1)

Reporting entities may group separate restructurings within a fiscal period for the same category of payables (for example, accounts payable or subordinated debentures) for disclosure purposes. For financial statement periods after the troubled debt restructuring, the borrower should disclose amounts contingently payable that are included in the carrying amount of restructured payables and the conditions under which those amounts would become payable or be forgiven. (ASC 470-60-50-2)

PRESENTATION AND DISCLOSURE EXAMPLES

Example 33.1: Debt Modification

During the year ended December 31, 20X1, the Company issued eight fixed-rate promissory notes totaling $2,192,250 for funding of $1,995,000 with original terms of two to six months and interest rates of 10% to 12%, default rates of 10% to 24% and for three of the notes, if the notes are not paid at maturity, an additional 2% per month for the next three months. On November 1, 20X1, the Company entered into debt modification agreements with two of the notes holders and extended the maturity date to November 1, 20X2. Management reviewed the guidance in ASC 470-60 Troubled Debt Restructurings and ASC 470-50 Debt Modifications and Extinguishments and concluded that the changes to the terms of its debts qualified for debt modification, which did not result in any gain or loss in the Company's statement of operation. As of December 31, 20X1, the balance on these notes amounts to $894,250 and none of the notes is past maturity.

Example 33.2: Troubled Debt Restructuring

(Dollars in thousands.) On July 8, 20X1, the Company entered into the fourth amendment to its existing credit agreement (the "Amendment to the Credit Agreement") with LRB, to renegotiate the terms of its 11.24%, $6,500 senior secured note. The Amendment to the Credit Agreement, among other provisions, (i) extended the maturity date to May 31, 20X3, (ii) reduced the applicable interest rate to 9.0%, and (iii) amended and restated certain other provisions. As consideration for these and other modifications, the principal amount owed to LRB was increased to $7,000.

The Company engaged an independent third party to assess the fair value of each of the derivative instruments included in the LRB Note. The results of the appraisal were that the conversion feature and the LRB Note should be bifurcated, and that the conversion option should be treated as a separate derivative liability. An initial fair value of $2,774 was assigned to the conversion option, which is included in "Derivative Liabilities" on the consolidated balance sheet and the B3D Note was assigned a fair value of $4,226 as of July 8, 20X1. The conversion option is marked to market at the end of each reporting period. The Company recorded a revaluation gain of approximately $1,012 that is included in "Other income (expense), net" for the year ended December 31, 20X1 for the change in the fair value of the conversion option. During the year ended December 31, 20X1, the Company recorded $724 of debt discount accretion expense that increased the carrying value of the LRB Note.

The modification to the terms included in the Credit Agreement Amendment were accounted for as a troubled debt restructuring in the Company's consolidated financial statements, in accordance with ASC 470-60, *Troubled Debt Restructurings by Debtors*. A debtor in a troubled debt restructuring involving only a modification of terms of a payable should account for the effects of the restructuring prospectively from the time of restructuring and not change the carrying amount of the payable at the time of the restructuring. The Company will pay interest monthly at the revised 9.0% rate over the life of the LRB Note. Since the future cash payments for principal and interest under the restructured LRB Note will be greater than the carrying value of the original note, no gain was recorded.

As a result of the extension of the maturity date to May 31, 20X3, the balance of the LRB Note was reclassified from current liabilities as of December 31, 20X0, to long-term liabilities on the Company's consolidated balance sheet as of December 31, 20X1.

The Company agreed on a $500 increase in the principal amount of the LRB Note, which will be amortized on a straight-line basis over the revised term of the LRB Note. The net balance of the deferred issuance costs was $370 as of December 31, 20X1, and is presented as a reduction of the LRB Note balance in the Company's consolidated balance sheet as of December 31, 20X1. Amortization expense from July 8, 20X1 through December 31, 20X1 was $130 and is included in "Interest expense" in the consolidated statement of operations and comprehensive loss.

The LRB Note is guaranteed on a full, unconditional, joint, and several basis, by the parent Company, Blake Industries, Inc., and all wholly owned subsidiaries of Holdings (the "Guarantor Subsidiaries"). Under the terms of a security and guarantee agreement dated July 8, 20X1, Blake Industries, Inc. (the parent company) and the Guarantor Subsidiaries each fully and unconditionally, jointly and severally, guarantee the payment of interest and principal on the LRB Note. Holdings pledged and granted to LRB a first priority security interest in, among other things, all of its equity interests in Holdings and all of its rights to receive distributions, cash or other property in connection with Holdings. The Company has not presented separate consolidating financial statements of Blake Industries, Inc., Holdings and Holdings' wholly owned subsidiaries, as each entity has guaranteed the LRB Note, so each entity is responsible for the payment.

Example 33.3: Troubled Debt Schedule and Policy

At December 31, 20X1, loans classified as troubled debt restructurings totaled $4.3 million compared to $5.4 million at December 31, 20X0. The following table presents information related to loans modified as troubled debt restructurings during the years ended December 31, 20X1 and 20X0.

(Dollars are in thousands)	# of Loans	Pre-Mod. Recorded Investment	Post-Mod. Recorded Investment	# of Loans	Pre-Mod. Recorded Investment	Post-Mod. Recorded Investment
		December 31, 20X1			*December 31, 20X0*	
Real estate secured:						
Commercial	1	$150	$150	—	$ —	$ —
Construction and land development	—	—	—	—	—	—
Residential one to four family	—	—	—	—	—	—
Multifamily	—	—	—	—	—	—
Farmland	1	205	305	—	—	—
Total real estate loans	2	455	455	—	—	—
Commercial	—	—	—	—	—	—
Agriculture	—	—	—	—	—	—
Consumer installment loans	—	—	—	—	—	—
All other loans	—	—	—	—	—	—
Total	2	$455	$455	—	$ —	$ —

During the year ended December 31, 20X1, the Company modified the terms of two loans for which the modification was considered to be a troubled debt restructuring. The interest rate was not modified on these loans; however, the payment terms and maturity date were changed. During the year ended December 31, 20X0, the Company did not modify any loans that were considered to be troubled debt restructurings.

Two loans modified as troubled debt restructurings defaulted during the year ended December 31, 20X1. No loans modified as troubled debt restructurings defaulted during the year ended December 31, 20X0. Generally, a troubled debt restructuring is considered to be in default once it becomes 90 days or more past due following a modification.

When determining the level of the allowance for loan losses, management considers troubled debt restructurings and subsequent defaults in these restructurings in its estimate. The Company evaluates all troubled debt restructurings for possible further impairment. As a result, the allowance may be increased, adjustments may be made in the allocation of the allowance, or charge-offs may be taken to further write down the carrying value of the loan.

Example 33.4: Revolving Credit Agreement

On December 11, 20X6, the Company entered into a new loan and security agreement (the "Loan and Security Agreement") with Chesapeake Bank, a division of Eastern Shore Bank, consisting of a $4,000,000 term loan and a $2,000,000 revolving credit facility. The proceeds from the term loan were used to repay all outstanding balances under its existing term loan with North Dakota Bank. Amounts outstanding under the new term loan shall bear interest at a per annum rate equal to the higher of (a) the prime rate (as published in the *Wall Street Journal*) plus 1.50% or (b) 6.50%. Under the terms of the Loan and Security Agreement the Company shall make interest-only payments through the twelve-month anniversary date after which the Company shall repay the new term loan in thirty-six equal and consecutive installments of principal, plus monthly payments of accrued interest. The term loan and revolving credit facility provide support for working capital, capital expenditures and other general corporate purposes, including permitted acquisitions. The outstanding term loan is secured by substantially all of our assets. Financing costs associated with the Loan and Security Agreement are being amortized over its term on a straight-line basis, which is not materially different from the effective interest method.

The new revolving credit facility has a maturity date of twenty-four months and advances shall bear interest at a per annum rate equal to the higher of (a) the Prime Rate (as published in the *Wall Street Journal*) plus 1.25% or (b) 6.25%. The revolving credit facility can be advanced based upon 80% of eligible accounts receivable, as defined in the Loan and Security Agreement.

The Loan and Security Agreement, as amended, includes financial covenants, including requirements that the Company maintain a minimum asset coverage ratio and certain other financial covenants, including requirements that the Company shall not deviate by more than 15% its revenue projections over a trailing three-month basis or the Company's recurring revenue shall not deviate by more than 20% over a cumulative year-to-date basis of its revenue projections. In addition, beginning on December 31, 20X6, the Company's Bank EBITDA, measured on a monthly basis over a trailing three-month period then ended, shall not deviate by the greater of 30% its projected Bank EBITDA or $150,000. The agreement also requires the Company to maintain a minimum Asset Coverage Ratio. The Asset Coverage Ratio is determined based on the ratio of unrestricted cash plus certain accounts that arise in the ordinary course the Company's business divided by all outstanding obligations to the bank. Pursuant to the terms of the new Loan and Security Agreement, the Company is required to maintain a minimum Asset Coverage Ratio of at least 0.75 to 1.00 from December 31, 20X6 through November 30, 20X7 and a minimum Asset Coverage Ratio of at least 1.50 to 1.00 each month thereafter. The Company was in compliance with the asset coverage ratio covenant, however, was not compliant with the EBITDA covenant, as described above. An appropriate waiver was received by

Chesapeake Bank for the covenant violation as of January 31, 20X7. Based upon the borrowing base formula set forth in the Loan and Security Agreement, as of January 31, 20X2, the Company had access to the full amount of the $2,000,000 revolving credit facility. As of January 31, 20X7, the Company had no outstanding borrowings under the revolving credit facility.

In connection with entering into the Loan and Security Agreement discussed above, effective December 11, 20X6 the Company terminated the Credit Agreement with North Dakota Bank, N.A., as administrative agent, and other lender parties thereto, dated November 21, 20X1, as amended from time to time, and repaid all outstanding amounts due thereunder.

As described in Note 14—Subsequent Events, in February 20X7 the Company prepaid the $4.0 million outstanding term loan with Chesapeake Bank in full with proceeds from the sale of the JMB Business, as required under the Loan and Security Agreement. Accordingly, we reclassified the term loan from noncurrent to current on the consolidated balance sheet as of January 31, 20X7.

Outstanding principal balances on debt consisted of the following at:

	January 31, 20X7	*January 31, 20X6*
Term loan	$ 4,000,000	$ 4,030,000
Deferred financing cost	(175,000)	(82,000)
Total	3,825,000	3,948,000
Less: Current portion	(3,825,000)	(597,000)
Noncurrent portion of debt	$ —	$ 3,351,000

Example 33.5: Debt Covenant Violation Penalty

During the year ended December 31, 20X1, the Company became subject to a penalty assessment of $17,500 due to a loan covenant violation. Such amount has been expensed as additional interest. Additionally, the fair value of the derivative liability associated with the penalty amounted to $29,265 and has been recorded as additional interest expense.

34 ASC 480 DISTINGUISHING LIABILITIES FROM EQUITY

AUTHORITATIVE LITERATURE

Subtopic

ASC 480, *Distinguishing Liabilities from Equity*, contains one Subtopic:

- ASC 480-10, *Overall*, which provides guidance on how an issuer classifies and measures financial instruments with characteristics of both liabilities and equity.

Scope and Scope Exceptions

ASC 480:

- Applies to all entities and to any freestanding financial instrument, including financial instruments that:
  - Comprise more than one option or forward contract.
  - Have characteristics of both a liability and equity and, in some circumstances, also has characteristics of an asset, including those composed of more than one option or forward contract embodying obligations that require or that may require settlement by transfer of assets.

- Does *not* address an instrument that has only characteristics of an asset. (ASC 480-15-2 and 15-3)

ASC 480 does *not* apply to:

1. A feature embedded in a financial instrument that is not a derivative instrument in its entirety. (ASC 480-10-15-5)
2. Mandatorily redeemable financial instruments that are:
   - Issued by nonpublic entities that are not SEC registrants, and
   - Mandatorily redeemable but not on fixed dates or not for amounts that are fixed or determined by reference to an interest rate index, currency index, or other external index.
   - Even if it is a nonpublic entity, SEC registrants are not eligible for the scope exception. (ASC 480-10-15-7A and 15-7B)
3. An obligation under share-based compensation arrangements if that obligation is accounted for under ASC 718. (ASC 480-10-15-8)
4. SEC registrants with mandatorily redeemable noncontrolling interests are subject to the scope exception in ASC 480-10-15-7F. However, those entities must still adhere to the disclosure requirements in ASC 480-10-50-1 through 50-3. (ASC 480-10-15-7F)
5. Registration payment arrangements in the scope of ASC 825-20. (ASC 480-10-15-8A)

ASC 480 does *not* apply to mandatorily redeemable noncontrolling interests as follows:

- The classification and measurement provisions do not apply to mandatorily redeemable noncontrolling interests that would not have to be classified as liabilities by the subsidiary, under the "only upon liquidation" exception in paragraphs 480-10-25-4 and 480-10-25-6, but would be classified as liabilities by the parent in consolidated financial statements.
- The measurement provisions do not apply to other mandatorily redeemable noncontrolling interests that were issued before November 5, 2003, both for the parent in consolidated financial statements and for the subsidiary that issued the instruments that result in the mandatorily redeemable noncontrolling interest. For those instruments, the measurement guidance for redeemable shares and noncontrolling interests in other predecessor literature continues to apply. (ASC 480-10-15-7E)

Entities should look to the guidance in ASC 805 for recognition and initial measure of consideration issued in a business combination. However, if a financial instrument in the scope of ASC 480 is issued as consideration, it should be classified under the guidelines in this Topic. (ASC 480-10-15-9 and 15-10)

Overview

ASC 480 addresses the needs to:

- Establish criteria for classification of certain instruments (e.g., mandatorily redeemable stock) that nominally are equity and have key characteristics of debt, but which will significantly impact corporate statements of financial position if a "substance over form" approach is strictly enforced; and
- Develop the methodology for disaggregating the constituent parts of compound instruments so that they may be accounted for as debt and as equity, respectively.

Initial Recognition and Measurement

The Codification emphasizes that to prevent the objectives of ASC 480 from being circumvented by the insertion of nonsubstantive or minimal features into financial instruments, these features should be disregarded in applying ASC 480's classification provisions. (ASC 480-10-25-1) Note that when analyzing an embedded feature as though it were a separate instrument, entities should not apply ASC 480-10-25-4 through 25-14, but should look to other guidance. (ASC 480-10-25-2)

Mandatorily Redeemable Financial Instruments A mandatory redemption clause requires common or preferred stock to be redeemed (retired) at a specific date or upon occurrence of an event which is uncertain as to timing, although ultimately certain to occur (for example, the death of the holder). (ASC 480-10-20) The obligation to transfer assets must be unconditional—that is, there is no specified event that is outside the control of the issuer that will release the issuer from its obligation. Thus, callable preferred shares, which are redeemable at the issuer's option, and convertible preferred shares, which are redeemable at the holder's option, are not mandatorily redeemable shares.

Mandatorily redeemable financial instruments are reported as liabilities. The only exception is for shares that are required to be redeemed only upon the liquidation or termination of the issuer, since the fundamental "going concern assumption" underlying GAAP financial statements means that such an eventuality is not given recognition. (ASC 480-10-25-4)

In determining if an instrument is mandatorily redeemable, the entity should consider all terms.

If shares have a conditional redemption feature, which requires the issuer to redeem the shares by transferring its assets upon an event not certain to occur, the shares become mandatorily redeemable—and, therefore, become a liability—if that event occurs, the event becomes certain to occur, or the condition is otherwise resolved. (ASC 480-10-25-5) The fair value of the shares is reclassified as a liability, and equity is reduced by that amount, recognizing no gain or loss. (ASC 480-10-30-2) An assessment must be made each reporting period to ascertain whether the triggering event has yet occurred. If it has, the conditionally mandatorily redeemable stock must be reclassified to liabilities. (ASC 480-10-25-7)

Mandatorily redeemable financial instruments are initially recognized at fair value. (ASC 480-30-1)

Obligations to Repurchase Shares Obligations to repurchase the issuer's equity shares by transferring assets include financial instruments, other than outstanding shares, that, at inception:

- Require or may require the issuers to settle the obligations by transferring assets.
- Embody obligations to repurchase the issuers' equity shares, or are indexed to the price of its own shares.
  (ASC 480-10-25-8)

These contracts should be reported as liabilities (or rarely, as assets, if the fair value of the contract is favorable to the issuer). (ASC 480-10-25-8)

Forward contracts that require physical settlement by repurchase of a fixed number of the issuer's equity shares in exchange for cash are measured initially at the fair value of the shares, as adjusted for any consideration or unstated rights or privileges. (ASC 480-10-30-3) Equity is reduced by this same amount. (ASC 480-10-30-5) Fair value in this context may be determined by reference to the amount of cash that would be paid under the conditions specified in the contract if the shares were repurchased immediately. Alternatively, the settlement amount can be discounted at the rate implicit at inception after taking into account any consideration or unstated rights or privileges that may have affected the terms of the transaction. (ASC 480-10-30-4)

Obligations to Issue a Variable Number of Shares If an entity enters into a contract that requires it or permits it at the entity's discretion to issue a variable number of shares upon settlement, that contract is recognized as a liability if at inception the monetary value of the obligation is based solely or predominantly on one of the following criteria:

- A fixed monetary amount known at inception.
- An amount that varies based on something other than the fair value of the issuer's equity shares.
- Variations inversely related to changes in the fair value of the entity's equity shares (i.e., a written put option that could be net share settled).
  (ASC 480-10-25-14)

Subsequent Measurement

Certain Physically Settled Forward Purchase Contracts and Mandatorily Redeemable Financial Instruments Subsequent measurement can be effected by either:

- Accretion (which is feasible only if the amount to be paid and the settlement date are both fixed), or
- By determining the amount of cash that would be paid under the conditions specified in the contract if settlement occurred at the reporting date (useful when either the amount to be paid or the settlement date vary based on defined conditions and terms).
  (ASC 480-10-35-3)

In either case, the change from the amount reported in the prior period is interest expense. If accretion is appropriate, the instruments should be measured subsequently at the present value of the amount to be paid at settlement, accruing interest cost using the rate implicit at inception.

Note that when redemption value is based on a notion of fair value, defined in the underlying agreement, the initial recognition of the difference between this computed amount and the corresponding book value will almost inevitably result in a surplus or deficit. In other words, the promised redemption amounts, measured at transition and again at the date of each statement of financial position, will not equal the book value of the equity which is subject to redemption. This discrepancy must be reflected in stockholders' equity, even though the redeemable equity is reclassified to a liability. In effect, the redemption arrangement will result in either a residual in equity (assuming that a redemption was to fully occur at the date of the statement of financial position) or a deficit, because the agreement provides that redeeming shareholders are entitled to more or less than their respective pro rata shares of the book value of their equity claims. If the redemption price of mandatorily redeemable shares is greater than the book value of those shares, the company should report the excess as a deficit (equity), even though the mandatorily redeemable shares are reported as a liability.

Common shares that are mandatorily redeemable are not included in the denominator when computing basic or diluted earnings per share. If any amounts, including contractual (accumulated) dividends, attributable to shares that are to be redeemed or repurchased have not been recognized as interest expense, those amounts are deducted in computing income available to common shareholders (the numerator of the calculation), consistently with the "two-class" method set forth in ASC 260. The redemption requirements for mandatorily redeemable shares for each of the next five years are required to be disclosed in the notes to the financial statements.

Contingent Consideration in a Business Combination If contingent consideration in a business combination is classified initially as a liability under the guidance in ASC 480, that consideration should be measured subsequently at fair value in accordance with the guidance in ASC 805-30. (ASC 480-10-35-4A)

All Other Financial Instruments All other financial instruments are recognized at fair value at the date of issuance and at every measurement date afterwards. (ASC 480-10-30-7) The changes in the fair value are recognized in earnings unless this subtopic or another specifies otherwise. (ASC 480-10-35-5)

Freestanding Instrument Involving Multiple Components That May Be Settled in a Variable Number of Shares If a freestanding instrument is composed of more than one option or forward contract and one of those contracts embodies an obligation to repurchase the issuer's shares that require or may require settlement by a transfer of assets, the financial instrument is a liability. In addition, if a freestanding instrument composed of more than one option or forward contract includes an obligation to issue shares, the various component obligations must be analyzed to determine if any of them would be obligations under ASC 480. If one or more would be obligations under this standard, then judgment must be used to determine if the monetary value of the obligations that would be liabilities is collectively predominant over the other component liabilities. If so, the instrument is a liability. If not, the instrument is outside the scope of ASC 480. (ASC 480-10-55-42 and 55-43)

Put Options ASC 480-10-55 provides examples of put options that are subject to only cash payment and also of those that could be settled by an issuance of stock. The former case is straightforward: the instrument must be classified as a liability if the share price at the reporting date is such that a cash payment would be demanded by the holders of the puttable warrants. If the share price at that date is such that exercise of the warrant would be elected over exercise of the put option, then the warrant would be included in equity, not in liabilities. In other words, classification would depend on current stock price and could change from period to period, although ASC 480-10-55 is not explicit on this point.

Other put arrangements call for settlement in shares. That is, if advantageous to do so, the warrant holders exercise the warrants and acquire shares, but if the strike price has not been attained at expiration date, the put is exercised and the reporting entity would have to settle, but instead of paying cash it would issue shares having an aggregate value equal to the put amount. Thus, at inception, the number of shares that the puttable warrant obligates the reporting entity to issue can vary, and the instrument must be examined under the provisions of ASC 480 that deal with obligations to issue a variable number of shares. The facts and circumstances must be considered in judging whether the *monetary value* of the obligation to issue a number of shares that varies is predominantly based on a fixed monetary amount known at inception; if so, it is a liability under ASC 480.

Put Warrant A detachable put warrant can either be put back to the debt issuer for cash or can be exercised to acquire common stock. These instruments should be accounted for in the same manner as a mezzanine security. The proceeds applicable to the put warrant ordinarily are to be classified as equity and should be presented between the liability and equity sections in accordance with SEC ASR 268. (ASC 480-10-S99)

In the case of a warrant with a put price substantially higher than the value assigned to the warrant at issuance, however, the proceeds should be classified as a liability since it is likely that the warrant will be put back to the company.

Warrant Yet another variation illustrated by ASC 480-10-55 is the warrant for the purchase of shares, where the shares are puttable. The holder can exercise the warrant and then immediately force the issuer to repurchase the shares issued. The price at which the shares could be put would be defined in the warrant, and the likelihood that the put option would be exercised would vary with the market value of the shares. Obviously, if the shares acquired by exercise of the warrant had a greater market value than the put price, the put would not be invoked. Accordingly, whether these warrants would be classified as equity or liability would depend on the market value of the underlying shares, and this could change from the date of one statement of financial position to that of the next. However, if the shares to be issued upon warrant exercise were to have a mandatory redemption feature, then the warrants would be reportable as liabilities in any case.

ASC 480 does not apply to or affect the timing of recognition of financial instruments issued as contingent consideration in a business combination, nor the measurement guidance for contingent consideration, as set forth in ASC 805. It also does not affect accounting for stock-based compensation or ESOP plans. (ASC 718)

PRACTICE ALERT

While SEC comments pertain to public entities, their comments can often provide valuable practice pointers for preparers of nonpublic entities. In the area of distinguishing liabilities from equity, the SEC has:

- Questioned how entities account for equity instruments, such as redeemable preferred stock, warrants, or convertible instruments.
- Asked for more details on the terms of the instruments.
- Requested entities provide information supporting the basis for its conclusion regarding classification of those instruments.
- Questioned the adequacy of disclosure about equity instruments
- Asked how redemption provisions affect the classification of preferred stock
- Requested more information when certain features may be triggered

PRESENTATION AND DISCLOSURE REQUIREMENTS

Presentation

Entities must present mandatorily redeemable preferred stock that does not contain a conversion option as a liability. (ASC 480-10-25-4) Items within the scope of ASC 480 should be presented as liabilities on the balance sheet, or sometimes assets and not as items in a mezzanine section between liabilities and equity. (ASC 480-10-45-1)

For entities having no equity instruments outstanding but having financial instruments in the form of shares, all of which are mandatorily redeemable financial instruments required to be classified as liabilities, the entity must present:

- A description on the statement of financial position of those instruments as shares subject to mandatory redemption.
- Payments to holders of those instrument and related accruals presented separately from payments to and interest due to other creditors in statements of cash flows and income.
  (ASC 480-10-45-2)

For entities not subject to the deferral in ASC 480-10-61-1, and if all of the entity's shares are subject to mandatory redemption:

- Where redemption price of the share exceeds the entity's equity balance, the entity should report an excess of liabilities over assets.
- Where the redemption price is less than book value, the entity should report as an excess of assets over liabilities.
  (ASC 480-10-45-2A)

For mandatorily redeemable shares not subject to the deferral in ASC 480-10-65-1, the entity should present the change in amount reported as interest cost and should be reflected in interest cost, amounts paid or to be paid to holders of the contracts in excess of the initial measurement. (ASC 480-10-45-2B and 45-3)

Entities should exclude from EPS common shares issued as mandatorily redeemable shares that require physical settlement in exchange for cash to be redeemed or repurchased. In calculating EPS consistent with the two-class method, deducted in computing available to common shareholders: amounts attributable to shares to be redeemed or repurchased are not recognized interest costs. (ASC 480-10-45-4)

Disclosure

For issuers of financial instruments within the scope of 480-10-25, the following must be disclosed:

- The nature and terms of the financial instruments.
- The rights and obligations embodied therein, including:
  - Settlement alternatives in the contract.
  - The entity that controls the settlement alternatives.
    (ASC 480-10-50-1)

Issuers of all outstanding financial instruments and for each settlement alternative must disclose:

- The amount that would be paid, or the number and fair value of shares that would be issued, determined under the conditions specified in the contract, if the settlement were to occur at the reporting date.
- How changes in the fair value of the issuer's equity shares would affect those settlement amounts.
- The maximum amount that the issuer could be required to pay to redeem the instrument by physical settlement.
- The maximum number of shares that could be required to be issued, if applicable.
- That a contract does not limit the amount that the issuer could be required to pay or the number of shares that the issuer could be required to issue, if applicable.
- For a forward contract or an option indexed to the issuer's equity shares,
  - the forward price or option strike price,
  - the number of issuer's shares to which the contract is indexed, and
  - the settlement date or dates of the contract, as applicable.
    (ASC 480-10-50-2)

For entities having no equity instruments outstanding but having financial instruments in the form of shares, all of which are mandatorily redeemable financial instruments required to be classified as liabilities disclosures must include:

- The components of the liability that would otherwise be related to shareholders' interest, and
- Other comprehensive income subject to the redemption feature.
  (ASC 480-10-50-4)

PRESENTATION AND DISCLOSURE EXAMPLES

Example 34.1: Presentation of Mandatorily Redeemable Shares in the Statement of Financial Position with Related Note

Total Assets	$ 3,600,000
Liabilities Other Than Shares	2,000,000
Shares Subject to Mandatory Redemption (Note 5)	1,600,000
Total Liabilities	$ 3,600,000

Note 5
Shares, all subject to mandatory redemption upon death of the holders, consist of:

Common Stock—$50 par value, 40,000 shares authorized, 20,000 shares issued and outstanding	$1,000,000
Retained earnings attributable to those shares	740,000
Accumulated other comprehensive income attributable to those shares	<140,000 >
	$1,600,000

Example 34.2: Accounting Policy—Shares Subject to Redemption

We account for our ordinary shares subject to possible conversion in accordance with the guidance in Accounting Standards Codification ("ASC") Topic 480, *Distinguishing Liabilities from Equity*. Ordinary shares subject to mandatory redemption are classified as a liability instrument and are measured at fair value. Conditionally redeemable ordinary shares (including ordinary shares that feature redemption rights that are either within the control of the holder or subject to redemption upon the occurrence of uncertain events not solely within our control) are classified as temporary equity. At all other times, ordinary shares are classified as shareholders' equity. Our ordinary shares feature certain redemption rights that are considered to be outside of our control and subject to occurrence of uncertain future events. Accordingly, ordinary shares subject to possible redemption are presented at redemption value as temporary equity, outside of the shareholders' equity section of our balance sheets.

Example 34.3: Accounting for Warrants at Fair Value

The Company accounts for its warrants issued in accordance with the GAAP accounting guidance under ASC 480, *Distinguishing Liabilities from Equity*. The Company estimated the fair value of these warrants at the respective balance sheet dates using the Black-Scholes option pricing based on the estimated market value of the underlying common stock at the valuation measurement date, the remaining contractual term, risk-free interest rate, and expected volatility of the price of the underlying common stock. There is a moderate degree of subjectivity involved when using option pricing models to estimate the warrants, and the assumptions used in the Black-Scholes option-pricing model are moderately judgmental.

Example 34.4: Derivative Liabilities—Change in Fair Value

Derivative liabilities include the fair value of instruments such as common stock warrants, preferred stock warrants and convertible features of notes, that are initially recorded at fair value and are required to be re-measured to fair value at each reporting period under provisions of ASC 480, *Distinguishing Liabilities from Equity,* or ASC 815, *Derivatives and Hedging*. The change in fair value of the instruments is recognized as a component of other income (expense) in the Company's statements of operations until the instruments settle, expire or are no longer classified as derivative liabilities. The Company estimates the fair value of these instruments using the Black-Scholes pricing model. The significant assumptions used in estimating the fair value include the exercise price, volatility of the stock underlying the instrument, risk-free interest rate, estimated fair value of the stock underlying the instrument and the estimated life of the instrument.

Example 34.5: Down-Round Features

In June and July 20X1, the Company issued convertible notes to ten investors with a principal amount of $2,388,889, receiving $1,791,666 in net cash proceeds (the "June 20X1 Notes"). The June 20X1 Notes had an original issue discount of $238,889, and the Company incurred an interest charge deducted from the gross proceeds of $358,333, based on a 15% stated rate. The total of $597,222 was recorded as debt discount. Additionally, the Company paid $132,848 of financing costs, which were recorded as a reduction of the carrying value of the debt. The deferred financing costs and debt discounts are being amortized using the effective interest method through the maturity of the June 20X1 Notes. The June 20X1 Notes mature on March 25, 20X2 and are convertible into the Company's common stock at a per share price of $0.35 at any time subsequent to the issuance date. The June 20X1 Notes contain a down-round feature, whereby any sale of common stock or common stock equivalent at a price per share lower than the conversion price of the June 20X1 Notes will result in the conversion price being lowered to the new price. As of December 31, 20X1, the June 20X1 Notes were convertible into 5,785,714 shares of common stock. The notes holders also received warrants to purchase a total of 3,685,714 shares of the Company's common stock at an exercise price of $0.35 per share for a term of five years. The warrants contain the same down round feature as the notes.

Example 34.6: Redeemable Preferred Stock

Pursuant to our Certificate of Incorporation we are authorized to issue 10,000,000 shares of $0.001 per share par value preferred stock. The authorized but unissued shares of preferred stock may be issued in designated series from time to time by one or more resolutions adopted by the Board. The Board has the authority to determine the preferences, limitations, and relative rights of each series of preferred stock.

During the year ended December 31, 20X1, the Company issued 14,000 shares of Series A Preferred in a series of private placement agreements. The Series A Preferred Shares were priced at $100.00/share and are convertible at any time at the holder's discretion into common shares whereby one preferred share converts at a price of $0.27/common share to 370.37 common shares. The conversion price was set at the closing price of the Company's common stock on March 12, 20X1, which was the day before announcement of the private placement. Upon maturity or full repayment of the Senior Convertible Notes and Promissory Notes currently outstanding, there will be mandatory redemption of the preferred shares in exchange for equivalent cash for the principal invested, plus any accrued and unpaid dividends. The holders of the Series A Preferred Shares are entitled to receive, when and if declared by the Board of Directors and in preference to the common stock, cumulative cash or in-kind dividends at a rate per annum of 5% of the original issue price. In the event of a liquidation, dissolution, or winding up of the Company, the proceeds would be distributed first to the holders of Series A Preferred Shares prior to any distributions to holders of other stock in an amount per share equal to the original issue price plus any declared but unpaid dividends. The holders of Series A Preferred Shares are entitled to vote, together with the holders of common stock, as if the Series A Preferred Shares had been converted to common stock on all matters submitted to stockholders for vote. In addition, the Series A Preferred Shares contains certain protective rights that require the vote or consent of the holders of at least a majority of the shares of Series A Preferred Shares.

Of the 14,000 shares issued during the year ended December 31, 20X1, 5,000 shares were issued to MTL. On May 29, 20X1, MTL assigned their interest in 4,500 of the shares to various investors in their entity. MTL retained 500 shares. In addition to the Series A Convertible Preferred Shares terms described in Note 1 above, MTL and their investors have a one-time right to require the Company to redeem all or a portion of the Series A Convertible Preferred Shares upon the receipt of a minimum of $5,000,000 from the close of Tranche 3 of the amended AMER Investment Agreement. MTL and their investors converted all of their preferred shares to 1,851,844 common shares during the fourth quarter of 20X1.

As the Series A Preferred Shares are redeemable upon maturity or full repayment of the Senior Convertible Notes and Promissory Notes, it has been classified as mezzanine equity in our Consolidated Balance Sheets. The Company recognizes change in the redemption value as they occur by adjusting the carrying amount of the mezzanine equity at each reporting date. The change in the redemption value of the Series A due to accrued and unpaid dividends since its issuance is insignificant.

On August 2, 20X1, the Company filed a Certificate of Designation of Series B Preferred Stock with the Delaware Secretary of State, designating 5,000 shares of preferred stock the Series B Convertible Preferred Shares. On August 5, 20X1, the Company executed the Series B Purchase Agreement with the Investors. Pursuant to the Series B Purchase Agreement, the Investors agreed to purchase up to $400,000 of Series B Convertible Preferred Shares. This transaction closed on August 7, 20X1.

The Series B Convertible Preferred Shares were issued at a price of $100.00 per share, and each Series B Convertible Preferred Share will be convertible at any time at the holder's discretion into 500 shares of common stock of the Company. The Series B Convertible Preferred Shares carry a 5% annual dividend, which may be paid, in the Company's sole discretion, in cash, additional shares of Series B Convertible Preferred Shares or a combination thereof. The Series B Convertible Preferred Shares, like the Series A Convertible Preferred Shares, are mandatorily redeemable at such time that the Company's $7.2 million Convertible Note debt currently outstanding become due and payable in accordance with their terms, as such terms may be modified from time to time.

On March 27, 20X2, the Company filed Certificates of Amendment to the Certificates of Designation for the Series A and B Convertible Preferred Stock clarifying that the private exchange offer completed by the Company in December 20X1, constituted a modification of the Old Notes for purposes of the mandatory redemption provisions of the Series A and B Preferred Shares. Accordingly, the Series A and B Preferred Shares are mandatorily redeemable on such date as a majority of the then-outstanding principal amount of the Exchange Notes become due and payable in accordance with their terms (as may be altered by modification, amendment, exchange or otherwise, from time to time).

35 ASC 505 EQUITY

AUTHORITATIVE LITERATURE

Subtopics

ASC 505 consists of five Subtopics:

- ASC 505-10, *Overall*, provides guidance on issues not addressed in the other ASC 505 subtopics.
- ASC 505-20, *Stock Dividends and Stock Splits*, provides guidance for the recipient and the issuer.
- ASC 505-30, *Treasury Stock*, provides guidance on an entity's repurchase of its own shares of outstanding common stock and the subsequent retirement of those shares.
- ASC 505-60, *Spin-offs and Reverse Spin-offs*, provides guidance on the distribution of nonmonetary assets in spin-off transactions.

Scope and Scope Exceptions

Guidance in ASC 505 generally applies to all entities unless more specific guidance is provided in other topics. (ASC 505-10-15-1) Specific exceptions follow.

ASC 505-20 applies to corporations and their stock dividends and stock splits, except it does *not* apply to distribution or issuance to shareholders of:

- Shares of another corporation held as an investment,
- Shares of a different class,
- Rights to subscribe for additional shares, and
- Shares of the same class where each shareholder is given an election to receive cash or shares with both of the following characteristics:
  - The shareholder can elect to receive the entire distribution in cash or shares of equivalent value and
  - There is a potential limitation on the total amount of cash that all shareholders can elect to receive in the aggregate.
  (ASC 505-20-15-1 through 3A)

ASC 505-30 applies to transactions involving the repurchase of an entity's own outstanding common stock and to the subsequent constructed or actual retirement of those shares. If other topics provide more specific guidance, then that guidance should be followed. (ASC 505-30-15-2)

ASC 505-60 does *not* apply to nonmonetary assets that do not constitute a business. (ASC 505-60-15-3)

Overview

CON 6 defines equity as the residual interest in the assets of an entity after deducting its liabilities. Stockholders' equity is comprised of all capital contributed to the entity plus its accumulated earnings less any distributions that have been made. There are three major categories within the equity section:

1. Paid-in capital. Paid-in capital represents equity contributed by owners.
2. Retained earnings. Retained earnings represents the sum of all earnings less those not retained in the business (i.e., what has been paid out as dividends).
3. Other comprehensive income. Other comprehensive income represents revenues, expenses, gains, and losses, which are included in comprehensive income because they

are not yet realized, but have been excluded from net income under applicable GAAP rules (e.g., accumulated translation gains or losses).

Comprehensive income is the change in equity (net assets) of a business entity from non-owner sources.

Depending on the laws of the jurisdiction of incorporation, distributions to shareholders may be subject to various limitations, such as on the amount of retained (accounting basis) earnings.

A major objective of the accounting for equity is the adequate disclosure of the sources from which the capital was derived. For this reason, a number of different paid-in capital accounts may be presented in the statement of financial position. The rights of each class of shareholder must be disclosed. Where shares are reserved for future issuance, such as under the terms of stock option plans, this fact must also be made known.

Legal Capital and Capital Stock

Legal capital typically refers to that portion of the stockholders' investment in a corporation that is permanent in nature and represents assets that will continue to be available for the satisfaction of creditor's claims. Traditionally, legal capital was comprised of the aggregate par or stated value of common and preferred shares issued. In recent years, however, many states have eliminated the requirement that corporate shares have a designated par or stated value. States that have adopted provisions of the Model Business Corporation Act[1] have eliminated the distinction between par value and the amount contributed in excess of par. In more than thirty states, the Model Act is the basis for business corporation statutes.

The specific requirements regarding the preservation of legal capital are a function of the business corporation laws in the state in which a particular entity is incorporated. Accordingly, any action by the corporation that could affect the amount of legal capital (e.g., the payment of dividends in excess of retained earnings) must be considered in the context of the relevant laws of the state where the company is chartered.

Ownership interest in a corporation is made up of common and, optionally, preferred shares. The common shares represent the residual risk-taking ownership of the corporation after the satisfaction of all claims of creditors and senior classes of equity.

Preferred Stock

Preferred shareholders are owners who have certain rights superior to those of common shareholders. Preferences as to earnings exist when the preferred shareholders have a stipulated dividend rate (expressed either as a dollar amount or as a percentage of the preferred stock's par or stated value). Preferences as to assets exist when the preferred shares have a stipulated liquidation value. If a corporation were to liquidate, these preferred holders would be paid a specific amount before the common shareholders would have a right to participate in any of the proceeds.

Convertible Preferred Stock

The treatment of convertible preferred stock at its issuance is no different than that of nonconvertible preferred. When it is converted, the book value approach is used to account for the conversion. Use of the market value approach would entail a gain or loss for which there is no

---

[1] The Model Business Corporation Act is a model created by the American Bar Association's Committee on Corporate Law and first published in 1950. It has since been extensively revised and is adopted in various forms in the majority of states.

theoretical justification, since the total amount of contributed capital does not change when the stock is converted. When the preferred stock is converted, the "Preferred stock" and related "Additional paid-in capital—preferred stock" accounts are debited for their original values when purchased, and "Common stock" and "Additional paid-in capital—common stock" (if an excess over par or stated value exists) are credited. If the book value of the preferred stock is less than the total par value of the common stock being issued, retained earnings are charged for the difference. This charge is supported by the rationale that the preferred shareholders are offered an additional return to facilitate their conversion to common stock. Many states require that this excess instead reduces additional paid-in capital from other sources.

Issuance of Shares The accounting for the sale of shares by a corporation depends upon whether the stock has a par or stated value. If there is a par or stated value, the amount of the proceeds representing the aggregate par or stated value is credited to the common or preferred stock account. The aggregate par or stated value is generally defined as legal capital not subject to distribution to shareholders. Proceeds in excess of par or stated value are credited to an additional paid-in capital account. The additional paid-in capital represents the amount in excess of the legal capital that may, under certain defined conditions, be distributed to shareholders.

A corporation selling stock below par value credits the capital stock account for the par value and debits an offsetting discount account for the difference between par value and the amount actually received. If the discount is on original issue capital stock, it serves to notify the actual and potential creditors of the contingent liability of those investors. As a practical matter, corporations avoid this problem by reducing par values to an arbitrarily low amount. This reduction in par eliminates the chance that shares would be sold for amounts below par.

Where the Model Business Corporation Act has been adopted or where corporation laws have been conformed to the guidelines of that Act, there is often no distinction made between par value and amounts in excess of par. In those jurisdictions, the entire proceeds from the sale of stock may be credited to the common stock account without distinction between the stock and the additional paid-in capital accounts.

Stock Subscriptions

A contract may be entered into between the corporation and prospective investors, where the investors agree to purchase specified numbers of shares to be paid for over some installment period. These stock subscriptions are not the same as actual stock issuances and the accounting differs.

The amount of stock subscriptions receivable by a corporation is occasionally accounted for as an asset on the statement of financial position and is categorized as current or noncurrent in accordance with the terms of payment. However, in accordance with SEC requirements, entities are required to use a contra equity account approach. Since subscribed shares do not have the rights and responsibilities of actual outstanding stock, the credit is made to a stock subscribed account instead of to the capital stock accounts.

If the common stock has par or stated value, the common stock subscribed account is credited for the aggregate par or stated value of the shares subscribed. The excess over this amount is credited to additional paid-in capital. No distinction is made between additional paid-in capital relating to shares already issued and shares subscribed for. This treatment follows from the distinction between legal capital and additional paid-in capital. Where there is no par or stated value, the entire amount of the common stock subscribed is credited to the stock subscribed account.

As the amount due from the prospective shareholders is collected, the stock subscriptions receivable account is credited and the proceeds are debited to the cash account. Actual issuance of the shares, however, must await the complete payment of the stock subscription. Accordingly, the debit to common stock subscribed is not made until the subscribed shares are fully paid for and the stock is issued.

When a subscriber defaults on an obligation under a stock subscription agreement, the accounting will follow the provisions of the state in which the corporation is chartered. In some jurisdictions, the subscriber is entitled to a proportionate number of shares based upon the amount already paid on the subscriptions, sometimes reduced by the cost incurred by the corporation in selling the remaining defaulted shares to other stockholders. In other jurisdictions, the subscriber forfeits the entire investment upon default. In this case, the amount already received is credited to an additional paid-in capital account that describes its source.

Additional Paid-in Capital

Additional paid-in capital represents all capital contributed to a corporation other than that defined as par, stated value, no-par stock, or donated capital. Additional paid-in capital can arise from proceeds received from the sale of common and preferred shares in excess of their par or stated values. It can also arise from transactions related to the following:

- Sale of shares previously issued and subsequently reacquired by the corporation (treasury stock)
- Retirement of previously outstanding shares
- Payment of stock dividends in a manner that justifies the dividend being recorded at the market value of the shares distributed
- Lapse of stock purchase warrants or the forfeiture of stock subscriptions, if these result in the retaining by the corporation of any partial proceeds received prior to forfeiture
- Warrants that are detachable from bonds
- Conversion of convertible bonds
- Other "gains" on the entity's own stock, such as that which results from certain stock option plans

When the amounts are material, the sources of additional paid-in capital should be described in the financial statements.

Donated Capital

Donated capital can result from an outright gift to the corporation (e.g., a major shareholder donates land or other assets to the company in a nonreciprocal transfer) or may result when services are provided to the corporation.

Donations should be reflected in the income statement, which means that, after the fiscal period has ended and the books have been closed, the effect of donations will be incorporated in the reporting entity's retained earnings. See the chapter on ASC 845, *Nonmonetary Transactions,* for more information.

Retained Earnings

Retained earning represents the accumulated amount of earnings of the corporation from the date of inception (or from the date of reorganization) less the cumulative amount of distributions made to shareholders and other charges to retained earnings (e.g., from treasury stock transactions). The distributions to shareholders generally take the form of dividend payments but may take other forms as well, such as the reacquisition of shares for amounts in excess of the original issuance proceeds.

ASC 505-20, *Stock Dividends and Stock Splits*

Dividends Dividends are the pro rata distribution of earnings to the owners of the corporation. Dividends only become a liability of the corporation when declared by the board of directors.

Three important dividend dates are:

1. The declaration date, when a legal liability is incurred by the corporation.
2. The record date, the point in time a determination is made as to which specific registered stockholders will receive dividends and in what amounts.
3. The payment date, the date the distribution of the dividend takes place.

Property Dividends If property dividends are declared, the paying corporation may incur a gain or loss. Since the dividend should be reflected at the fair value of the assets distributed, the difference between fair value and book value is recorded at the time the dividend is declared and charged or credited to a loss or gain account.

Scrip Dividends If a corporation declares a dividend payable in scrip that is interest bearing, the interest is accrued over time as a periodic expense. The interest is not a part of the dividend itself.

Liquidating Dividends Liquidating dividends are not distributions of earnings, but rather a return of capital to the investing shareholders. A liquidating dividend is normally recorded by the declarer through charging additional paid-in capital rather than retained earnings. The exact accounting for a liquidating dividend is affected by the laws of the states where the business is incorporated.

Stock Dividends Stock dividends represent neither an actual distribution of the assets of the corporation nor a promise to distribute those assets. For this reason, a stock dividend is not considered a legal liability or a taxable transaction.

Despite the recognition that a stock dividend is not a distribution of earnings, the accounting treatment of relatively insignificant stock dividends (generally less than 20% to 25% of the outstanding shares prior to declaration) is consistent with it being a real dividend. (ASC 505-20-25-3) Accordingly, retained earnings are debited for the fair market value of the shares to be paid as a dividend, and the capital stock and additional paid-in capital accounts are credited for the appropriate amounts based upon the par or stated value of the shares, if any. A stock dividend declared but not yet paid is classified as such in the stockholders' equity section of the statement of financial position. Because a stock dividend never reduces assets, it cannot be a liability.

Stock Splits When stock dividends are larger in magnitude, it is observed that per-share market value declines after the declaration of the dividend. (ASC 505-20-25-2) In such situations, it would not be valid to treat the stock dividend as an earnings distribution. Rather, logic suggests that it should be accounted for as a split. The precise treatment depends upon the legal requirements of the state of incorporation and upon whether the existing par value or stated value is reduced concurrent with the stock split.

Distributions to Shareholders Having Cash and Stock Components If a corporation makes a distribution to shareholders that allows them to elect to receive their distribution in either cash or shares of an equivalent value, and there is a limitation on the total amount of cash that shareholders can receive, then the stock portion of the distribution is considered a share issuance, not a stock dividend.

ASC 505-30, *Treasury Stock*

Treasury stock consists of a corporation's own stock that has been issued, subsequently reacquired by the firm, and not yet reissued or canceled. Treasury stock does not reduce the number of shares issued but does reduce the number of shares outstanding, as well as total stockholders' equity.

These shares are not eligible to receive cash dividends. Reacquired stock that is awaiting delivery to satisfy a liability created by the firm's compensation plan or reacquired stock held in a profit-sharing trust is still considered outstanding and would not be considered treasury stock. In such cases, the stock would be presented as an asset with the accompanying footnote disclosure. Accounting for excesses and deficiencies on treasury stock transactions is governed by ASC 505-30-30.

Three approaches exist for the treatment of treasury stock:

1. Cost,
2. Par value, and
3. Constructive retirement.

Cost Method Under the cost method, the gross cost of the shares reacquired is debited to a contra equity account (treasury stock) for the cost of the reacquisition. The treasury stock account is reported as a deduction from total paid-in capital and retained earnings. The equity accounts that were credited for the original share issuance (common stock, paid-in capital in excess of par, etc.) remain intact. When the treasury shares are reissued, proceeds in excess of cost are credited to a paid-in capital account. When proceeds are below cost, any deficiency is charged to retained earnings (unless paid-in capital from previous treasury share transactions exists, in which case the deficiency is charged to that account, with any excess charged to retained earnings). If many treasury stock purchases are made, a cost flow assumption (e.g., first-in, first-out (FIFO) or specific identification) should be adopted to compute excesses and deficiencies upon subsequent share reissuances. The advantage of the cost method is that it avoids identifying and accounting for amounts related to the original issuance of the shares and is, therefore, the simpler, more frequently used method.

Par Value Method Under the par value method, the treasury stock account is charged only for the aggregate par (or stated) value of the shares reacquired. Other paid-in capital accounts (excess over par value, etc.) are reported as a deduction in proportion to the amounts recognized upon the original issuance of the shares. The treasury share acquisition is treated almost as a retirement. However, the common (or preferred) stock account continues at the original amount, thereby preserving the distinction between an actual retirement and a treasury share transaction.

When the treasury shares accounted for by the par value method are subsequently resold, the excess of the sale price over par value is credited to paid-in capital. A reissuance for a price below par value does not create a contingent liability for the purchaser. It is only the original purchaser who risks this obligation to the entity's creditors.

Constructive Retirement Method The constructive retirement method is similar to the par value method, except that the aggregate par (or stated) value of the reacquired shares is charged to the stock account rather than to the treasury stock account.

If the shares had been resold for $6,500, the entry is:

Cost method		Par value method		Share retirement method	
Cash	6,500	Cash	6,500	Cash	6,500
Retained earnings*	500	Treasury stock	5,000	Common stock	5,000
Treasury stock	7,000	Additional paid-in capital— common stock	1,500	Additional paid-in capital— common stock	1,500

* "Additional paid-in capital—treasury stock" or "Additional paid-in capital—retired stock" of that issue would be debited first to the extent it exists.

Alternatively, under the par or constructive retirement methods, any portion of or the entire deficiency on the treasury stock acquisition may be debited to retained earnings without allocation to paid-in capital. Any excesses will always be credited to an "Additional paid-in capital—retired stock" account. (ASC 505-30-30-6)

Donated Stock In some circumstances, shares held by current stockholders may be donated back to the reporting entity. In accounting for donated treasury stock, the intentions of management regarding these reacquired shares is key; if these are to simply be retired, the common stock account should be debited for the par or stated value (if par or stated-value stock) or the original proceeds received (if no-par, no-stated-value stock). The current fair value of the shares should be credited to the "donated capital" account, and the difference should be debited or credited to a suitably titled paid-in capital account, such as "additional paid-in capital from share donations."

If the donated shares are to be sold, variations on the par and cost methods of treasury stock accounting can be employed, with "donated capital" being debited and credited, respectively, when shares are received and later reissued, instead of the treasury stock account employed in the previous illustrations. Note, however, that if the cost method is used, the debit to the donated capital account should be for the fair value of the shares, not the cost (a seeming contradiction). If the constructive retirement method is utilized instead, only a memorandum entry will be recorded when the shares are received; when reissued, the entire proceeds should be credited to "donated capital."

Other Treasury Stock Issues

Takeover Defense as Cost of Treasury Stock In certain instances an entity may incur costs to defend against an unwelcome or hostile attempted takeover. In some cases, in fact, putative acquirers will threaten a takeover struggle in order to extract so-called *greenmail* from the target entity, often effected through a buyback of shares held by the acquirer at a premium over-market value. ASC 505-30-30-3 states that the excess purchase price of treasury shares should not be attributed to the shares, but rather should be attributed to the other elements of the transaction and accounted for according to their substance, which could include the receipt of stated or unstated rights, privileges, or agreements. The SEC's position is that such excess is anything over the quoted market price of the treasury shares.

Accelerated Share Repurchase Programs Accelerated share repurchase programs are combinations of transactions that permit an entity to purchase a targeted number of shares immediately, with the final purchase price determined by an average market price over fixed periods of time. Such programs are intended to combine the immediate share retirement benefits (boosting earnings per share, etc.) of tender offers with the market impacts and pricing benefits of disciplined open market stock repurchase programs. (ASC 505-30-25-5)

An entity should account for an accelerated share repurchase program as two separate transactions:

1. As shares of common stock acquired in a treasury stock transaction recorded on the acquisition date, and
2. As a forward contract indexed to its own common stock.
   (ASC 505-30-25-6)

An entity would classify the forward contract in the previous example as an equity instrument because the entity will receive cash when the contract is in a gain position but pay cash or stock when the contract is in a loss position. Changes in the fair value of the forward contract would not be recorded, and the settlement of the forward contract would be recorded in equity.

The treasury stock transaction would result in an immediate reduction of the outstanding shares used to calculate the weighted-average common shares outstanding for both basic and diluted (EPS). The effect of the forward contract on diluted EPS would be calculated in accordance with ASC 260.

Own-Share Lending Arrangements Related to Convertible Debt Financing An entity may enter into a share-lending arrangement with an investment bank that is related to a convertible debt offering. (ASC 470-20-05) See the chapter on ASC 470 for more information.

Other Equity Accounts

A principle of GAAP financial reporting is that all items of income, expense, gain, or loss (other than transactions with owners) should flow through the income statement. In fact, however, a number of important exceptions have been made, including:

- Translation gains or losses (ASC 830),
- Certain adjustments for minimum pension obligations (ASC 715), and
- Unrealized gains and losses on available-for-sale portfolios of debt or equity investments. (ASC 320)

Hedging gains and losses qualifying under ASC 815 are also deferred for income measurement purposes.

ASC 505-60, Spin-offs and Reverse Spin-offs

Spin-offs A spin-off can involve the transfer of assets that constitute a business, by their holder (referred to as the spinnor), into a new legal entity (spinnee), the shares of which are distributed to the spinnor's shareholders. The distribution is nonreciprocal in that the shareholders of the spinnor are not required to surrender any of their stock in the spinnor in exchange for the shares of the spinnee. (ASC 505-60-05-2)

The accounting rules governing spin-offs and reverse spin-offs are found in ASC 505-60 and ASC 845-10-30.

Further, in accordance with ASC 845-10-30-10, a pro rata distribution to owners of an entity of shares of a subsidiary or other investee entity that has been or is being consolidated or accounted for under the equity method should be considered the equivalent of a spin-off. The distribution of shares of a wholly owned or consolidated subsidiary that constitutes a business to an entity's shareholders is recorded based on the carrying value of the subsidiary. Irrespective of whether the spun-off operations are to be sold immediately following the spin-off, management is not to account for the transaction as a sale of the spinnee followed by a distribution of the proceeds. (ASC 505-60-25-2)

Reverse Spin-offs Under certain circumstances, a spun-off subsidiary/spinnee will function as the continuing entity post-spin-off. When the spin-off of a subsidiary is structured in such a way that the legal form of the transaction does not represent its economic substance, this will be accounted for as a reverse spin-off whereby the legal spinnee is treated as if it were the spinnor for financial reporting purposes. (ASC 505-60-05-4)

The determination of whether reverse spin-off accounting is appropriate is a matter of professional judgment that depends on a careful analysis of all relevant facts and circumstances.

The guidance provides indicators to be considered in determining whether a spin-off should be accounted for as a reverse spin-off. No one indicator is to be considered presumptive or determinative:

- The relative sizes of the legal spinnor and the legal spinnee.
- The relative fair value of the legal spinnor and the legal spinnee.
- Retention of the majority of senior management.
- The length of the holding period.
  (ASC 505-60-25-8)

The guidance contains a rebuttable presumption that a spin-off should be accounted for based on its legal form. When the indicators are mixed, significant judgment is required to determine whether the rebuttable presumption has been overcome. The determination of the accounting spinnor and spinnee, respectively, has significant implications. In a spin-off, the net book value of the spinnee is treated, in effect, as a dividend distribution to the shareholders of the spinnor. Since the net book value of these entities will differ from each other, the amount of the reduction to retained earnings of the surviving reporting entity (the accounting spinnor) will be affected by this determination. ASC 505-60 offers several examples of fact patterns that support spin-off or reverse spin-off determinations.

Finally, the accounting for a reverse spin-off is further complicated by the fact that the determination of the accounting spinnor and spinnee significantly affects the reporting of discontinued operations in accordance with ASC 360. The accounting spinnee is reported as a discontinued operation by the accounting spinnor if the spinnee is a component of an entity and meets the conditions for such reporting contained in ASC 360.

PRACTICE ALERT

While not binding on nonpublic companies, SEC comments can be valuable in raising alerts on complex areas. Accounting for spin-offs is such an area. Preparers of financial instruments should be familiar with the legal arrangements and should be careful to properly allocate items such as pension and postretirement benefit plans, debt, contingencies, income taxes, goodwill and other intangible assets, and exercise care with intercompany transactions.

PRESENTATION AND DISCLOSURE REQUIREMENTS

Presentation

ASC 505-10-45-2 states that a contribution to a company's equity made in the form of a note receivable should generally not be reported as an asset except under the very limited circumstances when there is substantial evidence of both the ability and intent to pay in a reasonably short period of time. Public companies may want to refer to ASC 210-10-S99-1, paragraphs 27 through 29. The ASC notes that the most widespread practice is to report these notes as a reduction of equity. However, if the cash is received prior to the issuance of the financial statements, the note may be reported as an asset.

Notes received as a contribution to equity should be reported as a sale of capital stock, contribution to paid-in-capital, or as an asset if there is substantial evidence of the ability to pay within a short time or if collected in cash before the financial statements are issued or available to be issued. (ASC 505-10-45-2)

Appropriations of retained earnings are shown in the equity section and clearly identified. (ASC 505-10-45-3) Costs or losses should not be charged to an appropriation of retained earnings, and appropriation should not be transferred to income. (ASC 505-10-45-4)

Preparers should note that it is permissible to show separately treasury stock acquired for other than retirement or as a deduction from the capital stock total, additional paid-in capital, and retained earnings or cost of corporation's stock. (ASC 505-30-45-1)

The spinnor should report accounting for a spinnee as a discontinued operation if the spinnee meets the requirements in ASC 205-20-45-1A through 45-1C. (ASC 505-60-45-1)

Disclosure

In separate statements or in the basic financial statements or a note, if both financial position and results of operations are presented, the entity should disclose:

- Changes in the separate accounts comprising shareholders' equity (in addition to retained earnings).
- Changes in the number of shares of equity securities during at least the most recent annual fiscal period and any subsequent interim period presented.
  (ASC 505-10-50-2)

The entity should also disclose:

- Summary explanation within the financial statements of the pertinent rights and privileges of outstanding securities.
- The number of shares issued upon conversion, exercise, or satisfaction of required conditions during at least the most recent annual fiscal period and any subsequent interim period presented.
- Actual changes to conversion or exercise prices occurring during the reporting period, not including changes due to standard antidilution provisions.
  (ASC 505-10-50-3)
- For a financial instrument with a down round feature triggered during the reporting period where the effect has been recognized:
  ○ The fact that the feature has been triggered
  ○ The value of the effect of the down round feature that has been triggered
    (ASC 505-10-50-3)
- If a financial instrument has a down round feature that has been triggered during the reporting period and for which an entity has recognized the effect per the guidance in ASC 260-10-25-1, the following:
  ○ The fact that the feature has been triggered
  ○ The value of the effect of the down round feature that has been triggered
    (ASC 505-10-50-3A)
- For preferred stock (or other senior stock) that has a preference in involuntary liquidation considerably in excess of the par or stated value of the shares, the liquidation preference of the stock in the equity section of the statement of financial position in the aggregate, either parenthetically or in short.
  (ASC 505-10-50-4)

- Both of the following within the financial statements (either on the face of the statement of financial position or in the notes thereto):
  - Aggregate or per-share amounts at which preferred stock may be called or is subject to redemption through sinking-fund operations or otherwise.
  - Aggregate and per-share amounts of arrearages in cumulative preferred dividends. (ASC 505-10-50-5)
- The significant terms of the conversion features of the contingently convertible security that will enable users to understand the circumstances of the contingency and the potential impact of conversion. The following may be helpful in understanding both the nature of the contingency and the potential impact of conversion:
  - Events or changes in circumstances that would cause the contingency to be met and any significant features necessary to understand the conversion rights and the timing of those rights.
  - The conversion price and the number of shares into which a security is potentially convertible.
  - Events or changes in circumstances, if any, that could adjust or change the contingency, conversion price, or number of shares, including significant terms of those changes.
  - The manner of settlement upon conversion and any alternative settlement methods. (ASC 505-10-50-6)
- In order to meet the disclosure requirements of the preceding paragraph, the possible conversion prices and dates as well as other significant terms for each convertible instrument.
  (ASC 505-10-50-7)
- In the notes to its financial statements, the terms of the transaction, including the excess of the aggregate fair value of the instruments that the holder would receive at conversion over the proceeds received and the period over which the discount is amortized.
  (ASC 505-10-50-8)
- Whether the shares that would be issued if the contingently convertible securities were converted are included in the calculation of diluted EPS and the reasons why or why not. (ASC 505-10-50-9)
- Consider disclosures about derivative instruments entered into a connection with the issuance of the contingently convertible shares:
  - The terms of the instruments
  - How those instruments relate to the contingently convertible shares and
  - The number of shares underlying the derivative instruments
    (ASC 505-10-50-10)
- For an entity that issues redeemable stock, the amount of redemption requirements, separately by issue or combined, for all issues of capital stock redeemable at fixed or determinable prices on fixed or determinable dates in each of the five years following the date of the latest statement of financial position presented.
  (ASC 505-10-50-11)
- Where stock dividend in form is a stock split in substance, avoid the use of the word *dividend* in related corporate resolutions, notices, and announcements and, in those cases in

which because of legal requirements this cannot be done, describe the transaction as, for example, a stock split effected in the form of a dividend.
(ASC 505-20-50-1)

- State laws relating to an entity's repurchase of its own outstanding common stock that restrict the availability of retained earnings for payment of dividends or have other effects of a significant nature.
(ASC 505-30-50-2)
- Allocation of amounts paid in excess of current market price for repurchase of treasury shares and other elements of the transaction and the accounting treatment of such amounts.
(ASC 505-30-50-4)

PRESENTATION AND DISCLOSURE EXAMPLES

Example 35.1: Stockholders' Deficit

Stockholders' Deficit	*20X2*	*20X1*
Preferred stock; $0.0001 par value; 50,000,000 shares authorized; no shares issued and outstanding		
Common stock; $0.0001 par value; 250,000,000 shares authorized; 77,350,003 shares issued and outstanding at December 31, 20X2 and at December 31, 20X1	$ 7,735	$ 7,735
Additional paid-in capital	352,681	352,681
Accumulated deficit	(548,147)	(421,991)
Total Stockholders' Equity	$(187,731)	$ (61,575)

Example 35.2: Stockholders' Equity Deficit Results in Substantial Doubts about Going Concern

The accompanying financial statements have been prepared assuming that the Company will continue as a going concern, which contemplates the realization of assets and the liquidation of liabilities in the normal course of business. As at December 31, 20X1, the Company has a working capital deficit of $187,731 and has not earned any revenues to cover its operating costs. The Company intends to fund future operations through equity financing arrangements, which may be insufficient to fund its capital expenditures, working capital, and other cash requirements for the year ending December 31, 20X1.

The ability of the Company to realize its business plan is dependent upon, among other things, obtaining additional financing to continue operations, and development of its business plan. In response to these problems, management intends to raise additional funds through public or private placement offerings.

These factors, among others, raise substantial doubt about the Company's ability to continue as a going concern. The accompanying financial statements do not include any adjustments that might result from the outcome of this uncertainty.

Example 34.3: Preferred Stock—Rights and Privileges

The holders of our preferred stock have certain rights and privileges that are senior to our Common Stock, and we may issue additional shares of preferred stock without stockholder approval that could have a material adverse effect on the market value of the Common Stock. Our Board of Directors has the authority to issue a total of up to four million shares of preferred stock and to fix the rights, preferences, privileges, and restrictions, including voting rights, of the preferred stock, which typically are senior to the rights of the Common Stock, without any further vote or action by the holders of our Common Stock. The rights of the holders of our Common Stock will be subject to, and may be adversely affected by, the rights of the holders of the preferred stock that have been issued or might be issued in the future. Preferred stock also could have the effect of making it more difficult for a third party to acquire a majority of our outstanding voting stock. This could delay, defer, or prevent a change in control. Furthermore, holders of our preferred stock may have other rights, including economic rights, senior to the Common Stock. As a result, their existence and issuance could have a material adverse effect on the market value of the Common Stock. We have in the past issued and may from time to time in the future issue, preferred stock for financing or other purposes with rights, preferences, or privileges senior to the Common Stock. As of May 15, 20X3, we had three series of preferred stock outstanding: Series A Preferred, Series B Preferred, and Series C Preferred.

The provisions of our Series A Preferred prohibit the payment of dividends on our Common Stock unless the dividends on our preferred shares are first paid. In addition, upon a liquidation, dissolution or sale of our business, the holders of our Series A Preferred will be entitled to receive, in preference to any distribution to the holders of Common Stock, initial distributions of $1,000 per share, plus all accrued but unpaid dividends. As of December 31, 20X2 and 20X1, we had no cumulative undeclared dividends on our Series A Preferred.

The provisions of our Series B Preferred prohibit the payment of dividends on our Common Stock unless the dividends on our preferred shares are first paid. In addition, upon a liquidation, dissolution, or sale of our business, the holders of our Series B Preferred will be entitled to receive, in preference to any distribution to the holders of Common Stock, initial distributions of $2.50 per share, plus all accrued but unpaid dividends. As of December 31, 20X2 and 20X1, we had cumulative undeclared dividends on our Series B Preferred of approximately $8,000.

The provisions of our Series C Preferred prohibit the payment of dividends on our Common Stock unless the dividends on our preferred shares are first paid. In addition, upon a liquidation, dissolution or sale of our business, the holders of our Series C Preferred will be entitled to receive, in preference to any distribution to the holders of Common Stock, initial distributions of $10,000 per share, plus all accrued but unpaid dividends. As of December 31, 20X1, there were no shares of Series C Preferred outstanding. As of December 31, 20X2, we had no cumulative undeclared dividends on our Series C Preferred.

Example 34.4: Preferred Stock May Require Redemption

Upon the occurrence of certain events, we may be required to redeem all or a portion of our Series C Preferred. On September 10, 20X1, we filed the Series C COD with the Secretary of State of the State of Delaware, pursuant to which Holders of Series C Preferred may require us to redeem all or any portion of such Holder's shares of Series C Preferred at a price per share equal to the Stated Value plus all accrued and unpaid dividends at any time from and after the third anniversary of the issuance date or in the event of the consummation of a Change of Control (as such term is defined in the Series C COD). We cannot assure you that we will maintain sufficient cash reserves or that our business will generate cash flow from operations at levels sufficient to permit us to redeem our shares of Series C Preferred if and when required to do so. In the event we have insufficient cash available or do not have access to additional third-party financing on commercially reasonable terms or at all to complete such redemption, our business, results of operations, and financial condition may be materially adversely affected.

Example 34.5: Preferred Stock—Rights and Privileges—Large Shareholders

Certain large shareholders may have certain personal interests that may affect the Company. As a result of the securities issued to Lawson Capital Management and related entities controlled by Matthew Lawson, a member of our Board of Directors (together, "Lawson"), Lawson beneficially owns, in the aggregate, approximately 24% of the Company's outstanding voting securities as of May 12, 20X2. As a result, Lawson has the potential ability to exert influence over both the actions of the Board of Directors and the outcome of issues requiring approval by the Company's shareholders. This concentration of ownership may have effects such as delaying or preventing a change in control of the Company that may be favored by other shareholders or preventing transactions in which shareholders might otherwise recover a premium for their shares over current market prices.

Example 34.6: Common Stock Dividends

We do not expect to pay cash dividends on our Common Stock for the foreseeable future. We have never paid cash dividends on our Common Stock and do not anticipate that any cash dividends will be paid on the Common Stock for the foreseeable future. The payment of any cash dividend by us will be at the discretion of our Board of Directors and will depend on, among other things, our earnings, capital, regulatory requirements and financial condition. Furthermore, the terms of our Series A Preferred, Series B Preferred, and Series C Preferred directly limit our ability to pay cash dividends on our Common Stock.

Example 34.7: Schedule of Warrants to Acquire Outstanding Common Stock

Warrants—In connection with the issuance of convertible debt, preferred and common stock, and in connection with services provided, the Company has the 4,674,261 warrants to acquire the Company's common stock outstanding as of December 31, 20X1, as follows:

Expiring During the Year Ending December 31,	Warrant Shares	Exercise Price per Share	Weighted Average Exercises Price per Share
20X2	22,860	$3.50	$3.50
20X3	1,768,516	$1.80 to $ 3.30	$3.25
20X4	1,699,861	$1.80 to $ 5.00	$2.60
20X5	740,749	$1.80	$1.80
20X6	385,945	$1.80	$1.80
20X7	56,330	$2.25	$2.25

Example 34.8: Warrant Activity for the Reporting Year

The following table summarizes the outstanding warrant activity for the year ended December 31, 20X1:

Outstanding, January 1, 20X1	4,201,736
Issued	442,275
Issued as a result of common stock offering at $1.80 per share	30,250
Exercised	—
Expired	—
Outstanding, December 31, 20X1	**4,674,261**

Example 34.9: Modification of Exercise Price of Warrants to Acquire Stock Resulting in an Increase in Value

In connection with the confidentially marketed public offering that closed on September 9, 20X1 at a price per common share of $1.80, 70 warrants representing the right to acquire 1,992,325 shares with down-deal exercise price features were repriced to an exercise price of $1.80. In connection with the modification, the value of the warrants was recalculated based upon the value immediately prior to and immediately after the modification. In connection therewith the Company utilized Black-Scholes valuation models utilizing volatility of 50.56% and a risk-free rate of 1.51%, together with the contractual remaining terms of each warrant. This revaluation increased the value of the warrants by $405,324, which has been reflected as an increase in accumulated deficit and additional paid-in capital. In accordance with GAAP, this increased valuation is not charged to the consolidated statement of operations and comprehensive loss; however, it is included as an adjustment to net loss attributable to the parent in arriving at net loss per common share—basic and diluted.

Example 34.10: Statement of Stockholders' Equity

BIO-EN HOLDINGS CORP
STATEMENT OF STOCKHOLDERS' EQUITY
(in U.S. Dollars)

	Preferred Stock		Common Stock		Additional Paid-in Capital	Accumulated Deficit	Total Stockholders' Deficit
	Shares	Amount $	Shares	Amount $	$	$	$
Balance at January 1, 20X1	—	—	32,350,003	3,235	120,931	(333,606)	(209,440)
Stock issuance			45,000,000	4,500	231,750		236,250
Loss for the year	—	—	—	—	—	(88,385)	(88,385)
Balance at December 31, 20X1			77,350,003	7,735	352,681	(421,991)	(61,575)
Loss for the year						(126,156)	(126,156)
Balance at December 31, 20X9	—	—	77,350,003	7,735	352,681	(548,147)	(187,731)

Consolidated Statements of Changes in Stockholders' Equity Statement of Stockholders' Equity Attributable to Parent for the Years Ended December 31, 20X2 and 20X1:

	Preferred Stock		Common Stock		Additional Paid in Capital	Accumulated Comprehensive Other Loss	Accumulated Deficit	Total
	Shares	Amount	Shares	Amount				
Balance, January 1, 20X1	160,000	$ 699,332	9,598,208	$ 960	$ 17,752,990	$ (38,590)	$ (29,431,416)	$ (11,016,724)
Issuance of Series B preferred stock	268,333	1,068,039	—	—	273,626	—	—	1,341,665
Issuance of Series C preferred stock	427,500	3,050,142	—	—	1,360,681	—	—	4,410,823
Issuance of Series E preferred stock	714,519	1,886,330	—	—	—	—	—	1,886,330
Common stock issued for acquisition of Gold Medal Group	—	—	500,000	50	2,249,950	—	—	2,250,000
Share-based employee and director compensation	—	—	—	—	836,372	—	—	836,372
Exercise of employee options	—	—	16,527	2	61,975	—	—	61,977
Share-based professional services compensation	—	—	96,179	10	170,784	—	—	170,794
Conversion of debt into common stock	—	—	3,304,140	330	9,090,045	—	—	9,090,375
Interest on converted debt in common stock	—	—	196,050	20	915,680	—	—	915,700
Conversion of Series B preferred stock into common stock	(428,333)	(1,767,371)	480,067	48	1,767,323	—	—	—
Conversion of Series A preferred stock into common stock	—	—	118,542	11	533,434	—	—	533,445
Conversion of Series E preferred stock into common stock	(150,000)	(396,000)	150,000	15	395,985	—	—	—
Common stock issued in connection with debt financings	—	—	320,000	32	1,212,089	—	—	1,212,121
Warrants valued in connection with debt conversions and amendments	—	—	23,243	2	6,424,968	—	—	6,424,970
Foreign currency translation adjustment	—	—	—	—	—	43,611	—	43,611
Preferred stock dividends	—	—	—	—	407,061	—	(492,639)	(85,578)
Net loss	—	—	—	—	—	—	(14,670,330)	(14,670,330)

(continued)

	Preferred Stock		Common Stock		Additional Paid in Capital	Accumulated Comprehensive Other Loss	Accumulated Deficit	Total
	Shares	Amount	Shares	Amount				
Balance at December 31, 20X1	992,019	4,540,472	14,802,956	1,480	43,452,963	5,021	(44,594,385)	3,405,551
Issuance of registered common shares, net of offering costs	—		1,877,666	188	3,035,369	—	—	3,035,557
Series D preferred stock issuance	18,850	1,505,262	—	—	267,238	—	—	1,772,500
Series E preferred stock conversion	(300,000)	(792,000)	300,000	30	791,970	—	—	—
Share-based employee and director compensation	—		84,166	8	1,099,559	—	—	1,099,567
Issuance of restricted stock	—		75,000	8	205,492	—	—	205,500
Series A preferred stock conversion into common shares	—		50,000	5	89,995	—	—	90,000
Warrant modification	—		—	—	49,160	—	—	49,160
Deemed dividend on down round feature	—		—	—	405,324	—	(405,324)	—
Preferred stock dividends	—		111,111	11	199,989	—	(162,585)	37,415
Net loss	—		—	—	—	—	(7,622,948)	(7,622,948)
Foreign currency translation adjustment	—		—	—	—	(48,159)	—	(48,159)
Balance at December 31, 20X2	710,869	$ 5,253,734	17,300,899	$ 1,730	$ 49,597,059	$ (43,138)	$ (52,785,242)	$ 2,024,143

Example 34.12: Stockholders' Equity Attributable to Noncontrolling Interests

Statement of Stockholders' Equity Attributable to Noncontrolling Interests in Consolidated Subsidiaries for the Years Ended December 31, 20X2 and 20X1:

	Noncontrolling Equity Interest	Accumulated Deficit	Total
Balance, January 1, 20X1	$ –	$ –	$ –
Equity interest of noncontrolling equity holders of Entsorga West Virginia, LLC and Refuel America LLC and subsidiaries through December 13, 20X1	6,679,585	–	6,679,585
Net loss from December 14, 20X1 to December 31, 20X1	–	(76,890)	(76,890)
Balance at December 31, 20X1	6,679,585	(76,890)	6,602,695
Investment by noncontrolling interest	1,400,000	–	1,400,000
Net loss	–	(2,657,113)	(2,657,113)
Balance at December 31, 20X2	$ 8,079,585	$ (2,734,003)	$ 5,345,582

Example 34.13: Spin-off of Subsidiary

On October 1, 20X2, the Company completed the previously announced separation of its transitional and skilled nursing services, ancillary businesses, home health, and hospice operations and substantially all of its senior living operations into two separate, publicly traded companies:

- Commodore, which includes skilled nursing and senior living services, physical, occupational, and speech therapies, and other rehabilitative and healthcare services at 223 healthcare facilities and campuses, post-acute-related ancillary operations, and real estate investments; and
- The Flagship Group, Inc. (Flagship), which is a holding company of operating subsidiaries that provide home health, hospice, and senior living services.

The Company completed the separation through a tax-free distribution of all of the outstanding shares of common stock of Flagship to Commodore stockholders on a pro rata basis. Commodore stockholders received one share of Flagship common stock for every two shares of Commodore common stock held at the close of business on September 20, 20X2, the record date for the spin-off. The number of shares of Commodore common stock each stockholder owned and the related proportionate interest in Flagship did not change as a result of the spin-off. Each Commodore stockholder received only whole shares of Flagship common stock in the distribution, as well as cash in lieu of any fractional shares. The spin-off was effective from and after October 1, 20X2, with shares of Flagship common stock distributed on October 1, 20X2. Flagship is listed on the NASDAQ Global Select Market (NASDAQ) and trades under the ticker symbol "FLSP."

In connection with the spin-off, Flagship's operations consist of 63 home health, hospice, and home care agencies and 52 senior living communities. Commodore affiliates retained ownership of all the real estate, which includes the real estate of 29 of the 52 senior living operations that were contributed to Flagship. These assets are leased to Flagship on a triple-net basis. Flagship affiliates are responsible for all costs at the properties, including property taxes, insurance, and maintenance and repair costs. The initial terms range from 14 to 16 years. Annual rental income generated from the leases with Flagship is $12,164. The variable rent such as property taxes, insurance, and other items is not material for the year ended December 31, 20X2. Flagship's remaining 23 senior living operations are leasing the underlying real estate from unrelated third parties.

The Company received $11,600 from Flagship as a dividend payment in connection with the distribution of assets to Flagship. The Company used the funds to repay certain outstanding third-party bank debt. The assets and liabilities were contributed to Flagship based on their historical carrying values, which were as follows:

Cash and cash equivalents	$ 47
Accounts receivable, net	30,064
Prepaid expenses and other current assets	4,483
Property and equipment, net	13,728
Right-of-use assets	150,385
Goodwill and intangibles, net	74,747
Accounts payable	(4,725)
Accrued wages and related liabilities	(14,544)
Other accrued liabilities—current	(17,531)
Lease liabilities, net	(152,221)
Net contribution	$ 84,433

In accordance with Accounting Standards Codification (ASC) 505-60, *Equity Spin-offs and Reverse Spin-offs*, the accounting for the separation of the Company follows its legal form, with Commodore as the legal and accounting spinnor and Flagship as the legal and accounting spinnee, due to the relative significance of Commodore's healthcare business, the relative fair values of the respective companies, the retention of all senior management, and other relevant indicators.

As a result of the spin-off, the Company recorded a $71,181 reduction in retained earnings, which included net assets of $84,433 as of October 1, 20X2. The Company transferred cash of $47 to Flagship, with the remainder considered a noncash activity in the consolidated statements of cash flows. The spin-off also resulted in a reduction of noncontrolling interest of $13,252.

Commodore and Flagship entered into several agreements in connection with the spin-off, including a transition services agreement (TSA), a separation and distribution agreement, a tax matters agreement, and an employee matters agreement. Pursuant to the TSA, Commodore, Flagship, and their respective subsidiaries are providing various services to each other on an interim, transitional basis. Services being provided by Commodore include, among others, certain finance, information technology, human resources, employee benefits, and other administrative services. The TSA will terminate on September 30, 20X4. Billings by Commodore under the TSA were not material during the year ended December 31, 20X2.

Prior to the consummation of the spin-off, Flagship granted awards to certain employees and directors of Commodore under the Flagship Long-Term Incentive Plan (LTIP) in recognition of their performance in assisting with the spin-off. These awards were exchanged for Flagship common stock prior to the distribution.

Immediately after the spin-off, Commodore no longer consolidated the results of Flagship operations into its financial results. Flagship's assets, liabilities, operating results, and cash flows for all periods presented have been classified as discontinued operations within the consolidated financial statements. The following table presents the financial results of Flagship through the date of the spin-off for the indicated periods and does not include corporate overhead allocations:

	Year Ended December 31,		
	20X2	**20X1**	**20X0**
	(in thousands)		
Revenue/Expense	$ 249,039	$ 286,058	$ 250,991
Cost of services	187,560	209,423	184,252
Rent—cost of services	17,295	20,836	19,939
General and administrative expense	16,672	9,744	6,497
Depreciation and amortization	2,402	2,480	2,204
Total expenses	223,929	242,483	212,892
Income from discontinued operations	25,110	43,575	38,099
Interest income	26	47	—
Provision for income taxes	5,663	10,156	14,239
Income from discontinued operations, net of tax	19,473	33,466	23,860
Net income attributable to discontinued noncontrolling interests	629	595	160
Net income attributable to The Flagship Group, Inc.	$ 18,844	$ 32,871	$ 23,700

The Company incurred transaction costs of $9,119 related to the spin-off since commencing in 20X1, of which $7,909 and $746 are reflected in the Company's consolidated statement of operations as discontinued operations for the years ended December 31, 20X2 and 20X1, respectively. Transaction costs primarily consist of third-party advisory, consulting, legal, and professional services, as well as other items that are incremental and one-time in nature that are related to the separation. Transaction costs for 20X2 incurred prior to October 1, 20X2 are reflected in discontinued operations.

The following table presents the aggregate carrying amounts of the classes of assets and liabilities of the discontinued operations of Flagship:

	As of December 31, 20X1 *(in thousands)*
Assets	
Current assets:	
Cash and cash equivalents	$ 41
Accounts receivable—less allowance for doubtful accounts of $616	24,184
Prepaid expenses and other current assets	4,554
Total current assets as classified as discontinued operations on the consolidated balance sheet	28,779
Property and equipment, net	10,458
Restricted and other assets*	2,286
Intangible assets, net	78
Goodwill	30,892
Other indefinite-lived intangibles	25,136

	As of December 31, 20X1
Long-term assets as discontinued operations on the consolidated balance sheet	68,850
Total assets as discontinued operations on the consolidated balance sheet	$ 97,629
Liabilities	
Current liabilities:	
Accounts payable	4,390
Accrued wages and related liabilities	12,786
Other accrued liabilities	13,073
Total current liabilities as discontinued operations on the consolidated balance sheet	30,249
Other long-term liabilities	3,316
Long-term liabilities as discontinued operations on the consolidated balance sheet	3,316
Total liabilities as discontinued operations on the consolidated balance sheet	33,565

* Restricted and other assets is net of deferred tax liabilities.

36 ASC 605 REVENUE RECOGNITION

Authoritative Literature	409
Subtopics	409

AUTHORITATIVE LITERATURE

Subtopics

With the implementation of ASU 2014-09, *Revenue Recognition,* there is no revenue recognition guidance in ASC 605. The Topic does provide guidance on losses. ASC 605, *Revenue Recognition,* contains two Subtopics:

- ASC 605-20, *Revenue Recognition—Provision for Losses on Separately-Priced Extended Warranty and Product Maintenance Contracts*, which provides guidance on separately priced extended warranty and product maintenance contracts.
- ASC 605-35, *Revenue Recognition—Provision for Losses on Construction-Type and Production-Type Contracts*, which provides guidance on the accounting for a provision for losses on a contract for which a customer provides specifications for the production of facilities or the provision of related services.
  (ASC 605-10-05-02)

ASC 605 contains no presentation or disclosure sections.

37 ASC 606 REVENUE FROM CONTRACTS WITH CUSTOMERS

AUTHORITATIVE LITERATURE

Technical Alerts

ASU 2019-08 In November 2019, the FASB issued Accounting Standards Update 2019-08, *Compensation—Stock Compensation (Topic 718) and Revenue from Contracts with Customers (Topic 606): Codification Improvements—Share-Based Consideration Payable to a Customer*. The purpose of the ASU is to provide guidance on measuring share-based payment awards granted to a customer. Relevant changes are included in this chapter. For more information on the ASU, see the chapter on ASC 718.

ASU 2020-05 In June 2020, the FASB issued ASU 2020-05, *Revenue from Contracts with Customers (Topic 606) and Leases (Topic 842): Effective Dates for Certain Entities*, for entities that have not yet issued or made available to be issued financial statements reflecting the adoption of ASC 606. The ASU offers an option to extend the effective date of ASC 606. For those entities that choose the option, the effective date of ASC 606 will be for annual reporting periods beginning after December 15, 2019 and interim reporting periods within annual reporting periods beginning after December 15, 2020. Early application is still applicable.

Revenue *Influx or other enhancement of assets of an entity or settlements of liabilities (or a combination of both) from delivering or producing goods, rendering services, or other activities that constitute the entity's ongoing major or central operations. (ASC 606-10-20)*

Scope

ASC 606 affects all public companies, nonpublic companies, and nonprofit organizations and applies to contracts with customers.

Scope Exceptions The following are outside the scope of ASC 606:

- Lease contracts in the scope of ASC 840, *Leases*, and ASC 842, *Leases*, when implemented.
- Contracts issued within the scope of ASC Topic 944, *Financial Services—Insurance.*
- Financial instruments and other contractual rights or obligations in the scope of:
  - ASC 310, *Receivables*
  - ASC 320, *Investments—Debt Securities*
  - ASC 321, *Investments in Equity Securities* (when implemented)
  - ASC 323, *Investments—Equity-Method and Joint Ventures*
  - ASC 325, *Investments—Other*
  - ASC 405, *Liabilities*
  - ASC 470, *Debt*
  - ASC 815, *Derivatives and Hedging*
  - ASC 825, *Financial Instruments*
  - ASC 860, *Transfers and Servicing*
- Guarantees other than product or service warranties, in the scope of ASC 460, *Guarantees.* (Entities should look to ASC 815 for guidance on guarantees accounted for as derivatives.)
- Nonmonetary exchanges between entities in the same line of business to facilitate sales to customers or potential customers.
(ASC 606-10-15-2)

Revenue from transactions or events that do not arise from contracts with customers is not in the scope of ASC 606, such as:

- Dividends
- Non-exchange transactions, like donations or contributions
- Changes in regulatory assets and liabilities arising from alternative revenue programs for rate-regulated activities in the scope of ASC 930, *Regulated Operations*
(ASC 606-10-15-3)

Contracts Partially in Scope If a contract is partially within the scope of ASC 606 and partially within the scope of other guidance, the entity should apply the other guidance first. That is, if the other standard specifies how to separate or initially measure parts of the contract, then the entity should apply those requirements first. The remaining portion is accounted for under the requirements of the new standard. If the other standard does not have applicable separate and/ or initial measurement guidance, the entity should apply the revenue standard to separate and/or initially measure the contract. (ASC 606-10-15-4)

Sale or Transfer of Nonfinancial Assets Transactions that are not part of the entity's ordinary activities, such as the sale of property, plant, and equipment, nonetheless fall under certain aspects of ASC 606. An entity involved in such activities applies the guidance related to transfer of control and measurement of the transaction price to evaluate the timing and amount of the gain or loss. Entities should also apply the guidance in ASC 606 to determine whether the parties are committed to perform under the contract and, therefore, whether a contract exists.

Core Principle of ASC 606: . . . recognize revenue to depict the transfer of promised goods or services to customers in an amount that reflects the consideration to which the entity expects to be entitled in exchange for those goods or services. (ASC 606-10-05-3 et al.)

This core principle reflects the asset and liability approach that underlies ASC 606, recognizing revenue based on changes in assets and liabilities. The FASB believes that this is consistent with the conceptual framework approach to recognition and brings consistency to the measurement compared with the "earned and realized" criteria in previous standards.

Five Steps in the ASC 606 Revenue Model

To achieve the core principle, entities should follow these five steps:

1. Identify the contract with the customer. (ASC 606-10-25-1 through 25-13)
2. Identify performance obligations (promises) in the contract. (ASC 606-10-25-1 through 25-13)
3. Determine the transaction price. (ASC 606-10-32-2 through 32-27)
4. Allocate the transaction price. (ASC 606-10-32-28 through 25-41)
5. Recognize revenue when or as the entity satisfies a performance obligation by transferring promised goods or services to a customer. (ASC 606-10-25-23 through 25-30)

In reviewing a transaction, each of these five steps may not be needed, and they may not always be applied sequentially. Although the model is based on an assets and liabilities or control approach as opposed to the risk-and-rewards approach under previous standards, risks and rewards are a factor when determining control for point-in-time revenue recognition.

STEP 1: IDENTIFY THE CONTRACT WITH THE CUSTOMER

The Contract

Contract: Agreement between two or more parties that creates enforceable rights and obligations. (ASC 606-10-20)

Entities should first determine whether a contract is specifically excluded from the guidance in ASC 606 under the scope exceptions detailed earlier in this chapter. After determining that a contract is not specifically excluded, entities must identify the contracts that meet the criteria in Step 1 of the revenue recognition model. The agreement must not fall under one of the scope exceptions and must:

- Create enforceable rights and obligations, and
- Meet the five criteria listed in ASC 606.

If the entity determines that a contract does not meet the criteria for Step 1, the contract does not exist for purposes of ASC 606 and the entity does not apply Steps 2 through 5.

Enforceable Rights and Obligations

The enforceability of the contract:

- Is a matter of law
- Varies across legal jurisdictions, industries, and entities
- May vary within an entity
- May depend on the class of customer or nature of goods or services

The Five Contract Criteria

ASC 606 lists five criteria that are assessed at contract inception and that must be met for agreements to be considered contracts subject to the guidance of ASC 606. A contract exists if:

1. The contract has the approval and commitment of the parties
2. Rights of the parties are identifiable
3. Payment terms are identifiable
4. The contract has commercial substance
5. Collectibility of *substantially all of the consideration* is probable
   (ASC 606-10-25-1)

The assessment of the fifth criterion, collectibility, must reflect the customer's *ability and intent* to pay. This criterion acts as a collectibility threshold.

Collectibility Threshold

The Codification considers the customer's credit risk an important part of determining whether a contract is valid. It is not an indicator of whether revenue is recognized but, rather, an indicator of whether the customer is able to meet its obligation. (ASC 606-10-25-1(e))

To be accounted for under ASC 606, a contract must have commercial substance. To have commercial substance, the consideration must be collectible. So, the underlying objective of the collectibility assessment is to determine if there is a substantive transaction.

Collectibility is a "gating" question designed to prevent entities from applying ASC 606 to problematic contracts and recognizing revenue and an impairment loss at the same time.

Arrangements Where Contract Criteria Are Not Met

If the entity receives consideration from the customer, but the contract fails Step 1, the entity should apply what is sometimes referred to as the alternate recognition model and recognize the consideration received only when *one* of the following occurs:

a. The entity has no remaining obligations to transfer goods or services to the customers, and all or substantially all of the consideration promised by the customer has been received by the entity and is nonrefundable,
b. The contract has been terminated, and the consideration received from the customer is nonrefundable, or
c. The entity has transferred control of the goods or services to which the consideration that has been received relates, the entity has stopped transferring goods and services to the customer and has no obligation to transfer additional goods or services, and the consideration received from the customer is nonrefundable.
   (ASC 606-10-25-7)

If an arrangement does not meet the contract criteria in the revenue standard, consideration received should be accounted for as a liability until:

- "a," "b," or "c" above occur, or
- The arrangement meets the contract criteria.

The liability is measured at the amount of consideration received from the customer. The liability represents the entity's obligations to:

- Transfer goods or services in the future, or
- Refund the consideration received.
   (ASC 606-10-25-8)

The Portfolio Approach and Combining Contracts

A Practical Expedient An entity normally applies the revenue standard to individual contracts. However, in certain circumstances, an entity may use a practical expedient and apply the revenue standard to a group of contracts. This expedient allows for the portfolio approach—applying the revenue standard to a group of contracts or performance obligations under these conditions:

- The contracts must have similar characteristics, *and*
- The entity must reasonably expect that the effects of applying the guidance to a portfolio would not differ materially from applying it to individual contracts or performance obligations.
  (ASC 606-10-10-4)

Combination of Contracts Required Under certain circumstances ASC 606 requires a combination of contracts. The entity needs to assess whether the substance of the contract is that the pricing or economics of the contracts are interdependent. ASC 606 offers guidance to help make that judgment. The contracts should be accounted for as a single contract when the contracts are entered into at or near the same time with the same customers or parties related to the customer and if *any* of the following conditions are met:

a. The entity negotiates the contracts as a package with a single commercial objective.
b. The amount of consideration to be paid in the contract depends on the price or performance of the other contract.
c. The goods or services promised in the contracts (or some goods or services promised in the contracts) constitute a single performance obligation.
   (ASC 606-10-25-9)

Identifying the Customer

Customer: A party that has contracted with an entity to obtain goods or services that are an output of the entity's ordinary activities in exchange for consideration. (ASC 606-10-20)

Collaborative Arrangements A collaborative arrangement is not in the scope of ASC 606 unless the collaboration meets the definition of a customer. A collaborative arrangement requires careful analysis of the facts and circumstances. It is possible that portions of the contract will be a collaboration, while other portions will be a contract with a customer. The latter portion will be in the scope of the revenue standard. After a thorough analysis of the agreement, the entity should decide whether to apply the revenue standard and/or other guidance, such as ASC 808, *Collaborative Arrangements*.

STEP 2: IDENTIFY THE PERFORMANCE OBLIGATIONS

A performance obligation, the unit of account, is a promise in a contract with a customer to transfer to the customer either:

1. A good or service (or a bundle of goods and services) that is distinct.
2. A series of goods or services that are substantially the same and that have the same pattern of transfer to the customer.
   (ASC 606-10-20)

The purpose of the first part of the assessment is to identify the promises in the contract, taking note of terms and customary business practices. The entity must identify all promises, even if they seem inconsequential or perfunctory. An entity is not required to assess whether promised goods or services are performance obligations if they are immaterial in the context of the contract. (ASC 606-10-25-16A) In the second part of the assessment, the entity determines which of those promises are performance obligations that should be accounted for separately.

When identifying the promises in a contract, the entity must identify not only the explicit promises, but also the implicit promises and those activities associated with the contracts that do not meet the criteria for performance obligations.

Promised goods or services may include:

- Sale of goods produced by an entity
- Resale of goods purchased by an entity
- Resale of rights to goods or services purchased by an entity
- A contractually agreed-upon task for a customer
- Standing ready to provide goods or services
- Arranging for another party to transfer goods or services to a customer
- Rights to goods or services to be provided in the future that a customer can resell or provide to its customer
- Licenses
- Constructing, manufacturing, or developing an asset on behalf of a customer
- Options to purchase additional goods or services
  (ASC 606-10-25-18)

ASC 606 gives the entity the choice of whether to account for shipping and handling services performed after the customer takes control as a fulfillment cost. Entities electing this practical expedient must disclose it in accordance with ASC 606 disclosure requirements. (ASC 606-10-25-18A and 18B)

Determining Whether a Good or Service Is Distinct

To determine whether an entity has to account for multiple performance obligations, the entity must assess whether the good or service is distinct, that is, separately identifiable, from other promises in the contract. A good or service is distinct if it meets both these criteria:

1. It is capable of being distinct. The customer can benefit from the good or service on its own or together with other resources that are readily available to the customer, and
2. It is distinct within the context of the contract. The entity's promise to transfer the good or service to the customer is separately identifiable from other promises in the contract. (ASC 606-10-05-4B)

In some cases, even though a good or service is capable of being distinct, accounting for it as a separate performance obligation might not reflect the entity's performance in that contract. Therefore, the entity uses a two-part process for determining whether a promised good or service or bundle of goods or services is distinct:

1. Assess at the level of the good or service, that is, is the good or service inherently capable of being distinct? and
2. Assess in the context of the contract, that is, is the promise to transfer goods or services separately identifiable from other promises in the contract?
   (ASC 606-10-25-19)

If an entity determines that a promised good or service is not distinct, it must combine it with other promises in the contract until it identifies a bundle of goods or services that is distinct. The result may be that all the promises in a contract are accounted for as a single purchase obligation.

Series of Distinct Goods or Services That Are Substantially the Same and Have the Same Pattern of Transfer

There are two ways an entity may determine that two or more goods or services are a single performance obligation:

1. The entity determines that the goods or services are not distinct from each other.
2. The goods or services meet the criteria for being distinct, but may still be a single performance obligation.

The second category of performance obligations requires the entity to assess whether the performance obligations are a series of distinct goods or services that are "substantially the same or have the same pattern of transfer to the customer." (ASC 606-10-25-15)

STEP 3: DETERMINE THE TRANSACTION PRICE

The transaction price is:

The amount of consideration to which an entity expects to be entitled in exchange for transferring promised goods or services to a customer, excluding amounts collected on behalf of third parties (for example, some sales taxes). (ASC 606-10-20)

The transaction price should be determined at the inception of the contract. When determining the transaction price, the entity should look more widely than the contract terms and examine the entity's customary business practices, published policies, and specific statements. Also, the entity should assume that the terms of the contract will be fulfilled, that is, the goods or services will be transferred as promised and that the contract will not be canceled, renewed, or modified. (ASC 606-10-32-4)

Significant Financing Component

The entity must examine the facts and circumstances to determine if a significant financing component exists that must be accounted for. See the section that follows for more detail.

ASC 606 includes a practical expedient for significant financing components. The amount of consideration does not have to be adjusted if, at contract inception, the entity expects that there will be one year or less between:

- The transfer of goods or services, and
- Payment.
  (ASC-606-10-32-18)

The consideration recorded should reflect the price the customer would have paid if the customer paid cash when (or as) the goods or services transferred to the customer, that is, the objective is to reflect the cash selling price.

Variable Consideration The entity must examine the explicit and implicit terms of the contract to identify variable consideration. Variable consideration comes in two types:

1. Pricing adjustments for transactions that have already been completed, for instance, refunds, and
2. Incentive and performance-based fees.

Variable consideration may be explicitly stated in the contract or may be variable if either of the following exists:

- The customer has a valid expectation arising from an entity's customary business practices, published policies, or specific statements that the entity will accept an amount of consideration that is less than the price stated in the contract.
- Other facts and circumstances indicate that the entity's intention, when entering into the contract with the customer, is to offer a price concession to the customer. (ASC 606-10-32-7)

After estimating the amount of variable consideration, the entity then should apply the following constraint focused on the probability of a significant reversal of cumulative revenue recognized:

The entity should include some or all of the variable consideration in the transaction price to the extent that it is probable that a subsequent change in the estimate would not result in a significant reversal of cumulative revenue recognized. (ASC 606-10-32-11)

Sales-based or Usage-based Royalty Exception to Variable Constraint Guidance A narrow exception to the guidance on constraints in variable consideration involves sales-based or usage-based royalty consideration promised in exchange for a license of intellectual property only. For those types of consideration the entity should recognize only when (or as) the later of the following events occur:

- The subsequent sale or usage occurs.
- The performance obligation to which some or all of the sales-based or usage-based royalty allocated has been satisfied (or partially satisfied). (ASC 606-10-55-65)

The royalty in its entirety should be either within or not within the scope of the royalties exception. The royalties exception applies when the license of intellectual property is the predominant item to which the royalty relates. Determining when a license is the predominant item requires judgment on the part of the entity. In making this judgment, the entity may want to consider the value the customer places on the license in comparison with the other goods or services in the bundle. (ASC 606-10-55-65A-B)

Noncash Consideration

To determine the transaction price at contract inception, any noncash consideration promised by the customer should be measured at the fair value of the noncash consideration. If fair value cannot be reasonably estimated, the entity should measure the consideration indirectly by reference to the stand-alone selling price of the goods or services promised to the customer. (ASC 606-10-32-21 and 32-22)

In some cases the entity may receive goods or services, like materials, equipment, or labor, from the customer in order to facilitate delivery of the promised goods or services. In that case, the entity should assess whether it has control of those goods or services. If it does have control, the entity should account for them as noncash consideration received from the customer. (ASC 606-10-32-24)

Consideration Payable to the Customer

Unless consideration payable to a customer is for distinct goods or services received in return, it should be accounted for as a reduction of the transaction price. If the amount is variable, the entity should estimate the amount in accordance with the guidance on variable consideration. (ASC 610-10-32-25)

STEP 4: ALLOCATE THE TRANSACTION PRICE

In Step 4, the entity allocates the transaction price to each of the performance obligations (units of account). This is usually done in proportion to the stand-alone selling price, that is, on a relative stand-alone selling price basis. With some exceptions, discounts are allocated proportionately to the separate performance obligations.

This step is actually a two-part process:

1. Determine the stand-alone selling price.
2. Allocate the transaction price to the performance obligations.

Determining the Stand-alone Selling Price

> *Stand-alone Selling Price: The price at which an entity would sell a promised good or service separately to a customer. (ASC 606-10-20)*

The stand-alone selling price is determined at contract inception and is *not updated* for changes in selling prices between contract inception and when the performance under the contract is complete. If the entity enters into a *new* contract for the same good or service, it would reassess the stand-alone selling price and use the changed price for the new arrangement. A new contract may occur:

- When the entity enters into a new arrangement in the future, or
- As a result of a contract modification.

If the contract is modified and the modification is not treated as a separate contract, the entity updates the estimate of the stand-alone selling price at the time of the modification.

Unlike the stand-alone selling price, the transaction price may be updated. It must be reassessed, and, if necessary, updated at the end of each reporting period. Resulting changes to the transaction price should be allocated on the same basis as at contract inception.

Allocating the Transaction Price

In cases with more than one performance obligation, the entity must allocate, at contract inception, the transaction price to the performance obligations. The allocation is based on the fair value of each performance obligation. The best indicator of the fair value of the performance obligation is the observable, stand-alone selling price of the underlying good or service, sold in similar circumstances to similar customers. The transaction price, generally, should be allocated in proportion to the stand-alone selling prices. (ASC 606-10-30-31)

The amount the entity allocates to an unsatisfied performance obligation should be recognized in the period in which the transaction changes as:

- Revenue, or
- Reduction in revenue.

Changes in the Transaction Price

As uncertainties are resolved or new information becomes available, the entity should revise the amount of consideration it expects to receive. Transaction prices, including variable consideration and the related constraints, are updated at each reporting date. A change in transaction price not related to modification should be recognized as revenue or as a reduction in revenue in the period in which the change takes place. (ASC 606-10-32-43)

STEP 5: RECOGNIZE REVENUE WHEN (OR AS) THE ENTITY SATISFIES A PERFORMANCE OBLIGATION

An entity shall recognize revenue when (or as) the entity satisfies a performance obligation by transferring a promised good or service (that is, an asset) to a customer. An asset is transferred when (or as) the customer obtains control of the asset. (ASC 606-10-25-23)

To implement Step 5, the entity must determine at contract inception whether it will satisfy its performance obligation over time or at a point in time.

Control of an Asset

ASC 606 applies a single model, based on control, to allow entities to determine when revenue should be recognized. (ASC 610-10-25-25) To have control of an asset, entities must have the ability to:

- Direct the use of the asset, and
- Obtain substantially all of the remaining benefits of the asset.

Performance Obligations Satisfied Over Time

A performance obligation is satisfied over time if *any one* of the following three criteria is met (ASC 606-10-25-27):

1. The customer simultaneously receives and consumes the benefits as the entity performs. An indication that the customer receives and consumes the benefits is if another entity would not need to substantially reperform the work completed to date.
2. The entity creates or enhances an asset that the customer controls as the asset is created or enhanced.
3. This criterion consists of two parts:
   - The asset created by the entity does not have an alternative use to the entity, and
   - The entity has an enforceable right to payment for performance completed to date.

Performance Obligations Satisfied at a Point in Time

By default, if the performance obligation is not satisfied over time, it is satisfied at a point in time. To determine the point in time, the entity must consider when control has transferred and the customer has control of the assets. Indicators of control include when the customer has:

- A present obligation to pay
- Legal title
- Physical possession
- Risks and rewards of ownership
- Accepted the asset
  (ASC 606-10- 25-30)

Measuring Progress Toward Complete Satisfaction of a Performance Obligation

For each performance obligation satisfied over time:

> *... the objective when measuring progress is to depict an entity's performance in transferring control of goods or services promised to a customer (that is satisfaction of an entity's performance obligation). (ASC 606-10-25-31)*

Once the entity determines that a performance obligation is satisfied over time, it measures progress toward completion to determine the amount and timing of revenue recognition. The entity must apply a single method of measuring progress for each performance obligation that best reflects the transfer of control, that is, a measure that is consistent with the objective of depicting its performance. The entity should apply the method consistently to enhance comparability of revenue in different reporting periods. The entity must apply that method consistently to "similar performance obligations in similar circumstances," and the entity must be able to apply that method reliably. (ASC 606-10-25-32)

Practical Expedient If an entity has a right to consideration for an amount that corresponds directly to the value transferred to the customer of the entity's performance obligation completed to date, the entity may, as a practical expedient, recognize revenue for the amount the entity has a right to invoice. (ASC 606-10-55-18)

Methods for Measuring Progress To determine the best method, the entity should look at the nature of the promised goods and services and the nature of the entity's performance. Progress measures may be input or output methods.

Inability to Estimate Progress If an entity cannot reasonably estimate the progress toward completion, the entity may recognize revenue as the work is performed, but only to the extent of cost incurred if the entity expects to recover costs. However, no profit can be recognized. Once the entity is able to make a reasonable estimate of performance, it should make a cumulative catch-up adjustment for any revenue not previously recognized. This adjustment should be made in the period of the change in the estimate. (ASC 606-10-25-36 and 25-37)

OTHER ISSUES

Right of Return

Rights of return affect the transaction price by creating variability in the transaction price.

ASC 606 does not apply to exchanges for another product of the same type, quality, condition, and price. The guidance for warranties applies to returns of faulty goods or replacements.

At the time of initial sale, when revenue is deferred for the amount of the anticipated return, the entity recognizes a refund liability and a return asset. The asset is measured at the carrying amount of the inventory less the expected cost to recover the goods. If the realizable value of the item expected to be returned is expected to be less than the cost of the related inventory, the entity makes an adjustment to cost of goods sold.

At the end of the reporting period, the entity reassesses the measurement and adjusts for any changes in expected level of returns and decreases in the value of the returned products.

Once the entity determines that it has rights of return amounts, it records a liability and net revenue amount. In the revenue model, all variable consideration must be included in the top-line revenue number. In addition, the entity must record a returned asset outside of inventory and a contra amount against cost of sales. To measure the returned asset, the entity looks at the value of the inventory previously held and reduces it by the expected costs to recover that inventory. The entity also must test the returned asset for impairment, not as part of inventory, but as its own separate asset. This test must be done periodically, and estimates must be updated at each reporting period.

Warranties

Some warranties may simply provide assurance that the product will function as expected in accordance with certain specifications—assurance-type warranties. Other warranties provide customers with additional protection—service-type warranties. The type of warranty and the benefits provided by the warranty dictate the accounting treatment.

A warranty purchased separately is a separate performance obligation. Revenue allocated to the warranty is recognized over the warranty period. A warranty not sold separately may still be a performance obligation. Entities have to assess the terms of the warranty and determine under which category below the warranty falls:

- Category 1. These warranties, called assurance-type warranties, provide assurance that the product will function. A warranty that only covers the compliance of the product with agreed-upon specifications is termed "an assurance warranty." These warranties obligate the entity to repair or replace the product and are accounted for under the guidance in ASC 460, *Guarantees*.
- Category 2. These warranties, called service-type warranties, provide a service in addition to product assurance. The additional service is accounted for as a separate performance obligation.

When assessing whether the warranty, in addition to product assurance, provides a service that should be accounted for as a separate performance obligation, an entity should consider factors such as:

- Whether the warranty is required by law—If the entity is required by law to provide a warranty, the existence of the law indicates that the promised warranty is not a performance obligation because such requirements typically exist to protect customers from the risk of purchasing defective products.
- The length of the warranty coverage—The longer the coverage period, the more likely it is that the promised warranty is a performance obligation because it is more likely to provide a service in addition to the assurance that the product complies with agreed-upon specifications.
- The nature of the tasks that the entity promises to perform—If it is necessary for an entity to perform specific tasks to provide the assurance that the product complies with agreed-upon specifications (for example, a return shipping service for defective products), then those tasks likely do not give rise to a performance obligation. (ASC 606-10-55-33)

If a warranty is determined to be a performance obligation, the entity applies Step 4 of the revenue recognition model and allocates a portion of the transaction price to the warranty.

Principal versus Agent

More than one party may be involved in providing goods or services to a customer. In those situations, ASC 606 requires the entity to determine whether for each specified good or service it is a principal or an agent, whether the nature of its promise is a performance obligation:

- To provide the specified goods or services (principal), or
- To arrange for another party to provide them (agent).

Exhibit—Principal versus Agent

	Performance obligation to:	Report:
Principal	Provide the specified goods or services.	Gross, when or as the performance obligation is satisfied, for the consideration received from the customer.
Agent	Arrange for the specified goods or services to be provided by the other party.	Net for the fee the entity expects. (ASC 606-10-55-37B)
(ASC 606-10-55-37B and 55-38)		

Whether an entity is a principal or an agent depends on control. Before assessing control, the entity must identify the unit of account, that is, the specified good or service being provided to the customer. An entity may be a principal for one or more specified goods or services in a contract and an agent for others in the same contract. The entity must also determine the nature of each specified good or service:

- A good
- A service
- A right to a good or service from the other party that it then combines with other goods or services to provide a specified good or service to the customer (ASC 606-10-55-37A)

The entity must determine whether it has control of the goods or services before they are transferred. If the entity has control before transfer to the customer, it is the principal.

Customer Options to Purchase Additional Goods or Services

Some contracts give customers the option to purchase additional goods or services. These options are separate performance obligations if they provide a *material right* to the customer. A right is material if it results in a discount that the customer would not receive if not for entering into the contract, that is, it must be incremental to the discounts typically given for the good or service, to that class of customer, in that geographical area. (ASC 606-10-55-42)

Practical Alternative Estimating the stand-alone selling price may be difficult because the option may not be sold separately. ASC 606 provides a practical alternative. Instead of estimating the stand-alone selling price of the option, the entity can use the practical alternative and evaluate the transaction assuming the option will be exercised. The transaction price is determined by including any consideration estimated to be received from the optional goods and services. The transaction price is then allocated to all goods and services, including those under option. The alternative can be applied if the additional goods or service meet both of the following conditions:

1. They are similar to the original goods and services in the contract, and
2. They were provided in accordance with the original contract's terms. (ASC 606-10-55-45)

Customer's Unexercised Rights (Breakage)

Under some arrangements, a customer may make a nonrefundable prepayment. For that prepayment, the customer has a right to a good or service in the future, and the entity stands ready to deliver goods or services in the future. However, the customer may not actually exercise those rights. The most common examples of this situation are gift cards or vouchers. These unexercised rights are known as breakage.

Upon receipt of the customer's advance payment, the entity records a contract liability for the amount of the payment. When the contract performance obligations are satisfied, the entity recognizes revenue. A portion of the payment may relate to contractual rights that the entity does not expect the customer to exercise. The timing of revenue recognition related to breakage depends on whether the entity expects to be entitled to a breakage amount. To determine whether it expects to be entitled to a breakage amount, the entity should look to the guidance on constraining amounts of variable consideration found earlier in this chapter. The entity should recognize revenue for breakage proportionately as other balances are redeemed. Any changes in estimate breakage should be accounted for by adjusting the contract liability.

Nonrefundable Up-front Fees

An up-front fee relates to an activity that the entity must undertake to fulfill the contract. The activity occurs at or near inception of the contract, and the up-front fee is an advance payment for future goods or services.

Upon receipt of the fee, the entity should not recognize revenue, even if the fee is nonrefundable, if it does not relate to the performance obligation. Up-front fees are allocated to the transaction price and should be recognized as revenue when the related goods or services are provided. If there is an option to renew the contract and the option provides a material right, the entity should extend the revenue recognition period beyond the initial contract. (ASC 606-10-55-51)

If it is determined that the up-front fee should be accounted for as an advance payment for future goods or services, the entity may make use of the practical alternative mentioned in earlier in this chapter in "Customer Options to Purchase Additional Goods or Services." (ASC 606-10-55-45)

Some nonrefundable fees are intended to compensate an entity for costs incurred at the beginning of the contract. These costs may be, for example, for the hiring of additional personnel, systems set-up, or moving assets to the service site. These efforts usually do not satisfy performance obligations because goods or services are not transferred to the customer. The fees are advance payment for future goods or services. The underlying costs should not be factored into the measure of progress used for performance obligations satisfied over time if they do not depict the transfer of services to the customer. Some set-up costs might not meet the criteria for capitalization as fulfillment costs.

In some situations, a customer does not have to pay an additional up-front fee when the contract is renewed. Thus, the renewal option may give the customer a material right. If a material right is not provided, the fee would be recognized over the contract term. If a material right is provided, it is a performance obligation and the entity should allocate part of the transaction price to the material right. The entity has the option to apply the practical alternative for contract renewal if the criteria are met.

Licenses

An agreement that calls for the transfer of control of all the worldwide rights, exclusively, in perpetuity, for all possible applications of the intellectual property (IP) may be considered a sale rather than a license. If the use of the IP is limited by, for instance, geographic area, term, or type of application or substantial rights, then the transfer is probably a license. If the agreement represents a sale, the transaction is treated as a sale subject to the five-step model, including the guidance on variable constraint and the recognition constraint to any sale- or usage-based royalties.

A license arrangement establishes a customer's right to an entity's intellectual property and the entity's obligations to provide these rights.

Before identifying when the customer takes control of an asset, it is necessary to identify the nature of the entity's promise. Therefore, when accounting for a performance obligation that includes a license and other goods or services, the entity should consider the nature of its promise in granting a license. (ASC 606-10-55-57) ASC 606 classifies all distinct licenses of intellectual property into two categories:

1. *A right to access* the entity's intellectual property throughout the license period (or its remaining economic life, if shorter).
2. *A right to use* the entity's intellectual property as it exists at the point in time at which the license is granted.
   (Emphasis added.)
   (ASC 606-10-55-58)

Revenue from a license of IP that is a right to access should be recognized over time. Revenue from a license of IP that is a right to use should be recognized at a point in time. Revenue cannot be recognized from an IP license before:

- The entity has made available a copy of the IP to the customer, *and*
- The license period has begun.
  (ASC 610-10-55-58C)

Repurchase Agreements

A repurchase agreement is a contract in which an entity sells an asset and also promises or has the option (either in the same contract or another contract) to repurchase the asset. (ASC 606-10-55-66)

The repurchased asset may be:

- The asset that was originally sold to the customer,
- An asset that is substantially the same as that asset, or
- Another asset of which the asset that was originally sold is a component.

Agreements come in three forms:

1. A forward—the entity has an obligation to repurchase the asset.
2. A call option—the entity has a right to repurchase the asset.
3. A put option—the customer has the option to require the entity to repurchase the asset at a price that is lower than the original selling price.
   (ASC 606-10-55-67)

When the entity has an obligation (forward option) or right (call option) to repurchase the asset, the customer may have physical possession, but is limited in its ability to:

- Direct the use of the asset, and
- Obtain substantially all of the remaining benefits from the asset.

Therefore, the conditions as discussed in Step 5 for the customer to have control of the asset are not present, and the customer is deemed not to have control of the asset. The accounting treatment depends on the repurchase amount required. The entity should account for the contract as:

- A lease if the entity can or must repurchase the asset for a lower amount than the original selling price unless the contract is part of a sale-leaseback transaction. For a sale-leaseback transaction, the entity should account for the contract as a financing transaction and not as a sale-leaseback in accordance with ASC 840-40.
- A financing arrangement if the entity can or must repurchase the asset for an amount equal to or more than the original selling price of the asset.
  (ASC 606-10-55-68)

When assessing the repurchase price, the entity should consider the time value of money. If the contract is accounted for as a financing arrangement, the entity should continue to recognize the asset, but the entity also recognizes a financial liability for any consideration received. Interest and processing and holding costs, if applicable, are recognized for the difference between the consideration received and the amount of consideration to be paid to the customer. The entity derecognizes the asset and recognizes revenue if the option is not exercised. (ASC 606-10-55-69 through 55-71)

A put option gives the customer the right to require the entity to repurchase the asset. If the repurchase price is lower than the original selling price of the asset, the entity must evaluate at contract inception whether the customer has a significant economic incentive to exercise the option. The entity makes that judgment by considering the relationship of the repurchase price to the expected market value of the asset and the amount of time until the right expires.

If the entity concludes that the customer has a significant economic interest and anticipates that the option will be exercised, the option is accounted for as a lease, unless the agreement is part of a sale and leaseback transaction. (ASC 606-10-55-72) If not, the entity accounts for it as a sale with a right of return.

If the repurchase price is greater than or equal to the original selling price and is more than the expected market value of the asset, the entity accounts for the contract as a financing arrangement. The time value of money should be considered when comparing the repurchase price with the selling price. If the option expires unexercised, the entity derecognizes the liability and recognizes revenue.

Consignment Arrangements

Because control has not passed, the entity does not recognize revenue upon shipment or delivery to the consignee. Once control transfers, the entity recognizes revenue.

Bill-and-Hold Arrangements

In bill-and-hold arrangements, the entity must determine if the customer has control of the goods. ASC 606 provides four criteria, all of which an entity must meet in order to decide that control has passed to the customer:

1. The reason for the bill-and-hold is substantive.
2. The product must be identified in some way as belonging to the customer.

3. The product must be ready for physical transfer upon request from the customer.
4. The entity cannot have the ability to use the product or to direct it to another customer. (ASC 606-10-55-83)

The entity needs to consider whether it meets those criteria and if it is providing custodial services. If the entity is providing custodial services, part of the transaction price should be allocated to that performance obligation.

Contract Modifications

A contract modification is a change in the scope or price (or both) of a contract that is approved by the parties to the contract. (ASC 606-10-25-10) A contract modification must be approved by the parties. Like the original contract, the modification should be approved:

- In writing,
- Orally, or
- Implied by customary business practice.

Until the modification is approved, the entity should continue to apply the guidance to the existing contract. (ASC 606-10-25-10)

If the change in scope has been agreed to, but the price is not settled, the entity should estimate the change to the price in accordance with the guidance on estimating variable consideration and constraining estimates of variable consideration. (ASC 606-10-25-11)

When a modification occurs, entities must determine:

- If the modification has created a new contract and performance obligations, or
- If the existing contract has been modified.

If the entity determines that an existing, ongoing contract has been modified, then it must further analyze the modification to determine if the modification should be accounted for as:

1. A separate contract,
2. Effectively, a termination of the contract and execution of a new contract resulting in a prospective treatment,
3. Part of the original contract, which could result in a catch-up adjustment, or
4. A combination of 2 and 3 above.

The accounting treatment depends on what was changed. Entities must account for modifications on a:

- Prospective basis—when the additional goods or services are distinct, or
- Cumulative catch-up basis—when the additional goods or services are not distinct.

The entity must analyze the agreement and account for the modification as a separate contract if:

- The scope of the contract increases because of the addition of *distinct* promised goods or services, *and*
- The price of the contract increases by an amount of consideration that reflects the entity's stand-alone selling prices of the additional promised goods or services and any appropriate adjustment to that price to reflect the circumstances of the particular contract. (ASC 606-10-25-12)

Further, to be distinct, two criteria must be met:

1. The customer could benefit from the goods or services.
2. The promise to transfer a good or service is separately identifiable from other promises in the contract.
   (ASC 606-10-25-19)

If the entity determines that the modification should be accounted for as a separate contract, the next step is to assess the agreement using the five contract criteria detailed earlier in this chapter. If the contract meets the criteria, the company should account for the change prospectively, accounting for the change in the current period and in any future period affected. Previously reported results are not changed.

If the new goods or services are not distinct or not priced at the proper stand-alone selling price according to the criteria above, the changes are not treated as a separate contract. They are considered changes to the original contract, and the entity must then determine how to account for the remaining goods or services. That accounting depends on whether or not each of the remaining goods or services is distinct from the goods or services transferred on or before the date of the modification.

A change in transaction price may occur *after* a modification, but before fulfillment of performance obligations is completed. In that case, ASC 606 provides the following guidance:

- If the modification is accounted for as if it were a termination of the existing contract and the creation of a new contract, the entity allocates the change in the transaction price to the performance obligations identified in the contract before the modification if and to the extent that the change in transaction price is attributable to an amount of variable consideration promised before the modification.
- If the modification was not accounted for as a separate contract, the entity allocates the change in the transaction price to the performance obligations in the modified contract. These are the performance obligations that were not fully satisfied at the date of the modification.
  (ASC 606-10-32-45)

For more information on changes in transaction price, see the section on transaction prices earlier in this chapter.

PRACTICE ALERT

Revenue recognition is one of the topics that most often provokes comments from the SEC. The following comments are grouped by particular aspects of revenue recognition. Areas where significant judgment is needed are a particular focus of the SEC with comments on:

- Performance obligations
  - Significant payment terms
  - Significant financing components
  - Principal versus agent decisions
  - Whether maintenance, support, and warranty services are a single performance obligation

- ○ Whether multiple goods and services promised to a customer are distinct performance obligation
- ○ Identification of a measure of progress and why the methods used faithfully present the transfer of goods and services
- Disaggregation of revenue
  - ○ Determination of categories
  - ○ Determination of the transaction price
  - ○ Appropriateness of categories considering factors such as the entity's business, products or services, and geographic locations
  - ○ Analysis of payments made to partners
  - ○ Detail
  - ○ Clarification of whether guarantees of audience views are included in variable consideration
- Allocation of the transaction price
  - ○ Details about methods, inputs, and assumptions used to allocate prices
  - ○ How the stand-alone selling price was determined
- Timing of revenue recognition
  - ○ Significant judgments regarding transfer of control
  - ○ At what point revenue is recognized
  - ○ Identification of the appropriate recognition pattern and measure of progress
  - ○ How the entity determined whether to recognize revenue at a point in time or over time
  - ○ How the entity determined the appropriate point in time
  - ○ Timing of revenue recognition related to licensing agreements
  - ○ If a perpetual license and the hosting service are one combined performance obligation, the period of time over which revenue is recognized if the period is longer than the initial hosting period
- Contract costs
  - ○ Capitalization of contract costs
  - ○ Amortization period, including method
- Contract balances
  - ○ Significant payment terms

PRESENTATION AND DISCLOSURE REQUIREMENTS

Presentation

In the statement of financial position, if either party to a contract has performed, the reporting entity presents the contract as a contract asset or a contract liability. Unconditional rights to consideration are presented separately as a receivable. (ASC 606-10-45-1) If a customer pays consideration or an entity has a right to consideration that is unconditional and the entity has not transferred goods or services, the entity presents the contract as a contract liability. (ASC 606-10-45-2) If the opposite occurs and the entity transfers goods or services before payment is received, the contract is presented as a contract asset, exclusive of any amount presented as a receivable. (ASC 606-10-45-3) If there is a difference between the measurement of a receivable because of credit losses, it should be presented as a credit loss expense. (ASC 606-10-45-4)

Presentation of a Significant Financing Component The entity should separate the loan component from the revenue component. Interest income or expense resulting from a financing should be presented separately from the revenue component. Once a performance obligation is satisfied, the entity recognizes the present value of the consideration as revenue. The financing component (interest income or expense) is recognized over the financing period. The income or expense is recognized only to the extent that a contract asset, receivable, or contract liability, such as deferred revenue, is recognized for the customer contract. When accounting for the financing component, the entity should look to the relevant guidance on the effective interest method in ASC 835-30, *Interest—Imputation of Interest:*

- Subsequent measurement guidance in ASC 835-30-45-1A through 45-3
- Application of the interest method in ASC 835-30-55-2 and 55-3
  (ASC 606-10-32-20)

Disclosure

Disclosure Type	*Requirements*	*Disclosure Relief for Nonpublic Companies*[1]
Contract with customers	Revenue recognized from contracts with customers, disclosed separately from other sources of revenue. (ASC 606-10-50-4a)	
	Impairment losses recognized on receivables or contract assets, disclosed separately from other impairment losses. (ASC 606-10-50-4b)[2]	
Disaggregated revenue	Disaggregated into categories that show: How economic factors affect the amount, timing, and uncertainty of revenue and cash flows. (ASC 606-10-50-5)	May elect not to provide the quantitative disaggregation disclosure. If election is chosen, must disclose: Revenue disaggregated by timing of transfer of goods or services, and Qualitative information about how economic factors affect the nature, amount, timing, and uncertainty of revenue and cash flows (ASC 606-10-50-7)
	Information that enables users to understand the relationship between the disclosures of disaggregated information and segment information. (ASC 606-10-50-6)	May use the expedient in ASC 606-10-50-7 above.

(Continue)

Disclosure Type	Requirements	Disclosure Relief for Nonpublic Companies[1]
Contract balances	Opening and closing balances of receivables, contract assets, and contract liabilities. (ASC 606-10-50-8a)	
	Amount of revenue recognized in the current period that was included in the opening contract liability balance. (ASC 606-10-50-8b)	May elect not to make this disclosure. (ASC 606-10-50-11)
	Amount of revenue recognized in the current period from performance obligations satisfied or partially satisfied in the previous periods. (ASC 606-10-50-12A)	
	Explanation (may use qualitative information) of how the timing of performance obligations and the entity's contracts' payment terms will affect its contract asset and contract liability balances. (ASC 606-10-50-9)	May elect not to make this disclosure. (ASC 606-10-50-11)
	Qualitative and quantitative information about the significant changes in contract asset and liability balances. (ASC 606-10-50-10)	May elect not to make this disclosure. (ASC 606-10-50-11)
Performance obligations	Descriptive information about an entity's performance of obligations, including: When the entity typically satisfies its performance obligations, Significant payment terms, Nature of the goods or services promised to transfer (highlighting any performance obligations for another entity to transfer goods or services), Obligations for returns, refunds, and other similar obligations, Types of warrantees and related obligations (ASC 606-10-50-12)	
	Aggregate amount of the transaction price allocated to remaining performance obligations unsatisfied or partially satisfied.[3] (ASC 606-10-50-13a)	May elect not to make this disclosure. (ASC 606-10-50-16)
	Either a quantitative (using time bands) or a qualitative explanation of when the entity expects the aggregated amount of the transaction price allocated to remaining performance obligations unsatified or partially satisfied to be recognized as revenue. (ASC 606-10-50-13b)	May elect not to make this disclosure. (ASC 606-10-50-16)

(Continue)

Disclosure Type	Requirements	Disclosure Relief for Nonpublic Companies[1]
	Entities may elect not to disclose the information required by ASC 606-10-50-13 if: the related contract has an original expected duration of one year or less or the entity uses the practical expedient in ASC 606-10-55-18, recognizing revenue in the amount for which the entity has a right to invoice for performance obligations based on a right to consideration from a customer in an amount that corresponds directly with the value of the entity's performance completed to date. (ASC 606-10-50-14)	May elect not to make the disclosure in ASC 606-10-50-15. (ASC 606-10-50-16) This exemption cannot be applied to fixed consideration. (ASC 606-10-50-14B)
	Entities are not required to disclose information on variable consideration required by ASC 606-10-50-13 if the variable consideration is: based on a sales- or usage-based royalty promised in exchange for a license of intellectual property or allocated entirely to a wholly unsatisfied performance obligation or promise to transfer a distinct good or service that is part of a single performance obligation. (ASC 606-10-50-14A)	May elect not to make the disclosure in ASC 606-10-50-15. (ASC 606-10-50-16) This exemption cannot be applied to fixed consideration. (ASC 606-10-50-14B)
	Practical expedient: Entities may elect not to disclose the information required by IFRS 15.120 if the related contract has an original expected duration of one year or less or the entity recognizes revenue for the performance obligation in accordance with B16. An entity choosing this election should include qualitative explanation of whether any consideration is not included in the transaction price.	
	If applying the optional exemptions in ASC 606 in ASC 606-10-50-14 and 50-14A: • Which optional exemptions the entity is applying • Nature of the performance obligation • Remaining duration • Description of the variable consideration excluded from the information disclosed in accordance with ASC 606-10-50-13 • Whether any consideration from contracts with customers is not included in the transaction price (ASC 606-10-50-15)	May elect not to make the disclosure in ASC 606-10-50-15. (ASC 606-10-50-16)

(Continue)

Disclosure Type	Requirements	Disclosure Relief for Nonpublic Companies[1]
Significant judgments	Judgments and changes in judgment that affect the determination of the amount and timing of revenue recognition, particularly the timing of satisfaction of performance obligations, the transaction price and the amounts allocated to performance obligations. (ASC 606-10-50-17)	
	Methods used to recognize revenue for performance obligations satisfied over time. (ASC 606-10-50-18a)	
	Why the method used to recognize revenue over time provides a faithful depiction of the transfer goods or services. (ASC 606-10-50-18b)	May elect not to make this disclosure. (ASC 606-10-50-21)
	Significant judgments related to the transfer of control for performance obligations satisfied at a point in time. (ASC 606-10-50-19)	May elect not to make this disclosure. (ASC 606-10-50-21)
	Information about the methods, inputs, and assumptions used to determine and allocate transaction price (ASC 606-10-50-20a and c)	May elect not to make this disclosure. (ASC 606-10-50-21)
	Assessing whether an estimate of variable consideration is constrained. (ASC 606-10-50-20b)	
	Measuring obligations for returns, refunds, and other similar obligations. (ASC 606-10-50-20d)	May elect not to make this disclosure. (ASC 606-10-50-21)
Cost to obtain and to fulfill a contract	Judgments made to determine the cost to obtain or fulfill a contract and method of amortization. (ASC 340-40-50-2)	May elect not to make this disclosure. (ASC 340-40-50-4)
	Closing balances of assets and amount of amortization and impairment. (ASC 340-40-50-3)	May elect not to make this disclosure. (ASC 340-40-50-4)
Practical expedients	Use of the practical expedient regarding the existence of a significant financing component. (ASC 606-10-50-22)	May elect not to make this disclosure. (ASC 606-10-50-23)
	Use of the practical expedient for expensing incremental costs of obtaining a contract (ASC 340-40-50-5)	May elect not to make this disclosure. (ASC 340-40-50-6)

[1] For this purpose, nonpublic companies are entities except for public business entities, not-for-profit entities that have issued or are conduit bond obligors for securities that are traded, listed, or quoted on an exchange or an over-the-counter market, or employee benefit plans that file or furnish financial statements with or to the SEC.

2 Upon implementation of ASU 2016-13, *Financial Instruments—Credit Losses (Topic 326): Measurement of Credit Losses on Financial Instruments,* this item for U.S. GAAP reporters will be superseded by: "Credit losses recorded on any receivables or contract assets from contracts with customers, disclosed separately from credit loss from other contracts." The IFRS language will remain the same.

3 See discussion in this chapter for a practical expedient related to this requirement.

PRESENTATION AND DISCLOSURE EXAMPLES

Example 37.1: Adoption and Effect of ASU 2014-09

The Company adopted ASU No. 2014-09 and related standards (collectively, ASC 606, *Revenue from Contracts with Customers*), on January 1, 20X8 using the modified retrospective method of adoption. Prior periods have not been restated. Due to the cumulative net impact of adopting ASC 606, the January 1, 20X8 balance of retained earnings was increased by less than $2 million, primarily relating to the accelerated recognition for software installation service and training revenue. This cumulative impact reflects retrospective application of ASC 606 only to contracts that were not completed as of January 1, 20X8. Further, the Company applied the practical expedient permitting the effect of all contract modifications that occurred before January 1, 20X8 to be aggregated in the transition accounting. The impact of applying ASC 606 as compared with previous guidance applied to revenues and costs was not material for the year ended December 31, 20X8.

Example 37.2: Description of Revenue Sources

Revenue (Sales) Recognition The Company sells a wide range of products to a diversified base of customers around the world and has no material concentration of credit risk or significant payment terms extended to customers. The vast majority of LRB's customer arrangements contain a single performance obligation to transfer manufactured goods as the promise to transfer the individual goods is not separately identifiable from other promises in the contracts and, therefore, not distinct. However, to a limited extent LRB also enters into customer arrangements that involve intellectual property out-licensing, multiple performance obligations (such as equipment, installation, and service), software with coterminous post-contract support, services, and nonstandard terms and conditions.

Example 37.3: Sources of Revenue—Retail Product Sales and Rentals

The majority of our revenue relates to the sales of products through our bookstore locations, including virtual stores, and our store-affiliated ecommerce websites, and contains a single performance obligation. Revenue from sales of our products is recognized at the point in time when control of the products is transferred to our customers in an amount that reflects the consideration we expect to be entitled to in exchange for the products.

Example 37.4: Revenue Recognition Policy

Retail product revenue is recognized when the customer takes physical possession of our products, which occurs either at the point of sale for products purchased at physical locations or upon receipt of our products by our customers for products ordered through our websites and virtual stores. Wholesale product revenue is recognized upon shipment of physical products, at which point title passes and risk of loss is transferred to the customer.

Example 37.5: Revenue Recognition Policy—Transfer of Control

The Company recognizes revenue in light of the guidance of Accounting Standards Codification (ASC) 606, *Revenue from Contracts with Customers*. Revenue is recognized when control of goods has transferred to customers. For the majority of the Company's customer arrangements, control transfers to customers at a point in time when goods/services have been delivered as that is generally when legal title, physical possession and risks and rewards of goods/services transfers to the customer. In limited arrangements, control transfers over time as the customer simultaneously receives and consumes the benefits as LRB completes the performance obligation(s).

Example 37.6: Revenue Recognition Policy—Transaction Price, Including Sales Incentives

Revenue is recognized at the transaction price to which the Company expects to be entitled. When determining the transaction price, LRB estimates variable consideration applying the portfolio approach practical expedient under ASC 606. The main sources of variable consideration for LRB are customer rebates, trade promotion funds, and cash discounts. These sales incentives are recorded as a reduction to revenue at the time of the initial sale using the most-likely-amount estimation method. The most-likely-amount method is based on the single most likely outcome from a range of possible consideration outcomes. The range of possible consideration outcomes are primarily derived from the following inputs: sales terms, historical experience, trend analysis, and projected market conditions in the various markets served. Because LRB serves numerous markets, the sales incentive programs offered vary across businesses, but the most common incentive relates to amounts paid or credited to customers for achieving defined volume levels or growth objectives. There are no material instances where variable consideration is constrained and not recorded at the initial time of sale. Free goods are accounted for as an expense and recorded in cost of sales.

Example 37.7: Product Returns

Product returns are recorded as a reduction to revenue based on anticipated sales returns that occur in the normal course of business.

Example 37.8: Warranties

The company primarily has assurance-type warranties that do not result in separate performance obligations.

Example 37.9: Taxes

Sales, use, value-added, and other excise taxes are not recognized in revenue. The Company has elected to present revenue net of sales taxes and other similar taxes.

Example 37.10: Sales Taxes

Sales tax collected from our customers is excluded from reported revenues.

Example 37.11: Revenue Recognized Over Time

For substantially all arrangements recognized over time, the Company applies the "right to invoice" practical expedient. As a result, the Company recognizes revenue at the invoice amount when the entity has a right to invoice a customer at an amount that corresponds directly with the value to the customer of the Company's performance completed to date.

Example 37.12: Contracts with Multiple Performance Obligations

For contracts with multiple performance obligations, the Company allocates the contract's transaction price to each performance obligation using the Company's best estimate of the standalone selling price of each distinct good or service in the contract.

Example 37.13: Performance Obligations

The Company did not recognize any material revenue in the current reporting period for performance obligations that were fully satisfied in previous periods.

The Company does not have material unfulfilled performance obligation balances for contracts with an original length greater than one year in any years presented. Additionally, the Company does not have material costs related to obtaining a contract with amortization periods greater than one year for any year presented.

Example 37.14: Practical Expedients Used

LRB applies ASC 606 utilizing the following allowable exemptions or practical expedients:

- Exemption to not disclose the unfulfilled performance obligation balance for contracts with an original length of one year or less.
- Practical expedient relative to costs of obtaining a contract by expensing sales commissions when incurred because the amortization period would have been one year or less.
- Portfolio approach practical expedient relative to estimation of variable consideration.
- "Right to invoice" practical expedient based on LRB's right to invoice the customer at an amount that reasonably represents the value to the customer of LRB's performance completed to date.
- Election to present revenue net of sales taxes and other similar taxes.
- Sales-based royalty exemption permitting future intellectual property out-licensing royalty payments to be excluded from the otherwise required remaining performance obligations disclosure.

Example 37.15: Revenue Recognition for Rentals Recognized as Leases

The Company recognizes revenue from the rental of durable medical devices in light of the guidance of ASC 842, *Leases*.

Example 37.16: Contract Balances Recognized

Deferred revenue primarily relates to revenue that is recognized over time for one-year software license contracts. Approximately $600 million of the December 31, 20X2 balance was recognized as revenue during the year ended December 31, 20X3, while approximately $500 million of the December 31, 20X1 balance was recognized as revenue during the year ended December 31, 20X2.

Example 37.17: Schedule of Disaggregated Revenue Information by Product Type

The Company views the following disaggregated disclosures as useful to understanding the composition of revenue recognized during the respective reporting periods:

	Year ended December 31,		
Net Sales (Millions)	*20X3*	*20X2*	*20X1*
Safety and Industrial Business Products	$11,607	$12,494	$ 11,946
Transportation and Electronics Products	$ 9,602	$10,106	$ 9,861
Health Care Products	$ 7,431	$ 6,826	$ 6,635
Consumer Business Products	$ 5,089	$ 5,086	$ 5,006
Total Company	$32,136	$32,765	$31,657

Example 37.18: Disaggregation of Revenue by Year and Product Type

The following table disaggregates the revenue associated with our major product and service offerings.

	52 weeks ended		
	April 27, 20X3	*April 28, 20X2*	*April 29, 20X1*
Retail			
Product sales	$ 1,646,917	$ 1,753,528	$ 1,594,116
Rental income	195,883	219,145	232,481
Service and other revenue*	46,208	51,868	38,974
Retail total sales	$ 1,889,008	$ 2,024,541	$ 1,865,571
Wholesale sales	$ 223,374	$ 258,369	$ 14,758
DC sales**	$ 21,339	$ 15,762	$ —
Eliminations***	$ (99,078)	$ (95,055)	$ (5,967)
Total sales	$ 2,034,643	$ 2,203,617	$ 1,874,362

*Service and other revenue primarily relates to brand partnerships and other service revenues.
**DC sales primarily relate to direct-to-customer subscription-based revenue.
***The sales eliminations represent the elimination of Wholesale sales and fulfillment service fees to Retail and the elimination of Retail commissions earned from Wholesale.

Example 37.19: Disaggregation of Revenue by Geographic Location

	Year ended December 31, 20X3					
Net Sales (Millions)	*United States*	*Asia Pacific*	*Europe, Middle East, and Africa*	*Latin America and Canada*	*Other Unallocated*	*Worldwide Total*
Safety and industrial	$ 4,643	$ 2,877	$ 2,672	$ 1,419	$ (4)	$ 11,607
Transportation and electronics	2,304	5,228	1,472	601	(3)	9,602
Health care	3,597	1,490	1,743	603	(2)	7,431
Consumer	3,119	984	545	442	(1)	5,089
Corporate and unallocated	100	—	1	9	—	110
Elimination of dual credit	(604)	(783)	(207)	(109)	—	(1,703)
Total company	$ 13,159	$ 9,796	$ 6,226	$ 2,965	$ (10)	$ 32,136

| | | | Year ended December 31, 20X2 | | | |
Net Sales (Millions)	United States	Asia Pacific	Europe, Middle East, and Africa	Latin America and Canada	Other Unallocated	Worldwide Total
Safety and industrial	$ 4,921	$ 3,099	$ 3,001	$ 1,476	$ (3)	$ 12,494
Transportation and electronics	2,406	5,514	1,578	610	(2)	10,106
Health care	3,039	1,458	1,733	596	—	6,826
Consumer	3,045	1,021	574	447	(1)	5,086
Corporate and unallocated	48	—	—	3	(1)	50
Elimination of dual credit	(619)	(838)	(232)	(108)	—	(1,797)
Total company	$ 12,840	$ 10,254	$ 6,654	$ 3,024	$ (7)	$ 32,765

| | | | Year ended December 31, 20X1 | | | |
Net Sales (Millions)	United States	Asia Pacific	Europe, Middle East, and Africa	Latin America and Canada	Other Unallocated	Worldwide Total
Safety and industrial	$ 4,605	$ 2,981	$ 2,869	$ 1,497	$ (6)	$ 11,946
Transportation and electronics	2,372	5,328	1,550	615	(4)	9,861
Health care	3,037	1,346	1,667	587	(2)	6,635
Consumer	2,943	1,029	585	450	(1)	5,006
Corporate and unallocated	6	(1)	1	(4)	—	2
Elimination of dual credit	(591)	(874)	(216)	(112)	—	(1,793)
Total company	$ 12,372	$ 9,809	$ 6,456	$ 3,033	$ (13)	$ 31,657

Example 37.20: Determining Whether the Company Is Acting as Principal or Agent

For sales and rentals involving third-party products, we evaluate whether we are acting as a principal or an agent. Our determination is based on our evaluation of whether we control the specified goods or services prior to transferring them to the customer. There are significant judgments involved in determining whether we control the specified goods or services prior to transferring them to the customer, including whether we have the ability to direct the use of the good or service and obtain substantially all of the remaining benefits from the good or service. For those transactions where we are the principal, we record revenue on a gross basis, and for those transactions where we are an agent to a third party, we record revenue on a net basis.

Example 37.21: Revenue from Shipping Charges

Additional revenue is recognized for shipping charges billed to customers and shipping costs are accounted for as fulfillment costs within cost of goods sold.

Example 37.22: Rental Revenue, Including Buyout Option

Revenue from the rental of physical products, which contains a single performance obligation, is deferred and recognized over the rental period based on the passage of time commencing at the point of sale, when control of the product transfers to the customer. Rental periods are typically for a six-month period and are always less than one year in duration. We offer a buyout option to allow the purchase of a rented physical product at the end of the rental period if the customer desires to do so. We record the buyout purchase when the customer exercises and pays the buyout option price, which is determined at the time of the buyout. In these instances, we accelerate any remaining deferred rental revenue at the point of sale.

Revenue from the rental of digital products, which contains a single performance obligation, is recognized at the point of sale. A software feature is embedded within the content of our digital products, such that upon expiration of the rental term the customer is no longer able to access the content. While the digital rental allows the customer to access digital content for a fixed period of time, once the digital content is delivered to the customer, our performance obligation is complete.

Example 37.23: Returns Estimate

We estimate returns based on an analysis of historical experience. A provision for anticipated merchandise returns is provided through a reduction of sales and cost of goods sold in the period that the related sales are recorded.

Example 37.24: Gift Cards, Customer Loyalty Programs, Promotional Offers

We do not have gift card or customer loyalty programs. We do not treat any promotional offers as expenses.

Example 37.25: Payment Terms

Our payment terms are generally 30 days and do not extend beyond one year.

Example 37.26: Service Revenue

Service and other revenue primarily relates to direct-to-customer subscription-based writing service revenues and partnership marketing services, which include promotional activities and advertisements within our physical stores and web properties performed on behalf of third-party customers.

Example 37.27: Subscription-Based Revenue

Subscription-based revenue, which contains a single performance obligation, is deferred and recognized based on the passage of time over the subscription period commencing at the point of sale, when control of the service transfers to the customer. The majority of subscriptions sold are one month in duration.

Example 37.28: Partnership Marketing Agreements

Partnership marketing agreements often include multiple performance obligations which are individually negotiated with our customers. For these arrangements that contain distinct performance obligations, we allocate the transaction price based on the relative stand-alone selling price method by comparing the stand-alone selling price ("SSP") of each distinct performance obligation to the total value of the contract. The revenue is recognized as each performance obligation is satisfied, typically at a point in time for partnership marketing services and overtime for advertising efforts as measured based upon the passage of time for contracts that are based on a stated period of time or the number of impressions delivered for contracts with a fixed number of impressions.

Example 37.29: Contract Assets and Contract Liabilities, Including Schedule of Changes

Contract assets represent the sale of goods or services to a customer before we have the right to obtain consideration from the customer. Contract assets consist of unbilled amounts at the reporting date and are transferred to accounts receivable when the rights become unconditional. Contract assets (unbilled receivables) were $0 as of both April 27, 20X3 and April 28, 20X2 on our consolidated balance sheets.

Contract liabilities represent an obligation to transfer goods or services to a customer for which we have received consideration and consists of our deferred revenue liability (deferred revenue). Deferred revenue primarily consists of advanced payments from customers related to product rental and subscription-based performance obligations that have not yet been satisfied, as well as unsatisfied performance obligations associated with partnership marketing services. Deferred revenue is recognized ratably over the terms of the related rental or subscription periods, or when the contracted services are provided to our partnership marketing customers. Deferred revenue of $20,418 and $20,144 is recorded within Accrued Liabilities on our consolidated balance sheets for the periods ended April 27, 20X3 and April 28, 20X2, respectively. The following table presents changes in contract liabilities during the fiscal year ended April 27, 20X3:

(in thousands)	*Fiscal Year Ended April 27, 20X3*
Deferred revenue at the beginning of period	$ 20,144
Additions to deferred revenue during the period	212,424
Reductions to deferred revenue for revenue recognized during the period	(212,150)
Deferred revenue balance at the end of period	$ 20,418

As of April 27, 20X3, we expect to recognize $20,418 of the deferred revenue balance within in the next 12 months.

38 ASC 610 OTHER INCOME

AUTHORITATIVE LITERATURE

Subtopics

ASC 610, *Other Income*, contains three Subtopics:

1. ASC 610-10, *Overall*, which defines the scope of guidance on revenue recognized that is *not* in the scope of:
   - ASC 606, in other words, that is not from a contract with a customer,
   - Other topics, such as ASC 840 or 842 on leases and ASC 944 on insurance, or
   - Other revenue or income guidance.
2. ASC 610-20, *Gains and Losses from the Derecognition of Nonfinancial Assets*, applies to derecognition of nonfinancial assets with the scope of ASC 350 on intangibles and ASC 360 on property, plant, and equipment that is not in the scope of ASC 606. Nonfinancial assets are, for example, real estate, intangible assets, property, plant, and equipment.
3. ASC 610-30, *Gains and Losses on Involuntary Conversions*, applies to events and transactions in which nonmonetary assets are involuntarily converted to monetary assets that are then reinvested to other nonmonetary assets.

Scope and Scope Exceptions

ASC 610-10, *Overall* ASC 610-10 applies to all entities. (ASC 610-10-15-2)

ASC 610-20, *Gains and Losses from the Derecognition of Nonfinancial Assets* ASC 610-20 applies to all entities and the gain or loss recognized upon:

- The derecognition of nonfinancial assets and in substance nonfinancial assets.

For purposes of ASC 610, nonfinancial assets include intangible assets, land, buildings, material, and supplies that may have a zero carrying value. (ASC 610-20-15-1 and 15-2) These are further described below.

The term "in substance nonfinancial asset" is described in ASC 610-20-15-5 through 15-8. The Codification gives the example of a legal entity that holds only nonfinancial assets, for example, real estate, and points the reader to the Scope section for further guidance.

ASC 610-20 applies to a transfer of an ownership interest or a variable interest in a consolidated subsidiary, not a business or nonprofit activity, only if all of the assets in the subsidiary are nonfinancial assets or in substance nonfinancial assets. (ASC 610-20-15-3)

The guidance does not apply to the derecognition of:

- A transfer of a nonfinancial asset, including an in substance nonfinancial asset, in a contract with a customer
- A transfer of a subsidiary or group of assets that constitutes a business or nonprofit activity, except for an in substance nonfinancial asset
- Real estate or non-real estate sales-leaseback transactions, which are covered under ASC 360-20, 840-40, or 842-40 (the last upon implementation of ASU 2016-02)
- Conveyance of oil and gas mineral rights under ASC 932-360
- A transaction entirely accounted for under ASC 860
- A transfer of nonfinancial assets that comprise part of the consideration in a business combination under the guidance in ASC 805
- Transfer of nonfinancial assets to another entity in exchange for a noncontrolling ownership interest in that entity under ASC 845-10-30
- A nonmonetary exchange within the scope of ASC 845
- A lease contract
- An exchange of takeoff or landing slots under ASC 908-350
- A contribution of cash and other assets within ASC 720-25 and contributions within the scope of 958-605
- A transfer of an investment in a venture accounted for proportionally as described in ASC 810-10-45-11
- A transfer of nonfinancial or in substance nonfinancial assets between entities under common control

(ASC 610-20-15-4)

In substance nonfinancial assets. An in substance nonfinancial asset is a financial asset promised to a counterparty in a contract if substantially all of the fair value of the assets is concentrated in nonfinancial assets. In that case, then *all* of the financial assets are in substance nonfinancial assets. When evaluating a contract, if the contract includes the transfer of ownership interests in one or more consolidated subsidiaries that is not a business, the entity should consider the underlying assets in those subsidiaries. (ASC 610-20-15-5)

When a contract includes the transfer of ownership interests in one or more consolidated subsidiaries that is not a business and substantially all of the fair value of the assets promised to a counterparty in the contract is *not* concentrated in nonfinancial assets, an entity should evaluate whether substantially all of the fair value of the assets promised to the counterparty is concentrated in nonfinancial assets. If so, then the financial assets in that subsidiary are in substance nonfinancial assets. (ASC 610-20-15-6)

In making the determination of whether substantially all of the fair value of the assets is concentrated in nonfinancial assets, the entity should exclude cash or cash equivalents promised to the counterparty and disregard any liabilities assumed or relieved by the counterparty. (ASC 610-20-15-7)

If all of the assets promised to a counterparty in an individual consolidated subsidiary within a contract are not nonfinancial assets and/or in substance nonfinancial assets, an entity should apply the guidance in paragraph 810-10-40-3A(c) or 810-10-45-21A(b)(2) to determine the guidance applicable to that subsidiary. (ASC 610-20-15-8)

Contracts partially within the scope of other topics. If the counterparty's promises are not all nonfinancial assets or in substance nonfinancial assets, the contract may fall only partially within the scope of ASC 610. In that case, the entity should apply the guidance in ASC 606-10- 15-4 to determine how to measure the contract's elements. (ASC 610-20-15-9)

ASC 610-30, *Gains and Losses on Involuntary Conversions* ASC 610-30 applies to all entities and to events and transactions in which nonmonetary assets are involuntarily converted to monetary assets that are then reinvested in other nonmonetary assets.

ASC 610-10, *Overall*

This Subtopic establishes the pervasive scope of ASC 610 and provides a glossary. It does not include measurement, presentation, or other guidance.

ASC 610-20, *Gains and Losses from the Derecognition of Financial Assets*

Recognition If an entity has a gain or loss from the transfer of nonfinancial or in substance nonfinancial assets within the scope of ASC 610, it must determine whether to apply the guidance in ASC 810 or ASC 606. (ASC 10-20-25-1)

Measurement If the derecognition criteria are met, the selling entity should recognize a gain or loss equal to the difference between the consideration received and the carrying amount of the asset sold. (ASC 610-20-32-2) The consideration received is the transaction price determined under the guidance in ASC 606-10-32. (ASC 610-20-32-3) If a noncontrolling interest is received by the seller or retained in a partial sale, that noncontrolling interest received is noncash consideration measured at fair value under ASC 606. (ASC 610-20-32-4)

ASC 610-30, *Gains and Losses on Involuntary Conversions*

This subtopic provides guidance when nonmonetary assets are destroyed, stolen, condemned, or otherwise lost and the entity receives monetary assets such as insurance proceeds. The guidance makes clear that this type of transaction is a monetary transaction that results in a gain or loss.

Recognition, Measurement, and Presentation The cost of nonmonetary assets acquired is measured by the consideration paid, not affected by previous transactions. (ASC 610-30-30-1) The gain or loss recognized is classified under the provisions in ASC 225-20. (ASC 610-30-45-1)

If a nonmonetary asset is destroyed or damaged in one period and the amount of monetary assets to be received will not be determinable until a later period, gain or loss is recognized per the guidance in ASC 450. (ASC 610-30-25-4)

PRESENTATION AND DISCLOSURE REQUIREMENTS

Presentation

A gain or loss is recognized on the sale of a long-lived asset in accordance with ASC 360-10-45-5. (ASC 610-20-45-1)

If either party has performed, the entity should present the relationship between the entity's performance and the counterparty's payment in accordance with ASC 606-10-45 through 45-5. (ASC 610-20-45-2)

If the criteria in ASC 405-20-40-1 to derecognize a liability are assumed or relieved by a counterparty before transferring control, the entity should derecognize the liability and:

- A contract liability is recorded for the consideration received before transfer
- A contract asset to the extent the contract liability is included in the calculation of gain or loss
  (ASC 610-20-45-3)

A gain or loss on involuntary conversion of a nonmonetary asset to monetary assets should be classified in accordance with ASC 220-20. (ASC 610-30-45-1)

Disclosure

A gain or loss from the derecognition of a long-lived asset should be disclosed in accordance with ASC 360-10-50-3 through 50-3A. (ASC 610-20-50-1)

PRESENTATION AND DISCLOSURE EXAMPLES

Example 38.1: Effect of Adoption of ASC 610 on Real Estate Transactions

On January 1, 20X8, the Company adopted ASU 2014-09 ("Topic 606"), as subsequently amended, using the modified retrospective method and applied Topic 606 to those contracts that were not completed as of January 1, 20X8. Topic 606 added a new section, ASC 610, *Other Income—Gains and Losses from the Derecognition of Nonfinancial Assets*, which effectively superseded industry-specific accounting guidance applicable to real estate transactions.

As a result of the adoption of Topic 606 and ASC 610, the Company derecognized the underlying assets and liabilities associated with the contribution as of January 1, 20X8 and recognized the Company's investment in Adelaide under the equity method for the periods after December 31, 20X7.

The table below presents the real estate partnership investment in which the Company held an ownership interest (in thousands):

| Real estate partnership | Ownership Interest | The Company's Investment as of December 31, | |
		20X9	20X8
Adelaide*,**	81.4%	$34,097	$26,236
Total real estate partnership***		$34,097	$26,236

---

* The Company manages these real estate partnership investments and, where applicable, earns acquisition fees, leasing commissions, property management fees, and asset management fees.

** As of December 31, 20X7, the Company had a net deferred gain of $18.0 million relating to the sale of properties to Adelaide prior to the adoption of ASU 2017-05. These deferred gains were included in the Company's investment above. Upon adoption, the Company recorded a cumulative-effect adjustment of $19.1 million to its beginning accumulated deficit as of January 1, 20X8 on the Company's consolidated statements of changes in equity.

*** Representing eight property interests and 0.9 million square feet of GLA, as of December 31, 20X9, and 11 property interests and 1.3 million square feet of GLA, as of December 31, 20X8.

Example 38.2: Effect of Adoption of ASC 610 on Royalties

LRB transferred its co-commercialization rights to MTL in 20X5 in exchange for sales-based royalties through 20Z2. Royalties earned were $17 million in 20X7. As a result of the adoption of ASC 610 in the first quarter of 20X8, estimated future royalties resulting from the transfer of rights to MTL were recorded as a cumulative effect adjustment in retained earnings. A $23 million change in estimated future royalties was included in 20X9.

39 ASC 705 COST OF SALES AND SERVICES

Authoritative Literature   449

AUTHORITATIVE LITERATURE

ASC 705 does not contain any requirements for presentation and disclosure. ASC 705-10 only provides links to guidance in other Subtopics because the Codification's asset liability model generally results in the inclusion of that guidance in other Topics. ASC 705-20 only provides guidance on initial recognition.

40 ASC 710 COMPENSATION— GENERAL

AUTHORITATIVE LITERATURE

Subtopics

ASC 710, *Compensation—General,* contains one Subtopic:

- ASC 710-10, *Overall,* which is divided into two Subsections:
  - ○ *General*, which provides guidance on compensated absences, deferred compensation, and lump-sum payments under union contract
  - ○ *Deferred Compensation—Rabbi Trusts*

Scope and Scope Exceptions

ASC 710 applies to all entities, but it does *not* apply to the following transactions:

- Benefits paid to active employees other than compensated absences.
- Benefits paid at retirement or provided through a pension or postretirement benefit plan, including special or contractual termination benefits payable upon termination from a pension or other postretirement plan, that are covered by Subtopics 715-30 and 715-60.
- Individual deferred compensation contracts that are addressed by Subtopics 715-30 and 715-60, if those contracts, taken together, are equivalent to a defined benefit pension plan or a defined benefit other postretirement benefit plan, respectively.
- Special or contractual termination benefits that are not payable from a pension or other postretirement plan are covered by Topic 712.

- Stock compensation plans that are addressed by Topic 718.
- Other postemployment benefits (see Topic 712) that do not meet the conditions in paragraph 710-10-25-1 and are accounted for in accordance with Topic 450. (ASC 710-10-15-5)

In addition, the *Deferred Compensation—Rabbi Trusts* subsection does not address the accounting for stock appreciation rights even if they are funded through a rabbi trust. (ASC 710- 10-15-8)

Compensated Absences

Compensated absences refers to paid vacation, paid holidays, paid sick leave, and other paid leaves of absence. ASC 710 requires an employer to accrue a liability for employee's compensation for future absences if all of the following conditions are met:

1. The employee's right to receive compensation for future absences is attributable to employee services already rendered.
2. The right vests or accumulates.
3. Payment of the compensation is probable.
4. The amount of the payment can be reasonably estimated. (ASC 710-10-25-1)

Sick Pay ASC 710-10-25-7 allows an exception for employee paid sick days that accumulate but do not vest. No accrued liability is required for sick days that only accumulate. However, an employer is permitted to accrue these benefits if the four conditions (noted above) for compensated absences are met. FASB believed that these amounts are rarely material and the low reliability of estimates of future illness coupled with the high cost of developing these estimates indicates that accrual is not necessary. The required accounting should be determined by the employer's actual administration of sick pay benefits. If the employer routinely lets employees take time off when they are not ill and allows that time to be charged as sick pay, then an accrual is required. (ASC 710-10-25-6)

Bonus Payments

Bonus payments may require estimation since the amount of the bonus may be affected by:

- The entity's net income for the year,
- The income taxes currently payable, or
- Other factors.

Estimation may be challenging if bonus payments are accrued on a monthly basis for purposes of interim financial reporting but are determinable only annually by using a formula whose values are uncertain until shortly before payment.

Deferred Compensation Contracts

If the aggregate deferred compensation contracts with individual employees are equivalent to a pension plan, the contracts are accounted for under the guidance in ASC 715-30. All other deferred compensation contracts are accounted for according to ASC 710.

According to ASC 710, the amount to be accrued should not be less than the present value of the estimated payments to be made. This estimated amount is accrued in a systematic and rational manner. When elements of both current and future employment are present, only the portion attributable to the current services is accrued. (ASC 710-10-25-9) All requirements of the contract, such as continued employment for a specified period, availability for consulting services, and agreements not to compete after retirement, need to be met in order for the employee to receive future payments. Finally, the total amount is amortized to expense over the period from the date the contract is signed to the point when the employee is fully eligible to receive the deferred payments.

One benefit that may be found in a deferred compensation contract is for periodic payments to employees or their beneficiaries for life, with provisions for a minimum lump-sum settlement in the event of early death of one or all of the beneficiaries. The estimated amount to be accrued is based on the life expectancy of each individual concerned or on the estimated cost of an annuity contract, not on the minimum amount payable in the event of early death. (ASC 710-10-25-11)

Lump-Sum Payments Under Union Contracts

When signing a new union contract, the union may agree to lump-sum cash payments instead of pay increases. Sometimes these provisions eliminate base pay raises that would otherwise be required during the contract period. In these contracts, there is usually no requirement for the employee to reimburse the entity upon leaving the company. There is also an expectation that the employee would be replaced by another union worker at the same pay rate, but without additional lump-sum payments. (ASC 710-10-25-12)

Only when it is clear that the lump-sum payment will benefit a future period in the form of a lower base pay rate may it be deferred and amortized. (ASC 710-10-25-13)

Deferred Compensation—Rabbi Trusts

The chart below gives an overview of the guidance for rabbi trusts.

Trust	Description *(ASC 710-10-25-15)*	Accounting *(ASC 710-10-25-16 through 25-18)*
Plan A	Does not permit diversification. Must be settled by delivery of a fixed number of shares of employer stock.	Classify stock held by trust in equity, similar to treasury stock.
Plan B	Does not permit diversification. May be settled by delivery of cash or shares of employer stock.	Classify employee stock in equity in a manner similar to treasury stock. Classify deferred compensation obligation as a liability.
Plan C	Permits diversification, but the employee has not diversified.	Same as Plan B.
Plan D	Permits diversification, and the employee has diversified.	Assets accounted for in accordance with GAAP for the particular assets. Classify deferred compensation as a liability. Upon acquisition, debt securities may be classified as trading.

PRESENTATION AND DISCLOSURE REQUIREMENTS

Presentation

ASC 710 offers the following guidance for *Deferred Compensation—Rabbi Trusts.*

- Consolidate accounts of all types of plans with the financial statements of the employer. (ASC 710-10-45-1)
- Changes in fair value of Plan D should not be recorded in OCI. (ASC 710-10-45-2)
- Employer shares held by the rabbi trust should be treated as treasury stock for EPS purposes and excluded from the denominator in basic and diluted EPS calculations.
- The obligation under the deferred compensation arrangement is reflected in the denominator of the EPS computation. (ASC 710-10-45-3)
- If an obligation is required to be settled by delivery of share of employee stock (Plan A), include those shares in the calculation of basic and diluted EPS.
- If the obligation may be settled by delivery of cash, shares of employer stock, or diversified assets (other than Plan A), all those shares should be reflected in diluted EPS, but not in basic EPS. (ASC 710-10-45-4)

Disclosure

The following disclosure on compensated absences is only:

- If the employer's obligation is from services already rendered, the obligation vests or accumulates, and payment is probable but the amount cannot be estimated, that fact should be disclosed. (ASC 710-10-50-1)

PRESENTATION AND DISCLOSURE EXAMPLES

Example 40.1: Nonqualified Deferred Compensation Plans

We have three nonqualified deferred compensation plans: the Lucien Radcliffe Executive Deferral Plans I and II (collectively referred to as "LR") and the Lucien Radcliffe Directors' Deferral Plan ("LR"), which provides certain executives and Board of Directors members, respectively, the opportunity to defer a portion of their current-year salary or stock compensation to future years. A third party manages the investments of employee deferrals. Expenses related to investment results of these deferrals are based on the change in quoted market prices of the underlying investments elected by plan participants.

Example 40.2: Deferred Compensation—Rabbi Trust—Plan A

Obligations to participants who defer stock compensation through our deferral plans are satisfied only in company stock. There is no change in the vesting term for stock awards that are deferred into these plans. Obligations related to these deferred stock awards are treated as Plan A instruments, as defined by ASC 710. These obligations are classified as equity instruments within the Capital in excess of par value line of the Consolidated Balance Sheets. No subsequent changes in fair value are recognized in the Consolidated Financial Statements for these instruments. Participants earn share-based dividend equivalents in an amount equal to the value of per-share dividends paid to common shareholders. These dividends accumulate into additional shares of common stock, and are recorded through retained earnings in the period in which dividends are paid. Vested, deferred shares are included in the denominator of basic and diluted EPS in accordance with ASC 260, *Earnings Per Share*. The dilutive impact of unvested, deferred stock awards is included in the denominator of our diluted EPS calculation.

Example 40.3: Deferred Compensation—Rabbi Trust—Plan B

Participants who defer cash compensation into our deferral plans have a range of investment options, one of which is company stock. Obligations for participants who choose this investment election are satisfied only in shares of company stock, while all other obligations are satisfied in cash. These share-based obligations are treated as Plan B instruments, as defined by ASC 710. These deferred compensation obligations are recorded as liabilities on the Consolidated Balance Sheets, in the deferred compensation line. We record compensation cost for subsequent changes in fair value of these obligations. Participants earn share-based dividend equivalents in an amount equal to the value of per-share dividends paid to common shareholders. These dividends accumulate into additional shares of common stock, and are recorded as compensation cost in the period in which the dividends are paid. At December 31, 20X2, our deferred compensation obligation included $1,398 of share-based obligations, which represents 20,949 shares. The dilutive impact of these shares is included in the denominator of our EPS calculation. Compensation cost (benefit) recognized on the adjustment of fair value for deferred awards was immaterial in the current and prior year.

Example 40.4: Nonqualified Deferred Compensation—Accounting and Schedule

Supplemental Executive Retirement Plan: The Supplemental Executive Retirement Plan ("SERP") provides awards to a limited number of executives in the form of nonqualified deferred cash compensation. Gains and losses related to these benefits and the related investment results are recorded within the S,G&A caption in the Consolidated Statements of Net Income. The SERP is frozen and no further persons can be added, and funding was reduced to a nominal amount per year for the remaining participants.

Deferred compensation liabilities expected to be satisfied in the next 12 months are classified as current liabilities in the accrued wages and other liabilities line of the Consolidated Balance Sheets. Our deferred compensation liabilities as of December 31, 20X2 and December 31, 20X1 consisted of the following:

(In thousands)	*December 31, 20X2*	*December 31, 20X1*
Deferred cash obligations in LR and LR plans	$17,986	$12,845
Deferred cash obligations in SERP plan	5,830	6,271
Deferred liability for share-based obligations in LR and LR plans	1,398	673
Other noncurrent compensation arrangements	110	100
Total deferred compensation liabilities	21,234	19,889
Less current portion	(4,047)	(2,128)
Noncurrent deferred compensation liabilities	$17,277	$17,761

Employees who transferred to Lucien Radcliffe Enterprises as part of the Enterprises Transaction were treated as terminated employees in our deferred compensation plans and will receive payouts based on their distribution elections.

Example 40.5: Rabbi Trust Asset

Rabbi Trust Assets: The Rabbi Trust is intended to be used as a source of funds to match respective funding obligations in our nonqualified deferred compensation plans. Assets held by the Rabbi Trust are recorded on our Consolidated Balance Sheets, and include company-owned life insurance ("COLI") policies, short-term money market securities, and Lucien Radcliffe common stock. The COLI policies held by the Rabbi Trust are recorded at cash surrender value on the Rabbi Trust Assets line of the Consolidated Balance Sheets and totaled $22,353 and $20,662 as of December 31, 20X2, and December 31, 20X2, respectively. The cash receipts and payments related to the company-owned life insurance policies are included in cash flows from operating activities on the Consolidated Statements of Cash Flows and changes in the cash surrender value for these assets are reflected within the S,G&A line in the Consolidated Statements of Net Income.

The short-term securities held by the Rabbi Trust are recorded at their carrying value, which approximates fair value, on the prepaid expense and other current assets line of the Consolidated Balance Sheets and totaled $984 and $3,290 as of December 31, 20X2, and December 31, 20X1, respectively. All assets held by the Rabbi Trust are restricted to their use as noted above.

Net expenses associated with our nonqualified deferred compensation plans include expenses associated with investment returns of our plan participants as well as premiums and administrative fees associated with the plans and our Rabbi Trust, and are offset by the investment returns on our COLI policies. Net expenses associated with our deferred compensation plans totaled $1,031, $1,162, and $1,236 in fiscal years 20X2, 20X1, and 20X0, respectively, and are recorded within S,G&A.

Example 40.6: Compensated Absences—Inability to Estimate

Compensated Absences—Under our vacation policy, salaried employees are provided unlimited vacation leave. Therefore, we do not record an accrual for paid leave related to these employees since we are unable to reasonably estimate the compensated absences that these employees will take.

41 ASC 712 COMPENSATION—NONRETIREMENT POSTEMPLOYMENT BENEFITS

AUTHORITATIVE LITERATURE

ASC 712 provides guidance for employers that provide benefits for former or inactive employees after the employees' termination. These benefits may include counseling, pay continuation, continuation of health care benefits, and so on. The FASB sees these as benefits provided in exchange for service.

Subtopic

ASC 712, *Compensation—Nonretirement Postemployment Benefits*, contains one Subtopic:

- ASC 712-10, *Overall*, which provides guidance and links to other topics containing guidance on nonretirement postemployment benefits.

Initial Measurement and Recognition

ASC 712 applies the criteria set forth by ASC 710, *Compensation—General*, to accrue an obligation for postemployment benefits other than pensions if:

- Services have been performed by employees,
- Employees' rights accumulate or vest,
- Payment is probable, and
- The amount is reasonably estimable.

If these benefits do not vest or accumulate, ASC 450, *Contingencies*, applies. If neither ASC 710 nor ASC 450 is applicable because the amount is not reasonably estimable, this fact must be disclosed. (ASC 712-10-25-4 and 25-5)

Subsequent Measurement

To the extent they apply, entities may refer to ASC 715-30 and 715-60 for guidance in measuring their postemployment benefit obligations.

PRESENTATION AND DISCLOSURE REQUIREMENTS

Presentation

Note: ASC 712 does not have a "45" Section.

Disclosures

The disclosure requirements for termination benefits can be found in ASC 715-20-50-1. (ASC 712-10-50-1) If other postemployment benefits are not accrued because the amount cannot be reasonably estimated, the entity must disclose that fact. (ASC 712-10-50-2) Refer to the chapter on ASC 715 and the disclosure and presentation checklist at www.wiley.com/go/FSDM2021.

PRESENTATION AND DISCLOSURE EXAMPLES

Example 41.1: Severance and Termination Benefits Resulting from Restructuring

The Company accounts for restructuring costs in accordance with ASC 712 and ASC 420, as applicable. In connection with the consummation of the merger and the relocation of the Company's headquarters to New York, New York, the Company announced a restructuring plan that went into effect upon the closing of the merger. The Company recognized $0.1 million and $3.7 million of severance and transition bonus costs related to this restructuring within general and administrative expenses in the consolidated statements of operations for the years ended December 31, 20X2 and 20X1. Severance and transition bonus payments were $0.4 million and $5.5 million during the years ended December 31, 20X2, and 20X1.

Example 41.2: Restructuring Charges

On November 29, 20X9, following the completion of a strategic review of its business, the Company's board of directors approved a workforce reduction plan, or the Workforce Reduction, to reduce its workforce headcount by approximately 38%. The Company evaluated the related employee severance and other benefits to employees in connection with the Workforce Reduction to determine whether the benefits were within the scope ASC 712, *Compensation—Nonretirement Postemployment Benefits*, or within the scope of ASC 420, *Exit or Disposal Cost Obligations,* depending on the nature of the benefit and whether it is part of an ongoing benefit arrangement under ASC 712 or a one-time termination benefit unique to the Workforce Reduction. The Company recorded restructuring expense of $0.6 million at the time of the Workforce Reduction, pursuant to ASC 420, as the Company did not have an ongoing benefit arrangement under ASC 712. The Workforce Reduction was complete as of December 31, 20X9.

The following table outlines the components of the restructuring charges during the year ended December 31, 20X9 included in the consolidated statement of operations, and ending liability recorded in the balance sheet as at December 31, 20X9 (in thousands):

	Charges incurred during the year ended December 31, 20X9	Amount paid through December 31, 20X9	Remaining liability at December 31, 20X9
Employee severance, bonus, and other	$ 605	$ (232)	$ 373
Total restructuring charges	$ 605	$ (232)	$ 373

42 ASC 715 COMPENSATION— RETIREMENT BENEFITS

AUTHORITATIVE LITERATURE

Subtopics

ASC 715, *Compensation—Retirement Benefits*, contains six Subtopics:

- ASC 715-10, *Overall*, sets the objectives and the scope for ASC 715.
- ASC 715-20, *Defined Benefit Plans—General*, provides guidance on the presentation and disclosure requirements for single-employer defined benefit pension and other postretirement plans. (ASC 715-20-05-1)
- ASC 715-30, *Defined Benefit Plans—Pension*, provides accounting guidance related to single-employer defined benefit pension plans.
- ASC 715-60, *Defined Benefit Plans—Other Postretirement*, provides guidance on single-employer defined benefit plans other than postretirement benefit plans.
- ASC 715-70, *Defined Contribution Plans*, provides guidance on defined contribution plans.
- ASC 715-80, *Multiemployer Plans*, provides guidance on multiemployer plans as opposed to multiple employer plans. (ASC 715-10-05-2)

Overview

When an entity provides benefits that can be estimated in advance to its retired employees and their beneficiaries, the arrangement is a pension plan or a postretirement plan. These plans include unfunded, insured, trust fund, defined contribution and defined benefit plans, and deferred compensation contracts, if equivalent. Separate deferred profit sharing plans and pension payments to selected employees on a case-by-case basis are *not* considered pension or postretirement plans.

The typical plan is written and the amount of benefits can be determined by reference to the associated documents. The plan and its provisions can also be implied, however, from unwritten but established past practices.

The accounting for such arrangements is complex. In large part the complexity stems from a variety of "smoothing" features that necessitate the use of various accruals and deferrals, and the reporting of certain elements within other comprehensive income. Presentation of benefit plan expense and related items involves lengthy and complex notes.

Although the Codification is generally based on an asset and liability model, the foundation content of ASC 715 is based on an expense recognition model. Expense recognition models focus on remeasurement. Therefore, much of the guidance in ASC 715 is found in the subsequent measurement sections. (ASC 715-10-05-3)

Scope and Scope Exceptions

ASC 715 applies to all entities and many types of compensation arrangements including:

- Any arrangement that is in substance a postretirement benefit plan (regardless of its form or means or timing of funding),
- Written and unwritten plans,
- Deferred compensation contracts with individuals which taken together are the equivalent of a plan, and

- Health and other welfare benefits for employees on disability retirement.
  (ASC 715-10-15-3)

The guidance also applies to:

- Settlement of all or part of an employer's pension or other postretirement benefit obligation,
- Curtailment of a pension or other postretirement benefit plan, and
- Employers that provide pension or other postretirement benefits as part of a termination benefit not addressed in other Subtopics.
  (ASC 715-10-15-4)

ASC 715 does *not* apply to:

- Contracts with "selected employees under individual contracts with specific terms determined on an individual-by-individual basis" and
- Postemployment benefits paid after employment, but before retirement, like lay-off benefits.
  (ASC 715-10-15-5)

The ASC also provides guidance on the accounting treatment of contributions to the plan and significant events requiring a remeasurement occurring during the interim period between the month-end measurement date and the fiscal year-end.

ASC 715-20 follows the scope guidance in ASC 715-10 and applies to all single-employer defined benefit pension or other post-retirement benefit plans.

ASC 715-30 follows the same scope and scope exceptions as ASC 715-10 with the exceptions noted below. (ASC 715-30-15-1)

ASC 715-30 applies to defined benefit plans, including:

- Cash balance plans
- Termination benefits provided in the event of a voluntary or involuntary severance if the arrangement is in substance a termination
  (ASC 715-30-15-3)

This Subtopic does not apply to:

- Life insurance benefits provided outside a pension plan or
- Other postretirement health and welfare benefits. For health care benefits provided through a pension plan, look to the guidance in ASC 715-60.
  (ASC 715-30-15-4)

For plans with characteristics of defined benefit and defined contribution plans, entities should look to the guidance in ASC 715-70-15-2. (ASC 715-30-15-4A)

ASC 715-60 follows the scope guidance in ASC 715-10 with some qualifications. (ASC 715-60-15-1) It applies to single-employer plans. (ASC 715-60-15-6) It does not apply to:

- Pension or life insurance benefits provided through a pension plan. That guidance can be found in ASC 715-30.

- Disability benefits paid to former or inactive employees on disability retirement. That guidance is found in ASC 712.
- Disability benefits paid pursuant to a pension plan. See ASC 715-30 for guidance on those plans.
- COBRA benefits.
  (ASC 715-60-15-6)

The ASC 715-60 section on Medicare Prescription Drug, Improvement, and Modernization Act applies to single-employer defined benefit postretirement health plans. (ASC 715-60-15-11) The Subtopic does not address:

- Situations where the expected subsidy exceeds the employer's share of the cost on which the subsidy is based
- Multiemployer health and welfare benefit plans
  (ASC 715-60-15-12)

ASC 715-60 applies to:

- Settlement of all or a part of an employee's accumulated postretirement benefit obligation (APBO) or curtailment of a postretirement benefit plan
- Termination benefits not otherwise addressed by ASC 420, 710, 712, 715-30
  (ASC 715-60-15-15 and 15-18)

The guidance does not apply to a split-dollar life insurance arrangement that provides a specified benefit to an employee that is limited to the employee's active service period with an employer. (ASC 715-60-15-21)

The guidance in ASC 715-80 does not apply to multiple-employee plans, which are in substance aggregations of single-employee plans, combined to allow participants to pool plan assets for investment purposes or to reduce administrative costs. (ASC 715-80-15-3)

ASC 715-10, *Overall*

ASC 715-10 sets the objectives and scope for ASC 715. See the previous section for scope and scope exceptions.

ASC 715-20, *Defined Benefit Plans—General*

ASC 715-20, *Compensation—Retirement Benefits, Defined Benefits Plans, General*, provides disclosure and presentation guidance for defined benefit pension and other retirement benefit plans. The disclosure and presentation requirements for ASC 715-20 and can be found in the Presentation and Disclosure Requirements section later in this Chapter.

ASC 715-30, *Defined Benefit Plans—Pension*

ASC 715-30 specifies the accrual basis of accounting for pension costs. It includes three primary characteristics:

1. Delayed recognition. Changes are not recognized immediately but are subsequently recognized in a gradual and systematic way.
2. Reporting net cost. Various expense and income items are aggregated and reported as one net amount.
3. Offsetting assets and liabilities. Assets and liabilities are sometimes shown net.

Fundamentally, pension accounting includes:

- Measurement of net periodic pension costs and benefit obligations,
- Assumptions, and
- Measurement of plan assets.
  (ASC 715-30-05-6)

ASC 715-30 focuses directly on the terms of the plan to assist in the recognition of compensation cost over the service period of the employees. The full amount of under- and overfunding of pension plans is reported in the statement of financial position.

The principal emphasis of ASC 715-30 is the present value of the pension obligation and the fair value of plan assets. The main accounting issues revolve around the amount of expense to recognize on the income statement and the liability to be accrued on the statement of financial position. Because of the substantial use of smoothing, the periodic expense to be recognized under GAAP is a modified version of the actual economic consequence of the employer's commitment to pay future benefits. Theoretically, over the full-time horizon, which is measured in decades, all the expense should be recognized in results of operations.

ASC 715-30 also establishes standards to be followed by sponsors of defined benefit pension plans when:

- Obligations are settled,
- Plans are curtailed,
- Benefits are terminated,
- Events require adjustment, or
- Amounts previously recognized in AOCI should be recognized in earnings.
  (ASC 715-30-05-9)

The benefit formula, which is the basis for determining payments to plan participants, incorporates many factors including employee compensation, employee service longevity, employee age, and the like, and is considered to provide the best indication of pension obligations and costs. (ASC 715-30-20) It is used as the basis for determining the pension cost recognized in the financial statements each fiscal year.

Components of Net Periodic Pension Cost The benefits earned and costs recognized over the employees' service periods are computed by reference to the pension plan's benefit formula. Net periodic pension cost consists of the sum of the five components in the exhibit below. (ASC 715-30-35-4)

Exhibit—Five Components of Net Periodic Pension Cost

Component	Description	Effect on Pension Expense
1. Service cost	Expense from the increase in the PBO resulting from employee services rendered during the current year.	Increases
2. Interest cost on the liability, the PBO	Expense related to the PBO resulting from the discounted pension liability.	Increases
3. Actual return on plan assets	Adjustment for interest and dividends that the funds accumulated and increases and decreases in the fair value of the fund's assets.	Generally increases

Component	Description	Effect on Pension Expense
4. Amortization of any prior service cost included in AOCI	Allocation of prior service cost of providing retroactive benefits.	Generally increases
5. Gain or loss	Results from the difference between actual obligations different from assumptions, a change in assumptions, or a change in the value of either PBO or plan asset.	Decreases or increases

To provide smoothing of the effects of what are viewed as short-term fluctuations, the net gain or loss may be amortized. If gains and losses are not recognized immediately as a component of net periodic cost, they should be recognized in other comprehensive income as they occur, thus affecting the statement of financial position display in full, even as the expense recognition is deferred and amortized. (ASC 715-30-35-21)

Plan asset gains or losses result from both realized and unrealized amounts. They represent periodic differences between the actual return on assets and the expected return. (ASC 715-30-35-22)

The expected return is generated by multiplying the expected long-term rate of return by the market-related value of plan assets. (ASC 705-30-20) Market-related value is a concept unique to pension accounting. It results from the previously discussed actuarial smoothing techniques under ASC 715-30. Market-related value is either:

- The fair value of the plan assets or
- A calculated value that recognizes, in a systematic and rational manner, changes in fair value over not more than five years.
(ASC 715-30-20)

Net periodic pension costs—gain or loss Net periodic pension costs include only the expected return on plan assets. Any difference between actual and expected returns is deferred through the gain or loss component of net pension cost. If actual return is greater than expected return, net pension cost is increased to adjust the actual return to the lower expected return. If expected return is greater than actual return, the adjustment results in a decrease to net pension cost to adjust the actual return to the higher expected return. If the unrecognized net gain or loss is large enough, it is amortized. The full amount (measured by projected or accumulated benefit obligations, for pensions and other postretirement benefits, respectively) of over- or underfunding is recognized in the statement of financial position recognition, with the offsetting entry being to other comprehensive income. (ASC 715-30-25-1)

Cash Balance Plans Some employers have terminated classic defined benefit pension plans and replaced them with "cash balance" plans. The scope of ASC 715-30-15 includes plans that are characterized by defined principal-crediting rates as percentages of salary, and offer defined, noncontingent interest-crediting rates that entitle participants to future interest credits at stated, fixed rates until retirement. (ASC 715-30-15-3) The standard states that "cash balance" plans with the foregoing attributes should be deemed defined benefit plans. (ASC 715-30-20) This is true because an employer's contributions to a cash balance plan trust and the earnings on the invested plan assets may be unrelated to the principal and interest credits to participants' hypothetical accounts.

The benefit promise in the cash balance arrangement is not pay related and, accordingly, use of a projected unit credit method is neither required nor appropriate for purposes of measuring the benefit obligation and annual cost of benefits earned. The appropriate cost attribution approach, therefore, is the traditional unit credit method.

Reporting Funded Status When There Is More Than One Plan When the reporting entity has more than one plan, it is not acceptable to display one single net amount of over- or underfunding. Rather, all overfunded plans must be separately aggregated, as must underfunded plans. (ASC 715-30-25-2) The amount of overfunding is included in noncurrent assets, with no portion of the overfunding permitted to be displayed as a current asset. On the other hand, total underfunding is allocated between current and noncurrent liabilities, with the current portion computed (on a plan-by-plan basis) as the sum of the actuarial present value of benefits included in the benefit obligation payable over the ensuing twelve months, to the extent that it exceeds the fair value of plan assets.

Reporting Funded Status and Benefit Plan Transactions and Events in Comprehensive Income An employer must recognize all transactions and events affecting the over- or underfunded status of a defined benefit postretirement plan in comprehensive income (or changes in unrestricted net assets, if the entity is a not-for-profit organization) in the year in which they occur.

The reporting entity must recognize as a component of other comprehensive income the gains or losses and prior service costs or credits arising during that reporting period that are not recognized as components of net periodic benefit cost of the period pursuant to ASC 715-30 and ASC 715-60. For example, if a plan amendment is adopted that credits employees with prior service, this is not reflected immediately in benefit costs, but rather is subject to amortization (i.e., it is recognized as part of pension or other postretirement benefit plan cost over an extended period of time). These requirements make it necessary to record in other comprehensive income, in the year the amendment is effected, the full amount of the prior service cost less what is recognized in pension cost in that period. (ASC 715-30-35-11)

The effect of recording this debit in comprehensive income is balanced by recording an additional underfunding liability. Also, in accordance with ASC 740, this is treated as a temporary difference, since the liability has a different basis (carrying value) for financial reporting purposes than it does for tax purposes. The deferred tax asset (in the normal circumstances) or liability will be recorded. The deferred tax effects, in turn, will be allocated to other financial statement components, including comprehensive income. (ASC 715-30-25-3)

For each annual statement of income presented, these amounts should be recognized in accumulated other comprehensive income, showing *separately* the amounts ascribed to net gain or loss and net prior service cost or credit. Those amounts are separated into amounts arising during the period and reclassification adjustments of other comprehensive income as a result of being recognized as components of net periodic benefit cost for the period. (ASC 715-30- 35-63A)

Annuity and Insurance Contracts Benefits of annuity contracts and other insurance contracts that are equivalent in substance are excluded from plan assets and from the accumulated and projected benefit obligations if:

- They are valid and irrevocable,
- They transfer significant risks to an unrelated insurance company (not a captive insurer), and
- There is no reasonable doubt as to their payment.

Settlements Settlements include both the purchase of annuity contracts without participation rights and lump-sum cash payments. The following three criteria must all be met in order to constitute a pension obligation settlement:

1. It must be irrevocable.
2. It must relieve the obligor of primary responsibility for the obligation.
3. It must eliminate significant risks associated with the obligation and the assets used to effect it. (ASC 715-30-20)

Transactions that do not meet these three criteria do not qualify for treatment as a settlement under ASC 715-30.

If the entire projected benefit obligation is settled, any ASC 715-30 unrecognized net gain (loss) is immediately recognized. A pro rata portion is recognized in the case of partial settlement. If the obligation is settled by purchasing annuities with participation rights, the cost of the right of participation is deducted from the gain (but not from the loss) before recognition. (ASC 715-30-35-79)

If the cost of all settlements is greater than the sum of the service cost and interest components of net periodic pension cost, the entity must recognize the gain or loss in earnings. If the total of the interest cost and service cost components of the ASC 715-30 periodic pension cost is greater than or equal to the settlement costs during a given year, the recognition of the above gain (loss) is not required, but is permitted. However, a consistent policy must be followed in this regard. (ASC 715-30-35-82) The settlement cost is generally the cash paid, or the cost of annuities without participation rights purchased, or the cost of annuities with participation rights reduced by the cost of the right of participation.

The maximum gain or loss subject to recognition in earnings when an obligation is settled is the net gain or loss that is remaining in accumulated other comprehensive income (AOCI). The maximum gain or loss, first determined at the date of settlement, is fully reported in earnings only if the entire projected benefit obligation is settled; if it is only partially settled, only a pro rata portion of the maximum gain or loss can be recognized.

Under an annuity contract settlement, an unrelated insurance company unconditionally accepts an obligation to provide the required benefits. The following criteria must be met for this type of settlement:

- It must be irrevocable.
- It must involve a transfer of material risk to the insurance company.

There can be no reasonable doubt as to the ability of the insurance company to meet its contractual obligation. (ASC 715-30-35-86) The substance of any annuity contract with participation rights must relieve the employer of most of the risks and rewards or it does not meet the criteria. (ASC 715-30-35-87)

Curtailments Curtailments include early discontinuance of employee services or cessation or suspension of a plan. Additional benefits may not be earned, although future service time may be counted towards vesting. A curtailment must meet the following criteria:

- It must materially diminish present employees' future service, or
- It must stop or materially diminish the accumulation of benefits by a significant number of employees.
  (ASC 715-30-20)

A curtailment results in the elimination of future years of service. To the extent that prior service costs are included in AOCI, and this is associated with service years no longer expected to be rendered, this must be recognized currently as a loss. This would occur if prior service cost is being amortized over a term that no longer accurately reflects expected future service by the post-curtailment workforce. Prior service cost, in this context, includes that resulting from plan amendments. (ASC 715-30-35-92) The pro rata portions of any unrecognized cost of retroactive plan amendments are immediately recognized as a loss.

If curtailment results in a decrease in the projected benefit obligation, a gain is indicated. An increase in the projected benefit obligation (excluding termination benefits) indicates a loss. This indicated gain (loss) is then netted against the loss from unrecognized prior service cost recognized in accordance with the preceding paragraph. (ASC 715-30-35-93) The net result is the curtailment gain or curtailment loss. A gain is recognized upon actual employee termination or plan suspension. A loss is recognized when both the curtailment is probable and the effects are reasonably estimable. (ASC 715-30-35-94)

Termination Benefits Termination benefits may be categorized as special termination benefits for contractual termination benefits.

- Special short time period benefits require that a loss and a liability be recognized when the offer is accepted and the amount can be reasonably estimated.
- Contractual termination benefits require that a loss and a liability be recognized when it is probable that employees will receive the benefits and the amount can be reasonably estimated.
(ASC 715-30-25-10)

The cost of these benefits is the cash paid at termination and the present value of future payments. (ASC 715-30-25-11) Termination benefits and curtailments can occur together.

Component Disposal Gains or losses, that result because of a disposal of a component of the entity are recognized according to the provisions of ASC 360.

ASC 715-60, *Defined Benefit Plans—Other Postretirement*

ASC 715-60 contains the guidance for employers' accounting for other (than pension) postretirement employee benefits (commonly called OPEB). This guidance prescribes a single method for measuring and recognizing an employer's APBO. It applies to all forms of postretirement benefits, although the most material such benefit is usually postretirement health care coverage. (ASC 715-60-05-6) It uses the fundamental framework established by ASC 715-30. To the extent that the promised benefits are similar, the accounting provisions are similar. Only when there is a compelling reason is the accounting different. (ASC 715-60-05-7)

The guidance considers OPEB to be a form of deferred compensation and requires accrual accounting. The terms of the individual contract govern the accrual of the employer's obligation for deferred compensation and the cost is attributed to employee service periods until full eligibility to receive benefits is attained. The employer's obligation for OPEB is fully accrued when the employee attains full eligibility for all expected benefits.

Funded status is determined by the difference between the fair value of plan assets and the accumulated benefit obligation. (ASC 715-60-35-5)

Postretirement benefits can include tuition assistance, legal services, day care, housing subsidies, health insurance coverage (probably the most significant), and other benefits. The amount of benefits usually depends on a benefit formula. OPEB may be provided to current employees, former employees, beneficiaries, and covered dependents. The guidance applies to:

- Settlement of the APBO, and
- Curtailment of a plan as part of a special termination benefit offer.

The guidance also applies to deferred compensation contracts with individuals. Taken together, these contracts are equivalent to an OPEB plan. ASC 715-60 does not apply to benefits provided through a pension plan. If part of a larger plan with active employees, the OPEB is segregated and accounted for in accordance with this standard. If not materially different, estimates, averages, and computational shortcuts may be used.

The basic tenet of ASC 715-60 is that accrual accounting is better than cash basis accounting. Recognition and measurement of the obligation to provide OPEB is required in order to provide relevant information to financial statement users. Although funding and cash flow information is incorporated into the statement, the overall liability is the primary focus.

The guidance attempts, in accordance with the terms of the substantive plan, to account for the exchange transaction that takes place between the employer, who is ultimately responsible for providing OPEB, and the employee who provides services, in part at least, to obtain the OPEB. ASC 715-60 accounting requires that the liability for OPEB be fully accrued when the employee is fully eligible for all of the expected benefits. The fact that the employee may continue to work beyond this date is not relevant, since the employee has already provided the services required to earn the OPEB.

OPEB are considered to be deferred compensation earned in an exchange transaction during the time periods that the employee provides services. The expected cost generally is attributed in equal amounts (unless the plan attributes a disproportionate share of benefits to early years) over the periods from the employee's hiring date (unless credit for the service is only granted from a later plan eligibility or entry date) to the date that the employee attains full eligibility for all benefits expected to be received. This accrual is followed even if the employee provides service beyond the date of full eligibility.

Accounting for Postretirement Benefits The expected postretirement benefit obligation (EPBO) is the actuarial present value (APV) as of a specific date of the benefits expected to be paid to the employee, beneficiaries, and covered dependents. Measurement of the EPBO is based on the following:

- Expected amount and timing of future benefits.
- Expected future costs.
- Extent of cost sharing (contributions, deductibles, coinsurance provisions, etc.) between employer, employee, and others (i.e., the government). The APV of employee contributions reduces the APV of the EPBO. Obligations to return employee contributions, plus interest if applicable, are recognized as a component of EPBO.
  (ASC 715-60-35-2)

The EPBO includes an assumed salary progression for a pay-related plan. Future compensation levels represent the best estimate after considering the individual employees involved, general price levels, seniority, productivity, promotions, indirect effects, and the like.

The APBO is the APV as of a specific date of all future benefits attributable to service by an employee to that date. It represents the portion of the EPBO earned to date. After full eligibility is attained, the APBO equals the EPBO.

The APBO also includes an assumed salary progression for a pay-related plan. Thus, this term is more comparable to the projected benefit obligation (PBO) under ASC 715-30. The accumulated benefit obligation in ASC 715-30 has no counterpart in ASC 715-60.

Net periodic postretirement benefit costs include the following components:

- Service cost
- Interest cost—interest on the APBO
- Actual return on plan assets
- Gain or loss
- Amortization of unrecognized prior service cost
  (ASC 715-60-35-9)

Note that return on plan assets is included in the periodic expense determination, consistent with accounting for defined benefit pension plans. However, in virtually all cases, OPEB plans are unfunded, and thus there will be no asset return. If a trust has been established to fund these benefits, it does not necessarily have to be "bankruptcy proof," or insulated completely from the claims of general creditors, to qualify as plan assets in accordance with ASC 715-60-55. On the other hand, assets held in a trust that explicitly makes them available to the general creditors in bankruptcy do not qualify as plan assets under ASC 715-60. The funded status of other postretirement defined benefit plans must be formally reported in the statement of financial position, as described above.

Service costs and interest costs are defined and measured in the same manner by both ASC 715-60 and ASC 715-30. However, under ASC 715-60, interest increases the APBO while under ASC 715-30, interest increases the PBO.

Under ASC 715-60, a single method is required to be followed in measuring and recognizing the net periodic cost and the liability involved. That method attributes the EPBO to employee service rendered to the full eligibility date.

Assumptions ASC 715-60 requires the use of explicit assumptions using the best estimates available of the plan's future experience, solely with regard to the individual assumption under consideration. Plan continuity is to be presumed, unless there is evidence to the contrary. Principal actuarial assumptions include:

- Discount rates,
- Retirement age,
- Participation rates (contributory plans),
- Salary progression (pay-related plans), and
- Probability of payment (turnover, dependency status, mortality).
  (ASC 715-60-35-73a-e)

Present value factors for health care OPEB include:

- Cost trend rates,
- Medicare reimbursement rates, and
- Per capita claims cost by age.
  (ASC 715-60-35-73f)

Current interest rates, as of the measurement date, are used for discount rates in present value calculations. Examples include high-quality, fixed-income investments with similar amounts and timing and interest rates at which the postretirement benefit obligations could be settled. The EPBO, APBO, service cost, and interest cost components use assumed discount rates. (ASC 715-60-35-79)

The expected long-term rate of return on plan assets is an assumption about the average rate of return expected on contributions during the period and on existing plan assets. Current returns on plan assets and reinvestment returns are considered in arriving at the rate to be used. Related income taxes, if applicable, reduce the rate. Expected return on plan assets and the fair value of plan assets use this rate in their calculation. (ASC 715-60-35-84) Since the Employee Retirement Security Act of 1974 (ERISA) does not require OPEB plans to be funded via the separate trust vehicles used for pension plans, OPEB plans are often unfunded. Thus, there are no "plan assets." Instead, the sponsor pays benefits directly, as they become due, from general corporate assets.

Effect of the Prescription Drug Benefit on OPEB Computations The Medicare Prescription Drug, Improvement, and Modernization Act Subsections provide guidance on accounting for the effects of the Act. (ASC 715-60-05-8) Under ASC 715-60, the effects of the Act on current period measurements of postretirement benefit costs and the APBO must be accounted for, if defined criteria are met.

The guidance regarding accounting for the subsidiary set forth in ASC 715-60 applies only to sponsors of a single-employer defined benefit postretirement health care plan for which

1. The employers have concluded that prescription drug benefits available under the plan to some or all participants for some or all future years are "actuarially equivalent" to Medicare Part D and thus qualify for the subsidy under the Act, and
2. The expected subsidiaries will offset or reduce the employers' shares of the cost of the underlying postretirement prescription drug coverage on which the subsidies are based. (ASC 715-60-15-11)

ASC 715-60 also provides guidance for disclosures about the effects of the subsidy for employers that sponsor postretirement health care benefit plans that provide prescription drug coverage but for which the employers have not yet been able to determine actuarial equivalency.

The central question raised has been whether a subsidy is substantively similar to other Medicare benefits that existed when ASC 715-60 was issued—and therefore to be accounted for as a reduction of the APBO and net periodic postretirement benefit cost—or whether the subsidy represents a payment to the employer that is determined by reference to its plan's benefit payments but is not, in and of itself, a direct reduction of postretirement benefit costs. A secondary issue pertains to the timing of accounting recognition of the subsidy.

FASB concluded that the former interpretation is the correct one. That is, measures of the APBO and net periodic postretirement benefit cost on or after the date of enactment are to reflect the effects of the Act. When an employer initially accounts for the subsidy, its effect on the APBO is to be accounted for as an actuarial experience gain. Additionally, the subsidy reduces the service cost when it is recognized as a component of net periodic postretirement benefit cost. If the estimated expected subsidy changes, the effect is to be treated as an actuarial experience gain or loss.

Plan amendments will also affect the reporting of OPEB cost and the APBO. If prescription drug benefits currently available under an existing plan are deemed not actuarially equivalent as of the date of enactment of the Act, but the plan is later amended to provide actuarially equivalent benefits, the direct effect of the amendment on the APBO and the effect on the APBO from any resulting subsidy to which the employer is expected to be entitled as a result of the amendment are to be combined, and deemed to be an actuarial experience gain if it reduces APBO. On the other hand, if the combined effect increases the APBO, it is deemed to be prior service cost that is to be accounted for consistent with ASC 715-60.

Additionally, according to ASC 715-60, if a plan that provides prescription drug benefits that previously were deemed actuarially equivalent under the Act is subsequently amended to reduce its prescription drug coverage such that the coverage is not considered actuarially equivalent, any actuarial experience gain related to the subsidy previously recognized is unaffected. The combined net effect on the APBO of (1) the subsequent plan amendment that reduces benefits under the plan and thus disqualifies the benefits as actuarially equivalent, and (2) the elimination of the subsidy is to be accounted for as prior service cost (credit) as of the date the amendment is adopted.

In the periods in which the subsidy affects the employer's accounting for the plan, this will have no effect on any plan-related temporary difference accounted for under ASC 740, because the subsidy is exempt from federal taxation.

There may be a time lag before the employer is able to determine whether the benefits provided by its plan are actuarially equivalent. During the interim period, it is required to disclose the existence of the Act and the fact that measures of the APBO or net periodic postretirement benefit cost do not reflect any amount associated with the subsidy because the employer is unable to conclude whether the benefits provided by the plan are actuarially equivalent to Medicare Part D under the Act.

In interim and annual financial statements for the first period in which an employer includes the effects of the subsidy in measuring the APBO and the first period in which an employer includes the effects of the subsidy in measuring net periodic postretirement benefit cost, it is required to disclose the following:

- The reduction in the APBO for the subsidy related to benefits attributed to past service.
- The effect of the subsidy on the measurement of net periodic postretirement benefit cost for the current period. That effect includes (1) any amortization of the actuarial experience gain in (a) as a component of the net amortization called for by ASC 715-60, (2) the reduction in current period service cost due to the subsidy, and (3) the resulting reduction in interest cost on the APBO as a result of the subsidy.
- Any other disclosures required by ASC 715-20, specifically, disclosure of an explanation of any significant change in the benefit obligation or plan assets not otherwise apparent in the other disclosures required by that standard.

When ASC 715-60 is initially adopted, a remeasurement of the plan's assets and APBO, including the effects of the subsidy, if applicable, as well as the other effects of the Act, is to be made as of the earlier of (1) the plan's measurement date that normally would have followed enactment of the Act, or (2) the end of the employer's interim or annual period that includes the date of the Act's enactment. Alternatively, employers are permitted, but not required, to perform that remeasurement as of the date of enactment. The measurement of the APBO is to be based on the plan provisions in place on the measurement date (i.e., later amendments are not to be anticipated in the computation).

Deferred Compensation Contracts If the aggregate deferred compensation contracts with individual employees are equivalent to a pension plan, the contracts are accounted for according to ASC 715-30 and ASC 715-60. All other deferred compensation contracts are accounted for according to ASC 710.

ASC 715-60 states that the terms of the individual contract will govern the accrual of the employee's obligation for deferred compensation and the cost is to be attributed over the employee service period until full eligibility is attained.

ASC 715-70, *Defined Contribution Plans*

In the typical defined contribution plan, the contribution is either discretionary or derived from a formula, and that amount is the expense the sponsor should report in its financial statements for the year. Benefits are generally paid from the pool of accumulated contributions and are limited to the plan assets available to pay them. If, however, the defined contribution plan has defined benefits, the provision is calculated as required under ASC 715-30.

ASC 715-80, *Multiemployer Pension Plans*

A multiemployer plan is one to which two or more unrelated employers contribute, often pursuant to collectively bargained, union-sponsored agreements. For essentially practical reasons, the Codification requires that the contribution for the period be recognized as net pension cost and that any contributions due and unpaid be recognized as a liability. Thus, most of the complexities arising from smoothing are avoided in accounting for sponsors participating in multiemployer plans. Assets of all the employers sponsoring this type of plan are usually commingled and not segregated or restricted. A board of trustees usually administers these plans. If there is a withdrawal of an employer from this type of plan and if an obligation to make up any funding deficiency is either probable or reasonably possible, ASC 450 applies.

   The existence of an executed agreement does not require recognition by an employer of a liability beyond currently due and unpaid contributions. (ASC 715-80-55-2)

PRACTICE ALERT

While SEC comments pertain to public entities, they can often provide valuable practice pointers for preparers of nonpublic entities. In the area of retirement benefits, the SEC asked entities to provide detail about several items:

- The clarity of disclosures
- The discount rate used to determine the periodic benefit obligation
- Rates of return on fund investments
- Whether a corridor was used to amortize the actuarial gains or losses, how the corridor was determined, and the period for amortization of the actual gains and losses in excess of the corridor
- Reasons for the change in the expected return assumption
- Compliance with fair value disclosure requirements related determining the expected return on plan assets
- If a calculated value was used to determine the expected return on plan assets

PRESENTATION AND DISCLOSURE REQUIREMENTS

Defined Benefit Plan

Presentation

Balance Sheet The balance sheet must present the funded status of the plan. An overfunded plan is presented as a net benefit asset. An underfunded plan and an unfunded plan are presented as a net benefit liability. Plan benefits cannot be offset with another plan's net benefit liability. (ASC 715-30-25-6) The entity, however, must aggregate all overfunded plans with that recorded as a net benefit asset. Likewise, unfunded and underfunded plans should be aggregated as a net benefit liability. (ASC 715-20-45-2) Only assets that meet the definition of plan assets can offset the liability on the balance sheet. If that definition is not met, the assets are presented gross on the balance sheet.

Plan assets are measured on the balance sheet date or, as a practical expedient, on the calendar month end closest to the fiscal year-end. (ASC 715-30-35-62 and 35-63A)

The categorization of current or noncurrent is done on a plan-by-plan basis. The current liability is the amount by which the actuarial present value of benefits included in the benefit obligation payable in the next twelve months exceeds the fair value of plan assets. An overfunded plan is classified as noncurrent. (ASC 715-20-45-3)

Income Statement Entities should report:

- The service cost component in the same line item as other compensation costs arising from services rendered by the pertinent employees during the period, except for any amount being capitalized in connection with the production or construction of an asset such as inventory or property, plant, and equipment.
- The other components of net periodic pension cost, separately from the service cost compensation and outside a subtotal of income from operations.
  (ASC 715-20-45-3A)

Statement of Stockholders' Equity Gains and losses may be recognized in AOCI and subsequently amortized as a component of net periodic benefit cost. Prior service costs or credits are accounted for in a similar manner. (ASC 715-30-25-4)

Disclosure Public companies should disclose the items found in ASC 715-20-50-1. Public and nonpublic entities with two or more plans should follow the disclosure guidance in ASC 715-20-50-2 through 50-4. Disclosure for nonpublic entities can be found in ASC 715-20-50-5. Disclosure requirements for postretirement plans are, of necessity, voluminous and complex and generally focus on:

- Description of the plan
- The amounts recognized on the balance sheet
- A reconciliation of the benefit obligation and plan assets
- Plan assets, including strategies, classes, valuation, and concentrations of risk
- Net periodic benefit cost
- Other comprehensive income
- Expected cash flows
- Assumptions used in calculating the benefit obligation and the net periodic benefit cost

ASC 715 also offers guidance on disclosures for:

- Postretirement healthcare plans
- Medicare Prescription Drug, Improvement, and Modernization Act of 2003
- Curtailments and settlements
- Termination benefits
- Defined contribution plans
- Multiemployer plans

Details of the disclosures for public and nonpublic entities on the checklist can be found at www.wiley.com/go/FSDM2021.

PRESENTATION AND DISCLOSURE EXAMPLES

Example 42.1: Description of Pension and Postretirement Benefit Plans

During fiscal 20X2, we recognized an aggregate net benefit for employee defined benefit plans of $406. During fiscal 20X1, we recognized an aggregate net benefit for employee defined benefit plans of $973. During fiscal 20X0, we recognized an aggregate net expense for employee defined benefit plans of $1,505. The estimated income for these defined benefit plans for fiscal 20X3 is $200.

The Company recognizes the funded status of its defined benefit pension plans and other postretirement benefit plans, measured as the difference between the fair value of the plan assets and the benefit obligation. Benefit obligation balances reflect the projected benefit obligation ("PBO") for our pension plans and accumulated postretirement benefit obligations ("APBO") or our other postretirement benefit plans. The weighted average discount rate used to determine the pension benefit obligation was 3.50% and 3.90% as of March 31, 20X2 and 20X1, respectively. The fair value of the plan assets was $145,828 and $160,682 as of March 31, 20X2 and 20X1, respectively. The benefit obligation was $205,996 and $206,369 as of March 31, 20X2 and 20X1, respectively, resulting in an unfunded liability of $60,168 and $45,687 as of March 31, 20X2 and 20X1, respectively, which is primarily recorded within accrued pension and postemployment liabilities on the consolidated balance sheet.

Example 42.2: Description of Pension and Postretirement Benefit Plans

LRB has company-sponsored retirement plans covering substantially all employees. In total, LRB has three defined benefit plans. Pension benefits associated with these plans generally are based on each participant's years of service, compensation, and age at retirement or termination. The primary defined-benefit pension plan was closed to new participants effective January 1, 20X1. The Company also provides certain postretirement health care and life insurance benefits for its employees who reach retirement age while employed by the Company and were employed by the Company prior to January 1, 20X0.

The Company has made deposits for its defined benefit plans with independent trustees. Trust funds and deposits with insurance companies are maintained to provide pension benefits to plan participants and their beneficiaries. There are no plan assets in the nonqualified plan due to its nature. For its postretirement health care and life insurance benefit plans, the Company has set aside amounts at least equal to annual benefit payments with an independent trustee.

Example 42.3: Pension and Other Postretirement Benefit Liabilities Presented in Accumulated Other Comprehensive Income

Accumulated Other Comprehensive Loss The components of AOCL, net of income taxes, are as follows:

	March 31,	
	20X0	*20X9*
Derivatives	$ (1,426)	$ 735
Pension and other postretirement benefit liabilities	(93,353)	(74,670)
Cumulative translation adjustment	(6,215)	(9,032)
Total accumulated other comprehensive loss	$ (100,994)	$ (82,967)

Example 42.4: Schedule of Changes to Pension and Other Postretirement Benefits in Accumulated Other Comprehensive Income

The following table details the amounts reclassified from AOCI to earnings as well as the changes in derivatives, pension and other postretirement benefits, and foreign currency translation, net of income tax:

Years ended March 31,

	20X2				20X1			
	Derivatives	Pension and Other Postretirement Benefits	Cumulative Translation Adjustment	Total	Derivatives	Pension and Other Postretirement Benefits	Cumulative Translation Adjustment	Total
Beginning of year AOCI	$ 735	$ (74,670)	$ (9,032)	$ (82,967)	$ 1,904	$ (66,656)	$ (39,544)	$ (104,296)
Change in fair value of derivatives	(1,555)	—	—	(1,555)	(1,169)	—	—	(1,169)
Net gains reclassified from AOCI	(606)	—	—	(606)	—	—	—	—
Net actuarial losses reclassified from AOCI (1)	—	3,247	—	3,247	—	2,172	—	2,172
Prior service costs reclassified from AOCI*	—	(313)	—	(313)	—	(238)	—	(238)
Valuation adjustment for pension and postretirement benefit plans*	—	(21,617)	—	(21,617)	—	(9,948)	—	(9,948)
Currency translation gains reclassified from AOCI**	—	—	3,150	3,150	—	—	37,542	37,542
Net change in cumulative translation adjustment	—	—	(333)	(333)	—	—	(7,030)	(7,030)
End of year AOCI	$ (1,426)	$ (93,353)	$ (6,215)	$ (100,994)	$ 735	$ (74,670)	$ (9,032)	$ (82,967)

* Amounts related to our pension and other postretirement benefits that were reclassified from AOCI were recorded as a component of net periodic benefit cost for each period presented.

** Amounts related to the foreign currency translation gains realized upon the divestiture of our furniture business and eyewear brands in the second quarter of fiscal year 2020 and 2019, respectively.

Example 42.5: Curtailment Gain

In June 20X0, we announced changes to our qualified and nonqualified defined benefit pension plans. The benefits under the affected plans were determined by a cash balance formula that provides participating employees with an annual "pay credit" as a percentage of their eligible pay based on their age and eligible service. The changes were effective July 31, 20X0, with employees receiving a prorated pay credit for fiscal 20X0 and no future pay credits beginning in fiscal 20X1. However, a participating employee's benefit will continue to grow based on annual interest credits applied to the employee's cash balance account until commencement of the employee's benefit. As a result of the changes, we recognized a one-time curtailment gain of $5,783 during the quarter ended July 2, 20X0.

Example 42.6: Investment Strategy

The plan assets are invested in a variety of financial funds which have investments in a variety of financial instruments including equities, fixed income, and hedge funds. Plan assets are invested in various asset classes that are expected to produce a sufficient level of diversification and investment return over the long term. The investment goals are (1) to meet or exceed the assumed actuarial rate of return of 6.75% over the long term within reasonable and prudent levels of risk as of March 31, 20X2 and 20X1, and (2) to preserve the real purchasing power of assets to meet future obligations.

Example 42.7: Valuation of Funds

Investments in financial funds are valued by multiplying the fund's net asset value ("NAV") per share with the number of units or shares owned as of the valuation date. NAV per share is determined by the fund's administrator or the Company's custodian by deducting from the value of the assets of the fund all its liabilities and then dividing the resulting number by the outstanding number of shares or units. Investments held by the funds are valued on the basis of valuations furnished by a pricing service approved by the fund's investment manager, which determines valuations using methods based on market transactions for comparable securities and various relationships between securities that are generally recognized by institutional traders, or at fair value as determined in good faith by the fund's investment manager. For those assets that are invested within hedge funds there are certain restrictions on redemption of those assets including a one-year lockup period from initial investment and thereafter a 65-day notice period prior to redemption. There are no other significant restrictions on redemption of assets within other asset categories.

Example 42.8: Employer Contributions and Distributions

During fiscal 20X2, we made contributions of $3,600 directly to the pension trust, made no contributions to our other postretirement benefit plans, and distributed $1 directly to retirees under our nonqualified supplemental executive retirement plans. During fiscal 20X1, we contributed $1,200 directly to the pension trust, made no contributions to our other postretirement benefit plans, and made distributions of $293 directly to retirees under our nonqualified supplemental executive retirement plans. During fiscal 20X0, we contributed $13,800 directly to the pension trust, made no contributions to our other postretirement benefit plans, and made distributions of $11,110 to retirees under the nonqualified supplemental executive retirement plan.

Substantially all contributions made to our pension trust were required by local funding requirements. We expect to make mandatory contributions to the plans of approximately $6,642 during fiscal year 20X3.

The following benefit payments, which reflect expected future service, are expected to be paid primarily out of the pension trust:

	Pension Benefits
Fiscal 20X3	$ 13,184
Fiscal 20X4	12,769
Fiscal 20X5	12,960
Fiscal 20X6	13,077
Fiscal 20X7	13,407
Fiscal years 20X8 through 20YZ	$ 64,798

Example 42.9: 401(k) Plan

We sponsor a defined contribution retirement plan, a 401(k) savings plan. The plan is a tax-qualified retirement plan subject to the Employee Retirement Income Security Act of 1974 and covers most employees in the United States.

Total contributions in fiscal 20X2, 20X1, and 20X0 were $12,166, $14,607, and $19,865, respectively.

Example 42.10: 401(k) Plan with Benefit and Contribution Details

The Company sponsors employee savings plans under Section 401(k) of the Internal Revenue Code. These plans are offered to substantially all regular employees. For eligible employees hired prior to January 1, 20X1, employee 401(k) contributions of up to 5% of eligible compensation matched in cash at rates of 45% or 60%, depending on the plan in which the employee participates. Employees hired on or after January 1, 20X1, receive a cash match of 100% for employee 401(k) contributions of up to 5% of eligible compensation and receive an employer retirement income account cash contribution of 3% of the participant's total eligible compensation. All contributions are invested in a number of investment funds pursuant to the employees' elections. Employer contributions to the U.S. defined contribution plans were $186,000, $173,000, and $159,000 for 20X3, 20X2, and 20X0, respectively. LRB subsidiaries in various international countries also participate in defined contribution plans. Employer contributions to the international defined contribution plans were $96 million, $99 million, and $88 million for 20X2, 20X3, and 20X0, respectively.

Example 42.11: Special Termination Benefits

In May 20X2, (as part of the 20X2 restructuring actions) the Company began offering a voluntary early retirement incentive program to certain eligible participants of its U.S. pension plans who meet age and years of pension service requirements. The eligible participants who accepted the offer and retired by July 1, 20X2 received an enhanced pension benefit. Pension benefits were enhanced by adding one additional year of pension service and one additional year of age for certain benefit calculations.

Approximately 800 participants accepted the offer and retired before July 1, 20X2. As a result, the Company incurred a $35 million charge related to these special termination benefits in the second quarter of 20X2.

Example 42.12: Settlement Expense

In the fourth quarter of 20X2, the Company recognized a nonoperating $32 million settlement expense in its U.S. nonqualified pension plan. The charge is related to lump sum payments made to employees at retirement. The settlement expense is an accelerated recognition of past actuarial losses.

Example 42.13: Curtailment of Annuity Contract

In May 20X2, LRB modified the LRB Retiree Life Insurance Plan postretirement benefit to close it to new participants effective August 1, 20X2 (which results in employees who retire on or after August 1, 20X2 not being eligible to participate in the plan) and reducing the maximum life insurance and death benefit to $8,000 for deaths on or after August 1, 20X2. Due to these changes, the plan was remeasured in the second quarter of 20X2, resulting in a decrease to the accumulated projected benefit obligation liability of approximately $150 million and a related increase to shareholders' equity, specifically, accumulated other comprehensive income in addition to an immaterial income statement benefit prospectively.

Example 42.14: Reconciliation of Beginning and Ending Balances of the Benefit Obligation and the Fair Value of Plan Assets

The following tables include a reconciliation of the beginning and ending balances of the benefit obligation and the fair value of plan assets as of December 31 of the respective years. LRB also has certain nonqualified unfunded pension and postretirement benefit plans, inclusive of plans related to supplement/excess benefits for employees impacted by particular relocations and other matters, that individually and in the aggregate are not significant and that are not included in the tables. The obligations for these plans are included within other liabilities in the Company's consolidated balance sheet and aggregated less than $40 million as of December 31, 20X2 and 20X1.

(Millions)	Qualified and Nonqualified Pension Benefits		Postretirement Benefits	
	20X2	*20X1*	*20X2*	*20X1*
Change in benefit obligation				
Benefit obligation at beginning of year	$ 15,948	$ 17,360	$ 2,175	$ 2,410
Acquisitions/Transfers	—	—	—	—
Service cost	251	288	43	52
Interest cost	620	563	82	79
Participant contributions	—	—	—	—
Foreign exchange rate changes	—	—	—	(13)
Plan amendments	—	—	(171)	—
Actuarial (gain) loss	2,209	(1,226)	225	(244)
Benefit payments	(1,128)	(1,034)	(112)	(109)
Settlements, curtailments, special termination benefits, and other	35	(3)	—	—
Benefit obligation at end of year	$ 17,935	$ 15,948	$ 2,242	$ 2,175
Change in plan assets				
Fair value of plan assets at beginning of year	$ 14,803	$ 15,686	$ 1,260	$ 1,397
Acquisitions/Transfers	—	(4)	—	—
Actual return on plan assets	2,323	(95)	187	(32)
Company contributions	101	254	3	4
Participant contributions	—	—	—	—
Foreign exchange rate changes	—	—	—	—
Benefit payments	(1,128)	(1,034)	(112)	(109)
Settlements, curtailments, special termination benefits, and other	—	(4)	—	—
Fair value of plan assets at end of year	$ 16,099	$ 14,803	$ 1,338	$ 1,260
Funded status at end of year	$ (1,836)	$ (1,145)	$ (904)	$ (915)

Example 42.15: Schedule of Amounts Recognized in the Statement of Financial Position

(Millions)	Qualified and Nonqualified Pension Benefits		Postretirement Benefits	
	20X2	*20X1*	*20X2*	*20X1*
Amounts recognized in the consolidated balance sheet as of Dec. 31,				
Noncurrent assets	$ —	$ —	$ —	$ —
Accrued benefit cost				
Current liabilities	(48)	(60)	(4)	(3)
Noncurrent liabilities	(1,788)	(1,085)	(900)	(912)
Ending balance	$ (1,836)	$ (1,145)	$ (904)	$ (915)

(Millions)	Qualified and Nonqualified Pension Benefits		Postretirement Benefits	
	20X2	20X1	20X2	20X1
Amounts recognized in accumulated other comprehensive income as of Dec. 31,				
Net transition obligation (asset)	$ —	$ —	$ —	$ —
Net actuarial loss (gain)	5,899	5,374	663	584
Prior service cost (credit)	(128)	(152)	(262)	(123)
Ending balance	$ 5,771	$ 5,222	$ 401	$ 461

The pension accumulated benefit obligation represents the actuarial present value of benefits based on employee service and compensation as of the measurement date and does not include an assumption about future compensation levels. The accumulated benefit obligation of the pension plans was $17,125,000 and $15,033,000 at December 31, 20X2 and 20X1, respectively. The accumulated benefit obligation of the international pension plans was $7,355,000 and $6,438,000 at December 31, 20X2 and 20X1, respectively.

The following amounts relate to pension plans with accumulated benefit obligations in excess of plan assets as of December 31:

(Thousands)	Qualified and Nonqualified Pension Plans	
	20X2	20X1
Projected benefit obligation	$ 17,935	$ 593
Accumulated benefit obligation	17,125	521
Fair value of plan assets	16,099	9

Example 42.16: Components of Net Periodic Cost and Other Amounts Recognized in Other Comprehensive Income

The service cost component of defined benefit net periodic benefit cost is recorded in cost of sales, selling, general and administrative expenses, and research, development, and related expenses. The other components of net periodic benefit cost are reflected in other expense (income), net. Components of net periodic benefit cost and other supplemental information for the years ended December 31 follow:

(Millions)	Qualified and Nonqualified Pension Plans			Postretirement Benefits		
	20X2	20X1	20X0	20X2	20X1	20X0
Net periodic benefit cost (benefit)						
Operating expense						
Service cost	$ 251	$ 288	$ 268	$ 43	$ 52	$ 52
Nonoperating expense						
Interest cost	620	563	565	82	79	80

(Millions)	Qualified and Nonqualified Pension Plans			Postretirement Benefits		
	20X2	20X1	20X0	20X2	20X1	20X0
Expected return on plan assets	(1,040)	(1,087)	(1,035)	(81)	(84)	(86)
Amortization of prior service benefit	(24)	(23)	(23)	(33)	(40)	(53)
Amortization of net actuarial loss	366	503	388	34	61	56
Settlements, curtailments, special termination benefits, and other	70	—	2	5	—	(4)
Total nonoperating expense (benefit)	(8)	(44)	(103)	7	16	(7)
Total net periodic benefit cost (benefit)	$ 243	$ 244	$ 165	$ 50	$ 68	$ 45
Other changes in plan assets and benefit obligations recognized in other comprehensive (income) loss						
Prior service cost (benefit)	$ —	$ —	$ —	$ (171)	$ —	$ (1)
Amortization of prior service benefit	24	23	23	33	40	53
Net actuarial (gain) loss	926	(44)	607	119	(127)	69
Amortization of net actuarial loss	(366)	(503)	(388)	(34)	(61)	(56)
Foreign currency	—	—	—	(1)	(2)	—
Settlements and curtailments	(35)	—	(2)	(5)	—	—
Total recognized in other comprehensive (income) loss	$ 549	$ (524)	$ 240	$ (59)	$ (150)	$ 65
Total recognized in net periodic benefit cost (benefit) and other comprehensive (income) loss	$ 792	$ (280)	$ 405	$ (9)	$ (82)	$ 110

Example 42.17: Weighted-Average Assumptions Used to Determine Benefit Obligations

Weighted-average assumptions used to determine benefit obligations as of December 31:

	Qualified and Nonqualified Pension Benefits					
	United States			Postretirement Benefits		
	20X2	20X1	20X0	20X2	20X1	20X0
Discount rate	3.25%	4.36%	3.68%	3.27%	4.41%	3.79%
Compensation rate increase	3.21%	4.10%	4.10%	N/A	N/A	N/A

Weighted-average assumptions used to determine net cost for years ended December 31:

	Qualified and Nonqualified Pension Benefits United States			Postretirement Benefits		
	20X2	*20X1*	*20X0*	*20X2*	*20X1*	*20X0*
Discount rate—service cost	4.44%	3.78%	4.42%	4.53%	3.86%	4.50%
Discount rate—interest cost	4.02%	3.35%	3.61%	4.15%	3.52%	3.80%
Expected return on assets	7.00%	7.25%	7.25%	6.43%	6.53%	6.48%
Compensation rate increase	4.10%	4.10%	4.10%	N/A	N/A	N/A

Example 42.18: Description of Health Care Savings Plan

The Company provides eligible retirees in the U.S. postretirement health care benefit plans to a savings account benefits–based plan. The contributions provided by the Company to the health savings accounts increase 3% per year for employees who retired prior to January 1, 20X1 and increase 1.5% for employees who retire on or after January 1, 20X1. Therefore, the Company no longer has material exposure to health care cost inflation.

Example 42.19: Discount Rate Used to Measure Plan Liabilities

The Company determines the discount rate used to measure plan liabilities as of the December 31 measurement date for the pension and postretirement benefit plans, which is also the date used for the related annual measurement assumptions. The discount rate reflects the current rate at which the associated liabilities could be effectively settled at the end of the year. The Company sets its rate to reflect the yield of a portfolio of high-quality, fixed-income debt instruments that would produce cash flows sufficient in timing and amount to settle projected future benefits. Using this methodology, the Company determined a discount rate of 3.25% for the U.S. pension plans and 3.27% for the postretirement benefit plans as of December 31, 20X2, which is a decrease of 1.11 percentage points and 1.14 percentage points, respectively, from the rates used as of December 31, 20X1. A decrease in the discount rate increases the projected benefit obligation (PBO), the significant decrease in the discount rate as of December 31, 20X2 resulted in an approximately $2.0 billion higher PBO for the U.S. pension plans. For the international pension and postretirement plans, the discount rates also reflect the current rate at which the associated liabilities could be effectively settled at the end of the year. If the country has a deep market in corporate bonds, the Company matches the expected cash flows from the plan either to a portfolio of bonds that generate sufficient cash flow or a notional yield curve generated from available bond information. In countries that do not have a deep market in corporate bonds, government bonds are considered with a risk premium to approximate corporate bond yields.

Example 42.20: Measurement of Service Cost and Interest Cost

The Company measures service cost and interest cost separately using the spot yield curve approach applied to each corresponding obligation. Service costs are determined based on duration-specific spot rates applied to the service cost cash flows. The interest cost calculation is determined by applying duration-specific spot rates to the year-by-year projected benefit payments. The spot yield curve approach does not affect the measurement of the total benefit obligations as the change in service and interest costs offset in the actuarial gains and losses recorded in other comprehensive income.

Example 42.21: Assumption for the Expected Return on Plan Assets

For the primary U.S. qualified pension plan, the Company's assumption for the expected return on plan assets was 7.00% in 20X2. Projected returns are based primarily on broad, publicly traded equity and fixed-income indices and forward-looking estimates of active portfolio and investment management. As of December 31, 20X2, the Company's 20X3 expected long-term rate of return on plan assets is 6.75%. The expected return assumption is based on the strategic asset allocation of the plan, long-term capital market return expectations, and expected performance from active investment management. The 20X2 expected long-term rate of return is based on an asset allocation assumption of 23% global equities, 14% private equities, 47% fixed-income securities, and 16% absolute return investments independent of traditional performance benchmarks, along with positive returns from active investment management. The actual net rate of return on plan assets in 20X2 was 16.3%. In 20X1 the plan earned a rate of return of –0.5% and in 20X0 earned a return of 12.4%. The average annual actual return on the plan assets over the past 10 and 25 years has been 8.9% and 9.4%, respectively. Return on assets assumptions for international pension and other postretirement benefit plans are calculated on a plan-by-plan basis using plan asset allocations and expected long-term rate of return assumptions.

As of December 31, 20X2, the Company converted to the "Pri-20X2 Aggregate Mortality Table" and updated the mortality improvement scales to the Society of Actuaries Scale MP-20X2. The December 31, 20X2 update resulted in a small decrease to the U.S. pension PBO and U.S. accumulated postretirement benefit obligations.

Example 42.22: Contributions to Pension and Other Postretirement Plans

During 20X2, the Company contributed $207,000 to its pension plans and $3 million to its postretirement plans. During 20X1, the Company contributed $366,000 to its U.S. and international pension plans and $4,000,000 to its postretirement plans. In 20X3, the Company expects to contribute an amount in the range of $100,000 to $200,000 of cash to its retirement plans. The Company does not have a required minimum cash pension contribution obligation for its plans in 20X3. Future contributions will depend on market conditions, interest rates and other factors.

Example 42.23: Future Pension and Postretirement Benefit Payments

The following table provides the estimated pension and postretirement benefit payments that are payable from the plans to participants.

(Millions)	Qualified and Nonqualified Pension Benefits United States	Postretirement Benefits
20X3 benefit payments	$ 1,103	$ 121
20X4 benefit payments	1,096	128
20X5 benefit payments	1,104	136
20X6 benefit payments	1,106	142
20X7 benefit payments	1,111	148
Next five years	5,521	789

Example 42.24: Plan Asset Management

LRB's investment strategy for its pension and postretirement plans is to manage the funds on a going-concern basis. The primary goal of the trust funds is to meet the obligations as required. The secondary goal is to earn the highest rate of return possible, without jeopardizing its primary goal, and without subjecting the Company to an undue amount of contribution risk. Fund returns are used to help financfffe present and future obligations to the extent possible within actuarially determined funding limits and tax-determined asset limits, thus reducing the potential need for additional contributions from LRB. The investment strategy has used long-duration cash bonds and derivative instruments to offset a significant portion of the interest rate sensitivity of U.S. pension liabilities.

Normally, LRB does not buy or sell any of its own securities as a direct investment for its pension and other postretirement benefit funds. However, due to external investment management of the funds, the plans may indirectly buy, sell, or hold LRB securities. The aggregate amount of LRB securities is not considered to be material relative to the aggregate fund percentages.

Example 42.25: U.S. Pension Plans and Postretirement Benefit Plan Assets

The discussion references the fair value measurements of certain assets in terms of levels 1, 2, and 3. While the company believes that the valuation methods are appropriate and consistent with other market participants, the use of different methodologies or assumptions to determine the fair value of certain financial instruments could result in a different estimate of fair value at the reporting date.

In order to achieve the investment objectives in the pension plans and postretirement benefit plans, the investment policies include a target strategic asset allocation. The investment policies allow some tolerance around the target in recognition that market fluctuations and illiquidity of some investments may cause the allocation to a specific asset class to vary from the target allocation, potentially for long periods of time. Acceptable ranges have been designed to allow for deviation from strategic targets and to allow for the opportunity for tactical over- and underweights. The portfolios will normally be rebalanced when the quarter-end asset allocation deviates from acceptable ranges. The allocation is reviewed regularly by the named fiduciary of the plans. Approximately 50% of the postretirement benefit plan assets are in a 401(h) account. The 401(h) account assets are in the same trust as the primary pension plan and invested with the same investment objectives as the primary pension plan.

The fair values of the assets held by the U.S. pension plans by asset class are as follows:

(Millions) Asset Class	Fair Value Measurements Using Inputs Considered as						Fair Value at Dec. 31,	
	Level 1		Level 2		Level 3			
	20X2	20X1	20X2	20X1	20X2	20X1	20X2	20X1
Equities								
U.S. equities	$ 1,575	$ 1,369	$ —	$ —	$ —	$ —	$ 1,575	$ 1,369
Non-U.S. equities	1,585	1,234	—	—	—	—	1,585	1,234
Index and long/short equity funds*							417	372
Total Equities	$ 3,160	$ 2,603	$ —	$ —	$ —	$ —	$ 3,577	$ 2,975
Fixed Income								
U.S. government securities	$ 2,346	$ 1,889	$ 916	$ 732	$ —	$ —	$ 3,262	$ 2,621
Non-U.S. government securities			61	44	—	—	61	44
Preferred and convertible securities			52	44	—	—	52	44
U.S. corporate bonds	10	9	3,566	2,941	—	—	3,576	2,950
Non-U.S. corporate bonds			759	475	—	—	759	475
Derivative instruments	(5)	2	109	111	—	—	104	113
Other*								9
Total fixed income	$ 2,351	$ 1,900	$ 5,463	$ 4,347	$ —	$ —	$ 7,814	$ 6,256
Private Equity								
Growth equity	$ 80	$ 45	$ —	$ —	$ —	$ —	$ 80	$ 45
Partnership investments*							1,865	2,064
Total Private Equity	$ 80	$ 45	$ —	$ —	$ —	$ —	$ 1,945	$ 2,109
Absolute Return								
Fixed income and other	$ 1	$ 28	$ 117	$ 114	$ —	$ —	$ 118	$ 142
Hedge fund/fund of funds*							2,010	1,866
Partnership investments*							589	429
Total Absolute Return	$ 1	$ 28	$ 117	$ 114	$ —	$ —	$ 2,717	$ 2,437
Cash and Cash Equivalents								
Cash and cash equivalents	$ 20	$ 412	$ 5	$ 4	$ —	$ —	$ 25	$ 416
Repurchase agreements and derivative margin activity			(1)	(1)			(1)	(1)
Cash and cash equivalents, valued at net asset value*							480	870
Total Cash and Cash Equivalents	$ 20	$ 412	$ 4	$ 3	$ —	$ —	$ 504	$ 1,285
Total	$ 5,612	$ 4,988	$ 5,584	$ 4,464	$ —	$ —	$ 16,557	$ 15,062
Other items to reconcile to fair value of plan assets							$ (458)	$ (259)
Fair value of plan assets							$ 16,099	$ 14,803

* In accordance with ASC 820-10, certain investments that are measured at fair value using the net asset value (NAV) per share (or its equivalent) as a practical expedient have not been classified in the fair value hierarchy. The NAV is based on the fair value of the underlying assets owned by the fund, minus its liabilities, then divided by the number of units outstanding and is determined by the investment manager or custodian of the fund. The fair value amounts presented in this table are intended to permit reconciliation of the fair value hierarchy to the amounts presented in the fair value of plan assets.

The fair values of the assets held by the postretirement benefit plans by asset class are as follows:

(Millions) Asset Class	Fair Value Measurements Using Inputs Considered as						Fair Value at Dec. 31,	
	Level 1		Level 2		Level 3			
	20X2	20X1	20X2	20X1	20X2	20X1	20X2	20X1
Equities								
U.S. equities	$ 337	$ 356	$ —	$ —	$ —	$ —	$ 337	$ 356
Non-U.S. equities	77	58	—	—	—	—	77	58
Index and long/short equity funds*							33	34
Total Equities	$ 414	$ 414	$ —	$ —	$ —	$ —	$ 447	$ 448
Fixed Income								
U.S. government securities	$ 136	$ 112	$ 242	$ 213	$ —	$ —	$ 378	$ 325
Non-U.S. government securities	—	—	6	4	—	—	6	4
U.S. corporate bonds	—	—	203	162	—	—	203	162
Non-U.S. corporate bonds	—	—	46	32	—	—	46	32
Derivative instruments	—	—	5	5	—	—	5	5
Total Fixed Income	$ 136	$ 112	$ 502	$ 416	$ —	$ —	$ 638	$ 528
Private Equity								
Growth equity	$ 4	$ 2	$ —	$ —	$ —	$ —	$ 4	$ 2
Partnership investments*							92	101
Total Private Equity	$ 4	$ 2	$ —	$ —	$ —	$ —	$ 96	$ 103
Absolute Return								
Fixed income and other	$ —	$ 1	$ 5	$ 5	$ —	$ —	$ 5	$ 6
Hedge fund/fund of funds*							92	80
Partnership investments*							27	18
Total Absolute Return	$ —	$ 1	$ 5	$ 5	$ —	$ —	$ 124	$ 104
Cash and Cash Equivalents								
Cash and cash equivalents	$ 33	$ 47	$ 1	$ 5	$ —	$ —	$ 34	$ 52
Repurchase agreements and derivative margin activity	—		—				22	37
Cash and cash equivalents, valued at net asset value*								
Total Cash and Cash Equivalents	$ 33	$ 47	$ 1	$ 5	$ —	$ —	$ 56	$ 89
Total	$ 587	$ 576	$ 508	$ 426	$ —	$ —	$ 1,361	$ 1,272
Other items to reconcile to fair value of plan assets							$ (23)	$ (12)
Fair value of plan assets							$ 1,338	$ 1,260

* In accordance with ASC 820-10, certain investments that are measured at fair value using the NAV per share (or its equivalent) as a practical expedient have not been classified in the fair value hierarchy. The NAV is based on the fair value of the underlying assets owned by the fund, minus its liabilities, then divided by the number of units outstanding and is determined by the investment manager or custodian of the fund. The fair value amounts presented in this table are intended to permit reconciliation of the fair value hierarchy to the amounts presented in the fair value of plan assets.

Publicly traded equities are valued at the closing price reported in the active market in which the individual securities are traded.

Fixed income includes derivative instruments such as credit default swaps, interest rate swaps, and futures contracts. Corporate debt includes bonds and notes, asset-backed securities, collateralized mortgage obligations, and private placements. Swaps and derivative instruments are valued by the custodian using closing market swap curves and market derived inputs. U.S. government and government agency bonds and notes are valued at the closing price reported in the active market in which the individual security is traded. Corporate bonds and notes, asset-backed securities, and collateralized mortgage obligations are valued at either the yields currently available on comparable securities of issuers with similar credit ratings or valued under a discounted cash flow approach that utilizes observable inputs, such as current yields of similar instruments, but includes adjustments for certain risks that may not be observable, such as credit and liquidity risks. Private placements are valued by the custodian using recognized pricing services and sources.

The private equity portfolio is a diversified mix of derivative instruments, growth equity, and partnership interests. Derivative investments are written options that are valued by independent parties using market inputs and valuation models. Growth equity investments are valued at the closing price reported in the active market in which the individual securities are traded.

Absolute return consists primarily of partnership interests in hedge funds, hedge funds of funds, or other private fund vehicles. Corporate debt instruments are valued at either the yields currently available on comparable securities of issuers with similar credit ratings or valued under a discounted cash flow approach that utilizes observable inputs, such as current yields of similar instruments, but includes adjustments for certain risks that may not be observable, such as credit and liquidity risk ratings.

Other items to reconcile to fair value of plan assets include interest receivables, amounts due for securities sold, amounts payable for securities purchased, and interest payable.

The balances of and changes in the fair values of the U.S. pension plans' and postretirement plans' level 3 assets for the periods ended December 31, 20X2 and 20X3 were not material.

43 ASC 718 COMPENSATION— STOCK COMPENSATION

AUTHORITATIVE LITERATURE

The economic substance of share-based payment arrangements is to provide compensation for goods or services as they are received, resulting in costs that should be reported by the entity using the fair value method of accounting. (ASC 718-10-10-1) ASC 718 requires fair value accounting for all share-based payment plans, except for equity instruments held by employee stock ownership plans (ESOPs). (ASC 718-10-10-2)

Technical Alert

In November 2019, the FASB issued Accounting Standards Update 2019-08, *Compensation— Stock Compensation (Topic 718) and Revenue from Contracts with Customers (Topic 606) Codification Improvements—Share-Based Consideration Payable to a Customer.* The purpose of the ASU is to provide guidance on measuring share-based payment awards granted to a customer.

Guidance ASU 2019-08 clarifies the guidance in ASU 2018-07 by requiring entities to measure and classify share payment awards granted to a customer by applying the guidance in Topic 718. The amount recorded as a reduction of the transaction price must be measured on the basis of the grant-date fair value of the share-based payment award in accordance with Topic 718. (The grant date is the date at which grantor and grantee reach a mutual understanding of the key terms and conditions of a share-based payment award.) The classification and subsequent measurement of the award follow the guidance in Topic 718 unless the share-based payment award is subsequently modified and the grantee is no longer a customer.

Effective Dates The effective dates are as follows:

- For entities that have not yet adopted the amendments in ASU 2018-07:
  - Public business entities, in fiscal years beginning after December 15, 2019, and interim periods within those fiscal years, and
  - Other than public business entities, in fiscal years beginning after December 15, 2019, and interim periods within fiscal years beginning after December 15, 2020.
- For entities that have adopted the amendments in ASU 2018-07:
  - All entities, in fiscal years beginning after December 15, 2019, and interim periods within those fiscal years.

Early adoption is permitted, but not before the entity adopts the amendments in ASU 2018-07.

Transition An entity may adopt the amendments in ASU 2019-08 either in the same fiscal year that it adopts the amendments in ASU 2018-07 or in a fiscal year after the fiscal year that the entity adopts the amendments in ASU 2018-07 as follows:

- If an entity adopts the amendments in ASU 2019-08 in the same fiscal year that it adopts the amendments in ASU 2018-07, the entity should apply the amendments in ASU 2019-08 through a cumulative-effect adjustment to the opening balance of retained earnings at the beginning of the fiscal year in which it adopted the amendments in ASU 2018-07.
- If an entity adopts the amendments in ASU 2019-08 in a fiscal year after the fiscal year that the entity adopts the amendments in ASU 2018-07, the entity should apply the amendments in ASU 2019-08 through a cumulative-effect adjustment to the opening balance of retained earnings at the beginning of either:
  - The fiscal year in which it adopted the amendments in ASU 2018-07, or
  - The fiscal year in which it adopts the amendments in ASU 2019-08.

Subtopics

ASC 718, *Compensation—Stock Compensation*, provides guidance for employee and nonemployee share-based payments and contains five Subtopics:

- ASC 718-10, *Overall*, contains the high-level objectives and general guidance for the topic
- ASC 718-20, *Awards Classified as Equity*, deals with share-based payments classified as equity
- ASC 718-30, *Awards Classified as Liabilities*, deals with share-based payments classified as liabilities
- ASC 718-40, *Employee Stock Ownership Plans*, contains the following subsections:
  - General
  - Leveraged employee stock ownership plans
  - Nonleveraged employee stock ownership plans
- ASC 718-50, *Employee Share Purchase Plans*, contains guidance for compensatory and noncompensatory plans
  (ASC 718-10-05-1 and 15-2)

Note that ASC 718-20 and ASC 718-30 are interrelated with ASC 718-10. Generally, guidance that relates to both equity and liability instruments is included in ASC 718-10, while guidance specific to equity or liability instruments is in their respective Subtopics. (ASC 718-10-05-3)

Scope and Scope Exceptions

ASC 718 applies to all entities. It also applies to all share-based payment transactions where the entity acquires goods or services to be used or consumed in the grantor's own operations or provides consideration payable to a customer by issuing or offering to issue equity instruments or incurring liabilities to an employee or nonemployee that meet these conditions:

- The amounts are based in whole or in part on the price of the entity's shares or equity instruments
- The awards require or may require settlement by issuing the entity's equity instruments. (ASC 718-10-15-3)

Entities should look to ASC 323-10-25-3 through 25-5 for guidance on share-based compensation granted by an investor to the employees, or nonemployees of an equity method investee that provide goods or services to the investor that are used or consumed by the investee's operations. (ASC 718-10-15-3A)

If the purpose of awarding the shares is other than compensation, ASC 718 does not apply. (ASC 718-10-15-4) ASC 718 also does not apply to transactions involving share-based payment awards granted to a lender or an investor that provides financing to the issuer. (ASC 718-10-15-5)

If share-based payment awards are granted to a customer, as opposed to an employee, the awards should be:

- Measured and classified under the guidance in ASC 718
- Accounted for as a reduction of the transaction price and, therefore, of revenue, unless the consideration is in exchange for a distinct good or service. In that case, the entity should apply the guidance in ASC 606.
(ASC 718-10-15-5A)

For guidance on whether share-based payment awards issued in a business combination are part of a considerate transfer, see ASC 805-30-30-9. (ASC 718-10-15-6)

The guidance in ASC 718-20 applies to share-based payment awards that are classified in equity, and ASC 718-30 applies to share-based payment awards that are classified as liabilities. (ASC 718-20-15-3 and ASC 718-30-15-2)

ASC 718-10, *Overall*

Recognition Principle The entity recognizes the goods acquired or services received when obtained or received. The entity also recognizes a corresponding charge to equity or liabilities. (ASC 718-10-25-2)

The grant date is used to fix the value of equity-based awards. The grant date is when the parties have fixed the terms of their arrangement. This provides a meaningful measure of the cost to be incurred by the entity. This differs from the situation with equity-based compensation classified as a liability, where awards are settled for assets (e.g., cash from stock appreciation rights). In that scenario, the entity is obligated to distribute assets, so the relevant measure of compensation cost, ultimately, is the amount of assets disbursed.

1. The award is a unilateral grant and, therefore, the recipient does not have the ability to negotiate the key terms and conditions of the award with the grantor, and
2. It is expected that the key terms and conditions of the award will be communicated to an individual recipient within a relatively short time period from the date of approval. (ASC 718-10-25-5)

Classifying Awards as Liabilities or Equity Determining whether a share-based payment should be categorized as a liability requires close attention to the guidance of ASC 718. In turn, ASC 718 points to the classification criteria of ASC 480 to determine whether a freestanding financial instrument granted to a grantee is a liability or equity. (ASC 718-10-25-7)

Stock appreciation rights (SARs) pay employees the amount by which the share price at a defined date (say, three years hence) exceeds what it was at the measurement date. Depending on the plan, the award may be payable in the entity's shares, in cash, or in either at the option of the grantee. If the optionee has the right to demand cash or the SAR is payable in cash only, the grantor entity recognizes a liability for the accrued compensation.

An award may be indexed to a factor beyond the entity's share price. If that additional factor is not a market, performance, or service condition, the award is classified as a liability. In such a case, the additional factor is reflected in estimating the fair value of the award. (ASC 718-10-25-13)

If a broker is a related party of the entity, selling the shares in the open market for three days is generally sufficient for the award to qualify as equity. (ASC 718-10-25-17) Likewise, a provision for direct or indirect repurchase of shares issued upon exercise of options or the vesting of nonvested shares, with payment due employees withheld to meet the employer's withholding requirements, does not in and of itself result in liability classification of instruments otherwise classified as equity. However, if the amount of the withholding at the discretion of the employer is over the maximum tax rates in the employee's jurisdiction, the entire award should be classified as a liability. (ASC 718-10-25-18)

Valuation Models In the absence of an observable market price for an award, reporting entities must use a valuation technique that is:

- Applied consistently with ASC 718's fair value measurement objectives
- Based on established financial economic theory principles and is generally applied in that field

While ASC 718 does not dictate a valuation model, FASB points out that the binomial model or other so-called *lattice* models meet the requirements of ASC 718-10-55-16 and are preferred. The binomial model is favored over the closed-form model like the Black-Scholes-Merton formula, because the lattice model accommodates more potential post-vesting behaviors than the closed-form models. There are likely to be ranges of reasonable estimates for expected volatility, dividends, and option term.

ASC 718-40, *Employee Stock Ownership Plans*

ESOPs are defined contribution plans in which shares of the sponsoring entity are awarded to employees as additional compensation. ESOPs are created by a sponsoring corporation, which either funds the plan directly (unleveraged ESOP) or, more commonly, facilitates the borrowing of money either directly from an outside lender (directly leveraged ESOP) or from the employer, which in turn will borrow from an outside lender (indirectly leveraged ESOP).

ASC 718-50, *Employee Share Purchase Plans*

Employee share purchase plans are not compensatory if their terms are no more favorable than those available to all holders of the same class of shares and if all employees that meet limited employment qualifications may participate in the plan on an equitable basis. (ASC 718-50-25-1)

ASC 718-740, *Income Taxes*

Generally, it is inevitable that both the timing and the amounts of compensation expense related to share-based compensation will differ from the amounts and timing of compensation costs recorded in the financial statements. To the extent that these are timing differences, deferred tax accounting is appropriate. The cumulative amount of compensation cost that will result in a tax deduction should be considered a deductible temporary difference. This applies both for instruments classified as equity and for those categorized as liabilities. Any compensation cost recognized in the financial statements for instruments that will not result in a tax deduction should not be considered to result in a deductible temporary difference under ASC 740. (ASC 718-740-25-2 and 25-4)

In general, the fair value of stock-based compensation, which is computed at grant date and recognized over the vesting period as compensation cost in the financial statements, will not be tax deductible currently, giving rise to deferred tax benefits that are measured by the grantee with reference to the book compensation expense recognized. Ultimately, when the options vest and are exercised, the company is able to deduct the intrinsic value, measured by the spread between fair value on exercise date and exercise price. To the extent this exceeds or is less than the fair value of the stock-based compensation recognized as GAAP-basis expense, the tax effect is recognized as a tax expense or benefit in the income statement in the period in which the amount of the deduction is determined, usually when the award is exercised or expires in the case of share options or vests in the case of nonvested stock awards. (ASC 718-740-35-2)

PRACTICE ALERT

While SEC comments pertain to public entities, its comments can often provide valuable practice pointers for financial statement preparers of nonpublic entities. In the area of stock compensation, the SEC has cautioned entities to:

- Include the total intrinsic value of options exercised during the year
- Disclose the weighted average remaining contractual term of options currently exercisable
- Include the method used to estimate the fair value of options
- Include assumptions used to estimate the fair value of options
- Discuss the nature and reason for a modification in the award's terms
- Specify the number of awards expected to vest and assumptions used in calculating that number
- Indicate the valuation method, including significant assumptions
- Include the weighted average grant date fair value of equity instruments granted during the year
- Disclose the intrinsic value of options exercised
- Disclose the terms and conditions of awards
- Indicate whether any shares were repurchased

- Discuss significant assumptions used in valuation of awards, including volatility, expected term, and divided yield
- If used, disclose the simplified method was used

PRESENTATION AND DISCLOSURE REQUIREMENTS

Presentation

Balance Sheet Share-based compensation awards are classified as liabilities or equity. If liabilities, they are further categorized as current or noncurrent. If a vested award is payable on demand or if vesting is expected to occur within one year, the liability award is classified as current.

Income Statement Share-based compensation is included in the same line or lines as the cash compensation.

Disclosures

Critical ASC 718 disclosures include:

- A description of the share-based payment arrangements, including the terms of the awards. A nonpublic company should disclose its policy for measuring compensation cost.
- The most recent income statement should provide the number and weighted-average exercise prices of the share options and equity instruments.
- Each year for which an income statement is provided, a company should provide the weighted-average grant-date fair value of equity options and the intrinsic value of options exercised during the year.
- For fully vested share options and those expected to vest at the date of the latest statement of financial position, the company should provide the number, weighted-average exercise price, aggregate intrinsic value, and contractual terms of options outstanding and currently exercisable.
- If more than one share-based plan is in effect, the information should be provided separately for different types of awards.
- For each year for which an income statement is provided, companies should provide the following:
  - Companies that do not use the intrinsic value method should provide a description of the method of determining fair value and a description of the assumptions used.
  - Total compensation cost for share-based payment arrangements, including tax benefits and capitalization of compensation costs, should be stated.
  - Descriptions of significant modifications and numbers of employees affected should also be provided.
- On the date of the latest statement of financial position, the total compensation cost related to nonvested awards not yet recognized and the period over which they are expected to be recognized.
- The amount of cash received from exercise of share-based compensation and the amount of cash used to settle equity instruments should be disclosed.
- Description of the company's policy for issuing shares upon share options exercise, including the source of the shares.

The information needed to achieve disclosure objectives of ASC 718 can be found in detail at www.wiley.com/go/FSDM2021.

PRESENTATION AND DISCLOSURE EXAMPLES

Example 43.1: Share-Based Compensation Accounting Policy, Including Performance-Based and Time-Based Options

The Company accounts for share-based compensation in accordance with the provisions of ASC Topic 718, *Compensation—Stock Compensation*. Under ASC 718, share-based compensation cost is measured at the grant date, based on the calculated fair value of the award, and is recognized as an expense over the employee's requisite service period (generally the vesting period of the equity grant). The Company issues performance-based stock options, which vest only upon the Company's achievement of certain earnings per share targets on a calendar year basis, as determined by the Company's Board of Directors. These options were valued in the same manner as the time-based options. However, the Company only recognizes stock compensation expense to the extent that the targets are determined to be probable of being achieved, which triggers the vesting of the performance options.

Example 43.2: Share-Based Compensation Accounting Policy

Under the Company's Omnibus Incentive Plan ("the Plan") as in effect at March 31, 20X2, options exercisable for up to 19,865,000 shares of the Company's common stock may be granted over the life of the Plan to key employees, nonemployee directors, and consultants at exercise prices not less than the fair market value of the common stock on the date of grant. Options granted under the Plan are non-statutory stock options and generally vest 25% one year from the date of grant, with the remaining 75% vesting ratably each month for the next 36 months. The options granted to employees and the Company's Board of Directors expire at the end of five years and ten years from date of grant, respectively. All options granted in fiscal 20X2 and 20X1 were granted with an exercise price equal to the fair value of the Company's common stock on the grant date.

Example 43.3: Fair Value Estimation of Stock Options Using the Black-Scholes Model

The Company records compensation expense for employee stock options based on the estimated fair value of the options on the date of grant using the Black-Scholes option-pricing model with the assumptions included in the table below. The Company uses historical data, among other factors, to estimate the expected volatility, the expected dividend yield, and the expected option life. Upon adoption of ASU 2016-09, the Company accounts for forfeitures as they occur, rather than estimate expected forfeitures. The risk-free rate is based on the interest rate paid on a U.S. Treasury issue with a term similar to the estimated life of the option.

Example 43.4: Share-Based Compensation—Accounting Policy and Assumptions

The Company accounts for share-based compensation in accordance with the provisions of ASC Topic 718, *Compensation—Stock Compensation*. Under ASC 718, share-based compensation cost is measured at the grant date, based on the calculated fair value of the award, and is recognized as an expense over the employee's requisite service period (generally the vesting period of the equity grant). For the fiscal year ended March 31, 20X2, the Company recorded share-based compensation expense of $4,485,000.

The Company estimates the fair value of stock options using the Black-Scholes valuation model. Key input assumptions used to estimate the fair value of stock options include the exercise price of the award, the expected option term, the expected volatility of the Company's stock over the option's expected term, the risk-free interest rate over the option's term, and the Company's expected annual dividend yield. The Company issues performance-based stock options that vest only upon the Company's achievement of certain earnings per share targets on a calendar year basis, as determined by the Company's Board of Directors. These options were valued in the same manner as the time-based options. However, the Company only recognizes stock compensation expense to the extent that the targets are determined to be probable of being achieved, which triggers the vesting of the performance options. The Company's management believes that this valuation technique and the approach utilized to develop the underlying assumptions are appropriate in calculating the fair values of the Company's stock options granted in fiscal 20X2. Estimates of fair value are not intended to predict actual future events or the value ultimately realized by persons who receive equity awards.

The Company does not believe there is a reasonable likelihood that there will be a material change in the future estimates or assumptions that we use to determine stock-based compensation expense. However, if actual results are not consistent with our estimates or assumptions, we may be exposed to changes in stock-based compensation expense that could be material.

Example 43.5: Schedule of Estimate of Fair Value of Stock Option Grants

The fair value of each grant is estimated on the date of grant using the Black-Scholes option-pricing model. The following weighted average assumptions were used for the fiscal years ended March 31, 20X2, 20X1, and 20X0:

	Fiscal 20X2	*Fiscal 20X1*	*Fiscal 20X0*
Expected volatility	33%	34%	40%
Risk-free interest rate	1.42 to 2.33%	2.46 to 2.96%	1.88 to 2.56%
Dividend yield	0.0%	0.0%	0.0%
Weighted average option life	4.4 to 4.5 years	4.4 to 4.5 years	4.4 to 4.5 years

For the fiscal years ended March 31, 20X2, 20X1, and 20X0, the Company recorded share-based compensation expense of $4,485,000, $4,349,000, and $3,164,000, respectively. The table below shows the amounts recognized in the financial statements for the fiscal years ended March 31, 20X2, 20X1, and 20X0.

	Fiscal 20X2	*Fiscal 20X1*	*Fiscal 20X0*
Cost of revenue	$ 2,028,000	$ 1,896,000	$ 1,749,000
General and administrative	2,457,000	2,453,000	1,415,000
Total cost of stock-based compensation included in income before income taxes	4,485,000	4,349,000	3,164,000
Amount of income tax benefit recognized	985,000	1,048,000	1,105,000
Amount charged to net income	$ 3,500,000	$ 3,301,000	$ 2,059,000
Effect on basic earnings per share	$ 0.19	$ 0.18	$ 0.11
Effect on diluted earnings per share	$ 0.19	$ 0.17	$ 0.11

The following table summarizes information for all stock options for the fiscal years March 31, 20X2, 20X1, and 20X0:

	Fiscal 20X2	*Fiscal 20X1*	*Fiscal 20X0*
Options outstanding beginning of fiscal year	1,058,411	1,064,439	1,143,928
Options granted	271,575	290,300	334,200
Options exercised	(235,932)	(250,604)	(314,846)
Options canceled/forfeited	(64,951)	(45,724)	(98,843)
Options outstanding end of fiscal year	1,029,103	1,058,411	1,064,439

During the fiscal year, weighted average
exercise price of:

Options granted	$ 79.49	$ 57.27	$ 52.57
Options exercised	$ 38.34	$ 36.44	$ 27.59
Options canceled/forfeited	$ 59.87	$ 36.71	$ 35.59
At the end of fiscal year:			
Price range of outstanding options	$20.08–88.22	$12.71–62.31	$12.71–57.75
Weighted average exercise price per share	$ 54.87	$ 45.17	$ 39.45
Options available for future grants	316,691	523,415	260,961
Exercisable options	468,107	440,386	445,387

The following table summarizes the status of stock options outstanding and exercisable at March 31, 20X2:

Range of Exercise Prices	Number of Outstanding Options	Weighted Average Remaining Contractual Life(Years)	Outstanding Options: Weighted Average Exercise Price	Exercisable Options: Number of Exercisable Options	Exercisable Options: Weighted Average Exercise Price
$20.08 to 43.32	264,782	2.19	$ 31.41	247,798	$ 30.91
$43.33 to 57.75	363,979	2.91	52.58	185,609	51.83
$57.76 to 77.93	323,392	4.04	68.83	34,700	59.89
$77.94 to 88.22	76,950	5.50	87.76	—	—
Total	1,029,103	3.28	$ 54.87	468,107	$ 41.35

The following table summarizes the status of all outstanding options at March 31, 20X2, and changes during the fiscal year then ended:

	Number of Options	Weighted Average Exercise Price per Share	Weighted Average Remaining Contractual Life (Years)	Aggregate Intrinsic Value as of March 31, 20X2
Options outstanding, March 31, 20X1	1,058,411	$ 45.17		
Granted	271,575	79.49		
Exercised	(235,932)	38.34		
Canceled: forfeited	(60,466)	61.23		
Canceled: expired	(4,485)	41.63		
Options outstanding, March 31, 20X2	1,029,103	$ 54.87	3.28	$ 7,345,665
Options vested and expected to vest	877,664	$ 48.41	2.91	$ 4,465,053
Ending exercisable options	468,107	$ 41.35	2.42	$ 6,589,011

The weighted average fair value of options granted during fiscal 20X2, 20X1, and 20X0 was $22.99, $19.83, and $19.24, respectively. The total intrinsic value of options exercised during fiscal years 20X2, 20X1, and 20X0 was $10,281,000, $5,817,000, and $7,780,000, respectively.

Included in the above-noted stock option grants and stock compensation expense are performance-based stock options which vest only upon the Company's achievement of certain earnings per share targets on a calendar year basis, as determined by the Company's Board of Directors. These options were valued in the same manner as the time-based options. However, the Company only recognizes stock compensation expense to the extent that the targets are determined to be probable of being achieved, which triggers the vesting of the performance options. During the fiscal years ended March 31, 20X2, 20X1, and 20X0, the Company recognized stock compensation expense for performance-based options in the amount of $1,625,000, $1,631,000, and $649,000, respectively.

The Company received $8,147,000, $7,241,000, and $3,426,000 of cash receipts from the exercise of stock options during fiscal 20X2, 20X1, and 20X0, respectively. As of March 31, 20X2, $6,054,000 of total unrecognized compensation costs related to stock options is expected to be recognized over a weighted average period of 3 years.

44 ASC 720 OTHER EXPENSES

AUTHORITATIVE LITERATURE

Subtopics

ASC 720, *Other Expenses*, contains nine Subtopics and there is no relationship between the Subtopics:

- ASC 720-10, *Overall*
- ASC 720-15, *Start-Up Costs*
- ASC 720-20, *Insurance Costs*
- ASC 720-25, *Contributions Made*
- ASC 720-30, *Real and Personal Property Taxes*
- ASC 720-35, *Advertising Costs*
- ASC 720-40, *Electronic Equipment Waste Obligations*
- ASC 720-45, *Business and Technology Reengineering*
- ASC 720-50, *Fees Paid to the Federal Government by Pharmaceutical Manufacturers and Health Insurers*

ASC 720-10, *Overall*

ASC 720-10 provides no guidance. It merely lists all the Subtopics in Topic 720.

ASC 720-15, *Start-Up Costs*

ASC 720-15 applies to all nongovernmental entities. (ASC 720-15-15-1)

Start-up activities are based on the nature of the activity and not a time period. They include activities relating to organizing a new entity, and they may be called preoperating costs, preopening costs, and organization costs. (ASC 720-15-15-2 and 3)

This Subtopic lists the following specific activities that are *not* considered start-up costs and should be accounted for in accordance with other existing authoritative literature:

- Ongoing customer acquisition costs, such as policy acquisition costs (see Subtopic 944-30)
- Loan origination costs (see Subtopic 310-20)
- Activities related to routine, ongoing efforts to refine, enrich, or otherwise improve upon the qualities of an existing product, service, process, or facility
- Activities related to mergers or acquisitions
- Business process reengineering and information technology transformation costs addressed in Subtopic 720-45
- Costs of acquiring or constructing long-lived assets and getting them ready for their intended uses (however, the costs of using long-lived assets that are allocated to start-up activities (for example, depreciation of computers) are within the scope of this Subtopic)
- Costs of acquiring or producing inventory
- Costs of acquiring intangible assets (however, the costs of using intangible assets that are allocated to start-up activities (for example, amortization of a purchased patent) are within the scope of this Subtopic)
- Costs related to internally developed assets (for example, internal-use computer software costs)—however, the costs of using those assets that are allocated to start-up activities are within the scope of this Subtopic
- Research and development costs that are within the scope of Section 730-10-15
- Regulatory costs that are within the scope of Section 980-10-15
- Costs of fundraising incurred by not-for-profit organizations (NFPs)
- Costs of raising capital
- Costs of advertising
- Learning or start-up costs incurred in connection with existing contracts or in anticipation of future contracts for the same goods or services
- Costs incurred in connection with acquiring a contract
  (ASC 720-15-15-4)

ASC 720-15 provides guidance on financial reporting of start-up costs, including organization costs, and requires such costs to be expensed as incurred. (ASC 720-15-25-1) In addition to items mentioned above in the Scope section of this chapter, other costs outside the scope are store advertising, coupon giveaways within the scope of ASC 605 or ASC 606 when implemented, uniforms, furniture, cash registers, obtaining licenses, deferred financing costs, costs related to construction activities, such as security, property taxes, insurance, and utilities. (ASC 720-15-55-7)

ASC 720-20, *Insurance Costs*

ASC 720-20 applies to all entities. (ASC 720-20-15-2) The Subtopic contains Subsections with scope guidance as detailed below.

The Subsection on retroactive contracts applies to the following transactions:

- Those that meet the indemnification against loss or liability conditions of ASC 720-20-25-1
- Those that provide indemnification against loss or liability incurred related to a past event. (ASC 720-20-15-5)

The guidance in this Subsection does not apply to:

- Activities that legally extinguish the entity's liability
- Reinsurance transactions
  (ASC 720-20-15-6)

The Subsection on claims-made contracts does not apply to reinsurance transactions. (ASC 715-20-15-8)

The Subsection on multiple-year retrospectively rated contracts does not apply to a retrospectively rated insurance contract that is not a multiple-year contract or one that could be cancelled by either party without further obligations. (ASC 720-20-15-10)

ASC 720-20 provides guidance on:

- Retroactive contracts
- Claims-made contracts
- Multiple-year retrospectively rated contracts.

Guidance for each of the above is in a separate subsection. (ASC 720-20-05-1)

The premium paid minus the amount of the premium retained by the insurer is accounted for as a deposit by the insured. This is only to "the extent that an insurance contract or reinsurance contract does not, despite its form, provide for indemnification of the insured or the ceding entity by the insurer or reinsurer against loss or liability." (ASC 720-20-25-1)

Retroactive Contracts Amounts paid for retroactive insurance should be expensed when paid with a receivable established for expected recoveries. (ASC 720-20-25-3) If the amount paid for the insurance is less than the receivable, the entity should record a deferred gain. (ASC 720-20-25-4)

Claims-Made Contracts Retroactive and prospective provisions should be accounted for separately. If that is not practicable, the policy should be accounted for as a retrospective contract. (ASC 720-25-25-7 and 25-8)

Multiple-Year Retrospectively Rated Contracts For these contracts, the entity should recognize:

- A liability for the consideration the insured must pay
- An asset for any consideration the insurer must pay to the insured
  (ASC 720-20-25-15)

ASC 720-25, *Contributions Made*

ASC 720-25 applies to all entities. Not-for-profit entities should look to ASC 958-720 for additional guidance. (ASC 720-25-15-1) This Subtopic applies to contributions of cash and other assets, including promises to give made by resource providers, but it does not apply to items specified in ASC 958-605-15-6. (ASC 720-25-15-2 and 15-3)

Contributions made are expenses in the period when the contribution is made with the offsetting credit recorded as a decrease in assets or an increase in liabilities. Unconditional promises to give are recognized as payables and contribution expenses. ASC 958-605-25 contains guidance on conditional contributions. (ASC 720-25-25-1) Entities should recognize a gain or loss if a transferred asset's fair value differs from its carrying amount. (ASC 720-25-25-2)

ASC 720-30, *Real and Personal Property Taxes*

This Subtopic applies to all entities. (ASC 720-30-15-1)

Accrued real estate and personal property taxes represent the unpaid portion of an entity's obligation to a state, county, or other taxing authority that arises from the ownership of real or personal property, respectively. The most acceptable method of accounting for property taxes is a monthly accrual of property tax expense during the fiscal period of the taxing authority for which the taxes are levied. (ASC 720-30-25-7) The fiscal period of the taxing authority is the fiscal period that includes the assessment or lien date.

ASC 720-35, *Advertising Costs*

ASC 720-35 applies to all entities and to all advertising transactions and activities, except it does *not* apply to the following transactions:

- Direct-response advertising costs of an insurance entity (for guidance, see ASC 944-30).
- Advertising costs in interim periods (for guidance, see ASC 270-10-45-7).
- Costs of advertising conducted for others under contractual arrangements.
- Indirect costs that are specifically reimbursable under the terms of a contract.
- Fundraising by NFPs (however, ASC 720-35 does apply to advertising activities of NFPs).
- Customer acquisition activities, other than advertising.
- The costs of premiums, contest prizes, gifts, and similar promotions, as well as discounts or rebates, including those resulting from the redemption of coupons. (Other costs of coupons and similar items, such as the cost of newspaper advertising space, are considered advertising costs.)
  (ASC 720-35-15-3)

ASC 720-35 may or may not apply to activities, such as product endorsements and sponsorships of events, which may be performed pursuant to executory contracts. Generally, executory contract costs are recognized as the performance under the contract is received. If the costs are advertising costs, then this Subtopic applies. (ASC 720-35-15-4)

Except for the expenses detailed below in ASC 720-35-25-1A, the guidance offers two alternatives to accounting for the costs of advertising within the scope of the subtopic:

- Expensed as incurred
- Expensed the first time the advertising takes place, for example, the first time a television commercial airs or the first time a magazine appears for their intended purposes

Whichever alternative an entity chooses, it must apply it consistently to similar kinds of advertising. If the entity defers the costs, it must have the expectation that the advertising will occur. (ASC 720-35-25-1)

Advertising expenditures are sometimes made subsequent to the recognition of revenue (such as in "cooperative advertising" arrangements with customers). In order to achieve proper matching, these costs are estimated, accrued, and charged to expense when the related revenues are recognized. (ASC 720-35-25-1A)

Materials, such as sales brochures and catalogs, are accounted for as prepaid supplies until they are used. At that time, they are accounted for as advertising costs. (ASC 720-35-25-3)

ASC 720-35 has a separate guidance on communication advertising—television, airtime, and print advertising space. Costs associated with communication advertising are reported as advertising expense when the item or service has been received. (ASC 720-35-25-5)

Depreciation or amortization costs of a tangible asset used for advertising may be a cost of advertising. (ASC 720-35-35-1)

ASC 720-40, *Electronic Equipment Waste Obligations*

ASC 720-40 applies to all entities affected by Directive 2002/96 adopted by the European Union. (ASC 720-40-15-1) The guidance does not apply to:

- Historical costs from commercial users addressed in ASC 410-20, and
- New waste as defined in the Directive.
  (ASC 720-40-15-2)

ASC 720-40 contains "guidance on accounting for historical electronic equipment waste held by private households for obligations associated with Directive 2002/96/EC on Waste Electrical and Electronic Equipment adopted by the European Union." (ASC 720-40-05-01)

The Directive distinguishes between new and historical waste:

- New waste—put on the market after August 13, 2005
- Historical waste—put on the market on or before August 13, 2005

Only historical waste is dealt with by the Directive. (ASC 720-40-05-3) The Directive also distinguishes between waste from private households and commercial users. (ASC 720-45-05-4)

According to the Directive, producers in the markets should finance historical waste by private households. The obligation is not recognized before the beginning of a measurement period. (ASC 720-40-25-1) Producers bear the cost proportionally based on their share of the market as determine by each EU member country. (ASC 720-40-25-2) As the entity receives actual market share and program cost, it should adjust the liability. (ASC 720-40-35-1)

ASC 720-45, *Business and Technology Reengineering*

This Subtopic does not provide guidance for:

- Internal-use software costs (see ASC 350-40)
- The acquisition of property and equipment
  (ASC 720-45-15-2)

ASC 720-45 states that the cost of business process reengineering activities should be expensed as incurred. This includes internal efforts or third-party activities. (ASC 720-45-25-1)

These third-party costs should be expensed as incurred:

- Preparation of request for proposal
- Business current state assessment
- Business process reengineering
- Restructuring the workforce
  (ASC 720-45-25-2)

ASC 720-50, *Fees Paid to the Federal Government by Pharmaceutical Manufacturers and Health Insurers*

This Subsection applies to all pharmaceutical and health insurers subject to the annual fee described later in this chapter. (ASC 720-50-15-1)

ASC 720-50 provides guidance on certain provisions of the Patient Protection and Affordable Care Act, as amended by the Health Care and Education Reconciliation Act. Those acts require pharmaceutical manufacturers and health insurers to pay annual fees. (ASC 720-50-05-1 and 05-2)

The liability should be "estimated and recorded in full upon the first qualifying sale for pharmaceutical manufacturers or once the entity provides qualifying health insurance for health insurers in the applicable calendar year in which the fee is payable with a corresponding deferred cost that is amortized to expense using a straight-line method of allocation unless another method better allocates the fee over the calendar year that it is payable." (ASC 720-50-25-1)

PRACTICE ALERT

While SEC comments are addressed to registrants, the comments are insightful and reminders of items to address and decisions to document. In the area of start-up and advertising costs, the SEC staff has:

- Requested that the entity provide more detail in its disclosures about the current stage of the start-up, including:
  - The current status of development,
  - The steps taken towards planned operations,
  - The anticipated timeline, and
  - The steps that remain.
- Questioned the basis for accruing advertising costs.

PRESENTATION AND DISCLOSURE REQUIREMENTS

Presentation

Unless conditions for offsetting are met, offsetting prepaid insurance and receivables for expected recoveries against a recognized incurred but not reported liability or the liability incurred as a result of a past insurable event is not appropriate. (ASC 720-20-45-1)

Accrued liabilities for real and personal property taxes are included in current liabilities, described as estimated if subject to substantial uncertainty. (ASC 720-30-45-1)

An annual fee paid to the federal government by pharmaceutical manufacturers and health insurers is presented as an operating expense. (ASC 720-50-45-1)

Disclosure

For an entity that has changed from occurrence-based insurance to claims-made insurance or elects to significantly reduce or eliminate its insurance coverage, if it is at least reasonably possible that a loss has been incurred, consider possible disclosures with respect to unasserted claims. (ASC 720-20-50-1)

For advertising costs, entities should disclose:

- The accounting policy for reporting advertising, indicating whether such costs are expensed as incurred or expensed the first time the advertising takes place.
- The total amount charged to advertising expense for each income statement presented. (ASC 720-35-50-1)

PRESENTATION AND DISCLOSURE EXAMPLES

Example 44.1: Accounting Policy for Advertising Costs

Advertising costs are charged to operations in the period incurred, and totaled $348 million in 20X2, $396 million in 20X1, and $411 million in 20X0.

Example 44.2: Accounting Policy for Start-Up Costs

In accordance with ASC 720, *Start-Up Costs,* the Company expenses all costs incurred in connection with the start-up and organization of the Company.

Example 44.3: Organizational Costs Accounting Policy

In accordance with ASC 720, organizational costs, including accounting fees, legal fees, and costs of incorporation, are expensed as incurred.

45 ASC 730 RESEARCH AND DEVELOPMENT

AUTHORITATIVE LITERATURE

Overview

ASC 730 addresses the proper accounting and reporting for research and development costs. It identifies:

- Those activities that should be identified as research and development,
- The elements of costs that should be identified with research and development activities, and the accounting for these costs, and
- The financial statement disclosures related to them.
  (ASC 730-10-05-1)

The central issue in regard to research and development costs is that the future benefits related to these expenditures are uncertain. Given this uncertainty, it is generally difficult to justify classifying them as an asset. Generally, entities should charge them to expense as incurred. (ASC 730-10-05-2 and 05-3)

Subtopics

ASC 730, *Research and Development*, contains two Subtopics:

- ASC 730-10, *Overall*, which provides guidance on the activities, elements, costs, accounting, and disclosures for research and development
- ASC 730-20, *Research and Development Arrangements*, which provides guidance on arrangements used to finance research and development

Scope and Scope Exceptions

ASC 730 applies to all entities and to "activities aimed at developing or significantly improving a product or service (referred to as product) or a process or technique (referred to as process) whether the product or process is intended for sale or use." (ASC 710-30-15-3)

ASC 730 does *not* apply to:

- The costs of research and development activities conducted for others under a contractual arrangement
- Indirect costs
- Activities that are unique to entities in the extractive industries
- A process for use in an entity's selling or administrative activities
- Routine alterations to existing products and processes
- Market research
- Research and development assets acquired in an acquisition by not-for-profit entity or business combination
- Internally developed computer software and costs incurred to purchase or use computer software unless it is intended for use with R&D activities
  (ASC 730-10-15-4 and 5)

Note the following is effective upon implementation of ASU 2014-09, *Revenue from Contracts with Customers*: ASC 730-20 applies to arrangements for software development fully or partially funded by a party other than the vendor developing the software, and where technological feasibility has not been established. If the technological feasibility has been established before the arrangement is entered into, the guidance in ASC 730-20 does not apply to funded software arrangements. Neither does it apply to government research and development. (ASC 730-20-15-1A and 15-4)

ASC 730-10, *Research and Development—Overall*

There are three ways in which R&D costs are incurred by a business:

1. Purchase of R&D from other entities
2. Conducting R&D for others under a contractual arrangement
3. Conducting R&D activities for the benefit of the reporting entity

The accounting treatment relative to R&D depends upon the nature of the cost. R&D costs incurred in the ordinary course of operations consist of materials, equipment, facilities, personnel, and indirect costs that can be attributed to research or development activities. These costs are expensed in the period in which they are incurred unless they have alternative future uses. Examples of such R&D costs with alternative future uses include:

- Laboratory research to discover new knowledge
- Searching for applications of new research findings or other knowledge
- Formulation and design of product alternatives
- Testing for product alternatives
- Modification of products or processes
- Design, construction, and testing preproduction prototypes and models
- Design of tools, dies, etc. for new technology

- Pilot plants not capable of commercial production
- Engineering activity until the product is ready for manufacture
- Design and development tools used to facilitate research and development or components of a product or process that are undergoing research and development activities (ASC 730-10-55-1)

Examples of costs that are *not* considered R&D include:

- Engineering during an early phase of commercial production
- Quality control for commercial production
- Troubleshooting during a commercial production breakdown
- Routine, ongoing efforts to improve products
- Adaptation of existing capacity for a specific customer or other requirements
- Seasonal design changes to products
- Routine design of tools, dies, etc.
- Design, construction, start-up, etc. of equipment except that used solely for R&D
- Legal work related to patents or litigation (ASC 730-10-55-2)

ASC 730-20, *Research and Development Arrangements*

In many cases, entities will pay other parties to perform R&D activities on their behalf. Substance over form must be used in evaluating these arrangements. If costs are incurred to engage others to perform R&D activities that, in substance, could have been performed by the reporting entity itself, those costs must be expensed as incurred.

An alternative arrangement may consist of a business entering into a limited partnership where the limited partners provide funding and the business conducts the research under a contract with the partnership. Under such an arrangement, the partnership may retain legal ownership of the results of the research. The business may have an option to buy back the results of the research upon payment of a stipulated amount to the partnership.

On the other hand, if the payment is to acquire intangibles for use in R&D activities, and these assets have other uses, then the expenditure is capitalized and accounted for in accordance with ASC 350.

When R&D costs are incurred as a result of contractual arrangements, the nature of the agreement dictates the accounting treatment of the costs involved. The key determinant is the transfer of the risk associated with the R&D expenditures. Risk is not transferred to the other parties if there is a commitment by the business to repay the other parties.

If the business receives funds from another party to perform R&D and is obligated to repay those funds regardless of the outcome, a liability must be recorded and the R&D costs expensed as incurred. To conclude that a liability does not exist, the transfer of the financial risk must be substantive and genuine.

Nonrefundable Advance Payments Related to Future R&D Activities Nonrefundable advance payments are deferred and capitalized. (ASC 730-20-25-13) As the related goods are delivered and services performed, the capitalized amounts are to be recognized as expense. (ASC 730-20-35-1)

This is limited to nonrefundable advance payments for goods to be used or services to be rendered in future R&D activities pursuant to an executory contractual arrangement where the goods or services have no alternative future use.

PRACTICE ALERT

While SEC comments pertain to public entities, their comments can often provide valuable practice pointers for preparers of nonpublic entities. In the area of research and development, the SEC has commented on:

- The classification of research and development acquired as a result of a business consideration
- A change in the estimated fair value in contingent consideration as research and development expense in the consolidated statements of operations and why no portion was allocated to other costs

PRESENTATION AND DISCLOSURE REQUIREMENTS

Presentation

ASC 730 has no specific presentation requirements.

Disclosure

ASC 730-10 requires entities to disclose the total research and development costs expensed. This includes research and development costs incurred for a computer software product to be sold, leased, or otherwise marketed. (ASC 730-10-50-1)

If a research and development arrangement is accounted for a contract to perform research and development for others, the entity must disclose:

- The terms of significant arrangements, including:
  - Royalty arrangements
  - Purchase provisions
  - License agreements
  - Commitments to provide additional funding
- The amount of compensation earned and costs incurred under each contract (ASC 730-20-50-1)

ASC 730 does not require any specific disclosures for research and development arrangements accounted for as liabilities. The financial statement preparer may want to consider the guidance in ASC 440 on commitments.

PRESENTATION AND DISCLOSURE EXAMPLES

Example 45.1: Accounting Policy for Research and Development Costs

Research and development costs are charged to expense when incurred in accordance with FASB ASC 730, *Research and Development*. Research and development includes costs such as clinical trial expenses, contracted research and license agreement fees with no alternative future use, supplies and materials, salaries, share-based compensation, employee benefits, equipment depreciation, and allocation of various corporate costs. Purchased in-process research and development expense represents the value assigned or paid for acquired research and development for which there is no alternative future use as of the date of acquisition.

Example 45.2: Research and Development Costs Accounting Policy and Costs

In accordance with FASB ASC 730, research and development costs are expensed when incurred. Product and development costs were $237,658 and $867,887 for the years ended December 31, 20X2 and 20X1.

Example 45.3: Research and Development Incentive Income and Receivable

The Company recognizes other income from United Kingdom research and development incentives when there is reasonable assurance that the income will be received, the relevant expenditure has been incurred, and the consideration can be reliably measured. The small or medium-sized enterprise ("SME") research and development tax relief program supports companies that seek to research and develop an advance in their field and is governed through legislative law by HM Revenue & Customs as long as specific eligibility criteria are met.

Management has assessed the Company's research and development activities and expenditures to determine which activities and expenditures are likely to be eligible under the SME research and development tax relief program described above. At each period end management estimates the refundable tax offset available to the Company based on available information at the time. As the tax incentives may be received without regard to an entity's actual tax liability, they are not subject to accounting for income taxes. As a result, amounts realized under the SME R&D tax relief scheme are recorded as a component of other income.

The research and development incentive receivable represents an amount due in connection with the above program. The Company has recorded a research and development incentive receivable of approximately $444,000 as of December 31, 20X1 in the consolidated balance sheet and approximately $434,000 in other income in the consolidated statement of operations for the year then ended related to the SME research and development tax relief program.

Example 45.4: Research and Development Costs Increase Due to Acquisition

With the acquisitions of ABC in September 20X1 and XYZ in January 20X3, research and development ("R&D") costs factor more prominently into the Company's cost structure. Therefore, R&D costs are presented on the Consolidated Statement of Operations in order to provide transparency into these costs. Consistent with prior periods, the Company continues to account for R&D expenses in accordance with the provisions of ASC 730 and expense them as incurred.

46 ASC 740 INCOME TAXES

AUTHORITATIVE LITERATURE

Accounting Theory—A Balance Sheet Approach

When reporting income taxes, accounting theory has prioritized the statement of financial position. To compute deferred income taxes consistent with this balance sheet orientation requires use of the liability method. This method essentially ascertains, as of each date for which a statement of financial position is presented, the amount of future income tax benefits or obligations that are associated with the reporting entity's assets and liabilities existing at that time. Any adjustments necessary to increase or decrease deferred income taxes to the computed balance, plus or minus the amount of income taxes owed currently, determine the periodic income tax expense or benefit to be reported in the income statement. Put another way, income tax expense is the residual result of several other computations oriented to measurement in the statement of financial position.

There are two main objectives to accounting for income taxes:

1. Recognize the taxes payable or refundable on tax returns for the current year as a tax liability or asset
2. Recognize a deferred tax liability or asset for the estimated future tax effects attributable to temporary differences and carryforwards

ASC 740 provides guidance for:

- Recognizing and measuring the tax position taken in a tax return that affects amounts in financial statements
- Individual tax positions that do not meet the recognition thresholds required for the benefit of a tax position to be recognized in the financial statements
  (ASC 740-10-05-6)

Temporary differences, or differences between the tax basis for an asset or liability, result in taxable or deductible amounts in future years. Thus, these differences are often referred to as:

- Taxable temporary differences if they will result in taxable amounts in the future, or
- Deductible temporary differences if they will result in deductible amounts in the future.
  (ASC 740-10-05-7 and 05-8)

Technical Alert

In December 2019, the FASB issued ASU 2019-12, *Simplifying the Accounting for Income Taxes*. This ASU is part of the FASB's simplification initiative and is intended to simplify accounting for income taxes.

Guidance The ASU simplifies the accounting for income taxes by removing the following exceptions:

- Exception to the incremental approach for intraperiod tax allocation when there is a loss from continuing operations and income or gain from other items
- Exception to the requirement to recognize a deferred tax liability for equity method investments when a foreign subsidiary becomes an equity method investment
- Exception to the ability not to recognize a deferred tax liability for a foreign subsidiary when a foreign equity method investment becomes a subsidiary
- Exception to the general methodology for calculating income taxes in an interim when a year-to-date loss exceeds the anticipated loss for the year

The ASU is also designed to improve financial statement preparers' application of income tax–related guidance and simplify GAAP for:

- Franchise taxes that are partially based on income
- Transactions with a government that result in a step-up in the tax basis of goodwill
- Separate financial statements of legal entities that are not subject to tax
- Enacted changes in tax laws in interim periods

Subtopics

ASC 740, *Income Taxes*, consists of three Subtopics:

- ASC 740-10, *Overall*, which provides most of the guidance on accounting and reporting for income taxes.

- ASC 740-20, *Intraperiod Tax Allocation*, which provides guidance on the process of allocating income tax benefits or expenses to different components of comprehensive income and shareholders' equity. This includes allocating income tax expense or benefit to:
  - Continuing aspects
  - Discontinued operations
  - Other comprehensive income
  - Items charged or credited directly to shareholder's equity.
- ASC 740-30, *Other Considerations or Special Areas,* which provides guidance for specific limited exceptions, identified in ASC 740-10, related to investments in subsidiaries and corporate joint ventures arising from undistributed earnings or other causes.

Incremental guidance may also be found in other Topics, for example:

- Investments—Equity Method and Joint Ventures,
- Compensation—Stock Compensation,
- Business Combinations,
- Foreign Currency Matters,
- Reorganizations,
- Entertainment—Casinos,
- Extractive Activities—Oil and Gas,
- Financial Services—Depository and Lending,
- Financial Services—Insurance,
- Health Care Entities,
- Real Estate—Common Interest Realty Associations, and
- Regulated Operations.
  (ASC 740-10-05-4)

Scope and Scope Exceptions

The guidance in ASC 740-10 relating to uncertainty in income taxes includes any entity potentially subject to income taxes, including:

- Nonprofit organizations
- Flow-through entities (e.g., partnerships, limited liability companies, and S corporations)
- Entities whose income tax liabilities are subject to 100% credit for dividends paid, such as real estate investment trusts (REITs) and registered investment companies.
  (ASC 740-10-15-2AA)

ASC 740-10 does not apply directly or by analogy to:

- Other taxes.
- Franchise taxes or similar taxes to the extent based on capital or a non-income-based amount where no portion of the tax is based on income. The following guidance is added to ASC 740-10-15-4 by ASU 2019-12. (See Technical Alert at the beginning of this chapter.) If a franchise tax is partially based on income, deferred tax assets and liabilities should be recognized and accounted for under the guidance in ASC 740. When evaluating the realizability of its deferred tax assets, an entity should not consider the effect of potentially paying a non-income-based tax in future years. The amount of current tax expense equal to the amount that is based on income is accounted for under the

guidance in this Topic. Any incremental amount incurred is accounted for as a non-income-based tax.

- A withholding tax for the benefit of the recipients of a dividend.
(ASC 740-10-15-4)

The guidance in ASC 740-20 applies to basis differences arising from investments in subsidiaries and corporate joint ventures. The basic differences arise from exceptions to the general requirements in ASC 740-10 for the comprehensive recognition of deferred income taxes on temporary differences. (ASC 740-20-15-2 and 15-3)

Recognition

ASC 740 requires that all deferred income tax assets be given full recognition, whether arising from deductible temporary differences or from net operating loss or tax credit carryforwards. (ASC 740-10-25-2)

The only exceptions to applying the basic principles are:

- Where a deferred tax liability is not recognized for the following types of temporary differences unless it becomes apparent that they will reverse in the foreseeable future:
  - An essentially permanent difference in an excess of the amount for financial reporting over the tax basis of an investment for the foreign subsidiary or a foreign corporate joint venture
  - An essentially permanent difference in underestimated earnings of a domestic subsidiary or corporate joint venture that was in fiscal years beginning on or before December 15, 1992
  - For qualified thrift lenders, bad debt reserves for tax purposes that arose in tax years beginning before December 31, 1987
  - Policyholders of stock life insurance that arose in fiscal years beginning on or before December 15, 1992
- Upon implementation of ASC 842, the pattern of recognition of after-tax income for leveraged leases or the allocation of the purchase price in a purchase business combination of acquired leveraged leases
- A prohibition on recognition of
  - A deferred tax liability related to goodwill where amortization is not deductible for tax purposes
  - A deferred tax asset for the difference between the tax basis of inventory in the buyer's tax
  (ASC 740-10-25-3)

Under ASC 740 it is necessary to assess whether the deferred income tax asset is realizable. Testing for realization is accomplished by means of a "more-likely-than-not" criterion that indicates whether an allowance is needed to offset some or all of the recorded deferred income tax asset. (ASC 740-10-25-5) While the determination of the amount of the allowance may make use of the scheduling of future expected reversals, other methods may also be employed.

Basic Recognition Threshold The process of filing income tax returns requires management, in consultation with its tax advisors, to make judgments regarding how it will apply intricate and often ambiguous laws, regulations, administrative rulings, and court precedents. These judgments are called tax positions. If and when the income tax returns are audited by the taxing authority, sometimes years after they are filed, these judgments may be questioned or disallowed in their entirety or in part. As a result, management must make assumptions regarding the likelihood of success in defending its judgments in the event of audit in determining the accounting entries necessary to accurately reflect income taxes currently payable and/or refundable.

ASC 740-10 uses a two-step approach to recognition and measurement. The entity must evaluate each tax position as to whether, based on the position's technical merits, it is "more likely than not" that the position would be sustained upon examination by the taxing authority.

In making its evaluation, the entity is required to assume that the tax position will be examined by the taxing authority and that the taxing authority will be provided with all relevant facts and will have full knowledge of all relevant information. Thus, the entity is prohibited from asserting that a position will be sustained because of a low likelihood that the reporting entity's income tax returns will be examined. (ASC 740-10-25-7A)

For tax positions taken by management that do not meet the initial recognition criterion, the benefit becomes recognizable in the first interim period that the position meets any one of the following three conditions:

1. The more-likely-than-not threshold is met by the reporting date
2. The tax position is effectively settled through examination, negotiation, or litigation
3. The statute of limitations for the relevant taxing authority to examine and challenge the tax position has expired
   (ASC 740-10-25-8)

Tax Law Changes

If changes to income tax rates or other provisions of the income tax law are enacted, the effect of these changes must be recognized so that the deferred income tax assets and liabilities are fairly presented on the statement of financial position. (ASC 740-10-35-4)

When income tax rates are revised, this may impact not only the unreversed effects of items that were originally reported in the continuing operations section of the income statement, but also the unreversed effects of items first presented as discontinued operations or in other income statement captions. Furthermore, the impact of changes in income tax rates on the accumulated balance of deferred income tax assets or liabilities that arose through charges or credits to other comprehensive income (under ASC 220) is included in income tax expense associated with continuing operations.

Entities are permitted to reclassify stranded tax effects in accumulated other comprehensive income resulting from the Tax Cuts and Jobs Act to actual earnings. This provision does not affect other changes in tax law. (ASC 220-10-45-12A)

ASC 740-20, *Intraperiod Income Tax Allocation*

ASC 740-20 provides guidance on the allocation of intraperiod income tax expenses or benefits for a period to:

- Continuing operations
- Discontinued operations
- Other comprehensive income
- Items charged or credited directly to shareholders' equity
  (ASC 740-20-05-2)

The general principle is that the income statement presentation of the effects of income taxes should be the same as items to which the income taxes relate. A "with and without" approach is prescribed as the mechanism by which the marginal, or incremental, income tax effects of items other than those arising from continuing operations are to be measured.

ASC 730, *Other Consideration or Special Areas*

Undistributed Earnings of a Subsidiary While the timing of distribution of a subsidiary's net income to its parent may be uncertain, it will eventually occur, whether by means of dividends or via the disposal of the entity and realization of capital gains. Accordingly, deferred income taxes must be provided, but the amount will be dependent upon the anticipated means of realization. (ASC 740-30-25-3)

The magnitude of the income tax effects to be provided depends upon specific application of the income tax laws and management intent. (ASC 740-30-05-5) If the law provides a mechanism under which the parent can recover its investment tax-free, deferred income taxes are not provided.

In other cases, the minimization or avoidance of income taxes can be achieved only if the parent company owns a stipulated share of the subsidiary's stock. A parent owning less than this threshold level of its subsidiary may express its intent to utilize a tax planning strategy to acquire the necessary additional shares to realize this benefit. In evaluating this strategy, the cost of acquiring the additional shares must be considered, and the benefits to be recognized (i.e., a reduced deferred income tax liability) must be offset by the cost of implementing the strategy as discussed earlier in this chapter.

A distinction exists in the application of ASC 740-30 between differences in income tax and financial reporting basis that are considered "inside basis differences" versus "outside basis differences," and this is clarified by ASC 830-740-25.

Undistributed Earnings of an Investee When an entity has an equity method investee, it is presumed to be able to exercise significant influence, but lack control. Because the ability to indefinitely postpone income taxes on the investee's net income would be absent in such a case, GAAP requires full interperiod income tax allocation for the effects of undistributed investee net income. (ASC 740-30-25-15) The facts and circumstances involved in each situation, however, will be the final determinant of whether this temporary difference is assumed to be a future dividend or a capital gain for purposes of computing the deferred income tax effect.

PRACTICE ALERT

While SEC comments do not pertain to nonpublic entities, its comments can serve as pointers to presentation and disclosure problems of which nonpublic preparers should be aware. The SEC has focused its comment on reporting and disclosures for income taxes on:

- Compliance with disclosure requirements
  - Inclusion of transparent and complete disclosures
  - Omission of disclosures
  - Insufficient description of an accounting change or error
  - Tax elections
  - Amounts inconsistent with other information in the financial statements
  - Impact of temporary or permanent differences

- Valuation allowances
  - Realizability of deferred tax assets
  - Assessment of available positive and negative evidence used to determine the realizability of deferred tax assets
  - How the evidence was weighted
  - The objective verifiability of the evidence
  - Quantifying of projected taxable income, including time periods over which the tax assets will be used
  - Sources of future taxable income
  - The nature of tax strategies, uncertainties, risks, and assumptions
  - Whether the tax liabilities reverse in the same period and jurisdiction as the temporary benefits associated with the deferred tax assets
  - Significant estimates and assumptions used
  - Evidence for change in previously recorded valuation allowance and positive and negative evidence considered
- Significant or unusual events and their tax effects
  - The creation of temporary or permanent differences
  - Tax effect of the differences
  - Impact on future tax rates
- Impacts of recent tax legislation
  - Information that allows users to understand how the tax law changes are reflected in the financial statements
- Tax rate disclosures
  - Explanation of fluctuation in tax rates
  - Disclosures were unclear
  - Insufficient information about reconciling items and their underlying nature
  - Corrections of errors were incorrectly reflected as changes in estimates

PRESENTATION AND DISCLOSURE REQUIREMENTS

The *Disclosure and Presentation Checklist for Commercial Businesses*, found at www.wiley.com/go/FSDM2021, has a list of the interim and year-end presentation and disclosure requirements for this topic.

Presentation

Balance Sheet Balance sheet presentation considerations include:

- A reporting entity should present deferred tax assets and liabilities separate from income taxes payable or receivable on the balance sheet. (ASC 740-10-45-4)
- Deferred tax assets and liabilities and their valuation allowances are classified as noncurrent.
- A reporting entity can only offset deferred tax assets and liabilities within a jurisdiction. (ASC 740-10-45-6).
- A valuation allowance should be reflected as a reduction of the noncurrent deferred tax asset.
- The balance sheet classification of a liability for an unrecognized tax benefit as current versus noncurrent is determined based on the expected timing of cash payments. Balance sheet classification should be based on management's expectation of future cash payments. (ASC 740-10-45-11)

Income Statement—Classification of Interest and Penalties The decision as to whether to classify interest expense related to income taxes as a component of income tax expense or interest expense is an accounting policy election. Penalties are also allowed to be classified as a component of income tax expense or another expense classification (e.g., selling, general and administrative expense) depending on the reporting entity's accounting policy. Reporting entities are required to disclose their policy and the amount of interest and penalties charged to expense in each period, as well as the amounts accrued on the balance sheet for interest and penalties. (ASC 740-10-45-25)

The effects of changes in tax laws or rates are recognized in income from continuing operations in the period that includes the enactment date. (ASC 740-10-45-15) The tax effect of the enacted tax rates on current and deferred tax assets and liabilities should be determined at the date of enactment using temporary differences and currently taxable income existing as of the date of enactment. (ASC 740-10-45-17)

If a reporting entity experiences a change in tax status (e.g., change from a nontaxable partnership to a taxable corporation), the deferred tax effects of that change should be disclosed as a component of income tax expense attributable to continuing operations. (ASC 740-10-45-19)

Unrecognized tax benefits should be presented in the financial statements as a reduction to the deferred tax asset related to an NOL carryforward, a similar tax loss, or a tax credit carryforward. This presentation is not appropriate if:

- The NOL, similar tax loss, or tax credit carryforward is not available at the reporting date under the tax law of the applicable jurisdiction to settle any additional income generated by disallowance of a tax position, or
- The tax law does not require the entity to use, or the entity does not intend to use, the NOL, similar tax loss, or tax credit carryforward to offset additional income generated by disallowance of a tax position.

If either of these exceptions exists, the unrecognized tax benefit should be presented as a liability and not netted against the deferred tax asset for an NOL, similar tax loss, or tax credit carryforward. (ASC 740-10-45-10A and 45-10B)

Disclosures

Statement of Financial Position Critical balance sheet disclosures include:

- Total deferred tax assets and total deferred tax liabilities for each period a balance sheet is presented.
- The total valuation allowance and the net change in the valuation allowance for each period a balance sheet is presented. (ASC 740-10-50-2)
- The amounts and expiration dates of operating loss and tax credit carryforwards for tax purposes. (ASC 740-10-50-3a)
- Any portion of the valuation allowance for deferred tax assets for which subsequently recognized tax benefits will be credited directly to contributed capital. (ASC 740-10-50-3(b))
- Public entities must disclose the approximate tax effect of each type of significant temporary difference and tax carryforward that comprises deferred tax assets and liabilities (before allocation of valuation allowances). The assessment of what constitutes "significant" requires judgment. (ASC 740-10-50-6)

- A nonpublic company is not required to provide quantitative information regarding the types of temporary differences and carryforwards that give rise to significant deferred tax assets and liabilities. However, a nonpublic company must disclose the nature of significant items. (ASC 740-10-50-8)
- The nature and effect of any significant matters affecting comparability of information for all periods presented (unless otherwise evident from other disclosures). (ASC 740-10-50-14)
- The amount of income tax expense or benefit allocated to each component of other comprehensive income, including reclassification adjustments, either on the face of the statements in notes. (ASC 220-10-45-12)

Income Statement The significant components of income tax expense attributable to continuing operations for each year presented must be disclosed in the financial statements or notes. Those include:

- Current tax expense (or benefit)
- Deferred tax expense (or benefit) (exclusive of the effects of other components listed below)
- Investment tax credits
- Government grants (to the extent recognized as a reduction of income tax expense)
- The benefits of operating loss carryforwards
- Tax expense that results from allocating certain tax benefits directly to contributed capital
- Adjustments of a deferred tax liability or asset for enacted changes in tax laws or rates or a change in the tax status of the entity
- Adjustments of the beginning-of-the-year balance of a valuation allowance because of a change in circumstances that causes a change in judgment about the realizability of the related deferred tax asset in future years
  (ASC 740-10-50-9)

Reporting entities are required to disclose the amount of income tax expense or benefit allocated to continuing operations. (ASC 740-10-50-10) Reporting entities must also disclose amounts separately allocated to other categories of income in accordance with the intraperiod tax allocation provisions, such as discontinued operations and a cumulative effect of a change in accounting principle.

Income Tax Expense Compared to Statutory Expectations

Public Entities Public entities are required to provide a tax rate reconciliation that reconciles income tax expense attributable to continuing operations to the statutory Federal income tax rate applied to pretax income from continuing operations. Public entities can present the reconciliation using either dollar amounts or percentages. The reconciliation should include the estimated amount and the nature of each significant reconciling item. (ASC 740-10-50-12)

Nonpublic Entities A nonpublic company is not required to numerically reconcile the statutory and effective rates or provide the approximate tax effect of each type of temporary difference and carryforward that gives rise to significant deferred tax assets and liabilities. However, a nonpublic company must disclose the nature of significant reconciling items as well as a description of the significant temporary differences and carryforwards that affect comparability of information. (ASC 740-10-50-13)

Nonpublic companies are *not* required to include the following disclosures:

- Tabular reconciliation of the total amounts of unrecognized tax benefits at the beginning and end of the reporting date
- The net difference between the tax bases and the reported amounts of assets and liabilities when they are structured as nontaxable entities

Unrecognized Tax Benefit–Related Disclosures Reporting entities must disclose the nature of uncertain tax positions and related events if it is reasonably possible that the positions and events could change the associated recognized tax benefits within the next 12 months. This includes previously unrecognized tax benefits that are expected to be recognized upon the expiration of a statute of limitations within the next year. The following disclosures are required:

- Nature of the uncertainty
- Nature of the event that could occur within the next 12 months to cause the change
- Estimate of the range of the reasonably possible change, or statement that an estimate of the range cannot be made
  (ASC 740-10-50-15(d))

Reporting entities must disclose all tax years that remain open to assessment by a major tax jurisdiction. (ASC 740-10-50-15(e))

Public entities must include a reconciliation of the beginning and ending balances of the unrecognized tax benefits from uncertain positions that must disclose all unrecognized benefits. The reconciliations should cover all income statement periods presented and must disclose the total amount of unrecognized tax benefits that, if recognized, would impact the effective tax rate. (ASC 740-10-50-15A)

Policy-Related Disclosures Entities must disclose detail of the method of accounting used for investment tax credits and any material amounts involved. (ASC 740-10-50-20)

PRESENTATION AND DISCLOSURE EXAMPLES

Example 46.1: Accounting Policy for Income Taxes

The Company accounts for income taxes under the asset and liability method. Under the asset and liability method, deferred tax assets and liabilities are recognized for the future tax consequences attributable to differences between the financial statement carrying amounts of existing assets and liabilities and their respective tax bases. Deferred tax assets and liabilities are measured using enacted tax rates expected to apply to taxable income in the years in which those temporary differences are expected to be recovered or settled. The effect on deferred tax assets and liabilities of a change in tax rates is recognized in income in the period that includes the enactment date.

The Company records liabilities to address uncertain tax positions we have taken in previously filed tax returns or that we expect to take in a future tax return. The determination for required liabilities is based upon an analysis of each individual tax position, taking into consideration whether it is more likely than not that our tax position, based on technical merits, will be sustained upon examination. For those positions for which we conclude it is more likely than not the position will be sustained, we recognize the largest amount of tax benefit that is greater than 50% likely of being realized upon ultimate settlement with the taxing authority. The difference between the amount recognized and the total tax position is recorded as a liability. The ultimate resolution of these tax positions may be greater or less than the liabilities recorded.

The Company allocates tax expense among specific financial statement components using a "with-or-without" approach. Under this approach, the Company first determines the total tax expense or benefit (current and deferred) for the period. The Company then calculates the tax effect of pretax income from continuing operations only. The residual tax expense is allocated on a proportional basis to other financial statement components (i.e., discontinued operations, other comprehensive income).

Example 46.2: Accounting Policy for Income Taxes, Including Policy on Deferred Tax Assets

Current tax assets and liabilities are based upon an estimate of taxes refundable or payable for each of the jurisdictions in which the Company is subject to tax. In the ordinary course of business, there is inherent uncertainty in quantifying income tax positions. Toolkit software assesses income tax positions and records tax benefits for all years subject to examination based upon management's evaluation of the facts, circumstances, and information available at the reporting dates. For those tax positions where it is more likely than not that a tax benefit will be sustained, Toolkit records the largest amount of tax benefit with a greater than 50% likelihood of being realized upon ultimate settlement with a taxing authority that has full knowledge of all relevant information. For those income tax positions where it is not more likely than not that a tax benefit will be sustained, no tax benefit is recognized in the financial statements. When applicable, associated interest and penalties are recognized as a component of income tax expense. Accrued interest and penalties are included within the related tax asset or liability on the accompanying Consolidated Balance Sheets.

Deferred income taxes are provided for temporary differences arising from differences in bases of assets and liabilities for tax and financial reporting purposes. Deferred income taxes are recorded on temporary differences using enacted tax rates in effect for the year in which the temporary differences are expected to reverse. The effect of a change in tax rates on deferred tax assets and liabilities is recognized in income in the period that includes the enactment date. Deferred tax assets are reduced by a valuation allowance when, in the opinion of management, it is more likely than not that some portion or all of the deferred tax assets will not be realized.

Example 46.3: Provision for Income Taxes

The provision (benefit) for income taxes consists of the following:

(Amounts in thousands)	*20X2*	*20X1*	*20X0*
Current:			
Federal	$110.0	$117.9	$166.9
Foreign	38.1	52.4	41.1
State	29.5	30.4	30.6
Total current	177.6	200.7	238.6
Deferred:			
Federal	26.6	18.7	8.7
Foreign	1.5	(8.4)	2.9
State	6.1	3.4	0.7
Total deferred	34.2	13.7	12.3
Total income tax provision	$ 211.8	$ 214.4	$ 250.9

Example 46.4: Reconciliation of Federal Income Tax Rate to Effective Tax Rate

The following is a reconciliation of the statutory federal income tax rate to effective tax rate:

	20X2	*20X1*	*20X0*
Statutory federal income tax rate	21.0%	21.0%	35.0%
Increase (decrease) in tax rate resulting from:			
State income taxes, net of federal benefit	2.9	2.9	2.4
Noncontrolling interests	(0.4)	(0.4)	(0.6)
Repatriation of foreign earnings	(0.1)	(0.1)	(1.2)
Change in valuation allowance for deferred tax assets	0.4	0.3	0.1
Adjustments to tax accruals and reserves	(0.4)	(0.2)	(0.3)
Foreign rate differences	0.4	0.4	(2.4)
Domestic production activities deduction	—	—	(2.1)
Excess tax benefits related to equity compensation	(0.5)	(0.8)	(1.4)
U.S. tax reform, net impact	—	0.4	0.9
Other	(0.3)	0.1	0.1
Effective tax rate	23.0%	23.6%	30.5%

The Company's effective income tax rate on earnings was 23.4% in 20X2, 24.0% in 20X1, and 31.1% in 20X0. The effective tax rate for 20X2 and 20X1 reflects the reduction of the U.S. federal corporate income tax rate from 35% to 21%; 20X1 also included an additional nonrecurring net tax charge attributable to the prior year's U.S. tax reform changes. The effective tax rate for 20X0 included a one-time net tax costs associated with tax legislations, which was signed into law in the fourth quarter of 20X0, as well as tax benefits associated with certain legal charges.

Example 46.5: Tax Legislation

On December 22, 2017, the U.S. government passed the Tax Act. The Tax Act made broad and complex changes to the U.S. tax code, including, but not limited to (i) reducing the U.S. federal corporate tax rate from 35% to 21%; (ii) requiring companies to pay a one-time transition tax on certain unremitted earnings of foreign subsidiaries; and (iii) bonus depreciation that allows for full expensing of qualified property.

The Tax Act also established new tax laws that affect years after 2017, including, but not limited to (i) the reduction of the U.S. federal corporate tax rate discussed above; (ii) a general elimination of U.S. federal income taxes on dividends from foreign subsidiaries; (iii) a new provision designed to tax global intangible low-taxed income ("GILTI"); (iv) the repeal of the domestic production activity deductions; (v) limitations on the deductibility of certain executive compensation; (vi) limitations on the use of foreign tax credits to reduce the U.S. income tax liability; and (vii) a new provision that allows a domestic corporation an immediate deduction for a portion of its foreign derived intangible income ("FDII").

The Securities and Exchange Commission staff issued Staff Accounting Bulletin ("SAB") 118, which provided guidance on accounting for the tax effects of the Tax Act, for the Company's year ended December 30, 2017. SAB 118 provided a measurement period that should not extend beyond one year from the Tax Act enactment date for companies to complete the related accounting under ASC 740, *Income Taxes*. In accordance with SAB 118, a company must reflect the income tax effects of those aspects of the Tax Act for which the accounting under Accounting Standards Codification ("ASC") 740 is complete. To the extent that a company's accounting for a certain income tax effect of the Tax Act is incomplete, but the company is able to determine a reasonable estimate, it must record a provisional estimate in the financial statements. If a company cannot determine a provisional estimate to be included in the financial statements, it should continue to apply ASC 740 on the basis of the provisions of the tax laws that were in effect immediately before the enactment of the Tax Act.

The Company's accounting for certain elements of the Tax Act was incomplete as of December 30, 2017. However, the Company was able to make reasonable estimates of the effects and, therefore, recorded provisional estimates for these items. In connection with its initial analysis of the impact of the Tax Act, the Company recorded a provisional discrete net tax expense of $7.0 million in the fiscal year ended December 31, 2017. This provisional estimate consisted of a net expense of $13.7 million for the one-time transition tax and a net benefit of $6.7 million related to revaluation of deferred tax assets and liabilities, caused by the new lower corporate tax rate. To determine the transition tax, the Company must determine the amount of post-1986 accumulated earnings and profits of the relevant subsidiaries, as well as the amount of non-U.S. income taxes paid on such earnings. While the Company was able to make a reasonable estimate of the transition tax for 2017, it continued to gather additional information to more precisely compute the final amount reported on its 2017 U.S. federal tax return, which was filed in October 2018. The actual transition tax was $8.3 million greater than the Company's initial estimate and was included in income tax expense for 2018. Likewise, while the Company was able to make a reasonable estimate of the impact of the reduction to the corporate tax rate, it was affected by other analyses related to the Tax Act, including, but not limited to, the state tax effect of adjustments made to federal temporary differences. During 2018, the Company recorded additional net tax benefits of $4.4 million attributable to pension contributions made in 2018 that were deductible for 2017 at the higher 35% federal tax rate and other changes to the 2017 tax provision related to the Tax Act and subsequently issued tax guidance. Due to the complexity of the new GILTI tax rules, the Company continued to evaluate this provision of the Tax Act and the application of ASC 740 throughout 2018. Under GAAP, the Company is allowed to make an accounting policy choice to either (i) treat taxes due on future U.S. inclusions in taxable income related to GILTI as a current-period expense when incurred (the "Period Cost Method"); or (ii) factor in such amounts into the Company's measurement of its deferred taxes (the "Deferred Method"). The Company elected to apply the Period Cost Method to account for the new GILTI tax and treated it as a current-period expense for 2019 and 2018.

Example 46.6: Schedule of Temporary Differences

Temporary differences that give rise to the net deferred income tax asset as of 20X2, 20X1, and 20X0 year end are as follows:

(Amounts in millions)	*20X2*	*20X1*	*20X0*
Deferred income tax assets (liabilities):			
Inventories	$ 34.7	$ 33.6	$ 28.8
Accruals not currently deductible	62.4	72.9	61.7
Tax credit carryforward	2.0	1.8	2.1
Employee benefits	41.3	56.5	56.8
Net operating losses	40.4	40.9	44.0
Depreciation and amortization	(178.9)	(167.5)	(161.3)
Valuation allowance	(27.8)	(25.1)	(25.2)
Equity-based compensation	16.2	16.6	17.1
Undistributed non-U.S. earnings	(6.6)	(6.0)	—
Cash flow hedge	—	—	(0.3)
Other	(0.7)	(0.4)	(0.1)
Net deferred income tax asset (liability)	$ (17.0)	$ 23.3	$ 23.6

Example 46.7: Schedule of Net Operating Loss Carryforwards

As of 20X2 year end, the Company had tax net operating loss carryforwards totaling $209.6 million as follows:

(Amounts in thousands)	State	Federal	Foreign	Total
Year of expiration:				
20X3–20X7	$ 0.3	$ —	$ 59.0	$ 59.3
20X8–20Y2	—	—	9.4	9.4
20Y3–20Y7	74.4	—	—	74.4
20Y8–20Z2	—	—	—	—
20Z3–20Z7	—	—	34.1	34.1
Indefinite	—	—	32.4	32.4
Total net operating loss carryforwards	$ 74.7	$ —	$ 134.9	$ 209.6

Example 46.8: Deferred Income Tax Assets Valuation Allowance

A valuation allowance totaling $27.8 thousand, $25.1 thousand, and $25.2 thousand as of 20X2, 20X1, and 20X0 year end, respectively, has been established for deferred income tax assets primarily related to certain subsidiary loss carryforwards that may not be realized. Realization of the net deferred income tax assets is dependent on generating sufficient taxable income prior to their expiration. Although realization is not assured, management believes it is more likely than not that the net deferred income tax assets will be realized. The amount of the net deferred income tax assets considered realizable, however, could change in the near term if estimates of future taxable income during the carryforward period fluctuate.

Example 46.9: Reconciliations of Beginning and Ending Balances of Unrecognized Tax Benefits

The following is a reconciliation of the beginning and ending amounts of unrecognized tax benefits for 20X2, 20X1, and 20X0:

(Amounts in millions)	20X2	20X1	20X0
Unrecognized tax benefits at beginning of year	$ 11.1	$ 7.7	$ 9.4
Gross increases: tax positions in prior periods	—	1.3	1.4
Gross decreases: tax positions in prior periods	(0.6)	(0.1)	—
Gross increases: tax positions in the current period	0.5	2.8	1.0
Settlements with taxing authorities	—	—	(3.6)
Lapsing of statutes of limitations	(0.7)	(0.6)	(0.5)
Unrecognized tax benefits at end of year	$ 10.3	$ 11.1	$ 7.7

The unrecognized tax benefits of $10.3 million, $11.1 million, and $7.7 million as of 20X2, 20X1, and 20X0 year end, respectively, would impact the effective income tax rate if recognized. As of December 28, 20X2, unrecognized tax benefits of $1.2 million and

$9.1 million were included in Deferred income tax assets and Other long-term liabilities, respectively, on the accompanying Consolidated Balance Sheets. Interest and penalties related to unrecognized tax benefits are recorded in income tax expense. As of 20X2, 20X1, and 20X0 year end, the Company had provided for $1.1 million, $0.8 million, and $0.6 million, respectively, of accrued interest and penalties related to unrecognized tax benefits. During 20X2, the Company increased the reserve attributable to interest and penalties associated with unrecognized tax benefits by a net $0.3 million. As of December 28, 20X2, $1.1 million of accrued interest and penalties were included in Other long-term liabilities on the accompanying Consolidated Balance Sheets.

Example 46.10: Statute of Limitations and Its Effect on Tax Benefits

The Company and its subsidiaries file income tax returns in the United States and in various state, local, and foreign jurisdictions. It is reasonably possible that certain unrecognized tax benefits may either be settled with taxing authorities or the statutes of limitations for such items may lapse within the next 12 months, causing the Company's gross unrecognized tax benefits to decrease by a range of zero to $2.4 million. Over the next 12 months, the Company anticipates taking certain tax positions on various tax returns for which the related tax benefit does not meet the recognition threshold. Accordingly, the Company's gross unrecognized tax benefits may increase by a range of zero to $0.9 million over the next 12 months for uncertain tax positions expected to be taken in future tax filings.

Example 46.11: Tax Examinations

With few exceptions, the Company is no longer subject to U.S. federal and state/local income tax examinations by tax authorities for years prior to 20X1, and the Company is no longer subject to non-U.S. income tax examinations by tax authorities for years prior to 20X9.

Example 46.12: Effective Tax Rate

The following table summarizes our effective tax rate from income for the periods presented:

		For the Fiscal Year Ended	
	December 31, 20X2	*December 31, 20X1*	*December 31, 20X0*
		(Amounts in thousands)	
Income before income taxes	$ 30,821	$ 54,713	$ 12,801
Provision (benefit) for income taxes	(6,060)	9,813	13,395
Effective tax rate	(19.7)%	17.9%	104.6%

We are subject to income taxes in the United States and Australia. Our effective tax rate and provision for income taxes decreased from the fiscal year ended December 31, 20X1, to the fiscal year ended December 31, 20X2, primarily due to increased excess tax benefits from stock-based compensation, additional qualified activities for U.S. and Texas research and development tax credits, and the prior year Tax Act remeasurement of deferred tax assets that was not in effect for the current year.

Example 46.13: Financial Statement Presentation of Discontinued Operations with Provision for Income Taxes

Income Statement (ASC 740-270-55-52)

Net sales*		$xxxx
Other income*		xxx
Costs and expenses		
Cost of sales*	$xxxx	
Selling, general, and administrative expenses*	xxx	
Interest expense*	xx	
Other deductions*	xx	
Unusual items*	xxx	
Infrequently occurring items*	xxx	xxxx
Income (loss) from continuing operations before income taxes and other items listed below		xxxx
Provision for income taxes (benefit)**		xxx
Income (loss) from continuing operations before items listed below		xxxx
Discontinued operations:		
Income (loss) from operations of discontinued Division X (less applicable income taxes of $xxxx)	xxxx	
Income (loss) on reclassification of assets of Division X to held-for-sale (less applicable taxes of $xxxx)	xxxx	xxxx
Income (loss) before unusual items and cumulative effect of a change in accounting principle		xxxx
Unusual items (less applicable income taxes of $xxxx)		xxxx
Cumulative effect on prior years of a change in accounting principle (less applicable income taxes of $xxxx)***		xxxx
Net income (loss)		$xxxx

* *Components of ordinary income (loss).*
** *Consists of total income taxes (benefit) applicable to ordinary income (loss), unusual items, and infrequently occurring items.*
*** *This amount is shown net of income taxes. Although the income taxes are generally disclosed (as illustrated), this is not required.*

47 ASC 805 BUSINESS COMBINATIONS

AUTHORITATIVE LITERATURE

Historically, one of the most daunting problems facing accountants has been how to account for the acquisition of one enterprise by another, or other combination of two or more formerly unrelated entities, into one new enterprise.

U.S. GAAP requires the acquisition method of accounting for business combinations. The acquisition method requires that the actual cost of the acquisition be recognized, including any excess over the amounts allocable to the fair value of identifiable net assets, commonly known as "goodwill."

The major accounting issues in business combinations and in the preparation and presentation of consolidated or combined financial statements are:

- The proper accounting basis for the assets and liabilities of the combining entities
- The accounting for goodwill or negative goodwill (the gain from a bargain purchase)

The accounting for the assets and liabilities of entities acquired in a business combination is largely dependent on the fair values assigned to them at the transaction date. ASC 820, *Fair Value Measurements*, provides a framework for measuring fair value and important guidance when assigning values as part of a business combination. In essence, it favors valuations determined on the open market, but allows other methodologies if open market valuation is not practicable.

Techniques for Structuring Business Combinations

A business combination can be structured in a number of different ways that satisfy the acquirer's strategic, operational, legal, tax, and risk management objectives. Some of the more frequently used structures are:

- One or more businesses become subsidiaries of the acquirer. As subsidiaries, they continue to operate as legal entities.
- The net assets of one or more businesses are legally merged into the acquirer. In this case, the acquiree entity ceases to exist (in legal vernacular, this is referred to as a *statutory merger*, and normally the transaction is subject to approval by a majority of the outstanding voting shares of the acquiree).
- The owners of the acquiree transfer their equity interests to the acquirer entity or to the owners of the acquirer entity in exchange for equity interests in the acquirer.
- All of the combining entities transfer their net assets (or their owners transfer their equity interests) into a new entity formed for the purpose of the transaction. This is sometimes referred to as a *roll-up*, or put-together, transaction.
- A former owner or group of former owners of one of the combining entities obtains control of the combined entities collectively.
- An acquirer might hold a noncontrolling equity interest in an entity and subsequently purchase additional equity interests sufficient to give it control over the investee. These transactions are referred to as *step acquisitions*, or business combinations achieved in stages.
- A business owner organizes a partnership, S corporation, or LLC to hold real estate. The real estate is the principal location of the commonly owned business and that business entity leases the real estate from the separate entity.

Subtopics

ASC 805, *Business Combinations*, consists of six Subtopics:

- ASC 805-10, *Overall*, which provides guidance on transactions accounted for under the acquisition method
- ASC 852-20, *Identifiable Assets and Liabilities, and Any Noncontrolling Interest*, which deals with specific aspects of the acquisition method
- ASC 805-30, *Goodwill or Gain from Bargain Purchase, Including Consideration Transferred*, which, like ASC 805-20, deals with specific aspects of the acquisition method
- ASC 805-40, *Reverse Acquisitions*, which provides guidance on business combinations that are reverse acquisitions
- ASC 805-50, *Related Issues—Pushdown Accounting*, which offers guidance on two items that are similar, but not the same, as a business combination: acquisition of assets, and transactions between entities under common control
- ASC 805-740, *Income Taxes*, which provides "incremental guidance" on business combinations and on acquisitions by a not-for-profit (NFP) entity

Scope and Scope Exceptions

Transactions or other events that meet the definition of a business combination or an acquisition by a not-for-profit entity are subject to ASC 805. (ASC 801-10-15-3) Excluded from the scope of ASC 805, however, are:

- Formation of a joint venture
- Acquisition of an asset or group of assets that does not represent a business or a nonprofit activity
- Combinations between entities, businesses, or nonprofit activities under common control
- An acquisition by a NFP entity for which the acquisition date is before December 15, 2009, or a merger of NFP entities
- An event in which an NFP obtains control of a not-for-profit entity but does not consolidate that entity, as permitted or required by ASC 958-810-25-4
- If an NFP that obtained control in an event in which consolidation was permitted but not required decides in a subsequent annual reporting period to begin consolidating a controlled entity that it initially chose not to consolidate
- Financial assets and liabilities of a consolidated VIE that is a collateralized financing entity within the scope of 815-10
  (ASC 805-10-15-4)

Transactions and Events Accounted for as Business Combinations

A business combination results from the occurrence of a transaction or other event that results in an acquirer obtaining control of one or more businesses. This can occur in many different ways that include the following examples individually or, in some cases, in combination:

- Transfer of cash, cash equivalents, or other assets, including the transfer of assets of another business of the acquirer
- Incurring liabilities
- Issuance of equity instruments
- By providing more than one type of consideration

By contract alone without the transfer of consideration, such as when:

- An acquiree business repurchases enough of its own shares to cause one of its existing investors (the acquirer) to obtain control over it
- There is a lapse of minority veto rights that had previously prevented the acquirer from controlling an acquiree in which it held a majority voting interest
- An acquirer and acquiree contractually agree to combine their businesses without a transfer of consideration between them
  (ASC 805-10-55-2)

Qualifying as a Business

Clarifying the Definition of a Business The FASB Accounting Standards Codification presents an upfront, initial screen and a framework for financial reporters to use when determining whether a set of assets and activities is a business.

The Elements of a Business "A business is an integrated set of assets and activities that is capable of being conducted and managed for the purpose of providing a return in the form of dividends, lower cost, or other economic benefits directly to investors or other owners, members, or participants." (ASC 805-10-55-3A)

A business typically has:

- Inputs.
- Processes applied to those inputs. Documentation of processes is not required. The ASU clarifies that a process can be provided by the intellectual capacity of an organized workforce with the necessary skills and experience to use inputs to create outputs. For example, consulting firm employees may be capable of using the intellectual capacity to generate a product that can be sold to customers.
- Outputs that are used to generate a return to investors. However, outputs are not required for a set to be a business under both the extant and the new guidance. The new guidance defines an output as the result of inputs and processes applied to those inputs that provide:
  - Goods or services to customers,
  - Investment income (such as dividends or interest), or
  - Other revenues.
    (ASC 805-10-55-4)

The description of outputs focuses on revenue-generating activities, aligning the definition more closely with that in the revenue guidance in ASC 606.

Presence of Goodwill The existence of more than an insignificant amount of goodwill *may* indicate that a process included in the set is substantive. (ASC 805-10-55-9)

Accounting for Business Combinations Under the Acquisition Method

The acquirer accounts for a business combination using the *acquisition method*. (ASC 805-10-25-1)

The following steps are required to apply the acquisition method:

1. Identify the acquirer.
2. Determine the acquisition date.
3. Identify the assets and liabilities, if any, requiring separate accounting because they result from transactions that are not part of the business combination, and account for them in accordance with their nature and the applicable GAAP.

4. Identify assets and liabilities that require acquisition date classification or designation decisions to facilitate application of GAAP in postcombination financial statements and make those classifications or designations based on (a) contractual terms, (b) economic conditions, (c) acquirer operating or accounting policies, and (d) other pertinent conditions existing at the acquisition date.
5. Recognize and measure the identifiable tangible and intangible assets acquired and liabilities assumed.
6. Recognize and measure any noncontrolling interest in the acquiree.
7. Measure the consideration transferred.
8. Recognize and measure goodwill or, if the business combination results in a bargain purchase, recognize a gain.
(ASC 805-10-05-4)

Private Company Alternative for Accounting for Identifiable Intangible Assets in a Business Combination

If an entity adopts this alternative, it should no longer recognize and measure (and instead subsume into goodwill):

- Customer-related intangible assets, unless they are capable of being sold or licensed independently from the other assets of the business, and
- Noncompetition agreements.

An entity that elects the accounting alternative must adopt the private company alternative to amortize goodwill. (ASC 805-20-15-4) See the chapter on ASC 350, *Intangibles—Goodwill and Other*. However, an entity that elects the accounting alternative is not required to adopt the amendments in this topic.

Entities must decide whether or not to apply the accounting alternative upon the occurrence of the first transaction within the scope of this accounting alternative in fiscal years beginning after December 15, 2015. The elective adoption is effective for the fiscal year's first in-scope adoption annual financial reporting and all interim and annual periods thereafter. If the first in-scope transaction occurs in fiscal years beginning after December 15, 2016, the elective adoption is effective in the interim period that includes the date of that first in-scope transaction and subsequent interim and annual periods thereafter.

ASC 805-40, *Reverse Acquisitions*

A reverse acquisition is a stock transaction that occurs when one entity (the legal acquirer) issues so many of its shares to the former owners of another entity (the legal acquiree) that those former owners become the majority owners of the resultant consolidated enterprise. As a result of the transaction, the legal and accounting treatments will differ, with the legal acquiree being treated as the acquirer for financial reporting purposes. (ASC 805-40-20) While often the legal acquirer will adopt the acquiree's name, thus alerting users of the financial statements to the nature of the organizational change, this does not necessarily occur, and, in any event, it is critical that the financial statements contain sufficient disclosure so that users are not misled.

Following a reverse acquisition, just as in any business combination, consolidated financial statements must be presented. Although the financial statements will be identified as being those of the legal acquirer (which will be the legal owner of the legal acquiree), in substance these will be a continuation of the financial statements of the legal subsidiary/GAAP acquirer, with the assets, liabilities, revenues, and expenses of the legal acquirer being consolidated effective with the acquisition date.

Comparative financial statements for earlier periods, if presented, should be consistent, meaning that in order for them to be comparable to the postacquisition financial statements, these would also need to represent the financial statements of the legal acquiree. Since in some instances the acquiree's name is different from that shown in the heading, care must be taken to fully communicate with the readers. The fact that the prior period's financial information, identified as being that of the legal parent, is really that of the legal acquiree is obviously extremely pertinent to a reader's understanding of the financial statements.

If the legal parent/accounting subsidiary does not change its name to that of the accounting parent, it is essential that the financial statement titles be captioned in a way that clearly communicates the substance of the transaction to the readers. For example, the statements may be headed "ABC Company, Inc.—Successor to XYZ Corporation."

One adjustment to the financial statements is unique to a reverse acquisition. Management must retroactively adjust the capital of the legal acquiree/GAAP acquirer to reflect the legal capital of the legal acquirer/GAAP acquiree. The adjustment is necessary in order for the consolidated statement of financial position to reflect the capital of the legal parent/GAAP subsidiary. Information presented for comparative purposes in the consolidated financial statements should also be retroactively adjusted to reflect the legal parent's legal capital. (ASC 805-40-45-1)

The consolidated financial statements present the continuation of the financial statements of the legal subsidiary with the exception of its capital structure. Thus, those postcombination consolidated financial statements reflect the items detailed in ASC 805-40-45-2. (www.wiley.com/go/FSDM2021)

ASC 805-50, *Related Issues—Pushdown Accounting*

Under new basis (or *pushdown*) accounting, when an acquirer obtains control of an acquiree, an acquirer has the option of adjusting the amounts allocated to various assets and liabilities to reflect the arm's-length valuation reflected in a significant transaction, such as the sale of a majority interest in the entity. (ASC 805-50-25-4) The logic is that, as under accounting for business combinations, the most objective gauge of "cost" is that arising from a recent arm's-length transaction.

Pushdown accounting can be applied retrospectively as a change in accounting policy. Once applied, pushdown accounting cannot be undone. Pushdown accounting is optional for an entity each time an acquirer obtains control of the entity. The acquirer must still apply business combination accounting.

PRACTICE ALERT

While SEC comments do not pertain to nonpublic entities, preparers of nonpublic entities should review them and consider if any are relevant. In the area of business combinations, the SEC has asked for:

- Pro forma information
- An explanation of how the entity determined the fair value of acquired intangible assets
- An evaluation of whether the acquired assets are a business or an asset
- The reasons for the acquisition
- A table with the fair value of major classes of acquired assets and assumed liabilities
- Information on how the entity determined that identifiable assets have indefinite lives

- How the entity determined the useful lives of finite-lived intangible assets
- Qualitative descriptions of the factors that make up goodwill
- An analysis of how the acquirer was determined
- A description of a contingent consideration arrangement
- How the amount of consideration was determined
- An estimate of the range of outcomes related to contingent consideration
- The items for which the measurement period is still open
- The amount and classification of acquisition-related costs

PRESENTATION AND DISCLOSURE REQUIREMENTS

Presentation

Preparation and Presentation of Consolidated Financial Statements For consolidated financial statements prepared following a reverse acquisition, the financial statements are:

- Issued under the name of the legal parent
- Described in the notes as a continuation of the financial statements of the legal subsidiary
- Contain one adjustment: to retroactively adjust the acquirer's legal capital to reflect the legal capital of the acquiree
- Comparative information in the statements is retroactively adjusted to reflect legal capital of the legal parent
  (ASC 805-40-45-1)

Consolidated financial statements reflect:

- Assets and liabilities of the acquirer, recognized and measured at their precombination carrying amounts
- Assets and liabilities of the acquiree, recognized and measured in accordance with guidance in ASC 805 for business combinations
- Retained earnings and other equity balances of the legal subsidiary (accounting acquirer) before the business combination
- Equity interest, determined by adding the issued equity interest of the acquirer outstanding before the business combination to the fair value of the acquiree
- Noncontrolling interest's proportionate share of the acquirer's precombination carrying amounts of retained earnings and other equity interest
  (ASC 805-40-45-2)

Financial Statement Presentation in Period of Transfer Receiving entity reports results of operations for the period in which the transfer occurs as though the transfer had occurred at the beginning of the period. (ASC 805-50-45-2)

The statement of financial position and other financial information for the period in which the transfer occurs are presented as though the transfer had occurred at the beginning of the period. (ASC 805-50-45-4)

Comparative Financial Statement Presentation for Prior Years Financial statements and information presented for prior years:

- Is retrospectively adjusted
- Indicates the financial information of previously separate entities is combined

- Comparative information in prior years only adjusted for periods during which the entities were under common control (ASC 805-50-45-5)

Disclosures

Business Combinations Occurring During a Current Reporting Period or After the Reporting Date but Before the Financial Statements Are Issued Disclosures include information that enables the users to evaluate business combinations *occurring during the reporting period* or after the reporting date but before the financial statements are available to be issued. (ASC 805-10-50-1)

For each business combination that occurs during the reporting period, disclose:

a. Name and description of the acquiree.
b. Acquisition date.
c. Percentage of voting equity interest acquired.
d. Primary reasons for the business combination.
e. Description of how the acquirer obtained control over the acquiree.
f. For transactions that are recognized separately from the acquisition of assets and assumptions of liabilities in the business combination:
   ○ Description of each transaction,
   ○ How the acquirer accounted for each transaction,
   ○ Amounts recognized for each transaction and the line item in the financial statements in which each amount is recognized, and
   ○ If the transaction is the effective settlement of a preexisting relationship, the method used to determine the settlement amount.
g. For disclosures required in (f) above:
   ○ Amount of acquisition-related costs,
   ○ Amount recognized as an expense,
   ○ Line item or items in the income statement in which those expenses are recognized, and
   ○ Amount of any issuance costs not recognized as an expense and how they were recognized.
h. In a business combination achieved in stages, all of the following:
   ○ The acquisition-date fair value of the equity interest in the acquiree held by the acquirer immediately before the acquisition date.
   ○ The amount of any gain or loss recognized as a result of remeasuring to fair value the equity interest in the acquiree held by the acquirer immediately before the business combination (see paragraph 805-10-25-10) and the line item in the income statement in which that gain or loss is recognized.
   ○ The valuation techniques used to measure the acquisition-date fair value of the equity interest in the acquiree held by the acquirer immediately before the business combination.
   ○ Information that enables users of the acquirer's financial statements to assess the inputs used to develop the fair value measurement of the equity interest in the acquiree held by the acquirer immediately before the business combination.
i. If the acquirer is a public entity, all of the following:
   ○ The amounts of revenue and earnings of the acquiree since the acquisition date included in the consolidated income statement for the reporting period.

- ○ If comparative financial statements are not presented, the revenue and earnings of the combined entity for the current reporting period as though the acquisition date for all business combinations that occurred during the year had been as of the beginning of the annual reporting period (supplemental pro forma information).
- ○ If comparative financial statements are presented, the revenue and earnings of the combined entity as though the business combination(s) that occurred during the current year had occurred as of the beginning of the comparable prior annual reporting period (supplemental pro forma information).
- ○ The nature and amount of any material, nonrecurring pro forma adjustments directly attributable to the business combination included in the reported pro forma revenue and earnings.

j. If disclosure of any of the information required by (i) is impracticable, that fact and why the disclosure is impracticable. (ASC 805-10-50-2)

For individually immaterial business combinations occurring during the reporting period that are material collectively, the entity should disclose information required by (f) through (i) in the preceding paragraph in the aggregate. (ASC 805-10-50-3)

If the acquisition date is after the reporting date but before the financial statements are issued or available to be issued, the information required by FASB ASC 805-20-50-2 should be disclosed. If the accounting is incomplete at that time, describe which disclosures could not be made and why. (ASC 805-10-50-4)

The Financial Effects of Adjustments That Relate to Business Combinations That Occurred in the Current or Previous Reporting Periods Disclose financial effects of adjustments during the current period that relate to business combinations that occurred in the current or previous reporting periods. (ASC 805-10-50-5)

Disclose any other information needed for the users to evaluate the business combination per ASC 805-10-50-1. (ASC 805-10-50-7)

Business Combinations Occurring During a Current Reporting Period or After the Reporting Date but Before the Financial Statements Are Issued Make the following disclosures for identifiable assets and liabilities and any noncontrolling interest:

1. For indemnification assets:
    - The amount recognized as of the acquisition date.
    - A description of the arrangement and the basis for determining the amount of the payment.
    - An estimate of the range of outcomes (undiscounted) or, if a range cannot be estimated, that fact and the reasons why. If the maximum amount of the payment is unlimited, that fact.
2. For acquired receivables by major class of receivable, such as loans, direct finance leases under ASC 840, and any other class of receivables:
    - The fair value of the receivables.
    - The gross contractual amount of the receivables.
    - The best estimate at the acquisition date of the contractual cash flows not expected to be collected.

3. The amounts recognized as of the acquisition date for each major class of assets acquired and liabilities assumed.
4. For contingencies, the following:
   - For assets and liabilities arising from contingencies recognized at the acquisition date:
     ○ The amounts recognized at the acquisition date and the measurement basis applied (that is, at fair value or at an amount recognized in accordance with Topic 450 and Section 450-20-25).
     ○ The nature of the contingencies.
   - For contingencies that are not recognized at the acquisition date, the disclosures required by Topic 450 if the criteria for disclosures in that Topic are met.

Note: An acquirer may aggregate disclosures for assets and liabilities arising from contingencies that are similar in nature.

- For each business combination in which the acquirer holds less than 100% of the equity interest in the acquiree, the fair value of the noncontrolling interest in the acquiree and the valuation technique and significant inputs used to measure the fair value. (ASC 805-20-50-1)

If individually immaterial business combinations occurring during the reporting period are material collectively, the acquirer should disclose information above in the aggregate. (ASC 805-20-50-2)

If the acquisition date of a business combination is after the reporting date but before the financial statements are issued or are available to be issued, the information required in (1) above. If the initial accounting for the business combination is incomplete at the time the financial statements are issued or are available to be issued, describe which disclosures could not be made and the reason why. (ASC 805-20-50-3)

The Financial Effects of Adjustments That Relate to Business Combinations That Occurred in the Current or Previous Reporting Periods If the initial accounting is incomplete and, therefore, the amounts recognized related to the business combination are only provisional, disclose the:

- Reasons why the accounting is incomplete.
- Assets, liabilities, equity interests, or items for which the accounting is incomplete.
- Nature and amount of any adjustments recognized during the reporting period, including separately or on the face of the income statement the amount of adjustment to current period line items relating to the income effects that would have been recognized in previous periods if the adjustment to provisional amounts were recognized as of the acquisition date. (ASC 805-20-50-4A)

Note: The disclosure in ASC 805-20-50-4A above should also be made for individually material business combination and those that are material in the aggregate. (ASC 805-20-50-4)

Business Combinations Occurring During a Current Reporting Period or After the Reporting Date but Before the Financial Statements Are Issued For each business combination that occurs during the reporting period, disclose:

- A qualitative description of the factors that make up goodwill recognized.
- The acquisition-date fair value of the total consideration transferred and the acquisition-date fair value of each major class of consideration, such as cash, other tangible or intangible assets, liabilities incurred, and equity interests of the acquirer.
- For contingent consideration arrangements:
  ○ The amount recognized as of the acquisition date,
  ○ A description of the arrangement and the basis for determining the payment,
  ○ An estimate of the range of outcomes or the reason why a range cannot be estimated, and
  ○ If the maximum amount of the payment is unlimited.
- The total amount of goodwill that is expected to be deductible for tax purposes.
- If the acquirer is required to disclose segment information, the goodwill by segment.
- If the assignment of goodwill to reporting units has not been completed on the financial statements' issuance date, the acquirer discloses that fact.
- Bargain purchases:
  ○ The amount of gain recognized.
  ○ The line item in the income statement in which the gain is recognized.
  ○ A description of the reasons why the transaction resulted in a gain. (ASC 805-30-50-1)

If business combinations occurring during the reporting period are individually immaterial, but material collectively, disclose information required by the preceding paragraph in the aggregate. (ASC 805-30-50-2)

If the acquisition date of a business combination is after the reporting date but before the financial statements are issued or are available to be issued, disclose the information required by ASC 805-30-50-1 above.

If the accounting for the business combination is incomplete at the time the financial statements are issued or are available to be issued, describe which disclosures could not be made and the reason why they could not be made. (ASC 805-30-50-3)

The Financial Effects of Adjustments That Relate to Business Combinations That Occurred in the Current or Previous Reporting Policies For each material business combination or in the aggregate for individually immaterial business combinations that are material collectively, disclose:

- For each reporting period after the acquisition date until the entity collects, sells, or otherwise loses the right to a contingent consideration asset, or until the entity settles a contingent consideration liability or the liability is cancelled or expires, all of the following:
  ○ Any changes in the recognized amounts, including any differences arising upon settlement.
  ○ Any changes in the range of outcomes (undiscounted) and the reasons for those changes.
  ○ The fair value disclosures required by Section 820-10-50.
- A reconciliation of the carrying amount of goodwill at the beginning and end of the reporting period as required by paragraph 350-20-50-1. (ASC 805-30-50-4)

Transactions Between Entities Under Common Control Describe the nature of and effects on EPS of nonrecurring intra-entity transactions involving long-term assets and liabilities. (ASC 805-50-50-2)

In the notes to financial statements of the receiving entity, the following should be disclosed for the period in which the transfer of assets and liabilities or exchange of equity interests occurred:

- The name and brief description of the entity included in the reporting entity as a result of the net asset transfer or exchange of equity interests.
- The method of accounting for the transfer of net assets or exchange of equity interests. (ASC 805-50-50-3)

Pushdown Accounting For an entity electing pushdown accounting, provide information that enables users to evaluate the effect, which may include:

- Name and description of the acquirer.
- How the acquirer obtained control.
- Acquisition date.
- Fair value at the acquisition date of consideration transferred.
- As a result of applying pushdown accounting, amounts recognized by the acquiree for each major class of assets and liabilities.
- Reasons why initial accounting is incomplete.
- Qualitative description of the factors that make up recognized goodwill.
- Information to evaluate the effects of current reporting period adjustments related to pushdown accounting that occurred in the current or previous periods.
- Other information necessary for users to evaluate the effect of applying pushdown accounting.
  (ASC 805-50-50-5 and 50-6)

PRESENTATION AND DISCLOSURE EXAMPLES

Example 47.1: Accounting Policy for Business Acquisitions

The Company accounts for business acquisitions in accordance with ASC 805, *Business Combinations*. This standard requires the acquiring entity in a business combination to recognize all (and only) the assets acquired and liabilities assumed in the transaction and establishes the acquisition-date fair value as the measurement objective for all assets acquired and liabilities assumed in a business combination. Certain provisions of this standard prescribe, among other things, the determination of acquisition-date fair value of consideration paid in a business combination (including contingent consideration) and the exclusion of transaction and acquisition-related restructuring costs from acquisition accounting. In addition to business combinations, LRB periodically acquires certain tangible and/or intangible assets and purchases interests in certain enterprises that do not otherwise qualify for accounting as business combinations. These transactions are largely reflected as additional asset purchase and investment activity.

Example 47.2: Accounting Policy for Business Acquisitions, Including Research and Development, Acquisition, and Restructuring Costs, and Income Tax Changes

The Company accounts for acquisitions in accordance with guidance found in ASC 805, *Business Combinations* ("ASC 805"). This guidance requires consideration given (including contingent consideration), assets acquired, and liabilities assumed to be valued at their fair market values at the acquisition date. The guidance further provides that (1) in-process research and development will be recorded at fair value as an indefinite-lived intangible asset; (2) acquisition-related transaction costs will generally be expensed as incurred; (3) restructuring costs associated with a business combination will generally be expensed subsequent to the acquisition date; and (4) changes in deferred tax asset valuation allowances and income tax uncertainties after the acquisition date generally will effect income tax expense.

ASC 805 requires that any excess purchase price over fair value of assets acquired (including identifiable intangibles) and liabilities assumed be recognized as goodwill. Additionally, any excess fair value of acquired net assets over acquisition consideration results in a bargain purchase gain. Prior to recording a gain, the acquiring entity must reassess whether all acquired assets and assumed liabilities have been identified and must perform remeasurements to verify that the consideration paid, assets acquired, and liabilities assumed have all been properly valued.

Example 47.3: Business Combination

On July 7, 20X1, York Digital, Inc., entered into a Purchase Agreement to acquire substantially all of the assets comprising the consulting services business in the areas of master data management, data integration, and big data (the "Acquired Business") of InfoMatrix Inc., including all outstanding shares of InfoMatrix. The transaction was closed on July 13, 20X1.

Under the terms of the Purchase Agreement, the Company Entities paid at the closing of the acquisition $35.75 million in cash, less certain working capital adjustments that totaled $861,000. The Purchase Agreement also provided for contingent consideration of $19.25 million in deferred cash payments, with up to $8.25 million payable if the EBIT of the Acquired Business for the 12-month period beginning on August 1, 20X1 (the "Actual Year 1 EBIT"), equals $10.0 million and up to $11.0 million payable if the EBIT of the Acquired Business for the 12-month period beginning on August 1, 20X2 (the "Actual Year 2 EBIT"), equals $10.7 million. The deferred amount payments were subject to adjustments under the terms of the purchase agreements based upon, among other items, the amount of the Actual Year 1 EBIT and the amount of the Actual Year 2 EBIT.

To fund the acquisition, the Company entered into a new credit agreement on July 13, 20X1, with ABC Bank. The Credit Agreement provides for a total aggregate commitment of $65.0 million, consisting of (i) a revolving credit facility in an aggregate principal amount not to exceed $27.5 million, subject to increases to an aggregate amount not to exceed $37.5 million upon satisfaction of certain conditions; (ii) a $30.5 million term loan facility; and (iii) a $7.0 million delayed draw term loan facility to be used exclusively toward contingent consideration payments. In addition, the Company entered into Securities Purchase Agreements with Lucas Blake and Jean Sullivan (collectively, the "Investors") on July 7, 20X1, pursuant to which the Company issued and sold an aggregate 1.7 million shares (the "Shares") of its common stock, par value $0.01 per share (the "Common Stock"), to the Investors on July 13, 20X1, for $6.0 million in aggregate gross proceeds (the "Private Placement Transactions"). The Company used the proceeds from the Private Placement Transactions to fund a portion of the cash paid at the closing of the acquisition.

On April 20, 20X2, we entered into an amendment to the Credit Agreement. This amendment (i) reduced the aggregate commitment amount of the revolving credit facility from $27.5 million to $22.5 million, which amount is subject to increase to an aggregate commitment amount not exceeding $32.5 million upon satisfaction of certain conditions; (ii) increased the aggregate commitment amount of the swing loan sub-facility under the revolving credit facility from $3.0 million to $5.0 million; and (iii) amended the financial covenant in the Credit Agreement related to the Company's leverage ratio (as defined in the Credit Agreement) by increasing the maximum permitted leverage ratio for each of the fiscal quarters ending on or prior to September 30, 20X3. Our desired results of entering into this amendment were to increase our financial flexibility, lower our unused line fees, and improve the mechanics of how we manage our cash balances.

The acquisition was accounted for using the acquisition method of accounting. The acquisition method of accounting requires that the assets acquired and liabilities assumed be measured at their fair value as of the closing date.

Example 47.4: Table Summarizing the Fair Value of Consideration for the Acquired Business

The following table summarizes the fair value of consideration for the Acquired Business on the July 13, 20X1, closing date:

(Amounts in thousands)

Cash purchase price at closing	$ 35,750
Working capital adjustments	(861)
Estimated payout of contingent consideration*	17,125
Total fair value of consideration	$ 52,014

* Based on a valuation conducted by an independent third party, the fair value of contingent consideration at the closing date was determined to be $17,125,000.

Example 47.5: Details of Cash Paid at Closing

The cash purchase price at closing was paid by Digital with funds obtained from the following sources:

(Amounts in thousands)

Cash balances on hand	$ 341
Sale of common stock in private placement transactions	6,000
Term loan debt facility	30,500
Revolving line of credit	9,000
Payoff of Digital's previous credit facility	(10,091)
Cash paid at closing	$ 35,750

Example 47.6: Allocation of the Purchase Price

The allocation of the purchase price was based on estimates of the fair value of assets acquired and liabilities assumed as of July 13, 20X1, as set forth below. The excess purchase price over the fair values of the net tangible assets and identifiable intangible assets was recorded as goodwill, which includes value associated with the assembled workforce. Goodwill is expected to be largely deductible for tax purposes. The valuation of net assets acquired is as follows:

(Amounts in thousands)

Current assets	$ 6,909
Fixed assets and other	215
Identifiable intangible assets:	
Client relationships	16,671
Noncompete covenant	761
Trade name	1,221
Technology	1,209
Total identifiable intangible assets	19,862
Goodwill	27,417
Current liabilities	(2,389)
Net assets acquired	$ 52,014

The fair value of identifiable intangible assets has been estimated using the income approach through a discounted cash flow analysis. Specifically, the Company used the income approach through an excess earnings analysis to determine the fair value of client relationships. The value applied to the noncompete covenant was based on an income approach using a "with-or-without" analysis of this covenant in place. The trade name and technology were valued using the income approach—relief from royalty method. All identifiable intangibles are considered Level 3 inputs under the fair value measurement and disclosure guidance.

Example 47.7: Transaction Expenses

The Company incurred $2.0 million of transaction expenses related to the acquisition in 20X1. In 20X2 and 20X3, the Company reversed transaction expenses of $140,000 and $110,000, respectively, that did not materialize. This credit expense related to investment banker fees that were tied to the contingent consideration liability. These expenses are included in selling, general, and administrative expenses in the accompanying Consolidated Statement of Operations.

Example 47.8: Pro Forma Results

Included in the Consolidated Statement of Operations for year ended December 31, 20X1, are revenues of $9.2 million and net income of approximately $1.1 million applicable to the InfoMatrix operations from our July 13, 20X1, acquisition date through December 31, 20X1.

The following reflects the Company's unaudited pro forma results, had the results of InfoMatrix been included from January 1, 20X1, for all periods presented:

	Years Ended December 31		
	20X3	*20X2*	*20X1*
	(Amounts in thousands, except per share data)		
Revenue	$ 193,574	$ 177,164	$ 158,785
Net income	$ 11,145	$ 6,691	$ 2,388
Earnings per share, diluted	$ .99	$ .60	$ .22

The information above does not reflect all of the operating efficiencies or inefficiencies that may have resulted from the InfoMatrix acquisitions in those periods prior to the acquisition. Therefore, the unaudited pro forma information above is not necessarily indicative of results that would have been achieved had the business been combined during all periods presented.

Example 47.9: Business Acquisition Accounted for as a Purchase

On May 29, 20X1, the Company purchased a 51% membership interest in Ballarat Entertainment LLC, a talent management and television/film production company. The purchase price was approximately $166.6 million, of which 50% was paid in cash at closing, 32.5% was paid in the Company's Class B non-voting common shares at closing, and 17.5% was paid in the Company's Class B non-voting common shares on the one-year anniversary of closing. The number of shares issued was determined by dividing the dollar value of the portion of the purchase price to be paid by the daily weighted average closing price of the Company's Class B non-voting common shares on the New York Stock Exchange for the 20 consecutive trading days immediately preceding the closing date. A portion of the purchase price, up to $38.3 million, may be recoupable for a five-year period commencing on the acquisition date of May 29, 20X2, contingent upon the continued employment of certain employees, or the achievement of certain EBITDA targets, as defined in the Ballarat Entertainment acquisition and related agreements. Accordingly, $38.3 million was initially recorded as a deferred compensation arrangement within other current and noncurrent assets and is being amortized in general and administrative expenses over a five-year period.

The acquisition was accounted for as a purchase, with the results of operations of Ballarat Entertainment included in the Company's consolidated results from May 29, 20X2. Based on the purchase price allocation, $92.7 million was allocated to goodwill, $47.0 million was allocated to the fair value of finite-lived intangible assets, and $38.3 million was allocated to deferred compensation arrangements, as discussed above. The remainder of the purchase price was primarily allocated to cash and cash equivalents, accounts receivable, other assets, and accounts payable and accrued liabilities, and $15.8 million was recorded as a redeemable noncontrolling interest, representing the noncontrolling interest holders' 49% equity interest in Ballarat Entertainment (see Note 12). The acquired finite-lived intangible assets primarily represent customer relationships and are being amortized over a weighted average estimated useful life of 12 years. The Company incurred approximately $1.3 million of acquisition-related costs that were expensed in restructuring and other expenses during the fiscal year ended March 31, 20X3.

The Company used discounted cash flows ("DCF") analyses, which represent Level 3 fair value measurements, to assess certain components of its purchase price allocation, including acquired intangible assets and the redeemable noncontrolling interest. The acquisition goodwill arises from the opportunity for synergies of the combined companies to grow and strengthen the Company's television operations by expanding the Company's talent relationships and improving the Company's television production capabilities. The goodwill recorded as part of this acquisition is included in the Television Production segment. The goodwill is not amortized for financial reporting purposes, but is deductible for federal tax purposes.

Example 47.10: Acquisition, Including Goodwill

On August 7, 20X2, ToolMan acquired ABC Limited for a preliminary cash purchase price of $30.4 million (or $29.4 million, net of cash acquired). The preliminary purchase price is subject to change based upon finalization of a working capital adjustment that is expected to be completed in the first quarter of 20X3. ABC specializes in flexible, modular, and highly scalable Software as a

Service ("SaaS") products for OEM customers and their dealers, focused on the creation and delivery of service, diagnostics, parts, and repair information to the OEM dealers and connected vehicle platforms.

As of December 28, 20X2, the Company recorded, on a preliminary basis, the $11.4 million excess of the purchase price over the fair value of the net assets acquired in Goodwill on the accompanying Consolidated Balance Sheets. The Company anticipates completing the purchase accounting for the acquired net assets of Cognitran in the first half of 20X3.

On January 30, 20X0, ToolMan acquired XYZ for a cash purchase price of $9.2 million. XYZ designs and implements automotive vehicle inspection and management software for OEM franchise repair shops.

In fiscal 20X0, the Company completed the purchase accounting valuations for the acquired net assets of XYZ, including intangible assets. The $5.9 million excess of purchase price over the fair value of the net assets acquired was recorded in Goodwill on the accompanying Consolidated Balance Sheets.

For segment reporting purposes, the results of operations and assets of ABC and XYZ have been included in the Repair Systems & Information Group since the respective acquisition dates.

Pro forma financial information has not been presented for these acquisitions as the net effects, individually and collectively, were neither significant nor material to ToolMan's results of operations or financial position.

Example 47.11: Acquisitions Description for Three Recent Years

LRB makes acquisitions of certain businesses from time to time that are aligned with its strategic intent with respect to, among other factors, growth markets and adjacent product lines or technologies. Goodwill resulting from business combinations is largely attributable to the existing workforce of the acquired businesses and synergies expected to arise after LRB's acquisition of these businesses.

20X2 acquisitions:

In February 20X2, LRB completed the acquisition of all of the ownership interests of the technology business of ABC for $0.7 billion of cash, net of cash acquired, and assumption of $0.3 billion of ABC's debt. Based in Pittsburgh, Pennsylvania, ABC is a leading healthcare technology provider of cloud-based, conversational artificial intelligence-powered systems that help physicians efficiently capture and improve the patient narrative. The allocation of purchase consideration related to ABC was completed in the fourth quarter of 20X2. Net sales and operating loss (inclusive of transaction and integration costs) of this business included in LRB's consolidated results of operations in 20X2 were approximately $300 million and $25 million, respectively. ABC is reported within the Company's Health Care business.

In October 20X2, LRB completed the acquisition of all of the ownership interests of XYZ and its JKL subsidiaries for consideration of $4.5 billion net of cash acquired as shown in the table below, and assumption of $2.3 billion of debt. XYZ is a leading global medical technology company focused on advanced wound care and specialty surgical applications marketed under the JKL brand. The allocation of purchase consideration related to XYZ and its JKL subsidiaries is considered preliminary, with provisional amounts primarily related to intangible assets, working capital, and certain tax-related and contingent liability amounts. LRB expects to finalize the allocation of purchase price within the one-year measurement period following the acquisition. Net sales and operating loss (inclusive of transaction and integration costs) of this business included in LRB's consolidated results of operations in 20X2 were approximately $350 million and $45 million, respectively. XYZ is reported within the Company's Health Care business.

Example 47.12: Impact on the Consolidated Balance Sheet of Purchase Price Allocations

Pro forma information related to these acquisitions has not been included, as the impact on the Company's consolidated results of operations was not considered material. The following table shows the impact on the consolidated balance sheet of the purchase price allocations related to the 20X2 acquisitions and assigned finite-lived asset-weighted average lives.

Example 47.13: Purchased Identifiable Finite-Lived Intangible Assets

LRB purchased identifiable finite-lived intangible assets related to acquisitions, which closed in 20X2 and totaled $4.081 billion. The associated finite-lived intangible assets acquired will be amortized on a systematic and rational basis (generally straight line) over a weighted-average life of 14 years (lives ranging from 6 to 19 years).

20X1 acquisition:

There were no acquisitions that closed during 20X1.

20X0 acquisitions:

In September 20X0, LRB purchased all of the ownership interests of Edwin Technologies, LLC, a manufacturer of test kits that help enable food and beverage companies ensure their products are free from certain potentially harmful allergens such as peanuts, soy, or milk. Edwin is reported within the Company's health care business.

In October 20X0, LRB completed the acquisition of the underlying legal entities and associated assets of Lawson from Johnson Controls for $2.0 billion of cash, net of cash acquired. Lawson is a premier manufacturer of innovative products, including self-contained breathing apparatus systems, gas and flame detection instruments, and other safety devices that complement LRB's personal safety portfolio.

(Amounts in millions) Asset (Liability)	20X2 Acquisition Activity			Finite-lived intangible asset-weighted average lives (years)
	ABC	XYZ	Total	
Accounts receivable	$ 75	$ 295	$ 370	
Inventory	—	186	186	
Other current assets	2	65	67	
Property, plant, and equipment	8	147	155	
Purchased finite-lived intangible assets:				
Customer-related intangible assets	275	1,760	2,035	18
Other technology-based intangible assets	160	1,390	1,550	10
Definite-lived trade names	11	485	496	16
Purchased goodwill	517	2,952	3,469	
Other assets	58	73	131	
Accounts payable and other liabilities	(127)	(438)	(565)	

Interest-bearing debt	(251)	(2,322)	(2,573)
Deferred tax asset/(liability) and			
accrued income taxes	(24)	(288)	(312)
Net assets acquired	$ 704	$ 4,305	$ 5,009
Supplemental information:			
Cash paid	$ 708	$ 4,486	$ 5,194
Less: cash acquired	4	206	210
Cash paid, net of cash acquired	$ 704	$ 4,280	$ 4,984
Consideration payable	—	25	25
	$ 704	$ 4,305	$ 5,009

Example 47.14: Goodwill and Other Intangible Assets from Acquisition

The changes in the carrying amount of goodwill by segment for 20X3 and 20X2 are as follows:

(Amounts in millions)	*Commercial & Industrial Group*	*Snap-On Tools Group*	*Repair Systems & Information Group*	*Total*
Balance as of				
20X1 year end	$ 298.4	$ 12.5	$ 613.2	$ 924.1
Currency				
translation	(16.3)	—	(9.7)	(26.0)
Acquisitions	4.1	—	—	4.1
Balance as of				
20X2 year end	$ 286.2	$ 12.5	$ 603.5	$ 902.2
Currency				
translation	(6.4)	—	(1.1)	(7.5)
Acquisitions	6.4	—	12.7	19.1
Balance as of				
20X3 year end	$ 286.2	$ 12.5	$ 615.1	$ 913.8

Goodwill of $913.8 million as of 20X3 year end includes (i) $11.4 million, on a preliminary basis, from the acquisition of Cognitran; (ii) $6.4 million from the acquisition of Power Hawk; and (iii) $1.3 million from the acquisition of TMB. The goodwill from the Cognitran and TMB acquisitions is included in the Repair Systems & Information Group. The goodwill from the Power Hawk acquisition is included in the Commercial & Industrial Group.

Goodwill of $902.2 million as of 20X2 year end includes $2.6 million from the acquisition of Fastorq in 20X2. During 20X2, the purchase accounting valuations for the acquired net assets, including intangible assets, of Norbar and TCS were completed, resulting in an increase in goodwill of $1.4 million for Norbar and $0.1 million for TCS, which were both acquired in 20X1. As of 20X2 year end, goodwill includes $25.1 million from the acquisition of Norbar and $2.0 million from the acquisition of TCS. The goodwill from the Fastorq, Norbar, and TCS acquisitions is included in the Commercial & Industrial Group.

Additional disclosures related to other intangible assets as of 20X3 and 20X2 year end are as follows:

	20X3		20X2	
(Amounts in millions)	*Gross carrying value*	*Accumulated amortization*	*Gross carrying value*	*Accumulated amortization*
Amortized other intangible assets:				
Customer relationships	$ 182.9	$ (117.9)	$ 172.2	$ (107.6)
Developed technology	19.8	(18.9)	18.5	(18.3)
Internally developed software	168.0	(125.4)	156.6	(116.6)
Patents	38.5	(23.7)	35.7	(22.9)
Trademarks	3.5	(2.1)	3.2	(2.0)
Other	7.3	(3.1)	7.3	(2.9)
Total	420.0	(291.1)	393.5	(270.3)
Non-amortized trademarks	115.0	—	109.7	—
Total other intangible assets	$ 535.0	$ (291.1)	$ 503.2	$ (270.3)

As of year end 20X3, the gross carrying value of customer relationships includes $10.2 million related to the ABC acquisition and $0.9 million related to the Power Hawk acquisition. Additionally, the gross carrying value of intangible assets in 20X3 includes $6.5 million of non-amortized trademarks and $1.1 million of developed technology as a result of the ABC acquisition. There were no acquisitions during 20X2 that resulted in the recognition of other intangible assets as of year end 20X2.

Significant and unanticipated changes in circumstances, such as declines in profitability and cash flow due to significant and long-term deterioration in macroeconomic, industry, and market conditions, the loss of key customers, changes in technology or markets, significant changes in key personnel or litigation, a significant and sustained decrease in share price and/or other events, including effects from the sale or disposal of a reporting unit, could require a provision for impairment of goodwill and/ or other intangible assets in a future period. As of 20X3 year end, the company had no accumulated impairment losses.

The weighted-average amortization periods related to other intangible assets are as follows:

	Years
Customer relationships	15
Developed technology	2
Internally developed software	6
Patents	7
Trademarks	5
Other	39

LRB is amortizing its customer relationships on both an accelerated and straight-line basis over a 15-year weighted-average life; the remaining intangibles are amortized on a straight-line basis. The weighted-average amortization period for all amortizable intangibles on a combined basis is 12 years.

The company's customer relationships generally have contractual terms of three to five years and are typically renewed without significant cost to the company. The weighted-average 15-year life for customer relationships is based on the company's historical renewal experience. Intangible asset renewal costs are expensed as incurred.

The aggregate amortization expense was $22.3 million in 20X3, $25.3 million in 20X2, and $27.6 million in 20X1. Based on current levels of amortizable intangible assets and estimated weighted-average useful lives, estimated annual amortization expense is expected to be $21.4 million in 20X4, $18.9 million in 20X5, $15.4 million in 20X6, $13.2 million in 20X7, and $10.6 million in 20X8.

48 ASC 808 COLLABORATIVE ARRANGEMENTS

AUTHORITATIVE LITERATURE

A collaborative arrangement (sometimes referred to in practice as "line-item" joint ventures or "virtual" joint ventures) is a contractual agreement between two or more parties (participants) to jointly conduct business activities for their mutual benefit without the formation of a separate entity in which to conduct the activities.

Determining the proper accounting treatment for the various activities included in these endeavors is the subject of ASC 808, *Collaborative Arrangements*.

Technical Alert

In November 2018, the FASB issued ASU 2018-18, *Collaborative Arrangements (Topic 808): Clarifying the Intersection Between Topic 808 and Topic 606.* The ASU provides guidance on how to assess whether certain transactions between collaborative arrangement participants should be accounted for under ASC 606.

Guidance The new guidance provides more comparability in the presentation of revenue by allowing organizations to only present units of account in collaborative arrangements that are within the scope of ASC 606 together with the revenue accounted for under ASC 606. The new guidance affects the scope section of ASC 808. Those changes can be found in the Scope section below. Changes to the presentation and disclosure section can be found in the disclosure checklist at www.wiley.com/go/FSDM2021.

Effective Dates

The ASU is effective:

- For public companies:
  - Fiscal years beginning after December 15, 2019, and interim periods within those fiscal years
- For all other organizations:
  - Fiscal years beginning after December 15, 2020, and interim periods within fiscal years beginning after December 15, 2021

Early adoption is permitted.

Transition The changes should be applied retrospectively to the date of initial application of ASC 606. Entities are permitted to apply the amendments retrospectively to all contracts or only to contracts that are not completed at the date of initial application of ASC 606. The entity should disclose its elections. An entity may also elect to apply the practical expedient of the contract modifications allowed under ASC 606 for entities using modified retrospective transitions.

Subtopic

ASC 808-10, *Collaborative Arrangements*, contains one Subtopic:

- ASC 808-10, *Overall*, which defines collaborative arrangements and gives reporting requirements

Scope

Transactions and Events ASC 808-10 applies to all collaborative arrangements, except for those addressed in other topics. Specifically *excluded* from ASC 808 are arrangements for which the accounting treatment is addressed by other authoritative literature. (ASC 808-10-15-3)

A collaborative arrangement is not *primarily* conducted through a separate legal entity created for it. If a part of the arrangement is conducted through a legal entity, that part is accounted for under ASC 810, *Consolidations*; ASC 323-20, *Investments—Equity Method and Joint Ventures*; or other relevant accounting literature. A collaborative arrangement may involve various types of activities conducted or supervised by the participants. In some collaborative arrangements, a legal entity may be used for certain specified activities or in certain geographic jurisdictions due, for example, to legal restrictions imposed by the jurisdiction. (ASC 808-10-15-4)

It is important to note that ASC 808 does not address recognition or measurement of collaborative arrangements, including guidance regarding matters such as:

- Determining the appropriate units of accounting
- Determining the appropriate recognition requirements for a given unit of accounting
- The timing of when recognition criteria are considered to have been met (ASC 808-10-15-5)

Upon implementation of ASU 2018-18, the following scope requirements are effective:

- A collaborative arrangement within the scope of ASC 808 may be partially within the scope of other codifications topics, including ASC 606. (ASC 808-10-15-5A)

- An entity may have a collaborative arrangement that is partially within the scope of ASC 606 under the following circumstance: if a unit of account that is a promised good or service that is also distinct within the collaborative arrangement under the guidance in ASC 606 is with a customer, the entity should apply ASC 606 to a unit of account in the scope of ASC 606. Any position of a distinct bundle of goods or services that is not with a customer is not within the scope of ASC 606. (ASC 808-10-15-15B)
- If a collaborative arrangement is wholly or partially outside the scope of other topics, the unit of account recognition and measurement should be based on an analogy to authoritative accounting literature. If there is no appropriate analogy, a reasonable, rational, and consistently applied accounting policy election should be used. (ASC 808-10-15-5C)

What Constitutes a Collaborative Arrangement? A collaborative arrangement involves a joint operating activity. The activity upon which the participants collaborate is referred to as an "endeavor." The subject of a joint operating arrangement is characterized as a collaborative arrangement within the scope of ASC 808 if:

- The collaborative arrangement involves two or more parties.
- The parties are:
  ○ Active participants in the endeavor, and
  ○ Exposed to significant risks and rewards that depend on the endeavor's commercial success.
  (ASC 808-10-20)

Criteria for Collaborative Arrangements The description of collaborative arrangements included above lists two criteria:

1. Active involvement by participants
2. Exposure to risks and rewards
   (ASC 808-10-20)

Active involvement. In evaluating whether a participant is active with respect to an endeavor, management should consider the arrangement's specific facts and circumstances. Examples of involvement that could constitute active participation include, but are not limited to:

- Directing and executing the activities of the endeavor
- Participating on a steering committee or other oversight or governance body
- Possessing a legal or contractual right to the intellectual property that underlies the endeavor
  (ASC 808-10-15-8)

Solely providing financial resources to an endeavor would not constitute an active level of involvement for the purposes of ASC 808. (ASC 808-10-15-9)

Significant risks and rewards. Management of a participant should exercise its best judgment in evaluating whether the participant is exposed to significant risks and entitled to significant rewards. Consideration should be given to the terms and conditions of the arrangement and the facts and circumstances surrounding it. (ASC 808-10-15-10)

Examples of terms and conditions of an arrangement that may indicate that a participant is not exposed to significant risks or entitled to significant rewards include the following:

- Market rates are paid for services provided by the participant

- Ability of a participant to exit the arrangement without cause and recover all or most of its cumulative economic participation through the exit date
- Limits on the rewards that a participant is entitled to receive
- Allocation of initial profits from the endeavor to only one participant
  (ASC 808-10-15-11)

Other factors to consider are:

- The stage of the endeavor's life cycle at which the participant is commencing its involvement
- Management's expectations regarding the duration and extent of its financial participation in relation to the total expected duration and total expected value of the endeavor
  (ASC 808-10-15-12)

Frequently a collaborative arrangement will involve the license of intellectual property, with the participants to the arrangement exchanging consideration with respect to the license at the arrangement's inception. The existence of terms of this nature is not necessarily indicative of the participants not being exposed to significant risks or entitled to significant rewards. (ASC 808-10-15-13)

Timing and Assessment of Involvement A participant may become involved in a collaborative arrangement at any time during the life cycle of the endeavor. From the perspective of a participant, determination of whether an endeavor is a collaborative arrangement should be made at the inception of the arrangement or when the participant initially becomes involved in the arrangement based on the facts and circumstances existing at that time. A participant should reevaluate whether the arrangement continues to qualify as a collaborative arrangement any time there is a change in a participant's role in the arrangement or a change in a participant's exposure to risks or entitlement to rewards from the arrangement. (ASC 808-10-15-6)

Examples of Joint Operating Activities Collaborative arrangements are used to conduct many different types of business activities, including but not limited to research, development, branding, promotion, sales, marketing, order processing, package design, manufacturing, and distribution. Examples include:

- Two or more parties may agree to collaborate on joint operation of a facility, such as a hospital or long-term care nursing facility.
- Two professional services firms (e.g., architects, engineers, consultants) may choose to jointly submit a proposal to obtain a new engagement that neither would have the capacity and/or capability to perform on its own.
- A movie studio may collaborate with another studio because it wants to produce a film starring an actor who is under contract with another studio, or two studios may wish to spread the cost (and, of course, the risk) of producing a film.
- Frequently, in the pharmaceutical industry, two companies engage in a joint operating activity to research, develop, market, manufacture, and/or distribute a drug candidate, including the process of obtaining all necessary regulatory approvals in one or more geographic markets.
  (ASC 808-10-15-7)

The participants' roles and responsibilities vary between arrangements but can be structured where certain responsibilities are shared between the participants and other responsibilities are solely the responsibility of one of the participants.

PRACTICE ALERT

While SEC comments are directed at registrants, the staff comments can be useful practice pointers for all financial statement preparers. In the area of collaborative arrangements, the SEC has asked for:

- More detail on whether each partner assumes a proportionate share of risk
- Information on the separation, allocation, recognition, and disclosure principles used to account for payments between partners
- The rationale for concluding that the entity is the principal or agent in the transaction

PRESENTATION AND DISCLOSURE REQUIREMENTS

Presentation

A participant in a collaborative arrangement recognizes revenue earned and costs incurred in transactions with third parties (parties that are not participants to the collaborative arrangement) in its income statement based on whether the participant is serving as a principal or an agent in the transaction as determined under ASC 606-10-55-36 through 55-40. (ASC 808-10-45-1)

Disclosure

In the period in which a collaborative arrangement is entered into and in all annual periods thereafter, the participant should disclose:

- The nature and purpose of the arrangement
- The participant's rights and obligations under the collaborative arrangements
- The entity's accounting policy for collaborative arrangements
- The income statement classification amounts from transactions related to the arrangement
- Separately, information related to individually significant arrangements
  (ASC 808-10-50-1)

For details on disclosure and presentation requirements, see *Disclosure and Presentation Checklist for Commercial Businesses* (www.wiley.com/go/FSDM2021).

PRESENTATION AND DISCLOSURE EXAMPLES

Example 48.1: Detailed Analysis of Whether Arrangement Is within the Scope of ASC 808, Where Some Revenue Is within the Scope of ASC 606 and Some Is within the Scope of ASC 808

The Company analyzes its collaborative arrangements to assess whether it is within the scope of ASC 808, *Collaborative Arrangements* ("ASC 808") to determine whether such arrangements involve joint operating activities performed by parties that are both active participants in the activities and exposed to significant risks and rewards dependent on the commercial success of such activities. This assessment is performed throughout the life of the arrangement, based on changes in the responsibilities of all parties in the arrangement. For collaboration arrangements within the scope of ASC 808 that contain multiple elements, the Company first determines which elements of the collaboration are deemed to be within the scope of ASC 808 and those that are more reflective of a vendor-customer relationship (e.g., a licensing arrangement), where the contracted party has obtained goods or services that are an output of the Company's ordinary activities in exchange for a consideration and therefore within the scope of Topic 606. For those elements of the arrangement that are accounted for pursuant to Topic 606, including those to which Topic 606 is applied by analogy, the Company applies the five-step model described in the Company's revenue recognition policy. For elements of collaborative arrangements that are accounted for pursuant to ASC 808, an appropriate and rational recognition method is determined and applied consistently. Reimbursements from the counterparty that are the result of a collaborative relationship with the counterparty, instead of a customer relationship, such as co-development or clinical activities, are recorded as a reduction to research and development expense as the services are performed. Similarly, amounts that are owed to a collaboration partner related to the co-development clinical activities are recognized as research and development expenses.

The Company enters into out-licensing agreements that are within the scope of Topic 606. The terms of such out-license agreements include licenses to functional intellectual property ("IP"), given the functionality of the intellectual property is not expected to change substantially as a result of the licensor's ongoing activities. Such arrangements typically include payment of one or more of the following: nonrefundable upfront license fees; reimbursement of certain costs; development and regulatory milestone payments and milestone payments based on the level of sales; and royalties on net sales of licensed products.

The Company considers the economic and regulatory characteristics of the licensed IP; research, development, manufacturing, and commercialization capabilities of the licensee; and the availability of the associated expertise in the general marketplace to determine if it has standalone value at the inception of the licensing arrangement, which would make the license distinct. In addition, the Company considers whether the licensee can benefit from a promise for its intended purpose without the receipt of any additional goods or services promised in the contract, whether the value of the license is dependent on the remaining goods and services, whether there are other vendors that could provide the remaining promise, and whether the license is separately identifiable from the remaining goods and services. For licenses that are combined with other goods and services, the Company utilizes judgment to assess the nature of the combined performance obligation to determine whether the combined performance obligation is satisfied over time or at a point in time and, if over time, the appropriate method of measuring progress for purposes of recognizing revenue. The Company evaluates the measure of progress each reporting period and, if necessary, adjusts the measure of progress and related revenue recognition. The measure of progress, and thereby periods over which revenue should be recognized, are subject to estimates by management and may change over the course of the research and development and licensing agreement. Such a change could have a material impact on the amount of revenue the Company records in future periods.

Revenue is allocated to the licensed IP on a relative standalone selling price basis and, for functional IP, is recognized at a point when the licensed IP is made available for the customer's use and benefit, which generally occurs at the inception of the arrangement. However, in cases where the functionality of the IP is expected to substantively change as a result of activities of the Company that do not transfer additional promised goods or services, or in cases where there is an expectation that the Company will undertake activities to change the standalone functionality of the IP and the customer is contractually or practically required to use the latest version of the IP, revenue for the license to functional IP is recognized over time.

Development and regulatory milestone fees, which are a type of variable consideration, are recognized as revenue to the extent that it is probable that a significant reversal will not occur. The Company recognizes royalty revenue and sales-based milestones at the later of (i) when the related sales occur, or (ii) when the performance obligation to which the royalty has been allocated has been satisfied.

The Company has entered into a collaboration arrangement with Southern Star Pharma Inc. ("Southern"), as further described in Note 15 of its notes to unaudited consolidated financial statements.

Example 48.2: Collaboration Agreement

In July 20X3, the Company entered into a License and Collaboration Agreement with AllStar (the "AllStar Agreement"), under which the Company granted AllStar an exclusive, royalty-bearing, sub-licensable, nontransferable license to certain patent rights to research, develop, manufacture, have manufactured, use, seek and secure regulatory approval for, commercialize, offer for sale, sell, have sold and import, and otherwise exploit licensed products containing both a XYZ inhibitor and an ABC inhibitor (the "AllStar Licensed Products"), including the product candidate ST-228, outside of the United States. The Company also granted AllStar a right of first negotiation and a right of last refusal if it entered into any negotiation or agreement of any kind (other than an acquisition of all of the stock or assets of the Company) with any third party under which such third party would obtain the right to develop, manufacture, or commercialize AllStar Licensed Products in the United States.

The Company has agreed to conduct Phase 2a clinical studies in the United States. Upon the completion thereof, the Company and AllStar have agreed to jointly develop the AllStar Licensed Products, including carrying out joint studies. Each party has agreed to use commercially reasonable efforts to carry out development activities assigned to it under an agreed-upon development plan. AllStar has agreed to use commercially reasonable efforts to obtain regulatory approval for at least one AllStar Licensed Product in sensorineural hearing loss and in age-related hearing loss, in each case, in one major Asian country and one major European country. The Company has agreed to use commercially reasonable efforts to obtain regulatory approval for at least one AllStar Licensed Product in the United States. AllStar has the sole right to commercialize the AllStar Licensed Products outside of the United States, and the Company has the sole right to commercialize the AllStar Licensed Products in the United States. AllStar has agreed to use commercially reasonable efforts to commercialize AllStar Licensed Products in a major Asian country and a major European country following receipt of regulatory approval in such countries.

The collaboration is governed by a joint steering committee (JSC) established under the AllStar Agreement and shall be comprised of three representatives each from the Company and AllStar. The JSC shall oversee and coordinate the overall conduct of the development, manufacture, and commercialization of the AllStar Licensed Products. All decisions of JSC shall be taken through a unanimous vote, with each party's representatives collectively having one vote. Both the parties shall be responsible for carrying out the development and manufacturing activities in their defined territory in accordance with the plan as reviewed and approved in the JSC.

As consideration for the licensed rights under the AllStar Agreement, AllStar paid the Company an upfront payment of $80.0 million in July 20X2 and has agreed to pay potential development milestone payments up to $230.0 million and commercialization milestones of up to $315.0 million. Specifically, the Company would receive development milestone payments of $65.0 million and $25.0 million upon the first dosing of a patient in a Phase 2b clinical trial for LF228 in Europe and Asia, respectively, and $100.0 million and $40.0 million upon the first dosing of a patient in a Phase 3 clinical trial for LF228 in Europe and Asia, respectively. If the AllStar Licensed Products are successfully commercialized, the Company would be eligible for up to $315.0 million in potential commercial milestone payments and also tiered royalties at rates ranging from low- to mid-teen percentages. The parties shall share equally, on a 50-50 basis, all out-of-pocket costs and joint study costs for all the joint activities conducted pursuant to the development plans or the joint manufacturing plan.

The AllStar Agreement remains in effect until the expiration of all royalty obligations. Royalties are paid on a licensed product-by-licensed product and country-by-country basis until the latest of (i) the expiration of the last valid claim in the licensed patent rights with respect to such AllStar Licensed Product in such country or (ii) a set number of years from the first commercial sale of such AllStar Licensed Product in such country. AllStar may terminate the AllStar Agreement at will upon 60 days' written notice. Each party has the right to terminate the AllStar Agreement due to the other party's material breach if such breach remains uncured for 90 days (or 45 days in the case of nonpayment), or if the other party becomes bankrupt.

The AllStar Agreement is a collaborative agreement that is within the scope of ASC 808. The Company analyzed the joint research and development activities to assess whether they fall within the scope of ASC 808, and will reassess this throughout the life of the arrangement based on changes in the roles and responsibilities of the parties. Based on the terms of the arrangement as outlined above, both parties are deemed to be active participants in the collaboration. Each party is performing research and development activities in its defined territory and will be performing joint clinical studies in accordance with the development plan and the study protocol approved by the JSC. Additionally, AllStar and the Company are exposed to significant risks and rewards dependent on the commercial success of any product candidates that may result from the collaboration. As such, the collaboration arrangement is deemed to be within the scope of ASC 808.

The arrangement consists of two components: the license of IP and the research and development activities, including committee participation, to support the co-development and research plan. Under the provisions of ASC 808, the Company has determined that it will apply the guidance in ASC 606 to recognize the revenue related to the license, since that component of the arrangement is more reflective of a vendor-customer relationship. The Company determined that the license and the related research and development services associated with the Phase 2a clinical study were not distinct from one another, as the license has limited value to AllStar without the performance of the research and development activities and the Phase 2a study is essential to the use of the license. As such, the Company determined that these activities should be accounted for as a single combined performance obligation.

Revenue associated with this single performance obligation is being recognized as the research and development work is performed, using an input method on the basis of research and development costs incurred to date relative to total research and development costs expected to be incurred. The transfer of control occurs over this time period and, in management's judgment, is the best measure of progress toward satisfying the performance obligation. The Company has determined that the period of performance of the research and development services began upon the signing of the AllStar Agreement and will continue until the completion of the Phase 2a clinical trial of ST-228. The transaction price of $80.0 million has been allocated to the single combined performance obligation and will be recognized over such period. Management has analyzed the progress of the Phase 2a clinical trial and has estimated the completion date of such trial and the total costs it expects to incur in performing the trial and is recognizing the $80.0 million upfront fee as revenue over the period from July 20X2 until the estimated completion date using the input method. The Company regularly assesses its estimates and to the extent that facts and circumstances dictate, the Company revises its estimates of total cost or completion date and accounts for such change on a prospective basis. The estimated completion date of the Phase 2a clinical trial as of December 31, 20X2, has changed from the date used for accounting purposes as of September 30, 20X2. The Company was required to pay MIT a royalty of $16.0 million on the $80.0 million of sub-license revenues. The $16.0 million royalty was expensed in the third quarter of 20X2.

The $80.0 million upfront payment received from AllStar in July 20X2 was initially recorded as deferred revenue and is being recognized as revenue according to the policy described above. In the year ended December 31, 20X2, the Company recorded $28.9 million of revenue under the AllStar Agreement, which included $16.0 million related to the royalty payment to ABC and $12.9 million based upon the application of the input method to the remaining $64.0 million to be recognized over the estimated period to completion of the Phase 2a clinical trial for ST-228.

The potential development and regulatory milestone payments are fully constrained until the Company can conclude that achievement of the milestone is probable and that it is probable that recognition of revenue related to the milestone will not result in a significant reversal in the amount of cumulative revenue recognized when the uncertainty associated with the variable consideration is ultimately resolved, and as such these have been excluded from the transaction price. As part of its evaluation of the constraint, the Company considers numerous factors, including the fact that achievement of the milestones is outside the control of the Company and contingent upon the future success of clinical trials, the licensee's efforts, and the receipt of regulatory approval. Any consideration related to sales-based milestones (including royalties) will be recognized when the related sales occur, as these amounts have been determined to relate predominantly to the license granted to AllStar and therefore are recognized at the later of when the performance obligation is satisfied or when the related sales of licensed products occur. The Company reevaluates the transaction price, including its estimated variable consideration included in the transaction price and all constrained amounts, at each reporting period and as uncertain events are resolved or other changes in circumstances occur, and, if necessary, adjusts its estimate of the overall transaction price. Any such adjustments are recorded on a cumulative catch-up basis, which would affect revenues and earnings in the period of adjustment.

The AllStar Agreement contains joint research and development activities that are not within the scope of ASC 606. The Company will recognize research and development expense related to the joint study costs for all the joint activities in future periods and reimbursements received from AllStar will be recognized as an offset to research and development expense on the consolidated statement of operations during the development period. In the year ended December 31, 20X2, the Company received $186 from AllStar for joint costs.

Example 48.3: Collaborative Agreement, Contract Counterparty Not a Customer

On July 20, 20X1, our wholly owned subsidiary ABCTech Research and Development LLC ("ABCTech R&D") entered into a collaboration and option agreement ("Collaboration Agreement") with Kangaroo Bioscience AB ("Kangaroo"), pursuant to which ABCTech and Kangaroo will collaboratively develop COB.SLD-625, a lead bispecific antibody candidate simultaneously targeting 4-1BB (CD137), a member of the TNFR superfamily of a costimulatory receptor found on activated T-cells, and 5T4, a tumor antigen widely overexpressed in a number of different types of cancer. This product candidate is built on our novel ADAPTIR platform, which is designed to expand on the utility and effectiveness of therapeutic antibodies. Under this Collaboration Agreement, Kangaroo also granted to ABCTech a time-limited option to enter into a second agreement with Kangaroo for the joint development of a separate bispecific antibody.

Subject to certain exceptions for ABCTech's manufacturing and platform technologies, the parties will jointly own intellectual property generated in the performance of the development activities under the Collaboration Agreement. Under the terms of this Collaboration Agreement, the parties intend to share revenue received from a third-party commercialization partner equally, or, if the development costs are not equally shared under this Collaboration Agreement, in proportion to the development costs borne by each party.

The Collaboration Agreement also contains several points in development at which either party may elect to opt out (i.e., terminate without cause) and, following a termination notice period, cease paying development costs for this product candidate, which would be borne fully by the continuing party. Following an opt-out by a party, the continuing party will be granted exclusive rights to continue the development and commercialization of the product candidate, subject to a requirement to pay a percentage of revenue received from any future commercialization partner for this product, or, if the continuing party elects to self-commercialize, tiered royalties on the net sales of the product by the continuing party ranging from the low to mid-single digits, based on the point in development at which the opt-out occurs. The parties have also agreed on certain technical criteria, or "stage gates," related to the development of this product candidate that, if not met, will cause an automatic termination and wind-down of this Collaboration Agreement and the activities thereunder, provided that the parties do not agree to continue.

The Collaboration Agreement contains industry-standard termination rights, including for material breach following a specified cure period, and in the case of a party's insolvency.

ABCTech and Kangaroo have made a joint decision to delay submission of the clinical trial authorization ("CTA") for COB.SLD-625 previously planned for the fourth quarter of 2019. Kangaroo and ABCTech have made a joint decision to focus efforts on partnering COB.SLD-625 prior to Phase 1 clinical development. The adjustment to the development plan for COB.SLD-625 will allow both ABCTech and Kangaroo to align their resources with their respective ongoing clinical programs. The companies are initiating discussions with potential partners for the upcoming clinical development of COB.SLD-625.

We assessed the arrangement in accordance with ASC 606 and concluded that the contract counterparty, Kangaroo, is not a customer. As such the arrangement is not in the scope of ASC 606 and is instead treated as a collaborative agreement under ASC 808. For the year ended December 31, 20X3, we recorded a reduction in our research and development expense of $1.4 million, and for the year ended December 31, 20X2, we recorded a decrease in our research and development expense of $0.6 million, related to the collaboration arrangement.

Example 48.4: Joint Venture, Considered Collaborative Agreement

ABC entered into a Joint Venture Planting Agreement with the Seattle City Forestry Bureau on March 21, 2004, and certain Joint Venture Planting Agreements with an Oregon State–owned Bureau (the "Oregon Forest Bureau") in June 20X1 and May 20X2, respectively, which is considered a collaborative arrangement under U.S. GAAP. The purpose of this arrangement is to share some of the risks and rewards associated with this Joint Venture Planting Agreement. The Company's current share of profits is 80% for the collaborative agreement with the Seattle City Forestry Bureau and Oregon Forest Bureau dated June 20X1 and is 70% for the collaborative agreement with the Oregon Forest Bureau dated May 20X2. The Company accounts for this collaborative arrangement under ASC 808, *Collaborative Arrangements* and related topics, and will record revenue gross as the prime contractor. ASC Topic 808-10-15 defines collaborative arrangements and requires collaborators to present the result of activities for which they act as the principal on a gross basis and to report any payments received from (made to) the other collaborators based on other applicable authoritative accounting literature, and in the absence of other applicable authoritative literature, on the basis of a reasonable, rational, and consistent accounting policy that has been elected. The Company adopted the provisions of ASC 808-10-15. The adoption of this statement did not have an impact on the Company's consolidated financial position, results of operations, or cash flows. For the years ended December 31, 20X2 and 20X1, the Company has not generated any revenues or activity from this collaborative agreement.

Example 48.5: Analysis of Collaboration Agreements, Conclusion within Scope of ASC 606

The Company has entered into collaborative agreements with partners that typically include one or more of the following: (i) nonexclusive license fees; (ii) nonrefundable upfront fees; (iii) payments for reimbursement of research costs; (iv) payments associated with achieving specific development milestones; and (v) royalties based on specified percentages of net product sales, if any. At the initiation of an agreement, the Company has analyzed whether it results in a contract with a customer under Topic 606 or in an arrangement with a collaborator subject to guidance under ASC 808, *Collaborative Arrangements*.

The Company has considered a variety of factors in determining the appropriate estimates and assumptions under these arrangements, such as whether the elements are distinct performance obligations, whether there are determinable standalone prices, and whether any licenses are functional or symbolic. The Company has evaluated each performance obligation to determine if it can be satisfied and recognized as revenue at a point in time or over time. Typically, nonexclusive license fees, nonrefundable upfront fees, and funding of research activities have been considered fixed, while milestone payments have been identified as variable consideration, which must be evaluated to determine if it has been constrained and, therefore, excluded from the transaction price.

The Company's collaborative agreements that were not completed at the implementation of Topic 606 on April 1, 20X1, consisted of research collaboration and limited technology access licenses. These agreements provide the licensee with a nonexclusive, non-transferable, limited, royalty-free technology license, including access to the Company's proprietary bioprinter platform, training, and continued support by means of consumables and consultation throughout the duration of the contract. The Company has determined that the intellectual property license is not distinct from the continued support promised under the agreement and is therefore a single combined performance obligation. The Company recognized revenue for these combined performance obligations over time for the duration of the license period, as the combined performance obligation would not be fully satisfied until the end of the contract.

For the year ended March 31, 20X3, all collaborations and licenses revenue was within the scope of Topic 606 and recognized accordingly. As of September 30, 20X2, the Company completed its obligations under the existing agreements with respect to receipts of revenue and does not anticipate recording any further revenue.

Example 48.6: Guaranty

We have guaranteed the repayment by a third-party importer of its obligation under a bank credit facility that it uses in connection with its importation of our products in Russia. If the importer were to default on that obligation, which we believe is unlikely, our maximum possible exposure under the existing terms of the guaranty would be approximately $9 (subject to changes in foreign currency exchange rates). Both the fair value and carrying amount of the guaranty are insignificant.

As of April 30, 20X1, our actual exposure under the guaranty of the importer's obligation is approximately $5. We also have accounts receivable from that importer of approximately $8 at April 30, 20X1, which we expect to collect in full.

Based on the financial support we provide to the importer, we believe it meets the definition of a variable interest entity. However, because we do not control this entity, it is not included in our consolidated financial statements.

49 ASC 810 CONSOLIDATIONS

AUTHORITATIVE LITERATURE

The requirement to consolidate financial statements over which a reporting entity has control is a long-standing tenet of GAAP. There is a presumption that consolidated financial statements are more meaningful and are necessary for a fair presentation. Historically, the assessment of whether or not to consolidate was based on the voting interest the reporting entity held in the investee—the voting interest model.

Over the years, managers and their advisors devised many new and creative types of ownership structures, financing arrangements, financial instruments, and business relationships. Perhaps no such type of financial arrangement or structure has received the same level of negative publicity as the special purpose entity (SPE). An SPE is narrowly defined as a trust or other legal vehicle to which a transferor transfers a portfolio of financial assets, such as mortgage loans, commercial loans, credit card debt, automobile loans, and other groups of homogeneous borrowings.

Commonly, SPEs have been organized as trusts or partnerships (flow-through entities, to avoid double corporate income taxation), and the outside equity participant was ultimately defined as having as little as 3% of the total assets of the SPE at risk. No authoritative GAAP ever established this 3% threshold, but nevertheless it evolved somewhat by default and had been subject to varying interpretations under different sets of conditions.

In a process called a *securitization*, the SPE typically issues and sells securities that represent beneficial interests in the cash flows from the portfolio. The proceeds the SPE receives from the sale of these securities are used to purchase the portfolio from the transferor. The cash flows received by the SPE from the dividends, interest, redemptions, principal repayments, and/or realized gains on the financial assets are used to pay a return to the investors in the SPE's securities. By transferring packages of such loans to an SPE, these assets can be legally isolated and made "bankruptcy proof" (and thus made more valuable as collateral for other borrowings); various types of debt instruments can thus be used, providing the sponsor with fresh resources to fund future lending activities.

Technical Alert

In October 2018, the FASB issued ASU 2018-17, *Consolidation (Topic 810): Targeted Improvements to Related Party Guidance for Variable Interest Entities.*

The FASB issued the ASU in response to stakeholders' observations that ASC 810 could be improved by:

1. Applying the variable interest entity (VIE) guidance to private companies under common control
2. Considering indirect interests held through related parties under common control for determining whether fees paid to decision makers and service providers are variable interests

Guidance

The private company accounting alternative. The ASU allows a private company to elect not to apply VIE guidance to legal entities under common control (including common control leasing arrangements) if both the parent and the legal entity being evaluated for consolidation are not public business entities. The accounting alternative provides an accounting policy election that a private company will apply to all current and future legal entities under common control that meet the criteria for applying this alternative. Therefore, the alternative cannot be applied to select common control arrangements that meet the criteria for applying this accounting alternative. If the alternative is elected, a private company should continue to apply other consolidation guidance, particularly the voting interest entity guidance, unless another scope exception applies.

Under the accounting alternative, a private company should provide detailed disclosures about its involvement with and exposure to the legal entity under common control.

In effect, the amendments in the ASU expand the private company alternative provided by ASU 2014-07, not to apply the VIE guidance to qualifying common control leasing arrangements. Because the private company accounting alternative in the ASU applies to all common control arrangements that meet specific criteria and not just leasing arrangements, the amendments in ASU 2014-07 are superseded by the amendments in this Update.

Decision-making fees. Indirect interests held through related parties in common control arrangements should be considered on a *proportional* basis for determining whether fees paid to decision makers and service providers are variable interests. This is consistent with how indirect interests held through related parties under common control are considered for determining whether a reporting entity must consolidate a VIE. For example, if a decision maker or service provider owns a 20% interest in a related party and that related party owns a 40% interest in the legal entity being evaluated, the decision maker's or service provider's indirect interest in the VIE held through the related party under common control should be considered the equivalent of an 8% direct interest for determining whether its fees are variable interests.

This change should mean that fewer decision-making fees are variable interests. It should also reduce the risk that decision makers with insignificant direct and indirect interests could be considered to be the primary beneficiary (PB) of a VIE.

Effective Dates The ASU is effective as follows:

- For entities other than private companies:
  - Fiscal years beginning after December 15, 2019, and interim periods within those fiscal years
- For a private company:
  - Fiscal years beginning after December 15, 2020, and interim periods within fiscal years beginning after December 15, 2021

Early adoption is permitted.

Transition All entities are required to apply the amendments in this update retrospectively with a cumulative-effect adjustment to retained earnings at the beginning of the earliest period presented.

Subtopics

ASC 810, *Consolidations*, consists of two Subtopics:

- ASC 810-10, *Overall*, which has three Subsections:
  - General
  - Variable Interest Entities, which explains how to identify VIEs and when the reporting entity should consolidate the entity
  - Consolidation of Entities Controlled by Contract, which provides guidance for entities that are not VIEs but are controlled by contract, including physician practices and physician practice management entities
- ASC 810-30, *Research and Development Arrangements*, which provides direction on whether and how those arrangements should be consolidated

Scope and Scope Exceptions

All *legal* entities are included in the scope of ASC 810. The application to not-for-profit entities is subject to additional guidance in ASC 958-810. (ASC 810-10-15-4 and 15-5) Scope exceptions for ASC 810-10 follow the subsections and breakdown as follows:

- General, applying to all subtopics under ASC 810-10,
- Specific, applying to VIEs, and
- Consolidation of entities controlled by contracts that are not VIEs.

Applying the Scope Guidance If a reporting entity is within the scope of the VIE Subsection, that entity should apply the VIE guidance first. If not, then the reporting entity should determine whether it has a direct or indirect controlling financial interest. (ASC 810-10-15-3) For legal entities other than limited partnerships, this is defined as more than 50%. There are circumstances where an entity may hold a majority voting interest, but may not have a controlling interest, that is, the power to control the operations or assets of the investee. This is called a noncontrolling majority interest and may happen through a contract, lease, agreement with other stockholders, or court decrees. For limited partnerships, the usual condition for a controlling financial interest is ownership by one limited partner of more than 50% of the limited partnership's kick-out rights through voting interests. Control may also exist by contract, lease, agreement with partners, or by court decrees. (ASC 810- 10-15-8 and 15-8A)

Also see information below on VIEs within scope according to ASC 810-10-15-14.

If the reporting entity has a contractual management relationship that is not a VIE, the reporting entity should use the guidance in the 810-10 Subsections, *Consolidations of Entities Controlled by Contract*, to determine if the arrangement is a controlling financial interest. (ASC 810-10-15-3(c))

Exhibit—Determining Scope and Scope Exceptions (ASC 810-10-15-3)

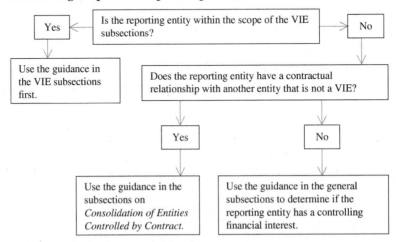

General Scope Exceptions A reporting entity with an explicit or implicit interest in a legal entity that is in the scope of the VIE Subsection follows the guidance in this Topic's VIE Subsections. (ASC 810-10-15-9) For entities that are not in the scope of the VIE subsection, a reporting entity should consolidate all entities in which the parent has a controlling financial interest, *except*:

- If the subsidiary:
  ◦ Is in a legal reorganization
  ◦ Is in bankruptcy
  ◦ Operates under "foreign exchange restrictions, controls, or other governmentally imposed uncertainties, so severe that they cast significant doubt on the parent's ability to control the subsidiary"
  ◦ Is a broker dealer within the scope of ASC 940 and control is likely to be temporary
- If the power of the majority voting interest shareholder or limited partner with majority of kick-out rights through voting interest is restricted by rights given to the noncontrolling shareholder or limited partners (noncontrolling rights) that are so restrictive that it is questionable whether control exists with majority owners
- If control exists other than through ownership of a majority voting interest or a majority of kick-out rights through voting interests
(ASC 810-10-15-10)

The guidance in ASC 810 does not apply to:

- An employee benefit plan subject to ASC 712, *Nonretirement Postemployment Benefits*, or to ASC 715, *Retirement Benefits*.
- An investment company within the scope of Topic 946 that is not an investment company, except if the investment company has an investment in an operating entity that provides services to the investment company. (ASC 946-810-45-3)
- A governmental organization.
- A financing entity established by a governmental organization, unless the financing entity meets both of the following conditions:
  ◦ It is not a governmental organization, and
  ◦ It is used by a business entity in a manner similar to a VIE to attempt to circumvent VIE accounting rules.
- Money market funds registered with the SEC pursuant to Rule 2a-7 of the Investment Company Act of 1940, that is, registered money market funds and those legal entities that are similar in purpose and design.
- Similar unregistered money market funds.
(ASC 810-10-15-12)

Variable Interest Entities within Scope VIEs follow the same scope and scope exceptions as in the General subsection, except as specified below. (ASC 810-10-15-13) The VIE model applies when the reporting entity has a variable interest in a legal entity. Any legal entity that, by design,[1] possesses one of the following characteristics is subject to consolidation under the VIE guidance:

- The entity is thinly capitalized. The total equity investment at risk is not sufficient to permit the entity to finance its activities without additional subordinated financial support from either the existing equity holders or other parties. Normally the equity provided by shareholders is sufficient to support operations. For this purpose, the total equity investment at risk:

---

[1] "By design" in this context applies to legal entities that meet the conditions in ASC 810-10-15-14 because of their structure.

- ○ Includes only equity investments in the entity that participate significantly in profits and losses, even if those investments do not carry voting rights.
- ○ Does not include equity interests that the entity issued in exchange for subordinated interests in other variable interest entities.
- ○ Does not include amounts provided to the equity investor directly or indirectly by the entity or by other parties involved with the entity (for example, by fees, charitable contributions, or other payments), unless the provider is a parent, subsidiary, or affiliate of the investor that is required to be included in the same set of consolidated financial statements as the investor.
- ○ Does not include amounts financed for the equity investor (for example, by loans or guarantees of loans) directly by the entity or by other parties involved with the entity, unless that party is a parent, subsidiary, or affiliate of the investor that is required to be included in the same set of consolidated financial statements as the investor.
- Equity holders lack the ability to direct the activities. For other than limited partnerships, that significantly affect the entity's economic performance, the investors do not have that ability through voting rights or similar rights if no owners hold voting rights or similar rights (such as those of a common stockholder in a corporation or a general partner in a partnership). Limited partners lack power if a simple majority is not able to exercise substantive kick-out rights or participating rights over the general partner.
- Reporting entity lacks the obligation to absorb the expected losses of the entity. Conventionally, the investors are exposed to the risks of ownership. The investor or investors do not have that obligation if they are directly or indirectly protected from absorbing the expected losses or are guaranteed a return by the entity itself or by other parties with whom the entity is involved.
- Reporting entity lacks the right to receive expected residual returns of the entity. Conventionally, the investors enjoy the benefit of ownership. The investors do not have that right if their benefits are limited to a specified maximum amount by the entity's governing documents or arrangements with other variable interest holders or with the entity.
- The entity was established with nonsubstantive voting interest. The guidance contains what can be thought of as an anti-abuse clause. This is designed to prevent an entity from structuring in a way that allows the sponsor to avoid consolidation under the VIE mode. This provision includes two conditions, both of which must be met:
  - ○ The distribution of economic benefits generated by the entity is proportional to equity ownership and voting rights, and
  - ○ Substantially all of the entity's activities either involve or are conducted on behalf of a party that has disproportionally low voting rights relative to economic interest. (ASC 810-10-15-14)

Variable Interest Entities Scope Exceptions As is clear from the above, a VIE differs from a voting interest entity because the VIE is structured in a way that voting rights are ineffective in determining which party has a controlling interest. In a VIE, control of an entity is achieved through arrangements that do not involve voting equity. The following are excluded from the scope of the subtopics and sections of ASC 810-10 governing VIEs:

- Not-for-profit entities, unless the entity was organized to avoid VIE status. It is important to note, however, that a not-for-profit organization can be a related party for the purpose of determining the primary beneficiary (parent) of a VIE by applying ASC paragraphs 810-10-25-42 through 44.

- Separate accounts of life insurance entities.
- An entity created prior to December 31, 2003, for which, after expending "exhaustive efforts," management of the variable interest holder is unable to obtain information needed to determine whether the entity is a VIE, to determine whether the holder is the primary beneficiary, or to make the required accounting entries required to consolidate the VIE.
- Entities that meet the definition of a business do not have to be evaluated by a variable interest holder to determine whether they are VIEs unless one or more of the following conditions exists:
    - The variable interest holder and/or its related parties/de facto agents[2] participated significantly in the design or redesign of the entity. This factor is not considered when the entity is an operating joint venture jointly controlled by the variable interest holder and either one or more independent parties, or a franchisee.
    - The design of the entity results in substantially all of its activities either involving or being conducted on behalf of the reporting entity and its related parties.
    - Based on the relative fair values of interests in the entity, the variable interest holder and its related parties provide more than half of its total equity, subordinated debt, and other forms of subordinated financial support.
    - The entity's activities relate primarily to one or both of the following:
        - Single-lessee leases, and
        - Securitizations or other forms of asset-backed financings.
        (ASC 810-10-15-17)

The above requirements for scope exceptions for businesses can be difficult to meet.

Private company alternative for common control arrangements A private company may elect not to apply VIE guidance to a lessor under common control when criteria (a) through (c) are met and in some situations (d) is not:

a. The private company lessee (the reporting entity) and the lessor legal entity are under common control,
b. The private company lessee has a leasing arrangement with the lessor legal entity,
c. Substantially all of the activity between the private company lessee and the lessor legal entity is related to the leasing activities (including supporting leasing activities) between those two entities, and
d. If the private company lessee explicitly guarantees or provides collateral for any obligation of the lessor legal entity related to the asset leased by the private company, then the principal amount of the obligation at inception of such guarantee or collateral arrangement does not exceed the value of the asset leased by the private company from the lessor legal entity.
(ASC 810-10-15-17AB)[3]

Instead of consolidating, the private company would make certain disclosures about the lessor and the leasing arrangement. If elected, the accounting alternative should be applied to all

---

[2] For this purpose, the term "de facto agent" would exclude a party with an agreement that it cannot sell, transfer, or encumber its interests in the entity without the prior approval of the variable interest holder when that right could constrain the other party's ability to manage the economic risks or realize the economic rewards from its interests in a VIE through the sale, transfer, or encumbrance of those interests.
[3] This paragraph is superseded upon implementation of ASU 2018-17.

leasing arrangements meeting the above conditions. If the conditions for applying the accounting alternative cease to be met, the private company should apply the VIE Subsection guidance prospectively at the date of change. The alternative should be applied retrospectively to all periods presented. (ASC 810-10-15-17B through 17C)[4]

A reporting entity that is a private company is not required to evaluate a legal entity if *all* of the following criteria are met:

a. The reporting entity and the legal entity are under common control.
b. The reporting entity and the legal entity are not under common control of a public business entity.
c. The legal entity under common control is not a public business entity.
d. The reporting entity does not directly or indirectly have a controlling financial interest in the legal entity when considering the General Subsection of this Topic. The VIE Subsection shall not be applied when making this determination.

If a private company elects to apply this accounting alternative, it must apply this alternative to all legal entities if the criteria above are met. A reporting entity that elects the accounting alternative and thus does not apply the guidance in the VIE Subsection shall continue to apply other accounting guidance (including guidance in the General Subsection of this Subtopic) unless another scope exception from this Topic applies. (ASC 810-10-15AD)[5]

For the purpose of applying paragraph 810-10-15-17AD(a) above to determine whether the private company reporting entity and the legal entity are under common control of a parent, the private company should consider only the parent's direct and indirect voting interest in the private company and the legal entity. That is, the guidance in the General Subsection of this Topic shall be considered when applying ASC 810-10-15-17AD(a). The guidance in the VIE Subsection should not be applied for making this determination. (ASC 810-10-15-17AE)[6]

If any of the criteria in ASC 810-10-15-17AD cease to be met, a private company should apply the guidance in the VIE Subsection at the date of change on a prospective basis, except for situations in which a reporting entity becomes a public business entity. When a reporting entity becomes a public business entity, it must apply the guidance in the VIE Subsection in accordance with ASC 250 on accounting changes and error corrections. (ASC 810-10-15-17AF)[7]

Collateralized Financing Entity—Alternative Approach Scope Criteria An entity may measure the financial assets and financial liabilities of a qualifying collateralized financial entity (CFE) using either the fair value of the financial assets or the financial liabilities, whichever is more observable. (ASC 810-10-30-11)

Entities that elect this option are relieved from independently measuring the fair value of the financial assets and financial liabilities. Entities that do not elect the alternative must attribute any differences in the fair value to the controlling interest holder in the consolidated income statement.

An entity may use the alternative if it meets both of the following conditions:

a. All of the financial assets and the financial liabilities of the collateralized financing entity are measured at fair value in the consolidated financial statements under other applicable Topics, other than financial assets and financial liabilities that are incidental

---

[4] Ibid.
[5] This paragraph is effective upon implementation of ASU 2018-17.
[6] Ibid.
[7] Ibid.

to the operations of the collateralized financing entity and have carrying values that approximate fair value (for example, cash, broker receivables, or broker payables).
b. The changes in the fair values of those financial assets and financial liabilities are reflected in earnings.
(ASC 810-10-15-17D)

This guidance is applied using:

- A modified retrospective approach by recording a cumulative-effect adjustment to equity as of the beginning of the annual period of adoption, or
- A retrospective approach by applying the changes retrospectively to all relevant prior periods beginning with the annual period of initial adoption.

ASC 810-30, *Research and Development Arrangements* ASC 810-30 is limited to those research and development arrangements in which all of the funds for the research and development activities are provided by the sponsor of the research and development arrangement. It does not apply to either:

- Transactions in which the funds are provided by third parties, which would generally be within the scope of Subtopic 730-20.
- Legal entities required to be consolidated under the guidance on variable interest entities. (ASC 810-30-15-3)

Consolidation Models—Introduction and Background

ASC 810 provides the primary authority for determining when presentation of consolidated financial statements is required. Consolidation is only required for legal entities within the scope of ASC 810. The rationale underlying ASC 810 is that when one enterprise directly or indirectly holds a controlling financial interest in one or more other enterprises, consolidated financial statements are more informative to users. There are two models for assessing whether a reporting entity has a controlling interest in the entity being evaluated for consolidation:

1. The voting interest model
2. The variable interest entity model

The VIE Model

Under the VIE model, the assessment of control differs from the voting interest model because control of a VIE can be achieved by other than ownership of shares. A controlling financial interest of a VIE requires:

- The power to direct the activities that most significantly impact the VIE's economic performance
- The obligation to absorb losses that could be significant to the VIE or the right to receive benefits from the VIE that could be potentially significant to the VIE. (ASC 810-10-05-8A)

Is the Reporting Entity the Primary Beneficiary? Once the reporting entity has determined that:

- A VIE scope exception does not apply, and
- The reporting entity has a variable interest in the legal entity (ASC 810-10-55-16), then the reporting entity applies the VIE model to determine if it is the primary beneficiary and, therefore, must consolidate the variable entity. (ASC 810-10-25-38)

Once it is determined that the reporting entity has a variable interest in a VIE, the reporting entity must determine whether it has a *controlling* financial interest. This assessment includes:

- The characteristics of the reporting entity's variable interests
- Other involvement, including related parties or de facto agents
- The involvement of other interest holders
- The VIE's purpose and design

The primary beneficiary must consolidate the VIE regardless of the extent of ownership (or lack of it) by that entity. More than one entity may have the obligation to absorb losses or the right to receive benefits, but only one reporting entity will have the *power* to direct those activities of the VIE that most significantly affect the VIE's performance and, therefore, be the primary beneficiary. (ASC 810-10-25-38A) Only one enterprise should be identified as the primary beneficiary, with the determining factor being the power to direct those activities of the VIE most significantly impacting its economic performance. It is possible that no primary beneficiary can be identified.

Shared power. ASC 810 includes the concept of shared power when evaluating a primary beneficiary. Power is shared:

- If two or more unrelated parties together have the power to direct the activities of a VIE that most significantly impact the VIE's economic performance, and
- If decisions about those activities require the consent of each of the parties.

If power is shared with other unrelated parties and no one party has the power to direct activities that most significantly impact the VIE's economic performance, then the reporting entity is *not* the primary beneficiary. (ASC 810-10-25-38D)

Fees paid to decision maker. In some arrangements, a legal entity may outsource all or some decision making over the entity's activities through a contractual arrangement. The fees received by those decision makers or service providers may represent variable interests. Decision makers or service providers may include oil and gas operators, real estate property managers, asset managers, and so forth. The decision maker or service provider must assess the fee arrangement to determine if it qualifies as a variable interest.

If a decision maker meets all three of the criteria below, it is not a variable interest.

Exhibit—Criteria to Determine Whether a Fee Paid to a Decision Maker or Service Provider Is a Variable Interest

ASC 810-10-25-55-37 paragraph:	The fees paid to a decision maker or service provider is a variable interest if:
A	The fees are compensation for services provided and are commensurate with level of effort required to provide those services.
C	The decision maker or service provider does not hold other economic interests in the VIE that individually, or in the aggregate, would absorb more than an insignificant amount of the VIE's expected losses or receive more than an insignificant amount of the VIE's expected residual returns.
D	The service arrangement includes only terms, conditions, or amounts that are customarily present in arrangements for similar services negotiated at arm's length.

Measurement

Initial measurement with common control. If the primary beneficiary of a VIE and the VIE itself are under common control, the primary beneficiary (parent) initially measures the assets, liabilities, and noncontrolling interests of the newly consolidated reporting entity at their carrying amounts in the accounting records of the entity that controls the VIE. (ASC 810-10-30-1)

Initial measurement absent common control. The rules governing the initial measurement of the assets and liabilities of a newly consolidated VIE conform closely to the rules governing other business combinations. The following table summarizes the rules:

Accounting by a Primary Beneficiary (Parent) for Initial Consolidation of a Variable Interest Entity

Recognition or measurement issue	Accounting treatment
1. Measurement date	Acquisition date, which is the date the acquirer/primary beneficiary obtains control of the acquiree/VIE. (ASC 805-10-25-6)
2. Measurement amount for assets, liabilities, and noncontrolling interests	The initial consolidation of a VIE that is a business is a business combination and should be accounted for as discussed previously in this chapter.
3. Measurement exception for enterprises under common control	Carrying value (net book value, or NBV) in the accounting records of the enterprise that controls the VIE with no "step-up."
4. Assets and liabilities transferred to the VIE by the PB at, after, or shortly before the date of initial consolidation where the VIE *is not a business*	The assets and liabilities are measured using the same amounts at which the assets and liabilities would have been measured if they had not been transferred. No gain or loss is recognized on account of the transfer.
5. Assets and liabilities transferred to the VIE by the PB at, after, or shortly before the date of initial consolidation where the VIE *is a business*	If the VIE is a business, it should follow ASC 805-10-25-20 et seq., *Determining What Is Part of the Business Combination Transaction*, to assess the substance of such transfers and whether they are to be considered part of the business combination.
6. Recognition and measurement of goodwill	If the VIE is a business, goodwill is recognized and measured identical to the manner described for other business combinations. If the VIE is not a business, goodwill is not to be recognized and, instead, is recognized as a loss in the period of initial consolidation. That loss, however, is not to be characterized as extraordinary.
7. Recognition of negative goodwill	Irrespective of whether the VIE is a business, negative goodwill is not used to reduce the carrying values of any of the acquired assets or liabilities; rather it is recognized and measured identically with the manner described for business combinations as a gain on bargain purchase with a prohibition against characterizing the gain as extraordinary.

After initial measurement, the assets, liabilities, and noncontrolling interests of a consolidated variable interest entity are accounted for as if the entity were consolidated based on majority voting interests.

Reconsideration of VIE Status Once an initial determination is made as to whether an entity is a variable interest entity (as opposed to a voting interest entity), that initial determination need not be reconsidered unless one or more of the following circumstances occurs:

- A change is made to the VIE's governing documents or contractual arrangements that results in changes in either the characteristics or sufficiency of the at-risk equity investment in the VIE.
- As a result of a return of some or all of the equity investment to the equity investors, other interests become exposed to the VIE's expected losses.
- There is an increase in the VIE's expected losses that results from the entity engaging in activities or acquiring assets that were not anticipated at either the inception of the entity or a later reconsideration date.
- There is a decrease in the VIE's expected losses due to the entity modifying or curtailing its activities.
- Additional at-risk equity is invested in the VIE.
- The equity investors, as a group, lose the power to direct the activities of the VIE that most significantly impact its economic performance.
(ASC 810-10-35-4)

The Voting Interest Model

The term "voting interest entity" is not defined explicitly in ASC 810. By default it means an entity that is not a variable interest entity. ASC 810 stipulates that the usual condition that best evidences which party holds a controlling financial interest is that the party holds a majority voting interest. Voting rights are the key driver in determining which party should consolidate the entity. Kick-out rights through voting interest are analogous to a shareholder's voting rights in a corporation. (ASC 810-10-25-1A) The voting interest model generally assumes the percentage of ownership determines the level of influence that the reporting entity has over an investee. Determination of whether the presumption of control of an investee with a majority voting interest or a limited partner with a majority of kick-out rights through voting interests is overcome is a "facts and circumstances" assessment to be made in each unique situation. Another important factor weighing on this determination is the relationships among limited and general partners (using ASC 850 related-party criteria). (ASC 810-10-25-5)

The exhibit below outlines the presumptive control based on voting interest. (Also, see the "Scope and Scope Exceptions" section at the beginning of this chapter for exceptions to the majority control presumption.)

Exhibit—Voting Interest Model

Percentage of Ownership	0 < 50	50	100
Presumptive Level of Influence	Little or none	Significant	Control
Valuation/Reporting Method	Fair value method	Equity method	Consolidation

Under the equity method, investments are shown as a single line in the statement of financial position and a single line item in the income statement. This is sometimes referred to as a one-line consolidation. In consolidated financial statements, details of all entities are reported in full.

Because of their unique design and purpose, the Codification offers specific guidance for limited partnerships and similar entities, like limited liability companies governed by a managing member, regarding voting rights. Kick-out rights are considered analogous to the voting rights held by a corporation's shareholders. To demonstrate that a limited partnership is a voting entity, the partners or members must have:

- Kick-out rights
- Participating rights
  (ASC 810-10-15-14)

The assessment of noncontrolling rights is made when a majority voting interest or a majority of kick-out rights through voting interests is obtained. The assessment is made again if there is a significant change to the terms or the exercisability of the noncontrolling shareholder's or limited partner's rights. (ASC 810-10-25-6)

Protective Rights Limited partners' rights (whether granted by contract or by law) that would allow the limited partners to block selected limited partnership actions would be considered protective rights. The presence of protective rights does not serve to overcome the presumption of control by the general partner(s). (ASC 810-10-15-20)

Substantive Participating Rights Substantive participating rights, on the other hand, do overcome the presumption of general partner control. Such rights could include:

- Selecting, terminating, and setting the compensation of management responsible for implementing the limited partnership's policies and procedures
- Establishing operating and capital decisions of the limited partnership, including budgets, in the ordinary course of business
  (ASC 810-10-25-11)

Kick-Out Rights If the limited partners have the *substantive ability* to dissolve (liquidate) the limited partnership or otherwise remove the general partners without cause—which is referred to as "kick-out rights"—then the general partners are deemed to lack control over the partnership. In such cases, consolidated financial reporting would not be appropriate, but equity method accounting would almost inevitably be warranted. To qualify, the kick-out rights must be exercisable by a single limited partner or a simple majority (or fewer) of limited partners. Thus, if a super-majority of limited partner votes is required to remove the general partner(s), this would not constitute a substantive ability to dissolve the partnership and would not thwart control by the general partner(s).

ASC 810-30, *Research and Development Arrangements*

Sponsored Research and Development Activities To illustrate the guidance in this section, ASC 810-30-55 discusses the accounting for a transaction in which a sponsor creates a wholly owned subsidiary with cash and rights to certain technology originally developed by the sponsor, and receives from the newly created subsidiary two classes of stock. The sponsor then distributes one of the classes of stock (e.g., Class A) to its stockholders. This class of stock has voting rights. Under a purchase option, the sponsor has the right, for a specified period of time, to repurchase all the Class A stock distributed to the stockholders for an exercise price approximating the fair value of the Class A shares. The class retained by the sponsor (e.g., Class B) conveys essentially no financial interest to the sponsor and has no voting rights other than certain blocking rights. The certificate of incorporation prohibits the subsidiary from changing its capital structure, from selling any significant portion of its assets, and from liquidating or merging during the term when the purchase option is outstanding.

The sponsor and the subsidiary enter into a development contract that requires the subsidiary to spend all the cash contributed by the sponsor for research and development activities mutually agreed upon with the sponsor. The subsidiary has no employees other than its CEO. The subsidiary contracts with the sponsor to perform, on behalf of the sponsor, all of the research and development activities under the development contract.

The sponsor accounts for the research and development contract as follows:

- The sponsor reclassifies the cash contributed to the subsidiary as restricted cash when the Class A shares are distributed to its stockholders.
- The distribution of the Class A shares by the sponsor to its stockholders is accounted for as a dividend based on the fair value of the shares distributed.
- In the financial statements of the sponsor, the Class A shares are presented similarly to a minority interest.
- The sponsor recognizes research and development expense as the research and development activities are conducted.
- The research and development expense recognized by the sponsor is not allocated to the Class A shares in determining net income or in calculating earnings per share.
- If the Class A purchase option is exercised, the sponsor accounts for the purchase as the acquisition of a minority interest.
- If the Class A purchase option is not exercised by its expiration date, the sponsor reclassifies the Class A stock to additional paid-in capital as an adjustment of the original dividend.

The effect of the above guidance is quite similar to what would be achieved by consolidating the subsidiary.

PRACTICE ALERT

While SEC comments pertain to financial statements of SEC filers, the staff comments can provide useful practice pointers for all preparers. In the area of consolidations, the SEC staff has asked preparers to:

- Explain how they determined an entity is a VIE
- Explain the entity's involvement with the VIE
- Provide a detailed analysis of how the entity determined that the reporting entity is the primary beneficiary, in particular about the activities that significantly impact the VIE's economic performance
- Provide information about how they evaluated details of the VIE arrangement and the company's involvement
- Give additional details about the entity's noncontrolling interests
- Submit the entity's calculation of ownership interests and net income or loss attributable to those interests
- Explain events that resulted in deconsolidation

PRESENTATION AND DISCLOSURE REQUIREMENTS

Presentation

Procedures In preparing consolidated financial statements, the parent eliminates 100% of the intercompany income or loss. This elimination is not affected by the existence of a noncontrolling interest since the consolidated financial statements present the financial position and economic performance of a single economic entity. The elimination of the intercompany income or loss may be allocated between the parent and noncontrolling interests.

Consolidated financial statements should not include gains or losses on transactions among entities in a consolidated group. (ASC 810-10-45-1) Retained earnings or deficit of a subsidiary at the acquisition date are not included in consolidated retained earnings. (ASC 810-10-45-2)

Consolidated financial statements include the subsidiary's revenues, expenses, gains, and losses only from the date of initial consolidation. (ASC 810-10-45-4) Consolidated financial statements reflect shares of the parent held by a subsidiary as treasury shares. (ASC 810-10-45-5)

Retained earnings in the consolidated financial statements reflect the accumulated earnings of the consolidated group not distributed to the owners of, or capitalized by, the parent. (ASC 810-10-45-9)

Combined Financial Statements In combined statements, intra-entity transactions and profits and losses are eliminated and noncontrolling interest, foreign operations, different fiscal periods, or income taxes are treated in the same manner as they are in consolidated statements. (ASC 810-10-45-10)

Noncontrolling Interest in a Subsidiary The noncontrolling interest in a subsidiary is reported in the consolidated statement of financial position within equity, but separately from the parent's equity, and is clearly identified and labeled. If noncontrolling interests are in more than one subsidiary, they are presented in the aggregate in the consolidated financial statements. (ASC 810-10-45-16)

Only the following may be presented as a noncontrolling interest in the consolidated financial statements:

- A financial instrument or an embedded feature issued by a subsidiary that is classified as equity in the subsidiary's financial statements, *or*
- A financial instrument or an embedded derivative issued by a parent or a subsidiary where the counterparty's payoff is based, at least in part, on the stock of a consolidated subsidiary considered indexed to the entity's own stock in the parent's consolidated financial statements and that is classified as equity. (ASC 810-10-45-16A)

An equity-classified instrument within the scope of ASC 815-40-15-5C should be presented as component of noncontrolling interest. (ASC 810-10-45-17A)

Attributing Net Income and Comprehensive Income to the Parent and the Noncontrolling Interest Net income and comprehensive income attributed to the parent and the noncontrolling interest are reported with the consolidated amounts, including amounts attributable to the owners of the parent and the noncontrolling interest: revenue, expenses, gains, losses, net income or loss, and other comprehensive income. (ASC 810-10-45-19) Net income or loss and other comprehensive income or loss are allocated to the parent and noncontrolling interest. (ASC 810-10-45-20)

If losses allocated to the parent and to the noncontrolling interest exceed their respective interests in the equity of the subsidiary and this continues to occur in subsequent periods, the excess as well as any further losses continue to be allocated to the parent and noncontrolling interest, even if this allocation results in a deficit balance in noncontrolling interest. (ASC 810-10-45-21)

Changes in a Parent's Ownership Interest in a Subsidiary ASC 810-10-45-22 through 45-24 below apply to:

- Transactions resulting in an increase in ownership of a subsidiary
- When the parent retains a controlling interest in the subsidiary, transactions that result in a decrease in ownership of either:
  i. A subsidiary that is a business or nonprofit activity, except for:
     a. A conveyance of oil or gas mineral rights
     b. A transfer of a good or service in a contract in the scope of ASC 606
- A subsidiary that is not a business or a nonprofit activity if the transaction is not addressed directly by guidance in other ASC topics, such as 606, 845, 860, 932, or 610-20.
  (ASC 810-10-45-21A)

The parent company may purchase or sell shares of the subsidiary after the acquisition date without affecting the determination that it controls the subsidiary. In addition, the subsidiary may issue new shares or repurchase some of its own shares as treasury stock or for retirement. (ASC 810-10-45-22)

The entity should account for changes in the parent's ownership interest that do not affect the determination that the parent retains a controlling financial interest in the subsidiary as equity transactions with no gain or loss recognized in consolidated net income or in other comprehensive income. The carrying amount of the noncontrolling interest in the subsidiary should be adjusted to reflect the change in ownership interest and the entity should recognize in equity attributable to the parent any difference between the fair value of the consideration received or paid in the transaction and the amount by which the noncontrolling interest is adjusted. (ASC 810-10-45-23)

In the case of a subsidiary that has accumulated other comprehensive income (AOCI), if there was a change in the parent's ownership interest, the carrying amount of AOCI is adjusted through a corresponding charge or credit to equity attributable to the parent. (ASC 810-10-45-24)

Variable Interest Entities The following are reported separately on the face of the statement of financial position:

- Assets of a consolidated VIE that can be used only to settle obligations of the consolidated VIE
- Liabilities of a consolidated VIE for which creditors (or beneficial interest holders) do not have recourse to the general credit of the primary beneficiary
  (ASC 810-10-45-25)

Presentation of the New Entity's Common Stock by the Sponsor The new research and development arrangement entity's Class A common stock is presented as noncontrolling interest of the sponsor classified as equity separate from the parent's equity. (ASC 810-30-45-1) Research and development expense recognized by the sponsor should not be allocated to the new entity's Class A common stock to determine net income or earnings available to the sponsor's common stockholders in the EPS calculation. (ASC 810-30-45-2)

Disclosure

Consolidation Policy The entity's consolidation policy should be described through the headings, other information, or in a note. (ASC 810-10-50-1)

Parent with a Less-Than-Wholly-Owned Subsidiary For each reporting period, a parent with one or more less-than-wholly-owned subsidiaries should disclose:

- Separately on the face of the consolidated financial statements:
  ○ The amounts of consolidated net income and consolidated comprehensive income, and
  ○ The related amounts of each attributable to the parent and the noncontrolling interest.

- Either on the face of the consolidated income statement or in the notes, amounts attributable to the parent for:
  ○ Income from continuing operations, and
  ○ Discontinued operations.
- Either in the consolidated statement of changes in equity if presented, or in the notes, a reconciliation of beginning of period and end of period carrying amounts of total equity, equity attributable to the parent, and equity attributable to the noncontrolling interest, separately disclosing:
  ○ Net income,
  ○ Transactions with owners acting in their capacity as owners, separately showing contributions and distributions, and
  ○ Each component of other comprehensive income.
- A separate schedule showing the effects of any changes in the parent's ownership interest in a subsidiary on the equity attributable to the parent.
  (ASC 810-10-50-1A)

Deconsolidation of a Subsidiary If a subsidiary is deconsolidated during the reporting period, in the parent's financial statements the entity should disclose:

- The amount of gain or loss recognized.
- The portion of any gain or loss that relates to the remeasurement to fair value of any investment retained by the former parent in its former subsidiary.
- The caption in the income statement in which the gain or loss is recognized, unless presented separately on the face of the income statement.
- the description of the valuation techniques used to measure the fair value of the former investment.
- Enough information for users to assess the inputs used in the development of fair value of the former investment.
- The nature of any continuing involvement with the entity acquiring the assets.
- Whether the transaction was with a related party.
- Whether the former subsidiary or entity acquiring the assets will be a related party after the deconsolidation.
  (ASC 810-10-50-1B)

A Change in the Difference Between Parent and Subsidiary Fiscal Year-Ends All entities that change (or eliminate) a previously existing difference between the reporting periods of a parent and a consolidated entity, or an investor and an equity method investee, should include the disclosures required by ASC 250. Note: This paragraph does not apply in situations in which a parent entity or an investor changes its fiscal year-end. (ASC 810-10-50-2)

Variable Interest Entities The following information should be provided by the primary beneficiary of a variable interest entity (unless that party also holds a majority voting interest) to provide the users of the financial statements with information to enable an understanding of:

- The significant judgments and assumptions made by management in determining whether it must consolidate a VIE and/or disclose information about its involvement in a VIE;
- The nature of restrictions on a consolidated VIE's assets and on the settlement of its liabilities reported by a reporting entity in its statement of financial position, including the carrying amounts of such assets and liabilities;

- The nature of, and changes in, the risks associated with the reporting entity's involvement with the VIE; and
- How a reporting entity's involvement with the VIE affects its financial position, financial performance, and cash flows.
(ASC 810-10-50-2AA)

Accounting Alternative For a private company lessee that elects the accounting alternative for one or more lessor legal entities (see 810-10-15-17A), the following information should be disclosed:

- Amount and key terms of liabilities that are recognized by the lessor and expose the lessee to providing financial support to the lessor legal entity.
- Qualitative description of circumstances not recognized by the lessor and that expose the private company lessee to providing financial support to the legal entity.
(ASC 810-10-50-2AD)[8]

In applying the requirements above, the lessee should consider exposures through implicit guarantees, including:

- The existence of an economic incentive for the lessee to act as guarantor or to make funds available.
- Those actions that have occurred in similar past situations.
- The lessor acting as guarantor or making funds available.
(ASC 810-10-50-2AE)[9]

The lessor legal entity information provided by the private company lessee should combine the disclosures with disclosures requested by other guidance, such as guarantees, related-party disclosures, and leases. Note: These can be combined in a single note or through cross-references. (ASC 810-10-50-2AF)[10]

Accounting Alternative for Entities Under Common Control In addition to disclosures required by other topics and in a single note or through cross-references, a reporting entity that does not consolidate or applies the VIE guidance to a legal entity because it meets the criteria for the accounting alternative should disclose:

- The nature and risks associated with involvement with the legal entity under common control
- How the involvement affects the reporting entity's financial position, cash flows, and financial performance
- Carrying amounts and classifications of assets and liabilities resulting from the involvement
- The maximum exposure to loss resulting from the involvement or the fact that the exposure cannot be quantified
- Qualitative and quantitative information about the exposure where the maximum exposure to loss exceeds carrying value of assets and liabilities, including explicit and implicit terms of the arrangement that could require the entity to provide financial support to the legal entity under common control
(ASC 810-10-50-2AG and 2AI)

---

[8] Upon implementation of ASU 2018-17, this paragraph is superseded.

[9] Ibid.

[10] Ibid.

Primary Beneficiary A primary beneficiary that is a business should include the disclosures required by other guidance. The primary beneficiary of a VIE that is not a business should disclose the amount of any gain or loss recognized on the initial consolidation of the VIE and all of the following:

a. The carrying amounts and classification of the VIE's assets and liabilities in the statement of financial position that are consolidated, including qualitative information about the relationships between those assets and liabilities.
b. Lack of recourse if creditors (or holders of beneficial interests) of a consolidated VIE have no recourse to the general credit of the PB.
c. Terms or arrangements, giving consideration to both explicit arrangements and implicit variable interests that could require the reporting entity to provide financial support to the VIE, including events or circumstances that could expose the reporting entity to a loss.
d. A business entity that issues voting equity interest and the entity holding the majority voting interest is the primary beneficiary, does not have to make disclosures (a) through (c) above.
(ASC 810-10-50-3)

In addition to disclosure required by other guidance, a reporting entity that holds a variable interest in a VIE but is not the VIE's primary beneficiary should disclose:

a. The carrying amounts and classification of the assets and liabilities in the statement of financial position of the reporting entity that relate to the reporting entity's variable interest in the VIE.
b. The entity's maximum exposure to loss as a result of its involvement with the VIE, including how the maximum exposure was determined and the significant sources of the reporting entity's exposure to the VIE. If management was unable to quantify the maximum exposure to loss, that fact.
c. A tabular comparison of the carrying amounts of the assets and liabilities, as required in (a) above, and the enterprise's maximum exposure to loss as required in (b) above. A reporting entity is to provide qualitative and quantitative information to enable financial statement users to understand the differences between the two amounts. The discussion includes, but not be limited to, the terms of arrangements, giving consideration to both explicit arrangements and implicit variable interests that could require the reporting entity to provide financial support to the VIE, and including events or circumstances that could expose the reporting entity to loss.
d. Information regarding any liquidity arrangements, guarantees, and/or other commitments by third parties that may affect the fair value or risk of the reporting entity's VIE is encouraged to be provided.
e. If applicable, significant factors and judgments made in determining the power to direct the activities of a VIE that most significantly impact the VIE's economic performance is shared.
(ASC 810-10-50-4)

Primary Beneficiaries or Other Holders of Interests in VIEs A reporting entity that is a primary beneficiary of a VIE or a reporting entity that holds a variable interest in a VIE but is not the entity's primary beneficiary should disclose:

- The methodology used to determine whether the reporting entity is the PB of a VIE, including significant judgments and assumptions made.
- If facts and circumstances change, resulting in a change in the conclusion to consolidate a VIE in the most recent financial statements, the primary factors that caused the change and the effect on the financial statements of the reporting entity.
- Whether the reporting entity has provided financial or other support (explicitly or implicitly) during the periods presented to the VIE that it was not previously contractually required to provide or whether the reporting entity intends to provide that support, including both of the following:
  i. The type and amount of support, including situations in which the reporting entity assisted the VIE in obtaining another type of support.
  ii. The primary reasons for providing the support.
- Qualitative and quantitative information about the reporting entity's involvement with the VIE (considering both explicit arrangements and implicit variable interest) including, but not limited to, the nature, purpose, size, and activities of the VIE, and how the VIE is financed.
  (ASC 810-10-50-5A)

A VIE may issue voting equity interests, and the entity that holds a majority voting interest also may be the primary beneficiary of the VIE. If so, and if the VIE meets the definition of a business and the VIE's assets can be used for purposes other than the settlement of the VIE's obligations, the disclosures in the preceding paragraph are not required. (ASC 810-10-50-5B)

Scope—Related Disclosures An enterprise that does not apply ASC 810 to one or more VIEs or potential VIEs because after exhaustive efforts it is unable to obtain the necessary information should provide the following information:

- The number of legal entities to which ASC 810 is not being applied and the reason why the information required to apply ASC 810 is not available.
- The nature, purpose, size (if the information is available), and activities of the VIE or potential VIE and the nature of the enterprise's involvement with those entities.
- The enterprise's maximum exposure to loss as a result of its involvement with the entity or entities.
- The amount of income, expense, purchases, sales, or other measure of activity between the reporting enterprise and the entity (entities) for all periods presented. (If not practicable to present the prior period information in the first set of financial statements to which this requirement applies, that prior period information may be omitted.)
  (ASC 810-10-50-6)

Aggregation of Certain Disclosures Disclosures about VIEs may be reported in the aggregate for similar entities if separate reporting would not provide more useful information to financial statement users. A reporting entity should disclose how similar entities are aggregated and shall distinguish between:

- VIEs that are not consolidated because the reporting entity is not the primary beneficiary but has a variable interest.
- VIEs that are consolidated.

The disclosures are presented in a manner that clearly explains to financial statement users the nature and extent of an entity's involvement with VIEs. (ASC 810-10-50-9)

Collateralized Financing Entities If a reporting entity consolidates a collateralized financing entity and measures the financing assets and liabilities using the measurement alternative in ASC 810-30-10 and ASC 810-10-35-6 through 35-8, it should disclose:

- Information on fair value measurement required by ASC 820 and ASC 825.
- For the less-observable fair value of the financial assets and liabilities measured in accordance with the measurement alternative, that the amount was measured on the basis of the more observable of the fair value of the financial assets and liabilities. (ASC 810-10-50-20 and 50-21)

PRESENTATION AND DISCLOSURE EXAMPLES

Example 49.1: Accounting Policy for VIEs

A variable interest entity ("VIE") is an entity that either (i) has insufficient equity to permit the entity to finance its activities without additional subordinated financial support, or (ii) has equity investors who lack the characteristics of a controlling financial interest. Under ASC 810, *Consolidations*, an entity that holds a variable interest in a VIE and meets certain requirements would be considered to be the primary beneficiary of the VIE and required to consolidate the VIE in its consolidated financial statements. In order to be considered the primary beneficiary of a VIE, an entity must hold a variable interest in the VIE and have both:

- The power to direct the activities that most significantly impact the economic performance of the VIE; and
- The right to receive benefits from, or the obligation to absorb losses of, the VIE that could be potentially significant to the VIE.

Example 49.2: Description of VIE and Determination of VIE Status and Primary Beneficiary

Effective September 1, 20X1, XYZ acquired a majority voting interest in substantially all of the assets and certain specified liabilities of ABC Inc. and ABC Corporation, a market leader of iris-based identity authentication solutions, through a newly formed entity, ABC LLC. The Company has issued ABC LLC a promissory note for the purposes of repaying protective advances and funding working capital requirements of the company. On June 2, 20X5, this promissory note was amended and restated to allow ABC LLC to borrow up to a maximum of $57,500. Through March 1, 20X4, interest on the outstanding principal of the loan accrued at 10%. From March 1, 20X4, forward, interest accrues at 2.5%. The amended and restated promissory note is due on August 31, 20X5. The outstanding principal balance of this promissory note is convertible at the sole option of XYZ into units of ABC LLC. If XYZ chooses not to convert into equity, the outstanding loan principal of the amended and restated promissory note will be repaid at a multiple of 1.50 based on the repayment date. The agreement includes customary events of default and is collateralized by all of the property of ABC LLC.

We have determined that we hold a variable interest in ABC LLC as a result of:

- Our majority voting interest and ownership of substantially all of the assets and certain liabilities of the entity; and
- The loan agreement with ABC LLC, which has a total outstanding principal balance of $54,074 as of February 29, 2020.

We concluded that we became the primary beneficiary of ABC LLC on September 1, 20X1, in conjunction with the acquisition. This was the first date that we had the power to direct the activities of ABC LLC that most significantly impact the economic performance of the entity because we acquired a majority interest in substantially all of the assets and certain liabilities of ABC Inc. and ABC Corporation on this date, as well as obtained a majority voting interest as a result of this transaction. Although we are considered to have control over ABC LLC under ASC 810, as a result of our majority ownership interest the assets of ABC LLC can only be used to satisfy the obligations of ABC LLC. As a result of our majority ownership interest in the entity and our primary beneficiary conclusion, we consolidated ABC LLC in our consolidated financial statements beginning on September 1, 20X1. Prior to September 1, 20X1, ABC Inc. and ABC Corporation were not required to be consolidated in our consolidated financial statements, as we concluded that we were not the primary beneficiary of these entities prior to that time.

Example 49.3: Schedule of Assets and Liabilities of a VIE

The following table sets forth the carrying values of assets and liabilities of ABC LLC that were included on our consolidated balance sheet as of February 29, 20X5 and February 28, 20X4:

(Amounts in thousands)	*February 29, 20X5*	*February 28, 20X4*
Assets		
Current assets:		
Cash and cash equivalents	—	$ 3
Accounts receivable, net	147	363
Inventory, net	2,052	(27)
Prepaid expenses and other current assets	313	322
Total current assets	2,512	661
Property, plant, and equipment, net	69	120
Intangible assets, net	2,600	33,064
Other assets	76	253
Total assets	$ 5,257	$ 34,098
Liabilities and Stockholders' Equity		
Current liabilities:		
Accounts payable	$ 2,086	$ 1,122
Interest payable to VOXX	9,994	8,729
Accrued expenses and other current liabilities	252	1,030
Due to VOXX	54,074	44,937
Total current liabilities	66,406	55,818
Other long-term liabilities	1,200	1,200
Total liabilities	67,606	57,018
Commitments and contingencies		
Partners' deficit:		
Capital	41,416	41,416
Retained losses	(103,765)	(64,336)
Total partners' deficit	(62,349)	(22,920)
Total liabilities and partners' deficit	$ 5,257	$ 34,098

The assets of ABC LLC can only be used to satisfy the obligations of ABC LLC.

Example 49.4: Schedule of Revenue and Expenses of a VIE

The following table sets forth the revenue and expenses of ABC LLC that were included in our consolidated statements of operations and comprehensive (loss) income for the years ended February 29, 20X5, February 28, 20X4, and February 28, 20X3:

	Year Ended February 29, 20X5	Year Ended February 28, 20X4	Year Ended February 28, 20X3
Net sales	$ 476	$ 668	$ 335
Cost of sales	826	309	455
Gross profit	(350)	359	(120)
Operating expenses:			
Selling	710	1,160	1,893
General and administrative	4,625	4,986	6,792
Engineering and technical support	5,144	7,487	7,159
Intangible asset impairment charges (Note X)	27,402	—	—
Total operating expenses	37,881	13,633	15,844
Operating loss	(38,231)	(13,274)	(15,964)
Other (expense) income:			
Interest and bank charges	(1,279)	(4,013)	(2,869)
Other, net	81	—	—
Total other expense, net	(1,198)	(4,013)	(2,869)
Loss before income taxes	(39,429)	(17,287)	(18,833)
Income tax expense	—	—	—
Net loss	$ (39,429)	$ (17,287)	$ (18,833)

Example 49.5: Variable Interest Entity and Guarantee

The Company has a 50% equity ownership in AXA. AXA distributes network management solutions provided by the Company and the other 50% owner to one customer. The Company holds equal voting control with the other owner. All actions of AXA are decided at the board level by majority vote. The Company evaluated ASC Topic 810, *Consolidations*, and concluded that AXA is a variable interest entity. The Company has concluded that it is not the primary beneficiary of AXA and therefore consolidation is not required. As of both March 31, 20X3, and 20X2, the carrying amount of the Company's investment in AKA was approximately $0.1 million, which is presented on the consolidated balance sheets under Other Assets.

The Company's revenue to AXA for fiscal years 20X3 and 20X2 was $1.3 million and $1.9 million, respectively. Accounts receivable from AXA is $0.2 million and $0.3 million, and deferred revenue relating to maintenance contracts is $0.5 million and $0.8 million, as of March 31, 20X3, and 20X2, respectively. The Company also has an unlimited guarantee for the performance of the other 50% owner in AXA, who primarily provides support and engineering services to the customer. This guarantee was put in place at the request of the AXA customer. The guarantee, which is estimated to have a maximum potential future payment of $0.7 million, will stay in place as long as the contract between AXA and the customer is in place. The Company would have recourse against the other 50% owner in AXA in the event the guarantee is triggered. The Company determined that it could perform on the obligation it guaranteed at a positive rate of return and, therefore, did not assign value to the guarantee. The Company's exposure to loss as a result of its involvement with AXA, exclusive of lost profits, is limited to the items noted above.

50 ASC 815 DERIVATIVES AND HEDGING

AUTHORITATIVE LITERATURE

The financial engineering efforts common in recent decades have resulted in the creation of a wide range of derivatives, from easily understood interest rate swaps (exchanging variable- or floating-rate debt for fixed-rate debt) and interest rate caps (limiting exposure to rising interest rates) to such complicated "exotics" as structured notes, inverse floaters, and interest-only strips. At one time, most of these were not given formal statement of financial position recognition, resulting in great accounting risk, that is, risk of loss in excess of amounts reported in the financial statements. The Codification includes extensive guidance on accounting for and reporting on derivatives and hedges.

ASC 815 requires that entities recognize derivative instruments, including certain derivatives embedded in other contracts, as assets or liabilities on the statement of financial position, measured at fair value. Entities may designate a derivative as:

- A fair value hedge
- A cash flow hedge
- A foreign currency exposure of:
  - An unrecognized firm commitment—a foreign currency fair value hedge
  - Available-for-sale debt security—a foreign currency fair value hedge
  - A forecasted transaction—a foreign currency cash flow hedge
  - A net investment in foreign operations

To be designated as a hedge, the instrument must meet specific requirements. (ASC 815-10-05-4)

In terms of gain or loss recognition on a hedged instrument, the entity generally recognizes:

- Changes in the fair value of the hedged asset or liability that are attributable to the hedged risk, and
- Earnings of the hedged forecasted transaction.
  (ASC 815-10-05-6)

Derivatives literature is exceedingly complex, which is largely a consequence of the rules establishing special accounting for hedging. Limited accounting relief for certain types of hedging activities may be provided by applying the simplified hedge accounting approach in ASC 825-20-25-133 through 25-138, *Financial Instruments: Fair Value Option*, and the "private company alternative" discussed later in this chapter.

Basic Principles of ASC 815

ASC 815 lists four principles, or cornerstones, that underlie its guidance:

1. Derivative instruments represent rights or obligations that meet the definitions of assets or liabilities and should be reported in financial statements as assets or liabilities.

2. Fair value is the most relevant measure for financial instruments and the only relevant measure for derivative instruments. Derivative instruments should be measured at fair value, and adjustments to the carrying amount of hedged items should reflect changes in their fair value (that is, gains or losses) that are attributable to the risk being hedged and that arise while the hedge is in effect.

3. Only items that are assets or liabilities should be reported as such in financial statements.

4. Special accounting for items designated as being hedged should be provided only for qualifying items. One aspect of qualification should be an assessment of the expectation of effective offsetting changes in fair values or cash flows during the term of the hedge for the risk being hedged. Gains and losses from hedges should be reported differently based on the type of hedge. (ASC 815-10-10-1)

Technical Alerts

ASU 2019-10

Guidance Regarding Effective Dates In November 2019, the FASB issued ASU 2019-10, *Financial Instruments—Credit Losses (Topic 326), Derivatives and Hedging (Topic 815), and Leases (Topic 842: Effective Dates)*. The ASU grants private companies, not-for-profit organizations, and certain small public company SEC filers additional time to implement recent FASB standards on current expected credit losses (CECLs).

ASU 2019-10: Effective Dates		
Topic	Public business entities that meet the definition of SEC filers, except smaller reporting companies (SRCs) as determined by the SEC as of November 15, 2019	All other entities
Derivatives— ASU 2017-12	Fiscal years beginning after December 15, 2019	Fiscal years beginning after December 15, 2021

ASU 2019-04 In April 2019, the FASB issued ASU 2019-04, *Codification Improvements to Topic 326, Financial Instruments—Credit Losses, Topic 815, Derivatives and Hedging, and Topic 825, Financial Instruments*.

Issue 3A: Partial-Term Fair Value Hedges of Interest Rate Risk The amendments clarify that an entity may measure the change in fair value of a hedged item using an assumed term only for changes attributable to interest rate risk. They also clarify that an entity may measure the change in the fair value of the hedged item attributable to interest rate risk using an assumed term when the hedged item is designated in a hedge of both interest rate risk and foreign exchange risk. In that instance, the change in carrying value of the hedged item attributable to foreign exchange risk must continue to be measured based on changes in the spot exchange rate in accordance with paragraph 815-25-35-18. In addition, the amendments clarify that one or more separately designated partial-term fair value hedging relationships of a single financial instrument can be outstanding at the same time, and for forward-starting partial-term fair value hedges, the issuance of the hedged item is assumed to occur on the date in which the first hedged cash flow begins to accrue.

Issue 3B: Amortization of Fair Value Hedge Basis Adjustments The amendments clarify that an entity may, but is not required to, begin to amortize a fair value hedge basis adjustment before the fair value hedging relationship is discontinued. They also clarify that if an entity elects to amortize the basis adjustment during an outstanding partial-term hedge, that basis adjustment should be fully amortized by the hedged item's assumed maturity date in accordance with ASC 815-25- 35-13B.

Issue 3C: Disclosure of Fair Value Hedge Basis Adjustments The amendments clarify that available-for-sale debt securities should be disclosed at their amortized cost and that fair value hedge basis adjustments related to foreign exchange risk should be excluded from the disclosures required by paragraph 815-10-50-4EE.

Issue 3D: Consideration of the Hedged Contractually Specified Interest Rate Under the Hypothetical Derivative Method The amendment clarifies that an entity should consider the contractually specified interest rate being hedged when applying the hypothetical derivative method.

Issue 3E: Scope for Not-for-Profit Entities The amendments clarify that a not-for-profit entity that does not separately report earnings may not elect the amortization approach for amounts excluded from the assessment of effectiveness for fair value hedging relationships. The amendments also update the cross-references in ASC 815-10-15-1 to further clarify the scope of ASC 815 for entities that do not report earnings separately.

Issue 3F: Hedge Accounting Provisions Applicable to Certain Private Companies and Not-for-Profit Entities The amendments clarify that a private company that is not a financial institution as described in paragraph 942-320-50-1 should document the analysis supporting a last-of-layer hedge designation concurrently with hedge inception. The amendments also clarify that not-for-profit entities (except for not-for-profit entities that have issued, or are a conduit bond obligor for, securities that are traded, listed, or quoted on an exchange or an over-the-counter market) qualify for the same subsequent quarterly hedge effectiveness assessment timing relief for which certain private companies qualify in accordance with ASC 815-20-25-142.

Issue 3G: Application of a First-Payments-Received Cash Flow Hedging Technique to Overall Cash Flows on a Group of Variable Interest Payments The amendments clarify that the application of the first-payments-received cash flow hedging technique to changes in overall cash flows on a group of variable interest payments continues to be permitted.

Issue 3H: Update to 2017-12 Transition Guidance

1. The amendment to paragraph 815-20-65-3(e)(1) clarifies that transition adjustments to amend the measurement methodology of the hedged item in a fair value hedge of interest rate risk should be made as of the date of initial application of Update 2017-12. The date of initial application differs from the date of adoption if an entity adopts the amendments in Update 2017-12 in an interim period. The amendments also clarify the following: An entity may rebalance its fair value hedging relationships of interest rate risk when it modifies the measurement methodology used for the hedged item from total contractual coupon cash flows to the benchmark rate component of the contractual coupon cash flows by any combination of increasing or decreasing the designated notional of the hedging instrument or increasing or decreasing the designated proportion of the hedged item. However, the entity may not add new hedged items or hedging instruments to the hedging relationship.

2. An entity may transition from a quantitative method of hedge effectiveness assessment to a method comparing the hedging relationship's critical terms in accordance with paragraphs 815-20-25-84 through 25-85 or paragraphs 815-20-25-129 through 25-129A without dedesignating the existing hedging relationship if the guidance in those paragraphs is met.

3. A debt security reclassified from held-to-maturity to available-for-sale in accordance with paragraph 815-20-65-3(e)(7):
   a. Does not call into question an entity's assertion to hold to maturity those debt securities that continue to be classified as held-to-maturity
   b. Is not required to be designated in a last-of-layer hedging relationship
   c. May be sold by an entity after reclassification

ASU 2017-12 In August 2017, the FASB issued ASU 2017-12, *Derivatives and Hedging (Topic 815): Targeted Improvements to Accounting for Hedging Activities.*

Guidance The amendments in this Update better align an entity's risk management activities and financial reporting for hedging relationships through changes to:

- The designation and measurement guidance for qualifying hedging relationships, and
- The presentation of hedge results.

The guidance aligns risk management activities and financial reporting in the following areas:

- Risk component hedging
- Accounting for the hedged item in fair value hedges of interest rate risk
- Recognition and presentation of the effects of hedging instruments
- Amounts excluded from the assessment of hedge effectiveness

Risk Component Hedging To address limitations on how an entity can designate the hedged risk in certain cash flow and fail value hedging relationships, the Update permits hedge accounting for risk components in hedging relationships involving nonfinancial risk and interest rate risk as follows:

1. For a cash flow hedge of a forecasted purchase or sale of a nonfinancial asset, an entity can designate as the hedged risk the variability in cash flows attributable to changes in a contractually specified component stated in the contract. The amendments remove the requirement in current GAAP that only the overall variability in cash flows or variability related to foreign currency risk could be designated as the hedged risk in a cash flow hedge of a nonfinancial asset.

2. For a cash flow hedge of interest rate risk of a variable-rate financial instrument, an entity can designate as the hedged risk the variability in cash flows attributable to the contractually specified interest rate. By eliminating the concept of benchmark interest rates for hedges of variable-rate instruments in current GAAP, the amendments remove the requirement to designate only the overall variability in cash flows as the hedged risk in a cash flow hedge of a variable-rate instrument indexed to a nonbenchmark interest rate.

3. For a fair value hedge of interest rate risk, the amendments add the Securities Industry and Financial Markets Association (SIFMA) Municipal Swap Rate as an eligible benchmark interest rate in the United States in addition to those already permitted under current GAAP (the U.S. Treasury Rate, the London Interbank Offered Rate [LIBOR] Swap Rate, and the Fed Funds Effective Swap Rate [or Overnight Index Swap Rate]). This allows an entity that issues or invests in fixed-rate tax-exempt financial instruments to designate as the hedged risk changes in fair value attributable to interest rate risk related to the SIFMA Municipal Swap Rate rather than overall changes in fair value.

Accounting for the Hedged Item in Fair Value Hedges of Interest Rate Risk To resolve issues with conflicts between an entity's risk management strategies and how an entity can account for hedges involving interest rate risk, the ASU changes the guidance for designating fair value hedges of interest rate risk and for measuring the change in fair value of the hedged item in fair value hedges of interest rate risk. Specifically, the amendments:

1. Permit an entity to measure the change in fair value of the hedged item on the basis of the benchmark rate component of the contractual coupon cash flows determined at hedge inception, rather than on the full contractual coupon cash flows as required by current GAAP.

2. Permit an entity to measure the hedged item in a partial-term fair value hedge of interest rate risk by assuming the hedged item has a term that reflects only the designated cash flows being hedged. Current GAAP does not allow this methodology when calculating the change in the fair value of the hedged item attributable to interest rate risk.

3. For prepayable financial instruments, permit an entity to consider only how changes in the benchmark interest rate affect a decision to settle a debt instrument before its scheduled maturity in calculating the change in the fair value of the hedged item attributable to interest rate risk.

4. For a closed portfolio of prepayable financial assets or one or more beneficial interests secured by a portfolio of prepayable financial instruments, permit an entity to designate an amount that is not expected to be affected by prepayments, defaults, and other events affecting the timing and amount of cash flows (the "last-of-layer" method). Under this designation, prepayment risk is not incorporated into the measurement of the hedged item.

Recognition and presentation of the effects of hedging instruments. The Board has determined that achieving the objective of better portraying the economic results of an entity's risk management activities in its financial statements can be accomplished only through a combination of changes to the designation and measurement guidance for qualifying hedging relationships and the method of presenting hedge results. To better portray in the financial statements the economic results of the entity's risk management activities, the ASU aligns the recognition and presentation of the effects of the hedging instrument and the hedged item in the financial statements to increase the understandability of the results of an entity's intended hedging strategies.

The ASU requires an entity to present the earnings effect of the hedging instrument in the same income statement line item in which the earnings effect of the hedged item is reported. This presentation enables users of financial statements to better understand the results and costs of an entity's hedging program. Also, relative to current GAAP, this approach simplifies the financial statement reporting for qualifying hedging relationships. Current GAAP provides special hedge accounting only for the portion of the hedge deemed to be "highly effective" and requires an entity to separately reflect the amount by which the hedging instrument does not offset the hedged item, which is referred to as the "ineffective" amount. However, the concept and the reporting of hedge ineffectiveness were difficult for financial statement users to understand and, at times, for preparers to explain. Thus, the Board decided on an approach that no longer separately measures and reports hedge ineffectiveness. To accomplish that objective, the amendments in this Update require the following recognition and presentation guidance for qualifying hedges:

1. For fair value hedges, the entire change in the fair value of the hedging instrument included in the assessment of hedge effectiveness is presented in the same income statement line that is used to present the earnings effect of the hedged item. The timing of recognition of the change in fair value of a hedging instrument included in the assessment of hedge effectiveness is the same as under current GAAP, but the presentation of hedge results could change because current GAAP does not specify a required presentation of the change in fair value of the hedging instrument.

2. For cash flow and net investment hedges, the entire change in the fair value of the hedging instrument included in the assessment of hedge effectiveness is recorded in other comprehensive income (for cash flow hedges) or in the currency translation adjustment section of other comprehensive income (for net investment hedges). Those amounts are reclassified to earnings in the same income statement line item that is used to present the earnings effect of the hedged item when the hedged item affects earnings. The timing of recognition

of the change in fair value of a hedging instrument could change relative to current GAAP because hedge ineffectiveness no longer is recognized currently in earnings. The presentation of hedge results also could change because current GAAP does not specify a required presentation of the change in fair value of the hedging instrument in the income statement.

Amounts Excluded from the Assessment of Hedge Effectiveness Current GAAP permits an entity to exclude option premiums and forward points from the assessment of hedge effectiveness. The amendments in this Update continue to allow an entity to exclude those components of a hedging instrument's change in fair value from the assessment of hedge effectiveness. Additionally, the amendments permit an entity to exclude the portion of the change in fair value of a currency swap that is attributable to a cross-currency basis spread from the assessment of hedge effectiveness.

For all types of hedges, if an entity excludes certain portions of a hedging instrument's change in fair value from the assessment of hedge effectiveness (excluded component), the amendments permit an entity to recognize in earnings the initial value of the excluded component using a systematic and rational method over the life of the hedging instrument. If an entity elects this method, any difference between the change in fair value of the excluded component and amounts recognized under the systematic and rational method is recognized in other comprehensive income, whereas for net investment hedges, the difference is recognized in the cumulative translation adjustment section of other comprehensive income. An entity also may elect to recognize all fair value changes in an excluded component currently in earnings, consistent with current GAAP.

For fair value and cash flow hedges, an entity should present amounts related to excluded components that are recognized in earnings in the same income statement line item that is used to present the earnings effect of the hedged item. For net investment hedges, the amendments do not specify a required presentation for excluded components.

Other Simplifications of Hedge Accounting Guidance The ASU also includes certain targeted improvements to ease the application of current guidance related to the assessment of hedge effectiveness. Current GAAP contains specific requirements for initial and ongoing quantitative hedge effectiveness testing and strict requirements for specialized effectiveness testing methods that allow an entity to forgo quantitative hedge effectiveness assessments for qualifying relationships (for example, the "shortcut" method and the "critical terms match" method). The amendments change effectiveness testing as follows:

1. In instances in which initial quantitative testing is required, an entity may perform subsequent assessments of hedge effectiveness qualitatively. An entity that makes this election is required to verify and document on a quarterly basis that the facts and circumstances related to the hedging relationship have not changed such that the entity can assert qualitatively that the hedging relationship was and continues to be highly effective. An entity may elect to perform qualitative assessments on a hedge-by-hedge basis.

2. For purposes of assessing whether the qualifying criteria for the critical terms match method are met for a group of forecasted transactions, an entity may assume that the hedging derivative matures at the same time as the forecasted transactions if both the derivative maturity and the forecasted transactions occur within the same 31-day period or fiscal month.

3. Entities will be able to perform the initial prospective quantitative assessment of hedge effectiveness at any time after hedge designation, but no later than the first quarterly effectiveness testing date, using data applicable as of the date of hedge inception.

4. To provide additional relief on the timing of hedge documentation, private companies that are not financial institutions and not-for-profit entities (except for not-for-profit entities that have issued, or are a conduit bond obligor for, securities that are traded, listed, or quoted on an exchange or an over-the-counter market) may select the method of assessing hedge effectiveness, and perform the initial quantitative effectiveness assessment and all quarterly hedge effectiveness assessments before the date on which the next interim (if applicable) or annual financial statements are available to be issued. This incremental relief does not affect the simplified hedge accounting approach for private companies.

5. If an entity that applies the shortcut method determines that use of that method was not or no longer is appropriate, the entity may apply a long-haul method for assessing hedge effectiveness as long as the hedge is highly effective and the entity documents at inception which long-haul methodology it will use.

Disclosures The ASU modifies disclosures required in current GAAP. Those modifications include a tabular disclosure related to the effect on the income statement of fair value and cash flow hedges and eliminate the requirement to disclose the ineffective portion of the change in fair value of hedging instruments. The amendments also require new tabular disclosures related to cumulative basis adjustments for fair value hedges.

Effective Dates The changes are effective as follows:

- For public business entities,
  - The amendments in this Update are effective for fiscal years beginning after December 15, 2018, and interim periods within those fiscal years.
- For all other entities, the effective date was extended by ASU 2019-10. The new dates are:
  - The amendments are effective for fiscal years beginning after December 15, 2020, and interim periods within fiscal years beginning after December 15, 2021.

Early application is permitted in any interim period after issuance of the Update.

All transition requirements and elections should be applied to hedging relationships existing (that is, hedging relationships in which the hedging instrument has not expired, been sold, terminated, or exercised or the entity has not removed the designation of the hedging relationship) on the date of adoption. The effect of adoption should be reflected as of the beginning of the fiscal year of adoption (that is, the initial application date).

Transition For cash flow and net investment hedges existing at the date of adoption, an entity should apply a cumulative-effect adjustment related to eliminating the separate measurement of ineffectiveness to accumulated other comprehensive income with a corresponding adjustment to the opening balance of retained earnings as of the beginning of the fiscal year that an entity adopts the amendments in the ASU. The amended presentation and disclosure guidance is required only prospectively.

If an entity elects to apply the proposed guidance in items 1–3 above, it would:

- Apply the guidance prospectively.
- Disclose the nature of and reason for electing the guidance in each interim financial statement of the fiscal year of change and the annual financial statement of the period of the change in accordance with Topic 250, *Accounting Changes and Error Corrections.*
- Cease applying the guidance as of January 1, 2023.

Subtopics

ASC 815, *Derivatives and Hedging*, contains eight Subtopics:

- ASC 815-10, *Overall*, which contains two Subsections:
  - General
  - Certain Contracts on Debt and Equity Securities
- ASC 815-15, *Embedded Derivatives*
- ASC 815-20, *Hedging—General*
- ASC 815-25, *Fair Value Hedges*
- ASC 815-30, *Cash Flow Hedges*
- ASC 815-35, *Net Investment Hedges*
- ASC 815-40, *Contracts in Entity's Own Equity*
- ASC 815-45, *Weather Derivatives*

ASC 815-40 and ASC 815-45 address guidance on accounting for contracts that have characteristics of derivative instruments but that are not accounted for as derivative instruments under ASC 815. The other Subtopics provide guidance on accounting for derivative instruments and hedging activities. ASC 815-10 focuses on whether a contract meets the definition of a derivative instrument. (ASC 815-10-05-2)

Scope—ASC 815-10

ASC 815 applies to all entities and to all derivative instruments, but contains extensive scope exceptions. Some of those exceptions relate to items that fall under other guidance; other exceptions are aimed at simplifying the guidance. If an entity, such as a not-for-profit or a defined benefit pension plan, does not report earnings as a separate option, the application of this subtopic to those entities can be found in ASC 815-10-35-3, 815-20-15-1, 815-25-35-19, and 815-30-15-3. (ASC 815-10-15-1)

Scope Exceptions The following instruments are *not* included in the ASC 815 guidance, provided they meet the specific exception criterion in ASC 815-10-15-14 through 15-42.

- Regular-way security trades
- Normal purchases and normal sales
- Certain insurance contracts and market risk benefits
- Certain financial guarantee contracts
- Certain contracts that are not traded on an exchange
- Derivative instruments that impede sales accounting
- Policyholders' investments in life insurance accounted for under ASC 325-30. This exclusion does not affect the accounting by the issuer of the life insurance contract. (ASC 815-10-15-67)
- Certain investment contracts accounted for under either ASC 960-325-35-1 or 35-3. This exclusion applies only to the party accounting for the contract under ASC 960. (ASC 815-10-15-68)
- Certain loan commitments
- Certain interest-only strips and principal-only strips
- Certain contracts involving an entity's own equity
- Leases
- Residual value guarantees subject to the requirements in ASC 840 or ASC 842 when implemented. (ASC 815-10-15-80)
- Registration payment arrangements within the scope of ASC 825-20.
- Certain fixed-odds wagering contracts for entities operating as a casino and for the casino operations of other entities; these contracts are in the scope of ASC 606. (815-10-15-82A) (ASC 815-10-15-13)

The following information expands on the list above and references the scope exceptions:

Regular-way security trades. Delivery of a security readily convertible to cash within the time period generally established by marketplace regulations or conventions where the trade takes place rather than by the usual procedure of an individual enterprise. Contracts for the delivery of securities that are not readily convertible to cash are not subject to ASC 815's provisions because net settlement would not be possible.

For example, most trades of equity securities in the United States require settlement in three business days. If an individual contract requires settlement in more than three business days (even if this is normal for a particular entity), this exception would not apply, unless the reporting entity is required, or has a continuing policy, to account for such transactions on a trade-date basis. (ASC 815-10-15-15) This exception also applies to when-issued and to-be-announced securities (except for those contracts accounted for on a trade-date basis), if there is no other way to purchase or sell them and if the trade will settle within the shortest period permitted.

Based on the foregoing, the following may be excluded:

- Forward purchases or sales of to-be-announced securities, and
- When-issued, as-issued, and if-issued securities. (ASC 815-10-15-17)

Note: Counterparties may reach different conclusions as to whether the contracts are derivative instruments. Asymmetrical results are acceptable (i.e., the exception may apply to one party but not the other). (ASC 815-10-15-24)

Normal purchases and normal sales. Contracts for purchase or sale of something, other than derivative instruments or financial instruments, that will be delivered in quantities expected to be used or sold over a reasonable time period in the normal course of business. (ASC 815-10-15-22) Terms must be consistent with normal transactions, and quantities must be reasonable in relation to needs. (ASC 815-10-15-27) To make that judgment, all relevant factors are to be considered. (ASC 815-10-15-28) An example would include contracts similar to binding purchase orders. However, take or pay contracts that require little or no initial net investment, and that have products readily convertible to cash that do not qualify as normal purchases, would be derivative instruments, and not exceptions. (See 815-20-25-7.)

The purpose of the "normal purchases and normal sales" definition is to exclude certain routine types of transactions from the required accounting as derivative instruments. This exemption includes certain contracts that contain net settlement or market mechanisms if it is judged probable, at the inception and throughout the duration of such contracts, that they will not in fact settle net and will instead result in physical delivery. Notwithstanding this more broadly based exemption from the accounting requirements of ASC 815, certain contracts will not qualify for exemption in any case. These include:

- Contracts whose price is based on an underlying that is not clearly and closely related to the assets being sold or purchased (ASC 815-10-15-30), and
- Contracts requiring cash settlement for any gains or losses or otherwise settled net on a periodic basis. (ASC 815-10-15-35)

The use of locational marginal pricing for certain contracts for the purchase or sale of electricity on a forward basis utilizing a nodal energy market does not, by itself, cause the contract to fail the physical delivery criterion of the normal purchases and normal sales elective scope exception in ASC 815. (ASC 815-10-15-36A) Documentary evidence is required to support the use of the expanded exemption from the ASC 815 provisions. (ASC 815-10-15-37)

On the other hand, a contract that meets the normal purchases and sales exceptions may qualify as a fair value or cash flow hedge if the requirements of ASC 815-20 are met. (ASC 815- 20-25-7)

Power purchase or sales agreements (whether forwards, options, or some combination thereof) pertaining to delivery of electricity qualify for this exception only if a series of conditions are met. The contracts cannot permit net settlement, but must require physical delivery, and must be capacity contracts, as differentiated from ordinary option contracts. For the seller, the quantities deliverable under the contracts must be quantities normally to be sold; for the buyer, quantities must be those to be used or sold in the normal course of business, and the buyer must be an entity that is contractually obligated to maintain sufficient capacity to meet the needs of its customers. Certain additional requirements, and further exceptions, are set forth by ASC 815-10-15-45.

Certain insurance contracts. Contracts where the holder is only compensated when an insurable event (other than price or rate change) takes place, and:

- The value of the holder's asset or liability is adversely changed, or
- The holder incurs a liability.

For example, contracts generally not considered to be derivative instruments include traditional life insurance and traditional property and casualty insurance policies. (ASC 815-10-15- 53)

Most traditional insurance contracts will not be derivative instruments. Some, however, can include embedded derivatives that must be accounted for separately. For example, embedded derivatives may be found in indexed annuity contracts, variable life and annuity contracts, and property and casualty contracts involving changes in currency rates. (ASC 815-10-15-54)

Certain financial guarantee contracts. Contracts that call for payments only to reimburse for a loss from debtor failure to pay when due. However, a credit-indexed contract requiring payment for changes in credit ratings (an underlying) would not be an exception. (ASC 815-10- 15-58)

Certain contracts that are not exchange traded contracts with underlyings based on one of the following:

- Climatic, geological, or other physical variable: for example, inches of rain or heating-degree days;
- Value or price involving a nonfinancial asset not readily converted to cash;
- Fair value of a nonfinancial liability that does not require delivery of an asset that is readily converted to cash; or
- Specified volumes of revenue of one of the parties: examples are royalty agreements or contingent rentals based on related sales.
  (ASC 815-10-15-59)

In the case of a mixture of underlyings, some of which are exceptions, the predominant characteristic of the combined variable of the contract is the determinant. If there is a high correlation with the behavior of the excepted variables above, it is an exception, and if there is a high correlation with the nonexcepted variables, it is a derivative instrument. (ASC 815-10-15-60)

Derivatives that serve as impediments to sales accounting. A derivative instrument that affects the accounting for the transfer of an asset. For example, a call option on transferred assets under ASC 860 would prevent accounting for the transfer as a sale. This exemption is necessary, because recognizing the call as a derivative instrument would result in double counting. (ASC 815-10-15-63)

In addition to the preceding, the following are not considered derivative instruments:

1. Certain contracts involving an entity's own equity issued or held that are both:
   - Indexed to the enterprise's own stock, and
   - Classified in shareholders' equity.

Derivative instruments are assets or liabilities. Items properly accounted for in shareholders' equity are thus excluded from the definition of derivatives. Contracts that can or must be settled through issuance of an equity instrument but that are indexed in part or in full to something other than the enterprise's own stock are considered derivative instruments if they qualify and they are to be classified as assets or liabilities.

2. Contracts issued in connection with stock-based compensation arrangements as addressed in ASC 718.
3. Any of the following:
   a. A contract between an acquirer and a seller to enter into a business combination,
   b. A contract to enter into an acquisition by a not-for-profit entity, and
   c. A contract between one or more NFPs to enter into a merger of not-for-profit entities.
4. Forward contracts that require settlement by the reporting entity's delivery of cash in exchange for a fixed number of its equity shares discounted for under ASC 480-10-30-3 through 30-5, 480-10-35-3, and 480-10-45-3.
   (ASC 815-10-15-74)

Note that for purposes of evaluating whether a financial instrument meets this exception, a down round feature is excluded from the consideration of whether the instrument is indexed to the entity's own stock. (ASC 815-10-15-75A)

The exceptions for the above four issued contracts are not applicable to the counterparties. (ASC 815-10-15-75)

Scope—ASC 815-15

The guidance in its entirety in 815-15 applies to all entities, but only to contracts that do not meet the definition of a derivative instrument. (ASC 815-15-15-1 and 15-2)

Scope Exceptions The guidance in ASC 815-15, *Embedded Derivatives*, does not apply to:

- Normal purchases and normal sales contracts
- Unsettled foreign currency transactions
- Plain-vanilla servicing rights
- Features involving certain aspects of credit risk
- Features involving certain currencies
  (ASC 815-15-15-3)

Under ASC 815-15, unsettled foreign currency transactions are not considered to contain embedded foreign currency derivatives if the transactions:

- Are monetary items,
- Have their principal payments, interest payments, or both denominated in a foreign currency, and
- Are subject to the requirement in ASC 830-20 to recognize any foreign currency gain or loss in earnings.
  (ASC 815-15-15-5)

The proscription in ASC 815-15-15-5 also applies to available-for-sale or trading debt securities that have cash flows denominated in a foreign currency. (ASC 815-15-15-6)

Scope—ASC 815-20

The guidance in ASC 815-20-15-1 applies to all entities except for:

- Entities that do not report entities separately cannot use cash flow hedge accounting under ASC 815-30 on cash flow hedges.
- Entities that do not report earnings separately cannot elect the amortization approach for amounts excluded from the assessment of effectiveness under fair value hedge accounting under the guidance in ASC 815-20-25-83A and 35-1a.

Scope—ASC 815-25

ASC 815-25 follows the scope and scope exceptions listed above.

Scope—ASC 815-30

ASC 815-30 follows the same scope and scope exceptions as those in ASC 815-20 above with the following exceptions:

- ASC 815-30 does not apply to entities that do not report earnings.
- This Topic does not offer guidance on how a not-for-profit should determine the components of an operating measure.
  (ASC 815-30-15-1 through 15-3)

Scope—ASC 815-35

ASC 815-35 follows the same scope and scope exceptions in ASC 815-20 above.

Scope—ASC 815-40

ASC 815-40 applies to all entities and to freestanding contracts that are indexed to and potentially settled in an entity's own stock. (ASC 815-40-15-1 and 15-2)

Scope Exceptions ASC 815-40 does not apply to:

a. Either the derivative instrument component or the financial instrument if the derivative instrument component is embedded in and not detachable from the financial instrument
b. Contracts that are issued to compensate grantees in a share-based payment arrangement
c. A written put option and a purchased call option embedded in the shares of a noncontrolling interest of a consolidated subsidiary if the arrangement is accounted for as a financing under the guidance beginning in paragraph 480-10-55-53
d. Financial instruments that are within the scope of ASC 480.
  (ASC 815-40-15-3)

ASC 815-40-15-13a above does not negate the applicability of this ASC 815-40 in analyzing the embedded feature under paragraphs 815-15-25-1(c) and 815-15-25-14 as though it were a freestanding instrument. (ASC 815-40-15-4)

Evaluating Whether an Instrument Is Considered Indexed to an Entity's Own Stock The guidance in ASC 815-40-15-5 through 15-8 applies to any freestanding financial instrument or embedded feature[1] that has all the characteristics of a derivative instrument. That guidance applies for the purpose of determining whether that instrument or embedded feature

---

[1] In this section, unless otherwise indicated, the assumption is that "financial instrument" means "financial instrument or embedded feature."

qualifies for the first part of the scope exception in ASC 815-10-15-74(a). That guidance does not address the second part of the scope exception in ASC 815-10-15-74(a). The guidance also applies to any freestanding financial instrument that is potentially settled in an entity's own stock, regardless of whether the instrument has all the characteristics of a derivative instrument for purposes of determining whether the instrument is within the scope of ASC 815-40. (ASC 815-40-15-5)

The guidance in ASC 815-40-15-5A through 15-8 does not apply to share-based payment awards within the scope of ASC 718 for purposes of determining whether instruments are classified as liability awards or equity awards. Equity-linked financial instruments issued to investors for purposes of establishing a market-based measure of the grant-date fair value of employee stock options are not within the scope of ASC 718. The guidance in ASC 815-40-15-5A through 15-8 applies to such market-based share-based payment stock option valuation instruments for purposes of making the determinations regarding the scope exception in ASC 815-10-15-74a. (ASC 815-40-15-5A)

The guidance in paragraphs 815-40-15-5 through 15-8 shall be applied to the appropriate unit of accounting, as determined under other applicable U.S. generally accepted accounting principles.

Another factor in determining whether an instrument is considered indexed to its own stock is if the subsidiary is a substantive entity:

- If it is, freestanding financial instruments (and embedded features) for which the payoff to the counterparty is based, in whole or in part, on the stock of a consolidated subsidiary are considered indexed to the entity's own stock in the consolidated financial statements of the parent.
- If it is not, the instrument or embedded feature should not be considered indexed to the entity's own stock.

If the subsidiary is considered to be a substantive entity, the guidance beginning in paragraph 815-40-15-5 should be applied to determine whether the freestanding financial instrument (or an embedded feature) is indexed to the entity's own stock and should be considered in conjunction with other applicable GAAP (for example, this Subtopic) in determining the classification of the freestanding financial instrument in the financial statements of the entity. The guidance in this paragraph applies to those instruments (and embedded features) in the consolidated financial statements of the parent, whether the instrument was entered into by the parent or the subsidiary. The guidance in this paragraph does not affect the accounting for instruments (or embedded features) that would not otherwise qualify for the scope exception in paragraph 815-10-15-74(a), that is, contracts issued or held by that reporting entity that are both:

- Indexed to its own stock, and
- Classified in stockholders' equity in its statement of financial position. (ASC 815-40-15-5C)

When classifying a financial instrument with a down round feature, the feature is excluded from the consideration of whether the instrument is indexed to the entity's own stock for the purposes of applying paragraphs 815-40-15-7C through 15-7I (Step 2 below).

The guidance in this paragraph applies to both the issuer and the holder of the instrument. Outstanding instruments within the scope of the guidance in paragraphs 815-40-15-5 through 15-8 should always be considered issued for accounting purposes, except lock-up options should not be considered issued for accounting purposes unless and until the options become exercisable. (ASC 815-40-15D)

An entity should evaluate whether an equity-linked financial instrument (or embedded feature), as discussed in paragraphs 815-40-15-5 through 15-8 is considered indexed to its own stock within the meaning of this Subtopic and paragraph 815-10-15-74(a) using the following two-step approach: (ASC 815-40-15-7)

1. Evaluate contingent exercise provisions.
2. Evaluate settlement provisions.

Evaluation of contingent exercise provisions (Step 1). An exercise contingency should not preclude an instrument (or embedded feature) from being considered indexed to an entity's own stock provided that it is not based on either:

- An observable market, other than the market for the issuer's stock (if applicable), or
- An observable index, other than an index calculated or measured solely by reference to the issuer's own operations (for example, sales revenue of the issuer; earnings before interest, taxes, depreciation, and amortization of the issuer; net income of the issuer; or total equity of the issuer).

If this Step 1 evaluation does not preclude an instrument from being considered indexed to the entity's own stock, the entity should proceed to Step 2 in ASC 815-40-15-7C. (ASC 815-40-15-7A)

If an instrument's strike price or the number of shares used to calculate the settlement amount would be adjusted upon the occurrence of an exercise contingency, the exercise contingency shall be evaluated under Step 1 and the potential adjustment to the instrument's settlement amount should be evaluated under Step 2, detailed below. (ASC 815-40-15-7B)

Evaluation of settlement provisions (Step 2). An instrument (or embedded feature) shall be considered indexed to an entity's own stock if its settlement amount will equal the difference between:

- The fair value of a fixed number of the entity's equity shares
- A fixed monetary amount or a fixed amount of a debt instrument issued by the entity (ASC 815-40-15-7C)

An instrument's strike price or the number of shares used to calculate the settlement amount are not considered fixed if its terms provide for any potential adjustment, regardless of the probability of such adjustment or whether such adjustments are in the entity's control. If the instrument's strike price or the number of shares used to calculate the settlement amount are not fixed, the instrument shall still be considered indexed to an entity's own stock if the only variables that could affect the settlement amount would be inputs to the fair value of a fixed-for-fixed forward or option on equity shares.

The settlement amount of a fixed-for-fixed forward or option on equity shares is equal to the difference between the price of a fixed number of equity shares and a fixed strike price. The fair value inputs of a fixed-for-fixed forward or option on equity shares may include the entity's stock price and additional variables, including all of the following:

- Strike price of the instrument
- Term of the instrument
- Expected dividends or other dilutive activities
- Stock borrow cost
- Interest rates
- Stock price volatility

- The entity's credit spread
- The ability to maintain a standard hedge position in the underlying shares

Determinations and adjustments related to the settlement amount, including the determination of the ability to maintain a standard hedge position, should be commercially reasonable. (ASC 815-40-15-7E)

An instrument should not be considered indexed to the entity's own stock if its settlement amount is affected by variables that are extraneous to the pricing of a fixed-for-fixed option or forward contract on equity shares. An instrument is not considered indexed to the entity's own stock if either:

- The instrument's settlement calculation incorporates variables other than those used to determine the fair value of a fixed-for-fixed forward or option on equity shares.
- The instrument contains a feature (such as a leverage factor) that increases exposure to the additional variables listed in the preceding paragraph in a manner that is inconsistent with a fixed-for-fixed forward or option on equity shares.
(ASC 815-40-15-7F)

Standard pricing models for equity-linked financial instruments contain certain implicit assumptions. One such assumption is that the stock price exposure inherent in those instruments can be hedged by entering into an offsetting position in the underlying equity shares. For purposes of applying Step 2, fair value inputs include adjustments to neutralize the effects of events that can cause stock price fluctuations, such as a merger agreement. (ASC 815-40-15-7G)

For purposes of applying Step 2, modifications that benefit the counterparty and give an entity the ability to unilaterally modify the terms of the instrument at any time, do not affect the determination of whether an instrument is considered indexed to an entity's own stock. (ASC 815-40-15-7H)

Strike price denominated in a foreign currency. The issuer of an equity-linked financial instrument incurs an exposure to changes in currency exchange rates if the instrument's strike price is denominated in a currency other than the functional currency of the issuer. An equity-linked financial instrument (or embedded feature) shall not be considered indexed to the entity's own stock if the strike price is denominated in a currency other than the issuer's functional currency (including a conversion option embedded in a convertible debt instrument that is denominated in a currency other than the issuer's functional currency). The determination of whether an equity-linked financial instrument is indexed to an entity's own stock is not affected by the currency (or currencies) in which the underlying shares trade. (ASC 815-40-15-7I)

Instruments classified as liabilities or assets. Instruments that do not meet the criteria to be considered indexed to an entity's own stock should be classified as a liability or an asset. (ASC 815-40-15-8A)

Distinguishing liabilities from equity. ASC 480 does not apply to a feature embedded in a financial instrument that is not a derivative instrument in its entirety. Therefore, entities should apply this Subtopic when evaluating those embedded features under ASC 815-15. (ASC 815-40-15-17)

ASC 815-10, *Overall*[2]

Derivative Financial Instruments Derivative financial instruments are financial instruments whose fair value correlates to a specified benchmark, such as stock prices, interest rates,

---

[2] Some of the items subject to the guidance in ASC 815-10 are financial instruments. For additional guidance on financial instruments, including the fair value option, see the chapter on ASC 825.

mortgage rates, currency rates, commodity prices, or some other agreed-upon reference. These are called "underlyings": that is, they derive their value from the underlyings. The two basic forms of derivatives are:

1. Option contracts, and
2. Forward contracts.

They can be either publicly or privately traded. Forward contracts have symmetrical gain and loss characteristics—that is, they provide exposure to both losses and gains from market movements, although generally there is no initial premium to be paid. Forward contracts are usually settled on or near the delivery date by paying or receiving cash, rather than by physical delivery. On the other hand, option contracts have asymmetrical loss functions: they provide little or no exposure to losses (beyond the premium paid) from unfavorable market movements, but can provide large benefits from favorable market movements. Both forwards and options have legitimate roles to play in hedging programs, if properly understood and carefully managed.

Subsequent Measurement Derivative instruments are measured subsequently at fair value. (ASC 815-10-35-1) The accounting for changes in fair value depends on whether the instrument is a designated hedge. If it is part of a hedging relationship, see the information in this chapter related to ASC 815-20, including the alternative approach for private companies discussed later in this chapter. If a derivative is not designated as a hedging instrument, any gain or loss on the change in fair value is recognized in earnings in the current period. (ASC 815-10-35-2)

Certain Contracts on Debt and Equity Securities Forward contracts and purchased options are measured according to their initial classification as outlined in the chart below:

Exhibit—Accounting Treatment—Forward Contracts and Purchased Options

Subsequent Accounting for Forward Contracts and Purchased Options on Securities				
	Debt Securities			**Equity Securities**
Event	Held-to-Maturity[3]	Available-for-Sale[4]	Trading	
Changes in fair value.	Recognize other than temporary declines in earnings. Otherwise, do not recognize.	Recognize other than temporary declines in earnings. Otherwise, a part of separate component of shareholders' equity per ASC 320.	Recognize in earnings as they occur.	Recognize in earnings as they occur.
Securities purchased under a forward contract.	Forward contract price at settlement date.	Recognize at fair value at settlement date.	Fair value at settlement date.	Fair value at settlement date.

(Continued)

---

[3] Upon implementation of ASU 2016-13, changes in the fair value of held-to-maturity forward contracts or purchased options are not recognized. However, credit losses on the underlying securities in a forward contract are recorded through an allowance account and measured at amortized cost. If the credit losses are on the underlying securities in a purchased option, they are recorded in an allowance account, but the losses are limited to the amount of the option premium.

[4] Upon implementation of ASU 2016-13, changes in fair value continue to be recognized as a separate component of shareholders' equity as they occur. However, credit losses on the underlying security in a forward contract are recorded in an allowance account and measured according to the guidance in ASC 326-30. If the credit losses are on the underlying securities in a purchased option, they are recorded in an allowance account, but the losses are limited to the amount of the option premium.

Subsequent Accounting for Forward Contracts and Purchased Options on Securities				
	Debt Securities			Equity Securities
Securities purchased by exercising an option.	The strike price plus any remaining carrying amount for the option premium at the exercise date.	Option strike price plus fair value of the option at the exercise date.	Fair value at settlement date.	Fair value at settlement date.
Option expires worthless and the same debt security is purchased in the market.	Market price plus any carrying amount for the option premium.	Market price plus any carrying amount for the option premium.		
Entity does not take delivery under the forward contract and purchases the same securities in the market.	If the option expires worthless, entity's intent to hold other debt securities to maturity would be called into question.			
	(ASC 815-10-35-5)			(ASC 815-10-35-6)

Derecognition Derecognition of derivatives is accounted for as follows:

- Liabilities—in accordance with ASC 405-20-40-1
- Assets—in accordance with ASC 860-10-40
  (ASC 815-10-40-1)

ASC 815-15, *Embedded Derivatives*

Recognition Embedded derivative instruments are defined as explicit or implicit terms affecting:

- The cash flows, or
- The value of other exchanges required by contract in a way similar to a derivative instrument.
  (ASC 815-15-20)

Separate Instrument Criteria An embedded derivative instrument must be separated from the host contract and accounted for separately as a derivative instrument by both parties if, and only if, *all* three following criteria are met:

1. Risks and economic characteristics are not clearly and closely related to those of the host contract;

2. The hybrid instrument is not required to be measured at fair value under GAAP with changes reported in earnings; and
3. A separate instrument with the same terms as the embedded derivative instrument, according to the guidance in ASC 815-10-15, would be accounted for as a derivative instrument. For this condition, the initial net investment of the hybrid instrument is not the same as that for the embedded derivative instrument.

Embedded Derivative Instrument Separated from Host

Recognition If the embedded derivative instrument cannot be reliably identified and measured separately, the contract cannot be designated as a hedging instrument, and the entire contract must be measured at fair value with the gain or loss recognized in income. (ASC 815-15-25-53)

If an embedded derivative instrument is separated from the host, the accounting is as follows:

- The embedded derivative instrument is accounted for based on ASC 815, and
- The host contract is accounted for based on GAAP for that instrument, without the embedded derivative instrument. (ASC 815-15-25-54)

Initial Measurement Both of the following should be measured initially at fair value:

- A hybrid financial instrument required to be separated into a host contract and a derivative instrument that an entity elects to irrevocably measure at fair value
- An entire hybrid instrument where the entity cannot identify and measure the embedded derivative
  (ASC 815-15-30-1)

Fair value measurements will often differ because they exclude transaction costs, which are included in many historical cost-based accounting entries; for example, the fair value of stock just purchased on an exchange is lower than its cost. ASC 815 holds that any difference at inception of a recognized hybrid financial instrument for which the fair value election is applied and the transaction price is *not* to be included in current earnings (and thus is retained in the asset carrying amount) unless estimated fair value has been determined:

- From a quoted price in an active market,
- From comparison to other observable current market transactions, or
- Using a valuation technique that incorporates observable market data.

Subsequent Measurement The changes in fair value are reported currently in earnings. (ASC 815-15-35-1)

ASC 815-20, *Hedging—General*

While ASC 815 requires that all derivatives be reported at fair value in the statement of financial position, the changes in fair value are reported in different ways depending on the nature and effectiveness of the hedging activities to which they are related, if held for hedging purposes. (ASC 815-20-35-1) ASC 815 identifies changes in the fair values of derivatives as being the result of:

- Effective hedging,
- Ineffective hedging, or
- Unrelated to hedging.

Furthermore, the hedging itself can be related to the fair value of an existing asset or liability or of a firm commitment, the cash flow associated with forecasted transactions, or foreign currency exposures.

Private Company Alternative ASC 815 allows for a simplified hedging accounting approach for private companies. This alternative applies to private companies, except for financial institutions.

The alternative allows private companies to apply a simplified hedge accounting method to hedging relationships. Certain criteria must be met and the relationships must involve receive-variable, pay-fixed interest rate swaps. This approach assumes no hedge ineffectiveness in a cash flow hedging relationship. (ASC 815-20-25-134) This alternative approach results in an income statement impact similar to what could have occurred had the company simply entered into a fixed-rate borrowing. This approach also allows private companies to measure the hedging interest rate swap at its settlement value, rather than at fair value, and gives private companies more time to put hedge documentation in place. (ASC 815-10-35-1A)

Hedges—Designation and Documentation Designation and documentation of a hedge at inception is required. (ASC 815-20-25-3)

Benchmark Interest Rate In each financial market, generally only the most widely used and quoted rates may be considered benchmark interest rates. In the United States, the following are considered to be benchmark interest rates:

- Interest rates on direct Treasury obligations of the U.S. government,
- The London Interbank Offered Rate (LIBOR) swap rate,
- The Fed Funds Effective Rate Overnight Index Swap Rate,
- The Securities Industry and Financial Markets Association (SIFMA) Municipal Swap Rate, and
- The Secured Overnight Financing Rate (SOFR) Overnight Index Swap Rate (ASC 815-20-25-6A)

ASC 815-25, *Fair Value Hedges* The change in the fair value of an entire financial asset or liability for a period is computed as the fair value at the end of the period, adjusted to exclude changes in fair value from:

- Payments received or made (partial recoveries or settlements), and
- The passage of time, minus the fair value at the beginning of the period.

ASC 815-30, *Cash Flow Hedges* The second major subset of hedging arrangements relates to uncertain future cash flows, as contrasted with hedged items engendering uncertain fair values. A derivative instrument may be designated as a hedge to the exposure of fluctuating expected future cash flows produced by a particular risk. The exposure may be connected with an existing asset or liability or with a forecasted transaction.

Foreign Currency Hedges Unlike ASC 830, ASC 815 allows hedges of forecasted foreign currency transactions, including some intercompany transactions. Hedging foreign currency intercompany cash flows with foreign currency options is a common practice. ASC 815 allows entities to use other derivative instruments (forward contracts, etc.), on the grounds that the accounting for all derivative instruments should be the same.

Designated hedging instruments and hedged items qualify for fair value hedge accounting or cash flow hedge accounting only if all of the criteria in ASC 815 for fair value hedge accounting and cash flow hedge accounting are met. Fair value hedges may be used for all recognized foreign currency-denominated asset or liability hedging situations, and cash flow hedges may be used for recognized foreign currency-denominated asset or liability hedging situations in which all of the variability in the functional currency-equivalent cash flows is eliminated by the effect of the hedge. (ASC 815-20-25-15) Remeasurement of the foreign currency-denominated assets and liabilities is based on the guidance in ASC 830-20-35-1, which requires remeasurement based on spot exchange rates, regardless of whether a fair value hedging relationship or a cash flow hedging relationship exists.

Hedged Items and Transactions Involving Foreign Exchange Risk ASC 815 provides complex hedging rules that permit the reporting entity to elect to obtain special accounting treatment relative to foreign currency risks with respect to the following items:

- Recognized foreign-currency-denominated assets or liabilities
- A forecasted functional-currency-equivalent cash flow associated with a recognized asset or liability
- Unrecognized firm commitments
- Foreign-currency-denominated forecasted transaction
- Net investment in a foreign operation
  (ASC 815-25-25-26)

Forward Exchange Contracts Foreign currency transaction gains and losses on assets and liabilities that are denominated in a currency other than the functional currency can be hedged if a U.S. entity enters into a forward exchange contract.

A general rule for estimating the fair value of forward exchange rates under ASC 815 is to use the changes in the forward exchange rates and discount those estimated future cash flows to a present-value basis. An entity will need to consider the time value of money if significant in the circumstances for these contracts.

Foreign Currency Net Investment Hedge Either a derivative instrument or a nonderivative financial instrument (which can result in a foreign currency transaction gain or loss under ASC 830) can be designated as a hedge of a foreign currency exposure of a net investment in a foreign operation. The gain or loss from the designated instrument to the extent that it is effective is reported as a translation adjustment. The hedged net investment is accounted for under ASC 830.

ASC 815-40, *Contracts in Entity's Own Equity*

Accounting for Contracts Held or Issued by the Reporting Entity That Are Indexed to Its Own Stock ASC 815-10-15 provides that the reporting entity is not to consider contracts issued or held by that reporting entity that are both:

- Indexed to its own stock, and
- Classified in stockholders' equity in its statement of financial position to be derivative instruments for purposes of ASC 815.
  (ASC 815-10-15-74)

The first part of this particular exemption (i.e., indexed to the entity's own stock) applies to any freestanding financial instrument or embedded feature that has all the characteristics of a derivative in ASC 815-10-15, for purposes of determining whether that instrument or embedded feature qualifies for the first part of the scope exception in ASC 815-10-15-74. It also applies to any freestanding financial instrument that is potentially settled in an entity's own stock, regardless of whether the instrument has all the characteristics of a derivative in ASC 815-10-15, for purposes of determining whether the instrument is within the scope of ASC 815-40.

An evaluation is made of whether an equity-linked financial instrument (or embedded feature), using the following two-step approach:

1. Evaluate the instrument's contingent exercise provisions, if any;
2. Evaluate the instrument's settlement provisions.
   (ASC 815-40-15-7)

An exercise contingency would not preclude an instrument (or embedded feature) from being considered indexed to an entity's own stock, provided that it is not based on:

- An observable market, other than the market for the issuer's stock (if applicable), or
- An observable index, other than an index calculated or measured solely by reference to the issuer's own operations (e.g., sales revenue of the issuer, EBITDA of the issuer, net income of the issuer, or total equity of the issuer).
  (ASC 815-40-15-7A)

An *exercise contingency* is a provision that entitles the entity, or counterparty, to exercise an equity-linked financial instrument (or embedded feature) based on changes in an underlying, including the occurrence (or nonoccurrence) of a specified event. Provisions that accelerate the timing of the entity's, or counterparty's, ability to exercise an instrument, and provisions that extend the length of time that an instrument is exercisable, are examples of exercise contingencies. If the evaluation of Step 1 does not preclude an instrument from being considered indexed to the entity's own stock, the analysis would proceed to Step 2, evaluating the settlement provisions.

An instrument (or embedded feature) would be considered indexed to an entity's own stock if its settlement amount will equal the difference between the fair value of a fixed number of the entity's shares and a fixed monetary amount or a fixed amount of a debt instrument issued by the entity. (ASC 815-40-15-7C)

An equity-linked financial instrument (or embedded feature) would not be considered indexed to the entity's own stock if the strike price is denominated in a currency other than the issuer's functional currency (including a conversion option embedded in a convertible debt instrument that is denominated in a currency other than the issuer's functional currency). (ASC 815-40-15-7I)

Freestanding financial instruments (and embedded features) for which the payoff to the counterparty is based, in whole or in part, on the stock of a consolidated subsidiary are not precluded from being considered indexed to the entity's own stock in the consolidated financial statements of the parent if the subsidiary is a substantive entity. (ASC 815-40-15-5C)

ASC 815-45, *Weather Derivatives*

ASC 815-45 applies to all weather derivatives that are not exchange-traded, and, therefore, not subject to the requirements of ASC 815-10. (ASC 815-45-15-2)

ASC 815-45 states that an entity that enters into a nonexchange-traded forward-based weather derivative in connection with nontrading activities is to account for the contract by applying an "intrinsic value method." The intrinsic value method computes an amount based on the difference between the expected results from an upfront allocation of the cumulative strike and the actual results during a period, multiplied by the contract price (for example, dollars per heating degree day). The use of external statistical sources, such as the National Weather Service, is necessary in applying this technique. (ASC 815-45-30-3 and 35-1 and 35-2)

Furthermore, an entity that purchases a nonexchange-traded option-based weather derivative in connection with nontrading activities is to amortize to expense the premium paid (or due) and apply the intrinsic value method to measure the contract at the date of each interim statement of financial position. The premium asset is to be amortized in a rational and systematic manner. (ASC 815-45-35-4)

Also, all entities that sell or write a nonexchange-traded option-based weather derivative are to initially recognize the premium as a liability and recognize any subsequent changes in fair value currently in earnings (the premium would not be amortized). (ASC 815-45-35-5)

In addition, a purchased or written weather derivative may contain an "embedded" premium or discount when the contract terms are not consistent with current market terms. In those circumstances, the premium or discount is to be quantified, removed from the calculated benchmark strike, and accounted for as noted above. (ASC 815-45-30-3A)

Finally, all weather derivative contracts entered into under trading or speculative activities are to be accounted for at their fair value, with subsequent changes in fair value reported currently in earnings.

PRACTICE ALERT

While SEC comments pertain to SEC filers, the staff comments can provide useful practice pointers for all preparers. SEC comments related to derivatives include asking for more information regarding:

- How the entity analyzed embedded conversion options
- How embedded conversion features were accounted for
- How conversion options were accounted for
- Where warrants were classified
- Whether embedded features should be bifurcated from the host
- How the entity determined the classification on the balance sheet

PRESENTATION AND DISCLOSURE REQUIREMENTS

Presentation

Balance Sheet Derivatives should be recognized on the balance sheet at fair value unless the entity elects the private company alternative.

Offsetting. If the entity does not intend to net the gross amounts, it may net if the derivatives are:

- With the same counterparty, and
- The reporting entity has the right to offset the amounts owed pursuant to a legally enforceable master netting arrangement.
  (ASC 815-10-45-5)

The entity has to exercise judgment when analyzing whether a transaction qualifies for offsetting. In any case, entities should disclose their policy.

Hybrid financial instruments reported at fair value. These instruments should be reported on the balance sheet separate from assets and liabilities not measured at fair value. (ASC 815-10-45-1) The entity may present:

- Separate line items for the fair value and non-fair-value amounts, or
- An aggregate amount with parenthetical disclosure of the amount at fair value.

Income Statement[5]

Gains and losses in fair value and cash flow hedges. The reporting entity should present the change in fair value of a derivative designated in a fair value or cash flow hedge in the same income statement line items as the hedged item. If the hedging instrument offsets changes in fair value or cash flows are presented in more than one income statement line item, the entity should present changes in fair value of the hedging instrument split among the line items that include the earnings effect of the hedged item.

Derivatives in net investment hedges. Entities should present, for qualifying net investment hedges, amounts reclassified from AOCI to earnings in the same income statement line item where the earnings effect of the hedged net investment is reported.

Disclosure The disclosure requirements for derivatives or nonderivative instruments that are designated and qualify as hedging instruments are extensive and designed to meet these obligations:

- How and why an entity uses derivative instruments
- How derivative instruments and related hedged items are accounted for under ASC 815
- How derivative instruments and related hedged items affect an entity's:
  - Financial position
  - Financial performance
  - Cash flows
  (ASC 815-10-50-1)

For a detailed list of disclosures, readers should consult the checklist at www.wiley.com/go/FSDM2021.

PRESENTATION AND DISCLOSURE EXAMPLES

Example 50.1: Accounting Policy for Derivatives

We account for derivative instruments in accordance with FASB ASC 815, *Derivatives and Hedging*, which requires all derivative instruments to be recognized in the financial statements and measured at fair value, regardless of the purpose or intent for holding them.

We do not qualify commodity derivatives or instruments used to manage foreign currency exchange exposures for hedge accounting treatment, and, as a result, the derivative gains and losses are immediately recognized in earnings. Although we do not perform the assessments required to achieve hedge accounting for derivative positions, we believe all of our derivatives are economic hedges of our risk exposure. The exposures hedged have a high inverse correlation to price changes of the derivative instrument. Thus, we would expect that over time any gain or loss in the estimated fair value of the derivatives would generally be offset by an increase or decrease in the estimated fair value of the underlying exposures.

We utilize derivative instruments to manage interest rate risk associated with anticipated debt transactions, as well as to manage changes in the fair value of our long-term debt. At the inception of an interest rate contract, the instrument is evaluated and documented for qualifying hedge accounting

---

[5] This section assumes the entity has adopted ASU 2017-12. See the Technical Alert at the beginning of this chapter.

treatment. If the contract is designated as a cash flow hedge, the mark-to-market gains or losses on the contract are deferred and included as a component of accumulated other comprehensive income (loss) and reclassified to interest expense in the period during which the hedged transaction affects earnings. If the contract is designated as a fair value hedge, the contract is recognized at fair value on the balance sheet, and changes in the fair value are recognized in interest expense. Generally, changes in the fair value of the contract are equal to changes in the fair value of the underlying debt and have no net import on earnings.

Example 50.2: Using Derivatives to Manage Foreign Currency and Interest Rate Risks

During fiscal 20X2, 20X1, and 20X0, we used derivative financial instruments to manage foreign currency and interest rate risks. We do not use derivative financial instruments for trading purposes. We account for these instruments in accordance with ASC 815, *Derivatives and Hedging* (ASC 815), which requires that every derivative instrument be recorded on the balance sheet as either an asset or liability measured at its fair value as of each reporting date. ASC 815 also requires that changes in our derivatives' fair values be recognized in earnings, unless specific hedge accounting and documentation criteria are met (i.e., the instruments are accounted for as hedges).

Example 50.3: Accounting for Changes in the Fair Value and Cash Flow Hedges

The accounting for changes in the fair value of a derivative depends on the intended use of the derivative and the resulting designation. For a derivative instrument designated as a fair value hedge, loss or gain attributable to the risk being hedged is recognized in earnings in the period of change with a corresponding earnings offset recorded to the item for which the risk is being hedged.

For a derivative instrument designated as a cash flow hedge, each reporting period we record the change in fair value of the derivative to accumulated other comprehensive loss ("AOCL") in our consolidated balance sheets, and the change is reclassified to earnings in the period the hedged item affects earnings.

Example 50.4: Description of Interest Rate Swap Agreements and Cross-Currency Interest Rate Swap Agreements

Our total borrowings were $71.6 million as of May 31, 20X3, consisting of $71.5 million of fixed-rate borrowings and $113,000 of other borrowings. As of May 31, 20X3, we held certain interest rate swap agreements that have the economic effect of modifying the fixed-interest obligations associated with our $1.5 million of 2.80% fixed-rate senior notes due July 20X4, so that the fixed-rate interest payable on these senior notes effectively became variable based on LIBOR. We have also entered into cross-currency interest rate swap agreements to manage the foreign currency exchange rate risk associated with our €750,000 of 3.125% fixed-rate senior notes due July 20X8 by effectively converting the fixed-rate, euro-denominated debt, including the annual interest payments and the payment of principal at maturity, to variable-rate, U.S. dollar–denominated debt based on LIBOR. The critical terms of the swap agreements match the critical terms of the July 20X4 Notes and July 20X8 Notes that the swap agreements pertain to, including the notional amounts and maturity dates. We do not use these swap arrangements for trading purposes. We are accounting for these swap agreements as fair value hedges pursuant to ASC 815, *Derivatives and Hedging*. The fair values of our outstanding fixed to variable interest rate swap agreements as of May 31, 20X3 and 20X2 were a $12 million net gain and a $17 million net loss, respectively. We estimate that the changes in the fair values of these swap agreements as of May 31, 20X3 and 20X2, respectively, were primarily attributable to a decrease and increase, respectively, in forward interest rate prices. If LIBOR-based interest rates would have been higher by 100 basis points as of May 31, 20X3 and 20X2, the change would have decreased the collective fair values of the fixed to variable swap agreements by $63,000 and $90,000, respectively.

By entering into the aforementioned swap arrangements, we have assumed risks associated with variable interest rates based upon LIBOR. Changes in the overall level of interest rates affect the interest expense that we recognize in our consolidated statements of operations. An interest rate risk sensitivity analysis is used to measure interest rate risk by computing estimated changes in cash flows as a result of assumed changes in market interest rates. As of May 31, 20X4 and 20X3, if LIBOR-based interest rates would have been higher by 100 basis points, the change would have increased our interest expense annually by approximately $24 million and $52 million, respectively, as it relates to our fixed to variable interest rate swap agreements and related borrowings, and as of May 31, 20X3, as it related to our floating-rate borrowings.

Example 50.5: Description of Foreign Currency Transaction Risk—Foreign Currency Forward Contracts

We transact business in various foreign currencies and have established a program that primarily utilizes foreign currency forward contracts to offset the risks associated with the effects of certain foreign currency exposures. Under this program, our strategy is to enter into foreign currency forward contracts so that increases or decreases in our foreign currency exposures are offset by gains or losses on the foreign currency forward contracts in order to mitigate the risks and volatility associated with our foreign currency transactions. We may suspend this program from time to time. Our foreign currency exposures typically arise from intercompany sublicense fees, intercompany loans and other intercompany transactions. Our foreign currency forward contracts are generally short-term in duration.

We neither use these foreign currency forward contracts for trading purposes nor do we designate these forward contracts as hedging instruments pursuant to ASC 815. Accordingly, we record the fair values of these contracts as of the end of our reporting period to our consolidated balance sheet with changes in fair values recorded to our consolidated statement of operations. Given the short duration of the forward contracts, amounts recorded generally are not significant. The balance sheet classification for the fair values of these forward contracts is prepaid expenses and other current assets for forward contracts in an unrealized gain position and other current liabilities for forward contracts in an unrealized loss position. The statement of operations classification for changes in fair values of these forward contracts is nonoperating income, net for both realized and unrealized gains and losses.

We expect that we will continue to realize gains or losses with respect to our foreign currency exposures, net of gains or losses from our foreign currency forward contracts. Our ultimate realized gain or loss with respect to foreign currency exposures will generally depend on the size and type of cross-currency transactions that we enter into, the currency exchange rates associated with these exposures and changes in those rates, the net realized gain or loss on our foreign currency forward contracts and other factors. The notional amounts of the forward contracts we held to purchase U.S. dollars in exchange for other major international currencies were $4.2 million and $3.8 million as of May 31, 20X3 and 20X2, respectively, and the notional amounts of forward contracts we held to sell U.S. dollars in exchange for other major international currencies were $3.9 million and $3.3 million as of May 31, 20X3 and 20X2, respectively. The fair values of our outstanding foreign currency forward contracts were nominal at May 31, 20X3 and 20X2. Net foreign exchange transaction losses included in nonoperating income, net in the accompanying consolidated statements of operations were $185,000 and $111,000 in fiscal 20X3 and 20X2, respectively. As a large portion of our consolidated operations are international, we could experience additional foreign currency volatility in the future, the amounts and timing of which are unknown.

Example 50.6: Description of Foreign Currency Translation Risk—Impact on Cash, Cash Equivalents and Marketable Securities

Fluctuations in foreign currencies impact the amount of total assets and liabilities that we report for our foreign subsidiaries upon the translation of these amounts into U.S. dollars. In particular, the amount of cash, cash equivalents and marketable securities that we report in U.S. dollars for a significant portion of the cash held by these subsidiaries is subject to translation variance caused by changes in foreign currency exchange rates as of the end of each respective reporting period (the offset to which is substantially recorded to AOCL on our consolidated balance sheets and is also presented as a line item in our consolidated statements of comprehensive income included elsewhere in this Annual Report).

As the U.S. dollar fluctuated against certain international currencies as of the end of fiscal 20X4, the amount of cash, cash equivalents and marketable securities that we reported in U.S. dollars for foreign subsidiaries that hold international currencies as of May 31, 20X4 decreased relative to what we would have reported using a constant currency rate from May 31, 20X3. As reported in our consolidated statements of cash flows, the estimated effects of exchange rate changes on our reported cash and cash equivalents balances in U.S. dollars was a decrease of $125,000 and $158,000 for fiscal 20X4 and 20X3, respectively. If overall foreign currency exchange rates in comparison to the U.S. dollar uniformly would have been weaker by 10% as of May 31, 20X4 and May 31, 20X3 the amount of cash, cash equivalents and marketable securities we would report in U.S. dollars would have decreased by approximately $491,000 and $434,000, respectively, assuming constant foreign currency cash, cash equivalents and marketable securities balances.

Example 50.7: Description of Fair Value Hedges—Interest Rate Swap Agreements and Cross-Currency Interest Rate Swap Agreements

In May 20X2, we entered into certain cross-currency interest rate swap agreements to manage the foreign currency exchange rate risk associated with our July 20X9 Notes by effectively converting the fixed-rate, euro-denominated 20X9 Notes, including the annual interest payments and the payment of principal at maturity, to variable-rate, U.S. dollar–denominated debt based on LIBOR. In July 20X0, we entered into certain interest rate swap agreements that have the economic effect of modifying the fixed-interest obligations associated with our July 20X5 Notes so that the interest payable on these senior notes effectively became variable based on LIBOR. The critical terms of the swap agreements match the critical terms of the July 20X9 Notes and July 20X5 Notes that the swap agreements pertain to, including the notional amounts and maturity dates.

We have designated the aforementioned swap agreements as qualifying hedging instruments and are accounting for them as fair value hedges pursuant to ASC 815. The changes in fair values of the cross-currency interest rate swap agreements associated with our July 20X9 Notes are recognized as interest expense and nonoperating income, net in our consolidated statements of operations with the corresponding amounts included in noncurrent assets or noncurrent liabilities in our consolidated balance sheets.

The changes in fair values of our interest rate swap agreements associated with our July 20X5 Notes are recognized as interest expense in our consolidated statements of operations with the corresponding amounts included in other noncurrent assets or other noncurrent liabilities in our consolidated balance sheets. The amount of net gain (loss) attributable to the interest rate risk being hedged is recognized as interest expense and amount of net gain (loss) attributable to the foreign exchange risk being hedged, as applicable, is recognized as nonoperating income, net in our consolidated statements of operations with the corresponding amount included in notes payable, current or notes payable, noncurrent. We exclude the portion of the change in fair value of cross-currency interest rate swap agreements attributable to the related cross-currency basis spread in our assessment of hedge effectiveness. The change in fair value of these cross-currency interest rate swap agreements attributable to the cross-currency basis spread is included in AOCL. The periodic interest settlements for the swap agreements for the July 20X9 Notes and July 20X5 Notes are recorded as interest expense and are included as a part of cash flows from operating activities and, for the swap agreements associated with the July 20X5 Notes, the cash flows that pertain to the principal balance are classified as financing activities.

Example 50.8: Description of Cash Flow Hedges—Cross-Currency Swap Agreements

In connection with the issuance of the January 20X5 Notes, we entered into certain cross-currency swap agreements to manage the related foreign currency exchange risk by effectively converting the fixed-rate, euro-denominated January 20X5 Notes, including the annual interest payments and the payment of principal at maturity, to fixed-rate, U.S. dollar–denominated debt. The economic effect of the swap agreements was to eliminate the uncertainty of the cash flows in U.S. dollars associated with the January 20X5 Notes by fixing the principal amount of the January 20X5 Notes at $1.6 million with a fixed annual interest rate of 3.53%. We have designated these cross-currency swap agreements as qualifying hedging instruments and are accounting for these as cash flow hedges pursuant to ASC 815. The critical terms of the cross-currency swap agreements correspond to the January 20X5 Notes including the annual interest payments being hedged, and the cross-currency swap agreements mature at the same time as the January 20X5 Notes.

We used the hypothetical derivative method to assess the effectiveness of our cross-currency swap agreements. The fair values of these cross-currency swap agreements are recognized as other current assets or other current liabilities in our consolidated balance sheets. We reflect the gains or losses on the effective portion of these cross-currency swap agreements in AOCL in our consolidated balance sheets and an amount is reclassified out of AOCL into nonoperating income, net in the same period that the carrying values of the euro-denominated January 20X5 Notes are remeasured and the interest expense is recognized. The cash flows related to the cross-currency swap agreements that pertain to the periodic interest settlements are classified as operating activities and the cash flows that pertain to the principal balance are classified as financing activities.

Example 50.9: Description of Foreign Currency Forward Contracts Not Designated as Hedges

We transact business in various foreign currencies and have established a program that primarily utilizes foreign currency forward contracts to offset the risks associated with the effects of certain foreign currency exposures. Under this program, our strategy is to enter into foreign currency forward contracts so that increases or decreases in our foreign currency exposures are offset by gains or losses on the foreign currency forward contracts in order to mitigate the risks and volatility associated with our foreign currency transactions. We may suspend this program from time to time. Our foreign currency exposures typically arise from intercompany sublicense fees, intercompany loans, and other intercompany transactions that are generally expected to be cash settled in the near term. Our foreign currency forward contracts are generally short term in duration. Our ultimate realized gain or loss with respect to currency fluctuations will generally depend on the size and type of cross-currency exposures that we enter into, the currency exchange rates associated with these exposures and changes in those rates, the net realized and unrealized gains or losses on foreign currency forward contracts to offset these exposures, and other factors.

We do not designate these forward contracts as hedging instruments pursuant to ASC 815. Accordingly, we recorded the fair values of these contracts as of the end of each reporting period to our consolidated balance sheets with changes in fair values recorded to our consolidated statements of operations. The balance sheet classification for the fair values of these forward contracts is other current assets for forward contracts in an unrealized gain position and other current liabilities for forward contracts in an unrealized loss position. The statement of operations classification for changes in fair values of these forward contracts is nonoperating income, net for both realized and unrealized gains and losses.

As of May 31, 20X4 and 20X3, the notional amounts of the forward contracts we held to purchase U.S. dollars in exchange for other major international currencies were $4.2 million and $3.8 million, respectively, and the notional amounts of forward contracts we held to sell U.S. dollars in exchange for other major international currencies were $3.9 million and $3.3 million, respectively. The fair values of our outstanding foreign currency forward contracts were nominal at May 31, 20X4 and 20X3. The cash flows related to these foreign currency contracts are classified as operating activities.

The effects of derivative instruments designated as hedges on certain of our consolidated financial statements were as follows, as of or for each of the respective periods presented below (amounts presented exclude any income tax effects):

Example 50.10: Schedule of Fair Values of Derivative Instruments Designated as Hedges in Consolidated Balance Sheets

(Amounts in hundreds of thousands)	Balance Sheet Location	Fair Value as of May 31 20X4	20X3
Derivative assets:			
Interest rate swap agreements designated as fair value hedges	Other noncurrent assets	$ 29	$ 5
Total derivative assets		$ 29	$ 5
Derivative liabilities:			
Cross-currency swap agreements designated as cash flow hedges	Other current liabilities	$ 251	$ —
Interest rate swap agreements designated as fair value hedges	Other current liabilities	—	$ 5
Cross-currency interest rate swap agreements designated as fair value hedges	Other noncurrent liabilities	$ 17	$ 17
Cross-currency swap agreements designated as cash flow hedges	Other noncurrent liabilities	—	$ 208
Total derivative liabilities		$ 268	$ 230

Example 50.11: Schedule of Effects of Fair Value Hedging Relationships on Hedged Items in Consolidated Balance Sheets

(Amounts in hundreds of thousands)	Year Ended May 31 20X4	20X3
Notes payable, current:		
Carrying amount of hedged item	$ —	$ 1,994
Cumulative hedging adjustments included in the carrying amount	—	(5)
Notes payable and other borrowings, noncurrent:		
Carrying amounts of hedged items	3,680	3,652
Cumulative hedging adjustments included in the carrying amount	75	44

Example 50.12: Schedule of Effects of Derivative Instruments Designated as Hedges on Income

	Year Ended May 31					
(Amounts in hundreds of thousands)	*20X4*		*20X3*		*20X2*	
	Nonoperating income, net	*Interest expense*	*Nonoperating income, net*	*Interest expense*	*Nonoperating income, net*	*Interest expense*
Consolidated statements of operations line amounts in which the hedge effects were recorded	$ 162	$ (1,995)	$ 815	$ (2,082)	$ 1,185	$ (2,025)
Gain (loss) on hedges recognized in income: Interest rate swaps designated as fair value hedges:						
Derivative instruments	$ —	$ 29	$ —	$ 31	$ —	$ (66)
Hedged items	—	(29)	—	(31)	—	66
Cross-currency interest rate swaps designated as fair value hedges:						
Derivative instruments	(7)	7	(38)	27	—	—
Hedged items	3	(7)	38	(27)	—	—
Cross-currency swap agreements designated as cash flow hedges: Amount of gain (loss) reclassified from accumulated OCI or OCL	(21)	—	(53)	—	51	—
Total gain (loss) on hedges recognized in income	$ (25)	$ —	$ (53)	$ —	$ 51	$ —

Example 50.13: Accounting Policy for Convertible Debt and Equity Securities

Features in several of our outstanding convertible debt and equity instruments are accounted for under Accounting Standards Codification 815, *Derivatives and Hedging* (ASC 815), as embedded derivatives. ASC 815 requires companies to bifurcate conversion options from their host instruments and account for them as freestanding derivative financial instruments according to certain criteria. The current fair value of the derivative is remeasured to fair value at each balance sheet date, with a resulting noncash gain or loss related to the change in the fair value of the derivative being charged to earnings (loss) in the statement of operations. We have determined that we must bifurcate and account for certain features of our convertible debt and equity instruments as embedded derivatives in accordance with ASC 815. We have recorded these embedded derivative liabilities as noncurrent liabilities on our consolidated balance sheet with a corresponding discount at the date of issuance that is netted against the principal amount of the applicable instrument. The derivative liabilities are remeasured to fair value at each balance sheet date, with a resulting noncash gain or loss related to the change in the fair value of the derivative liabilities being recorded in other income or expenses. There is no current observable market for this type of derivative and, as such, we determine the fair value of the embedded derivatives using the binomial lattice model. The valuation model uses the stock price, conversion price, maturity date, risk-free interest rate, estimated stock volatility, and estimated credit spread. Changes in the inputs for these valuation models may have a significant impact on the estimated fair value of the embedded derivative liabilities. For example, an increase in our stock price would result in an increase in the estimated fair value of the embedded derivative liabilities, if in this example, each of the other elements of the valuation model remained substantially unchanged from the last measurement date. The embedded derivative liabilities may have, on a U.S. GAAP basis, a substantial effect on our balance sheet from quarter to quarter and it is difficult to predict the effect on our future U.S. GAAP financial results, since valuation of these embedded derivative liabilities are based on factors largely outside of our control and may have a negative impact on our statement of operations and balance sheet. The effects of these embedded derivatives may cause our U.S. GAAP operating results to be below expectations, which may cause our stock price to decline.

51 ASC 820 FAIR VALUE MEASUREMENT

AUTHORITATIVE LITERATURE

ASC 820 provides:

- A unified definition of fair value,
- Related guidance on measurement, and
- Enhanced disclosure requirements to inform financial statement users about:
  - The fair value measurements included in financial statements,
  - The methods and assumptions used to estimate them, and
  - The degree of observability of the inputs used in management's estimation process.

Subtopic

ASC 820 contains one Subtopic:

- ASC 820-10, *Overall*, which defines fair value, describes a framework for measuring fair value, and details required disclosures

Scope and Scope Exceptions

ASC 820 does not require fair value measurements in addition to those required by other topics in the Codification.

In pursuing an incremental approach, ASC 820 contains scope exceptions for certain highly complex specialized applications. It does *not* apply to:

- Accounting principles for share-based payments in all ASC 718 Subtopics, except for transactions covered in ASC 718-40, which are within the scope of ASC 820
- Measurements that are similar to fair value but that are not intended to measure fair value, including:

- o Measurement models that are based on standalone selling price
- o Inventory
- Recognition and measurement of revenue from contracts with customers
- Recognition and measurement of gains and losses upon the derecognition of nonfinancial assets
(ASC 820-10-15-2)

In addition to the scope exceptions listed above, ASC 820 retains the practicability exceptions included in GAAP that apply when, in management's judgment, it is not practical to estimate fair value. In such instances, management is required to inform the reader in an explanatory note to the financial statements that it is unable to estimate fair value and the reasons that such an estimate cannot be made. (ASC 820-10-15-3) The practicability exception applies to certain measurements made in connection with the following matters:

GAAP measurement category	Primary GAAP
Asset retirement obligations	ASC 410-20, 440-10-50, and 440-10-55
Business combinations, for specific items where other measures are allowed	ASC 805-20-30-10
Financial assets or financial liabilities of a consolidated VIE when these items are measured using the measurement alternative	ASC 810-10-30-10 through 30-30 and 810-10-35-6 through 35-8
Guarantees, the use of an entry price at initial recognition	ASC 460
Nonmonetary transactions	ASC 845, 605-20-25, and 605-20-50
Participation rights	ASC 715-30 and 715-60
Restructuring obligations	ASC 420
Where the fair value cannot be reasonably estimated, such as noncash consideration	ASC 606-10-32-21 through 32-24
(ASC 820-10-15-3)	

If a reporting entity measures an investment's fair value using the net asset value per share (or an equivalent) practical expedient, the Codification provides those reporting entities with an option to measure the fair value of certain investments using net asset value instead of fair value. Thus, the Codification eliminates the requirement to classify the investment measured using the practical expedient within the fair value hierarchy based on whether the investment is:

- Does not have a readily determinable fair value,
- Is within the scope of ASC 946, or
- Is in a real estate fund for which it is industry practice to measure investments at fair value on a recurring basis and to issue financial statements consistent with ASC 946.
(ASC 820-10-15-4)

Definition of Fair Value

The term "fair value," rather than "market value," emphasizes that, even in the absence of active primary markets for an asset or liability, the asset or liability can be valued by reference to prices and rates from secondary markets. Over time, this concept has been expanded further to include the application of various fair value estimation models, such as the discounted probability-weighted expected cash flow model first introduced in *CON 7*.

Measurement Principles and Methodologies

ASC 820 contains a fair value measurement framework, which is used at both initial and subsequent measurement.

Initial Recognition When the reporting entity first acquires an asset or incurs (or assumes) a liability in an exchange transaction, the transaction price is an entry price, or the price paid to acquire the asset and the price received to assume the liability. Fair value measurements are based not on entry prices, but rather on exit prices—the price that would be received to sell the asset or paid to transfer the liability. While entry and exit prices differ conceptually, in many cases they may be identical and can be considered to represent fair value of the asset or liability at initial recognition. (ASC 820-10-30-2) This is not always the case, however, and in assessing fair value at initial recognition, management should consider transaction-specific factors and factors specific to the assets and/or liabilities that are being initially recognized. Examples of situations where transaction price might not represent fair value at initial recognition include:

- Related-party transactions, unless the entity has evidence that the transaction was entered into at market terms.
- Transactions taking place under duress or when the seller is forced to accept the price, such as when the seller is experiencing financial difficulties.
- Different units of account that apply to the transaction price and the assets/liabilities being measured. This can occur, for example, where the transaction price includes other elements besides the assets/liabilities that are being measured, such as unstated rights and privileges that are subject to separate measurement, or when the transaction price includes transaction costs (see discussion below).
- The exchange transaction takes place in a market different from the principal or most advantageous market in which the reporting entity would sell the asset or transfer the liability. An example of this situation is when the reporting entity is a securities dealer that enters into transactions with customers in the retail market, but the principal market for the exit transaction is with other dealers in the dealer market. (ASC 820-10-30-3A)

If another ASC topic requires or permits fair value measurement initially and the transaction price differs from fair value, the resulting gain or loss is recognized in earnings, unless otherwise specified. (ASC 820-10-30-6)

Subsequent Measurement

Transaction costs. Transaction costs are the incremental direct costs that would be incurred to sell an asset or transfer a liability. While, as previously discussed, transaction costs are considered in determining the market that is most advantageous, they are not used to adjust the fair value measurement of the asset or liability being measured. The FASB excluded them from the measurement because they are not characteristic of an asset or liability being measured. (ASC 820-10-35-9B)

Transportation costs. If an attribute of the asset or liability being measured is its location, the price determined in the principal or most advantageous market should be adjusted for the costs that would be incurred by the reporting entity to transport it to or from that market. (ASC 820-10-35-9C)

The measurement process. It is helpful to break down the measurement process under ASC 820 into a series of steps. Although not necessarily performed in a linear manner, the following procedures and decisions need to be applied and made, in order to value an asset or liability at fair value under ASC 820. The process in greater detail is as follows:

1. *Identify the item to be valued and the unit of account.* (ASC 820-10-35-2B through 2E)
2. *Determine the principal or most advantageous market and the relevant market participants.* (ASC 820-10-35-5A through 35-6C)
3. *Select the valuation premise to be used for asset measurements.* (ASC 820-10-35-10A through 10D)
4. *Consider the risk assumptions applicable to liability measurements.*
5. *Identify available inputs.* (ASC 820-10-35-16B through 16BB)
6. *Select the appropriate valuation approach(es).* (ASC 820-10-35-24A)
7. *Make the measurement.*
8. *Determine amounts to be recognized and information to be disclosed.*

Inputs   For the purpose of fair value measurements, inputs are the assumptions that market participants would use in pricing an asset or liability, including assumptions regarding risk. An input is either observable or unobservable. Observable inputs are either directly observable or indirectly observable. ASC 820 requires the evaluator to maximize the use of relevant observable inputs and minimize the use of unobservable inputs.

An observable input is based on market data obtainable from sources independent of the reporting entity. For an input to be considered relevant, it must be considered determinative of fair value. Even if there has been a significant decrease in the volume and level of market activity for an asset or liability, it is not to be automatically assumed that the market is inactive or that individual transactions in that market are disorderly (that is, are forced or liquidation sales made under duress).

An unobservable input reflects assumptions made by management of the reporting entity with respect to assumptions it believes market participants would use to price an asset or liability based on the best information available under the circumstances.

ASC 820 provides a fair value input hierarchy (see diagram below) to serve as a framework for classifying inputs based on the extent to which they are based on observable data.

Diagram

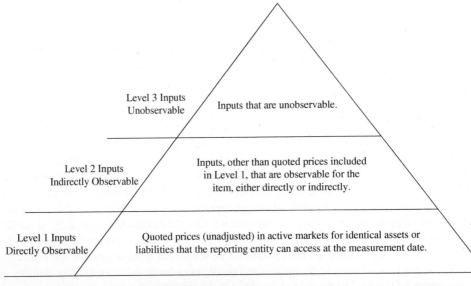

Level 1 inputs. Level 1 inputs are considered the most reliable evidence of fair value and are to be used whenever they are available. These inputs consist of quoted prices in active markets for identical assets or liabilities. (ASC 820-10-35-41BB) The active market must be one in which the reporting entity has the ability to access the quoted price at the measurement date. To be considered an active market, transactions for the asset or liability being measured must occur frequently enough and in sufficient volume to provide pricing information on an ongoing basis.

Level 2 inputs. Level 2 inputs are quoted prices for the asset or liability (other than those included in Level 1) that are either directly or indirectly observable. Level 2 inputs should be considered when quoted prices for the identical asset or liability are not available. If the asset or liability being measured has a contractual term, a Level 2 input must be observable for substantially the entire term. These inputs include:

- Quoted prices for *similar* assets or liabilities in active markets
- Quoted prices for identical or similar assets or liabilities in markets that are *not active*
- Inputs other than quoted prices that are observable for the asset or liability (e.g., interest rates and yield curves observable at commonly quoted intervals; implied volatilities; credit spreads; and market-corroborated inputs)
  (ASC 820-10-35-48)

Level 3 inputs. Level 3 inputs are unobservable inputs. These are necessary when little, if any, market activity occurs for the asset or liability. Level 3 inputs are assumptions that a market participant would use when pricing the asset or liability, including assumptions about risk. (ASC 820-10-35-53) The best information available in the circumstances should be used to develop the Level 3 inputs. This information might begin with internal data of the reporting entity. Cost/benefit considerations apply, in that management is not required to "undertake all possible efforts" to obtain information about the assumptions that would be made by market participants. Attention must be paid, however, to information available to management without undue cost and effort and, consequently, management's internal assumptions used to develop unobservable inputs should be adjusted if such information contradicts those assumptions.

Valuation Approaches In measuring fair value, management employs one or more valuation approaches consistent with the market approach, the income approach, and/or the cost approach. (ASC 820-10-35-24A) As previously discussed, the selection of a particular approach to measure fair value is to be based on its appropriateness to the asset or liability being measured, maximizing the use of observable inputs, and minimizing the use of unobservable inputs.

In certain situations, such as when using Level 1 inputs, use of a single valuation approach will be sufficient. In other situations, such as when valuing a reporting unit, management may need to use multiple valuation approaches. When doing so, the results yielded by applying the various approaches are evaluated considering the reasonableness of the range of values. The fair value is the point within the range that is most representative of fair value in the circumstances. (ASC 820-10-35-24B)

Management is required to consistently apply the valuation approaches it elects to use to measure fair value. It would be appropriate to change valuation approaches or how they are applied if the change results in fair value measurements that are equally or more representative of fair value. Situations that might give rise to such a change would be when new markets develop, new information becomes available, previously available information ceases to be available, valuation approaches improve, or market conditions change. (ASC 820-10-35-25) Revisions that result from either a change in valuation approach or a change in the application of a valuation approaches are to be accounted for as changes in accounting estimate under ASC 250. (ASC 820-10-35-26)

PRACTICE ALERT

While SEC comments pertain to SEC filers, non-filers can benefit from the staff comments. In the area for financial instruments, the SEC has raised questions about:

- The adequacy of disclosure related to equity instruments
- How entities accounted for equity instruments, including redeemable preferred stock, convertible instruments, and warrants
- The entities basis of conclusion for classifying of certain instruments
- The effect on classification of preferred stock of redemption provisions
- Disclosing additional information about rights, privileges, and preferences of warrants and preferred stock
- When features might be triggered
- Specific information about valuation techniques
- Additional information about inputs
- How the disclosure requirements apply to recurring and nonrecurring fair value measurements
- Procedures performed to validate fair value measurements obtained from third-party pricing services

PRESENTATION AND DISCLOSURE REQUIREMENTS

Disclosure

Substantial disclosures regarding fair value are required by various ASC topics. Those disclosures are often placed in different informative notes, including descriptions of the entity's accounting policies, financial instruments, impairment, derivatives, pensions, revenue recognition, share-based compensation, risks and uncertainties, certain significant estimates, and so forth. ASC 820 encourages preparers to combine disclosure requirements under ASC 820 with those of other subtopics. Plan assets of a defined benefit pension plan or other postretirement plans accounted for under ASC 715 are not subject to the ASC 820 requirements and should apply the disclosure requirements in the relevant paragraphs of ASC 715. A list of the required disclosures can be found at www.wiley.com/go/FSDM2021.

PRESENTATION AND DISCLOSURE EXAMPLES

Example 51.1: Accounting Policy—Fair Value of Financial Instruments

We apply the provisions of ASC 820, *Fair Value Measurement*, to our assets and liabilities that we are required to measure at fair value pursuant to other accounting standards, including our investments in marketable debt and equity securities and our derivative financial instruments.

Example 51.2: Accounting Policy—Fair Value Hierarchy

We perform fair value measurements in accordance with ASC 820. ASC 820 defines fair value as the price that would be received from selling an asset or paid to transfer a liability in an orderly transaction between market participants at the measurement date. When determining the fair value measurements for assets and liabilities required to be recorded at their fair values, we consider the principal or most advantageous market in which we would transact and consider assumptions that market participants would use when pricing the assets or liabilities, such as inherent risk, transfer restrictions, and risk of nonperformance.

ASC 820 establishes a fair value hierarchy that requires an entity to maximize the use of observable inputs and minimize the use of unobservable inputs when measuring fair value. An asset's or a liability's categorization within the fair value hierarchy is based upon the lowest level of input that is significant to the fair value measurement. ASC 820 establishes three levels of inputs that may be used to measure fair value:

- Level 1: quoted prices in active markets for identical assets or liabilities;
- Level 2: inputs other than Level 1 that are observable, either directly or indirectly, such as quoted prices in active markets for similar assets or liabilities, quoted prices for identical or similar assets or liabilities in markets that are not active, or other inputs that are observable or can be corroborated by observable market data for substantially the full term of the assets or liabilities; or
- Level 3: unobservable inputs that are supported by little or no market activity and that are significant to the fair values of the assets or liabilities.

Example 51.3: Schedule of Assets and Liabilities Measured at Fair Value on a Recurring Basis

Our assets and liabilities measured at fair value on a recurring basis consist of the following (Level 1 and Level 2 inputs are defined above):

(Amounts in millions)	May 31, 20X3 Fair Value Using Input Types			May 31, 20X2 Fair Value Using Input Types		
	Level 1	Level 2	Total	Level 1	Level 2	Total
Assets:						
Corporate debt securities and other	$ 4,036	$ 2,589	$ 6,625	$ 4,899	$ 17,343	$ 22,242
Commercial paper debt securities	—	5,640	5,640	—	—	—
Money market funds	18,587	—	18,587	5,700	—	5,700
Derivative financial instruments	—	29	29	—	5	5
Total assets	$ 22,623	$ 8,258	$ 30,881	$ 10,599	$ 17,348	$ 27,947
Liabilities:						
Derivative financial instruments	$ —	$ 268	$ 268	$ —	$ 230	$ 230

Our marketable securities investments consist of Tier 1 commercial paper debt securities, corporate debt securities, and certain other securities. Marketable securities as presented per our consolidated balance sheets included securities with original maturities at the time of purchase greater than three months, and the remainder of the securities were included in cash and cash equivalents. Our valuation techniques used to measure the fair values of our instruments that were classified as Level 1 in the table above were derived from quoted market prices and active markets for these instruments that exist. Our valuation techniques used to measure the fair values of Level 2 instruments listed in the table above, the counterparties to which have high credit ratings, were derived from the following: nonbinding market consensus prices that were corroborated by observable market data, quoted market prices for similar instruments, or pricing models, such as discounted cash flow techniques, with all significant inputs derived from or corroborated by observable market data, including LIBOR-based yield curves, among others.

Based on the trading prices of the $71.6 billion and $56.1 billion of senior notes and the related fair value hedges (refer to Notes 7 and 10 for additional information) that we had outstanding as of May 31, 20X3 and 20X2, respectively, the estimated fair values of the senior notes and the related fair value hedges using Level 2 inputs at May 31, 20X3 and 20X2 were $80.9 billion and $58.4 billion, respectively.

52 ASC 825 FINANCIAL INSTRUMENTS

AUTHORITATIVE LITERATURE

ASC 825-10 contains the fair value option, which encourages reporting entities to elect to use fair value to measure eligible assets and liabilities in their financial statements. The objective is to improve financial reporting by mitigating the volatility in reported earnings that is caused by measuring related assets and liabilities differently. Electing entities obtain relief from the onerous and complex documentation requirements that apply to certain hedging transactions under ASC 815. ASC 825-10 applies to businesses and not-for-profit organizations and provides management of these entities substantial discretion in electing to measure eligible assets and liabilities at fair value.

Subtopics

ASC 825, *Financial Instruments*, contains two Subtopics:

- ASC 825-10, *Overall*, which has two Subsections:
  - General, which provides guidance on the fair value option and some disclosures about financial instruments

- ○ Fair Value Option, which provides guidance on the circumstances under which entities may choose the fair value option and the related presentation and disclosure requirements (ASC 825-10-05-2)
- ASC 825-20, *Registration Payment Arrangements*, which provides guidance on financial instruments subject to registration payment arrangements

Scope and Scope Exceptions

The following items are eligible for the fair value option:

- All recognized financial assets and financial liabilities except for those listed in ASC 825-10-15-5 below.
- Firm commitments that would otherwise not be recognized at inception and that involve only financial instruments. An example is a forward purchase contract for a loan that is not readily convertible to cash. The commitment involves only financial instruments (the loan and cash) and would not be recognized at inception since it does not qualify as a derivative.
- A written loan commitment.
- Rights and obligations under insurance contracts or warranties that are not financial instruments[1] but whose terms permit the insurer (warrantor) to settle claims by paying a third party to provide goods and services to the counterparty (insured party or warranty claimant).
- A host financial instrument resulting from bifurcating an embedded nonfinancial derivative instrument from a nonfinancial hybrid instrument under ASC 815-15-25. An example would be an instrument in which the value of the bifurcated embedded derivative is payable in cash, services, or merchandise but the host debt contract is only payable in cash. (ASC 825-10-15-4)

Entities may *not* elect the fair value option for:

- Investments in subsidiaries required to be consolidated by the reporting entity
- Interests in variable interest entities required to be consolidated by the reporting entity[2]
- Employers' and plans' obligations (unfunded or underfunded liabilities) or assets (representing net overfunded positions) for:
  - ○ Pension benefits
  - ○ Other postretirement benefits (including health care and life insurance benefits)
  - ○ Postemployment benefits
  - ○ Other deferred compensation, termination, and share-based payment arrangements such as employee stock option plans; employee stock purchase plans; compensated absences; and exit and disposal activities
- Financial assets and financial liabilities under leases (this exception does not, however, apply to a guarantee of a third-party lease obligation or a contingent obligation associated with cancellation of a lease)
- Deposit liabilities, withdrawable on demand, of banks; saving and loan associations; credit unions; and other similar depository institutions

---

[1] Insurance contracts that require or permit the insurer to settle claims by providing goods or services instead of by paying cash are not, by definition, financial instruments. Similarly, warranties that require or permit the warrantor to settle claims by providing goods and services in lieu of cash do not constitute financial instruments.

[2] Under ASC 805, consolidated variable interest entities are referred to as subsidiaries in the same manner as consolidated voting interest entities.

- Financial instruments that are, in whole or in part, classified by the issuer as a component of stockholders' equity (including temporary equity), such as a convertible debt security with a noncontingent beneficial conversion feature (ASC 825-10-15-5)

The guidance in ASC 825-20 applies to all entities and the following transactions:

- A registration payment arrangement
- An arrangement that requires the issuer to obtain or maintain a listing on the stock exchange if the remaining characteristics of a registration payment are met (ASC 825-20-15-1 and 15-2)

The guidance in this subtopic does *not* apply to:

- Arrangements that require registration or listing of convertible debt instruments or convertible preferred stock if the form of consideration that would be transferred to the counterparty is an adjustment to the conversion ratio
- Arrangements in which the amount of consideration transferred is determined by reference to either:
  ○ An observable market other than the market for the issuer's stock
  ○ An observable index
- Arrangements in which the financial instrument or instruments subject to the arrangement are settled when the consideration is transferred (ASC 825-20-15-4).

ASC 825-10, *Overall*

ASC 825-10 provides management with substantial flexibility in electing the fair value option (FVO). Once elected, however, the election is irrevocable unless, as discussed later in this section, a new election date occurs. The election can be made for a single eligible item without electing it for other identical items subject to the following limitations:

1. If the FVO is elected with respect to an investment otherwise required to be accounted for under the equity method of accounting, the FVO election must be applied to all of the investor's financial interests in the same entity (equity and debt, including guarantees) that are eligible items.
2. If a single contract with a borrower (such as a line of credit or construction loan) involves multiple advances to that borrower and those advances lose their individual identity and are aggregated with the overall loan balance, the FVO is only permitted to be elected to apply to the larger overall loan balance and not individually with respect to each individual advance.
3. If the FVO is applied to an eligible insurance or reinsurance contract, it is also required to be applied to all claims and obligations under the contract.
4. If the FVO is elected for an eligible insurance contract (base contract) for which integrated or nonintegrated contract features or coverages (some of which are referred to as "riders") are issued either concurrently or subsequently, the FVO must be applied to those features and coverages. The FVO is not permitted to be elected for only the nonintegrated contract features and coverages, even though they are accounted for separately under ASC 944-30.[3] (ASC 825-10-25-7)

---

[3] ASC 944-30-20 defines a nonintegrated contract feature in an insurance contract as a feature in which the benefits provided are not related to or dependent on the provisions of the base contract. For the purposes of applying the FVO election, neither an integrated nor a nonintegrated contract feature or coverage qualifies as a separate instrument.

Other than as provided in (1) and (2) above, management is not required to apply the FVO to all instruments issued or acquired in a single transaction. (ASC 825-10-25-10) The lowest level of election, however, is at the single legal contract level. A financial instrument that is in legal form a single contract is not permitted to be separated into component parts for the purpose of electing the FVO. (ASC 825-10-25-11) For example, an individual bond is the minimum denomination of that type of debt security.

An investor in an equity security of a particular issuer may elect the FVO for its entire investment in that equity security, including any fractional shares issued by the investee in connection, for example, with a dividend reinvestment plan. (ASC 825-10-25-12)

Management of an acquirer, parent company, or primary beneficiary[4] decides whether to elect the FVO with respect to the eligible items of an acquiree, subsidiary, or consolidated variable interest entity. That decision, however, only applies in the consolidated financial statements. FVO choices made by management of an acquiree, subsidiary, or variable interest entity continue to apply in their separate financial statements should they choose to issue them. (ASC 825-10-25-6)

Management may elect the FVO for an eligible item on the date of occurrence of one of the following events:

- The entity initially recognizes the item.
- The entity enters into an eligible firm commitment.
- Financial assets previously required to be reported at fair value with unrealized gains and losses included in income due to the application of specialized accounting principles cease to qualify for that accounting treatment (e.g., a subsidiary subject to ASC 946 transfers a security to another subsidiary of the same parent that is not subject to the ASC).
- The accounting treatment for an investment in another entity changes because:
  - The investment becomes subject to the equity method of accounting.
  - The investor ceases to consolidate a subsidiary or variable interest entity but retains an interest in the entity.
- An event requires an eligible item to be remeasured at fair value at the time that the event occurs but does not require fair value measurements to be made at each subsequent reporting date.

Specifically excluded from being considered an eligible event are:

1. Recognition of impairment under lower-of-cost-or-market accounting, or
2. Other-than-temporary impairment.[5]
   (ASC 825-10-25-4)

Among the events that require initial fair value measurement or subsequent fair value remeasurements of this kind are:

- Business combinations,
- Consolidation or deconsolidation of a subsidiary or variable interest entity, and
- Significant modifications of debt, as defined in ASC 470-50, *Debt—Modifications and Extinguishments*.
  (ASC 825-10-25-5)

---

[4] Under ASC 805 a primary beneficiary is referred to as a parent in the same manner as a company that consolidates a voting interest entity.

[5] Upon implementation of ASU 2016-13, item 2 changes to "Accounting for Securities Under ASC 321 or ASC 326."

ASC 825-20, *Registration Payment Arrangements*

Entities must recognize registration payment arrangements as separate units of account from the financial instruments subject to those arrangements. Those financial instruments are recognized and initially measured in accordance with other applicable, relevant GAAP. Entities recognize contingent obligations to make future payments or otherwise transfer consideration under registration payment arrangements separately in accordance with ASC 450-20. (ASC 825-20-25-1 through 25-3, and 825-20-30-1 and 30-2)

A contingent obligation to make future payments or transfer consideration is measured separately using the guidance in ASC 450-20. (ASC 825-20-30-3) Using the measurement guidance in ASC 450-20, if the transfer of consideration is probable and reasonably estimable at inception, the contingent liability is included in the allocation of proceeds from the related financing transaction. The remaining periods are allocated using applicable GAAP. (ASC 825- 20-30-4)

The issuer's share price at the reporting date is used to measure the contingent liability under ASC 450-20 if all of the following are met:

- There is a requirement to deliver shares
- The transfer is probable
  (ASC 825-20-30-5)

After inception, if the consideration becomes probable and reasonably estimable, the charge is recognized in earnings. A sale equal to change in estimate is also recognized in earnings. (ASC 825-20-35-1)

PRACTICE ALERT

While non-SEC filers are not subject to SEC comments, those comments can provide valuable guidance and cautions. In the area of financial instruments, the SEC staff has asked preparers to:

- Describe how the entity accounts for specific instruments, such as redeemable preferred stock, warrants, and convertible instruments
- Explain the basis of conclusions regarding classification of permanent use temporary equity
- Review adequacy of disclosure
- Explain how the redemption provisions affect the classification of preferred stock
- Expand the disclosures to include additional information about the rights, privileges, and preferences of warrants and preferred stock
- Cite accounting guidance to support the entity's conclusion
- Describe valuation techniques used
- Provide information about significant unobservable imports

PRESENTATION AND DISCLOSURE REQUIREMENTS

Presentation

Statement of Financial Position In the note and on the face of the statement, financial assets and financial liabilities should be presented by:

- Category, and
- Form of financial asset.
  (ASC 825-10-45-1A)

Fair Value Option—Statement of Financial Position Assets and liabilities reported under the fair value option should be presented separately from the carrying value of those measured using another measurement attribute. (ASC 825-10-45-1B)

To accomplish that, the entity should:

- Present the aggregate of the fair value and non-fair-value amounts in the same line item and parenthetically the amount measured at fair value included in the aggregate amount, or
- Present two separate line items, displaying the fair value and non-fair-value carrying amounts.
  (ASC 825-10-45-2)

Statement of Cash Flows Classify cash receipts and cash payments related to items measured at fair value according to the nature and purpose following the guidance in ASC 230. (ASC 825-10-45-3)

Fair Value Option—Statement of Comprehensive Income In earnings, entities should report unrealized gains and losses for which the fair value option has been elected. (ASC 825-10-45-4)

For financial liabilities under the fair value option or embedded derivative guidance, entities should report:

- Qualifying changes in fair value recognized in net income, and
- Separately in other comprehensive income, the portion of the total change in fair value that is a result of a change in instrument-specific credit risk.
  (ASC 825-10-45-5)

Remeasurement of the component in fair value of a liability resulting from changes in instrument-specific credit risk is presented in AOCI. (ASC 825-10-45-5A) NOTE: ASC 825-10-45-5 does not apply to financial liabilities of a consolidated collateralized financing entity using the measurement alternative in ASC 810-10- 30-10 through 30-15 and 810-10-35-6 through 35-8. (ASC 825-10-45-7)

When a financial liability designated under the fair value option is derecognized, the entity should include in net income the cumulative amount of the gain or loss on the financial liability that resulted from changes in instrument-specific credit risk. (ASC 825-10-45-6)

The entity should present, in AOCI, the remeasurement of the component of the change in fair value of the liability resulting from the changes in investment-specific credit risk. (ASC 825-10-45-5A)

Disclosure

Entities For interim reporting periods, this disclosure guidance applies to all entities but is optional for those entities that do not meet the definition of a public business entity. (ASC 825-10-50-2A)

Transactions The disclosures about fair value prescribed in ASC 825-10-50-10 through 50-16 are not required for:

- Employers' and plans' obligations for pension benefits, other postretirement benefits including health care and life insurance benefits, postemployment benefits, employee stock option and stock purchase plans, and other forms of deferred compensation arrangements (see ASC 710, 712, 715, 718, and 960).

- Substantively extinguished debt is subject to the disclosure requirements of ASC 405-20.
- Insurance contracts, other than financial guarantees (including financial guarantee insurance contracts within the scope of ASC 944) and investment contracts, as discussed in ASC 944-20.
- Lease contracts as defined in ASC 840 or ASC 842 when implemented (a contingent obligation arising out of a cancelled lease and a guarantee of a third-party lease obligation are not lease contracts and are subject to the disclosure requirements in this subsection).
- Warranty obligations (see ASC 450 and the Product Warranties Subsections of ASC 460).
- Unconditional purchase obligations as defined in ASC 440-10-50-2.
- Investments accounted for under the equity method in accordance with the requirements of ASC 323.
- Noncontrolling interests and equity investments in consolidated subsidiaries (see ASC 810).
- Equity instruments issued by the entity and classified in stockholders' equity in the statement of financial position (see ASC 505).
- Receivable-variable, pay-fixed interest rate swaps for which the simplified hedge accounting approach is applied.
- Fully benefit-responsive investment contracts held by an employee benefit plan.
- Investments in equity securities accounted for under the measurement guidance for equity securities without readily determinable fair values (see ASC 321).
- Trade receivables and payables due in one year or less.
- Deposit liabilities with no defined or contractual maturities.
- Liabilities resulting from the sale of prepaid stored-value products within the scope of ASC 405-20-40-3.
  (ASC 825-10-50-8)

Fair Value of Financial Instruments The reporting entity should disclose:

- Either in the financial statements or the notes, the fair value of financial instruments.
- The level of the fair value hierarchy within which the fair value measurements are categorized in their entirety (Level 1, 2, or 3). (ASC 825-10-50-10)

For fair value disclosed in the notes, the entity should present fair value with the related carrying amount in a form that clarifies:

- Whether the fair value and carrying amount represent assets or liabilities, and
- How the carrying amounts relate to what is reported in the statement of financial position. (ASC 825-10-50-11)

If the fair value of financial instruments is disclosed in more than a single note, one of the notes should include a summary table. The summary table should contain the fair value and related carrying amounts and cross-references to the location(s) of the remaining disclosures required by this section. (ASC 825-10-50-12)

In disclosing the fair value of a financial instrument, the entity should not net that fair value with the fair value of other financial instruments—even if those financial instruments are of the same class or are otherwise considered to be related—except to the extent that the offsetting of carrying amounts in the statement of financial position is permitted under either of the following:

- The general principle in paragraph 210-20-45-1.
- The exceptions for master netting arrangements in ASC 815-10-45-5 and for amounts related to certain repurchase and reverse repurchase agreements in ASC 210-20-45-11 through 45-17.
  (ASC 825-10-50-15)

Concentrations of Credit Risk of All Financial Instruments An entity should disclose:

- All significant concentrations of credit risk arising from all financial instruments, whether from an individual counterparty or groups of counterparties. (ASC 825-10-50-20)
- Except as indicated in the following paragraph, all of the following about each significant concentration:
  ○ Information about the (shared) activity, region, or economic characteristic that identifies the concentration.
  ○ The maximum amount of loss due to credit risk that, based on the gross fair value of the financial instrument, the entity would incur if parties to the financial instruments that make up the concentration failed completely to perform according to the terms of the contracts and the collateral or other security, if any, for the amount due proved to be of no value to the entity.

With respect to collateral, all of the following:

- The entity's policy of requiring collateral or other security to support financial instruments subject to credit risk.
- Information about the entity's access to that collateral or other security.
- The nature and a brief description of the collateral or other security supporting those financial instruments.

With respect to master netting arrangements, all of the following:

- The entity's policy of entering into master netting arrangements to mitigate the credit risk of financial instruments.
- Information about the arrangements for which the entity is a party.
- A brief description of the terms of those arrangements, including the extent to which they would reduce the entity's maximum amount of loss due to credit risk.
  (ASC 825-10-50-21)

The requirements of the preceding paragraph do not apply to the following financial instruments, whether written or held:

- The financial instruments described in ASC 825-10-50-8(a); (c); (e); and (f), except for reinsurance recoverables and prepaid reinsurance premiums.
- Financial instruments of a pension plan, including plan assets, if subject to the accounting and reporting requirements of Topic 715.
- Financial instruments of a pension plan, other than the obligations for pension benefits, if subject to the accounting and reporting requirements of Topic 960, are subject to the requirements of ASC 825-10-50-20 through 50-21.
  (ASC 825-10-50-22)

Fair Value Option Entities that adopted the fair value option should disclose:

- The reasons that management elected the fair value option for each eligible item or group of similar eligible items.

- If management elected the fair value option for some but not all of the eligible items within a group of similar items:
  - A description of the items in the group and the reasons for the partial election.
  - Information sufficient to enable users to understand how the group of similar items relates to the individual line items presented on the statement of financial position.
- For each statement of financial position line item that included one or more items for which the fair value option was elected:
  - Information sufficient to enable users to understand how each statement of financial position line item relates to major categories of assets and liabilities presented in accordance with the fair value disclosure requirements of ASC 820 (see above) that provide the reader with information with respect to the level or levels within the fair value hierarchy in which the assumptions used to measure fair value (referred to as "inputs") are derived.
  - The aggregate carrying amount of items included in each statement of financial position line item, if any, that are not eligible for the fair value option.
- The difference between the aggregate fair value and the aggregate unpaid principal balance of:
  - Loans and long-term receivables (other than securities subject to ASC 820) with contractual principal amounts and for which the fair value option has been elected.
  - Long-term debt instruments that have contractual principal amounts and for which the fair value option has been elected.
- For loans held as assets for which the fair value option has been elected:
  - The aggregate fair value of loans that are 90 or more days past due.
  - The aggregate fair value of loans on nonaccrual status if the entity's policy is to recognize interest income separately from other changes in fair value.
  - The difference between the aggregate fair value and the aggregate unpaid principal balance for loans that are 90 or more days past due, in nonaccrual status, or both.
- For investments that, absent election of the fair value option, would have been accounted for under the equity method, the following disclosures from ASC 323 are to be made. The extent of disclosures necessary to inform the reader of the financial position and results of operations of an investee is based on management's evaluation of the significance of an investment to the financial position and results of operations of the reporting entity:
  - Parenthetical disclosure, or disclosure in the notes to the financial statements or in separate statements or schedules of:
    - The name of each investee and the percentage of ownership of its common stock held by the reporting entity.
    - The accounting policies of the investor with respect to investments in common stock.
  - When investments in common stock of corporate joint ventures or other investments accounted for under the equity method are, in the aggregate, material to the investor's financial position and results of operations, it may be necessary to present in the notes, or in separate statements, either individually or in groups, summarized information as to assets, liabilities, and results of operations of the investees. (ASC 825-10-50-28)

Required Disclosures for Each Period for Which an Interim or Annual Income Statement Is Presented For items for which the entity elected the fair value option, the entity should disclose:

- For each line item in the statement of financial position, the amounts of gains and losses from changes in fair value included in net income during the period and the specific line in the income statement on which those gains and losses are reported. ASC 825-10-25 permits management to meet this requirement by aggregating these disclosures with respect to items for which the fair value option was elected with the amounts of gains and losses from changes in fair value with respect to other items measured at fair value as required by other authoritative literature.
- A description of how interest and dividends are measured and where they are reported in the statement of income.
- With respect to gains and losses included in net income during the period attributable to changes in instrument-specific credit risk associated with loans and other receivables held as assets:
- The estimated amount of such gains or losses.
- How the gains or losses were determined.
- For liabilities, effects of the instrument-specific credit risk and changes in it:
  - The amount of change, during the period and cumulatively, in fair value of the liability attributable to changes in the instrument-specific credit risk.
  - How the gains and losses were determined.
  - If a liability is settled during the period, the amount, if any, recognized in other comprehensive income that was recognized in net income at settlement.
    (ASC 825-10-50-30)
- In annual financial statements only, the methods and significant assumptions used to estimate the fair value of items for which the fair value option was elected, except that the quantitative disclosures about significant unobservable inputs used in fair value measurements categorized within Level 3 of the fair value hierarchy are not required. (ASC 825-10-50-31)
- If management elects the fair value option upon the occurrence of an event where (1) an investment newly becomes subject to the equity method, (2) a subsidiary or a variable interest entity that the investor previously consolidated ceases to qualify for consolidation but the investor continues to hold common stock in the entity, or (3) an eligible item is required to be measured or remeasured at fair value at the time of the event but is not required to be subsequently remeasured at each succeeding reporting date, the following disclosures are required in the financial statements covering the period of the election:
  - Qualitative information about the nature of the event.
  - Quantitative information by statement of financial position line item indicating which line items in the income statement include the effect on net income of initially electing the fair value option for the item.
    (ASC 825-10-50-32)

The issuer of a registration payment arrangement should disclose the following information about each registration payment arrangement or each group of similar arrangements:

- The nature of the registration payment arrangement, including the approximate term of the arrangement, the financial instrument(s) subject to the arrangement, and the events or circumstances that would require the issuer to transfer consideration under the arrangement.
- Any settlement alternatives contained in the terms of the registration payment arrangement, including the party that controls the settlement alternatives.
- The maximum potential amount of consideration, undiscounted, that the issuer could be required to transfer under the registration payment arrangement (including the maximum

number of shares that may be required to be issued). If the terms of the arrangement provide for no limitation to the maximum potential consideration (including shares) to be transferred, that fact shall be disclosed.

- The fact, if so, that the terms of the arrangement provide for no limitation to the maximum potential consideration to be transferred.
- The current carrying amount of the liability representing the issuer's obligations under the registration payment arrangement and the income statement classification of any gains or losses resulting from changes in the carrying amount of that liability.
- The income statement classification of any gains or losses resulting from changes in the carrying amount of the liability representing the issuer's obligations under the registration payment arrangement.

(ASC 825-20-50-1)

PRESENTATION AND DISCLOSURE EXAMPLES

Example 52.1: Fair Value of Financial Instruments

The estimated fair value of financial instruments disclosed in the consolidated financial statements has been determined by using available market information and appropriate valuation methodologies. The carrying value of all current assets and current liabilities approximates fair value because of their short-term nature. The carrying value of the long-term debt obligations approximates fair value.

Example 52.2: Description and Fair Value of Financial Instruments

The Company's financial instruments include cash and cash equivalents, marketable securities, held-to-maturity debt securities, accounts receivable, certain investments, accounts payable, borrowings, and derivative contracts. The fair values of cash equivalents, accounts receivable, held-to-maturity debt securities, accounts payable, and short-term borrowings and current portion of long-term debt approximated carrying values because of the short-term nature of these instruments. Available-for-sale marketable securities, in addition to certain derivative instruments, are recorded at fair values as indicated in the preceding disclosures. To estimate fair values (classified as Level 2) for its long-term debt, the Company utilized third-party quotes, which are derived all or in part from model prices, external sources, market prices, or the third-party's internal records. Information with respect to the carrying amounts and estimated fair values of these financial instruments follow:

	December 31, 20X2		December 31, 20X1	
(Amounts in millions)	*Carrying Value*	*Fair Value*	*Carrying Value*	*Fair Value*
Long-term debt, excluding current portion	$ 17,518	$ 18,475	$ 13,411	$ 13,586

The fair values reflected above consider the terms of the related debt absent the impacts of derivative/hedging activity. The carrying amount of long-term debt referenced above is impacted by certain fixed-to-floating interest rate swaps that are designated as fair value hedges and by the designation of certain fixed rate Eurobond securities issued by the Company as hedging instruments of the Company's net investment in its European subsidiaries. A number of the Company's fixed-rate bonds were trading at a premium at December 31, 20X2 and 20X1 due to lower interest rates and tighter credit spreads compared to issuance levels.

Example 52.3: Determination of Fair Value

Fair value is defined as the price that would be received upon the sale of an asset or paid to transfer a liability in an orderly transaction between market participants on the measurement date. Valuation techniques used to measure fair value maximize the use of observable inputs and minimize the use of unobservable inputs. The fair value hierarchy defines a three-level valuation hierarchy for classification and disclosure of fair value measurements as follows:

Level 1: Quoted prices in active markets for identical assets or liabilities.

Level 2: Inputs other than Level 1 that are observable, either directly or indirectly, such as quoted prices for similar assets or liabilities; quoted prices in markets that are not active; or other inputs that are observable or can be corroborated by observable market data for substantially the full term of the assets or liabilities.

Level 3: Unobservable inputs that are supported by little or no market activity and that are significant to the fair value of the assets or liabilities.

Example 52.4: Fair Value Measurement of Acquisitions

On March 8, 20X1, the Company acquired Paragon. The Company estimated a contingent liability related to the revenue-based earnout of $72,177. The fair value of the contingent liability was measured using Level 3 inputs. Unobservable inputs for the probability-weighted model included weighted-average cost of capital (unobservable) and company-specific projected revenue and costs (unobservable). As of December 31, 20X1, Management determined revenue earnout would be $0, as the probability-weighted model has been updated based on the current updated forecast for the performance of the Paragon product portfolio. Beginning in Q4 20X1, in conjunction with subsidiary Spirit's Leadership change, Management reassessed the Paragon strategy relating to the roll-out of the commercial operating model, impact of physician reimbursement, and progression of third-party insurance reimbursement and its related impact on the long-term outlook for the business. These items resulted in revisions of our projections and a reduction of the fair value of the earnout liability. As a result, a gain of $72,177 was recognized and is included in gain on acquisition contingency in the consolidated statement of comprehensive (loss) income.

Example 52.5: Estimate of Fair Value of Contingent Liability Updated

On January 4, 20X0, the Company acquired Zylo. The Company estimates a contingent liability related to the clinical milestone and revenue-based earnout of $4,986. The fair value of the contingent liability was measured using Level 3 inputs. As of December 31, 20X1, there was a $3,856 reduction in the contingent liability estimate of the Zylo acquisition revenue-based earnout, as the probability-weighted model has been updated based on the current updated forecast for the performance of the Zylo product portfolio.

Example 52.6: Write Down to Fair Value of Long-Lived Assets

Long-lived assets, including property and equipment and intangible assets, subject to amortization were impaired and written down to their estimated fair values during the fourth quarter of 20X2 and the second quarter of 20X1. Fair value is measured as of the impairment date using Level 3 inputs. For the 20X2 impairments, the long-lived asset Level 3 fair value was measured based on orderly liquidation value for the property, plant and equipment, and other assets. The other intangible assets fair value was measured based on the income approach. Unobservable inputs for the orderly liquidation value included replacement costs (unobservable), physical deterioration estimates (unobservable), and market sales data for comparable assets and unobservable inputs for the income approach including forecasted cash flows generated from use of the intangible assets (unobservable). For the 20X1 impairments, the long-lived asset Level 3 fair value was determined using a market approach, which used inputs that included replacement costs (unobservable), physical deterioration estimates (unobservable), economic obsolescence (unobservable), and market sales data for comparable assets.

The following table summarizes impairments of long-lived assets and the related postimpairment fair values of the corresponding assets for the years ended December 31, 20X2 and 20X1:

	For the Year Ended December 31, 20X2	
	Impairment	*Fair Value*
Property, plant and equipment (net)	$ 11,655	$ —
Other intangible assets (net)	85,096	—
Other assets (net)	201	
	$ 96,952	$ —

	For the Year Ended December 31, 20X1	
	Impairment	*Fair Value*
Property, plant and equipment (net)	$ 1,797	$ —
Other intangible assets (net)	2,718	—
	$ 4,515	$ —

No impairments on long-lived assets were recorded for the years ended December 31, 20X0.

53 ASC 830 FOREIGN CURRENCY MATTERS

AUTHORITATIVE LITERATURE

To facilitate the proper analysis of foreign operations by financial statement users, transactions and financial statements denominated in foreign currencies must be expressed in a common currency (i.e., U.S. dollars). Preparing financial statements in a single currency requires the entity to recognize and measure changes in the relationship between different units of currency. The GAAP governing the translation of foreign currency financial statements and the accounting for foreign currency transactions are found in ASC 830.

The guidance in ASC 830 was issued in 1981 and has not changed significantly since that time. The guidance makes four assumptions. It assumes the reporting entity:

- Is located in the United States,
- Uses the U.S. dollar as its reporting currency,
- Is an operating company with a functional currency in U.S. dollars, and
- Provides support to its foreign operations.

However, in today's global economy, some U.S. reporting entities are merely holding companies with no significant operations. This has resulted in the four assumptions listed above no longer being true and has created challenges in applying the guidance. To prepare consolidated financial statements, amounts denominated in foreign currencies should be:

- Remeasured in the reporting currency, and/or
- Translated into the reporting currency.

These two processes are outlined in the exhibit below:

Subtopic	Process	Description of Process	Reporting Changes
ASC 830-20	Remeasurement	Used to measure amounts that are denominated in a foreign currency other than its functional currency.	Transaction gains and losses reflected in net income.
ASC 830-30	Translation	Used to translate a foreign entity's financial information to the reporting currency when the foreign entity's financial records are maintained in its functional currency.	Translation adjustments recorded in a cumulative translation account, a component of other comprehensive income.

The objectives of translation are to provide:

- Information relative to the expected economic effects of rate changes on an enterprise's cash flows and equity.
- Information in consolidated statements relative to the financial results and relationships of each individual foreign consolidated entity as reflected by the functional currency of each reporting entity.
  (ASC 830-10-10-2)

These are the steps in the process to achieve these goals:

Step 1	Determine the functional currency of each foreign entity.
Step 2	Remeasure into its functional currency the account balances of each entity not denominated in the entity's functional currency.
Step 3	Translate financial statements of foreign entities to the reporting currency of the parent company.
Step 4	Evaluate whether the cumulative translation account should be released into net income.

Subtopics

ASC 830 contains five Subtopics:

- ASC 830-10, *Overall*
- ASC 830-20, *Foreign Currency Transactions*
- ASC 830-30, *Translation of Financial Statements*
- ASC 830-250, *Statement of Cash Flows*
- ASC 830-740, *Income Taxes*

ASC 830 provides guidance about:

- Foreign currency transactions
- Translation of financial statements

Scope and Scope Exceptions

ASC 830 applies to all entities. ASC 830-20 does not apply to derivative instruments. Preparers should look to ASC 815 for guidance on derivatives.

Determining the Functional Currency

Before the financial statements of a foreign branch, division, or subsidiary are translated into U.S. dollars, the management of the U.S. entity must determine which currency is the functional currency of the foreign entity. Once determined, the functional currency cannot be changed unless economic facts and circumstances have clearly changed. Additionally, previously issued financial statements are not restated for any changes in the functional currency. (ASC 830-10-45-7) The functional currency decision is crucial, because different translation methods are applied that may have a material effect on the U.S. entity's financial statements.

The FASB defines functional currency but does not list definitive criteria that, if satisfied, would with certainty result in the identification of an entity's functional currency. Rather, realizing that such criteria would be difficult to develop, the FASB listed various factors that were intended to give management guidance in making the functional currency decision. These factors include:

- Cash flows
- Sales prices
- Sales markets
- Expenses
- Financing
- Intercompany transactions
  (ASC 810-10-55-5)

Translation When a Foreign Entity Maintains Financial Records in Its Functional Currency

Current Rate Method All assets and liabilities are translated at the exchange rate at the balance sheet date. Revenues and expenses are translated at rates in effect when the transactions occur, but those that occur evenly over the year may be translated at the weighted-average rate for the year. (ASC 830-30-45-3) The Codification allows averages or other approximations. (ASC 830-10-55-10)

Translation When a Foreign Entity Maintains Financial Records in a Currency Other Than Its Functional Currency

Remeasurement Method The remeasurement method has also been referred to as the monetary/nonmonetary method. This approach is used when the foreign entity's accounting records are *not* maintained in the functional currency. (ASC 830-10-55-17) This method translates monetary assets (cash and other assets and liabilities that will be settled in cash) at the current rate. Nonmonetary assets, liabilities, and stockholders' equity are translated at the appropriate historical rates.

Cessation of Highly Inflationary Condition

When a foreign subsidiary's economy is no longer considered highly inflationary, the entity converts the reporting currency values into the local currency at the exchange rates on the date of change on which these values become the new functional currency accounting bases for nonmonetary assets and liabilities. (ASC 830-10-45-15) Furthermore, ASC 830-740 states that when a change in functional currency designation occurs because an economy ceases to be highly inflationary, the deferred taxes on the temporary differences that arise as a result of a change in the functional currency are treated as an adjustment to the cumulative translation adjustments portion of stockholders' equity (accumulated other comprehensive income).

Applying ASC 740 to Foreign Entity Financials Restated for General Price Levels

Price level–adjusted financial statements are preferred for foreign currency financial statements of entities operating in highly inflationary economies when those financial statements are intended for readers in the United States. If this recommendation is heeded, the result is that the income tax bases of the assets and liabilities are often restated for inflation. ASC 830-740 provides guidance on applying the asset-and-liability approach of ASC 740 as it relates to such financial statements. It discusses (1) how temporary differences are to be computed under ASC 740, and (2) how deferred income tax expense or benefit for the year is to be determined.

With regard to the first issue, temporary differences are computed as the difference between the indexed income tax basis amount and the related price-level restated amount of the asset or liability. The consensus reached on the second issue is that the deferred income tax expense or benefit is the difference between the deferred income tax assets and liabilities reported at the end of the current year and those reported at the end of the prior year. The deferred income tax assets and liabilities of the prior year are recalculated in units of the current year-end purchasing power.

On a related matter, ASC 830-10-45-16 states that when the functional currency changes to the reporting currency because the foreign economy has become highly inflationary, ASC 740 prohibits recognition of deferred income tax benefits associated with indexing assets and liabilities that are remeasured in the reporting currency using historical exchange rates. Any related income tax benefits would be recognized only upon their being realized for income tax purposes. Any deferred income tax benefits that had been recognized for indexing before the change in reporting currency is effected are eliminated when the related indexed amounts are realized as income tax deductions.

Application of ASC 830 to an Investment to Be Disposed of That Is Evaluated for Impairment

Under ASC 830, accumulated foreign currency translation adjustments are reclassified to net income only when realized upon sale or upon complete or substantially complete liquidation of the investment in the foreign entity. ASC 830-30-45 addresses whether a reporting entity is to include the translation adjustments in the carrying amount of the investment in assessing impairment of an investment in a foreign entity that is held for disposal if the planned disposal will cause some or all of the translation adjustments to be reclassified to net income. The standard points out that an entity that has committed to a plan that will cause the translation adjustments for an equity-method investment or consolidated investment in a foreign entity to be reclassified to earnings is to include the translation adjustments as part of the carrying amount of the investment when evaluating that investment for impairment. An entity would also include the portion of the translation adjustments that represents a gain or loss from an effective hedge of the net investment in a foreign operation as part of the carrying amount of the investment when making this evaluation. (ASC 830-30-45-13)

Foreign Operations in the United States

With the world economy as interconnected as it is, entities in the United States are sometimes the subsidiaries of parent companies domiciled elsewhere in the world. The financial statements of the U.S. entity may be presented separately in the United States or may be combined as part of the financial statements in the foreign country.

In general, financial statements of U.S. companies are prepared in accordance with U.S. GAAP. However, adjustments may be necessary to conform these financial statements to the accounting principles of the foreign country of the parent entity where they will be consolidated.

Translation of Foreign Currency Transactions

According to ASC 830, a foreign currency transaction is a transaction ". . . denominated in a currency other than the entity's functional currency." Denominated means that the amount to be received or paid is fixed in terms of the number of units of a particular foreign currency regardless of changes in the exchange rate. From the viewpoint of a U.S. entity, a foreign currency transaction results when it imports or exports goods or services to or from a foreign entity or makes a loan involving a foreign entity and agrees to settle the transaction in currency other than the U.S. dollar (the functional currency of the U.S. entity). In these situations, the U.S. entity has "crossed currencies" and directly assumes the risk of fluctuating exchange rates of the foreign currency in which the transaction is denominated. This risk may lead to recognition of foreign exchange transaction gains or losses in the income statement of the U.S. entity. Note that transaction gains or losses can result only when the foreign transactions are denominated in a foreign currency. (ASC 830-20-35-1) When a U.S. entity imports or exports goods or services and the transaction is to be settled in U.S. dollars, the U.S. entity is not exposed to a foreign exchange gain or loss because it bears no risk due to exchange rate fluctuations.

PRACTICE ALERT

While non-SEC filers are not subject to SEC comments, those comments can provide valuable guidance and cautions. In the area of financial instruments, the SEC staff has asked preparers to:

- Explain how the indicator specified in ASC 830 suggested CAD or USD as the financial currency for the entity's initial assessment and the assessment adopted in the most recent financial statements.
- Clarify the significant changed economic facts and circumstances underlying each changed indicator.
- Disclose how the entity determined its functional currency as it relates to the primary economic environment in which it operates.

PRESENTATION AND DISCLOSURE REQUIREMENTS

Presentation

Unless these have been significant changes, the entity should use the functional currency consistently. Previously issued financial statements should not be restated for a change in functional currency. (ASC 830-10-45-7)

The entity should report in other comprehensive income the adjustment attributable to current-rate translation of nonmonetary assets as of the date of a change in functional currency from the reporting currency to a foreign currency. (ASC 830-10-45-9)

Disclosure

Aggregate transaction gain or loss included in the entity's net income should be disclosed in the notes. (ASC 830-20-50-1)

If significant, it may be necessary to disclose a rate change that occurred after the date of the reporting entity's financial statements and its effects on unsettled balances pertaining to foreign currency transactions. Included in the disclosure should be consideration of changes in unsettled transactions from the date of the financial statements to the date the rate changed. If it is not practicable to determine these changes, state that fact. (ASC 830-20-50-2)

To assist financial report users in understanding the implications of rate changes and to compare recent results with those of prior periods, entities are encouraged, but not required, to supplement required disclosures with an analysis and discussion of the effects of rate changes on the reported results of operations. (ASC 830-20-50-3)

The entity should include an analysis of changes in accumulated translation adjustments that are reported as other comprehensive income. At a minimum, the disclosures should include:

- Beginning and ending amounts of the translation adjustments account.
- Aggregate adjustment for the period resulting from translation adjustments, and gains and losses from certain hedges and intercompany balances.
- Amount of income taxes for the period allocated to translation adjustments.
- Amounts transferred from the translation adjustments account and included in determining net income as a result of the (partial) sale or liquidation of the foreign operation. (ASC 830-30-50-1)

Rate changes subsequent to the date of the financial statements or after the date of the foreign currency statements of a foreign entity should be disclosed if they are consolidated, combined, or accounted for by the equity method, and include, if significant, effects on unsettled foreign currency transactions. (ASC 830-30-50-2)

PRESENTATION AND DISCLOSURE EXAMPLES

Example 53.1: Foreign Currency

The reporting currency of the Company is the U.S. dollar. The Company determines the functional currency of each subsidiary in accordance with ASC 830, *Foreign Currency Matters*, based on the currency of the primary economic environment in which each subsidiary operates. Items included in the financial statements of such subsidiaries are measured using that functional currency.

For the subsidiaries where the U.S. dollar is the functional currency, foreign currency denominated monetary assets and liabilities are remeasured into U.S. dollars at current exchange rates and foreign currency denominated nonmonetary assets and liabilities are remeasured into U.S. dollars at historical exchange rates. Gains or losses from foreign currency remeasurement and settlements are included in other income (expense), net, in the consolidated statement of operations. For the years ended April 30, 20X3, 20X2, and 20X1, the Company recognized remeasurement loss of $2.2 million, $0.2 million, and $1.3 million, respectively.

For subsidiaries where the functional currency is other than the U.S. dollar, the Company uses the period-end exchange rates to translate assets and liabilities, the average monthly exchange rates to translate revenue and expenses, and historical exchange rates to translate shareholders' equity (deficit) into U.S. dollars. The Company records translation gains and losses in accumulated other comprehensive loss as a component of shareholders' equity in the consolidated balance sheet.

Example 53.2: Foreign Currency Translation

Transactions denominated in currencies other than the functional currency are translated into the functional currency at the exchange rates prevailing at the dates of the transaction. Monetary assets and liabilities denominated in currencies other than the functional currency are translated into the functional currency using the applicable exchange rates at the balance sheet dates. The resulting exchange differences are recorded in the statement of operations.

The reporting currency of the Company is the U.S. dollar ("USD"). The Company's subsidiary in Hong Kong maintains its books and records in its local currency, the Hong Kong dollar ("HKD"), which is the functional currency, as it is the primary currency of the economic environment in which this entity operates.

In general, for consolidation purposes, assets and liabilities of the Company's subsidiary, whose functional currency is not the USD, are translated into USD, in accordance with ASC 830, *Foreign Currency Matters*, using the exchange rate on the balance sheet date. Revenues and expenses are translated at average rates prevailing during the year. The gains and losses resulting from the translation of financial statements of foreign subsidiaries are recorded as a separate component of accumulated other comprehensive income within the statement of stockholders' equity.

Translation of amounts from HKD into USD has been made at the following exchange rates for the respective year:

	December 31	
	20X3	*20X2*
Year-end USD:HKD1 exchange rate	$ 0.128	$ 0.128
Annual average USD:HKD1 exchange rate	$ 0.128	$ 0.128

54 ASC 835 INTEREST

AUTHORITATIVE LITERATURE

ASC 835 provides guidance in two instances—where interest capitalization is in connection with an investment in an asset and where imputation of interest is required.

Per ASC 835-20, the recorded amount of an asset includes all of the costs necessary to get the asset set up and functioning properly for its intended use, including interest. The principal purposes accomplished by the capitalization of interest costs are:

- To obtain a more accurate measurement of the costs associated with the investment in the asset
- To achieve a better matching of costs related to the acquisition, construction, and development of productive assets to the future periods that will benefit from the revenues that the assets generate

ASC 835-30 specifies when and how interest is to be imputed when the receivable is non-interest-bearing or the stated rate on the receivable is not reasonable. It applies to transactions conducted at arm's length between unrelated parties, as well as to transactions in which captive finance companies offer favorable financing to increase sales of related companies.

Subtopics

ASC 835, *Interest*, contains three Subtopics:

- ASC 835-10, *Overall*, which merely points to other Topics with guidance on interest
- ASC 835-20, *Capitalization of Interest*, which provides guidance on capitalization of interest in connection with an asset investment
- ASC 835-30, *Imputation of Interest*, which provides guidance where imputation of interest is required

Scope and Scope Exceptions

All assets that require a time period to get ready for their intended use should include a capitalized amount of interest. However, accomplishing this level of capitalization would usually violate a reasonable cost-benefit test because of the added accounting and administrative costs that would be incurred. In many such situations, the effect of interest capitalization would be immaterial. Accordingly, interest cost is only capitalized as a part of the historical cost of the following types of assets (qualifying assets) when such interest is considered to be material. (ASC 835-20-15-2) Common examples include:

- Assets constructed for an entity's own use or for which deposit or progress payments are made
- Assets produced as discrete projects that are intended for lease or sale
- Equity-method investments when the investee is using funds to acquire qualifying assets for principal operations that have not yet begun
  (ASC 835-20-15-5)

Many entities use threshold levels to determine whether or not interest costs related to inventory or property, plant, and equipment should be capitalized. (ASC 835-20-15-4)

The capitalization of interest costs does not apply to the following situations:

- When the effects of capitalization would not be material, compared to the effect of expensing interest.
- When qualifying assets are already in use or ready for use.
- When qualifying assets are not being used and are not awaiting activities to get them ready for use.
- When qualifying assets are not included in a statement of financial position of the parent company and its consolidated subsidiaries.
- When principal operations of an investee accounted for under the equity method have already begun.
- When regulated investees capitalize both the cost of debt and equity capital.
- When assets are acquired with grants and gifts that are restricted by the donor (or grantor) to the acquisition of those assets, to the extent that funds are available from those grants and gifts. For this purpose, interest earned on the temporary investment of those funds that is subject to similar restriction is to be considered an addition to the gift or grant.
  (ASC 835-10-15-6)

All commitments to pay (and receive) money at a determinable future date are subject to present value techniques and, if necessary, interest imputation with the exception of the following:

- Normal accounts payable due within one year
- Amounts to be applied to purchase price of goods or services or that provide security to an agreement (e.g., advances, progress payments, security deposits, and retentions) except for amounts promised in a contract with a customer
- Amounts intended to provide security for one party
- Transactions between parent and subsidiary
- Obligations payable at some indeterminable future date (e.g., warranties)
- Lending and depositor savings activities of financial institutions whose primary business is lending money
- Transactions where interest rates are affected by prescriptions of a governmental agency (e.g., revenue bonds, tax exempt obligations, etc.)
- Estimates of contractual or other obligations assumed in connection with sales of property, goods, or services
- Receivables, contract assets, and contract liabilities in contracts with customers (ASC 835-30-15-3)

ASC 835-20, *Capitalization of Interest*

Interest Cost Generally, inventories and land that are not undergoing preparation for intended use are not qualifying assets. When land is being developed, it is a qualifying asset. If land is developed for lots, the capitalized interest cost is added to the cost of the land. The capitalized interest will then be properly matched against revenues when the lots are sold. If, however, the land is developed for a building, then the capitalized interest cost is added to the cost of the building, in which case the capitalized interest will be matched against related revenues as the building is depreciated.

The amount of interest to be capitalized. Interest cost includes the following:

- Interest on debt having explicit interest rates (fixed or floating)
- Interest related to capital leases
- Interest required to be imputed on payables (i.e., those due in over one year, per ASC 835-30)

Capitalization Interest Rate The most appropriate rate to use as the capitalization rate is the rate applicable to specific new debt resulting from the need to finance the acquired assets. If there is no specific new debt, the capitalization rate is a weighted-average of the rates of the other borrowings of the entity. This reflects the fact that the previously incurred debt of the entity could be repaid if not for the acquisition of the qualifying asset. The amount of interest to be capitalized is that portion that could have been avoided if the qualifying asset had not been acquired. Thus, the capitalized amount is the incremental amount of interest cost incurred by the entity to finance the acquired asset. (ASC 835-20-30-2)

Capitalizable Base Once the appropriate rate has been established, the base to which that rate is to be applied is the average amount of accumulated net capital *expenditures* incurred for qualifying assets during the relevant time frame. (ASC 835-20-30-3) Capitalized costs and expenditures are not the same terms. Theoretically, a capitalized cost financed by a trade payable for which no interest is recognized is not a capital expenditure to which the capitalization rate is applied. Reasonable approximations of net capital expenditures are acceptable, however, and capitalized costs are generally used in place of capital expenditures unless there is expected to be a material difference.

If the average capitalized expenditures exceed the specific new borrowings for the time frame involved, then the *excess* expenditures are multiplied by the weighted-average of rates and not by the rate associated with the specific debt. This requirement more accurately reflects the interest cost incurred by the entity to acquire the fixed asset. (ASC 835-20-30-3)

The amount capitalized cannot exceed the amount actually incurred during the period involved. On a consolidated basis, the ceiling is defined as the total of the parent's interest cost plus that of the consolidated subsidiaries. If financial statements are issued separately, the interest cost capitalized is limited to the amount that the separate entity has incurred, and that amount includes interest on intercompany borrowings. (ASC 835-20-30-6). The interest incurred is a gross amount and is not netted against interest earned except in cases involving externally restricted tax-exempt borrowings. (ASC 835-20-30-10)

Determining the Time Period for Interest Capitalization Three conditions must be met before capitalization commences:

1. Necessary activities are in progress to get the asset ready to function as intended
2. Qualifying asset expenditures have been made
3. Interest costs are being incurred
 (ASC 835-30-25-2)

Interest costs continue to be capitalized until the asset is ready to function as intended, even in cases where lower of cost or market rules are applicable and market is lower than cost. The required write-down is increased accordingly.

Capitalization of Interest Costs Incurred on Tax-Exempt Borrowings If qualifying assets have been financed with the proceeds from tax-exempt, externally restricted borrowings, and if temporary investments have been purchased with those proceeds, a modification is required. The interest costs incurred from the date of borrowing must be reduced by the interest earned on the temporary investment in order to calculate the ceiling for the capitalization of interest costs.

Assets Acquired with Gifts or Grants Qualifying assets that are acquired with externally restricted gifts or grants are not subject to capitalization of interest. The principal reason for this treatment is the concept that there is no economic cost of financing when a gift or grant is used in the acquisition.

ASC 835-30, *Imputation of Interest*

Receivables If a receivable is due on terms exceeding one year, the proper valuation is the present value of future payments to be received, determined by using an interest rate commensurate with the risks involved at the date of the receivable's creation. In many situations the interest rate commensurate with the risks involved is the rate stated in the agreement between the payee and the debtor. However, if the receivable is noninterest-bearing or if the rate stated in the agreement is not indicative of the market rate for a debtor of similar creditworthiness under similar terms, interest is imputed at the market rate. A valuation allowance is used to adjust the face amount of the receivable to the present value at the market rate. The balance in the valuation allowance is amortized as additional interest income so that interest income is recognized using a constant rate of interest over the life of the agreement. Initial recording of such a valuation allowance also results in the recognition of an expense, typically (for customer receivables) reported as selling expense or as a contra revenue item (sales discounts).

ASC 835-30-25 divides receivables into three categories for discussion:

1. Notes issued solely for cash,
2. Notes issued for cash and rights or privileges, and
3. Notes issued in exchange for property, goods, or services.

Note Issued Solely for Cash When a note is issued solely for cash, its present value is necessarily assumed to be equal to the cash proceeds. (ASC 835-30-25-4) The interest rate is that rate that equates the cash proceeds received by the borrower to the amounts to be paid in the future. (ASC 835-30-25-5)

Note Issued for Cash and Rights or Privileges When a note receivable that bears an unrealistic rate of interest is issued in exchange for cash, an additional right or privilege is usually granted, unless the transaction was not conducted at arm's length. If there was an added right or privilege involved, the difference between the present value of the receivable and the cash advanced is the value assigned to the right or privilege. It will be accounted for as an addition to the cost of the products purchased for the purchaser/lender, and as additional revenue to the debtor. (ASC 835-30-25-6)

Note Issued in Exchange for Property, Goods, or Services When a note is issued in exchange for property, goods, or services and the transaction is entered into at arm's length, the stated interest rate is presumed to be fair unless:

- No interest rate is stated,
- The stated rate is unreasonable,
- The face value of the note receivable is materially different from the fair value of the property, goods, or services received, or
- The face value of the note receivable is materially different from the current market value of the note at the date of the transaction.
(ASC 835-30-25-10)

Debt Issuance Costs

Costs may be incurred in connection with issuing bonds. Examples include legal, accounting, and underwriting fees; commissions; and engraving, printing, and registration costs. Debt issuance costs must be presented on the statement of financial position as a direct reduction of proceeds from debt and the costs must be amortized and reported as interest expense. (ASC 835- 30-45-1 through 45-3)

PRESENTATION AND DISCLOSURE REQUIREMENTS

Presentation

The discount or premium resulting from the determination of present value in cash or noncash transactions should reported in the balance sheet as a direct deduction from or addition to the face amount of the note, and debt issuance costs related to a note should be reported in the balance sheet as a direct deduction from the face amount of that note.

(ASC 835-30-45-1A) The description of the note should include the effective interest rate. The face amount also should be disclosed in the financial statements or in the notes to the statements. (ASC 835-30-45-2)

Amortization of discount or premium is reported as:

- Interest expense in the case of liabilities, or
- Interest income in the case of assets.

Amortization of debt issuance costs also should be reported as interest expense. (ASC 835-30-45-3)

Disclosure

The entity should disclose the following information related to interest cost in the financial statements or related notes:

- For an accounting period in which no interest cost is capitalized, the amount of interest cost incurred and charged to expense during the period
- For an accounting period in which some interest cost is capitalized, the total amount of interest cost incurred during the period and the amount thereof that has been capitalized.
  (ASC 835-20-50-1)

PRESENTATION AND DISCLOSURE EXAMPLES

Example 54.1: Accounting Policy for Capitalization of Interest

We follow the practice of capitalizing interest to real estate inventories during the period of development and to investments in unconsolidated joint ventures, when applicable, in accordance with ASC 835, *Interest* ("ASC 835"). Interest capitalized as a cost component of real estate inventories is included in cost of home sales as related homes or lots are sold. To the extent interest is capitalized to investment in unconsolidated joint ventures, it is included as a reduction of equity in net income (loss) of unconsolidated joint ventures when the related homes or lots are sold to third parties. In instances where the Company purchases land from an unconsolidated joint venture, the pro rata share of interest capitalized to investment in unconsolidated joint ventures is added to the basis of the land acquired and recognized as a cost of sale upon the delivery of the related homes or land to a third-party buyer. To the extent our debt exceeds our qualified assets as defined in ASC 835, we expense a portion of the interest incurred by us. Qualified assets represent projects that are actively selling or under development as well as investments in unconsolidated joint ventures accounted for under the equity method until such equity investees begin their principal operations.

Example 54.2: Amounts Outstanding Presented Net of Debt Issuance Costs

In accordance with ASC 835, *Interest*, the amounts outstanding under the Company's Term Loan are presented on the consolidated balance sheet net of related debt issuance costs, which were $11.4 million as of December 31, 20X1.

Example 54.3: Debt Discount Amortized to Interest Expense Using Effective Interest Method

The debt discount was being amortized to interest expense using the effective interest method in accordance with ASC 835 over the term of the agreement. For the year ended December 31, 20X2, approximately $313,000 was recognized as amortization of debt discount and is included in interest expense on the consolidated statement of operations and comprehensive loss.

Example 54.4: Amortization of Debt Issuance Costs and Debt Discounts

The Company accounts for debt issuance costs in accordance with ASC 835, *Interest*, which requires that costs paid directly to the issuer of a recognized debt liability be reported in the balance sheet as a direct deduction from the carrying amount of that debt liability, consistent with debt discounts. The Company amortizes the debt discount, including debt issuance costs, in accordance with ASC 835, *Interest*, over the term of the associated debt. See Note 13: Unsecured Promissory Notes and Warrants for a discussion of the Company's prior unsecured long-term note payable.

55 ASC 840 LEASES[1]

AUTHORITATIVE LITERATURE

Technical Alert

See the chapter on ASC 842, *Leases*, for information on the new standard on leases.

Subtopics

ASC 840, *Leases*, and its subtopics establish standards of accounting and reporting by lessees and lessors for leases overall, and for specific classifications of leases. ASC 840 contains four Subtopics:

- ASC 840-10, *Overall*
- ASC 840-20, *Operating Leases*
- ASC 840-30, *Capital Leases*
- ASC 840-40, *Sale-Leaseback Transactions*

Each of the Subtopics contains the following Subsections:

- General
- Lessees
- Lessors

Scope and Scope Exceptions

ASC 840 applies to all entities. However, to be considered a lease the right to use property, plant, or equipment must be transferred from one contracting party to the other. The definition of lease does not include contracts for services.

---

[1] The FASB has issued ASU 2016-02, *Leases*. See the chapter on ASC 842, *Leases*, for more information.

Variable Interest Entities

From the standpoint of the lessee, it is critical for the accountant to first determine whether the relationship between the entities requires consolidation as a VIE under ASC 810. This is discussed in detail in the Chapter on ASC 810. If consolidation is required, the effects of the lease recorded by the parties will be eliminated in the consolidated financial statements and the lease accounting will, in effect, be moot from the standpoint of the lessee.

In more complex situations or when qualitative analysis does not yield a conclusive answer, the holder of one or more variable interests may be required to estimate the present value of the probability-weighted expected cash flows associated with the entity in order to determine the expected variability of the entity's future cash flows as well as the portion of that expected variability that is allocable to the various holders of variable interests.

Lease or Sale—The Interplay of Lease and Revenue Recognition Accounting

ASC 840-10-35, *Determining Whether an Arrangement Contains a Lease* ASC 840 defines a lease as "an agreement conveying the right to use property, plant, or equipment (land and/or depreciable assets) usually for a stated period of time." ASC 840-10-35 provides guidance on determining when all or part of an arrangement constitutes a lease.

Scope of ASC 840-10-35. "Property, plant, or equipment," as the term is used in ASC 840, includes only land and/or depreciable assets. Therefore, inventory (including equipment parts inventory) cannot be the subject of a lease because inventory is not depreciable. (ASC 840-10-15-15) In addition, ASC 840 contains specific scope exceptions with respect to agreements concerning:

- Exploration or exploitation of natural resources (e.g., oil, gas, minerals, and timber)
- Intangible licensing rights (e.g., motion pictures, plays, manuscripts, patents, and copyrights)

Although specific property, plant, or equipment may be explicitly identified in an arrangement, it is not the subject of a lease if the arrangement can be fulfilled without using the specified property, plant, or equipment.

Lease treatment is not precluded in situations where the owner or manufacturer of the property has extended a product warranty that includes a provision for replacement of the property if it is not operating adequately. Similarly, if the arrangement includes a provision permitting the equipment owner the right to substitute other equipment on or after a specified date, irrespective of the reason, the arrangement can still qualify as a lease. (ASC 840-10-15-13)

Right to use property, plant, or equipment. The right to use the specified property, plant, or equipment is conveyed if any one of the following conditions is met:

- A *party* (for the purpose of this discussion, we will refer to this party, the potential lessee, as "the recipient" of the rights) has the ability or right to operate the property, plant, or equipment or direct others to do so as the recipient specifies, while attaining or controlling more than a minor portion of the output (or service utility),
- The recipient has the ability or right to control physical access to the specified property, plant, or equipment while attaining or controlling more than a minor portion of the output (or other service utility), or
- Analysis of the relevant facts and circumstances indicates that it is "remote" (as that term is used in ASC 450-20) that a party (or parties) other than the recipient will attain more

than a minor amount of the output (or other service utility) that will be produced or generated by the specified property, plant, or equipment during the term of the arrangement, *and* the price that the recipient will pay for the output is neither contractually fixed per unit of output nor equal to the market price per unit of output at the time delivery of the output is received.
(ASC 840-10-15-6)

Timing of initial assessment and subsequent reassessments. The assessment of whether an arrangement contains a lease is to be made at the inception of the arrangement. A reassessment of whether the arrangement contains a lease is to be made only if (a) the contractual terms are modified, (b) a renewal option is exercised or the parties to the arrangement agree on an extension of its term, (c) there is a change in the determination as to whether or not fulfillment of the arrangement is dependent on the property, plant, or equipment that was originally specified, or (d) the originally specified property and equipment undergoes a substantial physical change. (ASC 840-10-35-2) Remeasurement/redetermination is not permitted merely because of a change in an estimate made at inception (e.g., the number of expected units of output or the useful life of the equipment). (ASC 840-10-35-3)

Aggregation of separate contracts. There is a rebuttable presumption that separate contracts between the same parties (or related parties) that are executed on or near the same date were negotiated together as a package.

This presumption also provides accounting guidance for any recognized assets and liabilities existing at the time that an arrangement (or a portion of an arrangement) either ceases to qualify as a lease or commences to qualify as a lease due to a reassessment in the circumstances as described above.

Sales with a Guaranteed Minimum Resale Value ASC 606-10-25-30 states that transactions containing guarantees of resale value of equipment by a manufacturer should be accounted for as leases and not as sales. The minimum lease payments used to determine if the criteria have been met for lessor sales-type lease accounting are computed as the difference between the proceeds received from the transferee/lessee upon initial transfer of the equipment and the amount of the residual value guarantee on its first contractual exercise date.

If the lease is accounted for as an operating lease because it does not qualify for sales-type lease accounting, the manufacturer/lessor should record the proceeds received at inception as a liability, which is subsequently reduced by crediting revenue pro rata from the inception of the lease until the first guarantee exercise date so that, on that exercise date, the remaining liability is the guaranteed residual amount. If the lessee elects, under the terms of the arrangement, to continue to use the leased asset after the first exercise date, the manufacturer/lessor will continue to amortize the liability for the remaining residual amount to revenue to reduce it further to any remaining guarantee, if applicable.

Lessee Classification

For accounting and reporting purposes the lessee has two possible classifications for a lease:

1. Operating
2. Capital

The proper classification of a lease is determined by the circumstances surrounding the transaction. If substantially all of the benefits and risks of ownership have been transferred to the lessee, the lessee records the lease as a capital lease at its inception. Substantially all of the risks or benefits of ownership are deemed to have been transferred if any one of the following criteria is met:

- The lease transfers ownership to the lessee by the end of the lease term.
- The lease contains a bargain purchase option.
- The lease term is equal to 75% or more of the estimated economic life of the leased property, and the beginning of the lease term does not fall within the last 25% of the total economic life of the leased property.
- The present value of the minimum lease payments at the beginning of the lease term is 90% or more of the fair value to the lessor less any investment tax credit retained by the lessor. This requirement cannot be used if the lease's inception is in the last 25% of the useful economic life of the leased asset. The interest rate, used to compute the present value, is the incremental borrowing rate of the lessee unless the implicit rate is available and lower. For the purpose of this test, lease structuring fees or lease administration fees paid by the lessee to the lessor are included as part of the minimum lease payments.

If a lease agreement meets none of the criteria set forth above, it is classified as an operating lease by the lessee.

Lessor Classification

There are four possible classifications that apply to a lease from the standpoint of the lessor:

1. Operating
2. Sales-type
3. Direct financing
4. Leveraged

The conditions surrounding the origination of the lease determine its classification by the lessor. If the lease meets any one of the four criteria specified above for lessees and both of the qualifications set forth below, the lease is classified as either a sales-type lease, direct financing lease, or leveraged lease depending upon the conditions present at the inception of the lease.

1. Collectibility of the minimum lease payments is reasonably predictable.
2. No important uncertainties surround the amount of unreimbursable costs yet to be incurred by the lessor under the lease.

If a lease transaction does not meet the criteria for classification as a sales-type lease, a direct financing lease, or a leveraged lease as specified above, it is classified by the lessor as an operating lease. The classification testing is performed prior to considering the proper accounting treatment.

Distinctions Among Sales-Type, Direct Financing, and Leveraged Leases A lease is classified as a sales-type lease when the criteria set forth above have been met and the lease transaction is structured in such a way that the lessor recognizes a profit or loss on the transaction in addition to interest income. In order for this to occur, the fair value of the property must be different from the cost (carrying value). The essential substance of this transaction is that of a sale, and thus its name. Common examples of sales-type leases include (1) when a customer of an automobile dealership opts to lease a car in lieu of an outright purchase, and the re-lease of equipment coming off an expiring lease. Note, however, that a lease involving real estate must transfer title (i.e., criterion 1 in the preceding list) by the end of the lease term for the lessor to classify the lease as a sales-type lease.

A direct financing lease differs from a sales-type lease in that the lessor does not realize a profit or loss on the transaction other than interest income. In a direct financing lease, the fair value of the property at the inception of the lease is equal to the cost (carrying value). This type of lease transaction most often involves lessor entities engaged in financing operations. The lessor (a bank, or other financial institution) purchases the asset and then leases the asset to the lessee. This transaction merely replaces the conventional lending transaction in which the borrower uses the borrowed funds to purchase the asset. There are many economic reasons why the lease transaction is considered. They are as follows:

- The lessee (borrower) is able to obtain 100% financing.
- Flexibility of use for the tax benefits.
- The lessor receives the equivalent of interest as well as an asset with some remaining value at the end of the lease term.

One form of a direct financing lease is a leveraged lease. This type is mentioned separately because it receives a different accounting treatment by the lessor. A leveraged lease meets all the definitional criteria of a direct financing lease, but differs because it involves at least three parties: a lessee, a long-term creditor, and a lessor (commonly referred to as the equity participant). Other characteristics of a leveraged lease are as follows:

1. The financing provided by the long-term creditor must be without recourse to the general credit of the lessor, although the creditor may hold recourse with respect to the leased property. The amount of the financing must provide the lessor with substantial "leverage" in the transaction.
2. The lessor's net investment declines during the early years and rises during the later years of the lease term before its elimination.

PRESENTATION AND DISCLOSURE REQUIREMENTS

For detailed information on ASC's 840 presentation and disclosure requirements, see the financial statements disclosure checklist at www.wiley.com/go/FSDM2021.

PRESENTATION AND DISCLOSURE EXAMPLES

Example 55.1: Accounting Policy—Depreciation of Leased Property Under Capital Leases

Leased property and equipment under capital leases are depreciated using the straight-line method over the terms of the related leases.

Example 55.2: Accounting Policy for Leases

Leases are capitalized under the criteria set forth in ASC 840, *Leases*, which establishes the four criteria of a capital lease. At least one of the four following criteria must be met for a lease to be considered a capital lease: a transfer of ownership of the property to the lessee by the end of the lease term; a bargain purchase option; a lease term that is greater than or equal to 75% of the economic life of the leased property; present value of the future minimum lease payments equals or exceeds 90% of the fair market value of the leased property. If none of the aforementioned criteria are met, the lease will be treated as an operating lease.

Example 55.3: Leases—Accounting Policy and Description of Leases

Lease agreements are evaluated to determine whether they are capital leases or operating leases in accordance with ASC 840-10-25-1 of the FASB Accounting Standards Codification (Paragraph 840-10-25-1). Pursuant to ASC 840-10-25-1, "A lessee and a lessor shall consider whether a lease meets any of the following four criteria as part of classifying the lease at its inception under the guidance in the Lessees Subsection of this Section (for the lessee) and the Lessors Subsection of this Section (for the lessor):

a. Transfer of ownership. The lease transfers ownership of the property to the lessee by the end of the lease term. This criterion is met in situations in which the lease agreement provides for the transfer of title at or shortly after the end of the lease term in exchange for the payment of a nominal fee, for example, the minimum required by statutory regulation to transfer title.
b. Bargain purchase option. The lease contains a bargain purchase option.
c. Lease term. The lease term is equal to 75% or more of the estimated economic life of the leased property.
d. Minimum lease payments. The present value at the beginning of the lease term of the minimum lease payments, excluding that portion of the payments representing executory costs such as insurance, maintenance, and taxes to be paid by the lessor, including any profit thereon, equals or exceeds 90% of the excess of the fair value of the leased property to the lessor at lease inception over any related investment tax credit retained by the lessor and expected to be realized by the lessor."

In accordance with ASC 840-10-25-29 and 840-10-25-30, if at its inception a lease meets any of the four lease classification criteria in ASC 840-10-25-1, the lease shall be classified by the lessee as a capital lease; and if none of the four criteria in ASC 840-10-25-1 are met, the lease shall be classified by the lessee as an operating lease. Pursuant to ASC 840-10-25-31, a lessee shall compute the present value of the minimum lease payments using the lessee's incremental borrowing rate unless both of the following conditions are met, in which circumstance the lessee shall use the implicit rate:

a. It is practicable for the lessee to learn the implicit rate computed by the lessor.
b. The implicit rate computed by the lessor is less than the lessee's incremental borrowing rate.

Capital lease assets are depreciated on a straight-line method over the capital lease assets' estimated useful lives, consistent with the Company's normal depreciation policy for tangible fixed assets. Interest charges are expensed over the period of the lease in relation to the carrying value of the capital lease obligation.

Operating leases primarily relate to the Company's leases of office spaces. When the terms of an operating lease include tenant improvement allowances, periods of free rent, rent concessions, and/or rent escalation amounts, the Company establishes a deferred rent liability for the difference between the scheduled rent payment and the straight-line rent expense recognized, which is amortized over the underlying lease term on a straight-line basis as a reduction of rent expense.

Example 55.4: Operating Lease Expense

No assets under capital leases are included in machinery and equipment as of June 30, 20X2 or June 30, 20X1.

Operating lease expense was $2.3 million, $2.2 million, and $1.9 million in fiscal 20X2, 20X1, and 20X0, respectively. Future commitments under operating leases are as follows (in thousands):

Fiscal Year	
20X3	$ 2,204
20X4	2,040
20X5	1,876
20X6	1,614
20X7	1,685
Thereafter	2,191

Example 55.5: Capitalized Lease Obligations

Debt, including capitalized lease obligations, is comprised of the following (in thousands):

	June 30, 20X2	June 30, 20X1
Short-term and current maturities		
Loan and security agreement	$ 1,543	$ 1,474
Capitalized leases	—	78
	$ 1,543	$ 1,552
Long-term debt		
Loan and security agreement, net of current portion	$ 17,109	$ 18,552
	17,109	18,552
Total debt	$ 18,652	$ 20,104

Future maturities of debt are as follows (in thousands):

Fiscal Year	
20X3	$ 1,543
20X4	11,014
20X5	1,688
20X6	1,765
20X7	1,846
Thereafter	796
Total	$ 18,652

56 ASC 842 LEASES

AUTHORITATIVE LITERATURE

Lease transactions have become enormously popular over the years as businesses have sought new ways to finance long-lived assets. Leasing offers two attractive advantages: typically, 100% financing, coupled very often with off-the-books obligations.

A lease agreement involves at least two parties, a lessor and a lessee, and an asset that is to be leased. The lessor is the party that agrees to provide the lessee with right to use an asset for a specified period of time in return for consideration.

The lease transaction derives its accounting complexity from the number of alternatives available to the parties involved. Leases can be structured to allow differing assignments of income tax benefits associated with the leased asset to meet the objectives of the transacting parties. Leases can be used to transfer ownership of the leased asset, and they can be used to transfer control of the assets. In any event, the substance of the transaction dictates the accounting treatment, irrespective of its legal form. The lease transaction is probably the best example of the accounting profession's substance-over-form argument. If the transaction effectively transfers the control of the asset to the lessee, then the substance of the transaction is that of a sale and, accordingly, it is recognized as such for accounting purposes even though the transaction is legally structured as a lease.

Technical Alerts

ASU 2019-10 and ASU 2020-05—Deferrals in the Effective Dates The FASB deferred the effective date for ASU 2016-02, *Leases*, first in ASU 2019-10, *Financial Instruments—Credit Losses (Topic 326), Derivatives and Hedging (Topic 815), and Leases (Topic 842): Effective Dates*, and most recently in ASU 2020-05.

In June 2020, the FASB issued ASU 2020-05, *Revenue from Contracts with Customers (Topic 606) and Leases (Topic 842): Effective Dates for Certain Entities*. Because of the COVID-19 pandemic, the FASB in this ASU provides a deferral in the effective date for "all other" entities to fiscal years beginning after December 15, 2021, and interim periods beginning after December 15, 2022. These dates are reflected in the chart below and the term "all other" is defined in the chart.

The new standard is effective as follows:

	Public Companies	**All Other Entities**
Effective Date	Annual and interim periods in fiscal years beginning after December 15, 2018, including interim periods within those years.	Annual periods beginning on or after December 15, 2021, and interim period beginning after December 15, 2022.
Early Adoption	Yes	Yes

"Public companies" above refers to:

- Public business entities,
- Not-for-profit entities that have issued or are conduit bond obligors for securities that are traded, listed, or quoted on an exchange or over-the-counter market, and
- Employee benefit plans that file or furnish statements with or to the SEC.

Note that in order to capture comparative data, some companies will have to keep two sets of records for fiscal years beginning in 2017. Some entities may want to take advantage of the synergies between the new revenue recognition standard and the leases standard by early adopting and aligning processes.

ASU 2016-02—Putting It on the Balance Sheet

Guidance The objective of the standard is to improve information for financial statement users by increasing transparency and comparability among organizations. To accomplish this, the standard requires:

- Lessees to recognize lease assets (right-of-use assets) and lease liabilities on the balance sheet,
- Lessors to align with certain changes in the lessee model and the new revenue recognition standards, and
- Lessees and lessors to disclose significant information about lease transactions.

Lessees Under ASC 842, lessees recognize all leases other than short-term leases on the balance sheet. Lessees recognize a right-of-use (ROU) asset and a lease liability for those leases. Compared with ASC 840 guidance, this may significantly increase reported assets and liabilities for some lessees for some leases. For the first time, under ASC 842 long-term operating leases will appear on the balance sheet as non-debt liabilities. ASC 842 offers some relief to preparers by exempting leases with terms of less than 12 months. As a consequence, some lessees may request new or renewed leases with terms less than 12 months.

Lessors Under the guidance in ASC 842, the lessor accounting model is substantially unchanged. However, lessors will have to review their systems and processes to ensure that data will be available to management for the new required disclosures. The main focus of the FASB was specifically to improve the guidance for operating leases in the financial statements of lessees. Therefore, the Board decided not to make fundamental changes to lessor accounting. However, some changes were made to lessor guidance in order to conform and align it to the new guidance for lessees and the new revenue recognition guidance, ASU 2016-10, *Revenue from Contracts with Customers (Topic 606)*. The new leases standard is aligned with the revenue recognition standard, and those familiar with that standard will see some similarities in terminology and approach.

Effective Dates See the "Technical Alerts" section at the beginning of this chapter for deferrals of the effective dates.

Transition Like the revenue standard, the leases standard provides for a transition approach using the modified retrospective transition approach. The approach must be applied to all comparative periods presented.

Practical Expedients Again, as with the revenue recognition standard, the standard setters provide practical expedients to ease the transition. The expedients must be applied consistently to all leases. The expedients include:

- An entity may elect not to reassess:
  - ○ Whether expired or existing contracts contain leases under the new definition of a lease.
  - ○ Lease classification for expired or existing leases.
  - ○ Whether previously capitalized initial direct costs would qualify for capitalization under the new standard.

(The above expedients must be elected as a package at the date of adoption.)

- Use of hindsight when determining the lease term and in assessing impairment of right-to-use assets.

- Making an accounting policy election by class of underlying asset not to separate lease components from nonlease components. Lessors can make this election if:
  - The timing and pattern of transfer of the nonlease component and the associated lease component are the same, and
  - The lease component is classified as an operating lease on a standalone basis.

Entities making this election account for the nonlease components and the lease components as a single lease component.

To address concerns that it is costly to determine a discount rate, nonpublic entities may elect an accounting policy to use a risk-free rate to measure liabilities.

Note: For entities that have not yet adopted ASU 2016-02, the following ASUs have the same effective date as ASU 2016-02.

ASU 2018-01 In January 2018, the FASB issued ASU 2018-01, *Leases (Topic 842): Land Easements Practical Expedient for Transition to Topic 842*. The ASU adds an optional practical expedient upon transition for land easements that allows entities to continue applying their current accounting policy for certain land easements that exist on or expired before ASU 2018-01's effective date, which is the same as the new leases standard.

ASU 2018-10 In July 2018, the FASB issued ASU 2018-10, *Codification Improvements to Topic 842, Leases*. The ASU amends the following areas:

- Residual value guarantees
- Rate implicit in the lease
- Lessee reassessment of lease classification
- Lessor reassessments of lease term and purchase option
- Variable lease payments that depend on an index or a rate
- Investment tax credits
- Lease term and purchase option
- Transition guidance for amounts previously recognized in business combinations
- Certain transition adjustments
- Transition guidance for leases previously classified as capital leases under ASC 840
- Transition guidance for modifications to leases previously classified or direct financing or sales-type leases under ASC 840
- Transition guidance for sale and leaseback transactions
- Impairment of net investment in the lease
- Unguaranteed residual asset
- Effect of initial direct costs on rate implicit in the lease
- Failed sale and leaseback transaction

The changes are incorporated in this volume when appropriate.

ASU 2018-11 In July 2018, the FASB issued ASU 2018-11, *Leases (Topic 842): Targeted Improvements*. The ASU clarified:

- Transition requirements for initial adoption. See the transition requirements.
- Separating components of a contract.

The added guidance on separating components of a contract provides lessors with a practical expedient. It permits, by class of underlying asset, lessors to not separate nonlease components from the associated lease component. Instead, the lessor may account for those components as a single component if the nonlease components otherwise would be accounted for under the revenue guidance in ASC 606 and both of the following conditions are met:

- The timing and pattern of a transfer of the nonlease components and associated lease component are the same
- The lease component, if accounted for separately, would be classified as an operating lease
  (ASC 842-10-15-42A)

Certain disclosures are required, and those are included in the checklist found at www.wiley .com/go/FSDM2021.

ASU 2018-20 In December 2018, the FASB issued ASU 2018-20, *Narrow-Scope Improvements for Lessors*. To help lessors apply ASU 2016-02, the FASB issued amendments that permit lessors to make an accounting policy election not to evaluate whether sales taxes and other similar taxes imposed by a governmental authority on a specific lease revenue-producing transaction are the primary obligations of the lessor as owner of the underlying leased asset. If the lessor makes that election, it may exclude those taxes from the measurement of lease revenue and associated expense.

The ASU requires lessors to:

- Exclude lessor costs paid directly by lessees to third parties on the lessor's behalf from variable payments and thus lease revenue
- Include in the measurement of variable lease revenue and the associated expense lessor costs that are paid by the lessor and reimbursed by the lessee

When lessors allocate variable payments to lease and nonlease components, the ASU clarified that lessors are required to follow the recognition guidance in ASU 2016-02 for the lease component and other guidance for the nonlease component.

Certain disclosures are required and are included in the checklist at www.wiley.com/ go/FSDM2021.

ASU 2019-01 In March 2019, the FASB issued ASC 2019-01, *Leases (Topic 842): Codification Improvements*. The FASB clarified:

- The fair value of the underlying asset by lessors that are not manufacturers,
- The presentation of sale-type and direct financing leases on the statement of cash flows, and
- The transition disclosures under ASC 250.

These changes are incorporated in this chapter and in the checklist at www.wiley.com/go/ FSDM2021 as appropriate.

Subtopics—ASU 842

ASC 842 contains five Subtopics:

- ASC 842-10, *Overall,* which establishes the principles for reporting the amount, timing, and uncertainty of cash flows
- ASC 842-20, *Lessee,* which addresses accounting by lessees for finance and operating leases
- ASC 842-30, *Lessor,* which addresses accounting by lessors for sales-type, direct financing, and operating leases

- ASC 842-40, *Sale and Leaseback Transactions,* which addresses accounting for sale and leaseback transactions for leases accounted for under any of the above subtopics
- ASC 842-50, *Leveraged Lease Arrangements,* which provides guidance for leases defined as leveraged leases

Scope—ASU 842

ASC 842 applies to all leases. Because a lease conveys the right to control the use of an identified asset for a period of time in exchange for consideration, ASC 842 does not apply to leases of:

- Intangible assets,
- Biological assets, such as timber,
- Inventory,
- Assets under construction, or
- Leases to explore for and use minerals, oil, natural gas, and other similar resources. (ASC 842-10-15-1)

Determining Whether a Lease Is Present in the Contract The critical determination in applying the scope guidance is whether a contract contains a lease. A lease is present in the contract if the contract includes:

- An identified asset, that is,
  - The asset is explicitly or implicitly specified
  - The supplier has no practical ability to substitute or would not economically benefit from substituting
- The right to control the use of the asset during the term of the lease, that is,
  - The lessee has the ability to obtain substantially all economic benefit from the use of the asset
  - The lessee has decision-making authority over the use of the asset
    (ASC 842-10-15-9, 15-10, 15-20, and 15-17)

Economic benefit from the use of the asset. A portion of an asset is an identified asset if it is physically distinct. Examples include a floor of a building or a pipeline that connects a single customer to a large pipeline. However, if the portion is not physically distinct, like a capacity portion of a fiber optic cable, it is not an identified asset unless the portion represents substantially all of the asset giving the customer substantially all of the economic benefit. (ASC 842-10-15-16) When evaluating "substantially all," the entity should consider the economic benefits of the customer's right to use the asset as defined in the contract: for example, whether the lease of a vehicle is confined to a geographic area or number of miles. (ASC 842-10-15-18)

Direct the use of the asset The Codification identifies two subsections where the customer has the right to direct the use of the identified asset throughout the period of the leases:

- The customer can direct how and for what purpose the asset is used, and
- The decisions about use are predetermined, for example, by the terms of the lease or the design of the asset, and at least one of the following exists:
  - The customer can operate the asset without the supplier having the right to change the operating instructions, or
  - The customer designed the asset in a way that predetermines its use.
    (ASC 842-10-15-20 and 15-21)

Identifying the Separate Lease Components Once an entity concludes that a contract contains a lease, the entity must identify the separate lease components. The right to use an underlying asset is considered a separate component from any other components if:

- The lessee can benefit from the right-of-use either on its own or together with other resources readily available to the lessee, and
- The right-of-use is neither:
  - ◦ Highly dependent nor
  - ◦ Highly interrelated with other rights to use underlying assets in the contract.

If each right to use significantly affects the other, they are considered highly dependent or highly interrelated. (ASC 842-10-15-28)

Where the lease involves land and other assets, even if the conditions in ASC 842-10-15-28 are met, the entity accounts for the right to use land as a separate lease component. The only exception is if the accounting effect would be insignificant. (ASC 842-10-15-29)

Components of a contract include only those items that transfer a good or service to the lessee. Thus, the following are not components of a contract:

- Administrative taxes to set up a contract or initiate the lease
- Reimbursement or payment of the lessor's costs
  (ASC 842-10-15-30)

Nonlease components are accounted for under the relevant guidance. Each separate lease component is accounted for separately from the nonlease components unless the lessee elects the accounting policy in ASC 842-10-15-37 or in ASC 842-10-15-42A. (ASC 842-10-15-31)

Lessee Unless the lessor elects the practical expedient in ASC 842-10-15-42A, the next step in the process is to allocate the consideration to the separate lease and nonlease components by:

- Determining the relative standalone price of the lease and nonlease components based on their observable standalone prices or, if not available, an estimate of the standalone prices
- Allocating the contract's consideration on a relative standalone price basis to the separate contract components
  (ASC 842-10-15-33)

As a practical expedient, a lessee may elect, by class of underlying asset, not to separate nonlease from lease components. Instead, the lessee would account, as a single lease component, for each separate lease component associated with that lease component. (ASC 842-10-15-37)

Lessor Unless electing the accounting policy in ASC 842-10-15-42A, the lessor should allocate the contract's consideration to the separate lease and nonlease components. Capitalized costs should be allocated to the related separate lease or nonlease components. (ASC 842-10-15-38) The lessor may elect to exclude from the contract consideration and from variable payments not included in the contract consideration all taxes that are imposed on and concurrent with a specific lease revenue. Excluded from the election are taxes assessed on a lessor's total gross receipts or on the lessor as owner of the underlying asset. Excluded from the consideration and from variable payments not included in the contract consideration are all leases within the scope of the election. (ASC 842-10-15-39A)

A lessor may, as a practical expedient, elect by class of underlying asset to not separate nonlease from lease components. Instead, the lessor should account for the lease and nonlease components as a single component if the nonlease components would otherwise be accounted for under ASC 606, and:

- The timing and scope of the lease and nonlease components are the same, and
- If accounted for separately, the lease component would be accounted for as an operating lease.
  (ASC 842-10-15-42A)

Those familiar with the revenue recognition standard will recognize the concepts discussed above.

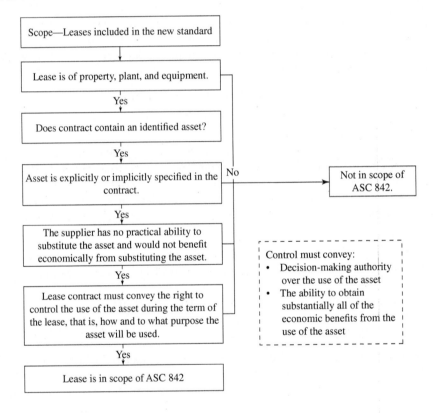

Lease Classification

Under ASC 840, the classification of a lease determines whether or not it is on the balance sheet. Because all leases are generally on the balance sheet, the classification of a lease determines how entities measure and present lease income and expenses and cash flows.

Lessees classify leases as either:

- Operating leases, or
- Financing leases.

Lessors retain the ASC 840 classifications:

- Sales-type
- Direct financing
- Operating leases

However, the leveraged lease classification is eliminated. Lessors should account for leveraged leases existing at the implementation date under the guidance in ASC 840.

For sales-type leases, in order to derecognize the asset and record revenue, collection of payments must be probable. Under ASC 840, the presence of upfront profit is the major difference between a sales-type lease and a direct financing lease. When upfront profit is present, the arrangement is a sales-type lease.

In a sales-type lease, the lessee needs to obtain control over the leased asset in order for the lessor to recognize upfront revenue and profit.

For a lease that otherwise would be a direct financing lease, collectibility uncertainties require that the lease be classified as an operating lease. In ASC 842, control is the key factor in lease classification. If the lease payments criterion has been met, at least in part, by the third-party residual value guarantee, the lease is classified as a direct financing lease.

Lessees should classify a lease as a finance lease, and lessors should classify a lease as a sales-type lease when the lease meets any of these criteria at lease commencement:

- The lease transfers ownership of the underlying asset to the lessee by the end of the lease term.
- The lease grants the lessee an option to purchase the underlying asset that the lessee is reasonably certain to exercise.
- The lease term is for the major part of the remaining economic life of the underlying asset. However, if the commencement date falls at or near the end of the economic life of the underlying asset, this criterion should not be used for purposes of classifying the lease.
- The present value of the sum of the lease payments and any residual value guaranteed by the lessee that is not already reflected in the lease payments in accordance with paragraph 842-10-30-5(f) equals or exceeds substantially all of the fair value of the underlying asset reduced by any related investment tax credit retained by the lessor and expected to be realized by the lessor.
- The underlying asset is of such a specialized nature that it is expected to have no alternative use to the lessor at the end of the lease term.
(ASC 842-10-25-2)

If none of the above criteria applies, a lessee classifies the lease as an operating lease and the lessor classifies the lease as a direct financing lease or an operating lease. The lessor classifies the lease as an operating lease unless both of the following criteria are met, in which case the lessor classifies the lease as a direct financing lease:

- The present value of the sum of the lease payments and any residual value guaranteed by the lessee that is not already reflected in the lease payments in accordance with paragraph 842-10-30-5(f) and/or any other third party unrelated to the lessor equals or exceeds substantially all of the fair value reduced by any related investment tax credit retained by the lessor and expected to be realized by the lessor of the underlying asset, and

- It is probable that the lessor will collect the lease payments plus any amount necessary to satisfy a residual value guarantee.
  (ASC 842-10-25-3)

The FASB clarified that for lessors who are not manufacturers or dealers, the fair value of the underlying asset at the commencement of the lease is its cost. The costs should reflect volume or trade discounts. However, if there is a significant amount of time between acquisition of the asset and commencement of the lease, the lessor should apply fair value. (ASC 842-30-55-17A)

Reassessment Lessees must reassess the lease term if a triggering event occurs that:

- Is under the lessee's control, or
- An option is exercised/not exercised as planned.

Any necessary reassessment should be made as of the date the reassessment is required. (ASC 842-10-25-1)

Modifications If the modification grants the lessee an additional right-of-use priced at market, a separate lease results. That lease should be classified at the lease modification date. (ASC 842-10-25-8) If the modification does not result in a separate lease, the entity should reassess the classification of the lease as of the effective date of the modification. (ASC 842-10-25-9)

Subsequent Measurement If a lessor changes its assessment regarding the possibility of exercising an option to extend a lease or actually exercises an option to terminate, the lessor should account for the exercise of that option as a lease modification. (ASC 842-10-35-3)

A lessee is required to remeasure the lease payment if any of the following occur:

a. The lease is modified.
b. A contingency affecting variable lease payments is resolved so that those payments meet the definition of lease payments. A change in a reference index or a rate used to calculate variable lease payments is not considered a resolution of a contingency.
c. A change in:
   - Lease term,
   - Assessment of whether a lessee is reasonably certain to exercise an option to purchase an underlying asset, or
   - Amounts probable of being owned by the lessee under residual value guarantees.
     (ASC 842-10-35-4)

If one of the events listed above under (a) or (c) occur or when a change unrelated to a reference index or rate under (b) above is resolved, variable lease payments dependent on an index or rate must be remeasured using the index or rate current as of the date the measurement is required. (ASC 842-10-35-5)

Sale-Leaseback Accounting ASC 842 brings sale-leaseback transactions onto the balance sheet by requiring seller-lessees to recognize a right-of-use asset and a lease liability for the leaseback.

A failed sale for the seller-lessee is not accounted for as a failed purchase by the buyer-lessor. ASC 842 requires buyer-lessors to evaluate whether they have purchased the underlying asset based on the transfer of control guidance in the new revenue recognition standard. The buyer-lessor must also account for a failed purchase as a financing arrangement.

A sale and leaseback transaction qualifies as a sale only if:

- It meets the sale guidance in the ASC 606,
- The leaseback is not a finance lease or a sales-type lease, and
- If there is a repurchase option:
  - The repurchase price is at the asset's fair value at the time of exercise, and
  - Alternative assets that are substantially the same as the transferred asset are readily available in the marketplace.
  (ASC 842-40-25-1 through 25-3)

If the transaction does not meet the qualifications for sale under the revenue recognition guidance, the seller-lessee accounts for it as a financing transaction. Purchase options preclude sale accounting unless:

- The strike price of the repurchase option is the fair value of the asset at the option exercise date, *and*
- Assets that are substantially the same as the underlying asset are readily available in the marketplace.

If the sale-leaseback transaction qualifies as a sale of the underlying asset, the seller-lessee recognizes the entire gain from the sale at the time of sale as opposed to recognition over the leaseback terms. The gain is the difference between the selling price and the carrying value of the amount of the underlying asset. The sale-leaseback guidance is the same for all assets, including real estate.

Build-to-Suit Lease Guidance While ASC 840's guidance is built on a risks and rewards model, the guidance in ASC 842 is built on control and ownership during the construction period, is based on the control model. ASC 842 states that a lessee is the owner for accounting purposes of an asset under construction if it controls the asset before the lease commencement date.

PRACTICE ALERT

While the SEC comments on reports from SEC filers, the staff comments can point to problems relevant to all financial statements. The SEC staff comments on leases have focused on disclosures and presentation, including:

- Completeness
- Transition
- Qualitative information, including significant judgments
- A description of terms or conditions
- The level of aggregation
- Discount rates and the significant judgments and assumptions used to determine the rates
- Presentation of lease-related cash flows

The staff has also commented on accounting for certain arrangements and their terms and conditions.

PRESENTATION AND DISCLOSURE REQUIREMENTS

Presentation—Using the Display Approach

To allow preparers to leverage existing standards and processes, the FASB designed the display approach for recognizing operating leases on the balance sheet. Using this approach, preparers can maintain their existing records and systems, use the information to create a period-end journal entry that conforms to the guidance in ASC 842, and then reverse the entry at the start of the next period. The following exhibit illustrates the journal entries:

Sample journal entries under the display approach for 12/31/X2:
Right-of-use asset
Accrued rent
Lease liability—current
Lease liability—long-term
Prepaid rent
Deferred initial direct costs—current
Deferred initial direct costs—long-term
Sample journal entries under the display approach for 1/1/X3:
Lease liability—current
Lease liability—long-term prepaid rent
Deferred initial direct costs—current
Deferred initial direct costs—long-term
Right-of-use asset
Accrued rent

Disclosures

The standard significantly expands qualitative and quantitative disclosures. The lessor's disclosures include:

- Qualitative information:
  - Information about the nature of variable payment arrangements and termination, renewal, or purchase options
  - Information about how the lessor manages residual asset risk, including about residual value guarantees and other means of limiting that risk
  - Significant accounting judgments and estimates
- Quantitative information:
  - Maturity analysis of lease receivables for sales-type and direct financing leases and of lease payments for operating leases
- Table of lease income, showing:
  - Selling profit or loss recognized at lease commencement and interest income for sales-type and direct financing leases
  - Operating lease income
  - Variable lease income

The lessee's disclosures include:

- Qualitative:
  - Nature of lease, such as terms and conditions of variable lease payments, extension and termination options, purchase options, and residual value guarantees
- Quantitative:
  - Operating lease costs
  - Amortization of finance lease right-of-use assets, and interest on finance lease liabilities
  - Variable lease cost
  - Weighted-average discount rate
  - Maturity analysis of lease liabilities
- Significant judgments
  - Such as whether a contract contains a lease, standalone price for lease and nonlease components, and the discount rate for the entities' leases
  - Information about the nature of leases

For detailed presentation and disclosure requirements, see the checklist at www.wiley.com/go/FSDM2021.

PRESENTATION AND DISCLOSURE EXAMPLES

Example 56.1: Adoption of New Accounting Standard ASU 2016-02

On March 1, 2019, ASU 2016-02, *Leases (Topic 842)* was adopted by the Company using the modified retrospective approach. The Company adopted the package of practical expedients that allows companies to not reassess historical conclusions related to contracts that contain leases, existing lease classification, and initial direct costs. It did not adopt the hindsight practical expedient. Adoption of the new standard resulted in the recording of additional lease assets and lease liabilities, which totaled $2,227 and $2,243, respectively, on March 1, 2019. The standard did not materially affect the Company's consolidated financial position, results of operations, or cash flows, and did not have an impact on the Company's debt-covenant compliance. The new guidance was applied to all operating and capital leases at the date of initial application. Leases historically referred to as capital leases are now referred to as finance leases under the new guidance.

Example 56.2: Adoption of New Accounting Standard ASU 2016-02, Including Effect

In February 2016, in an effort to increase transparency and comparability among organizations, the FASB issued ASU 2016-02, *Leases (Topic 842)*, which requires lessees to recognize a right-of-use asset and lease liability for all leases with a term of more than 12 months. We adopted the requirements of ASU 2016-02 and all related amendments on May 1, 2019, utilizing an optional transition method that allows for a cumulative-effect adjustment in the period of adoption with no restatement of prior periods. This transition method also does not require new lease disclosures for periods prior to the effective date. We elected certain practical expedients available under the guidance, including a package of practical expedients that allowed us to not reassess prior conclusions related to existing contracts containing leases, lease classification, and initial direct costs.

Adoption of ASU 2016-02 on May 1, 2019, resulted in the recognition of operating lease right-of-use assets and lease liabilities of $159,200 and $166,600, respectively, in our Consolidated Balance Sheet. The difference between the additional lease assets and lease liabilities was primarily due to an existing deferred rent balance that was reclassified to the operating lease liability. The new standard did not materially impact our Statement of Consolidated Income or Statement of Consolidated Cash Flows. The additional disclosures required are presented in Note X: Leases.

Example 56.3: Adoption of New Accounting Standards ASU 2016-02 and 2018-11

In February 2016, the FASB issued ASU 2016-02, *Leases (Topic 842)*. This update seeks to increase the transparency and comparability among entities by requiring public entities to recognize lease assets and lease liabilities on the balance sheet and disclose key information about leasing arrangements. To satisfy the standard's objective, a lessee will recognize a right-of-use asset representing its right to use the underlying asset for the lease term and a lease liability for the obligation to make lease payments. Both the right-of-use asset and lease liability will initially be measured at the present value of the lease payments, with subsequent measurement dependent on the classification of the lease as either a finance or an operating lease. For leases with a term of 12 months or less, a lessee is permitted to make an accounting policy election by class of underlying asset not to recognize lease assets and lease liabilities. If a lessee makes this election, it should recognize lease expense for such leases generally on a straight-line basis over the lease term.

In July 2018, the FASB issued ASU 2018-10, *Codification Improvements to Topic 842, Leases*, which contains several FASB Codification improvements for ASC Topic 842, including several implementation issues and ASU 2018-11, *Leases (Topic 842): Targeted Improvements*, which provides entities with an additional transition method for implementing ASC Topic 842. Entities have the option to apply the new standard at the adoption date, recognizing a cumulative-effect adjustment to the opening balance of retained earnings along with the modified retrospective approach previously identified, both of which include a number of practical expedients that companies may elect to apply. Under the cumulative-effect adjustment, comparative periods would not be restated. Under the modified retrospective approach, leases are recognized and measured under the noted guidance at the beginning of the earliest period presented. The new standard is effective for public companies for annual periods beginning after December 15, 2018, and interim periods within those years, with early adoption permitted. We adopted this guidance as of May 1, 2019, using the modified retrospective approach and elected the cumulative-effect adjustment practical expedient. As a result of the transition method selected, the Company did not restate previously reported comparable periods. Please refer to Note X for additional information regarding the Company's adoption of ASC 842.

Example 56.4: Accounting for a Finance Lease

Property under a finance lease is stated at the present value of minimum lease payments.

Example 56.5: Accounting Policy—Leases, Including Practical Expedients

The Company is a lessee in situations where we lease property and equipment, most commonly land or buildings, from a lessor. The Company is a lessor in situations where the Company owns land or buildings and leases a portion or all of the property or equipment to a tenant. In both situations, leases are reported in accordance with ASC 842, *Leases*. As a lessee, the Company recognizes a right-of-use asset representing its right to use the underlying asset for the lease term and a lease liability for the obligation to make lease payments. Both the right-of-use asset and lease liability are initially measured at the present value of the lease payments, with subsequent measurement dependent on the classification of the lease as either a finance or an operating lease. For leases with a term of 12 months or less, we have elected to not recognize lease assets and lease liabilities and will recognize lease expense on a straight-line basis over the lease term. The Company records the operating lease liability in accrued expenses and other long-term liabilities and records the finance lease liability within current maturities of long-term debt and finance lease obligations on the consolidated balance sheets. We have elected to adopt the package of practical expedients, as well as the land easement practical expedient. All lessor related activity is considered immaterial to the consolidated financial statements.

The leases initially recorded under ASC 842 were recognized, at the time of adoption, at an amount equal to the present value of the lease payments using the incremental borrowing rate of debt based upon the remaining term of the lease. New leases are recognized at the present value of the lease payments using the implicit rate in the lease agreement when it is readily determinable. In the case that the implicit rate is not readily determinable, the Company uses the incremental borrowing rate of debt based on the term of the lease.

Several leases have variable payment components of the lease, such as commission-based payments or payments for property taxes and insurance. For these leases the Company has not included those variable payments in the calculation of the lease liability, as the payments are not in-substance fixed and do not depend on an index or rate. These variable payments will be expensed as incurred. The Company also has options to renew or extend the current lease arrangement on many of our leases. In these situations, if it was reasonably certain the lease would be extended, we have included those extensions within the remaining lease payments at the time of measurement.

Example 56.6: Schedule of Lease Right-of-Use Assets

Lease right-of-use assets outstanding as of April 30, 20X1, consisted of the following (in thousands):

	Classification	*April 30, 20X1*
Operating lease right-of-use assets	Other assets	$ 21,143
Finance lease right-of-use assets	Property and equipment	$ 14,583

Example 56.7: Weighted-Average Remaining Lease Terms and Discount Rated and Supplementary Cash Flow Information

Weighted-average remaining lease terms, weighted-average discount rates, and supplementary cash flow information for outstanding leases were as follows:

	April 30, 20X1
Weighted-average remaining lease-term—finance lease	10.9
Weighted-average remaining lease-term—operating lease	20.4
Weighted-average discount rate—finance lease	5.34%
Weighted-average discount rate—operating lease	4.25%
Right-of-use assets obtained in exchange for new finance lease liabilities (in thousands)	$ 1,520
Right-of-use assets obtained in exchange for new operating lease liabilities (in thousands)	$ 2,840

Example 56.8: Schedule of Future Minimum Lease Payments

Future minimum payments under the finance leases and operating leases with initial or remaining terms of one year or more consisted of the following on April 30, 20X1 and April 30, 20X0:

(Amounts in Thousands)

Years ended April 30 20X1	Finance leases	Operating leases
20X2	$ 3,118	$ 1,829
20X3	3,110	1,814
20X4	3,116	1,717
20X5	2,565	1,683
20X6	1,167	1,686
Thereafter	10,764	25,335
Total minimum lease payments	23,840	34,064
Less amount representing interest	7,094	12,468
Present value of net minimum lease payments	$ 16,746	$ 21,596

Years ended April 30 20X0	Capital leases	Operating leases
20X1	$ 3,103	$ 1,703
20X2	3,109	1,547
20X3	3,096	1,354
20X4	3,098	1,228
20X5	2,548	1,066
Thereafter	9,215	10,438
Total minimum lease payments	24,169	$ 17,336
Less amount representing interest	7,689	
Present value of net minimum lease payments	$ 16,480	

Example 56.9: Sale and Leaseback Transaction

Effective during the third quarter of fiscal year 20X1, the Company, and the City of Indianapolis, Indiana ("Indianapolis") entered into an agreement in which Indianapolis agreed to issue up to $51.4 million of taxable industrial development revenue bonds for the purpose of acquiring, constructing, improving, purchasing, equipping, and installing a warehouse and distribution facility, which is to be developed and used by the Company. As title transfers to Indianapolis throughout development and the Company subsequently leases the related asset from Indianapolis, we have accounted for the transaction under the sale and leaseback guidance included in ASC 842-40. We have a purchase option included in the lease agreement for below the fair value of the asset, which prevents the transfer of the assets to Joplin from being recognized as a sale. Accordingly, we have not recognized any gain or loss related to the transfer. Furthermore, we have not derecognized the transferred assets and continue to recognize them in property and equipment on the consolidated balance sheets. The Company has the right and intends to set off any obligations to make payments under the lease with proceeds due from industrial revenue bonds. As of April 30, 20X1, we have $5,505 recognized as construction in process in property and equipment on the consolidated balance sheets related to this agreement.

Example 56.10: Accounting Policy—Leases

We determine whether an arrangement is a lease at inception. This determination generally depends on whether the arrangement conveys the right to control the use of an identified fixed asset explicitly or implicitly for a period of time in exchange for consideration. Control of an underlying asset is conveyed if we obtain the rights to direct the use of, and to obtain substantially all of the economic benefit from, the use of the underlying asset. Some of our leases include both lease and nonlease components, which are accounted for as a single lease component as we have elected the practical expedient in ASU 842-10-15-37. Some of our operating lease agreements include variable lease costs, including taxes, and common area maintenance or increases in rental costs related to inflation. Such variable payments, other than those dependent upon a market index or rate, are expensed when the obligation for those payments is incurred. Lease expense is recorded in operating expenses in the Consolidated Statements of Operations and Comprehensive (Loss) Income. The Company's lease agreements do not contain any material residual value guarantees or material restrictive covenants. Leases with an initial term of 12 months or less that do not include an option to purchase the underlying asset that the Company is reasonably certain to exercise are considered short-term leases and are not recorded on the balance sheet. The Company had no short-term leases during the year ended December 31, 20X1.

Right-of-use assets and lease liabilities are recognized at each lease's commencement date based on the present value of its lease payments over its respective lease term. When a borrowing rate is not explicitly available for a lease, our incremental borrowing rate is used based on information available at the lease's commencement date to determine the present value of its lease payments. Operating lease payments are recognized on a straight-line basis over the lease term.

We have operating leases for office equipment as well as offices, warehouses, and other facilities used for our operations. We also have finance leases composed primarily of computer hardware and machinery and equipment. Our leases have remaining lease terms of less than one year to seven years, some of which include renewal options. We consider these renewal options in determining the lease term used to establish our right-of-use assets and lease liabilities when it is determined that it is reasonably certain that the renewal option will be exercised.

Example 56.11: Sale and Leaseback Transaction

On September 30, 20X1, the Company, through its subsidiary Voice German Holdings, executed a sale leaseback transaction, selling its real property in Munich, Germany to Bendigo, Ltd. ("the Purchaser") for €10,920,000. Net proceeds received from the transaction were approximately $9,500,000 after transactional costs of $270,000 and repayment of the outstanding mortgage, which was $2,104,000 on September 30, 20X1. The transaction qualified for sale leaseback accounting in accordance with ASC 842, *Leases*. Concurrently with the sale, the Company entered into an operating lease arrangement ("lease") with the Purchaser for a small portion of the real property to continue to operate the combined Blake-Lawson sales office in Australia, with an initial lease term of five years. The Company recognized a gain related to the execution of the sale transaction of $4,057,000 for the year ended February 29, 20X2, which is recorded in Other income (expense) on the Consolidated Statements of Operations and Comprehensive (Loss) Income.

Example 56.12: Components of Lease Costs

The components of lease cost for the year ended February 29, 20X2, were as follows:

(Amounts in thousands)	*Year Ended February 29, 20X2*
Operating lease cost (a) (c)	$ 880
Finance lease cost:	
Amortization of right-of-use assets (a)	684
Interest on lease liabilities (b)	47
Total finance lease cost	$ 731

(a) *Recorded within Selling, General and Administrative; Engineering and Technical Support; and Cost of Sales on the Consolidated Statements of Operations and Comprehensive (Loss) Income.*
(b) *Recorded within Interest and Bank Charges on the Consolidated Statements of Operations and Comprehensive (Loss) Income.*
(c) *Includes immaterial amounts related to variable rent expense.*

Example 56.13: Supplemental Cash Flow Information

Supplemental cash flow information related to leases is as follows:

(Amounts in thousands)	*Year Ended February 29, 20X2*
Noncash investing and financing activities:	
Right-of-use assets obtained in exchange for operating lease obligations	$ 1,312
Property, plant, and equipment obtained in exchange for finance lease obligations	1,024
Upon the adoption of ASC 842:	
Right-of-use assets recorded in exchange for operating lease obligations	$ 2,227
Cash paid for amounts included in the measurement of lease liabilities:	
Operating cash flows from operating leases	$ 841
Operating cash flows from finance leases	47
Finance cash flows from finance leases	646

Example 56.14: Supplemental Balance Sheet Information Related to Leases

	February 29, 20X2
Operating Leases	
Operating lease, right-of-use assets	$ 3,143
Total operating lease right-of-use assets	$ 3,143
Accrued expenses and other current liabilities	$ 784
Operating lease liabilities, less current portion	2,391
Total operating lease liabilities	$ 3,175

Finance Leases

Property, plant, and equipment, gross	$ 2,503
Accumulated depreciation	(1,209)
Total finance lease right-of-use assets	$ 1,294
Accrued expenses and other current liabilities	$ 613
Finance lease liabilities, less current portion	720
Total finance lease liabilities	$ 1,333
Weighted-Average Remaining Lease Term	
Operating leases	4.4 years
Finance leases	3.9 years
Weighted-Average Discount Rate	
Operating leases	5.98%
Finance leases	3.87%

At February 29, 20X2, maturities of lease liabilities for each of the succeeding years were as follows:

	Operating Leases	*Finance Leases*
20X3	$ 948	$ 640
20X4	907	428
20X5	641	228
20X6	480	80
20X7	359	—
Thereafter	268	—
Total lease payments	3,603	1,376
Less imputed interest	428	43
Total	$ 3,175	$ 1,333

As of February 29, 20X2, the Company has not entered into any lease agreements that have not yet commenced.

At February 28, 20X1, the Company was obligated under noncancellable operating leases for equipment and warehouse facilities related to continuing operations for minimum annual rental payments for each of the succeeding fiscal years:

	Operating Leases
20X2	$ 946
20X3	604
20X4	391
20X5	154
20X6	10
Thereafter	—
Total minimum lease payments	$ 2,105

Rental expense for the above-mentioned operating lease agreements and other rental agreements on a month-to-month basis was $883 and $1,163 for the years ended February 28, 20X1 and February 28, 20X0, respectively.

The Company owns and occupies buildings as part of its operations. Certain space within these buildings may, from time to time, be leased to third parties from which the Company earns rental income as lessor. This leased space is recorded within Property, Plant and Equipment and was not material to the Company's Consolidated Balance Sheet at February 29, 20X2. Rental income earned by the Company for the years ended February 29, 20X2, February 28, 20X1, and February 28, 20X0, was $663, $517, and $553, respectively, which is recorded within Other Income (expense).

Example 56.15: Maturities of Long-Term Debt, Including Finance Leases

Listed below are the aggregate maturities of long-term debt, including finance lease obligations, for the five years commencing May 1, 20X0 and thereafter:

Years ended April 30	Finance Leases	Senior Notes	Total
20X1	$ 2,244	$ 569,000	$ 571,244
20X2	2,354	—	2,354
20X3	2,484	20,000	22,484
20X4	2,060	32,000	34,060
20X5	734	32,000	32,734
Thereafter	6,870	616,000	622,870
	$ 16,746	$ 1,269,000	$ 1,285,746

57 ASC 845 NONMONETARY TRANSACTIONS

AUTHORITATIVE LITERATURE

ASC 845, *Nonmonetary Transactions*, addresses those transactions in which no money changes hands. These transactions are most commonly associated with exchanges of fixed assets, but can also involve other items, such as inventory, liabilities, and ownership interests. They can also involve one-way, or nonreciprocal, transfers.

This Chapter sets forth the basic structure and concepts of nonmonetary transactions, including the concept of commercial substance, rules regarding similar and dissimilar exchanges, involuntary conversions, and how to handle exchanges that include a certain amount of monetary consideration.

Subtopics

ASC 845, *Nonmonetary Transactions*, has only one Subtopic:

- ASC 845-10, *Overall*, which includes five Subsections:
  - General
  - Purchases and sales of inventory with the same counterparty
  - Barter transactions
  - Exchanges involving monetary consideration
    (ASC 845-10-05-1)

Scope and Scope Exceptions

Several variants of noncash transactions are governed by ASC 845. ASC 845-10-15-4 lists scope exceptions. The following types of transactions are *not* treated as nonmonetary transactions:

1. A business combination accounted for by an entity according to the provisions of ASC 805 or a combination accounted for by a not-for-profit entity according to the provisions of ASC 958-805.
2. A transfer of nonmonetary assets solely between entities or persons under common control, such as between a parent and its subsidiaries or between two subsidiaries of the same parent, or between a corporate joint venture and its owners.
3. Acquisition of goods or services on issuance of the capital stock of an entity under ASC 718-10.
4. Stock issued or received in stock dividends and stock splits.
5. A pooling of assets in a joint undertaking intended to find, develop, or produce oil or gas from a particular property or group of properties.
6. The exchange of a part of an operating interest owned for a part of an operating interest owned by another party that is subject to ASC 932-360-55-6.
7. The transfer of a financial asset within the scope of ASC 860-10-15.
8. Involuntary conversions specified in ASC 610-30-15-2.
9. The transfer of goods or services in a contract with a customer within the scope of ASC 606 in exchange for noncash consideration.
10. The transfer of a nonfinancial asset within the scope of ASC 610-20 in exchange for noncash consideration. Noncash consideration promised in exchange for a nonfinancial asset that is a noncontrolling ownership interest is within the scope of ASC 845.
(ASC 845-10-15-4)

The guidance in the Purchases and Sales of Inventory with the Same Counterparty Subsections does not apply to inventory purchase and sales arrangements that are accounted for as derivatives under Topic 815, or involve exchanges of software or exchanges of real estate. (ASC 845-10-15-8)

The guidance in the Exchanges Involving Monetary Consideration Subsections does not apply to transfers between a joint venture and its owners. (ASC 845-10-15-14)

The guidance in the Exchanges of a Nonfinancial Asset for a Noncontrolling Ownership Interest Subsections does not apply to the following types of transfers:

- Transfers between a joint venture and its owners
- Capital contributions of real estate in return for an unconsolidated real estate investment (for guidance, see Subtopic 970-323)
- A deconsolidation of a subsidiary that is a business or nonprofit activity that is within the scope of Subtopic 810-10 (see paragraph 810-10-40-3A)
- A derecognition of a group of assets that constitutes a business or nonprofit activity that is within the scope of Subtopic 810-10 (see paragraph 810-10-40-3A)
(ASC 845-10-15-21)

Types of Nonmonetary Transactions

There are three types of nonmonetary transactions identified in ASC 845:

1. Nonreciprocal transfers with owners. Examples include dividends-in-kind, nonmonetary assets exchanged for common stock, split-ups, and spin-offs.

2. Nonreciprocal transfers with nonowners. Examples include charitable donations of property either made or received by the reporting entity and contributions of land by a state or local government to a private enterprise for the purpose of construction of a specified structure.
3. Nonmonetary exchanges. Examples include exchanges of inventory for productive assets, exchanges of inventory for similar products, and exchanges of productive assets. (ASC 845-10-05-3)

General Rule

The primary accounting issue in nonmonetary transactions is the determination of the amount to assign to the nonmonetary assets or services transferred to or from the reporting entity.

The general rule is to:

- Value the transaction at the fair value of the asset *given up*, unless the fair value of the asset *received* is more clearly evident, and
- Recognize gain or loss on the difference between the fair value and carrying value of the asset.

ASC 820 provides the guidance for fair value and provides that when one of the parties to a nonmonetary transaction could have elected to receive cash in lieu of the nonmonetary asset, the amount of cash that would have been received may be the best evidence of the fair value of the nonmonetary assets exchanged. The fair value of the asset surrendered should be used to value the exchange unless the fair value of the asset received is more clearly evident of the fair value. (ASC 845-10-30-1)

Modification of the General Rule

ASC 845-10-30-3 states that under certain circumstances a nonmonetary exchange should be measured based on the recorded amount (after reduction for any impairment) of the nonmonetary asset relinquished, and not on the fair values of the exchanged assets, if any of the following conditions apply:

1. The fair value of neither the asset received nor the asset relinquished is determinable within reasonable limits.
2. The transaction is an exchange of a product or property held for sale in the ordinary course of business for a product or property to be sold in the same line of business to facilitate sales to customers other than the parties to the exchange.
3. The transaction lacks commercial substance.

Note: ASC 845 states that a transfer of a nonmonetary asset will not qualify as an exchange if the transferor has substantial continuing involvement in the transferred assets that result in the transferee not obtaining the usual risks and rewards associated with ownership of the transferred assets.

Commercial Substance

As explained in ASC 845-10-30-4, a nonmonetary exchange is subjected to a test to determine whether or not it has "commercial substance." An exchange has commercial substance if cash flows change as a result of the exchange. If determined to have commercial substance, the exchange is recorded at the fair value of the transferred asset. If the transaction is determined not to have commercial substance, the exchange is recognized using the recorded amount of the exchanged asset or assets, reduced for any applicable impairment of value.

Entities should recognize losses incurred on all exchanges whether or not they have commercial substance. This is so that assets are not overstated. If an exchange has commercial substance, any gain should be recognized immediately. If an exchange has no commercial substance, the entity recognizes the gain through lower depreciation expense or when it sells the asset. However, if cash, or "boot," is received, the entity may recognize a portion of the gain even if there is no commercial substance.

Nonreciprocal Transfers

The valuation of most nonreciprocal transfers is based upon the fair value of the nonmonetary asset (or service) given up, unless the fair value of the nonmonetary asset received is more clearly evident. This will result in recognition of gain or loss on the difference between the fair value assigned to the transaction and the carrying value of the asset surrendered.

The valuation of nonmonetary assets distributed to owners of the reporting entity in a spin-off or other form of reorganization or liquidation is based on the recorded amounts, again, after first recognizing any warranted reduction for impairment. Other nonreciprocal transfers to owners are accounted for at fair value if:

- The fair value of the assets distributed is objectively measurable, and
- That fair value would be clearly realized by the distributing reporting entity in an outright sale at or near the time of distribution to the owners.

Nonmonetary Exchanges That Include Monetary Consideration (Boot)

A single exception to the nonrecognition rule for an exchange without commercial substance occurs when the exchange involves both a monetary and nonmonetary asset being exchanged for a nonmonetary asset. The monetary portion of the exchange is termed *boot*. When boot is at least 25% of the fair value of the exchange, the exchange is considered a monetary transaction. In that case, both parties record the exchange at fair value. When boot received is less than 25%, only the boot portion of the earnings process is considered to have culminated. The portion of the gain applicable to the boot is considered realized and is recognized in the determination of net income in the period of the exchange by the receiver of the boot. The payor does not record a gain. (ASC 845-10-25-6) The payor records the asset received at the monetary consideration received plus the recorded amount of the nonmonetary asset surrendered. Any loss in the exchange is recorded. (ASC 845-10-30-6)

Inventory Purchases and Sales with the Same Counterparty

Some enterprises sell inventory to another party from whom they also acquire inventory in the same line of business. These transactions may be part of a single or separate arrangements and the inventory purchased or sold may be raw materials, work-in-process, or finished goods. These arrangements require careful analysis to determine if they are to be accounted for as a single exchange transaction under ASC 845, *Nonmonetary Transactions*, and whether they are to be recognized at fair value or at the carrying value of the inventory transferred.[1]

---

[1] This guidance does not apply to arrangements accounted for as derivatives under ASC 815, or to exchanges of software or real estate.

ASC 845-10-15-6 states that inventory purchases and sales with the same counterparty should be treated as a single transaction when:

1. An inventory transaction is legally contingent upon the occurrence of another inventory transaction with the same counterparty, *or*
2. Two or more inventory purchase and sale transactions involving the same counterparties are entered into in contemplation of one another and are combined.

Measurement of the Exchange When management has determined that multiple transactions between the same counterparties within the same line of business are to be treated as a single exchange transaction, the measurement of the transaction depends on the type of inventory items exchanged.

Exchange of Product or Property Held for Sale for Productive Assets

An exchange of goods held for sale in the ordinary course of business for property and equipment to be used in the production process, even if they pertain to the same line of business, is recorded at fair value.

Barter Transactions

Through third-party barter exchanges, many commercial enterprises exchange their goods and services to obtain barter credits that can be used in lieu of cash to obtain goods and services provided by other members of the barter exchange.

If it subsequently becomes apparent that either of the following conditions exists, the reporting entity should recognize an impairment loss on the barter credits:

1. The carrying value of any remaining barter credits exceeds their fair value, or
2. It is probable that the entity will not use all of the remaining barter credits.
   (ASC 845-10-30-19)

If an exchange involves transfer or assumption of an operating lease for barter credits, impairment of the lease is to be measured as the amount of remaining lease costs (the discounted future rental payments plus the carrying amount of unamortized leasehold improvements) in excess of the fair value of the discounted amount of the probable future sublease rentals for the remaining lease term. (ASC 845-10-30-20)

PRACTICE ALERT

While SEC comments pertain to SEC filings, SEC staff comments can point to areas where all filers should exercise caution and perhaps document their decisions. In the area of nonmonetary transactions, the SEC has asked filers to:

- Explain how the company's purchases and sales on inventory with the same counterparty falls into one of the exceptions in ASC 845-10-30-3 to measurement at fair value
- Discuss why the company believes that its licensed content does not meet the definition of a productive asset and is more akin to inventory
- Clarify why record licenses are not recorded at historical cost in transactions where the company engages a noncash exchange of a license for the license of a customer
- Explain how you determined that the noncash exchange of a license for services should be accounted for under ASC 606 rather than ASC 845

PRESENTATION AND DISCLOSURE REQUIREMENTS

Presentation

The only guidance on presentation in ASC 845 is a note that the classification of inventory for purposes of the Purchases and Sales of Inventory with the Same Counterparty subsections is the same classification (new materials, WIP, and finished goods) that the entity uses for external reporting purposes. (ASC 845-10-45-1)

Disclosures

Reporting entities must disclose:

- The nature of the transaction,
- The basis of accounting for the assets transferred,
- Any gain or loss recognized,
- The amount of revenue and costs or gains and losses associated with inventory exchanges recognized at fair value.
  (ASC 845-10-50-1 and 50-3)

PRESENTATION AND DISCLOSURE EXAMPLES

Example 57.1: Accounting Policy for Noncash Exchanges

We apply ASC 845, *Accounting for Nonmonetary Transactions*, to account for products and services sold through noncash transactions based on the fair values of the products and services involved, where such values can be determined. Noncash exchanges would require revenue to be recognized at recorded cost or carrying value of the assets or services sold if any of the following conditions apply:

a. The fair value of the asset or service involved is not determinable.
b. The transaction is an exchange of a product or property held for sale in the ordinary course of business for a product or property to be sold in the same line of business to facilitate sales to customers other than the parties to the exchange.
c. The transaction lacks commercial substance.

We recognize revenue for noncash transactions at recorded cost or carrying value of the assets or services sold.

Example 57.2: Accounting Policy for Barter Transactions Related to Advertising

Barter transactions (advertising provided in exchange for goods and services) are reported at the estimated fair value of the products or services received. Revenue from barter transactions is recognized when advertisements are broadcast. Merchandise or services received are charged to expense when received or utilized. If merchandise or services are received prior to the broadcast of the advertising, a liability is recorded. If advertising is broadcast before the receipt of the goods or services, a receivable is recorded. Total revenues recognized related to barter transactions were $2.71 million, $3.1 million, and $2.8 million for each of the years ended December 31, 20X3, 20X2, and 20X1, respectively.

58 ASC 848 REFERENCE RATE REFORM

AUTHORITATIVE LITERATURE

Technical Alert

In March 2020, the FASB issued ASU 2020-04, *Reference Rate Reform (Topic 848): Facilitation of the Effects of Reference Rate Reform on Financial Reporting.* The ASU was issued in response to concerns about the structural risks of interbank-offered rates and the risks of cessation of LIBOR and is designed to provide relief from the potential accounting burden when transitioning from reference rates, like LIBOR, that may be discontinued. FASB stakeholders raised concerns about contract modifications, hedge accounting, and the volume of contracts, such as debt agreements, leases, and derivatives.

If certain criteria are met, the ASU's changes offer optional expedients and exceptions for applying the Codification to the contract, hedging relationships, and other matters. ASC 848 is unique in that the guidance sunsets in 2022. When certain benchmark rates are discontinued, contracts will be modified. The optional expedients and exceptions can be applied to contract modifications and hedging relationships entered into or evaluations made until December 31, 2022.

Effective Dates The amendments are effective as of March 12, 2020 through December 31, 2022. Once elected for a Topic or an industry Subtopic, the amendments must be applied prospectively for all eligible contract modifications for that Topic or industry Subtopics.

Contract modifications. An entity may elect to apply the guidance to contract modifications as of any date from the beginning of the interim period that includes or is subsequent to March 12, 2020, or it may apply the guidance prospectively from a date within an interim period that includes or is subsequent to March 12, 2020, up to the date when the financial statements are available to be issued.

Hedge accounting. The guidance related to hedges may be applied to eligible hedging relationships that either existed on, or were entered into after, the beginning of the interim period that includes March 12, 2020 (that is, January 1, 2020, for a calendar-year entity).

If an entity has not adopted the amendments in ASU 2017-12, *Derivatives and Hedging (Topic 815): Targeted Improvements to Accounting for Hedging Activities*, it is eligible to apply only certain of the optional expedients provided in ASC 848 for hedging relationships.

Sunset Provision

- The guidance in ASC 848 may not be applied to contract modifications made after December 31, 2022, or to new hedging relationships entered into after that date.
- In addition, the new guidance may not be applied to hedging relationships for periods after December 31, 2022, although hedging relationships existing at December 31, 2022, that apply the following expedients should retain those expedients through the end of the hedging relationship:
  - Expedient used to recognize in earnings the components excluded from the assessment of effectiveness in ASC 848-30-25-12
  - Expedient used to determine the rate to discount cash flows associated with the hedged item, as well as expedient used for any adjustment to the cash flows for the designated term or the partial term of the designated hedged item in a fair value hedge, in ASC 848-40-25-6
  - Expedient used to not periodically evaluate the conditions in ASC 815-20-25-104(d) and (g) when using the shortcut method for a fair value hedge in ASC 848-40-25-8

Subtopics

ASC 848 contains five Subtopics:

- ASC 848-10, *Overall*
- ASC 848-20, *Contract Modifications*, which provides optional expedients for contract modifications resulting from reference rate reform
- ASC 848-30, *Hedging—General*
- ASC 848-40, *Fair Value Hedges*
- ASC 848-59, *Cash Flow Hedges*
  (ASC 848-10-05-1)

ASC 848-10, *Overall*

Scope ASC 848 applies to all entities and, if elected, to contracts or other transactions that reference LIBOR or a reference rate that is expected to be discontinued as a result of reference rate reform. (ASC 848-10-15-2 and 15-3)

A reference rate is expected to be discontinued if any one of the following three conditions exists:

1. The reference rate administrator or its regulatory supervisor has announced its intention to discontinue the reference rate.
2. A significant number of market participants (or market participants representing a significant number of transactions) take the initiative to move away from the reference rate.
3. The method to calculate the reference rate is either fundamentally restructured or relies on another rate that is expected to be discontinued.
   (ASC 848-10-15-4)

Subsequent Measurement Entities have the option to use a one-time election to:

- Sell or transfer held-to-maturity (HTM) debt securities, or
- Both sell and transfer HTM to available-for-sale (AFS) or trading categories.

At the time of application of the election, the debt securities must:

- Reference a rate in the scope of ASC 848-10-15-3 above, and
- Be classified as HTM before January 1, 2020.

The election to sell and/or transfer HTM debt securities may be made at any time on or before December 31, 2022.
(ASC 848-10-35-1)

ASC 848-20, *Contract Modifications*

Scope and Scope Exceptions The guidance in ASC 848-20 applies only to a contract modification whose terms:

- Directly replace LIBOR or a reference rate that is expected to be discontinued as a result of reference rate reform
- Modify contract terms that change or have the potential to change the amount or timing of contractual cash flows, and is related to the replacement of LIBOR or another reference rate that is expected to be discontinued as a result of reference rate reforms
(ASC 848-20-15-2)

If a term is modified that changes or has the potential to change contractual cash flow, but is *unrelated* to reference rate reform, the guidance in ASC 848-20 does *not* apply. (ASC 848-20-15-3) An entity may adopt the guidance in this Subtopic even if contract modifications do not change the amount or timing of contractual cash flows, as long as they are made contemporaneously with modifications related to reference rate reform. (ASC 848-20-15-4)

The Codification offers examples of contract modifications that are considered either related or unrelated to reference rate reform.

- Examples of changes to terms that are related to the replacement of a reference rate:
  - Changes to the referenced interest rate index
  - Addition of or changes to a spread adjustment
  - Changes to the reset period, reset dates, day-count conventions, business-day conventions, payment dates, payment frequency, and repricing calculation
  - Changes to the strike price of an existing interest rate option
  - Addition of an interest rate floor or cap that is out of the money on the basis of the spot rate at the time of the amendment of the contract
  - Addition of a prepayment option for which exercise is contingent upon the replacement reference interest rate index not being determinable in accordance with the terms of the agreement
  - Addition of or changes to contractual fallback terms that are consistent with fallback terms developed by a regulator or by a private-sector working group convened by a regulator
  - Changes to terms that are necessary to comply with laws or regulations or to align with market conventions for the replacement rate.
  (ASC 848-20-15-5)

- Examples of changes to terms that are generally *unrelated* to the replacement of a reference rate in accordance with paragraph 848-20-15-3 include the following:
  - Changes to the notional amount or maturity date
  - Changes from a referenced interest rate index to a stated fixed rate
  - Changes to the loan structure
  - The addition of an underlying or variable unrelated to the referenced rate index
  - The addition of an interest rate floor or cap that is in the money on the basis of the spot rate at the time of the amendment of the contract
  - A concession granted to a debtor experiencing financial difficulty
  - The addition or removal of a prepayment or conversion option except for the addition of a prepayment option for which exercise is contingent upon the replacement reference interest rate index not being determinable in accordance with the terms of the agreement
  - The addition or removal of a feature that is intended to provide leverage
  - Changes to the counterparty except in accordance with paragraphs 815-20-55-56A, 815-25-40-1A, and 815-30-40-1A
  - Changes to the priority or seniority of an obligation in the event of a default or a liquidation event
  - The addition or termination of a right to use one or more underlying assets in a lease contract
  - Changes to renewal, termination, or purchase option provisions in a lease contract (ASC 848-20-15-6)

If the fallback terms in a modified contract are consistent with those developed by a regulator or by a private-sector working group convened by a regulator, then the addition or amendment of the fallback terms is presumed to be related to reference rate reform. (ASC 848-20-15-7) If not, then an entity should assess whether the new terms include, or have the potential to include, a term that is unrelated to reference rate reform in determining whether the modification is within the scope of ASC 848. (ASC 858-20-15-8)

A contract modification that directly replaces a reference rate index with a stated fixed rate is unrelated to reference rate reform. However, a replacement rate that is equal to the last published rate of a discontinued interest-rate index is not considered a stated fixed rate (that is, the replacement can be considered related to reference rate reform). (ASC 848-20-15-9)

Subsequent Measurement The election to apply the guidance in ASC 848-20 to contract modifications should be applied to all contract modifications that are accounted for within the scope of an ASC Topic or industry Subtopic. (ASC 848-20-35-1)

ASC 828-20 provides optional expedients for accounting for modifications of contracts accounted for in accordance with the following Topics that meet the scope of paragraphs 848-20-15-2 through 15-3:

- ASC 310 on receivables
- ASC 470 on debt
- ASC 840 or 842 on leases

Following is a summary of expedients under ASC 848 arranged by Codification topics:

- ASC 310, *Receivables*
  If the entity elects the optional expedient, the entity treats the modification as minor in accordance with ASC 310- 20-35-10 and the effective interest rate is adjusted prospectively. (848-20-35-6)

- ASC 470, *Debt*

  If the entity elects the optional expedient, the entity treats the modification as not substantial and it is accounted for prospectively by adjusting the effective interest rate in accordance with ASC 470-50.
  (848-20-35-8)

- ASC 842 and ASC 840, *Leases*

  The modification does not require lessees or lessors to reassess lease classification and the discount rate, to remeasure lease payments, or to make other reassessments or remeasurements that are required for a contract modification that is not accounted for as a separate contract. The lease is accounted for as a continuation of the existing lease.
  (848-20-35-11)

Following is a summary of potential outcomes of applying ASC 848-20-35-4 to contract modifications that meet the scope of ASC 848-20-15-2 and 15-3, but are not within the scope of ASC 848-20-35-4.

- ASC 815-15, *Derivatives and Hedging—Embedded Derivatives*

  The modification does not require entities to reassess the original conclusion about whether the contract contains an embedded derivative that is clearly and closely related to the economic characteristics and risks of the host contract under ASC 815-15-25-1(a).
  (848-20-35-14)

- ASC 815-10, *Derivatives*

  The modification does not require entities to reassess whether the modified instrument is a hybrid instrument and whether it includes a financing element under the guidance in (ASC 815-10-45-11 through 45-15). The modified instrument continues to be accounted for and presented in the same manner as the instrument before modification.

- ASC 944, *Financial Services*

  The modification does not require entities to reassess whether the insurance contract is substantially unchanged in accordance with ASC 944-30. The post-modification contract continues to be accounted for and presented in the same manner as the pre-modification contract.

- ASC 606, *Revenue from Contracts with Customers*

  The modification does not require entities to reassess the contract under modification guidance in ASC 606-10-25-10 through 25-13. The change in cash flows resulting from variability in the new reference rate is accounted for in the same manner as the variability that resulted from the original reference rate.

- ASC 810, *Consolidation*

  The modification is not a reconsideration event and therefore does not require a reporting entity to reconsider whether the counterparty to the contract is a variable interest entity.
  (848-20-55-2)

ASC 848-30, *Hedging—General*

ASC 848-30 allows the following optional expedients for different types of hedging relationships, which entities will generally elect on a hedge-by-hedge basis:

- For all types of hedging relationships (that is, fair value hedges, cash flow hedges, and net investment hedges):

- o The hedging relationship may continue without dedesignation of the hedging relationship if changes to the contractual terms of the hedging instrument, the hedged item, or the forecasted transaction are made due to reference rate reform.
- o If a component that is affected by reference rate reform is excluded from the assessment of hedge effectiveness, the entity can change the systematic and rational method used to recognize the excluded component in earnings. In addition, if the changes to a hedging instrument's contractual terms change the fair value of the excluded component, that change in fair value may be recognized in current earnings in the same income statement line item used to present the earnings' effect of the hedged item. (ASC 848-30-25-12 and 25-13)
- For a cash flow hedge:
  - o An entity may change to the method of assessing hedge effectiveness documented at hedge inception. This would not require dedesignation of the hedging relationship if both (1)
    - o The hedging instrument, hedged item, or hedged transaction references LIBOR or another rate that is expected to be discontinued, and (2)
    - o The new method designated for assessing hedge effectiveness is an optional expedient specified in ASC 848-50. (ASC 848-30-25-8)
- For a fair value hedge:
  - o If the entity makes a change to either the proportion of a designated hedging instrument or the proportion of the hedged item, the entity would not be require dedesignation of the hedging relationship. (ASC 848-30-25-9)
- For fair value and cash flow hedges:
  - o A change to the designated hedging instrument that combines and jointly designates two or more derivative instruments or proportions of those instruments in a hedging relationship would not require dedesignation of the hedging relationship.

ASC 848-40, *Fair Value Hedges*

ASC 848-40 allows the following optional expedients, which can be individually elected on a hedge-by-hedge basis. (ASC 848-40-25-1)

- A change to the designated benchmark interest rate that is expected to be impacted by the reference rate reform to a different eligible benchmark interest rate under ASC 815-20 would not require dedesignation of the hedging relationship if the hedge is expected to be highly effective. The guidance permits an entity to apply a method to change the designated benchmark interest rate that either adjusts the hedged item's cumulative fair value hedge-basis adjustment or maintains the cumulative basis adjustment. If the approach elected results in a change to the cumulative fair value hedge-basis adjustment, that change should be recognized in current earnings in the same income statement line item where the hedged item's effect on earnings is presented. The method applied to change the designated benchmark interest rate should be applied consistently across similar fair value hedging relationships.
- Entities that apply fair value hedge accounting using the shortcut method for assessing hedge effectiveness may disregard certain conditions for applying the shortcut method in

determining whether a hedge continues to qualify for the shortcut method when certain changes are made to the contractual terms of the hedging instrument. (ASC 848-40-25-1-8)

ASC 848-50, *Cash Flow Hedges*

ASC 848-50 permits the following optional expedients, which can be individually elected on a hedge-by-hedge basis for cash flow hedging relationships if the hedging instrument or hedged item includes a rate that is expected to be discontinued due to reference rate reform:

- Entities may disregard changes in the designated hedged interest rate risk when assessing whether the hedged forecasted transaction is probable, and may continue to apply hedge accounting if either the hedge remains highly effective or the entity elects to apply an optional expedient to subsequently assess hedge effectiveness under ASC 848-50-35.
- Entities may disregard certain conditions for (1) determining whether a cash flow hedge qualifies for the shortcut method to assess hedge effectiveness, (2) applying the simplified hedge accounting approach for eligible private companies, and (3) determining the presumption of perfect effectiveness in applying the change-in-variable-cash-flows method and the hypothetical derivative method.
- Entities may make certain adjustments to the quantitative methods of assessing hedge effectiveness described in ASC 815-30-35-10 through 35-32.
- An entity may make certain adjustments to the critical terms of a perfectly effective hypothetical hedging instrument to match the hedging instrument when assessing effectiveness based on an option's terminal value in accordance with ASC 815-20-25-126.
- For cash flow hedges of portfolios of forecasted transactions, an entity may disregard the requirement that the group of individual transactions must share the same risk exposure for which they are designated as being hedged.

PRESENTATION AND DISCLOSURE EXAMPLES

Example 58.1: Reference Rate Reform—Recent Accounting Pronouncement

In March 2020, the FASB issued ASU 2020-04, *Reference Rate Reform (Topic 848): Facilitation of the Effects of Reference Rate Reform on Financial Reporting*. This ASU provides optional guidance for a limited period of time to ease the burden in accounting for (or recognizing the effects of) reference rate reform on financial reporting. This would apply to companies meeting certain criteria that have contracts, hedging relationships, and other transactions that reference LIBOR or another reference rate expected to be discontinued because of reference rate reform. This standard is effective for use as of March 12, 2020 through December 31, 2022. We are currently assessing the impact the new guidance will have on our consolidated financial statements.

Example 58.2: Reference Rate Reform—New Accounting Pronouncement—Affected Loans Identified

In March 2020, the FASB issued ASU 2020-04, *Reference Rate Reform (Topic 848): Facilitation of the Effects of Reference Rate Reform on Financial Reporting*. These amendments provide temporary optional guidance to ease the potential burden in accounting for reference rate reform. The ASU provides optional expedients and exceptions for applying generally accepted accounting principles to contract modifications and hedging relationships, subject to meeting certain criteria, that reference LIBOR or another reference rate expected to be discontinued. It is intended to help stakeholders during the global market-wide reference rate transition period. The guidance is effective for all entities as of March 12, 2020 through December 31, 2022, and can be adopted as of any date from the beginning of an interim period that includes or is subsequent to March 12, 2020. The Company has identified loans and other financial instruments that are directly or indirectly influenced by LIBOR and does not expect the adoption of ASU 2020-04 to have a material impact on its consolidated financial statements.

59 ASC 850 RELATED-PARTY DISCLOSURES

AUTHORITATIVE LITERATURE

Subtopic

ASC 850 contains one Subtopic:

- ASC 850-10, *Overall*, which sets forth the disclosure requirements, certain significant related-party transactions, and control relationships

Scope

ASC 850 applies to all entities.

PRACTICE ALERT

While non-SEC filers are not subject to SEC comments, those comments can provide valuable guidance and cautions. In the area of financial instruments, the SEC staff has asked preparers to:

- Explain how the entity determined transactions could not be clearly identified as related-party
- Include a discussion regarding the use of advisors in the related-party discussions

PRESENTATION AND DISCLOSURE REQUIREMENTS

According to ASC 850, *Related-Party Disclosures*, financial statements are required to disclose material related-party transactions other than compensation arrangements, expense allowances, or other similar items that occur in the ordinary course of business.

A related party is essentially any party that controls or can significantly influence the management or operating policies of the company to the extent that the company may be prevented from fully pursuing its own interests. Related parties include affiliates, investees accounted for by the equity method, trusts for the benefit of employees, principal owners, management, and immediate family members of owners or management.

Transactions with related parties must be disclosed even if there is no accounting recognition made for such transactions (e.g., a service is performed without payment). Disclosures are not permitted to assert that the terms of related-party transactions were essentially equivalent to arm's-length dealings unless those claims can be substantiated. If the financial position or results of operations of the reporting entity could change significantly because of common control or common management, disclosure of the nature of the ownership or management control is required, even if there were no transactions between the entities.

The disclosures include:

1. The nature of the relationship
2. A description of transactions and the effects of those transactions reflected in the financial statements for each period for which an income statement is presented
3. The dollar amount of transactions for each period for which an income statement is presented and the effects of any change in the terms of such transactions as compared to the terms used in prior periods
4. Amounts due to and from related parties as of the date of each statement of financial position presented, together with the terms and manner of settlement

See the *Disclosure and Presentation Checklist for Commercial Businesses* (www.wiley.com/go/FSDM2021).

PRESENTATION AND DISCLOSURE EXAMPLES

Example 59.1: Accounting Policy for Related-Party Transactions

The Company follows ASC 850, *Related-Party Disclosures*, for the identification of related parties and disclosure of related-party transactions.

Example 59.2: Related-Party Transaction

On June 15, 20X1, the Company's two founding officers and directors, who were also major shareholders, resigned and Matthew Lawson was appointed as president, treasurer, secretary, and a director. Mr. Lawson is now the Company's sole director and officer. The resignations were not as a result of any disagreements on any matter relating to the Company's operations, policies, or practices. Mr. Lawson is the founder and president of Cornerstone Advisory Group, LLC, a private CFO-services firm, and Cornerstone Consulting, P.C., a registered CPA firm (collectively, "Cornerstone").

Commencing on June 15, 20X1, Cornerstone was engaged to provide accounting and advisory services to the Company in connection with audit coordination, financial statement preparation, and SEC filings. The Company pays customary fees for these services. During the year ended March 31, 20X2, the Company incurred fees of $13,179 to Eventus, and $1,861 is included in Accounts Payable to Related Party on the accompanying balance sheet as of March 31, 20X2.

The Company's principal office is at the offices of Cornerstone and does not pay Cornerstone rent for the use of these offices. In addition, Cornerstone paid certain bills on behalf of the Company, of which $3,085 is included as due to related parties on the accompanying balance sheet as of March 31, 20X2. The amounts are due on demand, unsecured, and do not bear interest.

Example 59.3: Accounting Policy for Related-Party Transactions

The Company follows ASC 850, *Related-Party Disclosures*, for the identification of related parties and disclosure of related-party transactions. In accordance with ASC 850, the Company's financial statements include disclosures of material related-party transactions, other than compensation arrangements, expense allowances, and other similar items in the ordinary course of business, as well as transactions that are eliminated in the preparation of financial statements.

Example 59.4: No Material Related-Party Transactions

Related-Party Activity: The Company does not have any material related-party activity.

Example 59.5: References to Other Notes

Related-Party Transactions

Related-Party Divestiture

See Note 13, Divestiture, for details regarding the sale of ABC to XYZ in December 20X1.

Related-Party Equity

See Note 7, Stockholders' Deficit, for details of these related-party equity transactions:

- November 20X2: XYZ securities purchase agreement
- August 20X2: Warrant transactions
- August 20X1: DSM offering
- May 20X1: Offerings
- May 20X1: Exchange of common stock for Series C convertible preferred stock
- July 20X0: DEF warrants
- Teaneck funding warrant

Related-Party Debt

See Note 5, Debt, for details of these related-party debt transactions:

- XYZ note (also see Note 13, Divestiture)
- February 20X0 private placement
- 20X0 Rule 144A convertible notes
- August 20X1 financing convertible notes
- R&D note

Example 59.6: Related-Party Debt Schedule

Related-party debt was as follows:

| (Amounts in thousands) | Years Ended December 31 | | | | | |
| | 20X8 | | | 20X7 | | |
	Principal	Unamortized Debt (Discount) Premium	Net	Principal	Unamortized Debt (Discount) Premium	Net
Total						
20X4 Rule 144A convertible notes	$ 9,705	$ (422)	$ 9,283	$ 9,705	$ (1,538)	$ 8,167
August 20X3 financing convertible notes	—	—	—	21,711	897	22,608
R&D note	—	—	—	3,700	(18)	3,682
	9,705	(422)	9,283	35,116	(659)	34,457
XYZ						
XYZ note	25,000	(6,311)	18,689	25,000	(8,039)	16,961
Other XYZ loan	—	—	—	393	—	393
	25,000	(6,311)	18,689	25,393	(8,039)	17,354
Biolding						
February 20X6 private placement	—	—	—	2,000	—	2,000
Foris						
20X4 Rule 144A convertible notes	5,000	(181)	4,819	5,000	(660)	4,340
Temasek						
20X4 Rule 144A convertible notes	10,000	(435)	9,565	10,000	(1,591)	8,409
	$ 49,705	$ (7,349)	$ 42,356	$ 77,509	$ (10,949)	$ 66,560

The fair value of the derivative liabilities related to the related-party R&D note, related party August 20X3 financing convertible notes (tranche notes) and related-party 20X4 Rule 144A convertible notes as of December 31, 20X8 and 20X7, was $0 and $0.2 million, respectively. The Company recognized (losses) gains from change in the fair value of these derivative liabilities of ($8.5) million and $0.6 million for the years ended December 31, 20X8 and 20X7, respectively; see Note 4, Fair Value Measurement.

At December 31, 20X8, Temasek was no longer a related party. However, the Company and Teaneck were related parties when they entered into the 20X4 Rule 144A convertible notes transaction, for which terms have remained unchanged since the borrowing date.

Example 59.7: Related-Party Revenue

The Company recognized revenue from related parties and from all other customers as follows:

(Amounts in thousands)

Years Ended December 31

	20X8				20X7 (as restated, Note 2)			
	Renewable Products	Licenses and Royalties	Grants and Collaborations	TOTAL	Renewable Products	Licenses and Royalties	Grants and Collaborations	TOTAL
Revenue from related parties								
XYZ	$18	$5,958	$4,735	$10,711	$—	$57,972	$1,679	$59,651
Total	342	—	—	342	(200)	—	—	(200)
Novvi	—	—	—	—	1,491	—	—	1,491
Subtotal revenue from related parties	360	5,958	4,735	11,053	1,291	57,972	1,679	60,942
Revenue from all other customers*	33,238	1,700	17,613	52,551	41,079	(9,269)	34,919	66,729
Total revenue from all customers	$33,598	$7,658	$22,348	$63,604	$42,370	$48,703	$36,598	$127,671

* Licenses and royalties revenue is negative for 20X7 due to the $13.1 million reversal of cumulative to date revenue as a result of entering into the 20X7 ABC partnership agreement. See Note 10, Revenue Recognition, for details of the Company's revenue agreements with XYZ.

Example 59.8: Related-Party Accounts Receivable

Related-party accounts receivable was as follows:

	Years Ended December 31	
(Amounts in thousands)	*20X8*	*20X7*
XYZ	$ 1,071	$ 12,823
Nova	188	1,607
Total	90	238
Related-party accounts receivable, net	$ 1,349	$ 14,668

In addition to the amounts shown above, there were the following amounts on the consolidated balance sheet at December 31, 20X8:

- A total of $8.0 million of unbilled receivables from XYZ, in the lines captioned "Contract assets—related party" and "Contract assets, noncurrent—related party"; and
- $4.3 million of contingent consideration receivable from XYZ in the line captioned "Other assets."

Example 59.9: Related-Party Accounts Payable

Amounts due to XYZ that were included in accounts payable and accrued and other current liabilities at December 31, 20X8 were $2.1 million and $0.6 million, respectively.

Example 59.10: Schedule of Related-Party XYZ Agreements with Note References

The Company is party to the following significant agreements (and related amendments) with related party DSM:

Related to	*Agreement*	*For Additional Information, See the Note Indicated*
Debt	XYZ Credit Agreement	5. Debt 10. Revenue Recognition
Debt	XYZ Note	5. Debt
Debt	November 20X8 XYZ Letter Agreement	5. Debt
Divestiture	November 20X7 Quota Purchase Agreement	13. Divestiture
Divestiture	December 20X7 XYZ Transition Services Agreement	13. Divestiture
Equity	May 20X7 Offerings	7. Stockholders' Deficit
Equity	August 20X7 XYZ Offering	7. Stockholders' Deficit
Equity	November 20X8 XYZ Securities Purchase Agreement	7. Stockholders' Deficit
Revenue	July and September 20X7 Collaboration and Licensing Agreements	10. Revenue Recognition
Revenue	December 20X7 XYZ Supply Agreement	10. Revenue Recognition
Revenue	December 20X7 XYZ Value Sharing Agreement, as Amended	10. Revenue Recognition
Revenue	December 20X7 XYZ Performance Agreement	10. Revenue Recognition
Revenue	November 20X7 Intellectual Property License Agreement	10. Revenue Recognition
Revenue	November 20X8 Supply Agreement Amendment	10. Revenue Recognition

Example 59.11: Related-Party Joint Venture

In December 20X6, the Company; JKL Chemicals Co., Ltd., an existing commercial partner of the Company; and MNO Industries Co., Ltd., an affiliate of JKL (collectively, "JKL") entered into a joint venture (the "Nova JV Agreement") pursuant to which the Company contributed certain assets, including certain intellectual property and other commercial assets relating to its business-to-business cosmetic ingredients business (the "Nova JV"), as well as its Lawson production facility. The Company also agreed to provide the Nova JV with exclusive (to the extent not already granted to a third party), royalty-free licenses to certain of the Company's intellectual property necessary to make and sell products associated with the Nova JV (the "Nova JV Products"). JKL purchased its 50% interest in the Nova JV in exchange for the following payments to the Company: (i) an initial payment of $10.0 million, and (ii) the profits, if any, distributed to JKL in cash as members of the Nova JV during the three-year period from 20X7 to 20X9, up to a maximum of $10.0 million.

The Nova JV operates in accordance with the Nova operating agreement, under which the Nova JV is managed by a board of directors consisting of four directors: two appointed by the Company and two appointed by JKL. In addition, JKL has the right to designate the chief executive officer of the Nova JV from among the directors and the Company has the right to designate the chief financial officer. The Company determined that it has the power to direct the activities of the Nova JV that most significantly impact its economic performance because of its (i) significant control and ongoing involvement in operational decision making, (ii) guarantee of production costs for certain Nova JV products, as discussed below, and (iii) control over key supply agreements, operational and administrative personnel, and other production inputs. The Company has concluded that the Nova JV is a variable interest entity (VIE) under the provisions of ASC 810, *Consolidations*, and that the Company has a controlling financial interest and is the VIE's primary beneficiary. As a result, the Company accounts for its investment in the Nova JV on a consolidation basis in accordance with ASC 810.

Under the Nova operating agreement, profits from the operations of the Nova JV, if any, are distributed as follows: (i) first, to the Company and JKL (the "Members") in proportion to their respective unreturned capital contribution balances, until each Member's unreturned capital contribution balance equals zero, and (ii) second, to the Members in proportion to their respective interests. In addition, any future capital contributions will be made by the Company and JKL on an equal (50%–50%) basis each time, unless otherwise mutually agreed.

Pursuant to the Nova JV Agreement, the Company and JKL agreed to make working capital loans to the Nova JV in the amounts of $0.5 million and $1.5 million, respectively, as described in more detail in Note 5, Debt, under Nova Working Capital Loans. In addition, the Company agreed to guarantee a maximum production cost for squalane and hemisqualane to be produced by the Nova JV and to bear any cost of production above such guaranteed costs.

In connection with the contribution of the Leland facility by the Company to the Nova JV, at the closing of the formation of the Nova JV, JKL made a loan to the Company in the principal amount of $3.9 million, and the Company in consideration therefore issued a promissory note to JKL in an equal principal amount, as described in more detail in Note 5, Debt under "JKL note."

The following presents the carrying amounts of the Nova JV's assets and liabilities included in the accompanying consolidated balance sheets. Assets presented below are restricted for settlement of the Nova JV's obligations and all liabilities presented below can only be settled using the Nova JV resources.

(Amounts in thousands)	*Years Ended December 31*	
	20X8	*20X7*
Assets	$ 12,904	$ 7,635
Liabilities	$ 2,364	$ 3,187

The Nova JV's assets and liabilities are primarily composed of inventory, property, plant and equipment, accounts payable, and debt, which are classified in the same categories in the Company's consolidated balance sheets.

There was no change in noncontrolling interest for the Nova JV for the years ended December 31, 20X8 and 20X7, due to profit-sharing provisions whereby the Company retains 100% of the profits from 20X7 to 20Y0.

Office Sublease: The Company subleases certain office space to Nova, for which the Company charged Nova $0.6 million and $0.5 million for the years ended December 31, 20X8 and 20X7, respectively.

See Note 16, Subsequent Events, for information regarding related-party transactions subsequent to December 31, 20X8.

60 ASC 852 REORGANIZATIONS

AUTHORITATIVE LITERATURE

Entities expected to reorganize as going concerns under Chapter 11 of the Bankruptcy Code employ so-called fresh-start accounting if:

1. The "reorganization value of the assets of the emerging entity immediately before the date of confirmation is less than the total of all postpetition liabilities and allowed claims, and
2. Holders of existing voting shares immediately before confirmation receive less than 50% of the voting shares of the emerging entity."
(ASC 852-10-45-19)

Subtopics

ASC 852, *Reorganizations*, contains two Subtopics:

- ASC 852-10, *Overall*, which provides guidance for entities that have filed petitions in the Bankruptcy Court and expect to reorganize under Chapter 11
- ASC 852-20, *Quasi Reorganizations*

Scope and Scope Exceptions

ASC 852-10 applies to all entities except governmental organizations but does *not* apply to debt restructurings outside of Chapter 11 and reorganizations consisting of liquidation or adoption of plans of liquidation under the Bankruptcy Code.

ASC 852-20 applies only to "readjustments in which the current income, or retained earnings or accumulated deficit account, or the income account of future years is relieved of charges that would otherwise be made against it." (ASC 852-20-15-2) Further, it does not apply to:

a. "Quasi reorganizations involving only deficit reclassifications
b. Charges against additional paid-in capital in other types of readjustments, such as readjustments for the purpose of correcting erroneous credits made to additional paid-in capital in the past
c. Financial reporting for entities that enter and intend to emerge from Chapter 11 reorganization, at the time of such reorganization."
(ASC 852-20-15-3)

Corporate Bankruptcy and Reorganizations

Entities Operating Under and Emerging from Protection of the Bankruptcy Laws The going concern assumption is one of the basic postulates underlying generally accepted accounting principles and is responsible for, among other things, the historical cost convention in financial reporting. For entities that have entered bankruptcy proceedings, however, the going concern assumption is no longer of central importance.

ASC 852 provides financial reporting standards for entities undergoing and emerging from reorganization under the bankruptcy laws. Under its provisions, assets are presented at estimated realizable values. Liabilities are set forth at the estimated amounts to be allowed in the statement of financial position, and liabilities subject to compromise are distinguished from those that are not. Furthermore, the Codification requires that in both the statements of income and cash flows that normal transactions be differentiated from those that have occurred as a consequence of the entity's being in reorganization. While certain allocations to the latter category are rather obvious, such as legal and accounting fees incurred, others are less clear. For example, the Codification suggests that if the entity in reorganization earns interest income on funds that would normally have been used to settle obligations owed to creditors, such income will be deemed to be income arising as a consequence of the bankruptcy action.

Another interesting aspect of ASC 852 is the accounting for the emergence from reorganization (known as confirmation of the plan of reorganization). The ASC provides for "fresh start" financial reporting in such instances. This accounting is similar to that applied in acquisitions, with the total confirmed value of the entity upon its emergence from reorganization being analogous to the purchase price in an acquisition. In both cases, this total value is allocated to the identifiable assets and liabilities of the entity, with any excess being allocated to goodwill. In the case of entities emerging from bankruptcy, goodwill (called reorganization value in excess of amounts allocable to identifiable assets) is measured as the excess of liabilities existing at the plan confirmation date, computed at present value of future amounts to be paid, over the reorganization value of assets. Reorganization value is calculated with reference to a number of factors, including forecasted operating results and cash flows of the new entity.

ASC 852 applies *only* to entities undergoing formal reorganization under the Bankruptcy Code. Less formal procedures may still be accounted for under quasi reorganization accounting procedures.

Quasi Reorganizations Generally, this procedure is applicable during a period of declining price levels. It is termed "quasi" because the accumulated deficit is eliminated at a lower cost and with less difficulty than with a legal reorganization.

Per ASC 852-20, the procedures in a quasi reorganization involve the:

1. Proper authorization from stockholders and creditors where required
2. Revaluation of assets to their current values: all losses are charged to retained earnings, thus increasing any deficit
3. Elimination of any deficit by charging paid-in capital:
   a. First, additional paid-in capital to the extent it exists
   b. Second, capital stock when additional paid-in capital is insufficient: the par value of the stock is reduced, creating the extra additional paid-in capital to which the remaining deficit is charged
   (ASC 852-20-25-4)

No retained earnings may be created by a reorganization. Any excess created by the reduction of par value is credited to "paid-in capital from quasi reorganization."

ASC 852-20-10-2 requires that retained earnings be titled for 10 years (less than 10 years may be justified under exceptional circumstances) after a quasi reorganization takes place. A title similar to "since quasi reorganization of June 30, 20XX" is appropriate.

PRESENTATION AND DISCLOSURE REQUIREMENTS

Presentation

While entering a reorganization proceeding is a significant event, the entity should normally not change its application of GAAP in its presentation of financial statements. (ASC 852-10-45-1) The financial statements during a Chapter 11 reorganization should distinguish between transactions and events that are directly associated with the reorganization and those that are not. (ASC 852-10-45-2)

If consolidated financial statements include entities in reorganization and entities not in reorganization proceedings, condensed financial statements of the entities in reorganization proceedings should be included. (ASC 852-10-45-14)

As of the confirmation date or as of a later date, entities whose plans have been confirmed by the court and thereby have emerged from Chapter 11 should include the effects of the plan in the financial statements and follow the guidance for fresh-start reporting if the entity meets the qualifications. (ASC 852-10-45-18)

If the entity does not qualify for fresh-start reporting, it should:

- Present liabilities compromised by confirmed plans at present value of amounts to be paid
- Report forgiveness of debt as an extinguishment of debt
  (ASC 852-10-45-29)

Disclosure

An entity in Chapter 11 should disclose:

- Claims not subject to reasonable estimation
- The principal categories of the claims subject to compromise

- The extent to which reported interest expense differs from stated contractual interest, either parenthetically or in the notes
- Intra-entity receivables and payables in the condensed financial statements (ASC 852-10-50-2 through 50-4)

When entities emerge from Chapter 11 reorganization and adopt fresh-start reporting, they should disclose additional information:

- Adjustments in the historical amounts of individual assets and liabilities
- The amount of debt forgiveness
- Significant matters relating to the determination of reorganization value, including:
  - The method used to determine reorganization value
  - Sensitive assumptions
  - Unless apparent, assumptions about anticipated conditions that are expected to be different from current conditions (ASC 852-10-50-7)

If an entity has a readjustment within the scope of the part of ASC 852-20 addressing quasi reorganizations, retained earnings previously accumulated cannot be earned forward and a new retained earnings account should be established, dated to show that it runs from the effective date of the readjustment. The dating should be disclosed in the financial statements. (ASC 852-20-50-2)

For more details on ASC 852 presentation and disclosure requirements, see the checklist at www.wiley.com/go/FSDM2021.

PRESENTATION AND DISCLOSURE EXAMPLES

Example 60.1: Voluntary Filing Under Chapter 11

On March 14, 20X2 (the "Petition Date"), the Company and certain of the Company's direct and indirect domestic subsidiaries (collectively, the "Debtors") filed voluntary petitions for relief (the "Chapter 11 Cases") under Chapter 11 of the United States Bankruptcy Code (the "Bankruptcy Code"), in the U.S. Bankruptcy Court for the Southern District of Texas, Houston Division (the "Bankruptcy Court"). LRB, Inc. ("LRB") and its direct and indirect subsidiaries did not file voluntary petitions for reorganization under the Bankruptcy Code and were not Debtors in the Chapter 11 Cases. On April 28, 20X2, the Company and the other Debtors filed a plan of reorganization (as amended, the "Plan of Reorganization") and a related disclosure statement with the Bankruptcy Court, which we subsequently amended by filing the second, third, fourth, and fifth amended Plan of Reorganization and amended versions of the disclosure statement. On January 22, 20X3, the Plan of Reorganization was confirmed by the Bankruptcy Court.

On May 1, 20X3 (the "Effective Date"), the conditions to the effectiveness of the Plan of Reorganization were satisfied and the Company emerged from Chapter 11 through (a) a series of transactions (the "Separation") through which its parent and its subsidiaries were separated from, and ceased to be controlled by, the Company and its subsidiaries, and (b) a series of transactions (the "Reorganization") through which the Company's debt was reduced from approximately $16 billion to approximately $5.8 billion and a global compromise and settlement among holders of claims ("Claimholders") in connection with the Chapter 11 Cases was effected. The compromise and settlement involved, among others, (i) the restructuring of the Company's indebtedness by (A) replacing its "debtor-in-possession" credit facility with a $450 million senior secured asset-based revolving credit facility (the "ABL Facility"), and (B) issuing to certain Claimholders, on account of their claims, an approximately $3.5 billion aggregate principal amount of new senior secured term loans (the "Term Loan Facility"), an approximately $1.45 billion aggregate principal amount of new 8.375% senior notes due in 2027 (the "Senior Unsecured Notes"), and an approximately $800 million aggregate principal amount of new 6.375% senior secured notes due in 2026 (the "6.375% Senior Secured Notes"); (ii) the Company's issuance of new Class A common stock, new Class B common stock, and special warrants to purchase shares of new Class A common stock and issue Class B common stock ("Special Warrants") to Claimholders, subject to ownership restrictions imposed by the Federal Communications Commission ("FCC"); (iii) the settlement of certain intercompany transactions; and (iv) the sale of the preferred stock of the Company's wholly owned subsidiary XYZ in connection with the Separation.

All of the Company's equity existing as of the Effective Date was canceled on such date pursuant to the Plan of Reorganization.

Example 60.2: Note 1—Application of Fresh-Start Accounting

Upon the Company's emergence from the Chapter 11 Cases, the Company adopted fresh-start accounting, which resulted in a new basis of accounting and the Company becoming a new entity for financial reporting purposes. As a result of the application of fresh-start accounting and the effects of the implementation of the Plan of Reorganization, the consolidated financial statements after the Effective Date are not comparable with the consolidated financial statements on or before that date. Refer to Note 3, Fresh-Start Accounting, for additional information.

References to "Successor" or "Successor Company" relate to the financial position and results of operations of the Company after the Effective Date. References to "Predecessor" or "Predecessor Company" refer to the financial position and results of operations of the Company on or before the Effective Date.

During the Predecessor period, the Company applied ASC 852, *Reorganizations* ("ASC 852") in preparing the consolidated financial statements. ASC 852 requires the financial statements, for periods subsequent to the commencement of the Chapter 11 Cases, to distinguish transactions and events that are directly associated with the reorganization from the ongoing operations of the business. Accordingly, certain charges incurred during 20X1 and 20X2 related to the Chapter 11 Cases, including the write-off of unamortized long-term debt fees and discounts associated with debt classified as liabilities subject to compromise, and professional fees incurred directly as a result of the Chapter 11 Cases are recorded as Reorganization items, net in the Predecessor period.

ASC 852 requires certain additional reporting for financial statements prepared between the bankruptcy filing date and the date of emergence from bankruptcy, including:

- Reclassification of Debtors' pre-petition liabilities that are unsecured or undersecured, or where it cannot be determined that the liabilities are fully secured, to a separate line item in the consolidated balance sheet called "Liabilities subject to compromise," and
- Segregation of Reorganization items, net, as a separate line in the consolidated statement of comprehensive loss, included within income from continuing operations.

The accompanying consolidated financial statements have been prepared assuming that the Company will continue as a going concern and contemplate the realization of assets and the satisfaction of liabilities in the normal course of business. During the Chapter 11 Cases, the Company's ability to continue as a going concern was contingent upon the Company's ability to successfully implement the Company's Plan of Reorganization, among other factors. As a result of the effectiveness and implementation of the Plan of Reorganization, there is no longer substantial doubt about the Company's ability to continue as a going concern.

Example 60.3: Note 2—Emergence from Voluntary Reorganization Under Chapter 11 Proceedings

---

As described in Note 1, on March 14, 20X0, the Company and the other Debtors filed the Chapter 11 Cases and on April 28, 20X0, the Company and the other Debtors filed a plan of reorganization, which was subsequently amended as the Plan of Reorganization and was confirmed on January 22, 20X1. The Debtors then emerged from bankruptcy upon effectiveness of the Plan of Reorganization on the Effective Date. Capitalized terms not defined in this note are defined in the Plan of Reorganization.

On or following the Effective Date and pursuant to the Plan of Reorganization, the following occurred:

- LRB was separated from and ceased to be controlled by the Company and its subsidiaries.
- The existing indebtedness of the Company of approximately $16 billion was discharged, the Company entered into the Term Loan Facility ($3,500 million) and issued the 6.375% Senior Secured Notes ($800 million) and the Senior Unsecured Notes ($1,450 million), collectively the "Successor Emergence Debt."
- The Company adopted an amended and restated certificate of incorporation and bylaws.
- Shares of the Predecessor Company's issued and outstanding common stock immediately prior to the Effective Date were canceled, and on the Effective Date, reorganized XYZ issued an aggregate of 56,861,941 shares of XYZ Class A common stock, 6,947,567 shares of Class B common stock, and special warrants to purchase 81,453,648 shares of Class A common stock or issue Class B common stock to holders of claims pursuant to the Plan of Reorganization.
- The following classes of claims received the Successor Emergence Debt and 99.1% of the new equity, as defined in the Plan of Reorganization:
  ○ Secured Term Loan/2019 PGN Claims (Class 4);
  ○ Secured Non-9.0% PGN Due 2019 Claims Other Than Exchange 11.25% PGN Claims (Class 5A);
  ○ Secured Exchange 11.25% PGN Claims (Class 5B);
  ○ XYZ 20X4/Legacy Notes Claims (Class 6); and
  ○ Guarantor Funded Debt Against Other Guarantor Debtors Other than DEF and ABC (Class 7).
- The holders of the Guarantor Funded Debt Unsecured Claims Against DEF (Class 7F) received their pro rata share of 100% of the LRB Interests held by the Debtors and Finest, LLC and Broad, LLC. Refer to the discussion below regarding the separation transaction.
- Settled the following classes of claims in cash:
  ○ General Unsecured Claims Against Non-Obligor Debtors (Class 7A); paid in full;
  ○ General Unsecured Claims Against TTWN Debtors (Class 7B); paid in full;
  ○ XYZ Unsecured Claims (Class 7D); paid 14.44% of allowed claim; and
  ○ Guarantor General Unsecured Claims (Class 7G); paid minimum of 45% and maximum of 55% of allowed claim.
- The LRB Due From Claims (Class 8) represent the negotiated claim between XYZ and LRB, which was settled in cash on the date of emergence at 14.44%.
- The Predecessor Company's common stockholders (Class 9) received their pro rata share of 1% of the new common stock; provided that 0.1% of the new common stock that otherwise would have been distributed to the Company's former sponsors was instead distributed to holders of Legacy Notes Claims.
- The Company entered into a new $450.0 million ABL Facility, which was undrawn at emergence.
- The Company funded the Guarantor General Unsecured Recovery Cash Pool for $17.5 million in order to settle the Class 7G General Unsecured Claims.
- The Company funded the Professional Fee Escrow Account.
- On the Effective Date, the XYZ, Inc. 20X1 Equity Incentive Plan (the "Post-Emergence Equity Plan") became effective. The Post-Emergence Equity Plan allows the Company to grant stock options and restricted stock units representing up to 12,770,387 shares of Class A common stock for key members of management and service providers and up to 1,596,298 for nonemployee members of the board of directors. The amounts of Class A common stock reserved under the

Post-Emergence Equity Plan were equal to 8% and 1%, respectively, of the Company's fully diluted and distributed shares of Class A common stock as of the Effective Date.

In addition, as part of the Separation, XYZ and LRB consummated the following transactions:

- The cash sweep agreement under the then-existing corporate services agreement and any agreements or licenses requiring royalty payments to XYZ by LRB for trademarks or other intellectual property ("Trademark License Fees") were terminated;
- XYZ and LRB entered into a transition services agreement (the "Transition Services Agreement"), pursuant to which the Company or its subsidiaries will provide administrative services historically provided to LRB by XYZ for a period of one year after the Effective Date, which may be extended under certain circumstances;
- The Trademark License Fees charged to LRB during the post-petition period were waived by XYZ;
- XYZ contributed the rights, title, and interest in and to all trade names, trademarks, service marks, common law marks, and other rights related to the Broad Channel trade name to LRB;
- XYZ paid $115.8 million to LRB, which consisted of the $149.0 million payment by XYZ to LRB, LRB's recovery of its claims under the Due from XYZ Note, partially offset by the $33.2 million net amount payable to XYZ under the post-petition intercompany balance between XYZ and LRB after adjusting for the post-petition Trademark License Fees, which were waived as part of the settlement agreement;
- XYZ entered into a revolving loan agreement with Broad Channel Outdoor, LLC, and Broad Channel International, Ltd., wholly owned subsidiaries of LRB, to provide a line of credit in an aggregate amount not to exceed $200 million at the prime rate of interest, which was terminated by the borrowers on July 30, 20X1, in connection with the closing of an underwritten public offering of common stock by LRB; and
- XYZ issued $60.0 million in preferred stock to a third party for cash (see Note 9, Long-Term Debt).

Example 60.4: Note 3—Fresh-Start Accounting

In connection with the Company's emergence from bankruptcy and in accordance with ASC 852, the Company qualified for and adopted fresh-start accounting on the Effective Date. The Company was required to adopt fresh-start accounting because (i) the holders of existing voting shares of the Predecessor Company received less than 50% of the voting shares of the Successor Company, and (ii) the reorganization value of the Company's assets immediately prior to confirmation of the Plan of Reorganization was less than the post-petition liabilities and allowed claims.

In accordance with ASC 852, with the application of fresh-start accounting, the Company allocated its reorganization value to its individual assets based on their estimated fair values in conformity with ASC 805, *Business Combinations*. The reorganization value represents the fair value of the Successor Company's assets before considering liabilities. The excess reorganization value over the fair value of identified tangible and intangible assets is reported as goodwill. As a result of the application of fresh-start accounting and the effects of the implementation of the Plan of Reorganization, the consolidated financial statements after May 1, 2019, are not comparable with the consolidated financial statements as of or prior to that date.

Example 60.5: Reorganization Value

As set forth in the Plan of Reorganization and the Disclosure Statement, the enterprise value of the Successor Company was estimated to be between $8.0 billion and $9.5 billion. Based on the estimates and assumptions discussed below, the Company estimated the enterprise value to be $8.75 billion, which was the midpoint of the range of enterprise value as of the Effective Date.

Management and its valuation advisors estimated the enterprise value of the Successor Company, which was approved by the Bankruptcy Court. The selected publicly traded companies analysis approach, the discounted cash flow analysis approach, and the selected transactions analysis approach were all utilized in estimating the enterprise value. The use of each approach provides corroboration for the other approaches. To estimate enterprise value utilizing the selected publicly traded companies analysis method, valuation multiples derived from the operating data of publicly traded benchmark companies were applied to the same operating data of the Company. The selected publicly traded companies analysis identified a group of comparable companies giving consideration to lines of business and markets served, size, and geography. The valuation multiples were derived based on historical and projected financial measures of revenue and earnings before interest, taxes, depreciation, and amortization and applied to projected operating data of the Company.

To estimate enterprise value utilizing the discounted cash flow method, an estimate of future cash flows for the period 20X1 to 20X4 with a terminal value was determined and the estimated future cash flows were discounted to present value. The expected cash flows for the period 20X1 to 20X4 with a terminal value were based upon certain financial projections and assumptions provided to the Bankruptcy Court. The expected cash flows for the period 20X1 to 20X4 were derived from earnings forecasts and assumptions regarding growth and margin projections, as applicable. A terminal value was included, calculated using the terminal multiple method, which estimates a range of values at which the Successor Company will be valued at the end of the Projection Period based on applying a terminal multiple to final year Adjusted EBITDA (referred to as "OIBDAN" in the documents filed with the Bankruptcy Court), which is defined as consolidated operating income adjusted to exclude noncash compensation expenses included within corporate expenses, as well as depreciation and amortization, impairment charges, and other operating income (expense), net.

To estimate enterprise value utilizing the selected transactions analysis, valuation multiples were derived from an analysis of consideration paid and net debt assumed from publicly disclosed merger or acquisition transactions, and such multiples were applied to the broadcast cash flows of the Successor Company. The selected transactions analysis identified companies and assets involved in publicly disclosed merger and acquisition transactions for which the targets had operating and financial characteristics comparable in certain respects to the Successor Company.

The following table reconciles the enterprise value per the Plan of Reorganization to the implied value (for fresh-start accounting purposes) of the Successor Company's common stock as of the Effective Date:

(Amounts in thousands, except per share data)	
Enterprise value	$ 8,750,000
Plus:	
Cash and cash equivalents	63,142
Less:	
Debt issued upon emergence	(5,748,178)
Finance leases and short-term notes	(61,939)
Mandatorily redeemable preferred stock	(60,000)
Changes in deferred tax liabilities*	(163,910)
Noncontrolling interest	(8,943)
Implied value of Successor Company common stock	$ 2,770,172
Shares issued upon emergence**	145,263
Per share value	$ 19.07

* *Difference in the assumed effect of deferred taxes in the calculation of enterprise value versus the actual effect of deferred taxes as of May 1.*

** *Includes the Class A common stock, Class B common stock, and Special Warrants issued at emergence. The reconciliation of the Company's enterprise value to reorganization value as of the Effective Date is as follows:*

(Amounts in thousands)

Enterprise value	$ 8,750,000
Plus:	
Cash and cash equivalents	63,142
Current liabilities (excluding current portion of long-term debt)	426,944
Deferred tax liability	596,850
Other long-term liabilities	54,393
Noncurrent operating lease obligations	818,879
Reorganization value	$ 10,710,208

Example 60.6: Consolidated Balance Sheet—Effect of Applying Fresh-Start Accounting

The adjustments set forth in the following consolidated balance sheet as of May 1, 20X2, reflect the effect of the Separation (reflected in the column Separation of LRB Adjustments), the consummation of the transactions contemplated by the Plan of Reorganization that are incremental to the Separation (reflected in the column Reorganization Adjustments) and the fair value adjustments as a result of applying fresh-start accounting (reflected in the column Fresh-Start Adjustments). The explanatory notes highlight methods used to determine fair values or other amounts of the assets and liabilities, as well as significant assumptions or inputs.

(Amounts in thousands)	*Predecessor*	*Separation of LRB Adjustments* *(A)*	*Reorganization Adjustments* *(B)*	*Fresh-Start Adjustments* *(C)*	*Successor*
CURRENT ASSETS					
Cash and cash equivalents	$ 175,811	$ —	$ (112,669) (1)	$ —	$ 63,142
Accounts receivable, net	748,326	—	—	(10,810) (1)	737,516
Prepaid expenses	127,098	—	—	(24,642) (2)	102,456
Other current assets	22,708	—	8,125 (2)	(1,668) (3)	29,165
Current assets of discontinued operations	1,000,753	(1,000,753) (1)	—	—	—
Total Current Assets	2,074,696	(1,000,753)	(104,544)	(37,120)	932,279

PROPERTY, PLANT, AND EQUIPMENT					
Property, plant, and equipment, net	499,001	—	—	333,991 (4)	832,992
INTANGIBLE ASSETS AND GOODWILL					
Indefinite-lived intangibles: licenses	2,326,626	—	—	(44,906) (5)	2,281,720
Other intangibles, net	104,516	—	—	2,240,890 (5)	2,345,406
Goodwill	3,415,492	—	—	(92,127) (5)	3,323,365
OTHER ASSETS					
Operating lease right-of-use assets	355,826	—	—	554,278 (6)	910,104
Other assets	139,409	—	(384) (3)	(54,683) (2)	84,342
Long-term assets of discontinued operations	5,351,513	(5,351,513) (1)	—	—	—
Total Assets	$ 14,267,079	$ (6,352,266)	$ (104,928)	$ 2,900,323	$ 10,710,208
CURRENT LIABILITIES					
Accounts payable	$ 41,847	$ —	$ 3,061 (4)	$ —	$ 44,908
Current operating lease liabilities	470	—	31,845 (7)	39,092 (6)	71,407
Accrued expenses	208,885	—	(32,250) (5)	2,328 (9)	178,963
Accrued interest	462	—	(462) (6)	—	—
Deferred revenue	128,452	—	—	3,214 (7)	131,666
Current portion of long-term debt	46,618	—	6,529 (7)	40 (6)	53,187
Current liabilities of discontinued operations	999,778	(999,778) (1)	—	—	—
Total Current Liabilities	1,426,512	(999,778)	8,723	44,674	480,131
Long-term debt	—	—	5,758,516 (8)	(1,586) (8)	5,756,930
Series A mandatorily redeemable preferred stock	—	—	60,000 (9)	—	60,000
Noncurrent operating lease liabilities	828	—	398,154 (7)	419,897 (6)	818,879

Deferred income taxes	—	—	575,341 (10)	185,419 (10)	760,760
Other long-term liabilities	121,081	—	(64,524) (11)	(2,164) (7)	54,393
Liabilities subject to compromise	16,770,266	—	(16,770,266) (7)	—	—
Long-term liabilities of discontinued operations	7,472,633	(7,472,633) (1)	—	—	—
Commitments and contingent liabilities (Note 10)					
STOCKHOLDERS' EQUITY (DEFICIT)					
Noncontrolling interest	13,584	(13,199) (1)	—	8,558 (11)	8,943
Predecessor common stock	92	—	(92) (12)	—	—
Successor Class A common stock	—	—	57 (13)	—	57
Successor Class B common stock	—	—	7 (13)	—	7
Predecessor additional paid-in capital	2,075,130	—	(2,075,130) (12)	—	—
Successor additional paid-in capital	—	—	2,770,108 (13)	—	2,770,108
Accumulated deficit	(13,288,497)	1,825,531 (1)	9,231,616 (14)	2,231,350 (12)	—
Accumulated other comprehensive loss	(321,988)	307,813 (1)	—	14,175 (12)	—
Cost of share held in treasury	(2,562)	—	2,562 (12)	—	—
Total Stockholders' Equity (Deficit)	(11,524,241)	2,120,145	9,929,128	2,254,083	2,779,115
Total Liabilities and Stockholders' Equity (Deficit)	$ 14,267,079	$ (6,352,266)	$ (104,928)	$ 2,900,323	$ 10,710,208

Example 60.7: Separation Adjustments

On May 1, 20X1, as part of the Separation, the outstanding shares of both classes of LRB common stock were consolidated such that DEF held all of the outstanding LRB Class A common stock that was held by subsidiaries of XYZ, through a series of share distributions by other subsidiaries that held LRB common stock and a conversion of LRB Class B common stock that DEF held to LRB Class A common stock. Prior to the Separation, XYZ owned approximately 89.1% of the economic rights and approximately 99% of the voting rights of LRB. To complete the Separation, LRB merged with and into DEF, with DEF surviving the merger and changing its name to Broad Channel Outdoor Holdings, Inc. ("New LRB"), and pre-merger shares of LRB Class A common stock (other than shares of LRB Class A common stock held by DEF or any direct or indirect wholly owned subsidiary of CCH) were converted into an equal number of shares of post-merger common stock of New LRB. XYZ transferred the post-merger common stock of New LRB it held to Claimholders pursuant to the Plan of Reorganization but retained 31,269,762 shares. Such retained shares were distributed to two affiliated Claimholders on July 18, 20X1. Upon completion of the merger and Separation, New LRB became an independent public company. Upon distribution of the shares held by XYZ, the Company does not hold any ownership interest in LRB.

The assets and liabilities of LRB have been classified as discontinued operations. The discontinued operations reflect the assets and liabilities of LRB, which are presented as discontinued operations as of the Effective Date. LRB's assets and liabilities are adjusted to (1) eliminate the balance on the Due from XYZ Note and the balance on the intercompany payable due to XYZ from LRB's consolidated balance sheet, which are intercompany amounts that were eliminated in consolidation; (2) eliminate LRB's noncontrolling interest and treasury shares; and (3) eliminate other intercompany balances.

Example 60.8: Reorganization Adjustments

In accordance with the Plan of Reorganization, the following adjustments were made:

1. The table below reflects the sources and uses of cash on the Effective Date from implementation of the Plan:

(Amounts in thousands)	
Cash at May 1, 20X1 (excluding discontinued operations)	$ 175,811
Sources:	
Proceeds from issuance of mandatorily redeemable preferred stock	$ 60,000
Release of restricted cash from other assets into cash	3,428
Total sources of cash	$ 63,428
Uses:	
Payment of mandatorily redeemable preferred stock issuance costs	$ (1,513)
Payment of new Term Loan Facility to settle certain creditor claims	(1,822)
Payments for Successor Emergence Debt issuance costs	(7,213)
Funding of the Guarantor General Unsecured Recovery Cash Pool	(17,500)
Payments for fully secured claims and general unsecured claims	(1,990)
Payment of contract cure amounts	(15,763)
Payment of consenting stakeholder fees	(4,000)
Payment of professional fees	(85,091)*
Funding of Professional Fee Escrow Account	(41,205)*
Total uses of cash	$ (176,097)
Net uses of cash	$ (112,669)
Cash upon emergence	$ 63,142

* Approximately $30.5 million of professional fees paid at emergence were accrued as of May 1, 20X1. These payments also reflect both the payment of success fees for $86.1 million and other professionals paid directly at emergence.

2. Pursuant to the terms of the Plan of Reorganization, on the Effective Date, the Company funded the Guarantor General Unsecured Recovery Cash Pool ("Cash Pool") account in the amount of $17.5 million, which was reclassified as restricted cash within other current assets. The Company made payments of $6.0 million through the Cash Pool at the time of emergence. Additionally, $3.4 million of restricted cash previously held to pay critical utility vendors was reclassified to cash.

3. Adjustments reflect the write-off of prepaid expenses related to the $2.3 million of prepaid premium for Predecessor Company's director and officer insurance policy, offset by the accrual of future reimbursements of $1.9 million for negotiated discounts related to the professional fee escrow account.

4. Adjustments reflect the reinstatement of $3.1 million of accounts payable included within liabilities subject to compromise to be satisfied in the ordinary course of business.

5. Adjustments reflect the reduction of accrued expenses related to the $21.2 million of professional fees paid directly, $9.3 million of professional fees paid through the Professional Fee Escrow Account, and other accrued expense items. Additionally, the Company reinstated accrued expenses included within liabilities subject to compromise to be satisfied in the ordinary course of business.

(Amounts in thousands)

Reinstatement of accrued expenses	$ 551
Payment of professional fees	(21,177)
Payment of professional fees through the escrow account	(9,260)
Impact on other accrued expenses	(2,364)
Net impact on accrued expenses	$ (32,250)

6. Adjustments reflect the write-off of the DIP facility accrued interest associated with the DIP facility fees paid at emergence.

7. As part of the Plan of Reorganization, the Bankruptcy Court approved the settlement of claims reported within liabilities subject to compromise in the Company's consolidated balance sheet at their respective allowed claim amounts. The table below indicates the disposition of liabilities subject to compromise:

(Amounts in thousands)

Liabilities subject to compromise pre-emergence	$16,770,266
To be reinstated on the Effective Date:	
Deferred taxes	$ (596,850)
Accrued expenses	(551)
Accounts payable	(3,061)
Finance leases and other debt	(16,867)*
Current operating lease liabilities	(31,845)
Noncurrent operating lease liabilities	(398,154)
Other long-term liabilities	(14,518)**
Total liabilities reinstated	$ (1,061,846)
Less amounts settled per the Plan of Reorganization	
Issuance of new debt	$ (5,750,000)
Payments to cure contracts	(15,763)
Payments for settlement of general unsecured claims from escrow account	(5,822)
Payments for fully secured and other claim classes at emergence	(1,990)
Equity issued at emergence to creditors in settlement of Liabilities subject to Compromise	(2,742,471)
Total amounts settled	(8,516,046)
Gain on settlement of Liabilities Subject to Compromise	$ 7,192,374

* Includes finance lease liabilities and other debt of $6.6 million and $10.3 million classified as current and long-term debt, respectively.

** Reinstatement of other long-term liabilities are indicated in the table below:

(Amounts in thousands)

Reinstatement of long-term asset retirement obligations	$ 3,527
Reinstatement of nonqualified deferred compensation plan	10,991
Total reinstated other long-term liabilities	$ 14,518

8. The exit financing consists of the Term Loan Facility of approximately $3.5 billion and 6.375% Senior Secured Notes totaling $800 million, both maturing seven years from the date of issuance, the Senior Unsecured Notes totaling $1.45 billion, maturing eight years from the date of issuance, and the $450 million ABL Facility with no amount drawn at emergence, which matures on June 14, 2023.

   Upon emergence, the Company paid cash of $1.8 million to settle certain creditor claims for which claims were designated to receive term loans pursuant to the Plan of Reorganization.

   The remaining $10.3 million is related to the reinstatement of the long-term portion of finance leases and other debt as described above.

(Amounts in thousands)	*Term*	*Interest Rate*	*Amount*
Term Loan Facility	7 years	LIBOR + 4.00%	$ 3,500,000
6.375% Senior Secured Notes	7 years	6.375%	800,000
Senior Unsecured Notes	8 years	8.375%	1,450,000
ABL Facility	4 years	Varies*	—
Total long-term debt: exit financing			$ 5,750,000
Less:			
Payment of Term Loan Facility to settle certain creditor claims			(1,822)
Net proceeds from exit financing at emergence			$ 5,748,178
Long-term portion of finance leases and other debt reinstated			10,338
Net impact on long-term debt			$ 5,758,516

* *Borrowings under the ABL Facility bear interest at a rate per annum equal to the applicable rate plus, at XYZ's option, either (x) a eurocurrency rate or (y) a base rate. The applicable margin for borrowings under the ABL Facility range from 1.25% to 1.75% for eurocurrency borrowings and from 0.25% to 0.75% for base-rate borrowings, in each case depending on average excess availability under the ABL Facility based on the most recently ended fiscal quarter.*

9. Adjustments reflect the issuance by XYZ operations of $60.0 million in aggregate liquidation preference of its Series A perpetual preferred stock, par value $0.001 per share. On May 1, 20Y2, the shares of the preferred stock will be subject to mandatory redemption for $60.0 million in cash, plus any accrued and unpaid dividends, unless waived by the holders of the preferred stock.

10. Adjustments reflect the reinstatement of deferred tax liabilities included within liabilities subject to compromise of $596.9 million, offset by an adjustment to net deferred tax liabilities of $21.5 million. Upon emergence from the Chapter 11 Cases, XYZ's federal and state net operating loss carryforwards were reduced in accordance with Section 108 of the U.S. Internal Revenue Code of 1986, as amended (the "Code"), due to cancellation of debt income, which is excluded from U.S. federal taxable income. The estimated remaining deferred tax assets attributed to federal and state net operating loss carryforwards upon emergence totaled $114.9 million. The adjustments reflect a reduction in deferred tax assets for federal and state net operating loss

carryforwards as described above, a reduction in deferred tax liabilities attributed to long-term debt as a result of the restructuring of our indebtedness upon emergence, and a reduction in valuation allowance.

11. Adjustments reflect the reinstatement of other long-term liabilities from liabilities subject to compromise, offset by the reduction of liabilities for unrecognized tax benefits classified as other long-term liabilities that were discharged and effectively settled upon emergence.

(Amounts in thousands)

Reinstatement of long-term asset retirement obligations	$ 3,527
Reinstatement of nonqualified pension plan	10,991
Reduction of liabilities for unrecognized tax benefits	(79,042)
Net impact to other long-term liabilities	$ (64,524)

12. Pursuant to the terms of the Plan of Reorganization, as of the Effective Date, all Predecessor common stock and stock-based compensation awards were canceled without any distribution. As a result of the cancellation, the Company recognized $1.5 million in compensation expense related to the unrecognized portion of share-based compensation as of the Effective Date.

13. Adjustments reflect the issuance of Successor Company equity, including the issuance of 56,861,941 shares of XYZ Class A common stock, 6,947,567 shares of Class B common stock, and special warrants to purchase 81,453,648 shares of Class A common stock or Class B common stock in exchange for claims against or interests in XYZ pursuant to the Plan of Reorganization.

(Amounts in thousands)

Equity issued to Class 9 Claimholders (prior equity holders)	$ 27,701
Equity issued to creditors in settlement of liabilities subject to compromise	2,742,471
Total equity issued at emergence	$ 2,770,172

14. The following table reflects the cumulative impact of the reorganization adjustments discussed above:

(Amounts in thousands)

Gain on settlement of liabilities subject to compromise	$ 7,192,374
Payment of professional fees upon emergence	(11,509)
Payment of success fees upon emergence	(86,065)
Cancellation of unvested stock-based compensation awards	(1,530)
Cancellation of Predecessor prepaid director and officer insurance policy	(2,331)
Write-off of debt issuance and mandatorily redeemable preferred stock costs incurred at emergence	(8,726)
Total Reorganization items, net	$ 7,082,213
Income tax benefit	$ 102,914
Cancellation of Predecessor equity	2,074,190*
Issuance of Successor equity to prior equity holders	(27,701)
Net impact on accumulated deficit	$ 9,231,616

* This value is reflective of Predecessor common stock, additional paid-in capital, and the recognition of $1.5 million in compensation expense related to the unrecognized portion of share-based compensation, less treasury stock.

Example 60.9: Fresh-Start Adjustments

We have applied fresh-start accounting in accordance with ASC 852. Fresh-start accounting requires the revaluation of our assets and liabilities to fair value, including both existing and new intangible assets, such as FCC licenses, developed technology, customer relationships, and trade names. Fresh-start accounting also requires the elimination of all predecessor earnings or deficits in accumulated deficit and accumulated other comprehensive loss. These adjustments reflect the actual amounts recorded as of the Effective Date as follows:

1. Adjustments reflect the fair value adjustment as of May 1, 20X1, made to accounts receivable to reflect management's best estimate of the expected collectability of accounts receivable balances.
2. Adjustments reflect the fair value adjustment as of May 1, 20X1, to eliminate certain prepaid expenses related to software implementation costs and other upfront payments. The Company historically incurred third-party implementation fees in connection with installing various cloud-based software products, and these amounts were recorded as prepaid expenses and recognized as a component of selling, general and administrative expense over the term of the various contracts. The Company determined that the remaining unamortized costs related to such implementation fees do not provide any rights that result in future economic benefits. In addition, the Company pays signing bonuses to certain of its on-air personalities, and these amounts were recorded as prepaid expenses and recognized as a component of direct operating expenses over the terms of the various contracts. To the extent these contracts do not contain substantive clawback provisions, these prepaid amounts do not provide any enforceable rights that result in future economic benefits. Accordingly, the balances related to these contracts as of May 1, 20X1, were adjusted to zero.
3. Adjustments reflect the fair value adjustment to eliminate receivables related to tenant allowances per certain lease agreements. These receivables were incorporated into the recalculated lease obligations per ASC 842.
4. Adjustments reflect the fair value adjustment to recognize the Company's property, plant, and equipment as of May 1, 20X1, based on the fair values of such property, plant, and equipment. Property was valued using a market approach comparing similar properties to recent market transactions. Equipment and towers were valued primarily using a replacement cost approach. Internally developed and owned software technology assets were valued primarily using the royalty savings method, similar to the approach used in valuing the Company's trade names and trademarks. Estimated royalty rates were determined for each of the software technology assets considering the relative contribution to the Company's overall profitability as well as available public market information regarding market royalty rates for similar assets. The selected royalty rates were applied to the revenue generated by the software technology assets. The forecasted cash flows expected to be generated as a result of the royalty savings were discounted to present value utilizing a discount rate considering overall business risks and risks associated with the asset being valued. For certain of the software technology assets the Company used the cost approach that utilized historical financial data regarding development costs and expected future profit associated with the assets. The adjustment to the Company's property, plant, and equipment consists of a $182.9 million increase in tangible property and equipment and a $151.0 million increase in software technology assets.
5. Historical goodwill and other intangible assets have been eliminated and the Company has recognized certain intangible assets at estimated current fair values as part of the application of fresh-start accounting, with the most material intangible assets being the FCC licenses related to the Company's 854 radio stations. The Company has also recorded customer-related and marketing-related intangible assets, including the XYZ trade name.

The following table sets forth estimated fair values of the components of these intangible assets and their estimated useful lives:

(Amounts in thousands)	*Estimated Fair Value*	*Estimated Useful Life*
FCC licenses	$ 2,281,720*	Indefinite
Customer/advertiser relationships	1,643,670**	5–15 years
Talent contracts	373,000**	2–10 years
Trademarks and trade names	321,928**	7–15 years
Other	6,808***	
Total intangible assets upon emergence	$ 4,627,126	
Elimination of historical acquired intangible assets	(2,431,142)	
Fresh-start adjustment to acquired intangible assets	$ 2,195,984	

* *FCC licenses: The fair value of the indefinite-lived FCC licenses was determined primarily using the direct valuation method of the income approach and, for smaller markets, a combination of the income approach and the market approach. The Company engaged a third-party valuation firm to assist it in the development of the assumptions and the Company's determination of the fair value of its FCC licenses.*

Under the direct valuation method, the fair value of the FCC licenses was calculated at the market level as prescribed by ASC 350. The application of the direct valuation method attempts to isolate the income that is properly attributable to the FCC licenses alone (that is, apart from tangible and identified intangible assets and goodwill). It is based upon modeling a hypothetical "greenfield" build-up to a "normalized" enterprise that, by design, lacks inherent goodwill and whose only other assets have essentially been paid for (or added) as part of the build-up process. Under the direct valuation method, it is assumed that rather than acquiring FCC licenses as part of a going concern business, the buyer hypothetically obtains FCC licenses and builds a new operation with similar attributes from scratch. Thus, the buyer incurs start-up costs during the build-up phase that are normally associated with going concern value. Initial capital costs are deducted from the discounted cash flow model, which results in value that is directly attributable to the FCC licenses. In applying the direct valuation method to the Company's FCC licenses, the licenses are grouped by type (e.g., FM licenses vs. AM licenses) and market size in order to ensure appropriate assumptions are used in valuing the various FCC licenses based on population and demographics that influence the level of revenues generated by each FCC license, using industry projections. The key assumptions used in applying the direct valuation method include market revenue growth rates, market share, profit margin, duration and profile of the build-up period, estimated start-up capital costs and losses incurred during the build-up period, the risk-adjusted discount rate ("WACC"), and terminal values. The WACC was calculated by weighting the required returns on interest-bearing debt and common equity capital in proportion to their estimated percentages based on a market participant capital structure.

For licenses valued using the market transaction method, the Company used publicly available data, which included sales of comparable radio stations and FCC auction data involving radio broadcast licenses to estimate the fair value of FCC licenses. Similar to the application of the income approach for the FCC licenses, the Company grouped licenses by type and market size for comparison to historical market transactions.

The historical book value of the FCC licenses as of May 1, 2019, was subtracted from the fair value of the FCC licenses to determine the adjustment to decrease the value of indefinite-lived intangible assets-licenses by $44.9 million.

** *Other intangible assets: Definite-lived intangible assets include customer/advertiser relationships, talent contracts for on-air personalities, trademarks and trade names, and other intangible assets. The Company engaged a third-party valuation firm to assist in developing the assumptions and determining the fair values of each of these assets.*

For purposes of estimating the fair values of customer/advertiser relationships and talent contracts, the Company primarily utilized the income approach (specifically, the multiperiod excess earnings method, or MPEEM) to estimate fair value based on the present value of the incremental after-tax cash flows attributable only to the subject intangible assets after deducting contributory asset charges. The cash flows attributable to each grouping of customer/advertiser relationships were adjusted for the appropriate contributory asset charges (e.g., FCC licenses, working capital, trade names, technology, workforce, etc.). The discount rate utilized to present-value the after-tax cash flows was selected based on consideration of the overall business risks and the risks associated with the specific assets being valued. Additionally, for certain advertiser relationships the Company used the cost approach, using historical financial data regarding the sales, administrative, and overhead expenses related to the Company's selling efforts associated with revenue for both existing and new advertisers. The ratio of expenses for selling efforts to revenue was applied to total revenue from new customers to determine an estimated cost per revenue dollar of revenue generated by new customers.

This ratio was applied to total revenue from existing customers to estimate the replacement cost of existing customer/ advertiser relationships. The historical book value of customer/advertiser relationships as of May 1, 20X1, was subtracted from the fair value of the customer/advertiser relationships determined as described above to determine the adjustment to increase the value of the customer/advertiser relationship intangible assets by $1,604.1 million.

For purposes of estimating the fair value of trademarks and trade names, the Company primarily used the royalty savings method, a variation of the income approach. Estimated royalty rates were determined for each of the trademarks and trade names considering the relative contribution to the Company's overall profitability as well as available public information regarding market royalty rates for similar assets. The selected royalty rates were applied to the revenue generated by the trademarks and trade names to determine the amount of royalty payments saved as a result of owning these assets. The forecasted cash flows expected to be generated as a result of the royalty savings were discounted to present value utilizing a discount rate considering overall business risks and risks associated with the asset being valued. The historical book values of talent contracts, trademarks and trade names, and other intangible assets as of May 1, 20X1, were subtracted from the fair values determined as described above to determine the adjustments as follows:

(Amounts in millions)		
Customer/advertiser relationships	$ 1,604.1	increase in value
Talent contracts	361.6	increase in value
Trademarks and trade names	274.4	increase in value
Other	0.8	increase in value
Total fair value adjustment	$ 2,240.9	increase in value

*** Included within other intangible assets are permanent easements, which have an indefinite useful life. All other intangible assets are amortized over the respective lives of the agreements, or over the period of time the assets are expected to contribute directly or indirectly to the Company's future cash flows.

The following table sets forth the adjustments to goodwill:

(Amounts in thousands)	
Reorganization value	$ 10,710,208
Less: Fair value of assets (excluding goodwill)	(7,386,843)
Total goodwill upon emergence	3,323,365
Elimination of historical goodwill	(3,415,492)
Fresh-start adjustment to goodwill	$ (92,127)

6. The operating lease obligation as of May 1, 20X1, had been calculated using an incremental bor-rowing rate applicable to the Company while it was a debtor-in-possession before its emergence from bankruptcy. Upon application of fresh-start accounting, the lease obligation was recalculated using the incremental borrowing rate applicable to the Company after emergence from bankruptcy and commensurate to its new capital structure. The incremental borrowing rate used decreased from 12.44% as of March 31, 20X1, to 6.54% as of May 1, 20X1. As a result of this decrease, the Company's operating lease liabilities and corresponding operating lease right-of-use assets increased by $541.2 million to reflect the higher balances resulting from the application of a lower incremental borrowing rate. The operating lease right-of-use-assets were further adjusted to reflect the resetting of the Company's straight-line lease calculation. In addition, the Company increased the operating lease right-of-use assets to recognize $13.1 million related to the favorable lease contracts.

7. Adjustments reflect the fair value adjustment to adjust deferred revenue and other liabilities as of May 1, 20X1, to its estimated fair value. The fair value of the deferred revenue was determined using the market approach and the cost approach. The market approach values deferred revenue based on the amount an acquirer would be required to pay a third party to assume the remaining performance obligations. The cost approach values deferred revenue utilizing estimated costs that will be incurred to fulfill the obligation plus a normal profit margin for the level of effort or assumption of risk by the acquirer. Additionally, a deferred gain was recorded at the time of the certain historical sale-leaseback transaction. During the implementation of ASC 842, the operating portion was written off as of January 1, 20X1. The financing lease deferred gain remained. As part of fresh-start accounting, this balance of $0.9 million was written off.

8. Adjustments reflect the fair value adjustment to adjust long-term debt as of May 1, 20X1. This adjustment is to state the Company's finance leases and other pre-petition debt at estimated fair values.

9. Adjustments reflect the fair value adjustment to adjust accrued expenses as of May 1, 20X1. This adjustment primarily relates to adjusting vacation accruals to estimated fair values.

10. Adjustments reflect a net increase to deferred tax liabilities for fresh-start adjustments attributed primarily to property, plant, and equipment and intangible assets, the effects of which are partially offset by a decrease in the valuation allowance. The Company believes it is more likely than not that its deferred tax assets remaining after the reorganization and emergence will be realized based on taxable income from reversing deferred tax liabilities primarily attributable to property, plant, and equipment and intangible assets.

11. Adjustments reflect the adjustment as of May 1, 20X1, to state the noncontrolling interest balance at estimated fair value.

12. The table below reflects the cumulative impact of the fresh-start adjustments as discussed above:

(Amounts in thousands)	
Fresh-start adjustment to accounts receivable, net	$ (10,810)
Fresh-start adjustment to other current assets	(1,668)
Fresh-start adjustment to prepaid expenses	(24,642)
Fresh-start adjustment to property, plant, and equipment, net	333,991
Fresh-start adjustment to intangible assets	2,195,984
Fresh-start adjustment to goodwill	(92,127)
Fresh-start adjustment to operating lease right-of-use assets	554,278
Fresh-start adjustment to other assets	(54,683)
Fresh-start adjustment to accrued expenses	(2,328)
Fresh-start adjustment to deferred revenue	(3,214)
Fresh-start adjustment to debt	1,546
Fresh-start adjustment to operating lease obligations	(458,989)
Fresh-start adjustment to other long-term liabilities	2,164
Fresh-start adjustment to noncontrolling interest	(8,558)
Total fresh-start adjustments impacting reorganization items, net	$ 2,430,944
Reset of accumulated other comprehensive income	(14,175)
Income tax expense	(185,419)
Net impact to accumulated deficit	$ 2,231,350

Example 60.10: Reorganization Items, Net

The tables below present the reorganization items incurred and cash paid for reorganization items as a result of the Chapter 11 Cases during the periods presented:

	Successor Company Period from May 2, 20X1 through December 31 20X1	Predecessor Company Period from January 1, 20X1 through May 1 20X1	Year Ended December 31 20X0
Write-off of deferred loans costs	$ —	$ —	$ (67,079)
Write-off of original issue discount	—	—	(131,100)
Debtor-in-possession refinancing costs	—	—	(10,546)
Professional fees and other bankruptcy-related costs	—	(157,487)	(147,119)
Net gain on settlement of liabilities subject to compromise	—	7,192,374	(275)
Impact of fresh-start adjustments	—	2,430,944	—
Other items, net	—	(4,005)	—
Reorganization items, net	$ —	$ 9,461,826	$ (356,119)
Cash payments for reorganization items, net	$ 18,360	$ 183,291	$ 103,727

As of December 31, 20X1, $0.4 million of Reorganization items, net, were unpaid and accrued in Accounts payable and Accrued expenses in the accompanying Consolidated Balance Sheet. As of December 31, 20X0, $47.5 million of professional fees were unpaid and accrued in Accounts payable and Accrued expenses in the accompanying Consolidated Balance Sheet. The Company incurred additional professional fees related to the bankruptcy, post-emergence, of $26.5 million for the period from May 2, 20X1 through December 31, 20X1, respectively, which are included within Other income (expense), net in the Company's Consolidated Statements of Comprehensive Income (Loss).

Example 60.11: Accounting Policy—Quasi Reorganization

During the fiscal year ended August 31, 20X1, the Company's shareholders approved a quasi reorganization which has been reflected in the accompanying financial statements by an elimination of the accumulated deficit of $3,478,477 as of August 31, 20X1, and a corresponding reduction of additional paid-in capital. As part of the reorganization the Company evaluated its assets to determine if any needed to be written down to fair market value as a part of the reorganization. The Company determined that all assets were currently being carried at fair value and no adjustment in value was required.

Example 60.12: Quasi Reorganization Not Completed, Correction of Error

In preparing the Company's September 30, 20X1, consolidated financial statements, the Company determined that events that would have allowed us to complete the previously disclosed quasi reorganization pursuant to Section 210 of the Codification of Financial Reporting Policies ("Quasi Reorg") effective June 30, 20X1, did not materialize during the subsequent quarter. As such we have subsequently determined that we do not meet all the requirements necessary to complete the Quasi Reorg during this period. The revision does not result in any change to total equity of the Company; it only affected individual equity account balances. The Company assessed the materiality of this misstatement in the June 30, 20X1, interim period financial statements in accordance with the SEC's Staff Accounting Bulletin ("SAB") No. 99, Materiality, codified in ASC 250, *Presentation of Financial Statements*, and concluded that the misstatement was not material to any interim period. In accordance with SAB 108, the Company has adjusted the quarter ended June 30, 20X1, financial statements. There was no impact to the statement of operations or cash flows.

	June 30, 20X1		
	As Originally Reported	*Adjustment*	*As Corrected*
Series A preferred stock	$ 5.00	$ —	$ 5.00
Common stock	158,461	—	158,461
Additional paid-in-capital	1,000,226	110,652,881	111,653,107
Accumulated deficit	—	(110,652,881)	(110,652,881)
Treasury stock	—	—	—
Total stockholders' equity (deficit)	$ 1,158,692	$ —	$ 1,158,692

Example 60.13: Presentation of Stockholders' Equity in Quasi Reorganization

	As of December 31, 20X2	*As of December 31, 20X1*
Stockholders' Equity		
Pref Stock—$0.001 par value; 5,000,000 shares auth, consisting of Series 4 convertible pref stock—10,415 shares auth; 1 and 1 issued, and 1 and 1 outstanding as of Dec. 31, 20X2, and Dec. 31, 20X1, respectively, Series 5 convertible pref stock—12,000 shares auth; 126 and 0 issued, and 126 and 0 outstanding as of Dec. 31, 20X2 and Dec. 31, 20X1, respectively.	—	—
Common stock—$0.001 par value; 250,000,000 shares authorized; 4,234,922 and 35,159 issued and 4,234,922 and 35,158 outstanding as of December 31, 20X2 and December 31, 20X1, respectively.	4	—
Additional paid-in capital	158,382	123,226
Treasury stock, at cost, 1 share	(695)	(695)
Accumulated other comprehensive income	94	26
Accumulated deficit (excluding $2,442 reclassified to additional paid-in capital in quasi reorganization)	(151,763)	(117,773)
Stockholders' equity attributable to The Company	6,022	4,784
Noncontrolling interest	26	18
Total Stockholders' Equity	6,048	4,802
Total Liabilities and Stockholders' Equity	$ 21,219	$ 12,178

61 ASC 853 SERVICE CONCESSION ARRANGEMENTS

AUTHORITATIVE LITERATURE

ASC 853 addresses a narrow issue and limits the scope of the guidance to arrangements in which the grantor is a public-sector entity.

Subtopic

ASC 853, *Service Concession Arrangements*, contains one Subtopic:

- ASC 853-10, *Overall*, which addresses the accounting for service concession arrangements between a public sector entity grantor and an operating entity where the operating entity operates the grantor's infrastructure

Scope

ASC 853 applies to the accounting:

- By operating entities
  - Of a service concession arrangement
  - Under which a public-sector entity grantor enters into a contract with an operating entity
  - To operate the grantor's infrastructure

The operating entity also may provide the construction, upgrading, or maintenance services of the grantor's infrastructure. (ASC 853-10-15-2)

It is important to note that a service concession arrangement within the scope of ASC 853 must meet *both* of the following conditions:

a. The grantor controls or has the ability to modify or approve the services that the operating entity must provide with the infrastructure, as well as to whom it must provide them and at what price.
b. The grantor controls, through ownership, beneficial entitlement, or otherwise, any residual interest in the infrastructure at the end of the term of the arrangement.
(ASC 853-10-15-3)

Scope Exception

A service concession arrangement meeting the scope criteria in Topic 980 on regulated operations should apply the guidance in Topic 980.

Accounting for Service Concession Arrangements

The Topic has two main provisions:

- Service concession arrangements in scope are accounted for in accordance with ASC 606 to recognize revenue on construction, upgrade, or operation services. The grantor is the customer for ASC 853 service concession arrangements. Operating entities should look to other Topics to account for other aspects of service concession arrangements. (ASC 853- 20-25-1)
- The infrastructure involved in the arrangements should not be recognized as the operating entity's property, plant, and equipment. Service concession arrangements within the scope of ASC 853 are not within the scope of ASC 840 or ASC 842. (ASC 853-10-25-2)

Service Concession Arrangements The infrastructure that an entity operates may be airports, roads, bridges, hospitals, prisons, and so forth. The operating entity may also provide construction or maintenance services to the grantor's infrastructure. A key feature of a service concession arrangement is that it is generally for the public good. The operator usually receives payment for the services performed over a specified time. The operator may have the right to charge users of the infrastructure. The arrangement may include unconditional guarantees for guaranteed minimum payments.

Economic Substance The grantor controls or has the ability to modify or approve the services provided and the price charged for the service. The grantor controls any residual interest in the infrastructure at the end of the term. This control is important in deciding the economic substance of the transaction and the reason why it is not appropriate for the operating entity to recognize a lease of property, plant, and equipment. (ASC 853-10-05-01 and 05-02)

PRESENTATION AND DISCLOSURE REQUIREMENTS

ASC 853 contains no presentation or disclosure requirements.

PRESENTATION AND DISCLOSURE EXAMPLES

Example 61.1: Contracts Considered Service Concession Arrangements—Accounting Policy

The Company's 50-year firm fixed-price contracts with the U.S. government are considered service concession arrangements under ASC 853, *Service Concession Arrangements*. Accordingly, the services under these contracts are accounted for under Topic 606, *Revenue from Contracts with Customers*, and the water and/or wastewater systems are not recorded as property, plant, and equipment on Registrant's balance sheet. For the Company, performance obligations consist of (i) performing ongoing operation and maintenance of the water and/or wastewater systems and treatment plants for each military base served, and (ii) performing construction activities (including renewal and replacement capital work) on each military base served. The transaction price for each performance obligation is either delineated in, or initially derived from, the applicable 50-year contract and/or any subsequent contract modifications. Depending on the state in which operations are conducted, the Company's military utility privatization subsidiaries are also subject to certain state non–income tax assessments, which are accounted for on a gross basis and have been immaterial to date.

The ongoing performance of operation and maintenance of the water and/or wastewater systems and treatment plants is viewed as a single performance obligation for each 50-year contract with the U.S. government. Registrant recognizes revenue for operations and maintenance fees monthly using the "right to invoice" practical expedient under ASC Topic 606. The Company has a right to consideration from the U.S. government in an amount that corresponds directly to the value to the U.S. government of the Company's performance completed to-date. The contractual operations and maintenance fees are firm-fixed, and the level of effort or resources expended in the performance of the operations-and-maintenance-fees performance obligation is largely consistent over the 50-year term. Therefore, Registrant has determined that the monthly amounts invoiced for operations and maintenance performance are a fair reflection of the value transferred to the U.S. government. Invoices to the U.S. government for operations and maintenance service, as well as construction activities, are due upon receipt.

Example 61.2: Contracts Considered Service Arrangements—Accounting Before and After Adoption of ASC 606

Other real estate assets are accounted for in accordance with ASC 853, *Service Concession Arrangements*. ASC 853 stipulates that the facilities subject to the standard may not be accounted for as a lease, nor should the infrastructure used in the service concession arrangement be recognized as property and equipment by the operating entity. Instead, the contracts should be accounted for under the applicable revenue standards. The Company owns four facilities that are accounted for as service concession arrangements. The facilities accounted for under ASC 853 were constructed in periods prior to 2013.

On January 1, 2018, the Company adopted ASU 2014-09, *Revenue from Contracts with Customers* and its subsequent corresponding update, ASC 606. For facilities that the Company constructed for the public entity, two separate and distinct performance obligations exist. Service revenue is recognized as provided. All revenues and costs related to the construction of the facilities were recognized upon adoption of ASC 606. Revenue recognized related to the construction of the facilities for which cash has not yet been received is recorded as a contract asset and is amortized and evaluated for impairment on an ongoing basis. For facilities contributed to a service contract, the cost of the facility is accounted for as costs to fulfill the service contract and the cost is recognized over the term of the service contract. The costs related to contract assets and costs to fulfill the service contracts are recoverable if the contract is terminated or not renewed due to the existence of residual interest options.

Prior to the adoption of ASC 606, other real estate assets were stated at cost, net of accumulated amortization. These assets represent the cost of all infrastructure to be transferred to the public entity grantors should the grantors exercise their residual interest. The costs related to the facilities constructed for a governmental entity were deferred as an other real estate asset, and the deferred costs were amortized in proportion to revenue recognized over the term of the related services arrangement. The costs related to the facilities that were constructed before entering into the service concession arrangement were amortized in proportion to revenue recognized over the term of the related service contract as an investment in the service contract.

62 ASC 855 SUBSEQUENT EVENTS

AUTHORITATIVE LITERATURE

ASC 855 describes the circumstances under which an entity should recognize events or transactions in its financial statements that occur subsequent to the balance sheet date but before the financial statements are available to be issued. This can have a potentially significant impact on loss contingencies.

Subtopic

ASC 855, *Subsequent Events*, consists of one Subtopic:

- ASC 855-10, *Overall*, which provides guidance for events or transactions occurring after the balance sheet date

Scope and Scope Exceptions

ASC 855 applies to all entities and all transactions except for those covered in other Codification Topics.

Types of Subsequent Events

The statement of financial position is dated as of the last day of the fiscal period, but a period of time usually elapses before the financial statements are issued. During this period, significant events or transactions may have occurred that materially affect the company's financial position. These events and transactions are called "subsequent events." The omission of disclosure of significant events occurring between the date of the statement of financial position and issuance date of the financial statements could mislead the reader who is otherwise unaware of those events.

SEC filers and conduit bond obligors for conduit debt securities traded in a public market are required to evaluate subsequent events through the date the financial statements are issued. All other entities must evaluate subsequent events through the date the financial statements are *available* to be issued. (ASC 855-10-25-1A and 25-2)

There are two types of subsequent events, which relate to when the event or transaction occurred and determine the accounting treatment:

1. *Existing conditions.* Additional evidence may arise about a condition that existed as of the balance sheet date. If so, recognize these changes within the financial statements.
2. *Subsequent events.* Evidence may arise about conditions that did not exist as of the balance sheet date, but which occurred later. Entities should not recognize these changes within the financial statements.

The following table presents a variety of sample situations occurring after the balance sheet date but before the financial statements are available to be issued that apply to these two types of subsequent events:

Event	Accounting Treatment
Litigation is settled for an amount different from the recorded liability	(1)
Loss of assets due to a natural disaster	(2)
Changes in estimated credit losses on receivables from conditions arising after the balance sheet date	(2)
Changes in the fair value of assets or liabilities	(2)
Issuing significant guarantees	(2)
(ASC 855-10-55-1 and 55-2)	

1. *Recognize within the financial statements if they are not yet available to be issued.*
2. *Do not recognize until the next reporting period.*

PRACTICE ALERT

While non-SEC filers are not subject to SEC comments, those comments can provide valuable guidance and cautions. In the area of financial instruments, the SEC staff has asked preparers to:

- Disclose the date through which subsequent events were evaluated
- Explain how the entity determined that an item is a second-quarter event and that the year-end financial statements should not be revised
- Explain how the entity considered the guidance in ASC 855 in concluding the disclosures in the year-end financial statements

PRESENTATION AND DISCLOSURE REQUIREMENTS

Presentation

Nonrecognized Subsequent Events See ASC 855-10-50-3 below for situations in which an entity should consider presenting pro forma financial statements.

Disclosures

Date Through Which Subsequent Events Have Been Evaluated For non-SEC filers, the following:

- The date through which subsequent events have been evaluated.
- Whether that date is either of the following:
  - The date the financial statements were issued.
  - The date the financial statements were available to be issued.
  (ASC 855-10-50-1)

Nonrecognized Subsequent Events For nonrecognized subsequent events whose disclosure, by their nature, is necessary in order to prevent the financial statements from being misleading, disclose the following:

- The nature of the event.
- An estimate of the financial effect of the event or a statement that an estimate cannot be made.
  (ASC 855-10-50-2)

If the nonrecognized subsequent event is so significant that disclosure is best made by presenting pro forma financial data, management should consider supplementing the historical financial statements with that data that would give effect to the event as if it had occurred on the date of the statement of financial position. In some situations, management should also consider presenting pro forma statements, usually a statement of financial position only, in columnar form on the face of the historical financial statements. (ASC 855-10-50-3)

Revised Financial Statements For non-SEC filers, disclose the date through which management evaluated subsequent events and whether that date represents the date the financial statements were issued or the date the financial statements were available to be issued. (ASC 855-10-50-4)

If the financial statements are reissued, disclose the date through which subsequent events were evaluated with respect to both the originally issued financial statements and the revised financial statements. (ASC 855-10-50-5)

See the *Disclosure and Presentation Checklist for Commercial Businesses* at www.wiley.com/go/FSDM2021 for ASC 855 presentation and disclosure requirements.

PRESENTATION AND DISCLOSURE EXAMPLES

Example 62.1: Subsequent Events, Including Events Related to COVID-19

The Company evaluated all events and transactions that occurred after December 31, 2019, and through the date of this filing in accordance with FASB ASC 855, *Subsequent Events*. The Company determined that it does have material subsequent events to disclose as follows:

Subsequent Events

- On January 4, 2020, the Company's ABC subsidiary entered into another future receivable purchase agreement with XYZ Funding and received $14,500. This agreement provides for payment over 70 business days and carried a fee of $4,850. This obligation is not convertible under any terms into Company stock.

- On January 16, 2020, SwissCO agreed to purchase an additional 53,000 Series B preferred shares for $53,000 under the same terms as its prior purchases.
- On January 24, 2020, the Company's Monday Morning subsidiary entered into a first future receivable purchase agreement with Vox Funding and received $14,500. This agreement provides for payment over 3.5 months and carried a fee of $4,850. This obligation is not convertible under any terms into Company stock.
- In March 2020, as a subsequent event and as part of the Company's streamlining operations and as a result of COVID-19, the Company filed a Chapter 11 reorganization of its retail group.
- On March 16, 2020, the President of the United States of America issued stay-at-home instructions and a business closure directive in response to the COVID-19 pandemic. Management took steps to promptly close all of its RedWing stores and Fashion Group operations, laying off the vast majority of its employees. The Company's landlords and Ameri and XYZ have agreed to collections deferment of an indeterminate duration. The Fashion Group continues limited operations in creating and producing PPE materials.
- On March 27, 2020, the Congress of the United States passed the CARES Act, allowing companies to apply for SBA loans under the Paycheck Protection Program (PPP). These loans provide for certain funding based on previous employment, which in part may be forgivable under certain conditions. The remaining portion needs to be repaid over two years and carries a 1% annual interest rate with a six-month moratorium on payments. These loans require no collateral or personal guarantees. During the period from May 5, 2020 to May 22, 2020, the Company's subsidiaries qualified and received an aggregate of $294,806.78 in PPP loans.

Example 62.2: Subsequent Events—Sale of OEM Business

The Company evaluated subsequent events as of the issuance date of the consolidated financial statements as defined by FASB ASC 855, *Subsequent Events*.

On January 13, 20X2, we entered into the Equity Purchase Agreement, as amended by that certain First Amendment to Equity Purchase Agreement dated March 6, 20X2, and that certain Second Amendment to Equity Purchase Agreement dated April 27, 20X2 (as amended, the "OEM Purchase Agreement"), with LRB Ltd., a Delaware corporation and an entity affiliated with Lawson Private Equity LLP, for the sale (the "Sale") of the Company's business of providing original equipment manufacturing ("OEM"), including the design, development, and manufacture of private label and custom biological-, metal-, and polymer-based implants (the "OEM Business"), provided that the OEM Business shall not be deemed to include the marketing, sale, or direct distribution of surgical implants, instruments, or biologics used in the treatment of conditions affecting the spine (x) as represented by the Company's Spine or International lines of business and (y) as otherwise described in the Company's Annual Report on Form 10-K for the year ended December 31, 20X0, filed with the SEC on March 5, 20X1, for a purchase price of $440,000, subject to certain adjustments. More specifically, pursuant to the terms of the OEM Purchase Agreement, the Company will sell all of the issued and outstanding shares of the Company's OEM, LLC (which, prior to the sale, is required to convert to a corporation).

The OEM Purchase Agreement contemplates that, prior to the closing (the "OEM Closing") of the sale and each of the agreements ancillary to the OEM Purchase Agreement (the "Contemplated Transactions"), we will undergo an internal reorganization, pursuant to which, in addition to certain inter-company transfers and mergers, the Company and its subsidiaries will transfer to the OEM group companies (the "OEM Group Companies") the assets primarily used in the operation of the OEM Business and the OEM Group Companies will assume certain liabilities that are related to the OEM Business (collectively, the "Reorganization").

The Contemplated Transactions are subject to customary closing conditions, including, among other things, the approval of the Contemplated Transactions by the Company's stockholders. The parties currently expect to close the Contemplated Transactions in the third quarter of 20X2. Following the OEM Closing, the Company will focus exclusively on the design, development, and distribution of spinal implants to the global market.

Example 62.3: Subsequent Event—Effect of COVID-19

The COVID-19 pandemic has directly and indirectly adversely impacted the Company's business, financial condition, and operating results. The extent to which these adverse impacts will continue will depend on numerous evolving factors that are highly uncertain and rapidly changing and that cannot be predicted with precision or certainty at this time. The spread of COVID-19 has caused many hospitals and other health care providers to refocus their care on the surge of the COVID-19 cases and to postpone elective and non-emergent procedures, restrict access to health care facilities, and in some cases reallocate scarce resources to their critically ill patients.

These efforts have impacted and could continue to impact our business activities, including our product sales, as many of our products are used in connection with elective surgeries. Many of our employees have been furloughed, and although our operations are beginning to increase towards normal levels, we continue to have many employees working remotely. Additionally, these measures are hindering our ability to recruit, vet, and hire personnel for key positions. It is unknown how long these disruptions could continue. Due to the challenges created by the furloughs and remote working conditions, on May 11, 2020, we filed a Current Report on Form 8-K to avail ourselves of an extension to file our Quarterly Report on Form 10-Q for the quarterly period ended March 31, 2020, originally due on May 11, 2020, relying on an order issued by the Securities and Exchange Commission on March 25, 2020, pursuant to Section 36 of the Securities Exchange Act of 1934, as amended (Release No. 34-88465), regarding exemptions granted to certain public companies.

As noted above, our product sales have been materially reduced as a result of COVID-19. While we are continuing to monitor and evaluate the impact on our business of COVID-19, we have not at this point identified any material impairments, increases in allowances for credit losses, restructuring charges, other expenses, or changes in accounting judgments that have had or are reasonably likely to have a material impact on our financial statements specifically due to the COVID-19 pandemic. However, as the global outbreak of COVID-19 continues to rapidly evolve, it could continue to materially and adversely affect our revenues, financial condition, profitability, and cash flows for an indeterminate period of time.

Example 62.4: Subsequent Event—Stockholder Litigation

There is currently ongoing stockholder litigation related to the Investigation. A class action complaint was filed by Jean Blake against the Company, and certain current and former officers of the Company, in the U.S. District Court for the Northern District of Illinois on March 23, 20X2, demanding a jury trial. A shareholder derivative lawsuit was filed by Summers on behalf of the Company against certain current and William Hobart former directors and officers of the Company in the U.S. District Court for the Northern District of Illinois on June 5, 20X2, demanding a jury trial. In the future, we may become subject to additional litigation or governmental proceedings or investigations that could result in additional unanticipated legal costs regardless of the outcome of the litigation. If we are not successful in any such litigation, we may be required to pay substantial damages or settlement costs. Based on the current information available to the Company, the impact that current or any future stockholder litigation may have on the Company cannot be reasonably estimated.

63 ASC 860 TRANSFERS AND SERVICING

AUTHORITATIVE LITERATURE

Transfers with continuing involvement raise questions about whether the assets have been sold or remain as assets. (ASC 860-10-05-4) ASC 860 describes the proper accounting for sales of financial assets to third parties and the use of financial assets as collateral in secured borrowings. Importantly, ASC 860 sets forth the guidelines for a transferor to derecognize transfers from the transferor's statement of financial position. This chapter also includes ASC 860's standards for repurchase agreements and securities lending. Although those two types of transfers usually involve investments, the guidance is contained in ASC 860 because the same underlying theory—the financial components approach—is used for those transactions as is used for transfers involving receivables.

Transfers of financial assets may involve a sale or a transfer where the transferor has some continuing involvement with the transferred financial assets. Arrangements where the transferor has continuing involvement include:

- Servicing arrangements, such as resource and guarantee arrangements
- Agreements to purchase or redeem transferred financial assets

- Options written or held
- Pledges of collateral
- The transferor's beneficial interest in the transferred financial asset
  (ASC 860-10-05-4)

ASC 860 covers:

- Securitizations
- Factoring
- Transfers of receivables with recourse
- Securities lending transactions
- Repurchase agreements
- Loan participations
- Banker's acceptances
  (ASC 860-10-05-6)

Subtopics

ASC 860 contains four Subtopics:

- ASC 860-10, *Overall,* which together with the other three Subtopics provides guidance on transfers and servicing of financial assets and transfers of servicing rights
- ASC 860-20, *Sales of Financial Assets,* provides guidance on a transfer that satisfies the conditions for a sale and if a transferor regains control of assets previously sold
- ASC 860-30, *Secured Borrowing and Collateral,* provides guidance for secured borrowings with a transfer of collateral
- ASC 860-50, *Servicing Assets and Liabilities,* provides guidance for servicing assets and for servicing liabilities
  (ASC 860-10-05-2)

Scope and Scope Exceptions

ASC 860 applies to all entities and to transfers and servicing of noncash financial assets. A transfer includes:

- Selling a receivable,
- Transferring a receivable to a trust, or
- Using a receivable as security for a loan.

A transfer does *not* include:

- The origination of a receivable,
- The settlement of a receivable, or
- The restructuring of a receivable in a troubled debt restructuring.
  (ASC 860-10-15-2 and 20-20)

Those transactions are transfers involving the issuer of the receivable.
Among the types of transfers of financial assets for which ASC 860 provides guidance are:

- All loan participations
- Transfers of equity method and cost-method investments (ASC 860-10-55-3)
- Financial instruments
- Financial assets
- Collateral

- Transfers of receivables with recourse (factoring with recourse)
- Transfers of options to repurchase individual financial assets
- Transfers of receivables with servicing retained
- Transfers of lease receivables under sales-type and direct financing leases
- Putting a receivable into a securitization trust
- Repurchase agreements
- Dollar rolls
- Securities lending transactions
- Posting a receivable as collateral
- Banker's acceptances
  (ASC 860-10-55-43)

ASC 860-10-15-4 *excludes* the following items from the scope of ASC 860:

- Except for transfers of servicing assets (see ASC 860-50-40) and for the transfers noted in the following paragraph, transfers of nonfinancial assets
- Transfers of unrecognized financial assets, for example, lease payments to be received under operating leases
- Transfers of custody of financial assets for safekeeping
- Contributions
- Transfers of in-substance nonfinancial assets
- Investments by owners or distributions to owners of a business entity
- Employee benefits subject to the provisions of ASC 712
- Leveraged leases subject to ASC 840 (ASC 842 upon implementation)
- Money-over-money and wrap-lease transactions involving nonrecourse debt subject to ASC 840 (ASC 842 upon implementation)

The guidance in ASC 860-30 applies to transactions in which cash is obtained in exchange for financial assets with an obligation for an opposite exchange later, such as repurchase agreements, dollar rolls, and securities lending transactions. (ASC 860-30-15-3)

The guidance in ASC 860-50 applies to transactions:

- In which servicing assets are obtained and servicing liabilities are incurred, including transactions in which loans are transferred and servicing retained by the transferor, and in which servicing assets are transferred with loans retained by the transferor.
  (ASC 860-50-15-3)

ASC 860-10, *Overall*

If receivables or other financial assets are transferred to another entity and the transferor has no continuing involvement with the transferred assets or with the transferee, it is clear that:

- A sale has taken place,
- The asset should be derecognized, and
- A gain or loss on the sale is to be measured and recognized.

However, in some situations, the transferor may have some form of continuing involvement with the transferred assets. It may:

- Sell the receivables with recourse for uncollectible amounts,
- Retain an interest in the receivables, or
- Agree to service the receivables after the sale.

The more control that the transferor retains over the receivables, the more the transfer appears to be in substance a secured borrowing rather than a sale. ASC 860 establishes the criteria and procedures used to determine whether a transfer of financial assets is a sale or a secured borrowing.

In a sale or other transfer, financial assets and liabilities may be disaggregated into components, which become separate assets and liabilities. (ASC 860-10-05-5) ASC 860 uses a financial components approach, in which a single financial asset is viewed as a mix of component assets (controlled economic benefits) and component liabilities (obligations for probable future sacrifices of economic benefits). The focus is on who controls the components, and, therefore, the economic benefits of the asset, and whether that control has changed as a result of a given transfer:

- If the transferor has surrendered control of the transferred assets, the transfer is a sale, and the assets should be derecognized.
- If the transferor retains control of the transferred assets, the transfer is a secured borrowing, with the asset pledged as collateral to secure an obligation of the transferor, and derecognition is not appropriate.

Derecognition of financial liabilities by a debtor can be properly reflected only if the obligation is extinguished, which requires that either:

- The debt is retired (paid off), or
- The debtor is legally released from being the primary obligor by either the counterparty or by judicial action (e.g., in bankruptcy proceedings).

Transferors and transferees should use symmetrical reporting, that is, account for transfers of financial assets in a similar way.

The conditions for sale, transfer, and derecognition are discussed in the following sections.

Conditions for a Sale of a Financial Asset A transfer of financial assets (or a component of a financial asset) is recognized as a sale if the transferor surrenders control over those assets in exchange for consideration. The conditions for accounting as a sale a transfer of an entire financial asset, a group of entire financial assets, or a participating interest in an entire financial asset where control has been surrendered are described in ASC 860-10-40-5:

a. Isolation of transferred financial assets
b. Pledge or exchange rights
c. Effective control

A repurchase to maturity transaction is accounted for as a secured borrowing as if the transferor maintains effective control. (ASC 860-10-40-5A)

ASC 860-20, *Sales of Financial Assets*

This Subtopic provides guidance for transfers of financial assets that satisfy the conditions in ASC 860-10-40-5 listed earlier in this chapter. (ASC 860-20-05-1) Any participating interest(s) obtained, other assets obtained, and any liabilities incurred should be recognized and initially measured at fair value.[1] (ASC 860-20-30-2)

---

[1] Upon implementation of ASU 2016-13, this guidance makes an exception for a purchased financial asset with credit deterioration and a beneficial interest that meets the criteria in paragraph 325-40-30-1A. In those cases, entities should apply the guidance in ASC 326 on measurement of credit losses to determine the initial amortized cost basis.

Measuring Assets and Liabilities after Completion of a Transfer Financial assets, except for instruments that are within the scope of Subtopic 815-10, that can contractually be prepaid or otherwise settled in such a way that the holder would not recover substantially all of its recorded investment, should be subsequently measured like investments in debt securities classified as available for sale or trading under ASC 320. Therefore, all relevant provisions of ASC 320 should be applied. (ASC 860-20-35-2)

Sale of a Participating Interest When a transfer of a participating interest that satisfies the conditions above in ASC 860-10-40-05 has been completed, the transferor (*seller*) should:

- Allocate the previous carrying amount of the entire financial asset between the participating interests sold and the participating interest that continues to be held by the transferor, on the basis of relative fair values as of the date of the transfer;
- Derecognize the participating interest(s) sold;
- Recognize and initially measure at *fair value* servicing assets, servicing liabilities, and any other assets obtained and liabilities incurred in the sale;
- Recognize in earnings any gain or loss on the sale; and
- Report any participating interest or interests that continue to be held by the transferor as the difference between the previous carrying amount of the entire financial asset and the amount derecognized (i.e., the initial amount is allocated book value).
  (ASC 860-20-40-1A)

Sale of an Entire Financial Asset or Group of Entire Financial Assets If, instead of a participating interest, the entire financial asset or group of financial assets is transferred, in a manner that complies with the requirements (as set forth above) for sale accounting, then the transferor (seller) is required to:

- Derecognize all transferred financial assets;
- Recognize and initially measure at fair value servicing assets, servicing liabilities, and any other assets obtained (including a transferor's beneficial interest in the transferred financial assets) and liabilities incurred in the sale; and
- Recognize in earnings any gain or loss on the sale.

The transferee furthermore is to recognize all assets obtained and any liabilities incurred and initially measure them at fair value (which, in the aggregate, presumptively equals the price paid). (ASC 860-20-40-1B)

If the transfer is accounted for as a secured borrowing, there is no adjustment to carrying value and no gain recognition.

ASC 860-30, *Secured Borrowing and Collateral*

This Subtopic provides guidance on secured borrowings with transfers of collateral. (ASC 860-30-01-1)

ASC 860-30-35-2 provides subsequent measurement guidance for pledged assets required to be reclassified that are accounted for as secured borrowings. For those assets, the transferor should follow the same measurement principles as before the transfer.

ASC 860-50, *Servicing Assets and Liabilities*

Interests Retained by the Transferor Interests in transferred assets that are not a part of the proceeds of a sale are considered retained interests that are still under the control of the transferor. Retained interests include:

- Participating interests for which control has not been given up by the transferor,
- Servicing assets and liabilities, and
- Beneficial interests in assets transferred in a securitization in a transaction that can be accounted for as a sale.

In general, the more extensive an interest that the transferor of assets retains, the less likely the transaction will be classified as a sale and the more likely the transaction will be classified as a secured borrowing. If a determination cannot be made between classification as proceeds of a sale or as retained interests, the asset is classified as proceeds and measured at fair value.

Overcollateralization is the other principal residual interest held by transferors. To enhance the creditworthiness of the securities issued by the trust, it is commonly found that placing a surfeit of collateral (i.e., the underlying mortgage or other loans) into the trust (say, $100 of loans receivable for each $90 of debt to be issued by the trust) will result in a significantly reduced net interest cost incurred by the trust, and hence a greater yield spread that will ultimately revert to the transferor. Additionally, an overcollateralization structure will garner a better rating for the trust securities, making them more readily marketable (in addition to having lower coupon rates), thus insuring the ability to fully fund the trust.

Servicing assets and servicing liabilities are measured by allocating the carrying value of the transferred assets before the transfer between the assets sold (if any) and the assets retained based on their relative fair values on the date of transfer. ASC 860-50-35 specifies that the carrying value allocated should be exclusive of any amounts included in an allowance for loan losses. Any gain recognized upon a partial sale of a loan is not to exceed the gain that would be recognized if the entire loan were sold. If the transferor retains a servicing contract, a portion of the carrying value is allocable to either a servicing asset retained or a servicing liability. If the initial measure is zero, the servicing contract does not result in a servicing asset or liability. (ASC 860-50-30-2)

The retained interests continue to be the transferor's assets, since control of these assets has not been transferred. Thus, the retained interest is considered continuing control over a previously owned asset (although the form may have changed). It is not to be remeasured at fair value, nor is a gain or loss recognized on it.

The Nature of Servicing Servicing of financial assets can include such activities as:

- Collecting payments (principal, interest, and escrows)
- Paying taxes and insurance from escrows
- Monitoring delinquencies
- Foreclosing
- Investing funds temporarily prior to their distribution
- Remitting fees to guarantors, trustees, and service providers
- Accounting for and remitting distributions to holders of beneficial interests (ASC 860-50-05-3)

Securitizations

Entities that generate a large number of similar receivables, such as mortgages, credit card receivables, or car loans, sometimes securitize those receivables. Securitization is the transformation of the receivables into securities that are sold to other investors. (ASC 860-10-05-7) Transfers in securitization transactions must be evaluated for sale accounting treatment by the criteria in ASC 860 and must be evaluated for consolidation by the usual GAAP criteria applicable to variable interest entities, set forth at ASC 810. If consolidation of the securitization entity is necessitated by the circumstances, gain cannot be recognized on the transfer.

Repurchase Agreements Repurchase agreements are used to obtain short-term use of funds. (ASC 860-10-05-9) Under the terms of a repurchase agreement, the transferor transfers financial assets to a transferee in exchange for cash. Concurrently, the transferor agrees to reacquire the financial assets at a future date for an amount equal to the cash exchanged and an interest factor. Many repurchase agreements are for short terms, often overnight.

It is necessary to determine whether the repurchase agreement meets the requirements for effective control through both a right and an obligation. Usually the critical determination is whether the repurchase agreement gives the transferor effective control over the transferred assets. If a transferor does not maintain control over the transferred assets and other criteria in ASC 860 are met, the transfer is accounted for as a sale and a forward commitment.

Accounting for Collateral Accounting for collateral depends both on whether the secured party has the right to sell or repledge the collateral and on whether the debtor has defaulted. Ordinarily, the transferor should carry the collateral as an asset and the transferee does not record the pledged asset.

The collateral provisions of ASC 860 apply to all transfers (repurchase agreements, dollar roll, securities lending, etc.) of financial assets pledged as collateral and accounted for as a secured borrowing. The provisions do not apply to the accounting for cash in secured borrowing transactions.

If the secured party (transferee) has the right to sell or repledge the collateral, then the debtor (transferor) reclassifies the asset used as collateral and reports it in the statement of financial position separately from other assets not similarly encumbered. That is, the debtor (transferor) continues to hold the collateral assets as its own, and the secured party (transferee) does not recognize the collateral asset. If the secured party (transferee) sells the collateral, it recognizes the proceeds from the sale and the obligation to return the collateral to the debtor (transferor).

Although collateral is required to be reclassified and reported separately by the transferor if the transferee has the right to sell or repledge the collateral, that requirement does not change the transferor's measurement of the collateral. The same measurement principles are to be used as before the transfer and the collateral is not derecognized. The subsequent measurement of the transferee's obligation to return the collateral in securities borrowing and resale agreement transactions is not addressed by ASC 860.

If the transferor defaults and is not entitled to the return of the collateral, it is to be derecognized by the transferor. If not already recognized, the transferee records its asset at fair value.

PRACTICE ALERT

While SEC comments relate to SEC filings, the staff comments can be important practice reminders. Regarding ASC 860, the staff comments required the following:

- Explain how your accounting treatment, presentation, and related disclosures for other financing receivables that you intend to sell is consistent with ASC 860.
- Provide your accounting analysis regarding the sale of loans.
- Provide the following information related to an SBA loan sale:
  - The fair value of the portion of the loans sold and the portion retained,
  - How the previous carrying amount was allocated based on the relative fair values at the date of transfer,
  - How the gain or sale was calculated in accordance with ASC 860-20-40-1A, and
  - The journal entry recorded.

- Review the accounting policy disclosure to more accurately describe the accounting related to the sale of the guaranteed portion of SBA loans consistent with ASC 860-20-40-1A.
- Revise the disclosure to include the carrying amount of financing receivables pledged as collateral to secure your nonrecourse revolving time-share receivable credit facility in accordance with ASC 860-30-50-1A(b)).

PRESENTATION AND DISCLOSURE REQUIREMENTS

ASC 860-10, *Overall*

ASC 860's presentation and disclosure requirements are detailed and comprehensive and are designed to meet its disclosure objectives to give users an understanding of:

- A transferor's continuing involvement with transferred financial assets
- The nature of any retractions on assets reported that relate to a transferred financial asset
- How servicing assets and servicing liabilities are reported under ASC 860
- How the following affects an entity's financial position, performance, and cash flows
- Transfers of financial assets accounted for as sales if a transferor has continuing involvement with the transferred financial asset
- Transfer of financial assets accounted for as secured borrowings
  (ASC 860-10-50-2)

If separate reporting of each transfer does not provide financial statement users with information that is more useful, an entity may aggregate disclosures for multiple transfers having similar characteristics. (ASC 860-10-50-4A)

When determining how to aggregate, the entity should consider:

- The nature of the transferor's continuing involvement
- The types of assets transferred
- Risks attributable to the transferred assets that the transferor continues to bear and how that risk changed because of the transfer
- Information regarding risks and uncertainties required to be disclosed in ASC 310-10-50-25
- Concentrations involving loan product terms
  (ASC 860-10-50-5)

The disclosures should clearly and fully explain:

- The transferor's risk exposure
- Any restrictions on the assets because of these transactions
  (ASC 860-10-50-6)

ASC 860-20, *Sales of Financial Assets*

ASC 860-20-50 requires additional disclosures if transfers are accounted for as a sale and the transferor has continuing involvement with the transferred financial assets, including:

- Characteristics of the transfer
- Information about initial fair value measurements of assets obtained and liabilities incurred with the transfer

- Cash flows between the transferor and the transferee
(ASC 860-20-50-2 and 50-3)

For each statement of financial position, the transferor must disclose the following about its ongoing involvement:

- Qualitative and quantitative information
- Information about subsequent measurements of assets and liabilities attributable to the reporting entity's continuing involvement with transferred financial assets
- The hypothetical impact on the fair value of a transferor's interests in the transferred asset
- Asset quality of transferred financial assets
(ASC 860-20-50-4)

ASC 860-30, *Secured Borrowing and Collateral*

As a secured party with the right by contract to sell or repledge collateral received, the transferor must report the collateralized asset separately from other assets that are not encumbered or pledged. (ASC 860-30-45-1)

ASC 860-30 requires entities to disclose on the financial statements or notes that assets are pledged as collateral and:

- The carrying amount and classifications of:
  ○ Assets pledged as collateral that are not reclassified separately reported in the statement of financial position
  ○ Associated liabilities
- Qualitative information about the relationships between those assets and associated liabilities
(ASC 860-30-50-1A(b))

If liabilities incurred by the obligor arise from securities lending transactions or repurchase agreements, they should be classified separately. (ASC 860-30-45-2)

The following information about the collateral pledged and the associated risks to which the transferor continues to be exposed should be disclosed for each interim and annual period:

- Disaggregation of the gross obligation by the class of collateral pledged
- The remaining contractual maturity of the repurchase agreements, securities lending transactions, and repurchase-to-maturity transactions
- A discussion of the potential risks associated with the agreements and related collateral pledged
(ASC 860-30-50-7)

ASC 860-50, *Servicing Assets and Liabilities*

Servicing assets should be reported separately from servicing liabilities, distinguishing between those subsequently measured at fair value and those measured using the amortization method. (ASC 860-50-45-1)

The Codification offers two options for meeting the separate reporting requirement:

- Present separate line items for amounts measured at fair value
- Present all amounts on one line with parenthetical disclosure of the amount measured at fair value
(ASC 860-50-45-2)

Entities must disclose for all servicing assets and liabilities:

- Management's basis for determining the classes of servicing assets and liabilities
- A description of the risks inherent in servicing assets and liabilities
- The instruments used in mitigating the income statement effect of changes in fair value
- The amount of contractually specified servicing, late, and ancillary fees for each period including a description of where each is reported
- Quantitative and qualitative information about assumptions used to estimate fair value (ASC 860-50-50-2)

ASC 860-50 also requires, for each period, disclosures for servicing assets and liabilities subsequently measured under the amortization method. Those and other disclosure details can be found in the checklist at www.wiley.com/go/FSDM2021.

PRESENTATION AND DISCLOSURE EXAMPLES

Example 63.1: Receivables Securitization Program

In fiscal 20X2 and fiscal 20X3, we entered into receivables purchase agreements (the "Receivables Purchase Agreements") with ABC Bank, Ltd. Under these agreements, ABC acts as an agent to facilitate the sale of certain of the The Company's receivables (the "Receivables") to certain unaffiliated financial institutions (the "Purchasers"). The sale of the Receivables is accounted for as a sale of assets under the provisions of ASC 860, *Transfers and Servicing*. We utilize NG Funding III and NG Funding IV to facilitate the sale to fulfill requirements within the agreement.

Sales of the Receivables occur daily and are settled with the Purchasers on a monthly basis. The proceeds from the sale of these Receivables comprise a combination of cash and a deferred purchase price ("DPP") receivable. The DPP receivable is ultimately realized by the Company following the collection of the underlying Receivables sold to the Purchasers. The amount available under the Receivables Purchase Agreement fluctuates over time based on the total amount of eligible Receivables generated during the normal course of business, with maximum availability of $200,000 as of April 25, 20X3, of which $200,000 was utilized.

We have no retained interests in the transferred Receivables, other than our right to the DPP receivable and collection and administrative service fees. We consider the fees received adequate compensation for services rendered, and accordingly have recorded no servicing asset or liability. The DPP receivable is recorded at fair value within the consolidated balance sheets within prepaid expenses and other current assets. The DPP receivable was $117,327 as of April 25, 20X3, and $57,238 as of April 27, 20X2. The difference between the carrying amount of the Receivables and the sum of the cash and fair value of the DPP receivable received at time of transfer is recognized as a gain or loss on sale of the related Receivables. We recorded a loss on sale of Receivables within operating expenses in the consolidated statements of operations and other comprehensive (loss) income during fiscal 20X3 and 20X2 of $7,242 and $7,622, respectively.

Example 63.2: Accounting Policy for Receivables Sold Under Receivable Securitization Facilities and Receivables Sales Facilities

ABC uses receivables securitization facilities or receivables sales facilities in the normal course of business as part of managing its cash flows. The Company accounts for receivables sold under these facilities as a sale of financial assets pursuant to ASC 860, *Transfers and Servicing*, and derecognizes these receivables, as well as the related allowances, from its balance sheets. Generally, the fair value of the sold receivables approximates the book value due to the short-term nature and, as a result, no gain or loss on sale of receivables is recorded. Under the receivables securitization facility, the deferred purchase price receivable is recorded at fair value, which is determined by calculating the expected amount of cash to be received based on unobservable inputs consisting of the face amount of the receivables adjusted for anticipated credit losses.

Example 63.3: Accounting Policy for Cash Flows

The Company reflects cash flows related to its beneficial interests in securitization transactions, which is the deferred purchase price (the "DPP") recorded in connection with the Company's Receivables Securitization Facility, within investing activities in its statements of cash flows.

Example 63.4: Accounting Policy for Factoring Arrangements

The Company accounts for the transfer of accounts receivable to a third party under a factoring type arrangement in accordance with ASC 860, *Transfers and Servicing*. ASC 860 requires that several conditions be met in order to present the transfer of accounts receivable as a sale. Even though the Company has isolated the transferred (sold) assets and has the legal right to transfer its assets (accounts receivable), it does not meet the third test of effective control because its accounts receivable sales agreement with a third-party factor requires it to be liable in the event of default by one of its customers. Because it does not meet all three conditions, it does not qualify for sale treatment of its accounts receivable, and its debt thus incurred is presented as a secured loan liability, entitled "Loan payable: factor" on its balance sheet. The Company recorded a sales discount of $13,000 on December 31, 20X9 and 20X8, respectively.

Example 63.5: Lines of Credit

On October 19, 20X0, XYZ Digital entered into a 12-month agreement with a third party to pledge the rights to amounts due from our customers, in exchange for a borrowing facility in amounts up to a total of $500,000. The agreement was amended on April 12, 20X1, which increased the allowable borrowing amount by $250,000, to a maximum of $750,000. The proceeds from the facility are determined by the amounts we invoice our customers. We evaluated this facility in accordance with ASC 860, classifying it as a secured borrowing arrangement. As such, we record the amounts due from customers in accounts receivable and the amount due to the third party as a liability, presented under "Lines of credit" on the balance sheet. During the term of this facility, the third-party lender has a first priority security interest in XYZ Digital, and therefore we will require such third-party lender's written consent to obligate it further or pledge our assets against additional borrowing facilities. Because of this position, it may be difficult for XYZ Digital to secure additional secured borrowing facilities. The cost of this secured borrowing facility is 0.05% of the daily balance. During the year ended December 31, 20X2 and 20X1, the Company included $85,291 and $78,566, respectively, in interest expense related to this secured borrowing facility, and as of December 31, 20X2 and December 31, 20X1, the outstanding balances were $258,646 and $96,512, respectively.

Example 63.6: Mortgage Servicing Rights

Mortgage servicing rights ("MSRs") are the rights to receive a portion of the interest coupon and fees collected from the mortgagors for performing specified mortgage servicing activities, which consist of collecting loan payments, remitting principal and interest payments to investors, managing escrow accounts, performing loss mitigation activities on behalf of investors, and otherwise administering the loan servicing portfolio. MSRs are initially recorded at fair value. Changes in fair value subsequent to the initial capitalization are recorded in the Company's results of operations. The Company recognizes MSRs on all loans sold to investors that meet the requirements for sale accounting and for which servicing rights are retained.

The Company applies fair value accounting to MSRs, with all changes in fair value recorded to net revenue in accordance with FASB ASC 860-50, *Servicing Assets and Liabilities*. The fair value of MSRs is based on the present value of the expected future cash flows related to servicing these loans. The revenue components of the cash flows are servicing fees, interest earned on custodial accounts and other ancillary income. The expense components include operating costs related to servicing the loans (including delinquency and foreclosure costs) and interest expenses on servicer advances that are consistent with the assumptions major market participants use in valuing MSRs. The expected cash flows are primarily impacted by prepayment estimates, delinquencies and market discounts. Generally, the value of MSRs is expected to increase when interest rates rise and decrease when interest rates decline, due to the effect those changes in interest rates have on prepayment estimates. Other factors noted above as well as the overall market demand for MSRs may also affect the valuation.

	March 28, 20X2	*March 30, 20X1*
Number of loans serviced with MSRs	4,688	4,557
Weighted average servicing fee (basis points)	31.12	31.59
Capitalized servicing multiple	67.19%	77.97%
Capitalized servicing rate (basis points)	20.91	24.63
Serviced portfolio with MSRs (in thousands)	$ 585,777	$ 556,934
Mortgage servicing rights (in thousands)	$ 1,225	$ 1,372

INDEX